Windows Programmer's Guide to

ObjectWindows® Library

Guide to ObjectWindows® Library

Namir Clement Shammas

SAMS

A Division of Prentice Hall Computer Publishing
11711 North College, Carmel, Indiana 46032 USA

To my aunt Berthie, who cultivated my enthusiasm for math and algebra at an early age

Copyright © 1992 by Sams Publishing

FIRST EDITION
FIRST PRINTING—1992

All rights reserved. No part of this book shall be reproduced, stored in a retrieval system, or transmitted by any means, electronic, mechanical, photocopying, recording, or otherwise, without written permission from the publisher. No patent liability is assumed with respect to the use of the information contained herein. Although every precaution has been taken in the preparation of this book, the publisher and author assume no responsibility for errors or omissions. Neither is any liability assumed for damages resulting from the use of the information contained herein. For information, address Sams Publishing, 11711 N. College Ave., Carmel, IN 46032.

International Standard Book Number: 0-672-30106-7
Library of Congress Catalog Card Number: 92-71755

95 94 93 92   8 7 6 5 4 3 2 1

Interpretation of the printing code: the rightmost double-digit number is the year of the book's printing; the rightmost single-digit number is the number of the book's printing. For example, a printing code of 92-1 shows that the first printing of the book occurred in 1992.

Composed in New Baskerville and MCPdigital by
Prentice Hall Computer Publishing

Printed in the United States of America

Screen reproductions in this book were created by means of the program Collage Plus from Inner Media, Inc., Hollis, NH.

Publisher
Richard K. Swadley

Managing Editor
Neweleen A. Trebnik

Acquisitions Editor
Joseph B. Wikert

Product Development Specialists
Jennifer Flynn
Stacy Hiquet

Production Editor
Andy Saff

Copy Editors
Hugh Vandivier
Colleen Flanagan

Editorial Coordinators
Becky Freeman
Bill Whitmer

Editorial Assistants
Rosemarie Graham
Lori Kelley

Technical Editor
Bob Aronson

Cover Illustrator
Kathy Hanley

Director of Production and Manufacturing
Jeff Valler

Production Manager
Corinne Walls

Book Designer
Michele Laseau

Production Analyst
Mary Beth Wakefield

Page Layout Coordinator
Matthew Morrill

Proofreading/Indexing Coordinator
Joelynn Gifford

Graphic Image Specialist
Dennis Sheehan

Production
Keith Davenport (Book Shepherd), Christine Cook, Jerry Ellis, Dennis Hager, Carla Hall-Batton, John Kane, Carrie Keesling, Betty Kish, Linda Quigley, Sandra Shay, Angie Trzepacz, Sue VandeWalle, Julie Walker, Lisa Wilson, Allan Wimmer, Christine Young

Indexer
Jeanne Clark

Overview

	Acknowledgments xiii	
	Introduction xv	
1	ObjectWindows Basics 2	
2	Creating Basic ObjectWindows Applications 60	
3	Creating Basic Windows 100	
4	Windows Editing Classes 188	
5	ObjectWindows Controls 224	
6	Grouped Controls 290	
7	Scroll Bars, List Boxes, and Combo Boxes 322	
8	Dialog Boxes 402	
9	MDI Windows 502	
10	ObjectWindows Streams 530	
11	Controls Resource Script 580	

Contents

1 ObjectWindows Basics 2
    Common Windows Data Types 3
    The ObjectWindows Data-Typing Convention 5
    The ObjectWindow Hierarchy 6
        The `Object` Class 8
        The `TModule` Class 9
        The `TApplication` Class 10
        The `TWindowsObject` Class 12
        The `TDialog` Class 15
        The `TFileDialog` Class 17
        The `TInputDialog` Class 18
        The `TSearchDialog` Class 18
        The `TWindow` Class 19
        The `TControl` Class 21
        The `TScrollBar` Class 22
        The `TStatic` Class 23
        The `TEdit` Class 24
        The `TListBox` Class 25
        The `TComboBox` Class 26
        The `TGroupBox` Class 28
        The `TButton` Class 28
        The `TCheckBox` Class 29
        The `TRadioButton` Class 30
        The `TEditWindow` Class 31
        The `TFileWindow` Class 33
        The `TMDIFrame` Class 34
        The `TMDIClient` Class 36
        The `TScroller` Class 37
    Streams and ObjectWindows Classes 39
    Borland Windows Custom Controls (BWCC) 40
    Windows API Functions 40
        Windows Manager Interface Functions 41
        Graphics Device Interface (GDI) Functions 42
        System Services Interface Functions 44
    Invoking Windows API Functions 45

ObjectWindows Library

Windows Messages	48
Windows-Management Messages	49
Initialization Messages	50
Input Messages	50
System Messages	51
Clipboard Messages	51
System Information Messages	52
Control Manipulation Messages	52
Control Notification Messages	52
Scroll Bar Notification Messages	52
Nonclient Area Messages	52
Multiple Document Interface (MDI) Messages	53
Responding to Messages	53
Sending Messages	56
User-Defined Messages	57
Summary	58

2 Creating Basic ObjectWindows Applications … 60

Creating a Minimal ObjectWindows Application	62
Extending the Window Operations	69
Adding A Menu	72
Building Menu Resources	74
Creating a Sample Menu	77
Responding to Menu Selections	81
Creating Multiple Instances	89
Closing a Window	95
Summary	99

3 Creating Basic Windows … 100

Creating a Read-Only Text Window	101
Writing Text in a Window	107
Creating Windows	113
Window Class Registration	120
Changing the Cursor	134
Creating Child Windows	141
Scrolling Through Text	149
The Auto Scroll and Track Modes	155
Changing the Scroll Bar Metrics	162
Internally Induced Scrolling	172
Summary	185

4 Windows Editing Classes 188
- The `TEditWindow` Class 189
  - The Free-Form Calculator 192
  - The Typewriter Application 202
- The `TFileWindow` Class 209
  - An Enhanced Text Editor 212
- Summary 222

5 ObjectWindows Controls 224
- The Static Text Control 225
  - The `TStatic` Class 225
  - Static Text Sampler 228
- The Edit Control 242
  - The `TEdit` Class 242
  - Menu-Driven Commands and the Clipboard 244
  - Edit Controls for Text Queries 244
  - Altering the Edit Controls 248
  - The Command-Oriented Calculator Application (COCA) 249
- The Push Button Control 263
  - The `TButton` Class 264
  - Handling Button Messages 264
  - Manipulating Buttons 265
  - The Modified Calculator Application 266
  - The Button Manipulation Tester 279
- Summary 289

6 Grouped Controls 290
- The Check Box Control 291
  - The `TCheckBox` Class 292
  - Responding to Check Box Messages 294
- The Radio Button Control 295
  - The `TRadioButton` Class 295
- The Group Control 296
  - The `TGroupBox` Class 296
  - Responding to Group Box Messages 297
- The Updated Calculator Application 298
  - Experimenting with the Application 300
  - The Application's Code 301
- Summary 320

ObjectWindows Library

7 Scroll Bars, List Boxes, and Combo Boxes 322
The Scroll Bar Control 323
The `TScrollBar` Class 324
Responding to Scroll Bar Notification Messages 326
The Countdown Timer 327
The Timer's Code 328
The List Box Controls 336
The `TListBox` Class 336
Responding to List Box Notification Messages 342
The Simple List Manipulation Tester 344
The Single-List Application Code 345
Synchronized Scrolling of Lists 356
The Synchronized Lists Program 356
The Scrolling Lists Code 358
Handling Multiple-Selection Lists 365
The Multiple-Selection List Tester 366
The Multiple-Selection List Tester Code 368
The Combo Box Control 378
The `TComboBox` Class 378
Responding to Combo Box Notification Messages ... 381
Combo Boxes as History List Boxes 381
The COCA Version 4 Application 382
The Code for the COCA Version 4 Application 383
Summary 400

8 Dialog Boxes 402
Constructing Dialog Boxes 404
Executing Modal Dialog Boxes 404
Minimizing Resource File Contribution 414
Creating Modeless Dialog Boxes 418
Using Dialog Boxes as Windows 433
Transferring Control Data 445
The Transfer Buffer Type 446
The `Transfer` Member Function 448
The Transfer Buffer 452
Data Transfer Rules 453
Data Transfer Examples 454
A Simple Modal Dialog Box 454
A Complex Modal Dialog Box 462
A Modeless Dialog Box 469
Initialization of Window Controls 480

Declaring the `TInputDialog` Class 487
Using the `TFileDialog` Class 493
The `TSearchDialog` Class 499
Summary 500

9 MDI Windows 502

The MDI Application Features and Components 503
Basics of Building an MDI Application 504
The `TMDIFrame` Class 505
Building MDI Frame Windows 508
The `TMDIClient` Class 509
Building MDI Child Windows 510
Managing MDI Messages 510
A Simple Text Viewer 511
The Revised Text Viewer 518
Summary 529

10 ObjectWindows Streams 530

The ObjectWindows Stream Hierarchy 531
    The `pstream` Class 532
    The `fpbase` Class 534
    The `ipstream` Class 534
    The `opstream` Class 536
    The `iopstream` Class 538
    The `ofpstream` Class 539
    The `fpstream` Class 539
    The `ifpstream` Class 540
    The `TStreamable` Class 541
Making a Class Streamable 541
    Step One: Using the `__link` Macro 542
    Step Two: Declaring the Descendant Class 542
    Step Three: Declaring Public Constructors 542
    Step Four: Declaring the Protected
    Stream Constructor 543
    Step Five: Declaring the `build` Member Function 543
    Step Six: Declaring the `write` Member Function 544
    Step Seven: Declaring the `read` Member Function ... 546
    Step Eight: Declaring the `streamableName`
    Member Function 548
    Step Nine: Declaring the << and >> Operators 548
    Step Ten: Registering the Streamable Class
    with the Stream Manager 549

ObjectWindows Library

  Making a Simple Class Streamable: An Example 549
  Storing Controls in a Stream 560
  Constructing Controls from Streams 567
  Summary 577

11 Controls Resource Script 580
  The Dialog Box Resource 581
  The DIALOG Option Statements 582
   The STYLE Statement 583
   The CAPTION Statement 583
   The MENU Statement 583
   The CLASS Statement 584
   The FONT Statement 584
  The Dialog Box Control Resources 585
   The CONTROL Statement 585
   The LTEXT Statement 587
   The RTEXT Statement 588
   The CTEXT Statement 588
   The CHECKBOX Statement 589
   The PUSHBUTTON Statement 589
   The DEFPUSHBUTTON Statement 590
   The LISTBOX Statement 590
   The GROUPBOX Statement 590
   The RADIOBUTTON Statement 591
   The EDITTEXT Statement 591
   The COMBOBOX Statement 592
   The SCROLLBAR Statement 592
  Summary 593

Index 595

Acknowledgments

I would like to acknowledge the participation of the many people who made this book possible. I would like to thank Publisher Richard Swadley and Publishing Manager Joseph Wikert for their vision of this Windows Programmer's Guide series. Many thanks to Developmental Editor Jennifer Flynn, Production Editor Andy Saff, and Copy Editors Hugh Vandivier and Colleen Flanagan for their patience and labor of love. Also, I would like to thank Technical Editor Bob Aronson for his valuable comments and corrections. Many thanks to Borland's Nan Borreson for promptly ensuring that I got beta copies hot off the Borland's disk copying machines. Finally, I would like to thank all those who are involved in producing the book at Sams Publishing.

Trademarks

All terms mentioned in this book that are known to be trademarks or service marks are listed below. In addition, terms suspected of being trademarks or service marks have been appropriately capitalized. Sams Publishing cannot attest to the accuracy of this information. Use of a term in this book should not be regarded as affecting the validity of any trademark or service mark.

> Apple and Macintosh are registered trademarks of Apple Computer, Inc.
>
> IBM is a registered trademark of International Business Machines Corporation.
>
> Microsoft C Compiler and Microsoft Windows are registered trademarks of Microsoft Corporation.
>
> Norton Desktop is a registered trademark of Symantec.
>
> Borland C++, ObjectWindows, Turbo C++, and Turbo Pascal are registered trademarks of Borland International.

Introduction

Programming Windows applications is without a doubt more elaborate than programming DOS applications. While DOS held the spotlight, most programmers did not worry about horror stories shared by the early Windows programmers. The most common of these was that a Windows program required an enormous number of lines just to say "Hello World." The popularity of Windows 3.0 has brought most programmers face to face with the new programming techniques involved in creating Windows applications. The Microsoft SDK for the C compiler is not much consolation. The good news is that you need not suffer too much—the advent of the object-oriented C++ language brings with it some relief. The use of C++ is greatly enhanced by Windows interface class hierarchies, such as the Borland ObjectWindows library (OWL).

Who Should Use This Book?

This book shows you how to write Windows applications using the ObjectWindows library. For you to use this book effectively, I assume the following:

- You are familiar with C++.
- You are familiar with Windows.
- You are new to programming Windows applications.

The focus of this book is to present the various components of ObjectWindows using a practical hands-on approach. However, ObjectWindows classes do not cover all aspects of Windows programming, such as printing and graphics. Therefore, I use and discuss some of the Windows API functions needed to complement ObjectWindows applications. Selecting these Windows API functions is a judgment call. If I included most or all of the API functions, you would end up with a general Windows book with only a few chapters on ObjectWindows!

 ObjectWindows Library

 Note: In this book the Windows API functions are distinguished with a bold monospace font, as in `MessageBox`. ObjectWindows functions appear in regular monospace, as in `TranslateMessage`.

What Does This Book Include?

This book comprises 11 chapters that present the various aspects of programming with the ObjectWindows library.

Chapter 1 introduces you to the ObjectWindows classes and teaches you how to use Windows API functions and manage messages. This chapter gives you the background information for creating Windows applications with the ObjectWindows library.

Chapter 2 presents simple OWL programs to demonstrate their basic components. The chapter also discusses using menus and menu resources, creating multiple instances of an OWL application, and closing a window safely.

Chapter 3 takes a more detailed look at manipulating application windows. The chapter presents more details about creating nondefault windows and Windows class registrations. It also discusses writing and maintaining text to a window and scrolling the text in a window.

Chapter 4 is an epilogue to Chapter 3. It presents the OWL classes that implement text editors and text-file editors. The chapter also discusses how to use Windows API functions to send text to the system's printer.

Chapter 5 is the first of three chapters that present the various window controls. This chapter discusses the static text, edit box, and push button controls. Chapter 6 presents the group box, check box, and radio button controls. These controls enable you to fine-tune the action of Windows applications. Chapter 7 discusses the scroll bar, list box, and combo box controls. The chapter also examines how to handle multiple-selection list boxes, synchronize the scrolling of list boxes, and make a combo box work like a history list control.

INTRODUCTION

Chapter 8 discusses both modal and modeless dialog boxes. It examines the creation and execution of various dialog boxes, the use of a dialog box as an application window, and the transfer of data. This chapter offers several examples of transferring data between an application and a dialog box or window.

Chapter 9 presents the multiple document interface (MDI) windows. This chapter examines the various components of an MDI-compliant application and offers two sample applications. These examples show the typical and enhanced MDI windows.

Chapter 10 discusses using streams to store and recall both OWL and non-OWL objects. This chapter examines the steps required to make a class streamable. The chapter also demonstrates the use of streams in storing control instances in one application and then their use in other applications to construct the controls of the application window.

Chapter 11 presents the resource script syntax for creating controls. To create OWL dialog boxes, you need to know the non-OWL information presented in this chapter.

> **Caution:** Programming with the ObjectWindows library is certainly easier than using the Microsoft SDK package. However, creating sophisticated OWL applications requires some effort. Although OWL classes and the Windows API functions enable you to achieve your desired program functionality in more ways than one, you most likely will meet a dead end with some techniques—not every programming approach that makes sense actually works!

The book includes a companion disk that contains two self-extracting archive files: CPPOWL30.EXE and CPPOWL31.EXE. Extract the files from CPPOWL30.EXE if you have the Borland C++ 3.0 compiler. Extract the files from the CPPOWL31.EXE if you are using the Borland C++ 3.1 compiler. Both archived files contain the .H, .RC, .RES, .PRJ, and .CPP files that are related to the programs in this book.

To install the files, first create the directory CPPOWL as a subdirectory of \BORLANDC\OWL. Make the CPPOWL the current directory and then invoke CPPOWL30.EXE or CPPOWL31.EXE. These simple steps unpack the book's files in the directory \BORLANDC\OWL\CPPOWL.

ObjectWindows Library

Additional Features in This Book

As you have already seen in this introduction, from time to time I highlight important information for you. Watch for the following icons:

Note: These notes bring important information to your attention.

Tip: These tips can save you time and give you important clues on how to improve your code.

Caution: Watch for these warnings, which can save you some frustration.

In addition to the Notes, Tips, and Cautions, you will find programmer's templates for important code. These templates are boxed as in the following example:

```
void _TWinApp_::InitInstance()
{
   TApplication::InitInstance();
   // put additional statements here
}
```

CHAPTER 1

ObjectWindows Basics

The ObjectWindows library provides you with a powerful tool that will assist you in developing Windows applications. Without such a library, coding Windows applications becomes a more difficult, frustrating, and an increasingly code-intensive process. The ObjectWindows library succeeds in combining object-oriented and event-driven programming concepts, and exemplifies how well these two programming disciplines work together. This chapter introduces you to the ObjectWindows class library and some basic information related to Windows. In this chapter you learn about the following concepts:

- Common Windows data types
- The ObjectWindows data-typing convention
- The ObjectWindows hierarchy
- Windows API functions
- How to respond to Windows messages
- How to send messages
- User-defined messages

The information in this chapter should prepare you to create Windows applications with the ObjectWindows library. Although the ObjectWindows library provides an excellent tool for developing Windows applications, it does not encompass all of the Windows API functions. Therefore, you still should learn about some of these API functions.

Common Windows Data Types

Windows programming comprises a large number of data types. In this section, I focus on the most relevant data types. Becoming familiar with these data types will enable you to better understand the declarations of ObjectWindows classes. The Windows data types involve a number of simple

data types as well as a group of structures. The simple data types include many that are typedefs, which declare aliases with more meaningful names. These aliases clarify the declarations of functions and variables. Table 1.1 shows a selection of the most frequently used Windows data types.

Table 1.1. The most frequently used Windows data types.

Data Type	Meaning
char	Signed 8-bit character.
int	Signed 16-bit integer.
long	Signed 32-bit integer.
short	Signed 16-bit integer.
void	Untyped value.
BOOL	16-bit integer that represents Boolean values.
BYTE	Unsigned 8-bit integer.
DWORD	Unsigned 32-bit integer or a segment/offset address.
UINT	Unsigned 32-bit integer for future compatibility.
FAR	Data-type attribute used to create far pointers.
FARPROC	Long pointer to a function.
HANDLE	General handle.
HINSTANCE	Replaces HANDLE in Borland C++ 3.1.
HDC	Handle to a display context.
HWND	Window handle.
LONG	Same as the long type.
LPSTR	Long pointer to a character string.
LPVOID	Long pointer to a void type.
PWORD	Pointer to the WORD type.
WORD	Unsigned 16-bit integer.

In addition to the simple data types shown in Table 1.1, Windows programming involves many structures. Two of these structures, POINT and RECT, are simple, yet important. The POINT structure stores the x and y coordinates of a point and is declared as follows:

```
struct POINT {
    int x;
    int y;
};
```

The RECT structure defines the coordinates of the top-left and bottom-right corners of a rectangle, and is declared as follows:

```
struct RECT {
    int left;
    int top;
    int right;
    int bottom;
};
```

The ObjectWindows Data-Typing Convention

ObjectWindows employs a data-typing convention that makes it easy to identify the data type. Table 1.2 shows the general syntax of the data-typing convention. Table 1.3 describes specific data types frequently used by ObjectWindows classes, which apply the data-typing convention.

Table 1.2. The ObjectWindows data-typing convention.

Convention	Meaning
Pclass	Pointer type to the class class.
Rclass	Reference type to the class class.
RPclass	Reference to a pointer to the class class.
PCclass	Pointer type to a const class class.
RCclass	Reference type to a const class class.

Table 1.3. The data types frequently used by ObjectWindows classes, which apply the data-typing convention.

Data Type	Meaning
PCchar	Pointer to a char constant.
Pchar	Pointer to the char type.
PCvoid	Pointer to a void constant.
Pint	Pointer to the int type.
Pvoid	Pointer to the void type.
RCObject	Reference to a constant Object.
Rint	Reference to an int type.
Ripstream	Reference to an ipstream type.
Ropstream	Reference to an opstream type.
RPvoid	Reference to a pointer to a void type.

The ObjectWindow Hierarchy

The ObjectWindows library is a hierarchy of classes that streamlines the creation of applications' user interfaces. Figure 1.1 shows the ObjectWindows class hierarchy. Borland C++ 3.1 considers the classes TBWindow, TBButton, TBCheckBox, and others (not shown in Figure 1.1) as part of the ObjectWindows hierarchy. In Borland C++ 3.0, they are also available but considered bonus classes. This ObjectWindows hierarchy has two base classes:

> Class Object, the primary base
>
> Class TStreamable, the secondary base class

Only the TModule class and its subclass, TApplication, are solely derived from the Object class. The other ObjectWindows classes inherit from both bases classes. With this multiple inheritance, classes can be included in input/output streams for persistent object support.

ObjectWindows Basics

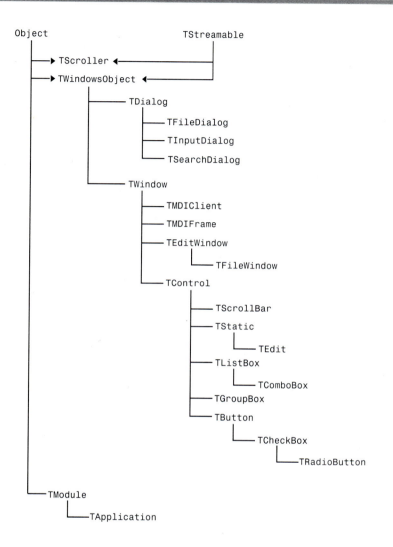

Figure 1.1. The Object-Windows class hierarchy.

With the ObjectWindows hierarchy, you can reduce significantly the amount of coding involved when you create the user-interface of Windows applications. This section presents the class declarations of the various Object Windows members and briefly discusses the functionality supported by each class.

The Object Class

The Object class lies at the root of the ObjectWindows hierarchy. As such, Object is an abstract class that defines the general structure and functionality common to the ObjectWindows classes. The following shows the declaration of the Object class:

```
class _CLASSTYPE Object {
public:
    virtual ~Object() {}
    virtual classType isA() const = 0;
    virtual char _FAR *nameOf() const = 0;
    virtual hashValueType hashValue() const = 0;
    virtual int isEqual(const Object _FAR &) const = 0;
    virtual int isSortable() const { return 0; }
    virtual int isAssociation() const { return 0; }
    void _FAR *operator new(size_t s);
    virtual void forEach(iterFuncType, void _FAR *);
    virtual Object _FAR & firstThat(condFuncType, void _FAR *) const;
    virtual Object _FAR & lastThat(condFuncType, void _FAR *) const;
    virtual void printOn(ostream _FAR &) const = 0;
    static Object _FAR *ZERO;
    static Object _FAR & ptrToRef(Object _FAR *p)
        { return p == 0 ? *ZERO : *p; }
    friend ostream _FAR& operator << (ostream _FAR&,
                                      const Object _FAR&);
};
```

This declaration indicates that the Object class is not a highly abstract object with a minimal number of members. A highly abstract class is one with dummy methods. This is not the case with Object. On the contrary, the class defines a number of virtual member functions that provide container class properties. Such member functions include forEach, firstThat, lastThat, isSortable, and isAssociation. The static pointer-typed data member ZERO is the address returned by the new operator when allocation fails. The isA and nameOf member functions are abstract functions that return the class category and the specific class name. Such member functions are useful when you query the class name or category of an instance.

Note: The _CLASSTYPE identifier is a special smart macro because it expands into either huge, far, or near, based on the data model being used.

ObjectWindows Basics

> **Note:** The ObjectWindows class declarations usually include the _CLASSDEF macro. This macro declares pointer and reference typedefs that are related to the declared class.
>
> The _CLASSDEF macro defines these typedefs using a series of other macros that result in the following declarations:
>
> ```
> typedef classname _FAR * Pclassname
> typedef classname _FAR & Rclassname
> typedef classname _FAR * _FAR & RPclassname
> typedef const classname _FAR * PCclassname
> typedef const classname _FAR & RCclassname
> ```
>
> where the _FAR macro is automatically defined as far when appropriate. The _FAR macro expands to far if the __DL__ or _CLASSDLL is set.

The TModule Class

The TModule class is a direct descendant of the Object class. TModule models dynamic-link libraries (DLLs) and contributes its members to ObjectWindows applications (through its child class, TApplication). The following is the declaration of the TModule class:

```
class _EXPORT TModule : public Object {
public:
    // Lib and WinMain args
    HINSTANCE hInstance;
    LPSTR    lpCmdLine;
    int Status;
    LPSTR Name;
    TModule(LPSTR AName, HINSTANCE AnInstance, LPSTR ACmdLine);
    virtual ~TModule();
BOOL LowMemory();
void RestoreMemory();
virtual PTWindowsObject ValidWindow(PTWindowsObject AWindowsObject);
virtual PTWindowsObject MakeWindow(PTWindowsObject AWindowsObject);
virtual int ExecDialog(PTWindowsObject ADialog);
HWND GetClientHandle(HWND AnHWindow);
virtual PTWindowsObject GetParentObject(HWND ParentHandle);
virtual void Error(int ErrorCode);
// define pure virtual functions derived from Object class
virtual classType isA() const
```

```
        { return moduleClass; }
virtual Pchar nameOf() const
        { return "TModule"; }
virtual hashValueType hashValue() const
        { return hashValueType(hInstance); }
virtual int isEqual(RCObject module)  const
        { return (hInstance == ((RTModule)module).hInstance); }
virtual void printOn(Rostream outputStream) const
        { outputStream << nameOf() << "{ hInstance = "
            << hInstance << " }\n"; }
};
```

The _EXPORT macro conditionally expands to _EXPORT if a DLL is created (__DL__ is set). Otherwise, the _EXPORT macro expands to _CLASSTYPE.

The class constructor creates an instance of TModule with the arguments of the application/DLL name, the application/DLL handle, and the command line.

The member functions LowMemory and RestoreMemory perform memory management tasks. The MakeWindow member function creates a window, a process involving the object-validating ValidWindow member function. After the member function ValidWindow verifies the validity of the invoked object, the ExecDialog member function executes a modal dialog box. The ExecDialog function works with the Execute member function of the invoked dialog box. Also notice that the isA and nameOf member functions return the moduleClass enumerated value and the "TModule" string, respectively.

The TApplication Class

The TApplication class is a subclass of TModule and is also the parent class of every ObjectWindows application you develop. The members of TApplication, together with the members inherited from TModule, provide the basic data components and operations to support a minimal Windows application. Such an application features a window and responds to a minimal set of commands.

The following listing shows the declaration of the TApplication class:

```
class _EXPORT TApplication : public TModule {
public:
    // WinMain arguments
    HINSTANCE hPrevInstance;
    int      nCmdShow;
    PTWindowsObject MainWindow;
```

ObjectWindows Basics

```
        HINSTANCE HAccTable;
        PTWindowsObject KBHandlerWnd;
        TApplication(LPSTR AName, HINSTANCE AnInstance,
                     HINSTANCE APrevInstance, LPSTR ACmdLine, int ACmdShow);
        ~TApplication();
        virtual void Run();
        virtual BOOL CanClose();
        void SetKBHandler(PTWindowsObject AWindowsObject);
        // define pure virtual functions derived from Object class
        virtual classType isA() const
            { return applicationClass; }
        virtual Pchar nameOf() const
            { return "TApplication"; }
    protected:
        virtual void InitApplication();  // "first"-instance initialization
        virtual void InitInstance();     // each-instance initialization
        virtual void InitMainWindow();   // init application main window
        virtual void MessageLoop();
        /* IdleAction may be redefined in derived classes to do
        some action when there are no messages pending. */
        virtual void IdleAction() {}
        virtual BOOL ProcessAppMsg(LPMSG PMessage);
        virtual BOOL ProcessDlgMsg(LPMSG PMessage);
        virtual BOOL ProcessAccels(LPMSG PMessage);
        virtual BOOL ProcessMDIAccels(LPMSG PMessage);
};
```

The class constructor creates an instance of `TApplication` based on the supplied application name, the instance handle, the handle of the previous instance (0 if none exists), the command-line string, and an integer code that determines how to display the window (normal, maximized, or minimized). Multiple member functions initialize the instances of `TApplication`:

- The `InitMainWindow` function initializes the main window of the ObjectWindows application.

- The `InitApplication` function initializes the first instance of the ObjectWindows application.

- The `InitInstance` function initializes every instance of the ObjectWindows application.

The instances of `TApplication` and their descendants manage the various messages by using a set of member functions. The Windows messages are managed by the `MessageLoop` function, which, as the name suggests, oversees

the application's message loop. The `MessageLoop` function works with the `ProcessAppMsg` member function to process the incoming messages. The `IdleAction` function enables the application to perform any background processing (such as sorting data) while the application is idle. To handle keyboard input, the `ProcessDlgMsg` manages particular modeless dialog boxes and window message processing. The `Run` member function initializes and executes the instances of an ObjectWindows application.

The TWindowsObject Class

The `TWindowsObject` class is a very important abstract class derived from the `Object` and `TStreamable` classes. The `TWindowsObject` class is the parent of the various interface classes in the ObjectWindows hierarchy. This includes windows, dialog boxes, and controls. The following listing is the declaration of the `TWindowsObject`. As the declaration indicates, `TWindowsObject` is a sophisticated class with public, protected, and private data members and member functions.

```
class _EXPORT TWindowsObject : public Object, public TStreamable { public:
    int Status;
    HWND HWindow;   // handle to associated MS-Windows window
    LPSTR Title;
    PTWindowsObject Parent;
    TWindowsObject(PTWindowsObject AParent, PTModule AModule = NULL);
    virtual ~TWindowsObject();
    void SetFlags(WORD Mask, BOOL OnOff);
    /* Determines whether the flag whose mask is passed has been set,
       returning a BOOL indicator -- True = On, False = Off. */
    BOOL IsFlagSet(WORD Mask) { return((Flags & Mask) == Mask); }
    PTWindowsObject FirstThat(TCondFunc Test, Pvoid PParamList);
    void ForEach(TActionFunc Action, Pvoid PParamList);
    PTWindowsObject FirstThat(
          BOOL (TWindowsObject::* _FAR Test)(Pvoid, Pvoid),
          Pvoid PParamList);
    void ForEach(
          void (TWindowsObject::* _FAR Action)(Pvoid, Pvoid),
          Pvoid PParamList);
    PTWindowsObject Next();
    PTWindowsObject GetFirstChild() { return ChildList->SiblingList;}
    PTWindowsObject GetLastChild() { return ChildList; }
    PTWindowsObject Previous();
    void EnableKBHandler();
    void EnableAutoCreate();
```

ObjectWindows Basics

```
        void DisableAutoCreate();
        void EnableTransfer();
        void DisableTransfer();
        PTModule GetModule() { return Module; }
        PTApplication GetApplication() { return Application; }
        FARPROC GetInstance() { return Instance; }
        virtual BOOL Register();
/* Pure virtual function, placeholder for derived classes */
/* to redefine to create an MS_Windows element to be associated */
/* with an OWL window object */
        virtual BOOL Create() = 0;
        virtual void Destroy();
        virtual int GetId();
        PTWindowsObject ChildWithId(int Id);
        virtual PTMDIClient GetClient();
        virtual void SetParent(PTWindowsObject NewParent);
        void Show(int ShowCmd);
        void SetCaption(LPSTR ATitle);
        virtual BOOL CanClose();
        void SetTransferBuffer(Pvoid ATransferBuffer)
            { TransferBuffer = ATransferBuffer; }
        virtual WORD Transfer(Pvoid DataPtr, WORD TransferFlag);
        virtual void TransferData(WORD Direction);
        virtual void DefWndProc(RTMessage Msg);
        virtual void BeforeDispatchHandler() {}
        virtual void AfterDispatchHandler() {}
        virtual void DispatchAMessage(WORD AMsg, RTMessage AMessage,
            void (TWindowsObject::* _FAR)(RTMessage));
        void CloseWindow();
        void GetChildren(Ripstream is);
        void PutChildren(Ropstream os);
        BOOL CreateChildren();
        virtual void ShutDownWindow();
        virtual void DrawItem(DRAWITEMSTRUCT far & DrawInfo);
        virtual void ActivationResponse(WORD Activated, BOOL IsIconified);
        // define pure virtual functions derived from Object class
        virtual classType isA() const = 0;
        virtual Pchar nameOf() const = 0;
        virtual hashValueType  hashValue() const
            { return hashValueType(HWindow); }
        virtual int isEqual(RCObject testwin) const
            { return this ==  &(RTWindowsObject)testwin; }
        virtual void printOn(Rostream outputStream) const
            { outputStream << nameOf() << "{ HWindow = "
                           << HWindow << " }\n"; }
```

```
            static PTStreamable build();
    protected:
        FARPROC DefaultProc;
        Pvoid TransferBuffer;
        virtual void GetWindowClass(WNDCLASS _FAR & AWndClass);
        virtual LPSTR GetClassName() = 0;
        void RemoveClient()
            { RemoveChild((PTWindowsObject)GetClient()); }
        void GetChildPtr(Ripstream is, RPTWindowsObject P);
        void PutChildPtr(Ropstream os, PTWindowsObject P);
        void GetSiblingPtr(Ripstream is, RPTWindowsObject P);
        void PutSiblingPtr(Ropstream os, PTWindowsObject P);
        virtual void DefCommandProc(RTMessage Msg);
        virtual void DefChildProc(RTMessage Msg);
        virtual void DefNotificationProc(RTMessage Msg);
        virtual void SetupWindow();
        virtual void WMVScroll(RTMessage Msg) = [WM_FIRST + WM_VSCROLL];
        virtual void WMHScroll(RTMessage Msg) = [WM_FIRST + WM_HSCROLL];
        void DispatchScroll(RTMessage Msg);
        virtual void WMCommand(RTMessage Msg) = [WM_FIRST + WM_COMMAND];
        virtual void WMDrawItem(RTMessage Msg) = [WM_FIRST + WM_DRAWITEM];
        virtual void WMClose(RTMessage Msg) = [WM_FIRST + WM_CLOSE];
        virtual void WMDestroy(RTMessage Msg) = [WM_FIRST + WM_DESTROY];
        virtual void WMNCDestroy(RTMessage Msg) =
                    [WM_FIRST + WM_NCDESTROY];
        virtual void WMActivate(RTMessage Msg) = [WM_FIRST + WM_ACTIVATE];
        virtual void WMQueryEndSession(RTMessage Msg) =
                    [WM_FIRST + WM_QUERYENDSESSION];
        virtual void CMExit(RTMessage Msg) = [CM_FIRST + CM_EXIT];
        TWindowsObject(StreamableInit) {};
        virtual void write (Ropstream os);
        virtual Pvoid read (Ripstream is);
    private:
        FARPROC Instance;
        PTApplication Application;
        PTModule Module;
        WORD Flags;
        WORD CreateOrder;
        BOOL OrderIsI(Pvoid P, Pvoid I);
        BOOL CreateZeroChild(Pvoid P, Pvoid I);
        void AssignCreateOrder();
        PTWindowsObject ChildList, SiblingList;
        void AddChild(PTWindowsObject AChild);
        void RemoveChild(PTWindowsObject AChild);
        int IndexOf(PTWindowsObject P);
```

```
    PTWindowsObject At(int APosition);
    virtual const Pchar streamableName() const
            { return "TWindowsObject"; }
};
```

The operations supplied by the TWindowsObject class include managing the various instances of an ObjectWindows application, streamlining incoming messages, and closing windows.

> **Note:** The declaration of the message-handling member functions is followed by a special syntax (such as = [WM_FIRST + WM_VSCROLL]) that defines the message handled by that function. The WM_xxxx identifiers are unsigned integer constants that represent message numbers and offset values. The WM_xxxx constants and messages are discussed later in this chapter.

The TDialog Class

The TDialog class, a child of TWindowsObject, serves both as a functioning user-interface class and as a parent class for more specialized dialog box classes (namely the TFileDialog file selection, TInputDialog line input, and TSearchDialog search dialog boxes). The TDialog class supports instances that represent either modal or modeless dialog boxes. The instances of TDialog contain instances of control classes, such as the radio button and the check box. The following is the declaration of the TDialog class:

```
class _EXPORT TDialog : public TWindowsObject {
public:
    TDialogAttr Attr;
    BOOL IsModal;
    TDialog(PTWindowsObject AParent, LPSTR AName,
            PTModule AModule = NULL);
    TDialog(PTWindowsObject AParent, int ResourceId,
            PTModule AModule = NULL);
    virtual ~TDialog();
    virtual BOOL Create();
    virtual int Execute();
    virtual void CloseWindow(int ARetValue);
    virtual void CloseWindow();
    virtual void ShutDownWindow(int ARetValue);
```

```
    virtual void ShutDownWindow();
    virtual void Destroy(int ARetValue);
    virtual void Destroy();
    void SetCaption(LPSTR ATitle);
    // Returns the handle of the dialog's control with the passed Id
    HWND GetItemHandle(int DlgItemID)
       { return GetDlgItem(HWindow, DlgItemID); }
    // Sends the passed message to the dialog box's control
    // that has the Id DlgItemID.
    DWORD SendDlgItemMsg(int DlgItemID, WORD AMsg,
                         WORD WParam, DWORD LParam)
       { return SendDlgItemMessage(HWindow, DlgItemID,
                                   AMsg, WParam, LParam); }
    virtual classType isA() const { return dialogClass; }
    virtual Pchar nameOf() const { return "TDialog"; }
    static PTStreamable build();
protected:
    virtual void GetWindowClass(WNDCLASS _FAR & AWndClass);
    virtual LPSTR GetClassName();
    virtual void SetupWindow();
    virtual void Ok(RTMessage Msg) = [ID_FIRST + IDOK];
    virtual void Cancel(RTMessage Msg) = [ID_FIRST + IDCANCEL];
    virtual void WMInitDialog(RTMessage Msg) =
                [WM_FIRST + WM_INITDIALOG];
    virtual void WMQueryEndSession(RTMessage Msg) =
                [WM_FIRST + WM_QUERYENDSESSION];
    virtual void WMClose(RTMessage Msg) = [WM_FIRST + WM_CLOSE];
    TDialog(StreamableInit) : TWindowsObject(streamableInit) {};
    virtual void write (Ropstream os);
    virtual Pvoid read (Ripstream is);
private:
    virtual const Pchar streamableName() const { return "TDialog"; }
};
```

The TDialog class has three constructors. The first two constructors are similar except for the second parameter. The common parameters are a pointer to the parent window's object and a pointer to the associated module. The first constructor contains the name of the resource used to create the dialog box. In the second constructor, the second parameter is an equivalent integer-typed resource ID. The third class constructor creates an instance of TDialog from data supplied by a stream.

The modal instances of TDialog are created with the Execute member function (or better yet, the safer TModule::ExecuteDialog member function). Modal dialog boxes are created and executed. They return control to other windows only when the user finishes with them. You create instances of modeless dialog boxes by using the `TModule::MakeWindow` member function. The `TDialog` class uses the `Destroy` member function to remove dialog boxes.

The TFileDialog Class

The `TFileDialog` class brings a practical and much needed specialization to dialog boxes. The instances of `TFileDialog` enable you to select a file for various input and output operations. The following is the declaration of `TFileDialog`:

```
class _EXPORT TFileDialog : public TDialog {
public:
    LPSTR FilePath;
    char PathName[MAXPATH];
    char Extension[MAXEXT];
    char FileSpec[FILESPEC];
    TFileDialog(PTWindowsObject AParent, int ResourceId,
                LPSTR AFilePath, PTModule AModule = NULL);
    virtual BOOL CanClose();
    void SelectFileName();
    void UpdateFileName();
    BOOL UpdateListBoxes();
    static PTStreamable build();
protected:
    virtual void SetupWindow();
    virtual void HandleFName(RTMessage Msg) = [ID_FIRST + ID_FNAME];
    virtual void HandleFList(RTMessage Msg) = [ID_FIRST + ID_FLIST];
    virtual void HandleDList(RTMessage Msg) = [ID_FIRST + ID_DLIST];
    TFileDialog(StreamableInit) : TDialog(streamableInit) {};
private:
    virtual const Pchar streamableName() const
                { return "TFileDialog"; }
};
```

The `TFileDialog` class has two constructors. The first constructor enables you to create an instance from scratch. Of particular interest is the `AFilePath` parameter that supplies the path containing the sought files. The `ResourceID` parameter enables you to specify whether the file dialog box handles file input or output. The second class constructor enables you to create an instance by reading its data from a stream.

The `TInputDialog` Class

The `TInputDialog` class implements a general-purpose dialog box in which you can type text. The following listing declares the `TInputDialog` class:

```
class _EXPORT TInputDialog : public TDialog {
public:
    LPSTR Prompt;
    LPSTR Buffer;
    WORD BufferSize;
    TInputDialog(PTWindowsObject AParent, LPSTR ATitle,
                 LPSTR APrompt, LPSTR ABuffer, WORD ABufferSize,
                 PTModule AModule = NULL);
    void TransferData(WORD Direction);
    static PTStreamable build();
protected:
    virtual void SetupWindow();
    TInputDialog(StreamableInit) : TDialog(streamableInit) {};
    virtual void write (Ropstream os);
    virtual Pvoid read (Ripstream is);
private:
    virtual const Pchar streamableName() const
        { return "TInputDialog"; }
};
```

The public class constructor contains the parameters `ATitle`, `APrompt`, and `ABuffer`, which specify the dialog box title, the prompt message, and the default input, respectively. With the protected class constructor, you can create instances by reading them from a stream.

The `TSearchDialog` Class

The `TSearchDialog` class creates the frequently used text search and replace dialog boxes. This class is another example of a practical specialization of the parent class `TDialog`. The following is the declaration of the `TSearchDialog` class:

```
class _EXPORT TSearchDialog : public TDialog {
public:
  TSearchDialog(PTWindowsObject AParent, int ResourceId,
                TSearchStruct _FAR &SearchStruct,
                PTModule AModule = NULL);
};
```

> **Note:** The declaration for `TSearchDialog` consists only of a class constructor. This short declaration demonstrates the code-reduction achieved by object-oriented programming. The `TSearchDialog` class inherits all the required data members and member functions. The `TSearchDialog` uses the `TSearchStruct` structure to pass data to and from the search dialog boxes. This feature enables you to preserve your most recent input.

The TWindow Class

The `TWindow` class, a child of `TWindowsObject`, implements generic windows. These windows contain a caption, the Control menu (also known as the System menu), and maximize/minimize icons. You can move, resize, minimize, and maximize the instances of `TWindow`. The following is the declaration of the `TWindow` class:

```
class _EXPORT TWindow : public TWindowsObject {
public:
    TWindowAttr  Attr;
    PTScroller Scroller;
    HINSTANCE FocusChildHandle;
    TWindow(PTWindowsObject AParent, LPSTR ATitle,
            PTModule AModule = NULL);
    TWindow(HWND AnHWindow, PTModule AModule = NULL);
    virtual ~TWindow();
    virtual BOOL AssignMenu(LPSTR MenuName);
    virtual BOOL AssignMenu(int MenuId);
    virtual BOOL Create();
    virtual void ActivationResponse(WORD Activated, BOOL IsIconified);
    virtual classType isA() const { return windowClass; }
    virtual Pchar nameOf() const { return "TWindow"; }
    static PTStreamable build();
protected:
    virtual LPSTR GetClassName()
        { return "OWLWindow"; }
    virtual void GetWindowClass(WNDCLASS _FAR & AWndClass);
    virtual void SetupWindow();
    virtual void WMCreate(RTMessage Msg) = [WM_FIRST + WM_CREATE];
    virtual void WMMDIActivate(RTMessage Msg) =
                [WM_FIRST + WM_MDIACTIVATE];
```

```
    virtual void WMHScroll(RTMessage Msg) = [WM_FIRST + WM_HSCROLL];
    virtual void WMVScroll(RTMessage Msg) = [WM_FIRST + WM_VSCROLL];
    virtual void WMPaint(RTMessage Msg) = [WM_FIRST + WM_PAINT];
    virtual void Paint(HDC PaintDC, PAINTSTRUCT _FAR & PaintInfo);
    virtual void WMSize(RTMessage Msg) = [WM_FIRST + WM_SIZE];
    virtual void WMMove(RTMessage Msg) = [WM_FIRST + WM_MOVE];
    virtual void WMLButtonDown(RTMessage Msg) =
                [WM_FIRST + WM_LBUTTONDOWN];
    TWindow(StreamableInit) : TWindowsObject(streamableInit) {};
    virtual void write (Ropstream os);
    virtual Pvoid read (Ripstream is);
private:
    virtual const Pchar streamableName() const { return "TWindow"; }
};
```

The `Attr` data member stores the attributes of the `TWindow` instances. Another interesting data member is `Scroller`, which is a pointer to an instance of class `TScroller` that helps scroll the contents of a window. You can create visual vertical and horizontal scroll bars by assigning special styles to the `Attr.Style` member. These attributes are represented by the `TWindowAttr` structure, which is declared as follows:

```
struct _CLASSTYPE TWindowAttr {
    DWORD Style;
    DWORD ExStyle;
    int X, Y, W, H;    // dimensions
    LPSTR Menu;        // Menu name
    int Id ;           // Child identifier
    LPSTR Param;
 };
```

This structure defines the style, extended style, position, size, menu handle, and control ID.

The `TWindow` class contains member functions that respond to create, paint, move, size, vertical scroll, horizontal scroll, mouse-down, and activate-MDI-window messages.

Fortunately, registration is a *transparent* process—that is, ObjectWindows classes manage the process in the background. Chapter 3, "Creating Basic Windows," demonstrates how you can fine-tune the registration of a window.

ObjectWindows Basics

Note: The Create member function manages the registration and creation of a window. Registration is an important process that requires the following steps:

1. Declare a WNDCLASS-typed variable.

2. Assign values to the data fields of the WNDCLASS-typed variable that you declared.

3. Call the RegisterClass function with the pointer to the WNDCLASS-typed variable as the sole argument.

The TControl Class

The TControl class is a child of TWindow. It provides common data members and member functions to its own derived class that implement specialized visual controls (such as combo boxes, push buttons, list boxes, check boxes, and radio buttons). The following is the declaration of class TControl:

```
class _EXPORT TControl : public TWindow {
public:
    TControl(PTWindowsObject AParent, int AnId, LPSTR ATitle, int X,
            int Y, int W, int H, PTModule AModule = NULL);
    TControl(PTWindowsObject AParent, int ResourceId,
            PTModule AModule = NULL);
    virtual int GetId() { return Attr.Id; }
protected:
    TControl(StreamableInit) : TWindow(streamableInit) {};
    virtual void WMPaint(RTMessage Msg) = [WM_FIRST + WM_PAINT];
    virtual void WMDrawItem(RTMessage Msg) = [WM_FIRST + WM_DRAWITEM];
    virtual void ODADrawEntire(DRAWITEMSTRUCT far & DrawInfo);
    virtual void ODAFocus(DRAWITEMSTRUCT far & DrawInfo);
    virtual void ODASelect(DRAWITEMSTRUCT far & DrawInfo);
};
```

The TControl class declares a relatively small number of member functions. These functions handle the paint and draw messages and manage the appearance of an owner-drawable control when that control is selected, has gained focus, has lost focus, or needs to be drawn.

The TScrollBar Class

The TScrollBar is a child of TControl and provides windows with vertical and horizontal scroll bars. Each scroll bar defines a range of values and uses the visual scroll bar thumb to display the currently selected value. You can move the scroll bar thumb in small increments (line increments) or in large increments (page increments). The following listing declares the TScrollBar class:

```
class _EXPORT TScrollBar : public TControl {
public:
    int LineMagnitude, PageMagnitude;
    TScrollBar(PTWindowsObject AParent, int AnId, int X, int Y, int W,
              int H, BOOL IsHScrollBar, PTModule AModule = NULL);
    TScrollBar(PTWindowsObject AParent, int ResourceId,
              PTModule AModule = NULL);
    void GetRange(Rint LoVal, Rint HiVal);
    int GetPosition();
    void SetRange(int LoVal, int HiVal);
    void SetPosition(int ThumbPos);
    int DeltaPos(int Delta);
    virtual WORD Transfer(Pvoid DataPtr, WORD TransferFlag);
    static PTStreamable build();
protected:
    virtual LPSTR GetClassName() { return "SCROLLBAR"; }
    virtual void SetupWindow();
    virtual void SBLineUp(RTMessage Msg) = [NF_FIRST + SB_LINEUP];
    virtual void SBLineDown(RTMessage Msg) = [NF_FIRST + SB_LINEDOWN];
    virtual void SBPageUp(RTMessage Msg) = [NF_FIRST + SB_PAGEUP];
    virtual void SBPageDown(RTMessage Msg) = [NF_FIRST + SB_PAGEDOWN];
    virtual void SBThumbPosition(RTMessage Msg) =
                                [NF_FIRST + SB_THUMBPOSITION];
    virtual void SBThumbTrack(RTMessage Msg) =
                                [NF_FIRST + SB_THUMBTRACK];
    virtual void SBTop(RTMessage Msg) = [NF_FIRST + SB_TOP];
    virtual void SBBottom(RTMessage Msg) = [NF_FIRST + SB_BOTTOM];
    TScrollBar(StreamableInit) : TControl(streamableInit) {};
    virtual void write (Ropstream os);
    virtual Pvoid read (Ripstream is);
private:
    virtual const Pchar streamableName() const { return "TScrollBar"; }
};
```

The data members LineMagnitude and PageMagnitude store the displacement in the scroll bar thumb for the line and page increments, respectively. The member functions GetRange and GetPosition return the range of values and the current thumb value, respectively. The `SetRange`, `SetPosition`, and `DeltaPos` member functions set the range of values, the new absolute thumb position, and the new relative thumb position, respectively. The family of `SBxxxx` member functions moves the thumb up or down (left or right for horizontal scroll bars) by lines, by pages, or to either extreme end of the scroll bar's range.

The TStatic Class

The `TStatic` class is a child of `TControl` and provides static text objects for windows and dialog box controls. Keep in mind that static text is *not* text carved in stone. You can change static text internally if the Windows application warrants it. The following is the declaration of the `TStatic` class:

```
class _EXPORT TStatic : public TControl {
public:
    WORD TextLen;
    TStatic(PTWindowsObject AParent, int AnId, LPSTR ATitle,
            int X, int Y, int W, int H, WORD ATextLen,
            PTModule AModule = NULL);
    TStatic(PTWindowsObject AParent, int ResourceId, WORD ATextLen,
            PTModule AModule = NULL);
    /* Returns the length of the control's text. */
    int GetTextLen() { return GetWindowTextLength(HWindow); }
    /* Fills the passed string with the text of the associated text
       control.  Returns the number of characters copied. */
    int GetText(LPSTR ATextString, int MaxChars)
        { return GetWindowText(HWindow, ATextString, MaxChars); }
    /* Sets the contents of the associated static text control to
       the passed string. */
    void SetText(LPSTR ATextString)
        { SetWindowText(HWindow, ATextString); }
    /* Clears the text of the associated static text control. */
    void Clear() { SetText(""); }
    virtual WORD Transfer(Pvoid DataPtr, WORD TransferFlag);
    virtual Pchar nameOf() const { return "TStatic"; }
    static PTStreamable build();
protected:
    virtual LPSTR GetClassName() { return "STATIC"; }
    TStatic(StreamableInit) : TControl(streamableInit) {};
    virtual void write (Ropstream os);
    virtual Pvoid read (Ripstream is);
private:
    virtual const Pchar streamableName() const { return "TStatic"; }
};
```

The first two class constructors create static text that is associated with a descendant of the TWindowsObject (which includes TWindow, TDialog, and their own descendants). The constructors enable you to assign the text for TStatic instances, and the SetText member function enables you to alter that text. TStatic instances are attached to (or owned by) descendents of TWindowsObject. The GetText and GetTextLen member functions return the text of a TStatic instance and its length, respectively.

The TEdit Class

The TEdit class is a child of TStatic that implements an edit control that can edit the contents of a window. The edit control can handle single and multiple lines (in the latter, lines are separated by sequences of ASCII 10 and ASCII 13 characters). The following is the declaration of the TEdit class:

```
class _EXPORT TEdit : public TStatic {
public:
    TEdit(PTWindowsObject AParent, int AnId, LPSTR AText, int X,
          int Y, int W, int H, WORD ATextLen, BOOL Multiline,
          PTModule AModule = NULL);
    TEdit(PTWindowsObject AParent, int ResourceId, WORD ATextLen,
          PTModule AModule = NULL);
    void Undo();
    BOOL CanUndo();
    void Paste();
    void Copy();
    void Cut();
    int GetNumLines();
    int GetLineLength(int LineNumber);
    BOOL GetLine(LPSTR ATextString, int StrSize, int LineNumber);
    void GetSubText(LPSTR ATextString, int StartPos, int EndPos);
    BOOL DeleteSubText(int StartPos, int EndPos);
    BOOL DeleteLine(int LineNumber);
    void GetSelection(Rint StartPos, Rint EndPos);
    BOOL DeleteSelection();
    BOOL IsModified();
    void ClearModify();
    int GetLineFromPos(int CharPos);
    int GetLineIndex(int LineNumber);
    void Scroll(int HorizontalUnit, int VerticalUnit);
    BOOL SetSelection(int StartPos, int EndPos);
    void Insert(LPSTR ATextString);
    int Search(int StartPos, LPSTR AText, BOOL CaseSensitive);
```

ObjectWindows Basics

```
        static PTStreamable build();
protected:
    virtual LPSTR GetClassName() { return "EDIT"; }
    virtual void SetupWindow();
    virtual void CMEditCut(RTMessage Msg) = [CM_FIRST + CM_EDITCUT];
    virtual void CMEditCopy(RTMessage Msg) = [CM_FIRST + CM_EDITCOPY];
    virtual void CMEditPaste(RTMessage Msg) =
                                    [CM_FIRST + CM_EDITPASTE];
    virtual void CMEditDelete(RTMessage Msg) =
                                    [CM_FIRST + CM_EDITDELETE];
    virtual void CMEditClear(RTMessage Msg) =
                                    [CM_FIRST + CM_EDITCLEAR];
    virtual void CMEditUndo(RTMessage Msg) = [CM_FIRST + CM_EDITUNDO];
    virtual void ENErrSpace(RTMessage Msg) = [NF_FIRST + EN_ERRSPACE];
    TEdit(StreamableInit) : TStatic(streamableInit) {};
private:
    virtual const Pchar streamableName() const { return "TEdit"; }
};
```

The TEdit class contains member functions that enable the class instances to cut, copy, paste, delete, and clear text, and to undo the last text changes. Other member functions provide services related to editing lines, substrings, and selected text.

The TListBox Class

The TListBox is a child of TControl that provides list box controls for Windows applications. The list box enables you to select from a list of strings. The operations of the TListBox instances including adding, inserting, deleting, and searching for strings in the list boxes. The string search can be either exact or partial. Other list box operations include clearing the list, returning the number of strings stored, and making single or multiple selections. The following is the declaration of the TListBox class:

```
class _EXPORT TListBox : public TControl {
public:
    TListBox(PTWindowsObject AParent, int AnId, int X, int Y,
            int W, int H, PTModule AModule = NULL);
    TListBox(PTWindowsObject AParent, int ResourceId,
            PTModule AModule = NULL)
            : TControl(AParent, ResourceId, AModule){};
    int AddString(LPSTR AString);
    int InsertString(LPSTR AString, int Index);
    int DeleteString(int Index);
```

```
        void ClearList();
        virtual WORD Transfer(Pvoid DataPtr, WORD TransferFlag);
        int GetCount();
        int FindString(LPSTR AString, int SearchIndex);
        int FindExactString(LPSTR AString, int SearchIndex);
        int GetString(LPSTR AString, int Index);
        int GetStringLen(int Index);
        // next four functions only for single-selection
        // list boxes (and combo boxes).
        int GetSelString(LPSTR AString, int MaxChars);
        int SetSelString(LPSTR AString, int SearchIndex);
        int GetSelIndex();
        int SetSelIndex(int Index);
        int GetSelCount();
        // next four functions only for multiple-selection list boxes.
        int GetSelStrings(LPSTR *Strings, int MaxCount, int MaxChars);
        int SetSelStrings(LPSTR *Prefixes, int NumSelections,
                          BOOL ShouldSet);
        int GetSelIndexes(Pint Indexes, int MaxCount);
        int SetSelIndexes(Pint Indexes, int NumSelections,
                          BOOL ShouldSet);
        static PTStreamable build();
protected:
        virtual LPSTR GetClassName()
            { return "LISTBOX"; }
        virtual WORD GetMsgID(WORD AMsg);
        TListBox(StreamableInit) : TControl(streamableInit) {};
private:
        virtual const Pchar streamableName() const { return "TListBox"; }
};
```

The member functions of the TListBox class implement its functionality, including functions that manage single and multiple selections. The instance of TListBox should be created in the instances of TWindow (or their descendants).

The TComboBox Class

The TComboBox class is a child of TListBox and provides the combo box controls. This control combines an input text box and a list box, enabling you to either select an item from the list box or type a string not found in the list. When your Windows program creates TComboBox instances, it can create one of three types of combo boxes: simple, drop-down, and drop-down list.

ObjectWindows Basics

Caution: The simple combo box includes the edit text box and the list box that is always displayed. The drop-down combo box differs from the simple type in that the list box appears only when you click the down scroll arrow. The drop-down list combo box supports only selecting an entry from the list, but the other list boxes can be either from the list or the edit control.

The following listing is the declaration of the `TComboBox` class:

```
class _EXPORT TComboBox : public TListBox {
public:
    WORD TextLen;
    TComboBox(PTWindowsObject AParent, int AnId, int X, int Y, int W,
             int H, DWORD AStyle, WORD ATextLen,
             PTModule AModule = NULL);
    TComboBox(PTWindowsObject AParent, int ResourceId, WORD ATextLen,
             PTModule AModule = NULL);
    /* Returns the length of the associated edit control's text. */
    int GetTextLen() { return GetWindowTextLength(HWindow); }
    /* Fills the supplied string with the text of the associated
       edit control. Returns the number of characters copied. */
    int GetText(LPSTR AString, int MaxChars)
        { return GetWindowText(HWindow, AString, MaxChars); }
    void SetText(LPSTR AString);
    /* Selects characters in the edit control of the combo box
       that are between StartPos and EndPos. Returns CB_ERR if
       the combo box does not have an edit control. */
    int SetEditSel(int StartPos, int EndPos)
        { return (int)SendMessage(HWindow, CB_SETEDITSEL,
                    0, MAKELONG(StartPos, EndPos)); }
    int GetEditSel(Rint StartPos, Rint EndPos);
    /* Clears the text of the associated edit control. */
    void Clear() { SetText(""); }
    void ShowList();
    void HideList();
    virtual WORD Transfer(Pvoid DataPtr, WORD TransferFlag);
    virtual Pchar nameOf() const { return "TComboBox"; }
    static PTStreamable build();
protected:
    virtual LPSTR GetClassName() { return "COMBOBOX"; }
    virtual WORD GetMsgID(WORD AnId);
    virtual void SetupWindow();
    TComboBox(StreamableInit) : TListBox(streamableInit) {};
```

```
    virtual void write (Ropstream os);
    virtual Pvoid read (Ripstream is);
private:
    virtual const Pchar streamableName() const { return "TComboBox"; }
};
```

The TGroupBox Class

The TGroupBox class is a special child of TControl that serves as a visual grouping placeholder and contains other ObjectWindows controls. The instances of class TGroupBox enable you to group check box and radio button controls visually and logically. This grouping is more significant to the mutually exclusive radio button controls—within a group, you can only check one radio button at any time. Here is the declaration of the TGroupBox class:

```
class _EXPORT TGroupBox : public TControl {
public:
    BOOL NotifyParent;
    TGroupBox(PTWindowsObject AParent, int AnId, LPSTR AText, int X,
              int Y, int W, int H, PTModule AModule = NULL);
    TGroupBox(PTWindowsObject AParent, int ResourceId,
              PTModule AModule = NULL);
    virtual void SelectionChanged(int ControlId);
    static PTStreamable build();
protected:
    virtual LPSTR GetClassName() { return "BUTTON"; }
    TGroupBox(StreamableInit) : TControl(streamableInit) {};
    virtual void write (Ropstream os);
    virtual Pvoid read (Ripstream is);
private:
    virtual const Pchar streamableName() const { return "TGroupBox"; }
};
```

The SelectionChanged member function updates the state of the controls in a group (when appropriate).

The TButton Class

The TButton class is a versatile child of TControl that offers the Windows push button controls. In addition, TButton is the parent and grandparent class for the TCheckBox and TRadioButton classes. Buttons are popular controls in Windows applications. A window can contain multiple buttons, of which only one

ObjectWindows Basics

can be designated as the default control (the button activated when you press the Enter key). The default control appears with a thicker border than the other buttons. The following is the declaration of the TButton class:

```
class _EXPORT TButton : public TControl {
public:
    BOOL IsDefPB;
    TButton(PTWindowsObject AParent, int AnId, LPSTR AText,
            int X, int Y, int W, int H, BOOL IsDefault,
            PTModule AModule = NULL);
    TButton(PTWindowsObject AParent, int ResourceId,
            PTModule AModule = NULL);
    static PTStreamable build();

protected:
    BOOL IsCurrentDefPB;
    virtual LPSTR GetClassName() { return "BUTTON"; }
    virtual void SetupWindow();
    virtual void WMGetDlgCode(RTMessage Msg) =
                        [WM_FIRST + WM_GETDLGCODE];
    virtual void BMSetStyle(RTMessage Msg) = [WM_FIRST + BM_SETSTYLE];
    TButton(StreamableInit) : TControl(streamableInit) {};

private:
    virtual const Pchar streamableName() const { return "TButton"; }
};
```

The Boolean data members IsDefPB and IsCurrentDefPB indicate whether the instance of TCheckBox is the initial and current default push button, respectively.

The TCheckBox Class

The TCheckBox class is a child of TButton and offers the check box interface used in Windows applications. Typically, a check box has two states, checked and unchecked. However, in Windows a check box can have a third, so-called grayed state (the check box appears with a gray background color). This third state can indicate, visually and logically, that a check box is disabled, for example. Check boxes can be used individually or in groups. Each check box usually represents an on/off state. Combining check boxes in a group enables your Windows applications to offer several mutually nonexclusive options. The following listing shows the declaration of the TCheckBox class:

```
class _EXPORT TCheckBox : public TButton {
public:
    PTGroupBox Group;
    TCheckBox(PTWindowsObject AParent,int AnId, LPSTR ATitle, int X,
             int Y ,int W, int H, PTGroupBox AGroup,
          PTModule AModule = NULL);
    TCheckBox(PTWindowsObject AParent, int ResourceId,
             PTGroupBox AGroup, PTModule AModule = NULL);
    void Check();
    void Uncheck();
    void Toggle();
    WORD GetCheck();
    void SetCheck(WORD CheckFlag);
    virtual WORD Transfer(Pvoid DataPtr, WORD TransferFlag);
    static PTStreamable build();
protected:
    virtual void BNClicked(RTMessage Msg) = [NF_FIRST + BN_CLICKED];
    /* Override TButton's processing so drawable check boxes and radio
       buttons work properly. */
    virtual void WMGetDlgCode(RTMessage Msg) =
                    [WM_FIRST + WM_GETDLGCODE] { DefWndProc(Msg); }
    TCheckBox(StreamableInit) : TButton(streamableInit) {};
    virtual void write (Ropstream os);
    virtual Pvoid read (Ripstream is);
private:
    virtual const Pchar streamableName() const { return "TCheckBox"; }
};
```

The TCheckBox class declares the data member Group to make the class instances with group controls. The same data member is inherited by the descendants of TCheckBox to play a similar role. In addition, TCheckBox has a number of member functions to set, query, and toggle the state of a check box instance. The BNClicked member function handles the clicked messages occurring when you click a check box.

The TRadioButton Class

The TRadioButton class is a child of TButton and represents the interface object that contains the radio buttons in a Windows application. A radio button is either checked or unchecked. Typically, multiple radio buttons are grouped together to offer a set of alternate choices. When you check a radio button in a group, all the other radio buttons in that same group are automatically unchecked—the radio buttons in a group object are mutually exclusive. The radio button control earned its name because it resembles the buttons on a car radio, which enables you to select only one station at a time. The following listing gives the declaration of the TRadioButton class:

```
class _EXPORT TRadioButton : public TCheckBox {
public:
    TRadioButton(PTWindowsObject AParent, int AnId, LPSTR ATitle,
             int X, int Y, int W, int H, PTGroupBox AGroup,
             PTModule AModule = NULL);
    TRadioButton(PTWindowsObject AParent, int ResourceId,
             PTGroupBox AGroup, PTModule AModule = NULL)
             : TCheckBox(AParent, ResourceId, AGroup, AModule) {};
    static PTStreamable build();
protected:
    virtual void BNClicked(RTMessage Msg) = [NF_FIRST + BN_CLICKED];
    TRadioButton(StreamableInit) : TCheckBox(streamableInit) {};
private:
    virtual const Pchar streamableName() const
        { return "TRadioButton"; }
};
```

The TRadioButton class inherits many of the members it needs. The class declares three constructors and three member functions. The first two constructors, which are public, enable you to create radio buttons that are part of a group. The third constructor, which is protected, creates the required instances by reading their data from a stream. The BNClicked member function handles the click messages.

The TEditWindow Class

The TEditWindow class implements a special class of windows that support the input and editing of text. The TEditWindow instances include menu selection that enables you to search for and replace text. The following listing is the declaration of the TEditWindow class:

```
class _EXPORT TEditWindow : public TWindow {
public:
    PTEdit Editor;
    TSearchStruct SearchStruct;
    BOOL IsReplaceOp; // True if the search is a search and replace.
```

```
        TEditWindow(PTWindowsObject AParent, LPSTR ATitle,
                    PTModule AModule = NULL);
        void DoSearh();
        static PTStreamable build();
    protected:
        virtual void WMSize(RTMessage Msg) = [WM_FIRST + WM_SIZE];
        virtual void WMSetFocus(RTMessage Msg) = [WM_FIRST + WM_SETFOCUS];
        virtual void CMEditFind(RTMessage Msg) = [CM_FIRST + CM_EDITFIND];
        virtual void CMEditFindNext(RTMessage Msg) =
                                [CM_FIRST + CM_EDITFINDNEXT];
        virtual void CMEditReplace(RTMessage Msg) =
                                [CM_FIRST + CM_EDITREPLACE];
        TEditWindow(StreamableInit) : TWindow(streamableInit) {};
        virtual void write (Ropstream os);
        virtual Pvoid read (Ripstream is);
    private:
        virtual const Pchar streamableName() const
                { return "TEditWindow"; }
    };
```

The TEditWindow class contains the Editor and SearchStruct data members of type PTEdit and TSearchStruct, respectively. The Editor data member is a pointer to an instance of TEdit that handles text editing capabilities. SearchStruct is a structured data member that manages data for searching and replacing text.

The set of CMxxxx member functions implement command-handling C++ member functions that deal with searching and replacing text. These C++ member functions invoke the DoSearch member function. The value assigned to the IsReplaceOp data member determines whether the DoSearch function searches for text or replaces it. The WMxxxx member functions handle messages for resizing and setting the focus to the window instance.

> **Caution:** The instances of TEditWindow can transfer text between their window and the outside world only through the Clipboard! The descendants of TEditWindow that you create must include member functions that at least send the text to an output device (such as a file), the printer, or the communication ports.

The TFileWindow Class

The TFileWindow class is a child of TEditWindow and extends the functionality of its parent class by handling text in files. The added operations include Open, Read, Write, Save, and Save As. In addition, the instances of TFileWindow use dialog boxes to open and save files. The instances of TFileWindow offer text editors with limited capability. The declaration of the TFileWindow class is as follows:

```cpp
class _EXPORT TFileWindow : public TEditWindow {
public:
    LPSTR FileName;
    BOOL IsNewFile;
    TFileWindow(PTWindowsObject AParent, LPSTR ATitle, LPSTR AFileName,
                PTModule AModule = NULL);
    virtual ~TFileWindow();
    virtual BOOL CanClear();
    virtual BOOL CanClose();
    void NewFile();
    void Open();
    BOOL Read();
    void ReplaceWith(LPSTR AFileName);
    BOOL Save();
    BOOL SaveAs();
    void SetFileName(LPSTR AFileName);
    BOOL Write();
    static PTStreamable build();
protected:
    virtual void SetupWindow();
    virtual void CMFileNew(RTMessage Msg) = [CM_FIRST + CM_FILENEW];
    virtual void CMFileOpen(RTMessage Msg) = [CM_FIRST + CM_FILEOPEN];

    virtual void CMFileSave(RTMessage Msg) = [CM_FIRST + CM_FILESAVE];
    virtual void CMFileSaveAs(RTMessage Msg) = [CM_FIRST + CM_FILESAVEAS];
    TFileWindow(StreamableInit) : TEditWindow(streamableInit) {};
    virtual void write (Ropstream os);
    virtual Pvoid read (Ripstream is);
private:
    virtual const Pchar streamableName() const
        { return "TFileWindow"; }
};
```

The protected CMxxxx member functions respond to the file-manipulation commands (New, Open, Save, and Save As) and accordingly invoke the public member functions that open, close, and save a file.

> **Note:** The Multiple Document Interface (MDI) is a specification for Windows applications that manage multiple windows within a single application. The Program Manager, the File Manager, and the Turbo C++ for Windows integrated development environment (IDE) are examples of MDI applications. The main window of an MDI application resembles any ordinary application window—it has a title bar, a control menu icon, a menu, a sizing border, and minimize/maximize icons. The main application is called the *frame window,* and the area inside the window is the workspace. The *workspace* is intended to contain zero or more child windows (also called *client windows*). The client windows resemble the frame window (and may even have scroll bars) with one important exception: they have no menus. The main menu of the frame window manipulates the client windows. At any one time, only one client window can be selected. Client windows can be maximized and minimized. The latter case results in icons appearing inside the workspace that represent the client windows.

The TMDIFrame Class

The `TMDIFrame` class models the instances of MDI frame windows. The operations of this class include the creation of both frame and client windows. Client windows are modeled by the `TMDIClient` class. The following listing is the declaration of the `TMDIFrame` class:

```
class _EXPORT TMDIFrame : public TWindow {
public:
    PTMDIClient ClientWnd;       // MDI client window
    int ChildMenuPos;            // menu position for child menu
    PTWindow ActiveChild;
    TMDIFrame(LPSTR ATitle, LPSTR MenuName, PTModule AModule = NULL);
    TMDIFrame(LPSTR ATitle, int MenuId, PTModule AModule = NULL);
    TMDIFrame(HWND AnHWindow, HWND ClientHWnd, PTModule AModule = NULL);
    virtual ~TMDIFrame();
    /* Constructs the TMDIFrame's MDI client window. */
    virtual void InitClientWindow()
        { ClientWnd = new TMDIClient(this); }
    /* Returns a pointer to the TMDIFrame's MDI client window. */
    virtual PTMDIClient GetClient() { return ClientWnd; }
    /* Constructs a new MDI child window object.  By default,
       constructs an instance of TWindow as an MDI child window object.
```

ObjectWindows Basics

```cpp
     Will almost always be redefined by descendants to construct an
     instance of a user-defined TWindow descendant as an MDI child
     window object. */
   virtual PTWindowsObject InitChild()
       { return new TWindow(this, ""); }
   virtual PTWindowsObject CreateChild();
   /* Tiles the MDI child windows by calling the TileChildren method
     of the MDI client window object. */
   virtual void TileChildren() { ClientWnd->TileChildren(); }
   /* Cascades the MDI child windows by calling the CascadeChildren
     method of the MDI client window object. */
   virtual void CascadeChildren() { ClientWnd->CascadeChildren(); }
   /* Arranges iconized MDI child windows by calling the
     ArrangeIcons method of the MDI client window object. */
   virtual void ArrangeIcons() { ClientWnd->ArrangeIcons(); }
   virtual BOOL CloseChildren();
   static PTStreamable build();
protected:
   virtual void GetWindowClass(WNDCLASS _FAR & AWndClass);
   virtual LPSTR GetClassName() { return "OWLMDIFrame"; }
   virtual void SetupWindow();
   /* Because an MDI child doesn't get MDIACTIVATE messages when the
     frame gets (de)activated, call its ActivationResponse here. */
   virtual void WMActivate(RTMessage Msg)
       { TWindow::WMActivate(Msg);
         if (ActiveChild)
           ActiveChild->ActivationResponse(
               Msg.WParam, IsIconic(ActiveChild->HWindow)); }
   /* Responds to an incoming "CreateChild" command (with a
     CM_CREATECHILD command identifier) by calling CreateChild to
     construct and create a new MDI child. */
   virtual void CMCreateChild(RTMessage) =
               [CM_FIRST + CM_CREATECHILD] { CreateChild(); }
   /* Responds to an incoming "Tile" command (with a CM_TILECHILDREN
     command identifier) by calling TileChildren to tile the MDI
     child windows. */
   virtual void CMTileChildren(RTMessage) =
               [CM_FIRST + CM_TILECHILDREN] { TileChildren(); }
   /* Responds to an incoming "Cascade" command (with a
     CM_CASCADECHILDREN command identifier) by calling CascadeChildren
     to cascade the MDI child windows. */
   virtual void CMCascadeChildren(RTMessage) =
               [CM_FIRST + CM_CASCADECHILDREN] { CascadeChildren(); }
   /* Responds to an incoming "Arrange" command (with a
     CM_ARRANGEICONS command identifier) by calling ArrangeIcons
```

```
            to arrange the icons of the MDI child windows. */
        virtual void CMArrangeIcons(RTMessage) =
                    [CM_FIRST + CM_ARRANGEICONS] { ArrangeIcons(); }
        /* Responds to an incoming "CloseAll" command (with a
           CM_CLOSECHILDREN command identifier) by calling CloseChildren
           to close the MDI child windows. */
        virtual void CMCloseChildren(RTMessage) =
                    [CM_FIRST + CM_CLOSECHILDREN] { CloseChildren(); }
        TMDIFrame(StreamableInit) : TWindow(streamableInit) {};
        virtual void write (Ropstream os);
        virtual Pvoid read (Ripstream is);
private:
        virtual const Pchar streamableName() const { return "TMDIFrame"; }
};
```

The `MDIFrame` class consists of member functions that respond to messages involved with managing the client windows. These messages include arranging the icons of client windows and closing, cascading, tiling, and creating new client windows.

The TMDIClient Class

The `TMDIClient` class works with the `TMDIFrame` class in handling the individual client window of an MDI ObjectWindows application. The following is the declaration of the `TMDIClient` class:

```
class _EXPORT TMDIClient : public TWindow {
public:
    LPCLIENTCREATESTRUCT ClientAttr;
    TMDIClient(PTMDIFrame AParent, PTModule AModule = NULL);
    TMDIClient(PTMDIFrame AParent, HWND AnHWindow,
               PTModule AModule = NULL);
    virtual ~TMDIClient();
    /* Arranges iconized MDI child windows. */
    virtual void ArrangeIcons()
    { SendMessage(HWindow, WM_MDIICONARRANGE, 0, 0); }
    /* Cascades the MDI child windows. */
    virtual void CascadeChildren()
    { SendMessage(HWindow, WM_MDICASCADE, 0, 0); }
    /* Tiles the MDI child windows. */
    virtual void TileChildren()
    { SendMessage(HWindow, WM_MDITILE, 0, 0); }
    static PTStreamable build();
protected:
```

ObjectWindows Basics

```cpp
        virtual LPSTR GetClassName() { return "MDICLIENT"; }
        /* Override TWindow::WMPaint and instead call DefWndProc */
        virtual void WMPaint(RTMessage Msg) = [WM_FIRST + WM_PAINT]
            { DefWndProc(Msg); }
        /* Override TWindow::WMMDIActivate, instead just call DefWndProc. */
        virtual void WMMDIActivate(RTMessage Msg) =
                [WM_FIRST + WM_MDIACTIVATE] { DefWndProc(Msg); }
        TMDIClient(StreamableInit) : TWindow(streamableInit) {}
        virtual void write (Ropstream os);
        virtual Pvoid read (Ripstream is);
private:
        virtual const Pchar streamableName() const { return "TMDIClient"; }
};
```

The member functions of the `TMDIClient` class help create, cascade, tile, paint, and activate a client window.

The TScroller Class

The `TScroller` class is a child of classes `Object` and `TStreamable`. The instances of `TScroller` are invisible objects that assist the instances of `TWindow` in scrolling their contents. The `TWindow::Scroller` data member is linked to an instance of `TScroller` and offers support to the window's scroll bars. The following listing declares the `TScroller` class:

```cpp
class _EXPORT TScroller : public Object, public TStreamable {
public:
    PTWindow Window;
    long XPos, YPos;       // current pos in horz/vert scroll units
    long XRange, YRange;   // # of scrollable horz/vert scroll units
    int XUnit, YUnit;      // logical device units per horz/vert
                           // scroll unit
    int XLine, YLine;      // # of horz/vert scroll units per line
    int XPage, YPage;      // # of horz/vert scroll units per page
    BOOL AutoMode;         // auto scrolling mode
    BOOL TrackMode;        // track scroll mode
    BOOL AutoOrg;          // indicates Scroller offsets origin
    BOOL HasHScrollBar;
    BOOL HasVScrollBar;
    TScroller(PTWindow TheWindow, int TheXUnit, int TheYUnit,
              long TheXRange, long TheYRange);
    ~TScroller();
    void SetUnits(int TheXUnit, int TheYUnit);
    virtual void SetPageSize();
```

```
        virtual void SetSBarRange();
        void SetRange(long TheXRange, long TheYRange);
        virtual void BeginView(HDC PaintDC, PAINTSTRUCT _FAR & PaintInfo);
        virtual void EndView();
        virtual void VScroll(WORD ScrollEvent, int ThumbPos);
        virtual void HScroll(WORD ScrollEvent, int ThumbPos);
        virtual void ScrollTo(long X, long Y);
        // Scrolls to a position calculated using the passed Delta values.
        void ScrollBy(long Dx, long Dy) { ScrollTo(XPos + Dx, YPos + Dy); }
        virtual void AutoScroll();
        /* Returns a BOOL value indicating whether or not the passed
           area (in units) is currently visible. */
        BOOL IsVisibleRect(long X, long Y, int XExt, int YExt)
            { return (X + XExt >= XPos) && (Y + YExt >= YPos) &&
                (X < XPos + XPage) && (Y < YPos + YPage); }
        /* Converts a horizontal range value from the scroll bar to a
           horizontal scroll value. */
        int XScrollValue(long ARangeUnit)
            { return (int)LongMulDiv(ARangeUnit, MaxInt, XRange); }
         /* Converts a vertical range value from the scroll bar to
            a vertical scroll value. */
        int YScrollValue(long ARangeUnit)
            { return (int)LongMulDiv(ARangeUnit, MaxInt, YRange); }
        /* Converts a horizontal scroll value from the scroll bar to
           a horizontal range value. */
        long XRangeValue(int AScrollUnit)
            { return LongMulDiv(AScrollUnit, XRange, MaxInt); }
        /* Converts a vertical scroll value from the scroll bar to
           a vertical range value. */
        long YRangeValue(int AScrollUnit)
            { return LongMulDiv(AScrollUnit, YRange, MaxInt); }
        // Defines a pure virtual functions derived from Object class
        virtual classType isA() const { return scrollerClass; }
        virtual Pchar nameOf() const { return "TScroller"; }
        virtual hashValueType hashValue() const
            { return InstanceHashValue; }
        virtual int isEqual(RCObject testobj)  const
            { return (this == &(RTScroller)testobj); }
        virtual void printOn(Rostream outputStream) const
            { outputStream << nameOf() << "{ Window = "
                        << Window <<" }\n";}
        static PTStreamable build();
    protected:
        TScroller(StreamableInit) {};
        virtual void write (Ropstream os);
```

```
    virtual Pvoid read (Ripstream is);
    hashValueType InstanceHashValue;
    static hashValueType ClassHashValue;
private:
    virtual const Pchar streamableName() const { return "TScroller"; }
};
```

The TScroller class has a rather large number of data members to store various data that manages the type and movements of a scroll bar. The class member functions scroll the thumb by using absolute or relative displacement, set the scroll bar range and the logical scroll units, and convert between horizontal/vertical range values of the scroll bar to horizontal/vertical range values.

Streams and ObjectWindows Classes

The ObjectWindows classes define the << and >> stream operators for the TButton, TCheckBox, TComboBox, TDialog, TEdit, TEditWindow, TFileDialog, TFileWindow, TInputDialog, TGroupBox, TListBox, TMDIClient, TMDIFrame, TRadioButton, TScrollBar, TScroller, TStatic, TWindow, and TWindowsObject classes. The << and >> stream operators enable your ObjectWindows application to read and write the instances of these classes (and their descendants) to streams. Using the C++ overloading feature, ObjectWindows declares two versions of the << and >>— these declarations are located in the header files for the ObjectWindows classes and appear as inline functions. I discuss ipstream and opstream functions in Chapter 10, "ObjectWindows Streams."

The general form for declaring the operator >> is as follows:

```
Ripstream operator >> (Ripstream is, RTclassName cl);
Ripstream operator >> (Ripstream is, RPTclassName cl);
```

These two general forms of declaration differ in the data type associated with the second parameter. The first version uses a reference to the class type, and the second version uses the reference to the pointer to the class type.

Similarly, there are two general forms for declaring the operator <<:

```
Ropstream operator << (Ropstream os, RTclassName cl);
Ropstream operator << (Ropstream os, RPTclassName cl);
```

The various forms of both stream operators return a reference to stream types. Such an operator type enables you to chain << or >> operators.

Borland Windows Custom Controls (BWCC)

Borland C++ 3.1 offers additional ObjectWindows classes. These extended classes provide your ObjectWindows applications with controls that resemble the colors and the look of the controls in the Turbo Pascal for Windows IDE and in the Borland C++ for Windows IDE. These extended classes add little to the functionality of their parent classes. The names of the extended classes are also derived from their parent classes. The naming convention inserts a B (for Borland) after the letter T in the class name. For example, the ObjectWindows TButton is the parent of the TBButton extended class. To find out more about these classes, consult th file BWCC-OWL.DOC in directory \BORLAND\OWL\DOC.

> **Note:** If you are familiar with Windows API functions, you can skip the next section. If not, read on. The following section is for the reader who is new to programming Windows applications. I use the API functions of Windows 3.0 not because they are the state of the art but because they are a good starting point for gradually becoming familiar with Windows API functions in general. Windows 3.1 contains even more functions. I discuss the Windows 3.0 functions to avoid overwhelming you.

Windows API Functions

Windows 3.0 consists of about 600 API functions. Windows 3.1 raises that number to just over 1,000, adding support for multimedia and pen computers. (Somehow that .1 version difference comes across as a major understatement!) The high number of API functions becomes very frustrating because it lengthens the learning curve for the average Windows application programmer. Windows 3.0 includes three groups of API functions: Windows Manager interface, graphics device interface (GDI), systems services interface.

Windows Manager Interface Functions

These functions manage message processing, create windows, move and alter windows, and create system output. Table 1.4 shows the types of Windows Manager interface functions. Although ObjectWindows handles most of these functions, you will still most likely call on some of them (especially the Message functions).

Table 1.4. The types of Windows Manager interface functions.

API Functions Type	Purpose
Message	Reads and processes Windows messages in an application's queue.
Window-creation	Creates, destroys, alters, and retrieves information about windows.
Display and movement	Shows, hides, moves, and returns information regarding the number and positions of windows on the screen.
Input	Controls the system devices, disables input from system devices, and specifies the special action of Windows when an application receives input from the system devices.
Hardware*	Alters and queries the state of input devices (Windows employs the mouse and the keyboard as input devices).
Painting*	Prepares a window for painting and offers practical general graphics functions.
Dialog-box	Creates, changes, tests, and removes dialog boxes and the controls inside them.
Scrolling	Controls the scrolling of a window and of the window's scroll bars.
Menu	Creates, alters, and removes menus.

continues

Table 1.4. continued

API Functions Type	Purpose
Information*	Retrieves information about the number and location of windows on-screen.
System*	Returns information about the system metrics, color, and time.
Clipboard	Exchanges data between Windows applications and the Clipboard.
Error*	Displays system errors and requests a response from the user to handle the error.
Caret*	Creates, removes, displays, hides, and changes the blink time of the caret.
Cursor*	Sets, moves, shows, hides, and restricts the cursor movements.
Hook*	Manages system hooks.
Property*	Creates and retrieves the window's property list.
Rectangle*	Sets and queries information about rectangles in a window's client area.

* This function has no equivalent in ObjectWindows.

Graphics Device Interface (GDI) Functions

These functions perform device-independent graphics operations for Windows applications. Operations include drawing a wide assortment of lines, text, and bitmapped images on several output devices. Table 1.5 shows the types of GDI functions. The operations of these functions are not implemented in the ObjectWindows hierarchy. Consequently, if you plan to develop Windows applications that use graphics, you should become more familiar with the GDI functions.

Table 1.5. The types of graphics device interface (GDI) functions.

API Functions Type	Purpose
Device-context	Creates, deletes, and restores device contexts (which link a Windows application, a device driver, and an output device).
Drawing-tool	Creates and removes the drawing tools that the GDI uses when it generates output on a device.
Color-palette	Provides a device-independent method for accessing colors of a display device.
Drawing-attribute	Influences a Windows application's output image (which can appear as a brush, line, bitmap, or text).
Mapping	Sets and queries GDI mapping mode information.
Coordinate	Converts between custom and screen coordinates and determines the location of an individual point.
Region	Creates, modifies, and obtains information about regions. A region is an elliptic or polygonal area within a window that can be supplied with graphical output.
Clipping	Creates, changes, and tests clipping regions.
Line-output	Creates both simple and complex line output by using a selected pen drawing tool.
Ellipse and polygon	Draws ellipses and polygons.
Bitmap	Displays bitmaps.
Text	Writes text on a device of display surface, obtains text information, changes text alignment, and modifies text justification.
Fonts	Selects, creates, deletes, and obtains information about fonts.
Metafile	Creates, copies, closes, removes, retrieves, plays, and obtains information about metafiles.
Printer-control	Obtains the printer's capabilities and alters its initialization state.
Printer-escape	Permits an application to access the facilities of a specific device not directly available through GDI.
Environment	Sets and queries information related to the environment of the output device.

System Services Interface Functions

These functions access code and data in modules, allocate local and global memory, manage tasks, load program resources, manipulate strings, change Windows initialization files, offer debugging aid, perform port communication and file I/O, and create sound. Table 1.6 shows the types of system services interface functions. Most of the system services interface functions are not included in the ObjectWindows hierarchy.

Table 1.6. The types of system services interface functions.

API Functions Type	Purpose
Module-management	Sets and queries information regarding Windows modules.
Memory-management	Manages global and local system memory.
Segment	Allocates, deallocates, locks, and unlocks memory segments.
OS interrupt	Enables assembly language programs to carry out certain DOS and NETBIOS interrupts without directly coding the interrupts.
Task	Changes the execution status of a task (a *task* is a single Windows application call), retrieves information related to a task, and obtains information about the environment within which a task is executing.
Resource-management	Locates and loads application resources (limited to cursor, icon, bitmap, string, and font) from a Windows executable file.
String-manipulation	Offers frequently used string-manipulation functions, such as string copy, comparison, case conversion, and character test.
Atom-management	Creates and manages atoms (an *atom* is a unique integer-index to a string).
Initialization-file	Sets and queries information from the WIN.INI Windows initialization file or any other private initialization file (usually with .INI extension).

ObjectWindows Basics

API Functions Type	Purpose
Communications	Performs serial and parallel communications through the system's ports.
Sound	Creates sound and music for the system's sound generator.
Utility macros	Obtains the contents of bytes, words, and long integers. Also creates unsigned long integers and structures.
File I/O	Creates, opens, closes, reads from, and writes to files.
Debugging	Assists in catching errors in Windows applications and modules.
Optimization-tool	Manages how the Windows Profiler and Swap software development tools (available in the Microsoft Windows SDK) interact with a Windows application that is being developed.
Application-exec	Allows one Windows application to execute another Windows program.

Invoking Windows API Functions

The ObjectWindows hierarchy is valuable because it uses C++ classes to package many Windows interface functions. This packaging operation relieves you from including many repetitive sequences of Windows function calls. This does not mean that your ObjectWindows application will be completely without any Windows API function calls. You can invoke many functions that perform a variety of useful tasks to complement your ObjectWindows code. This section presents a couple Windows API functions as examples.

The following code fragment includes the `Polyline`, `MessageBeep`, and `MessageBox` API functions. The code's main purpose is to plot a polygon, which involves the following steps:

1. Start a loop that attempts to draw a polygon.
2. Call a user-defined routine to obtain the number of points in the polygon.
3. Invoke the Boolean function **Polyline**.
4. If the result of function **Polyline** is FALSE, call the API function **MessageBeep** to sound a beep, and then invoke the **MessageBox** function. This function pops up an error message box that asks whether you want to try a new set of points to plot. The message box shows the Yes button, No button, and the lowercase *i* icon.

The following is the code for these steps:

```
const MAX_POINTS = 10;
POINT points[MAX_POINTS];
HDC hDC;
int answer = IDNO;
// other declarations
// other statements
do {
    read_points(points); // get the data for the points
    if (!Polyline(hDC, points, MAX_POINTS)) {
        MessageBeep(0); // beep
        // show error message box
        answer = MessageBox(
                    HWindow,                // window handle
                    "Error! Try again",     // error message
                    "Polygon Plot Error!",  // message box title
                    MB_YESNO |              // message box options
                    MB_ICONINFORMATION);
    }
} while (answer == IDYES);
// other statements
```

The **Polyline** function is declared as follows:

```
BOOL Polyline(HDC hDC, LPPOINT lpPoints, int nCount)
```

where hDC is the handle of the device context. The lpPoints is the pointer to a POINT-typed array. The nCount is the number of points in the array used to draw the polygon (the number must be at least two).

The **MessageBeep** function is a simple function declared as follows:

```
void MessageBeep(WORD wType)
```

The value 0 assigned to the wType parameter supplies the only required argument.

ObjectWindows Basics

The `MessageBox` function is an important API function that enables you to communicate with the end user of your Windows applications. Many ObjectWindows programs in this book use the `MessageBox` function. That's why I discuss the function's parameters in detail. The following is the declaration of the `MessageBox` function:

```
int FAR PASCAL MessageBox(HWND hWndParent, LPSTR lpText,
                LPSTR lpCaption, WORD wType)
```

The first parameter is the handle to the parent window. The second and third parameters are the message and caption strings. The last parameter specifies the buttons and the icons that appear in the message box. Table 1.7 shows most of the values for the message box `wType` parameter. In the preceding code fragment, the argument for `wType` is

```
MB_YESNO | MBICONINFORMATION
```

which causes the message box to display the Yes and No buttons and also include the lowercase *i* icon.

Table 1.7. Most of the values for the message box `wType` parameter.

Value	Meaning
MB_ABORTRETRYIGNORE	Shows three buttons in the message box: Abort, Retry, and Ignore.
MB_DEFBUTTON1	Sets the first button as the default. If no `MB_DEFBUTTONx` identifier is specified, the message box makes the first button the default.
MB_DEFBUTTON2	Sets the second button as the default.
MB_DEFBUTTON3	Sets the third button as the default.
MB_ICONASTERISK	Includes an icon with a lowercase *i* within a circle in the message box. (Same as `MB_ICONINFORMATION`.)
MB_ICONEXCLAMATION	Includes an exclamation point icon in the message box.
MB_ICONHAND	Includes a stop sign icon in the message box. (Same as `MB_ICONSTOP`.)
MB_ICONINFORMATION	Includes an icon with a lowercase *i* within a circle in the message box.
MB_ICONQUESTION	Includes a question mark icon in the message box.
MB_ICONSTOP	Includes a stop sign icon in the message box.

continues

Table 1.7. continued

Value	Meaning
MB_OK	Includes an OK button in the message box.
MB_OKCANCEL	Includes OK and Cancel buttons in the message box.
MB_RETRYCANCEL	Includes Retry and Cancel buttons in the message box.
MB_YESNO	Includes Yes and No buttons in the message box.
MB_YESNOCANCEL	Includes Yes, No, and Cancel buttons in the message box.

The `MessageBox` function returns a value that reflects the user's choice. Table 1.8 lists the identifiers that represent the function's values.

Table 1.8. The identifiers representing values returned by the `MessageBox` function.

Identifier	Meaning
IDABORT	The user pressed the Abort button.
IDCANCEL	The user pressed the Cancel button.
IDIGNORE	The user pressed the Ignore button.
IDNO	The user pressed the No button.
IDOK	The user pressed the OK button.
IDRETRY	The user pressed the Retry button.
IDYES	The user pressed the Yes button.

Windows Messages

Windows applications contain various types of interface elements that use messages to interact with each other in response to events. The Windows metaphor resembles the working office comprising employees, managers, departments, and material resources (computers, typewriters, photocopying machines, phones, faxes, and so on). Each employee (who, for the sake of the discussion, corresponds to a Windows object) plays a role as defined in the job description (which corresponds to a class declaration).

Events from the outside world, events directed to the outside world, and internal events stimulate the activities of an office. To respond to these events, the various employees and departments must communicate with each other through messages. Similarly, the Windows environment and its applications interact with each other and with the outside world by using messages (which corresponds to I/O devices). The following sources can generate these messages:

- ☐ User-generated events (such as typing on the keyboard, moving the mouse, and clicking the mouse button) result in user-generated messages.
- ☐ A Windows application can call Windows functions, which results in Windows sending messages back to the application.
- ☐ A Windows application can send internal messages intended for specific program components.
- ☐ The Windows environment can send messages to a Windows application.
- ☐ Two Windows applications can send dynamic data exchange (DDE) messages to share data.

The types of message categories listed in this section are available in Windows 3.0.

Windows-Management Messages

Windows sends these messages to an application when the state of a window is altered. Table 1.9 lists a selection of Windows-management messages.

Table 1.9. A selection of Windows-management messages.

Message	Meaning
WM_ACTIVATE	Sent when a window becomes active or inactive.
WM_CLOSE	Sent when a window is closed.
WM_MOVE	Sent when a window is moved.
WM_PAINT	Sent when either Windows or an application requests to repaint part of an application's window.
WM_QUIT	Signifies a request to end an application.
WM_SIZE	Sent after a window is resized.

Initialization Messages

Windows sends these messages when an application constructs a menu or a dialog box. Table 1.10 lists the initialization messages.

Table 1.10. The initialization messages.

Message	Meaning
WM_INITDIALOG	Sent right before a dialog box is displayed.
WM_INITMENU	Requests the initialization of a menu.
WM_INITMENUPOPUP	Sent right before a pop-up menu is displayed.

Input Messages

Windows sends these messages in response to an input through the mouse, keyboard, scroll bars, or system timer. Table 1.11 lists a selection of some of these input messages.

Table 1.11. A selection of input messages.

Message	Meaning
WM_COMMAND	Sent when you select a menu item.
WM_HSCROLL	Sent when you click the horizontal scroll bar with the mouse.
WM_KEYDOWN	Sent when a nonsystem key is pressed.
WM_KEYUP	Sent when a nonsystem key is released.
WM_LBUTTONDBLCLK	Sent when you double-click the left mouse button.
WM_LBUTTONDOWN	Sent when you press the left mouse button.
WM_LBUTTONUP	Sent when you release the left mouse button.
WM_MOUSEMOVE	Sent when you move the mouse.
WM_RBUTTONDBLCLK	Sent when you double-click the right mouse button.
WM_RBUTTONDOWN	Sent when you press the right mouse button.
WM_RBUTTONUP	Sent when you release the right mouse button.
WM_TIMER	Sent when the timer limit set for a specific time has elapsed.
WM_VSCROLL	Sent when you click the vertical scroll bar with the mouse.

System Messages

Windows sends these messages to an application when you access the Windows Control menu, scroll bars, or size box. Most Windows applications do not respond to these messages and instead pass them to the `DefWindowProc` API function for default processing.

Clipboard Messages

Windows sends these messages to an application when other applications attempt to access the Clipboard of a window.

System Information Messages

Windows sends these messages when a system-level change is made that affects other Windows applications. Among such changes are those that affect the fonts, color palette, system color, time, and the contents of the WIN.INI file.

Control Manipulation Messages

Windows applications send these messages to a control object, such as the push button, list box, combo box, and edit control. The control messages perform a specific task and also return a value indicating the outcome.

Control Notification Messages

These messages notify the parent window of a control that actions have occurred within that control.

Scroll Bar Notification Messages

These messages include the WM_HSCROLL and WM_VSCROLL messages. The scroll bars send these messages to their parent windows when you click the scroll bars.

Nonclient Area Messages

Windows sends these messages to create and update the *nonclient area* (that is, the area outside the working or client area of a window). You seldom will need to override the default responses to these messages in your ObjectWindows application.

Multiple Document Interface (MDI) Messages

MDI frame windows send these messages to a child client window. These messages result in operations such as activating, deactivating, creating, removing, arranging, and restoring client windows.

Responding to Messages

The various Windows messages are packaged in special data structure that contains the transmitted message and any required additional information. The ObjectWindows hierarchy uses the TMessage structure to transmit messages. The following listing declares TMessage:

```
struct TMessage {
    HWND Receiver;
    WORD Message;
    union {
        WORD WParam;
        struct tagWP {
            BYTE Lo;
            BYTE Hi;
        } WP;
    };
    union {
        DWORD LParam;
        struct tagLP {
            WORD Lo;
            WORD Hi;
        } LP;
    };
    long Result;
};
```

The TMessage structure contains four data members. The Receiver data member is a handle of the window that receives the message. The Message data member is assigned the Windows message. The WParam member is a WORD-typed

member that contains additional data. The `TMessage` structure enables you to access easily the low and high bytes of `WParam` by enclosing the `WParam` and the equivalent members of the `WP` structure in an untagged union. The `LParam` is a `DWORD`-type parameter that contains additional data (such as the x,y coordinates of a mouse click). The `Lo` and `Hi` members of the `LP` structure (which is enclosed in an untagged union with the `LParam` member) readily accesses the low and high `WORD`s of `LParam`. The ObjectWindows hierarchy internally uses the `Result` data member to query the outcome of the processed message.

ObjectWindows performs a lot of background work, including retrieving and routing messages and providing default responses for the messages received. To animate your ObjectWindows application, declare derived classes that offer the desired response to specific messages. These responses are offered by message response member functions, which you declare. The general syntax for such a member function follows:

```
class _TWinApp_ : public _ObjectWindows_class_ {
public:
    // declarations of data members
    virtual void _my_response_(RTMessage Msg) =
        [ _base_msg_num_ + _msg_offset_num_ ];
    // other member functions};
};
```

The `_TWinApp_` application class is derived from an ObjectWindows class. It declares the member function `_my_response_` that responds to the message number (`_base_msg_num_` + `_msg_offset_num_`). Later in this chapter I explain the general form for adding the two components of a message. Notice that the response function has an `RTMessage`-type parameter (a reference type to the `TMessage` structure). This reference data type enables two-way communication between the message dispatcher and the message response member function.

Now you'll apply the preceding general syntax to a simple example. Say you want to create an ObjectWindows application that displays a `"Hello World"` message when you click a free window client area (one that is not covered by a control). You would declare a derived class, call it `TAppWindow`, and call the sought member function `WMLButtonDown`:

```
class TAppWindow : public TWindow {
public:
    virtual void WMLButtonDown(RTMessage Msg) =
                [WM_FIRST + WM_LBUTTONDOWN];
};
```

The message response member function handles the `WM_LBUTTONDOWN` message generated when you click the left mouse button. Notice that the name of the message response member function is derived from the message it handles. Borland recommends this convention, which makes such member functions more readable.

So, what about the code for the response of function `WMLButtonDown`? The easiest way to display a message is to call the Windows API function, **MessageBox**, and display the intended message:

```
void TWinApp::WMLButtonDown(RTMessage Msg)
{
    MessageBox(HWindow, "Hello World", "Greetings!", MB_OK);
}
```

The `HWindow` is the handle of the window that received the mouse click message.

Now, what about the `_base_msg_num_` and the `WM_FIRST` identifier? The answer lies in the unsigned integer `WORD` type, which you use when you type Windows messages. `WORD` offers up to 65,536 messages! You must use the good old divide-and-conquer approach to manage this large number of messages. In addition, you must consider and catalog several kinds of messages, including Windows messages, programmer-defined window messages, programmer-defined child ID messages, programmer-defined notification messages, programmer-defined command messages, and multiple sets of internal messages. Table 1.12 lists the ObjectWindows constants that define the various ranges of messages. Each constant defines the base value for a particular message range. ObjectWindows also declares the other message constants as offset values to be added to the base values.

Table 1.12. The ranges of Windows messages.

Constant	Value	Message Range	Meaning
WM_FIRST	0x0000	0x0000–0x03FF	Windows messages.
WM_USER	0x0400	0x0400–0x6EFF	Programmer-defined window messages.
WM_INTERNAL	0x7F00	0x7F00–0x7FFF	Reserved for internal use.
ID_FIRST	0x8000	0x8000–0x8EFF	Programmer-defined child ID messages.
ID_INTERNAL	0x8F00	0x8F00–0x8FFF	Reserved for internal use.
NF_FIRST	0x9000	0x9000–0x9EFF	Programmer-defined notification messages.

continues

Table 1.12. continued

Constant	Value	Message Range	Meaning
NF_INTERNAL	0x9F00	0x9F00–0x9FFF	Reserved for internal use.
CM_FIRST	0xA000	0xA000–0xFEFF	Programmer-defined command messages.
CM_INTERNAL	0xFF00	0xFF00–0xFFFF	Reserved for internal use.

Sending Messages

Windows lets your application send messages to itself, other applications, or to Windows itself. The Windows API functions **SendMessage**, **PostMessage**, and **SendDlgItemMessage** provide important tools for sending messages. The **SendMessage** function sends a message to a window and requires that window to handle the message. The **SendMessage** is declared as follows:

DWORD SendMessage(HWND hWnd, WORD wMsg, WORD wParam, LONG lParam)

The parameter hWnd is the handle of the window that receives the message. The parameter wMsg specifies the message sent. The wParam and lParam parameters designate additional optional information. The **SendMessage** function communicates with other windows and controls (the descendants of TControl). TControl offers many such communications through its members.

PostMessage is similar to **SendMessage**, except it lacks the sense of urgency—the message is posted in the window's message queue. The targeted window handles the message later when it is convenient for that window. The following is the declaration of the Boolean **PostMessage** function:

BOOL PostMessage(HWND hWnd, WORD wMsg, WORD wParam, LONG lParam)

The hWnd parameter is the handle of the window that receives the message. The wMsg parameter specifies the message sent. The wParam and lParam parameters designate additional optional information.

The **SendDlgItemMessage** function sends a message to a particular item in a dialog box. The following is the declaration of the **SendDlgItemMessage** function:

DWORD SendDlgItemMessage(HWND hDlg, int nIDDlgItem,
                WORD wMsg, WORD wParam, LONG lParam)

ObjectWindows Basics

The `hDlg` parameter is the handle of the dialog box containing the targeted control. The `nIDDlgItem` parameter indicates the integer identifier of the dialog box item that receives the message. The `wMsg` parameter specifies the message sent. The `wParam` and `lParam` parameters designate other optional information.

User-Defined Messages

ObjectWindows enables you to define your own messages. The constant `WM_USER` is associated with the number of the first message. You should declare constants that represent the offset values for your custom messages. For example, you can use the `#define` directive to define your own messages:

```
#define WM_USER1 0
#define WM_USER2 1
#define WM_USER3 2
```

or you can use the constant declarations to create similar constants:

```
constant WORD WM_USER1 = 0;
constant WORD WM_USER2 = 1;
constant WORD WM_USER3 = 2;
```

These user-defined messages can be used in the following example class and its user-defined message response member functions:

```
class TWinApp : public TWindow {
public:
    // declarations of data members
    virtual void WMUser1(RTMessage Msg) =
        [WM_USER + WM_USER1];
    virtual void WMUser2(RTMessage Msg) =
        [WM_USER + WM_USER2];
    virtual void WMUser3(RTMessage Msg) =
        [WM_USER + WM_USER3];
    // other member functions
};
```

To send the preceding user-defined messages, you can use the **SendMessage** API function. For example, the following statement sends the `WM_USER2` message:

```
SendMessage(HWindow, WM_USER2, wordVar, longVar);
```

Summary

This chapter presents basic information regarding the ObjectWindows class hierarchy as well as Windows-related information. Topics include the following:

- Popular Windows data types, including simple data types (such as BYTE, WORD, and LONG) and data structures (such as RECT and POINT).
- The ObjectWindows data-typing convention that creates reference, pointer, reference to pointers, and reference to constants data types. The chapter also presents frequently used ObjectWindows reference and pointer data types.
- The ObjectWindows hierarchy, including the various classes that make up the ObjectWindows library.
- The Windows API functions. There are three general categories: the Window Manager, GDI, and system services functions.
- How to invoke Windows API functions, such as `MessageBox`, `MessageBeep`, and `Polyline`.
- The various categories of Windows messages.
- How to respond to Windows messages in your own ObjectWindows applications. This process involves declaring descendant ObjectWindows classes that contain one or more message response member functions. The latter functions provide the required response.
- How to use a few Windows API functions to send messages.
- How to define your own messages, send these messages, and then respond to them.

Chapter 2, "Creating Basic ObjectWindows Applications," presents the basics of building an ObjectWindows application and attaching menus to it.

ObjectWindows Basics

CHAPTER 2

Creating Basic ObjectWindows Applications

The last chapter provided you with much background information regarding the ObjectWindows classes, Windows API functions, and Windows messages. In this chapter you start building very simple ObjectWindows applications, and you learn about the following topics:

- Creating a minimal ObjectWindows application
- Extending the operations of the application's window
- Adding a menu to an ObjectWindows application
- Responding to menu selections
- Alternating between different menus
- Creating multiple instances of an ObjectWindows application
- Closing a window

These topics also demonstrate the power and functionality of ObjectWindows. This functionality includes default characteristics and responses. Building your own ObjectWindows application involves extending the basic characteristics and functionality of ObjectWindows.

Note: Every ObjectWindows application you develop begins with the declaration of a descendant of the TApplication class. Even the most trivial ObjectWindows applications require this step. Extending the other ObjectWindows classes depends on the features of your applications. The other required component for an ObjectWindows application is the WinMain function—similar to the main() function in a non-Windows C or C++ program.

Creating a Minimal ObjectWindows Application

You first must consider the `WinMain` function, because it is the entry point for executing an ObjectWindows application. The following listing is the general template for the `WinMain` function:

```
int PASCAL WinMain(HINSTANCE hInstance, HINSTANCE hPrevInstance,
                   LPSTR lpCmdLine, int nCmdShow)
{
  _TWinApp_ _WinApp_(_window_title_, hInstance,
                    hPrevInstance, lpCmdLine, nCmdShow,
                    _optional_additional_parameters_);
 _WinApp_.Run(); // run OWL application
  return _WinApp_.Status; // return application status
}
```

Note: If you are using Borland C++ 3.0 or the backward compatiblity header files, you need to use the `HANDLE` data type rather than `HINSTANCE`. These types are used mostly in declaring the application class `TWinApp` and the `WinMain` function. The companion disk contains a special set of archived files that are compatible with version 3.0. Another important difference between versions 3.0 and 3.1 is that the latter version requires that you use the WIN30 or WIN31 macros in the Compiler options to indicate that your application is for Windows 3.0 or 3.1, respectively. In addition, Borland C++ 3.1 enables you to define the STRICT macro in the Compiler options to request strict compiler type checking. The project files that are also included in the archived files have the WIN31 macro defined for version 3.1.

The `WinMain` function uses the Pascal convention for passing parameters. Windows passes arguments to its parameters. The `hInstance` parameter is the handle for the current instance. The `hPrevInstance` parameter is the handle for the previous instance and is 0 for the instance created. The `lpCmdLine` parameter passes the arguments of the command line to the created instance. The `nCmdShow` parameter specifies whether the application's window is normal, maximized, or minimized.

Creating Basic ObjectWindows Applications

The _TWinApp_ class is the template of the application class derived from TApplication. The _WinApp_ variable is the template for the application instances. You create these instances with the same parameters of WinMain plus a string of characters that specifies the application name. You can also use this name as the window title. The _optional_additional_parameters_ is a template for additional parameters needed by the application class constructor.

The WinMain function contains two additional statements. The _WinApp_.Run statement executes the application. The last statement returns the value of the Status data member to indicate whether the application terminated without error. The WinMain function might contain additional statements to accommodate other special initialization.

> **Note:** The Run member function is responsible for invoking other member functions that initialize the various instances of an ObjectWindows application and process incoming messages.

The Run member function invokes the previous member functions in the following order:

1. Run invokes the InitApplication member function to initialize the first instance of the ObjectWindows application. The code for the member function TApplication::InitApplication is as follows:

   ```
   void TApplication::InitApplication()
   {
   }
   ```

   The previous member function performs no task—it's just a dummy function that you override when performing special initialization to the application.

2. Run calls the InitInstance member function to initialize every other instance of the ObjectWindows application. To show you how InitInstance works, here is the code for TApplication::InitInstance:

   ```
   void TApplication::InitInstance()
   {
     InitMainWindow();
     MainWindow = MakeWindow(MainWindow);
     if ( MainWindow )
       MainWindow->Show(nCmdShow);
     else
   Status = EM_INVALIDMAINWINDOW;
   }
   ```

This example demonstrates that `InitInstance` calls `InitMainWindow`. So, every time you create an instance of an ObjectWindows application, you invoke these two functions.

> **Note:** If you plan to perform additional steps in initializing the instances of an application, you must declare your own `InitInstance`.
>
> To declare your own `InitInstance`, use the following general form:
>
> ```
> void _TWinApp_::InitInstance()
> {
>    TApplication::InitInstance();
>    // put additional statements here
> }
> ```
>
> You must call `TApplication::InitInstance` first and then perform your own additional initialization.

3. `Run` invokes the `InitMainWindow` member function to initialize the main window of each instance. The `TApplication::InitMainWindow` member function is defined as follows:

   ```
   void TApplication::InitMainWindow()
   {
      MainWindow = new TWindow(NULL, Name);
   }
   ```

   This function uses the application's name (stored in the data member `Name`) as the window's title. The NULL argument indicates that the window has no parent window. The function creates a `TWindow` instance, which provides the bare bones of ObjectWindows functionality. You must declare your version of `InitMainWindow` for the custom ObjectWindows application you develop.

4. `Run` calls the `MessageLoop` member function to process any incoming messages. The following is the code for `TApplication::MessageLoop`:

   ```
   void TApplication::MessageLoop()
   {
     MSG Message;
     while ( TRUE )
     {
        if ( PeekMessage(&Message, 0, 0, 0, PM_REMOVE) )
   ```

Creating Basic ObjectWindows Applications

```
      {
        if ( Message.message == WM_QUIT )
          break;
        if ( !ProcessAppMsg(&Message) )
        {
          TranslateMessage(&Message);
          DispatchMessage(&Message);
        }
      }
      else    // No message waiting.
        IdleAction();
    }
    Status = Message.wParam;
}
```

As you can see, the code for `MessageLoop` is not terribly complicated. The function lives up to its name by using an open `while` loop to process incoming messages. Notice that the `WM_QUIT` message causes the loop to stop iterating. Also notice the calls to the **TranslateMessage** and **DispatchMessage** API functions. The first function translates virtual key messages. The second function dispatches the messages to the proper message response member function. You can declare your own version of `MessageLoop` if you need to handle incoming messages a bit differently—but you must do so with extreme care.

To give you a clearer idea of how `Run` works, here is the code for the member function `TApplication::Run`:

```
void TApplication::Run()
{
  if ( !hPrevInstance )
    InitApplication();
  if (Status == 0 )
    InitInstance();
  if (Status == 0)
    MessageLoop();
  else
    Error(Status);
}
```

This code demonstrates that `InitApplication` is called once—when the first instance of the application is created. The `InitInstance` (and `InitMainWindow`, which is called by `InitInstance`) and the `MessageLoop` member functions are called if the operation has progressed without error.

65

Now look at the creation of the application classes that are descendants of `TApplication`. The following is the template for an application class:

```
class _TWinApp_ : public TApplication
{
public:
  // public data members declarations
    _TWinApp_(LPSTR    AName,              // application name
              HINSTANCE hInstance,          // instance handle
              HINSTANCE hPrevInstance,      // previous instance handle
              LPSTR    lpCmdLine,           // command-line arguments
              int      nCmdShow,            // display command
              _other_params_) :             // additional parameters
          TApplication(AName, hInstance, hPrevInstance,
                       lpCmdLine, nCmdShow)
              { /* initialization statements */ };
// other constructors
// class destructors
// other member functions
protected:
  // protected data members
  virtual void InitMainWindow();
  virtual void InitInstance();        // optional
  virtual void InitApplication();     // optional
  virtual BOOL CanClose();            // optional
  // other protected member functions
private:
  // private data members
  // other private member functions
};
```

As this template indicates, your application classes should declare an `InitMainWindow` member function. The declaration of the member functions `InitInstance`, `InitApplication`, and `CanClose` (more about this function later in this chapter) is needed only to fine-tune the operations of these inherited functions in your ObjectWindows application. This fact also applies to the declaration of other constructor parameters, data members (public, protected, and private), and member functions (public, protected, and private).

Listing 2.1 is the source code for a minimal ObjectWindows application that uses this template. Notice that the application class `TWinApp` declares a constructor and the `InitMainWindow` member function. The `InitMainWindow` creates an instance of `TWindow`, which is accessed by the inherited pointer-typed data member `MainWindow`. The instances of `TWindow` can have a Control menu and can be moved, resized, minimized, and maximized. Figure 2.1 displays a sample

Creating Basic ObjectWindows Applications

session with the MINWINAP.EXE application. To close the application window, use the Close option in the Control menu.

Caution: To create the MINWINAP.EXE file, you must first create the MINWINAP.PRJ project file and add the MINWINAP.CPP and OWL.DEF (found in the directory \BORLANDC\OWL\LIB). All of the files that I have created for this book are located in the directory \BORLANDC\OWL\CPPOWL. Make sure that you create the CPPOWL subdirectory and attach it to the \BORLANDC\OWL directory. To compile the project, you also need to set the following directory paths in the Options/Directories dialog box:

- Set the Include Directory to

   \BORLANDC\INCLUDE;\BORLANDC\OWL\INCLUDE;\BORLANDC\CLASSLIB\INCLUDE

- Set the Library Directory to

   \BORLANDC\LIB;\BORLANDC\OWL\LIB\BORLANDC\CLASSLIB\LIB

- Set the Output Directory to

   \BORLANDC\OWL\CPPOWL

Maintain these settings for the other project files in this book.

For the Options | Linker | Library dialog box, set the three library options (ObjectWindows, Classes, and Run-time) to `static`.

Listing 2.1. The source code in the MINWINAP.CPP file.

```
#include <owl.h>

// declare the custom application class as
// a subclass of TApplication

class TWinApp : public TApplication
{
public:
  TWinApp(LPSTR  AName,              // application name
          HINSTANCE hInstance,       // instance handle
          HINSTANCE hPrevInstance,   // previous instance handle
```

continues

Listing 2.1. continued

```
          LPSTR   lpCmdLine,     // command-line arguments
          int     nCmdShow) :    // display command
          TApplication(AName, hInstance, hPrevInstance,
                  lpCmdLine, nCmdShow) {};

protected:
  virtual void InitMainWindow();

};

void TWinApp::InitMainWindow()
{
  MainWindow = new TWindow(NULL, Name);
}

int PASCAL WinMain(HINSTANCE hInstance, HINSTANCE hPrevInstance,
              LPSTR lpCmdLine, int nCmdShow)
{
  TWinApp WinApp("Minimal OWL Application", hInstance,
              hPrevInstance, lpCmdLine, nCmdShow);
  WinApp.Run(); // run OWL application
  return WinApp.Status; // return application status
}
```

The OWL.H header file is included to ensure that all the required Windows and ObjectWindows declarations are available to the compiler.

> **Caution:** Figure 2.1 was shot on a system running Norton Desktop. This program attaches additional selections to menus to help make the running of Windows programs more convenient. When you compile and run the MINWINAP.EXE application, your menu will not contain the Launch Manager, Launch List, and Task List options unless you use Norton Desktop also.

Creating Basic ObjectWindows Applications

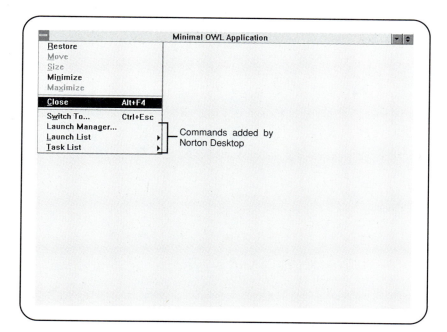

Figure 2.1.
A sample session with the MINWINAP.EXE application.

Extending the Window Operations

After building a minimal ObjectWindows application, you'll now write a new application that adds some functionality to the application's window. The next program, shown in Listing 2.2, performs the following main tasks:

☐ Responds to the left button mouse click (when the mouse is inside the application window) by displaying a message box with an OK button.

☐ Responds to the right button mouse click by displaying a message box asking whether you want to close the window.

These tasks require that the application declares a descendant of TWindow to implement the desired options. Listing 2.2 shows the declaration of the TAppWindow class, a descendant of TWindow. The new class declares a constructor and two message response member functions. The TAppWindow constructor

69

simply calls the `TWindow` constructor, because no additional class instantiation is needed. The `WMLButtonDown` and `WMRButtonDown` member functions respond to the `WM_LBUTTONDOWN` and `WM_RBUTTONDOWN` messages, respectively. The extended C++ syntax indicates this response and defines the messages handled by these member functions.

The declaration of class `TAppWindow` precedes the macro `_CLASSDEF(TAppWindow)`, which declares related reference and pointer types.

The `WMLButtonDown` member function simply calls the **MessageBox** API function to display the string `You clicked the left button!` in a message box with the caption `Mouse Click Event!` The box includes the OK button that you click to resume program execution. The `HWindow` argument is the handle for the window you just clicked.

The code for the `WMRButtonDown` is a bit more elaborate. The function first invokes the **MessageBeep** API function to sound a beep. The function then calls the **MessageBox** API function to display a box with the caption `Query`, the message `Want to close this application`, Yes and No buttons, and a question mark icon. The `WMRButtonDown` function stores the result of the **MessageBox** function in the local variable result. The last statement is an `if` statement that compares the contents of the variable result with the constant `IDYES`. When the test is positive, the function calls the **SendMessage** API function to close the window by using the `WM_CLOSE` message.

The application class is very similar to the one in file MINWINAP.CPP. The exception is that the `InitMainWindow` member function creates a new instance of `TAppWindow` rather than `TWindow`.

To compile the program in Listing 2.2, include the SECAPP.CPP and OWL.DEF files in your SECAPP.PRJ file. Figure 2.2 shows a sample session with the SECAPP.EXE application.

Listing 2.2. The source code of file SECAPP.CPP.

```
#include <owl.h>

// declare the custom application class as
// a subclass of TApplication

class TWinApp : public TApplication
{
public:
  TWinApp(LPSTR  AName,            // application name
```

```
              HINSTANCE hInstance,      // instance handle
              HINSTANCE hPrevInstance,  // previous instance handle
              LPSTR    lpCmdLine,      // command-line arguments
              int      nCmdShow) :     // display command
              TApplication(AName, hInstance, hPrevInstance,
                      lpCmdLine, nCmdShow) {};

protected:
  virtual void InitMainWindow();

};


// use the _CLASSDEF macro to declare reference and pointer
// types related to the new TAppWindow class
_CLASSDEF(TAppWindow)

// expand the functionality of TWindow by deriving class TAppWindow
class TAppWindow : public TWindow
{
public:
  TAppWindow(PTWindowsObject AParent, LPSTR ATitle) :
           TWindow(AParent, ATitle) {};

  // handle the left mouse button click
  virtual void WMLButtonDown(RTMessage Msg)
       = [WM_FIRST + WM_LBUTTONDOWN];

  // handle the right mouse button click
  virtual void WMRButtonDown(RTMessage Msg)
       = [WM_FIRST + WM_RBUTTONDOWN];

};

void TAppWindow::WMLButtonDown(RTMessage Msg)
{
  MessageBox(HWindow, "You clicked the left button!",
          "Mouse Click Event!", MB_OK);
}

void TAppWindow::WMRButtonDown(RTMessage Msg)
{
  int result;
  MessageBeep(0); // beep
```

continues

Listing 2.2. continued

```
  // prompt user if he or she want to close the application
  result = MessageBox(HWindow, "Want to close this application",
                      "Query", MB_YESNO | MB_ICONQUESTION);

  // if the user clicked the Yes button send a WM_CLOSE message
  // to the application's window
  if (result == IDYES)
     SendMessage(HWindow, WM_CLOSE, 0, 0);
}

void TWinApp::InitMainWindow()
{
  MainWindow = new TAppWindow(NULL, Name);
}

int PASCAL WinMain(HINSTANCE hInstance, HINSTANCE hPrevInstance,
                   LPSTR lpCmdLine, int nCmdShow)
{
  TWinApp WinApp("A Simple OWL Application", hInstance,
                 hPrevInstance, lpCmdLine, nCmdShow);
  WinApp.Run(); // run OWL application
  return WinApp.Status; // return application status
}
```

Caution: The `WMLButtonDown` and `WMRButtonDown` member causes a compile-time warning, because the `Msg` parameter is not referenced inside the functions. This is true for any response message handler that does not use the `Msg` parameter.

Adding A Menu

Most Windows applications include menus. The MINWINAP.EXE and SECAPP.EXE applications contain only the Control menu. This section demonstrates how to use a resource file to build a menu that can be attached to the application's window. The menus are regarded as attributes of a window

Creating Basic ObjectWindows Applications

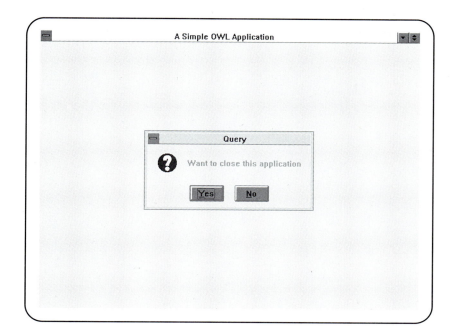

Figure 2.2.
A sample session with the SECAPP.EXE application.

rather than as separate objects. That's why there is no ObjectWindows class that models menus. The `TWindow::Attr` data member accesses menus. This data member contains the `TWindowAttr` type, which is declared as follows:

```
struct _CLASSTYPE TWindowAttr {
    DWORD Style;       // window style
    DWORD ExStyle;     // the extended style
    int X, Y, W, H;    // location and dimensions of the window
    LPSTR Menu;        // resource ID name
    int Id;            // resource ID number
    LPSTR Param;       // values passed by Windows
};
```

Note: It might seem strange to make menus an attribute of a window that is loaded from a resource, because this seems to deviate from the philosophy of using classes to build the various instances that make up an ObjectWindows application. The fact that you can handle menus this way demonstrates the nature and flexibility of resources. *Resources* are components that are created and compiled outside a Windows or ObjectWindows application. Applications use resources

continues

by simply loading them. Resources only define the appearance of visual objects; they do not control the behavior of these objects. That is the task of the Windows or ObjectWindows application. The advantage of resources is that you can modify them without recompiling the application. For example, you can change the wording of menu items or alter the location of a button. A more impressive example is the ability to change the language used in the various menus, dialog boxes, and other controls. This enables a software developer to easily maintain and update a single version of the application while using different versions of the resources for each language. Apple Computer applied this approach when designing the Apple Macintosh computer to work in different languages, including Arabic!

Building Menu Resources

The menu resource file (which is usually stored in a .RC file extension) can contain MENU, MENUITEM, POPUP, MENUITEM SEPARATOR, and ACCELERATORS statements.

The MENU Statement

The MENU statement defines the contents of a menu resource. The general syntax for the MENU statement is

```
menuID MENU [load options] [mem options]
BEGIN
     item definitions
END
```

The menuID is the unique name or integer ID of the menu resource. The keywords associated with a resource file appear in uppercase letters. This convention is optional, because the keywords are not case-sensitive. However, using uppercase letters makes it easier to distinguish between resource keywords and nonkeywords. The load options are

- PRELOAD, which loads the resource immediately.
- LOADONCALL, which loads the resource as needed. This is the default option.

The `mem options` are

- `FIXED`, which keeps the resource in a fixed memory location.
- `MOVABLE`, which moves the resource when needed for the sake of memory compaction. This option is selected by default.
- `DISCARDABLE`, which discards the resource when no longer needed. This option is also selected by default.

The MENUITEM Statement

The `MENUITEM` statement defines the name and attributes of an actual menu item. The general syntax for the `MENUITEM` statement is

```
MENUITEM text, result [, option list]
```

The `text` field accepts a string literal (enclosed in double quotation marks) that designates the name of the menu item. To define a hot key for a menu item, place the ampersand before the letter you want to designate as a hot key (the selection is *not* case-sensitive). To display the ampersand as part of the menu name, use a sequence of two ampersand characters (`&&`). You can also include the `\t` sequence to insert a tab in the menu item name. You can insert the `\a` sequence to align all text that follows it and flush it right.

The `result` field contains an integer, usually a `CM_xxxx` constant, that represents the command sent by the menu item.

The `option list` can include the following items:

- `CHECKED` displays a check mark next to the menu item.
- `GRAYED` displays the menu item in a gray color to indicate that it is inactive.
- `HELP` places a vertical separator bar to the left of the menu item.
- `INACTIVE` displays the menu item but prevents its selection. This option is usually combined with the `GRAYED` option to provide a better visual indication that the menu item is inactive.
- `MENUBARBREAK` places the menu item on a new line for static menu bar items. In the case of pop-up menu items, `MENUBARBREAK` separates the new and old columns with a vertical line.
- `MENUBREAK` places the menu item on a new line for static menu bar items. For the pop-up menus (presented next), `MENUBREAK` places the menu item in a new column, without any dividing line between the columns.

The POPUP Statement

The POPUP statement defines the beginning of a pop-up menu. The general syntax for the POPUP statement is

```
POPUP text [,option list]
BEGIN
      item definitions
END
```

The text and option list fields are similar to their counterparts in the MENUITEM statement. The item definitions field consists of MENUITEM and other POPUP statements. The latter statements enable you to create nested menus.

The MENUITEM SEPARATOR Statement

MENUITEM SEPARATOR is a special form of the MENUITEM statement that creates an inactive menu item and displays a horizontal bar between two active menu items.

The ACCELERATORS Statement

The ACCELERATORS statement defines one or more accelerators for an ObjectWindows application. An *accelerator* is a keystroke defined to give the application user a quick way to select a menu item and carry out a specific task. The general syntax for the ACCELERATORS statement is

```
accTableName ACCELERATORS
BEGIN
      event, idValue, [type] [NOINVERT] [ALT] [SHIFT] [CONTROL]
END
```

The accTableName field defines a unique name or integer ID that distinguishes an accelerator resource from any other type of resource. The event field specifies the keystroke used as an accelerator. The keystroke can be one of the following:

- A single ASCII character enclosed in double quotation marks. You can place a caret symbol before the character to indicate that it is a control character. In this case, the type field is not required.

- An integer value that designates the ASCII code of a character. In this case, the type field must be the ASCII keyword.

- An integer value that represents a virtual key. In this case, the type field must be the keyword VIRTKEY.

The `idValue` field is an integer that identifies the accelerator. The `type` field is required only when the `event` field is an ASCII character code or a virtual key.

The `NOINVERT` option prevents a top-level menu item from being highlighted when the accelerator is used. The `ALT`, `SHIFT`, and `CONTROL` options activate the accelerator when the Alt, Shift, and Ctrl keys are pressed.

The following is an example of an accelerator resource:

```
"EditKeys" ACCELERATORS
BEGIN
    "h",        IDDHEADING                      ; The H key
    "H",        IDDHOLD                         ; The Shift-H keys
    "^B",       IDDBOLD                         ; The Control-B keys
    64,         IDDADD                          ; The Shift-A keys
    97,         IDDAPPEND                       ; The A key
    "s",        IDDSEARCH, ALT                  ; The Alt-S keys
    VK_F7,      IDDSAVE, VIRTKEY                ; The F7 function key
    VK_F2,      IDDLOAD, SHIFT, VIRTKEY         ; The Shift-F2 keys
    VK_F3,      IDDSAVEAS, CONTROL, VIRTKEY     ; The Ctrl-F3 keys
    VK_F1,      IDDNEW, ALT, SHIFT, VIRTKEY     ; The Alt-Shift-F1 keys
END
```

Creating a Sample Menu

Armed with the information from the last section, I present the contents of the menu resource file MENU1.RC in Listing 2.3. This file contains a single menu definition with the `OPTIONS` name ID. The menu contains three main menu items: File, Edit, and Help. The File and Edit menu items are pop-up menus. The Edit menu options contain the Delete menu item, which is also a pop-up menu. The menu items include horizontal separator bars. All the menu names use the ampersand to define their corresponding hot keys.

The various `MENUITEM` statements contain `CM_xxxx` constants that define the result of selected menu items. Most of the `CM_xxxx` constants are already defined in the WINDOWS.H header file. The `CM_HELP` and `CM_EDITDELETE_BLOCK` constants are customized values that are declared in the MENUS.H header file, shown in Listing 2.4.

With the .RC resource files, you can easily build and update the menus you want to include in an application. Resource files also enable you to build other controls, such as dialog boxes. I discuss the resource script statements for dialog boxes and their various controls in their respective chapters. The UDE for Borland C++ 3.1 automatically compiles the .RC resource files included in a projected file. If you are using version 3.0, you need to compile the resource file before you compile your project file.

To compile the resource file, you can use either the Windows Resource Compiler (a command-line tool) or the Resource Workshop. Using the resource compiler is a very easy and straightforward process: you exit to DOS from Windows, move to the \BORLANDC\OWL\CPPOWL directory, and invoke a simple batch file (call it DORC.BAT) that contains the following command:

```
rc -i\borlandc\include -i\borlandc\owl\include
   -i\borlandc\owl\cppowl -r %1.rc
```

The `rc` command invokes the resource compiler. The `-i` is the include directive, and the `-r` directive tells the resource compiler simply to compile your .RC file into .RES file. (Otherwise, the resource compiler will try to include the resulting .RES file in the application's .EXE file.) This attempt generates a resource compiler error because you haven't yet compiled your application.

Listing 2.5 contains the source code for the MENU1.CPP ObjectWindows application. I derived this program from SECAPP.CPP by adding the `AssignMenu("OPTIONS")` statement to the `TAppWindow` constructor. The `AssignMenu` member function loads the menu with the name `OPTIONS` to the inherited `Twindow::Attr` data member. If a window is already assigned to `Attr`, the old one is removed. In the MENU1.CPP application, the `AssignMenu` function completes the action of the `TAppWindow` constructor.

To compile this application, include the MENU1.CPP, MENU1.RC, and OWL.DEF files in the MENU1.PRJ project file.

Listing 2.3. The source code for the MENU1.RC resource file.

```
#include <windows.h>
#include <owlrc.h>
#include "menus.h"

OPTIONS MENU LOADONCALL MOVEABLE PURE DISCARDABLE
BEGIN
  POPUP "&File"
  BEGIN
    MENUITEM "&New", CM_FILENEW
    MENUITEM "&Open", CM_FILEOPEN
    MENUITEM "&Save", CM_FILESAVE
    MENUITEM "Save&As", CM_FILESAVEAS
```

```
      MENUITEM SEPARATOR
      MENUITEM "E&xit", CM_EXIT
    END
    POPUP "&Edit"
    BEGIN
      MENUITEM "&Undo", CM_EDITUNDO
      MENUITEM SEPARATOR
      MENUITEM "C&ut", CM_EDITCUT
      MENUITEM "C&opy", CM_EDITCOPY
      MENUITEM "&Paste", CM_EDITPASTE
      POPUP "&Delete"
      BEGIN
         MENUITEM "&Line", CM_EDITDELETE
         MENUITEM "&Block", CM_EDITDELETE_BLOCK
      END
      MENUITEM "&Clear", CM_EDITCLEAR
    END
    MENUITEM "&Help", CM_HELP
END
```

Listing 2.4. The contents of the MENUS.H header file.

```
#define CM_HELP 201
#define CM_EDITDELETE_BLOCK 202
```

Listing 2.5. The source code of the MENU1.CPP.

```
#include <owl.h>

// declare the custom application class as
// a subclass of TApplication

class TWinApp : public TApplication
{
public:
  TWinApp(LPSTR   AName,              // application name
          HINSTANCE hInstance,        // instance handle
          HINSTANCE hPrevInstance,    // previous instance handle
          LPSTR   lpCmdLine,          // command-line arguments
          int     nCmdShow) :         // display command
          TApplication(AName, hInstance, hPrevInstance,
                    lpCmdLine, nCmdShow) {};
```

continues

Listing 2.5. continued

```
protected:
  virtual void InitMainWindow();

};


// use the _CLASSDEF macro to declare reference and pointer
// types related to the new TAppWindow class
_CLASSDEF(TAppWindow)

// expand the functionality of TWindow by deriving class TAppWindow
class TAppWindow : public TWindow
{
public:
  TAppWindow(PTWindowsObject AParent, LPSTR ATitle) :
             TWindow(AParent, ATitle)
             { AssignMenu("OPTIONS"); };

  // handle the left mouse button click
  virtual void WMLButtonDown(RTMessage Msg)
      = [WM_FIRST + WM_LBUTTONDOWN];

  // handle the right mouse button click
  virtual void WMRButtonDown(RTMessage Msg)
      = [WM_FIRST + WM_RBUTTONDOWN];

};

void TAppWindow::WMLButtonDown(RTMessage Msg)
{
  MessageBox(HWindow, "You clicked the left button!",
             "Mouse Click Event!", MB_OK);
}

void TAppWindow::WMRButtonDown(RTMessage Msg)
{
  int result;
  MessageBeep(0); // beep

  // prompt user whether he or she want to close the application
  result = MessageBox(HWindow, "Want to close this application",
                      "Query", MB_YESNO | MB_ICONQUESTION);

  // if the user clicked the Yes button, send a WM_CLOSE message
```

```
  // to the application's window
  if (result == IDYES)
     SendMessage(HWindow, WM_CLOSE, 0, 0);
}

void TWinApp::InitMainWindow()
{
  MainWindow = new TAppWindow(NULL, Name);
}

int PASCAL WinMain(HINSTANCE hInstance, HINSTANCE hPrevInstance,
                   LPSTR lpCmdLine, int nCmdShow)
{
  TWinApp WinApp("A Menu-Driven OWL Application", hInstance,
                 hPrevInstance, lpCmdLine, nCmdShow);
  WinApp.Run(); // run OWL application
  return WinApp.Status; // return application status
}
```

Figure 2.3 shows a sample session with the MENU1.EXE application. The figure shows the nested menus defined in the MENU1.RC resource file. The program responds to the left and right mouse button clicks in the same way as the SECAPP.EXE program. The menu items of the MENU1.EXE program are mute, so expect the Exit menu item to which a default response occurs. The Exit menu works because ObjectWindows defines a CMExit response function.

Responding to Menu Selections

Listing 2.5 demonstrates how to build a nested menu and load it into an application. However, selecting the menu items (except for Exit) resulted in no action. This section basically answers the question, "How does an application respond to a menu selection, and can that response load a different menu?"

Look at the contents of resource file MENU2.RC, shown in Listing 2.6. The resource file defines two menus, tagged LONGMENU and SHORTMENU. As the names suggest, the first menu is the longer version of the second one. These menus

Figure 2.3.
A sample session with the MENU1.EXE application.

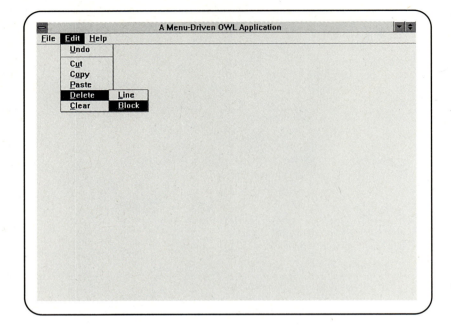

differ from the ones in MENU1.RC in that they are not as nested and use the INACTIVE and GRAYED options. Notice that these two options do not appear with every menu item—they are assigned to the menu items that I include, but keep inactive. As a result, the names of the menu items appear in a gray color and cannot be selected. There are no corresponding C++ message response member functions. By contrast, the menu items without INACTIVE and GRAYED options can be selected and will generate a response, albeit a simple one.

Listing 2.6. The resource script in file MENU2.RC.

```
#include <windows.h>
#include <owlrc.h>
#include "menu2.h"

LONGMENU MENU LOADONCALL MOVEABLE PURE DISCARDABLE
BEGIN
  POPUP "&File"
  BEGIN
    MENUITEM "&New", CM_FILENEW, INACTIVE, GRAYED
    MENUITEM "&Open", CM_FILEOPEN, INACTIVE, GRAYED
    MENUITEM "&Save", CM_FILESAVE, INACTIVE, GRAYED
    MENUITEM "Save&As", CM_FILESAVEAS, INACTIVE, GRAYED
    MENUITEM SEPARATOR
```

```
      MENUITEM "Short &Menus", CM_SHORTMENU
      MENUITEM SEPARATOR
      MENUITEM "E&xit", CM_EXIT
    END
    POPUP "&Edit"
    BEGIN
      MENUITEM "&Undo", CM_EDITUNDO, INACTIVE, GRAYED
      MENUITEM SEPARATOR
      MENUITEM "C&ut", CM_EDITCUT
      MENUITEM "C&opy", CM_EDITCOPY
      MENUITEM "&Paste", CM_EDITPASTE
      MENUITEM "&Delete", CM_EDITDELETE, INACTIVE, GRAYED
      MENUITEM "&Clear", CM_EDITCLEAR, INACTIVE, GRAYED
    END
    MENUITEM "&Help", CM_HELP
END

SHORTMENU MENU LOADONCALL MOVEABLE PURE DISCARDABLE
BEGIN
    POPUP "&File"
    BEGIN
      MENUITEM "&Open", CM_FILEOPEN, INACTIVE, GRAYED
      MENUITEM "Save&As", CM_FILESAVEAS, INACTIVE, GRAYED
      MENUITEM SEPARATOR
      MENUITEM "&Long Menus", CM_LONGMENU
      MENUITEM SEPARATOR
      MENUITEM "E&xit", CM_EXIT
    END
    POPUP "&Edit"
    BEGIN
      MENUITEM "C&ut", CM_EDITCUT
      MENUITEM "C&opy", CM_EDITCOPY
      MENUITEM "&Paste", CM_EDITPASTE
    END
    MENUITEM "&Help", CM_HELP
END
```

The menu items in Listing 2.6 contain two interesting members. The Short &Menus item in menu LONGMENU results in the CM_SHORTMENU command that selects the short menu. The SHORTMENU menu contains a complementary menu item, &Long Menus, that results in the CM_LONGMENU command which selects the long menu.

The user-defined CM_xxxx constants CM_HELP, CM_SHORTMENU, and CM_LONGMENU are defined in the MENU2.H header file, shown in Listing 2.7.

Listing 2.7. The contents of the MENU2.H header file.

```
#define CM_HELP 201
#define CM_SHORTMENU 202
#define CM_LONGMENU 203
```

The source code for the application appears in Listing 2.8.

Listing 2.8. The source code in the file MENU2.CPP.

```
#include <owl.h>
#include "menu2.h"

// declare the custom application class as
// a subclass of TApplication

class TWinApp : public TApplication
{
public:
  TWinApp(LPSTR    AName,            // application name
          HINSTANCE hInstance,        // instance handle
          HINSTANCE hPrevInstance,    // previous instance handle
          LPSTR    lpCmdLine,         // command-line arguments
          int      nCmdShow) :        // display command
          TApplication(AName, hInstance, hPrevInstance,
                       lpCmdLine, nCmdShow) {};
protected:
  virtual void InitMainWindow();

};

// use the _CLASSDEF macro to declare reference and pointer
// types related to the new TAppWindow class
_CLASSDEF(TAppWindow)

// expand the functionality of TWindow by deriving class TAppWindow
class TAppWindow : public TWindow
{
public:
  TAppWindow(PTWindowsObject AParent, LPSTR ATitle) :
              TWindow(AParent, ATitle)
                { AssignMenu("LONGMENU"); };
  // handle the left mouse button click
  virtual void WMLButtonDown(RTMessage Msg)
```

```
                    = [WM_FIRST + WM_LBUTTONDOWN];

    // handle the right mouse button click
    virtual void WMRButtonDown(RTMessage Msg)
                    = [WM_FIRST + WM_RBUTTONDOWN];

    // load the long menu
    virtual void CMLongMenu(RTMessage Msg)
                    = [CM_FIRST + CM_LONGMENU];

    // load the short menu
    virtual void CMShortMenu(RTMessage Msg)
                    = [CM_FIRST + CM_SHORTMENU];

    // exit the application
    virtual void CMExit(RTMessage Msg)
                    = [CM_FIRST + CM_EXIT];

    // get online help
    virtual void CMHelp(RTMessage Msg)
                    = [CM_FIRST + CM_HELP];

    // handle the Cut menu option
    virtual void CMEditCut(RTMessage Msg)
                    = [CM_FIRST + CM_EDITCUT];
    // handle the Copy menu option
    virtual void CMEditCopy(RTMessage Msg)
                    = [CM_FIRST + CM_EDITCOPY];

    // handle the Paste menu option
    virtual void CMEditPaste(RTMessage Msg)
                    = [CM_FIRST + CM_EDITPASTE];

private:
    // display a message "Feature not implemented"
    void notImplemented();
    // prompt user to quit the application
    void promptToQuit();
};

void TAppWindow::WMLButtonDown(RTMessage Msg)
{
    MessageBox(HWindow, "You clicked the left button!",
               "Mouse Click Event!", MB_OK);
```

continues

Listing 2.8. continued

```
}

void TAppWindow::WMRButtonDown(RTMessage Msg)
{
  promptToQuit();
}

// assign the long menu
void TAppWindow::CMLongMenu(RTMessage Msg)
{
  AssignMenu("LONGMENU");
}

// assign the short menu
void TAppWindow::CMShortMenu(RTMessage Msg)
{
  AssignMenu("SHORTMENU");
}

void TAppWindow::CMExit(RTMessage Msg)
{
  promptToQuit();
}

void TAppWindow::CMEditCut(RTMessage Msg)
{
  notImplemented();
}

void TAppWindow::CMEditCopy(RTMessage Msg)
{
  notImplemented();
}

void TAppWindow::CMEditPaste(RTMessage Msg)
{
  notImplemented();
}

void TAppWindow::CMHelp(RTMessage Msg)
{
  MessageBox(HWindow,
    "This a sample one line help (that leaves more to be desired)",
    "Help", MB_OK | MB_ICONINFORMATION);
}
```

```
void TAppWindow::notImplemented()
{
  MessageBox(HWindow, "This feature is not implemented",
             "Information", MB_OK);
}

void TAppWindow::promptToQuit()
{
  int result;
  MessageBeep(0); // beep

  // prompt user if he or she want to close the application
  result = MessageBox(HWindow, "Want to close this application",
                      "Query", MB_YESNO | MB_ICONQUESTION);

  // if the user clicked the Yes button send a WM_CLOSE message
  // to the application's window
  if (result == IDYES)
     SendMessage(HWindow, WM_CLOSE, 0, 0);
}

void TWinApp::InitMainWindow()
{
  MainWindow = new TAppWindow(NULL, Name);
}

int PASCAL WinMain(HINSTANCE hInstance, HINSTANCE hPrevInstance,
                   LPSTR lpCmdLine, int nCmdShow)
{
  TWinApp WinApp("Multi-Menu Application", hInstance,
                 hPrevInstance, lpCmdLine, nCmdShow);
  WinApp.Run(); // run OWL application
  return WinApp.Status; // return application status
}
```

First, notice that the header file MENU2.H appears in an `#include` directive. With this inclusion, the program can work with the user-defined CM_*xxxx* constants in the message response member functions. The source code declares the application class TWinApp and the window class TAppWindow. The second class responds to the various messages. The TAppWindow class declares a constructor and a series of message response member functions. The class constructor calls the TWindow constructor and then AssignMenu with the LONGMENU argument. Consequently, the application's window begins with the long menu.

The `TAppWindow` class declares two private functions, `notImplemented` and `promptToQuit`. The first function displays a message box containing the note. This feature is not implemented. In fact, this message box is the common response to most menu items. The `promptToQuit` function prompts you to close the application with a message box containing Yes and No buttons.

Now look at the message response member functions of `TAppWindow`. The first two functions are identical to those in the previous applications—they respond to mouse clicks on the window. The current version of the `WMRButtonDown` function now calls the `promptToQuit` function.

Note: Menus are part of a window and therefore menu messages are sent to the window; therefore, the command response methods must be in the window subclass.

The `CMLongMenu` member function responds to the user-defined `CM_LONGMENU` command. The extended syntax of the member function declaration includes the expression `CM_FIRST + CM_LONGMENU` to indicate that the function responds to a command message. The `CMLongMenu` calls the `AssignMenu` with the `LONGMENU` argument to load the long menu. The `CMShortMenu` is coded similarly and responds to the `CM_SHORTMENU` command to load the short menu.

The `CMExit` member function provides a new response to the Exit menu selection (which generates the `CM_EXIT` command). In the last program, when you select Exit, the application closes without any confirmation. The `CMExit` function calls the private member function `promptToQuit`, which confirms your request to close the application.

The `CMHelp` member function responds to the user-defined `CM_HELP` command by providing a one-line help message box. The message box appears with an OK button and an information icon (an *i* enclosed in a circle).

The member functions `CMEditCut`, `CMEditCopy`, and `CMEditPaste` all invoke the private member function `notImplemented`. This is the common (and symbolic) response that I provide for the `CM_EDITCUT`, `CM_EDITCOPY`, and `CM_EDITPASTE` commands.

To create the application, include MENU2.CPP, MENU2.RC, and OWL.DEF files in the MENU2.PRJ project file. Figure 2.4 shows a sample session with the MENU2.EXE application. When you run the application, use the Long Menu and Short Menu selections to toggle between the two forms of menus. In addition, select the Help item to call the one-line help message box. Select the Edit Cut, Edit Copy, and Edit Paste items to view the response. Notice the inactive menu items when you navigate through the various menus.

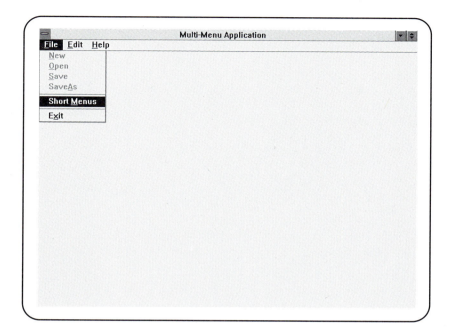

Figure 2.4. A sample session with the MENU2.EXE application.

Creating Multiple Instances

One of the powerful advantages of Windows is the ability to run multiple instances of the same application. This feature is backed by a smart scheme that saves memory and other system resources by pooling common code and data segments. Thus, you can load, for example, three instances of a scientific calculator and work independently with them. This section discusses how to create multiple instances of an ObjectWindows application. To make the example application more interesting, the first instance has a different window title and menu than all the other instances. Listing 2.9 shows the resource script file MENU3.RC and Listing 2.10 shows the source code for the MENU3.CPP ObjectWindows application file.

Listing 2.9. The resource script in file MENU3.RC.

```
#include <windows.h>
#include <owlrc.h>
#include "menus.h"
```

continues

Listing 2.9. continued

```
  MAINMENU MENU LOADONCALL MOVEABLE PURE DISCARDABLE
BEGIN
POPUP "&File"
  BEGIN
    MENUITEM "&New", CM_FILENEW, INACTIVE, GRAYED
    MENUITEM "&Open", CM_FILEOPEN, INACTIVE, GRAYED
    MENUITEM "&Save", CM_FILESAVE, INACTIVE, GRAYED
    MENUITEM "Save&As", CM_FILESAVEAS, INACTIVE, GRAYED
    MENUITEM SEPARATOR
    MENUITEM "E&xit", CM_EXIT
  END
  POPUP "&Edit"
  BEGIN
    MENUITEM "&Undo", CM_EDITUNDO, INACTIVE, GRAYED
    MENUITEM SEPARATOR
    MENUITEM "C&ut", CM_EDITCUT
    MENUITEM "C&opy", CM_EDITCOPY
    MENUITEM "&Paste", CM_EDITPASTE
    MENUITEM "&Delete", CM_EDITDELETE, INACTIVE, GRAYED
    MENUITEM "&Clear", CM_EDITCLEAR, INACTIVE, GRAYED
  END
  MENUITEM "&Help", CM_HELP
END
SECONDMENU MENU LOADONCALL MOVEABLE PURE DISCARDABLE
BEGIN
  POPUP "&File"
  BEGIN
    MENUITEM "&Open", CM_FILEOPEN, INACTIVE, GRAYED
    MENUITEM "Save&As", CM_FILESAVEAS, INACTIVE, GRAYED
    MENUITEM SEPARATOR
    MENUITEM "E&xit", CM_EXIT
  END
  POPUP "&Edit"
  BEGIN
    MENUITEM "C&ut", CM_EDITCUT
    MENUITEM "C&opy", CM_EDITCOPY
    MENUITEM "&Paste", CM_EDITPASTE
  END
  MENUITEM "&Help", CM_HELP
END
```

Listing 2.10. The source code for the file MENU3.CPP.

```cpp
#include <owl.h>
#include <string.h>
#include "menu2.h"
// declare the custom application class as
// a subclass of TApplication

class TWinApp : public TApplication
{
public:
  TWinApp(LPSTR   AName,            // application name
          HINSTANCE hInstance,      // instance handle
          HINSTANCE hPrevInstance,  // previous instance handle
          LPSTR   lpCmdLine,        // command-line arguments
          int     nCmdShow);        // display command

protected:
  char WinCaption[30]; // title of window
  virtual void InitMainWindow();
  virtual void InitApplication();
};
// use the _CLASSDEF macro to declare reference and pointer
// types related to the new TAppWindow class
_CLASSDEF(TAppWindow)

// expand the functionality of TWindow by deriving class TAppWindow
class TAppWindow : public TWindow
{
public:
  TAppWindow(PTWindowsObject AParent,
             LPSTR ATitle);

  // handle the left mouse button click
  virtual void WMLButtonDown(RTMessage Msg)
      = [WM_FIRST + WM_LBUTTONDOWN];

  // handle the right mouse button click
  virtual void WMRButtonDown(RTMessage Msg)
      = [WM_FIRST + WM_RBUTTONDOWN];

  // exit the application
  virtual void CMExit(RTMessage Msg)
      = [CM_FIRST + CM_EXIT];
```

continues

Listing 2.10. continued

```
    // get online help
  virtual void CMHelp(RTMessage Msg)
       = [CM_FIRST + CM_HELP];

  // handle the Cut menu option
  virtual void CMEditCut(RTMessage Msg)
       = [CM_FIRST + CM_EDITCUT];
// handle the Copy menu option
  virtual void CMEditCopy(RTMessage Msg)
       = [CM_FIRST + CM_EDITCOPY];

  // handle the Paste menu option
  virtual void CMEditPaste(RTMessage Msg)
       = [CM_FIRST + CM_EDITPASTE];

private:
  // display a message "Feature not implemented"
  void notImplemented();
  // prompt user to quit the application
  void promptToQuit();
};

TAppWindow::TAppWindow(PTWindowsObject AParent,
                       LPSTR ATitle) :
                       TWindow(AParent, ATitle)
{
  if (GetApplication()->hPrevInstance == 0)
    AssignMenu("MAINMENU");
  else
    AssignMenu("SECONDMENU");

};

void TAppWindow::WMLButtonDown(RTMessage Msg)
{
  MessageBox(HWindow, "You clicked the left button!",
             "Mouse Click Event!", MB_OK);
}

void TAppWindow::WMRButtonDown(RTMessage Msg)
{
  promptToQuit();
}

void TAppWindow::CMExit(RTMessage Msg)
```

```cpp
{
  promptToQuit();
}

void TAppWindow::CMEditCut(RTMessage Msg)
{
  notImplemented();
}

void TAppWindow::CMEditCopy(RTMessage Msg)
{
  notImplemented();
}

void TAppWindow::CMEditPaste(RTMessage Msg)
{
  notImplemented();
}

void TAppWindow::CMHelp(RTMessage Msg)
{
  MessageBox(HWindow,
    "This a sample one line help (that leaves more to be desired)",
    "Help", MB_OK | MB_ICONINFORMATION);
}

void TAppWindow::notImplemented()
{
  MessageBox(HWindow, "This feature is not implemented",
             "Information", MB_OK);
}

void TAppWindow::promptToQuit()
{
  int result;
  MessageBeep(0); // beep

  // prompt user whether he or she want to close the application
  result = MessageBox(HWindow, "Want to close this application",
                      "Query", MB_YESNO | MB_ICONQUESTION);

  // if the user clicked the Yes button send a WM_CLOSE message
  // to the application's window
  if (result == IDYES)
     SendMessage(HWindow, WM_CLOSE, 0, 0);
}
```

continues

Listing 2.10. continued

```
TWinApp::TWinApp(LPSTR  AName, HINSTANCE hInstance,
                 HINSTANCE hPrevInstance, LPSTR  lpCmdLine,
                 int nCmdShow) :
          TApplication(AName, hInstance, hPrevInstance,
                       lpCmdLine, nCmdShow)
{
  strcpy(WinCaption, "A Secondary Window");
};

void TWinApp::InitApplication()
{
  strcpy(WinCaption, "The Main Window");
}

void TWinApp::InitMainWindow()
{
  MainWindow = new TAppWindow(NULL, WinCaption);
}

int PASCAL WinMain(HINSTANCE hInstance, HINSTANCE hPrevInstance,
                   LPSTR lpCmdLine, int nCmdShow)
{
  TWinApp WinApp("Multi-Menu Multi-Window Application",
                 hInstance, hPrevInstance, lpCmdLine,
                 nCmdShow);
  WinApp.Run(); // run OWL application
  return WinApp.Status; // return application status
}
```

How can you create a different first instance? In this case, the first instance possesses a different window title and menu than all other instances. To implement this feature, recall the following sequence that calls to the application class constructor and member functions:

1. The `TWinApp` application class constructor is automatically called to create an instance of the application. This initialization should include a statement that stores the default window title (used for all instances except the first one) in the special data member. Call this special data member `WinCaption`.

2. Declare the protected `TWinApp::InitApplication` member function to assign the special window title to the `WinCaption` member of the first instance. This assignment overwrites the default window title previously assigned to data member `WinCaption`.

3. Include the following special menu assignment code in the constructor of the custom window class:

```
TAppWindow::TAppWindow(PTWindowsObject AParent,
                       LPSTR ATitle) :
                       TWindow(AParent, ATitle)
{
  if (GetApplication()->hPrevInstance == 0)
    AssignMenu("MAINMENU");
  else
    AssignMenu("SECONDMENU");
};
```

With the expression `GetApplication()->hPrevInstance`, you can access the `hPrevInstance` data member of the current application. Comparing this expression with 0 tests whether there is a previous instance. If the test is TRUE, the window class constructor is dealing with the first instance and then assigns the special menu for that first instance. If the test is FALSE, the constructor assigns the default menu for all other instances.

The MENU3.RC defines two menus, MAINMENU and SECONDMENU. These menus are similar to the menus LONGMENU and SHORTMENU found in MENU2.RC, except they do not contain the toggle menu items.

The first instance has the window title The Main Window. Every other instance has the window title A Secondary Window. In MENU3.CPP, notice that the application name (which is supplied to the TWinApp constructor) is not the window title.

The instances of TWinApp respond to the mouse button click in a manner similar to the MENU3.EXE program. Likewise, the menu options produce a similar response to MENU3.EXE. Figure 2.5 shows a sample session with four instances of the MENU3.EXE ObjectWindows application.

Closing a Window

Recall that the MENU1.EXE enabled the user to exit the application and close its window by simply selecting the Exit menu item. Using the default response, the application quickly terminates the program. Although this abrupt exit is harmless for the MENU1.EXE program, it is a feature that—if maintained—will drown software developers with hate letters from application users! Therefore, a Windows application should close its window only after making sure that the user does not lose data. In addition, the application should make any other appropriate shutdown operations.

Figure 2.5.
A sample session with the MENU3.EXE application.

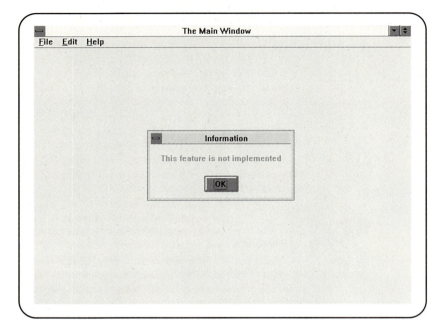

Note: Both Windows and ObjectWindows offer a sophisticated sequence for carefully closing down an application to include all of the child windows. In fact, the process resembles a query of all related objects that can veto the closing of the target window in response to the WM_CLOSE message. You need to know about your contribution to the process of closing your application's window. By declaring the member function CanClose in your custom window classes, you provide your application with an additional say (or vote, if you prefer) in the matter of closing a window. The CanClose member function that you declare focuses on the special closing criteria of your own application. In most cases, make sure the user does not exit the application if there is new or altered data that has not been saved. Other criteria might include the deallocation of special dynamic data.

To demonstrate the inclusion of the CanClose member function and how that inclusion can streamline the closing of a window, consider the source code in Listing 2.11. The ObjectWindows program is a revised version of SECAPP.CPP. The most important change is the declaration of the Boolean member function CanClose in the custom window class TAppWindow:

```
BOOL TAppWindow::CanClose()
{
return MessageBox(HWindow, "Want to close this application",
                  "Query", MB_YESNO | MB_ICONQUESTION) == IDYES;
}
```

Listing 2.11. The source code for the MENU4.CPP program file.

```
#include <owl.h>

// declare the custom application class as
// a subclass of TApplication

class TWinApp : public TApplication
{
public:
   TWinApp(LPSTR    AName,              // application name
           HINSTANCE hInstance,         // instance handle
           HINSTANCE hPrevInstance,     // previous instance handle
           LPSTR    lpCmdLine,          // command-line arguments
           int      nCmdShow) :         // display command
           TApplication(AName, hInstance, hPrevInstance,
                     lpCmdLine, nCmdShow) {};

protected:
   virtual void InitMainWindow();

};


// use the _CLASSDEF macro to declare reference and pointer
// types related to the new TAppWindow class
_CLASSDEF(TAppWindow)

// expand the functionality of TWindow by deriving class TAppWindow
class TAppWindow : public TWindow
{
public:
   TAppWindow(PTWindowsObject AParent, LPSTR ATitle) :
                 TWindow(AParent, ATitle)
                 { AssignMenu("OPTIONS"); };

   // handle the left mouse button click
   virtual void WMLButtonDown(RTMessage Msg)
       = [WM_FIRST + WM_LBUTTONDOWN];
```

continues

Listing 2.11. continued

```
  // handle the right mouse button click
  virtual void WMRButtonDown(RTMessage Msg)
      = [WM_FIRST + WM_RBUTTONDOWN];

  virtual BOOL CanClose();
};

void TAppWindow::WMLButtonDown(RTMessage Msg)
{
  MessageBox(HWindow, "You clicked the left button!",
           "Mouse Click Event!", MB_OK);
}

void TAppWindow::WMRButtonDown(RTMessage Msg)
{
  SendMessage(HWindow, WM_CLOSE, 0, 0);
}

BOOL TAppWindow::CanClose()
{
  return MessageBox(HWindow, "Want to close this application",
                  "Query", MB_YESNO | MB_ICONQUESTION) == IDYES;
}

void TWinApp::InitMainWindow()
{
  MainWindow = new TAppWindow(NULL, Name);
}

int PASCAL WinMain(HINSTANCE hInstance, HINSTANCE hPrevInstance,
                LPSTR lpCmdLine, int nCmdShow)
{
  TWinApp WinApp("A Simple OWL Application", hInstance,
              hPrevInstance, lpCmdLine, nCmdShow);
  WinApp.Run(); // run OWL application
  return WinApp.Status; // return application status
}
```

The code for `CanClose` is very simple in this case and consists of a straightforward call to the API function `MessageBox`. The message box displays its query message along with Yes and No buttons and an information icon. The `CanClose` function compares the result of `MessageBox` with the constant `IDYES` and returns the Boolean result.

Declaring the `CanClose` member function also enables the programmer to rewrite the statement for the `WMRButtonDown` member function. The new version has a simple code—one that relies on the `CanClose` function. The `WMRButtonDown` member function simply sends a `WM_CLOSE` message to its own window by using the API function `SendMessage` and lets the `CanClose` member function handle the message. If you add a menu with the Exit option (which results in the `CM_EXIT` command), the `CanClose` function will also handle the created message by selecting the Exit menu item. There is no need for a `CMExit` member function because the application uses the default `CMExit` function.

Summary

This chapter examined the basics of creating ObjectWindows applications. In this chapter you learned about the following topics:

- Creating a minimal ObjectWindows application that offers predefined operations and default responses.

- Extending the window operations to handle mouse clicks that result in the display of simple message boxes.

- Adding a menu with nested menu structures to demonstrate the use of resource script files in building sophisticated menus.

- Responding to menu selections that included changing menu structures at run-time.

- Creating multiple instances of an ObjectWindows application and giving the first instance a different window title and menu structure.

- Closing a window using the special `CanClose` member function to confirm a window's closing.

This chapter begins to give you a feel of how the components of an ObjectWindows application work together like the employees of a company. The simple interaction provided by the various programs only scratched the surface of the complex world of Windows and ObjectWindows. The next chapter focuses more on the window classes and presents applications that place text in the windows.

CHAPTER 3

Creating Basic Windows

The most relevant aspect of the Windows environment, as the name suggests, is the use of windows. Typically, a window is a visible part of the screen that contains specific information. Windows are the placeholders of information. In this chapter, I discuss the attributes used in creating windows and altering their components (including scroll bars). You will learn about the following:

- Creating a read-only text window
- Writing text in a window
- Registering a window class
- Changing a cursor at run-time
- Creating child windows
- Scrolling through text using scroll bars
- Investigating the auto scroll and track modes of a scroll bar
- Changing the scroll bar metrics (including the units, line size, page size, and ranges of a scroll bar)
- Examining internally induced scrolling
- Optimizing the `Paint` member function

Creating a Read-Only Text Window

The last chapter, "Creating Basic ObjectWindows Applications," presented a number of menu-driven ObjectWindows applications. However, these programs could not display any information inside their windows. This section

presents an ObjectWindows application that displays read-only text in its window. The basic notion of the application is similar to read-only online help windows.

The program demonstrates how to display text and maintain that text after one or more of the following has occurred:

- Resizing the window
- Minimizing and then normalizing or maximizing the window
- Moving a modal dialog box over the text area
- Moving another window that was covering the read-only text

The main tools required to implement the application's features are the `TextOut` API function and the `Paint` member function. The `TextOut` function writes a character string on the specified display. The text appears in the currently selected font and at the specified window coordinates. The general syntax of the `TextOut` function is

```
TextOut(HDC hDC, int X, int X, LPSTR lpString, int nCount)
```

The `hDC` parameter specifies the device context. The `X` and `Y` parameters identify the window location where the first character will appear. The `lpString` parameter points to the string that will be displayed in the window. The `nCount` parameter indicates the leading number of characters of `lpString` to display. The argument for the last parameter is usually the size of the displayed string argument.

By itself, the `TextOut` API function displays text once. This means that altering the viewing area of the window or moving another window over the displayed text erases it. You need a mechanism to update the display of text in the window. Enter the `Paint` member function, which enables you to display and maintain the contents of a window (both text and graphics). The `Paint` function is versatile because it is called by `WMPaint` whenever the window and its viewing area are altered. This update feature includes the initial creation of the window (after all, it is resized from nothing). Consequently, the versatility of `Paint` includes setting the initial display as well as maintaining it.

The parameters of member function `Paint` enable you to display text and draw graphics with various tools. The member function `TWindow::Paint` has no statements. Therefore, your own version of `Paint` does not need to call `TWindow::Paint` before performing its own window displaying and updating tasks.

Now look at the program source code. Listing 3.1 shows the script for the resource file WINDOW1.RC. This resource file defines a menu with a single menu item, Exit, to exit the application.

> **Note:** You need to declare a Paint member function in your window class. The code you place inside your version of the Paint function determines what information appears, remains, and disappears. In the case of this ObjectWindows application, I am displaying the same information from start to finish. The protected TWindow::Paint member function is declared as follows:
>
> virtual void Paint(HDC PaintDC, PAINTSTRUCT _FAR & PaintInfo)

Listing 3.1. The script for the resource file WINDOW1.RC.

```
#include <windows.h>
#include <owlrc.h>

EXITMENU MENU LOADONCALL MOVEABLE PURE DISCARDABLE
BEGIN
    MENUITEM "E&xit", CM_EXIT
END
```

Listing 3.2 shows the source code for the WINDOW1.CPP program file. The part of the program relevant to this application is the TAppWindow class and its member functions. The window class declares a constructor and three member functions: WMLButtonDown, CanClose, and Paint. The constructor invokes the constructor of the parent class and calls the AssignMenu member function to load the EXITMENU menu resource.

Listing 3.2. The source code for the WINDOW1.CPP program file.

```
#include <string.h>
#include <owl.h>

// declare the custom application class as
// a subclass of TApplication

class TWinApp : public TApplication
{
public:
  TWinApp(LPSTR    AName,         // application name
          HINSTANCE hInstance,    // instance handle
```

continues

Listing 3.2. continued

```
           HINSTANCE hPrevInstance, // previous instance handle
           LPSTR     lpCmdLine,     // command-line arguments
           int       nCmdShow) :    // display command
      TApplication(AName, hInstance, hPrevInstance,
                   lpCmdLine, nCmdShow) {};

protected:
  virtual void InitMainWindow();

};


// use the _CLASSDEF macro to declare reference and pointer
// types related to the new TAppWindow class
_CLASSDEF(TAppWindow)

// expand the functionality of TWindow by deriving class TAppWindow
class TAppWindow : public TWindow
{
public:

  TAppWindow(PTWindowsObject AParent, LPSTR ATitle);

  // handle the left mouse button click
  virtual void WMLButtonDown(RTMessage Msg)
       = [WM_FIRST + WM_LBUTTONDOWN];

  // handle closing the window
  virtual BOOL CanClose();

protected:
  // handle painting the window
  void Paint(HDC DC, PAINTSTRUCT& P);

};

TAppWindow::TAppWindow(PTWindowsObject AParent, LPSTR ATitle) :
                 TWindow(AParent, ATitle)
{
  AssignMenu("EXITMENU");
}

void TAppWindow::WMLButtonDown(RTMessage Msg)
{
```

```
    MessageBox(HWindow, "You clicked the left mouse button",
               "Information!", MB_OK | MB_ICONINFORMATION);
}

void TAppWindow::Paint(HDC DC, PAINTSTRUCT& P)
{

  const MAX_LINES = 3;
  const LINE_INCR = 20;
  char Lines[3][40] = {"This is line 1",
                       "This is line 2",
                       "This is line 3"};

  for (BYTE i = 0; i < MAX_LINES; i++)
    TextOut(DC, 0, i * LINE_INCR,
            Lines[i], strlen(Lines[i]));
}

BOOL TAppWindow::CanClose()
{
  return MessageBox(HWindow, "Want to close this application",
                    "Query", MB_YESNO | MB_ICONQUESTION) == IDYES;
}

void TWinApp::InitMainWindow()
{
  MainWindow = new TAppWindow(NULL, Name);
}

int PASCAL WinMain(HINSTANCE hInstance, HINSTANCE hPrevInstance,
                   LPSTR lpCmdLine, int nCmdShow)
{
  TWinApp WinApp("A Simple Read-Only Text Window",
                 hInstance, hPrevInstance, lpCmdLine, nCmdShow);
  WinApp.Run(); // run OWL application
  return WinApp.Status; // return application status
}
```

The Paint function is the main point of interest, for it declares two constants and a three member string array. This array contains the three displayed text lines. The Paint function displays these lines using a for loop and the TextOut API function. Notice the arguments of the TextOut function. The first argument is DC, the handle to a display context, which is also the first parameter of the Paint function. The arguments for placing the text are 0 (for parameter X) and i * LINE_INCR (for parameter Y). These values display the text, starting with

the left margin of the window. The constant `LINE_INCR` represents the total height of a line, taking into account both the height of the displayed characters and the line spacing.

To create the WINDOW1.EXE ObjectWindows application, you need to create a make file that contains the WINDOW1.CPP, WINDOW1.RC, and OWL.DEF files.

Compile and run the application. Notice that the three lines of text appear when the window is created. You can alter the size of the window by resizing it, minimizing it, maximizing it, and restoring it back to normal. The lines of text are always visible (or at least a portion of them) as long as the top-left portion of the screen is not obscured by another window. You can also click the left mouse button to display a message box. Drag that message box over the text lines and release the mouse. Then drag the message box away from the text location. What do you see? The text lines reappear—`Paint` is constantly at work. Figure 3.1 shows a sample session with the WINDOW1.EXE application.

Figure 3.1.
A sample session with the WINDOW1.EXE application.

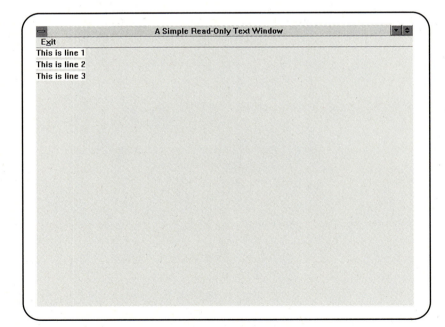

Writing Text in a Window

The WINDOW1.EXE program only displayed fixed text by using `TextOut` and `Paint`. This section presents an application that lets you place your own text on-screen by following these steps:

1. Move the mouse to the location where you want to place your text.
2. Click the left mouse button. This results in the appearance of an input dialog box.
3. Type (and edit) the text you want to appear.
4. When you are finished entering text, click the OK button or press the Enter key. The text you typed in the input dialog box appears in the window at the location of the mouse click. To abort this step, click the Cancel button.

The application enables you to enter up to 10 strings, each of which can be 40 characters long. If you attempt to enter an 11th string, the program beeps.

This application introduces new elements that use an input dialog box and store the various texts that you type. The dialog box is a resource defined in the INPUTDIA.DLG file, which is located by default in the \BORLANDC\ OWL\INCLUDE directory.

Listing 3.3 provides the script for the resource file WINDOW2.RC. This file declares a menu with two items, Clear and Exit. The Clear menu item issues the predefined `CM_EDITCLEAR` command to clear the window. The Exit menu item sends a `CM_EXIT` command to close the window. Notice that the .RC file also contains an include directive for the INPUTDIA.DLG resource file.

Listing 3.3. The script for the resource file WINDOW2.RC.

```
#include <windows.h>
#include <owlrc.h>
#include <inputdia.dlg>

MAINMENU MENU LOADONCALL MOVEABLE PURE DISCARDABLE
BEGIN
    MENUITEM "&Clear", CM_EDITCLEAR
    MENUITEM "E&xit", CM_EXIT
END
```

Listing 3.4 contains the source code for the WINDOW2.CPP program file. Notice that the file includes the INPUTDIA.H header file that contains the declaration of the ObjectWindows `TInputDialog` class. The functionality of the `TInputDialog` class supports the required input dialog box. The program also declares global constants that define the maximum number of strings, maximum length of a string (excluding the space required for the ASCII 0 delimiter character), and the height of a text line.

Listing 3.4. The source code for the WINDOW2.CPP program file.

```
#include <string.h>
#include <owl.h>
#include <inputdia.h>

const MAX_STRINGS = 10;
const MAX_STRING_LEN = 40;
const LINE_INCR = 20;

// declare the custom application class as
// a subclass of TApplication

class TWinApp : public TApplication
{
public:
  TWinApp(LPSTR     AName,           // application name
          HINSTANCE hInstance,       // instance handle
          HINSTANCE hPrevInstance,   // previous instance handle
          LPSTR     lpCmdLine,       // command-line arguments
          int       nCmdShow) :      // display command
          TApplication(AName, hInstance, hPrevInstance,
                  lpCmdLine, nCmdShow) {};
protected:
  virtual void InitMainWindow();

};

// use the _CLASSDEF macro to declare reference and pointer
// types related to the new TAppWindow class
_CLASSDEF(TAppWindow)

// expand the functionality of TWindow by deriving class TAppWindow
class TAppWindow : public TWindow
{
public:
```

```
    TAppWindow(PTWindowsObject AParent, LPSTR ATitle);

    // handle the left mouse button click
    virtual void WMLButtonDown(RTMessage Msg)
        = [WM_FIRST + WM_LBUTTONDOWN];

    // handle clearing the window
    virtual void CMEditClear(RTMessage Msg)
        = [CM_FIRST + CM_EDITCLEAR];

    // handle closing the window
    virtual BOOL CanClose();

protected:
    int numStrings; // current number of strings
    POINT Coord[MAX_STRINGS]; // array of coordinates
    char Lines[MAX_STRINGS][MAX_STRING_LEN+1]; // array of strings

    // handle painting the window
    virtual void Paint(HDC DC, PAINTSTRUCT& P);
};

TAppWindow::TAppWindow(PTWindowsObject AParent, LPSTR ATitle) :
                 TWindow(AParent, ATitle)
{
    AssignMenu("MAINMENU");
    numStrings = 0;
    for (int i = 0; i < MAX_STRINGS; i++)
        Lines[i][0] = '\0';
}

void TAppWindow::WMLButtonDown(RTMessage Msg)
{
    HDC DC;

    if (numStrings < MAX_STRINGS) {
        if (GetApplication()->ExecDialog(
            new TInputDialog(this, "Text Input", "Enter a string",
                             Lines[numStrings],
                             sizeof(Lines[numStrings]))) == IDOK)
        {
            // store the coordinates of the mouse click
            Coord[numStrings].x = Msg.LP.Lo;
            Coord[numStrings].y = Msg.LP.Hi;
            DC = GetDC(HWindow);
```

continues

Listing 3.4. continued

```
      TextOut(DC, Msg.LP.Lo, Msg.LP.Hi,
              Lines[numStrings], strlen(Lines[numStrings]));
      ReleaseDC(HWindow, DC);
      numStrings++;
    }
  }
  else
    MessageBeep(0);
}

void TAppWindow::CMEditClear(RTMessage Msg)
{
  // clear the strings
  while (numStrings > 0)
    Lines[--numStrings][0] = '\0';
  InvalidateRect(HWindow, NULL, TRUE);
}

void TAppWindow::Paint(HDC DC, PAINTSTRUCT& P)
{
  if (numStrings > 0)
    for (BYTE i = 0; i < numStrings; i++)
      TextOut(DC, Coord[i].x, Coord[i].y,
              Lines[i], strlen(Lines[i]));
}

BOOL TAppWindow::CanClose()
{
  return MessageBox(HWindow, "Want to close this application",
                    "Query", MB_YESNO | MB_ICONQUESTION) == IDYES;
}

void TWinApp::InitMainWindow()
{
  MainWindow = new TAppWindow(NULL, Name);
}

int PASCAL WinMain(HINSTANCE hInstance, HINSTANCE hPrevInstance,
                   LPSTR lpCmdLine, int nCmdShow)
{
  TWinApp WinApp("A SimpleText Window",
                 hInstance, hPrevInstance, lpCmdLine, nCmdShow);
  WinApp.Run(); // run OWL application
  return WinApp.Status; // return application status
}
```

Creating Basic Windows

Concerning the classes declared in the application, the application window class, TAppWindow, provides the desired operations. The declaration of the TAppWindow class includes a class constructor, three public message response member functions, and the protected Paint member function. The protected section also contains the declaration of the data members numStrings, Coord, and Lines. The numStrings member stores the current number of strings. The POINT-typed array Coord stores the coordinates of the left button mouse clicks. The member Lines stores the text that you type.

The class constructor performs a few tasks, which include loading the MAINMENU menu resource, assigning zero to the data member numString, and assigning null strings to the members of the Lines array.

The WMLButtonDown member function prompts you to enter text and writes that text at the location where you clicked the left mouse button. The member function first checks whether you have run out of string space. If not, the function performs the following tasks:

- Invokes a dynamic instance (on the heap) rather than a static instance (in the program's data or stack segment) of TInputDialog to execute a modal input dialog box. The box displays the caption Text Input and the prompt message of Enter a string. Enter some text and click the OK button to proceed.

- Stores the coordinates of the mouse click in a member of array Coord. The x and y coordinates are given by the expressions Msg.LP.Lo and Msg.LP.Hi, respectively.

- Calls the GetDC API function to create a device context for writing the string you just entered. The device context is now associated with the HWindow window handle.

- Invokes the TextOut API function to display the text at the mouse click location.

> **Caution:** At this point, the WMLButtonDown function releases the device context DC associated with the window handle HWindow. This step is very important, because it prevents your system from running out of memory.

- Increments the number of current strings, stored in data member numStrings.

The `CMClear` member function clears the window by performing the following tasks:

- Assigns zero to the `numStrings` data member.
- Clears the members of the array `Lines`.

> **Note:** At this point, `WMLButtonDown` invokes the API function **`InvalidateRect`** to clear the application's window.

The `Paint` member function redraws all the currently available strings. The `numString` data member provides the count for the current number of strings to be drawn. The member function invokes the **`TextOut`** API function by using the arguments `Coord[i].x` and `Coord[i].y` to specify the coordinates of the output text. In addition, the function uses the arguments `Lines[i]` and `strlen(Lines[i])` to specify the output text and the number of output characters, respectively.

> **Note:** This version of `Paint` shows how the function decides what to display and what not to display.

To create the WINDOW2.EXE ObjectWindows application, create a resource file that contains the WINDOW.CPP, WINDOW2.RC, and OWL.DEF files. You also need to compile the resource file before linking the application's .OBJ file.

Compile and run the application. Initially, the window is clear. Click the left mouse button to pop up an input dialog box. Next, type your name and click the OK button. Your name appears at the location where you clicked the left mouse button. Repeat this process a few times, entering more text. When a few strings are visible, shrink and expand the size of the window. What do you see? The visible part (based on the current window size) of the text you typed is still there. Once again, you witness the power of `Paint`. Click the Clear menu item to clear the window and repeat the process. Figure 3.2 shows a sample session with the WINDOW2.EXE application.

Creating Basic Windows

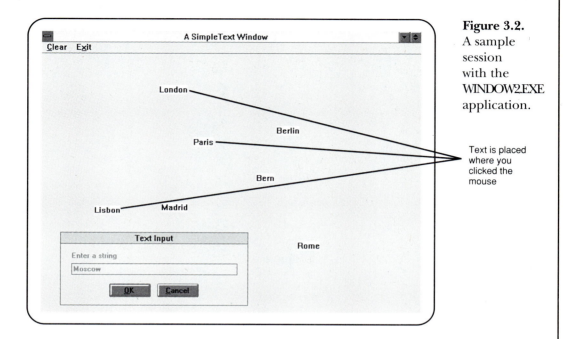

Figure 3.2. A sample session with the WINDOW2.EXE application.

Text is placed where you clicked the mouse

Creating Windows

Whether you program with or without ObjectWindows, you can still create windows that have various attributes and styles. For example, you can incorporate vertical and horizontal scroll bars. You can also include or exclude a caption. These attributes are assigned to newly created windows and are stored in the TWindow::Attr data member that has the TWindowAttr type. The latter type is declared in file WINDOW.H as follows:

```
struct _CLASSTYPE TWindowAttr {
    DWORD Style;
    DWORD ExStyle;
    int X, Y, W, H;
    LPSTR Menu;    // Menu name
    int Id ;       // Child identifier
    LPSTR Param;
};
```

The Style data member specifies the style of the created window. Table 3.1 shows some of the window styles. You can combine a number of window styles (assuming they do not conflict with each other) by using the bitwise OR operator. The `ExStyle` data member designates the extended window styles. Under Windows 3.0, there are only two extended styles, `WS_EX_DLGMODALFRAME` and `WS_EX_NOPARENTNOTIFY`. Windows 3.1 has five extended styles, adding `WS_EX_ACCEPTFILES`, `WS_EX_TOPMOST`, and `WS_EX_TRANSPARENT`. These extended styles are beyond the scope of this book. Consult the Microsoft Windows API documentation to learn more about the extended window styles.

Table 3.1. The window styles.

Style	*Meaning*
`WS_BORDER`	Creates a window that has a border.
`WS_CAPTION`	Creates a window that has a caption. This style requires that the `WS_BORDER` style is also selected.
`WS_CHILD`	Creates a child window. Cannot be selected with the `WS_POPUP` style.
`WS_CHILDWINDOW`	Creates a child window with the `WS_CHILD` style.
`WS_CLIPCHILDREN`	Excludes the area held by child windows when drawing inside the parent window. You use this style when creating the parent window.
`WS_CLIPSIBLINGS`	Clips child windows relative to each other.
`WS_DISABLED`	Creates a window that is initially disabled.
`WS_HSCROLL`	Creates a window that has a horizontal scroll bar.
`WS_ICONIC`	Creates a window that is originally iconic (that is minimized). This style is used only with the `WS_OVERLAPPED` style.
`WS_MAXIMIZED`	Creates a window that has a maximum size.
`WS_MAXIMIZEBOX`	Creates a window that has a maximize box.
`WS_MINIMIZE`	Creates a window that has a minimum size.
`WS_MINIMIZEBOX`	Creates a window that has a minimize box.
`WS_OVERLAPPED`	Creates an overlapped window with a caption and a border.
`WS_POPUP`	Creates a pop-up window. This style cannot be used with the `WS_CHILD` style.
`WS_POPUPWINDOW`	Creates a window with the `WS_OVERLAPPED`, `WS_CAPTION`, `WS_SYSMENU`, `WS_THICKFRAME`, `WS_MINIMIZEBOX`, and `WS_MAXIMIZEBOX` styles.

Style	Meaning
WS_SYSMENU	Creates a window with the Control menu box. This style is utilized only with windows that have title bars.
WS_THICKFRAME	Creates a window that has a thick frame, which is used for resizing.
WS_VISIBLE	Creates a visible window.
WS_VSCROLL	Creates a window that has a vertical scroll bar.

The X and Y data members specify the initial location of the window. These data members represent the initial location of the top-left corner of the created window. The H and W data members specify the height and width of the window, respectively. By setting the X, Y, H, and W data members, you determine the initial location and dimensions of a new window. As you move and resize the window, these data members change as well.

> **Tip:** The Menu data member is a pointer to a string that identifies the menu resource. With the ObjectWindows AssignMenu member function, you can easily select the initial menu and change it at will during the program's execution. Therefore, there is little incentive to use the Windows API functions that load and select the menu resources.

The Id data member specifies the child window ID. The child and parent windows use this ID to communicate. I discuss child windows later in this chapter.

The Param data member points to a value passed to the window at the time of its creation.

To get a good idea of how the TWindow constructor—the one I have been using—initializes a window, here is the constructor's code:

```
TWindow::TWindow(PTWindowsObject AParent,
            LPSTR ATitle, PTModule AModule)
          : TWindowsObject(AParent, AModule)
{
  Title = _fstrdup(ATitle ? ATitle : "");
  DefaultProc = (FARPROC)DefWindowProc;
  if ( !AParent )
```

```
      Attr.Style = WS_OVERLAPPEDWINDOW;
  else
    if ( AParent->IsFlagSet(WB_MDIFRAME) )
    {
      /* Set WB_MDICHILD by default, change this if you want a
         non-mdi child as a child of your TMDIFrame window. */
      SetFlags(WB_MDICHILD, TRUE);
      Attr.Style = WS_CLIPSIBLINGS;
    }
    else
      Attr.Style = WS_VISIBLE;
  Attr.ExStyle = 0;
  Attr.X = CW_USEDEFAULT;
  Attr.Y = 0;
  Attr.W = CW_USEDEFAULT;
  Attr.H = 0;
  Attr.Param = NULL;
  Attr.Menu = NULL;
  Attr.Id = 0;
  Scroller = NULL;
  FocusChildHandle = 0;
}
```

This code indicates that when a parent window is created, the `Style` data member of the `Attr` member is assigned `WS_OVERLAPPEDWINDOW`. This style creates a window with a caption and borders. By contrast, the code assigns `WS_VISIBLE` to the non-MDI child window. (Chapter 9, "MDI Windows," discusses MDI child windows in more detail.) The code also shows that the extended style, `Y`, and `H` data members are all assigned 0. The `X` and `W` data members are assigned `CW_USEDEFAULT`. These assignments create a window with a default size. The `Menu` data member of `Attr` is assigned NULL to indicate that no menu is associated with the window.

Armed with the information about the `Style`, `X`, `Y`, `W`, and `H` data members of the `Attr` data member, you are now ready for the next ObjectWindows application. Each instance creates a window with randomly selected values for these data members. Therefore, you will see windows that vary in location, size, and style.

Listing 3.5 shows the source code for the WINDOW3.CPP program file. This program uses the menu resource defined in the WINDOW1.RC file (see Listing 3.1). The program displays three short lines of text and responds to the left mouse button click.

Listing 3.5. The source code for the WINDOW3.CPP program file.

```cpp
#include <string.h>
#include <time.h>
#include <owl.h>

// declare the custom application class as
// a subclass of TApplication

class TWinApp : public TApplication
{
public:
  TWinApp(LPSTR    AName,           // application name
          HINSTANCE hInstance,      // instance handle
          HINSTANCE hPrevInstance,  // previous instance handle
          LPSTR    lpCmdLine,       // command-line arguments
          int      nCmdShow) :      // display command
          TApplication(AName, hInstance, hPrevInstance,
                    lpCmdLine, nCmdShow) {};

protected:
  virtual void InitMainWindow();

};

// use the _CLASSDEF macro to declare reference and pointer
// types related to the new TAppWindow class
_CLASSDEF(TAppWindow)

// expand the functionality of TWindow by deriving class TAppWindow
class TAppWindow : public TWindow
{
public:

  TAppWindow(PTWindowsObject AParent, LPSTR ATitle);

  // handle the left mouse button click
  virtual void WMLButtonDown(RTMessage Msg)
      = [WM_FIRST + WM_LBUTTONDOWN];

  // handle closing the window
  virtual BOOL CanClose();

protected:
  // handle the window painting
  virtual void Paint(HDC DC, PAINTSTRUCT& P);
```

continues

Listing 3.5. continued

```
};

TAppWindow::TAppWindow(PTWindowsObject AParent, LPSTR ATitle) :
                TWindow(AParent, ATitle)
{
  // generate random window locations and sizes for the
  // different instances
  randomize();
  Attr.X = 10 + random(501);
  Attr.Y = 10 + random(501);
  Attr.H = 70 + random(101);
  Attr.H = 70 + random(101);
  switch (random(7)) {
    case 0:
      Attr.Style |= WS_OVERLAPPEDWINDOW;
      break;
    case 1:
      Attr.Style |= WS_HSCROLL | WS_VSCROLL;
      break;
    case 2:
      Attr.Style |= WS_HSCROLL;
      break;
    case 3:
      Attr.Style |= WS_VSCROLL;
      break;
    case 4:
      Attr.Style |= WS_MINIMIZE;
      break;
    case 5:
      Attr.Style |= WS_MAXIMIZE;
      break;
    case 6:
      Attr.Style |= WS_POPUPWINDOW;
      break;
  }
  AssignMenu("EXITMENU");
}

void TAppWindow::WMLButtonDown(RTMessage Msg)
{
    MessageBox(HWindow, "You clicked the left mouse button",
              "Information!", MB_OK | MB_ICONINFORMATION);
}
```

```
void TAppWindow::Paint(HDC DC, PAINTSTRUCT& P)
{

  const MAX_LINES = 3;
  const LINE_INCR = 20;
  char Lines[3][40] = {"This is line 1",
                       "This is line 2",
                       "This is line 3"};

  for (BYTE i = 0; i < MAX_LINES; i++)
    TextOut(DC, 0, i * LINE_INCR,
            Lines[i], strlen(Lines[i]));
}

BOOL TAppWindow::CanClose()
{
  return MessageBox(HWindow, "Want to close this application",
                    "Query", MB_YESNO | MB_ICONQUESTION) == IDYES;
}

void TWinApp::InitMainWindow()
{
  MainWindow = new TAppWindow(NULL, Name);
}

int PASCAL WinMain(HINSTANCE hInstance, HINSTANCE hPrevInstance,
                   LPSTR lpCmdLine, int nCmdShow)
{
  TWinApp WinApp("A Simple Read-Only Text Window",
                 hInstance, hPrevInstance, lpCmdLine, nCmdShow);
  WinApp.Run(); // run OWL application
  return WinApp.Status; // return application status
}
```

The most relevant part of the program is the TAppWindow constructor. The constructor uses the random function to assign values to the following data members of Attr:

- ☐ Assigns a random number between 10 and 510 to the data member X.
- ☐ Assigns a random number between 10 and 510 to the data member Y.
- ☐ Assigns a random number between 70 and 170 to the data member H.
- ☐ Assigns a random number between 70 and 170 to the data member W.

■ Uses a random number to choose between various combinations of window styles. The constructor uses the random function and the `switch` statement to pick the random selection.

To create the WINDOW3.EXE ObjectWindows application, you must first create a resource file that contains the WINDOW3.CPP, WINDOW1.RC, and OWL.DEF files.

Compile and run the application. You can either run several instances simultaneously or sequentially. In each case, notice the different location, size, and style of the created windows. Figure 3.3 shows a sample session with the WINDOW3.EXE application.

Figure 3.3.
A sample session with the WINDOW3.EXE application.

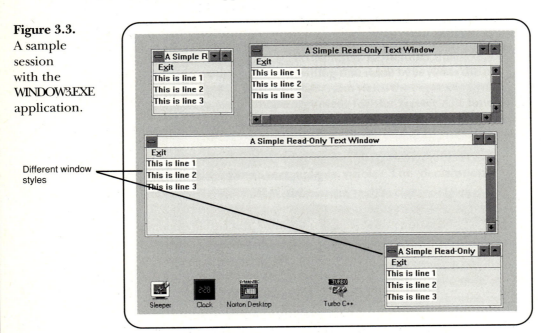

Different window styles

Window Class Registration

The last section presented the attributes that create individual windows. These attributes specify the window style, location, width, height, and menu. Consequently, these attributes are called creation attributes. The WINDOW3.EXE ObjectWindows application demonstrates how you can create a family of windows where each window possesses a unique combination of creation attributes.

120

> **Note:** In addition to the creation attributes, a window has another set of attributes that are more fixed or permanent. These attributes are related to the window classes. The term *window class* should not be confused with any ObjectWindows or any other object-oriented class. In fact, the term *window class* really means Windows category of windows. Microsoft coined the term while developing Windows with C and assembly language in the absence of object-oriented programming tools. A window class is a set of fixed attributes applying to all windows that are members of that class.

The process that defines a window class (or category, if you prefer) and sets its attributes is called *registration*. If you have programmed with C for Windows, you are all too familiar with this process. Fortunately, ObjectWindows handles the process of registering window classes in a manner that is invisible to you. The action of ObjectWindows includes supplying the window class with default registration attributes. These attributes include the window class style (which is different from the window style presented in the last section), icon, cursor, background color, and default menu.

In most cases, the window class registration that ObjectWindows performs is very adequate—you need not take any further steps. However, in case you do want to alter some or all of the registration attributes, you must declare the `GetClassName` and `GetWindowClass` member functions in your Windows class. The latter is by far the more relevant of the two member functions.

The `GetClass` member function returns the name of the default window class. The general syntax is:

```
LPSTR _TAppWindow_::GetClassName()
{
     return _class_name_string_;
}
```

The name of the class returned by the `GetClassName` member function might not match the application window class. Usually the returned name either matches or is a close derivation of the application window class.

The `GetWindowClass` member function takes a special structure, `WNDCLASS`, that contains the data fields representing the registration attributes. Here is the general syntax for the `GetWindowClass` member function:

```
void _TAppWindow_::GetWindowClass(WNDCLASS& AWndClass)
{
    TWindow::GetWindowClass(AWndClass);
    // insert statements to assign new attribute settings
}
```

Caution: This syntax indicates that your own version of `GetWindowClass` should first call the `TWindow::GetWindowClass` member function before assigning new values to specific registration attributes. This sequence enables you to safely build or override the default attribute settings supplied by ObjectWindows.

Now take a look at the WNDCLASS structure, which is declared in WINDOWS.H as follows:

```
typedef struct tagWNDCLASS
    {
    WORD        style;
    LONG        (FAR PASCAL *lpfnWndProc)( HWND, WORD, WORD, LONG );
    int         cbClsExtra;
    int         cbWndExtra;
    HINSTANCE   hInstance;
    HICON       hIcon;
    HCURSOR     hCursor;
    HBRUSH      hbrBackground;
    LPSTR       lpszMenuName;
    LPSTR       lpszClassName;
    } WNDCLASS;
```

The style field specifies the class style, which can be a combination of individual style identifiers (using the bitwise OR operator). Table 3.2 shows a selection of style values. The following statement shows the default ObjectWindows setting for the style field:

```
AWndClass.style = CS_HREDRAW | CS_VREDRAW;
```

Table 3.2. A selection of style values.

Value	Meaning
CS_CLASSDC	Provides the window class with its own display context.
CS_DBLCLKS	Sends double-click messages to a window.
CS_HREDRAW	Redraws the entire window when the horizontal size is altered.
CS_NOCLOSE	Restricts the close option on the Control menu.
CS_OWNDC	Provides each window instance with its own display context. (**Warning!** This style uses about 800 bytes of memory for each display context.)
CS_PARENTDC	Shares the parent window's display context with the window class.
CS_VREDRAW	Redraws the entire window when the vertical size is altered.

The hIcon field of WNDCLASS is a HICON handle to the icon resource. Table 3.3 shows the icon values used with the **LoadIcon** API function.

Table 3.3. Icon values predefined for Windows.

Value	Meaning
IDI_APPLICATION	The default application icon (an empty white rectangle).
IDI_ASTERISK	The asterisk (usually appears in information messages).
IDI_EXCLAMATION	The exclamation point (usually appears in warning messages).
IDI_HAND	The stop sign (usually appears in warning messages).
IDI_QUESTION	The question mark (usually appears in prompting messages).

The **LoadIcon** API function has the following declaration:

HICON LoadIcon(HINSTANCE hInstance, LPSTR lpIconName);

The hInstance parameter specifies an instance of the module whose executable file contains the icon. To access the predefined icons that Windows uses, pass a NULL argument to the hInstance parameter. The lpIconName points to the string containing the name of the icon resource. Table 3.3 comprises the predefined values for lpIconName when hInstance is NULL. You can also use the MAKEINTRESOURCE macro to create additional icons. The default ObjectWindows setting for the hIcon field loads the empty white rectangle icon using the following statement:

AWndClass.hIcon = LoadIcon(NULL, IDI_APPLICATION);

The hCursor field in WNDCLASS is the HCURSOR handle to the cursor resource. Table 3.4 shows the cursor values that are used with the **LoadCursor** API function. The **LoadCursor** API function has the following declaration:

HCURSOR LoadCursor(HINSTANCE hInstance, LPSTR lpCursorName);

The hInstance parameter specifies an instance of the module that includes the executable file containing the icon. To access the predefined cursors used by Windows, pass a NULL argument to the hInstance parameter. The lpCursorName points to the string that contains the name of the cursor resource. Table 3.4 contains the predefined values for lpCursorName when hInstance is NULL.

Table 3.4. Window's predefined cursor type values.

Value	Meaning
IDC_ARROW	The standard arrow cursor
IDC_CROSS	The cross hair cursor
IDC_IBEAM	The I beam cursor
IDC_ICON	The empty icon
IDC_SIZE	The special cursor with four arrows pointing north, east, south, and west
IDC_SIZENESW	The double-pointed cursor with arrows pointing northeast and southwest
IDC_SIZENS	The double-pointed cursor with arrows pointing north and south

Value	Meaning
IDC_SIZENWSE	The double-pointed cursor with arrows pointing northwest and southeast
IDC_SIZEWE	The double-pointed cursor with arrows pointing west and east
IDC_UPARROW	The vertical arrow cursor
IDC_WAIT	The hourglass cursor

You can also use the MAKEINTRESOURCE macro to create additional cursor. The default ObjectWindows setting loads the arrow cursor by using the following statement:

```
AWndClass.hCursor = LoadCursor(NULL, IDC_ARROW);
```

The hbrBackground field is a HBRUSH handle that sets the background color of the window class. The following are the various COLOR_xxxx constants that offer the settings for hbrBackground:

COLOR_ACTIVEBORDER	COLOR_INACTIVEBORDER
COLOR_ACTIVECAPTION	COLOR_INACTIONCAPTION
COLOR_APPWORKSPACE	COLOR_MENU
COLOR_BACKGROUND	COLOR_MENUTEXT
COLOR_BTNFACE	COLOR_SCROLLBAR
COLOR_BTNTEXT	COLOR_WINDOW
COLOR_CAPTIONTEXT	COLOR_WINDOWFRAME
COLOR_GRAYTEXT	COLOR_WINDOWTEXT
COLOR_HIGHLIGHT	

hbrBackground can be any color; the COLOR_ constants just define a convenient way to get to the system colors. Use the following general form with the COLOR_xxxx constants:

```
(HBRUSH)(COLOR_xxxx + 1)
```

The default ObjectWindows setting uses the COLOR_WINDOW constant in the following statement:

```
AWndClass.hbrBackground = (HBRUSH)(COLOR_WINDOW + 1);
```

The `lpszMenuName` is the pointer to the default resource name of the menu that all windows in the class share. The default ObjectWindows setting is NULL. To assign a default menu, supply the `MAKEINTRESOURCE` macro with the integer resource ID of the desired menu, in the following general form:

```
AWndClass.lpszMenuName = MAKEINTRESOURCE(_integer_resource_ID_)
```

Using the ObjectWindows `AssignMenu` member function is just as convenient and flexible. You do not gain any significant advantage by assigning a menu resource to the `lpszMenuName` field.

The next ObjectWindows application builds instances with varying window class style, icons, cursor shapes, background colors, and menus. Each instance has a main menu with two simple selections. The first selection provides a token help message, and the second selection enables you to exit the application. Listing 3.6 shows the WINDOW4.H header file that defines the `CM_HELPx` command constants.

Listing 3.6. The source code for the WINDOW4.H header file.

```
#define CM_HELP1 201
#define CM_HELP2 202
#define CM_HELP3 203
```

Listing 3.7 contains the script for the WINDOW4.RC resource file. The script defines three menus with the ID numbers of 101, 102, and 103. The menus differ in their first menu items.

Listing 3.7. The script for the resource file WINDOW4.RC.

```
#include <windows.h>
#include <owlrc.h>
#include "window4.h"

101 MENU LOADONCALL MOVEABLE PURE DISCARDABLE
BEGIN
    MENUITEM "&Menu 101", CM_HELP1
    MENUITEM "E&xit", CM_EXIT
END

102 MENU LOADONCALL MOVEABLE PURE DISCARDABLE
BEGIN
    MENUITEM "&Menu 102", CM_HELP2
    MENUITEM "E&xit", CM_EXIT
END
```

```
103 MENU LOADONCALL MOVEABLE PURE DISCARDABLE
BEGIN
    MENUITEM "&Menu 103", CM_HELP3
    MENUITEM "E&xit", CM_EXIT
END
```

Listing 3.8 shows the source code for the WINDOW4.CPP program file. The source code declares two classes, `TWinApp` and `TAppWindow`. The second class contains the declarations that are relevant to this discussion.

Listing 3.8. The source code for the WINDOW4.CPP program file.

```
#include <time.h>
#include <stdlib.h>
#include <string.h>
#include <owl.h>

#include "window4.h"

// declare the custom application class as
// a subclass of TApplication

class TWinApp : public TApplication
{
public:
  TWinApp(LPSTR     AName,           // application name
          HINSTANCE hInstance,       // instance handle
          HINSTANCE hPrevInstance,   // previous instance handle
          LPSTR     lpCmdLine,       // command-line arguments
          int       nCmdShow) :      // display command
          TApplication(AName, hInstance, hPrevInstance,
                    lpCmdLine, nCmdShow) {};

protected:
  virtual void InitMainWindow();

};

// use the _CLASSDEF macro to declare reference and pointer
// types related to the new TAppWindow class
_CLASSDEF(TAppWindow)
```

continues

Listing 3.8. continued

```cpp
// expand the functionality of TWindow by deriving class TAppWindow
class TAppWindow : public TWindow
{
public:
  TAppWindow(PTWindowsObject AParent, LPSTR ATitle) :
           TWindow(AParent, ATitle) {};

  // handle the left mouse button click
  virtual void WMLButtonDown(RTMessage Msg)
      = [WM_FIRST + WM_LBUTTONDOWN];

  // handle the left mouse button click
  virtual void WMRButtonDown(RTMessage Msg)
      = [WM_FIRST + WM_RBUTTONDOWN];

  // handle the CM_HELP1 command
  virtual void CMHelp1(RTMessage Msg)
      = [CM_FIRST + CM_HELP1];

  // handle the CM_HELP2 command
  virtual void CMHelp2(RTMessage Msg)
      = [CM_FIRST + CM_HELP2];

  // handle the CM_HELP3 command
  virtual void CMHelp3(RTMessage Msg)
      = [CM_FIRST + CM_HELP3];

  // handle closing the window
  virtual BOOL CanClose();

protected:
  // return the name of this class
  LPSTR GetClassName() { return "TAppWindow"; }

  // assign the attributes to the Windows class WNDCLASS
  virtual void GetWindowClass(WNDCLASS& W);

  // handle painting the window
  virtual void Paint(HDC DC, PAINTSTRUCT& P);
};

void TAppWindow::GetWindowClass(WNDCLASS& W)
{
  TWindow::GetWindowClass(W);
```

```
randomize();
// select a window style using at random
switch (random(4)) {
  case 0:
        W.style = CS_HREDRAW;
        break;
  case 1:
        W.style = CS_VREDRAW;
        break;
  case 2:
        W.style = CS_HREDRAW | CS_VREDRAW;
        break;
  case 3:
        W.style = CS_HREDRAW | CS_VREDRAW | CS_NOCLOSE;
        break;
}

// select a color at random
switch (random(6)) {
  case 0:
    W.hbrBackground = (HBRUSH)(COLOR_WINDOW + 1);
    break;
  case 1:
    W.hbrBackground = (HBRUSH)(COLOR_GRAYTEXT + 1);
    break;
  case 2:
    W.hbrBackground = (HBRUSH)(COLOR_HIGHLIGHT + 1);
    break;
  case 3:
    W.hbrBackground = (HBRUSH)(COLOR_HIGHLIGHTTEXT + 1);
    break;
  case 4:
    W.hbrBackground = (HBRUSH)(COLOR_ACTIVECAPTION + 1);
    break;
  case 5:
    W.hbrBackground = (HBRUSH)(COLOR_ACTIVEBORDER + 1);
    break;
}

// select an application icon at random
switch (random(5)) {
  case 0:
      W.hIcon = LoadIcon(NULL, IDI_APPLICATION);
      break;
```

continues

Listing 3.8. continued

```
    case 1:
        W.hIcon = LoadIcon(NULL, IDI_ASTERISK);
        break;
    case 2:
        W.hIcon = LoadIcon(NULL, IDI_EXCLAMATION);
        break;
    case 3:
        W.hIcon = LoadIcon(NULL, IDI_HAND);
        break;
    case 4:
        W.hIcon = LoadIcon(NULL, IDI_QUESTION);
        break;
}

// select a cursor shape at random
switch (random(11)) {
  case 0 :
        W.hCursor = LoadCursor(NULL, IDC_ARROW);
        break;
  case 1 :
        W.hCursor = LoadCursor(NULL, IDC_CROSS);
        break;
  case 2 :
        W.hCursor = LoadCursor(NULL, IDC_IBEAM);
        break;
  case 3 :
        W.hCursor = LoadCursor(NULL, IDC_ICON);
        break;
  case 4 :
        W.hCursor = LoadCursor(NULL, IDC_SIZE);
        break;
  case 5 :
        W.hCursor = LoadCursor(NULL, IDC_SIZENESW);
        break;
  case 6 :
        W.hCursor = LoadCursor(NULL, IDC_SIZENS);
        break;
  case 7 :
        W.hCursor = LoadCursor(NULL, IDC_SIZENWSE);
        break;
  case 8 :
        W.hCursor = LoadCursor(NULL, IDC_SIZEWE);
        break;
```

```cpp
    case 9 :
        W.hCursor = LoadCursor(NULL, IDC_UPARROW);
        break;
    case 10 :
        W.hCursor = LoadCursor(NULL, IDC_WAIT);
        break;
  }

  // select a default menu at random
  W.lpszMenuName = MAKEINTRESOURCE(101 + random(3));
}

void TAppWindow::Paint(HDC DC, PAINTSTRUCT& P)
{

  const MAX_LINES = 3;
  const LINE_INCR = 20;
  char line[3][40] = {"This is line 1",
                      "This is line 2",
                      "This is line 3"};

  for (BYTE i = 0; i < MAX_LINES; i++)
    TextOut(DC, 0, i * LINE_INCR,
            line[i], strlen(line[i]));
}

void TAppWindow::WMLButtonDown(RTMessage Msg)
{
  MessageBox(HWindow, "You clicked the left button!",
             "Mouse Click Event!", MB_OK);
}

void TAppWindow::WMRButtonDown(RTMessage Msg)
{
  SendMessage(HWindow, WM_CLOSE, 0, 0);
}

void TAppWindow::CMHelp1(RTMessage Msg)
{
  MessageBox(HWindow, "This menu has an ID of 101",
             "HELP", MB_OK | MB_ICONINFORMATION);
}

void TAppWindow::CMHelp2(RTMessage Msg)
{
```

continues

Listing 3.8. continued

```
  MessageBox(HWindow, "This menu has an ID of 102",
             "HELP", MB_OK | MB_ICONINFORMATION);
}

void TAppWindow::CMHelp3(RTMessage Msg)
{
  MessageBox(HWindow, "This menu has an ID of 103",
             "HELP", MB_OK | MB_ICONINFORMATION);
}

BOOL TAppWindow::CanClose()
{
  MessageBeep(0); // beep
  // prompt user whether he or she want to close the application
  return MessageBox(HWindow, "Want to close this application",
                    "Query", MB_YESNO | MB_ICONQUESTION) == IDYES;
}

void TWinApp::InitMainWindow()
{
  MainWindow = new TAppWindow(NULL, Name);
}

int PASCAL WinMain(HINSTANCE hInstance, HINSTANCE hPrevInstance,
                   LPSTR lpCmdLine, int nCmdShow)
{
  TWinApp WinApp("Windows Class Registration Demo", hInstance,
                 hPrevInstance, lpCmdLine, nCmdShow);
  WinApp.Run(); // run OWL application
  return WinApp.Status; // return application status
}
```

The `TAppWindow` class declares a constructor and a number of member functions. The relevant member functions are `GetClassName`, `GetWindowClass`, `CMHelp1`, and `CMHelp2`. The `GetClassName` member function returns the name of the class, `TAppWindow`. The `GetWindowClass` function is the most relevant member, and it performs the following tasks:

- Invokes the parent `GetWindowClass` member function.
- Randomizes the random number generator seed.
- Selects a window style at random from four alternate styles. Two of these styles combine the `CS_xxxx` styles shown in Table 3.2.

Creating Basic Windows

- Selects a background color at random from six alternate values.
- Selects the application icon at random. Aside from the IDI_APPLICATION, the other icons are actually meant to be used in various message dialog boxes. I am using these icons simply for the sake of demonstration.
- Selects the cursor shape at random from the 11 IDC_xxxx values. Some of these shapes—like the ones used to resize or move a window—are very rarely suitable for an application. I am including them here for the sake of the demonstration.
- Selects the default menu at random from the three possible menus, using the MAKEINTRESOURCE macro.

The CMHelp1 and CMHelp2 member functions display a token help message in a message box.

To create the WINDOW4.EXE ObjectWindows application, you must create a make file that contains the WINDOW4.CPP, WINDOW4.RC, and OWL.DEF files.

Run multiple instances of the WINDOW4.EXE application. Notice that each instance has a different combination of icons, cursor shapes, background colors, and menus. The different window styles are less obvious. Figure 3.4 shows a sample session with the WINDOW4.EXE application.

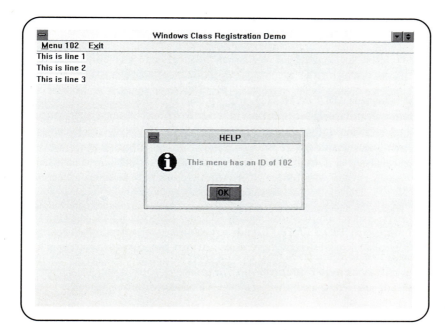

Figure 3.4. A sample session with the WINDOW4.EXE application.

Changing the Cursor

In Chapter 2, "Creating Basic ObjectWindows Applications," I demonstrated how to use the `AssignMenu` member function to alter menus at run-time. In this section, I discuss changing the cursor shape at run-time. Typically, the shape of the cursor changes in two cases: positional change (that is, by moving the cursor to a specific area) or incidental change (a cursor leading to a certain task). A typical example of the positional change is moving the mouse cursor to a hypertext link in the online help system window. A typical example of the incidental change is altering the cursor to the hourglass when performing time-consuming file I/O. The next example demonstrates both types of cursor changes.

Listing 3.9 shows the source code for the WINDOW5.CPP application.

Listing 3.9. The source code for the WINDOW5.CPP program file.

```
#include <string.h>
#include <owl.h>
#include "window4.h"

// declare an enumerated type of the cursor types used
// in this application.
enum cursorShape { isArrow = 1, isCross, isIBeam,
                   isIcon, isUpArrow, isWait };


// declare the custom application class as
// a subclass of TApplication

class TWinApp : public TApplication
{
public:
  TWinApp(LPSTR    AName,           // application name
          HINSTANCE hInstance,      // instance handle
          HINSTANCE hPrevInstance,  // previous instance handle
          LPSTR    lpCmdLine,       // command-line arguments
          int      nCmdShow) :      // display command
          TApplication(AName, hInstance, hPrevInstance,
                  lpCmdLine, nCmdShow) {};
```

```
  protected:
    virtual void InitMainWindow();

};

// use the _CLASSDEF macro to declare reference and pointer
// types related to the new TAppWindow class
_CLASSDEF(TAppWindow)

// expand the functionality of TWindow by deriving class TAppWindow
class TAppWindow : public TWindow
{
public:

  TAppWindow(PTWindowsObject AParent, LPSTR ATitle) :
            TWindow(AParent, ATitle) {};

 // handle the left mouse button click
  virtual void WMLButtonDown(RTMessage Msg)
      = [WM_FIRST + WM_LBUTTONDOWN];

  // handle the left mouse button click
  virtual void WMRButtonDown(RTMessage Msg)
      = [WM_FIRST + WM_RBUTTONDOWN];

  // handle the left mouse button click
  virtual void WMMouseMove(RTMessage Msg)
      = [WM_FIRST + WM_MOUSEMOVE];

  // handle the CM_HELP1 command
  virtual void CMHelp1(RTMessage Msg)
      = [CM_FIRST + CM_HELP1];

  // handle closing the window
  virtual BOOL CanClose();

protected:
  HCURSOR hCursorArrow;
  HCURSOR hCursorIBeam;
  HCURSOR hCursorCross;
  HCURSOR hCursorIcon;
  HCURSOR hCursorUpArrow;
  HCURSOR hCursorWait;
  cursorShape CursorIndex;
```

continues

Listing 3.9. continued

```cpp
  // return the name of this class
  LPSTR GetClassName() { return "TAppWindow"; }

  // assign the attributes to the Windows class WNDCLASS
  virtual void GetWindowClass(WNDCLASS& W);

  // handle painting the window
  virtual void Paint(HDC DC, PAINTSTRUCT& P);

  // cursor selection member functions
  void selectNextCursor();
  void selectPrevCursor();
  void selectCursor(cursorShape newCursorIndex);
};

void TAppWindow::GetWindowClass(WNDCLASS& W)
{
  TWindow::GetWindowClass(W);
  randomize();
  // select a window style
  W.style = CS_HREDRAW | CS_VREDRAW;

  // select a color
  W.hbrBackground = (HBRUSH)(COLOR_WINDOW + 1);

  // select an application icon
  W.hIcon = LoadIcon(NULL, IDI_EXCLAMATION);

  // load the various cursor icons
  hCursorArrow = LoadCursor(NULL, IDC_ARROW);
  hCursorIBeam = LoadCursor(NULL, IDC_IBEAM);
  hCursorCross = LoadCursor(NULL, IDC_CROSS);
  hCursorIcon = LoadCursor(NULL, IDC_ICON);
  hCursorUpArrow = LoadCursor(NULL, IDC_UPARROW);
  hCursorWait = LoadCursor(NULL, IDC_WAIT);
  CursorIndex = isArrow;
  W.hCursor = NULL;

  // select a default menu
  W.lpszMenuName = MAKEINTRESOURCE(101);
}

void TAppWindow::Paint(HDC DC, PAINTSTRUCT& P)
{
```

```
  const MAX_LINES = 3;
  const LINE_INCR = 20;
  char line[3][40] = {"This is line 1",
                      "This is line 2",
                      "This is line 3"};

  for (BYTE i = 0; i < MAX_LINES; i++)
    TextOut(DC, 0, i * LINE_INCR,
            line[i], strlen(line[i]));
}

void TAppWindow::WMLButtonDown(RTMessage Msg)
{
  if ((Msg.LP.Lo > 100 ¦¦ Msg.LP.Hi > 100) &&
      Msg.LP.Lo < 400)
    selectNextCursor();
}
void TAppWindow::WMRButtonDown(RTMessage Msg)
{
  if ((Msg.LP.Lo > 100 ¦¦ Msg.LP.Hi > 100) &&
      Msg.LP.Lo < 400)
    selectPrevCursor();
}

void TAppWindow::WMMouseMove(RTMessage Msg)
{
  if (Msg.LP.Lo <= 100 && Msg.LP.Hi <= 100)
    selectCursor(isCross);
  else if (Msg.LP.Lo >= 400)
    selectCursor(isUpArrow);
  else
    selectCursor(CursorIndex);
}

void TAppWindow::CMHelp1(RTMessage Msg)
{
  MessageBox(HWindow, "This menu has an ID of 101",
             "HELP", MB_OK ¦ MB_ICONINFORMATION);
}

BOOL TAppWindow::CanClose()
{
  MessageBeep(0); // beep
```

continues

Listing 3.9. continued

```cpp
  // prompt user whether he or she want to close the application
  return MessageBox(HWindow, "Want to close this application",
                    "Query", MB_YESNO | MB_ICONQUESTION) == IDYES;
}

void TAppWindow::selectNextCursor()
{
  CursorIndex = cursorShape(CursorIndex % isArrow + 1);
  selectCursor(CursorIndex);
}

void TAppWindow::selectPrevCursor()
{
  CursorIndex = cursorShape((CursorIndex == isArrow) ?
                            isWait : --CursorIndex);
  selectCursor(CursorIndex);
}

void TAppWindow::selectCursor(cursorShape newCursorIndex)
{
  switch (newCursorIndex) {
    case isArrow:
      SetCursor(hCursorArrow);
      break;
    case isCross:
      SetCursor(hCursorCross);
      break;
    case isIBeam:
      SetCursor(hCursorIBeam);
      break;
    case isIcon:
      SetCursor(hCursorIcon);
      break;
    case isUpArrow:
      SetCursor(hCursorUpArrow);
      break;
    case isWait:
      SetCursor(hCursorWait);
      break;
  }
}

void TWinApp::InitMainWindow()
{
```

Creating Basic Windows

```
  MainWindow = new TAppWindow(NULL, Name);
}

int PASCAL WinMain(HINSTANCE hInstance, HINSTANCE hPrevInstance,
                   LPSTR lpCmdLine, int nCmdShow)
{
  TWinApp WinApp("An Icon Test OWL Application", hInstance,
                 hPrevInstance, lpCmdLine, nCmdShow);
  WinApp.Run(); // run OWL application
  return WinApp.Status; // return application status
}
```

This program uses menu 101 of the WINDOW4.RC file and displays three short text lines. The application changes its cursor shape to the cross hair when you move it to the square area defined by (0,0) and (100,100) as the top-left and bottom-right corners. The cursor also changes shape to the vertical arrow when you move beyond the x coordinate value of 400. I will call the area outside these two zones the "free area."

To demonstrate the incidental change, I made the left and right mouse buttons select the next and previous cursor shapes, respectively. The program enables you to pick from a set of six cursor shapes: arrow, cross hair, I beam, icon, vertical arrow, and hourglass. In addition, the program prevents the incidental and positional cursor changes from conflicting with each other. Resolving this conflict involves monitoring where the mouse button is clicked to detect whether the click location is inside the special areas that demonstrate the positional cursor changes.

The basic tools for changing the cursor are the **LoadCursor** and **SetCursor** API functions. The **LoadCursor** loads the cursor resources and assigns them to an HCURSOR handle. The **SetCursor** function uses an HCURSOR handle to set the current cursor.

The program declares the cursorShape enumeration type to represent the six types of cursor shapes used in the program. The program also declares two classes, TWinApp and TAppWindow. The TWinApp application class creates the main window. The TAppWindow class contains the relevant member function for the cursor shape changes. The TAppWindow class declares the member functions that are also found WINDOW4.CPP and adds a few data members and member functions. The WMMove public member function handles the WM_MOUSEMOVE mouse movement message. The new data members include six protected HCURSOR handles to access the six cursor shapes previously mentioned. In

addition, the class declares the protected `CursorIndex` as an enumerated member that stores the cursor shape appearing in the free area. The new protected member functions are `selectNextCursor`, `selectPrevCursor`, and `selectCursor`. These functions select the next, previous, or specific cursor shape.

The `GetWindowClass` member function influences the window class registration and performs the following tasks:

- Selects the style, icon, background color, and menu for the `TAppWindow` window class
- Loads the icon resources and ties them to the six data member handles
- Assigns the enumerated value `isArrow` to the data member `CursorIndex`
- Assigns NULL to the `hCursor` handle

The positional cursor change is implemented with the `WMMouseMove` message response member function. This function monitors the movement of the mouse. The expressions `Msg.LP.Lo` and `Msg.LP.Hi` provide the x and y coordinates of the mouse. The function tests the following conditions:

- If the mouse is located in the upper square area bound by (0,0), (100,100), the function calls `selectCursor` with an `isCross` argument. This call produces a cross hair cursor.
- If the x coordinate exceeds 399, the function calls `selectCursor` with an `isUpArrow` argument. This call produces a vertical arrow cursor.
- If the previous two conditions fail (the mouse cursor is now located in the free area), the function displays the current cursor by calling `selectCursor` with the `CursorIndex` argument.

While the mouse cursor is in the free area, the left and right mouse clicks implement the incidental cursor change. The `WMLButtonDown` and `WMRButtonDown` member functions first verify that the cursor is indeed in the free area before calling the `selectNextCursor` and `selectPrevCursor` functions, respectively.

The `selectNextCursor` and `selectPrevCursor` functions both update the `CursorIndex` data member and call `selectCursor`, but the latter function actually sets the new cursor shape. The `selectCursor` uses a `switch` statement to pick the cursor shape and to invoke the **SetCursor** API function that performs the required task.

To create the WINDOW5.EXE ObjectWindows application, you must first create a make file that contains the WINDOW5.CPP, WINDOW4.RC, and OWL.DEF files. Compile and run the program. Experiment with moving the cursor in the window. Observe the change in the cursor shape as you move to special areas that demonstrate the positional changes in the cursor shape. Move the cursor to the free area, click either mouse button, and observe the change in cursor shape.

Creating Child Windows

The windows of an application are placeholders for visible objects. This includes dialog boxes, controls (such as the list box, the push button, and the check box), and even other windows. In this section, I discuss the creation of non-MDI child windows within a parent window. Before presenting the specifics of creating child windows, I need to highlight an important concept used in Windows.

> **Note:** The concept of ownership and parent-child relation is very important in Windows and any other similar user-interface. So far, I have presented ObjectWindows applications that display a single window. The code for these programs typically declares two classes: one for the application and one for the window interface. Usually, the application class contains an `InitMainWindow` member function that creates the window instance and assigns it to the `MainWindow` pointer. In doing so, the application instance is the owner of the window instance. This ownership occurs between an invisible object (the application) and a visible interface object (the window).
>
> As one of the results of this relationship, when you close the application, it in turn closes the window that it owns. Another result becomes clear when you start placing visible objects (dialog boxes, controls, and other windows) inside a window. The parent-child relationship among these visible objects builds on the ownership concepts by incorporating the management of the flow of messages among these objects. The parent-child links are maintained by a list of pointers to the various objects. As an example of how the ownership and parent-child links work, when you close the parent window, all of the child windows are automatically closed. The parent window is the owner of the child window and ensures that the parent-child link is empty before the parent window is closed.

Child windows are confined to the space provided by their parent window. The `TModule::MakeWindow` member function creates child windows. This function is called in the following form:

```
GetModule()->MakeWindow(_window_pointer_)
```

The `MakeWindow` attempts to create a window and returns its pointer. If the window creation fails, the `MakeWindow` returns NULL. To give you an idea of how the `MakeWindow` function works, here is its code:

```
PTWindowsObject TModule::MakeWindow(PTWindowsObject AWindowsObject)
{
  if ( AWindowsObject && ValidWindow(AWindowsObject) )
    if ( (AWindowsObject->Create()) )
      return AWindowsObject;
    else
    {
      Error(AWindowsObject->Status);
      AWindowsObject->ShutDownWindow();
    }
  return NULL;
}
```

The `MakeWindow` function first tests whether the window object (the invisible part) is successfully created by calling the `ValidWindow` member function. The `ValidWindow` function ensures that adequate heap space is available for the creation of the window object. If the window is indeed created, the `MakeWindow` function invokes the window object's `Create` member function to construct the visual components of that window. By contrast, if the window creation experiences problems, the `MakeWindow` deallocates any heap space and raises an error condition.

The next ObjectWindows application uses `MakeWindow` to demonstrate the creation of child windows. Listing 3.10 shows the source code for the WINOBJ1.CPP program file. The program uses the menu resource defined in the MENU3.RC file. Selecting the Help menu item creates child help windows. Actually, the program creates two types of child windows. The first type has a thick frame that enables you to resize the window. The second type has a simple fixed frame. Each child window contains a number in its title. Only the odd child windows have the thick frames.

Listing 3.10. The source code for the WINOBJ1.CPP program file.

```cpp
#include <stdio.h>
#include <string.h>
#include <owl.h>
#include "menus.h"

// declare the custom application class as
// a subclass of TApplication

class TWinApp : public TApplication
{
public:
  TWinApp(LPSTR    AName,           // application name
          HINSTANCE hInstance,      // instance handle
          HINSTANCE hPrevInstance,  // previous instance handle
          LPSTR    lpCmdLine,       // command-line arguments
          int      nCmdShow) :      // display command
          TApplication(AName, hInstance, hPrevInstance,
                    lpCmdLine, nCmdShow) {};
protected:
  virtual void InitMainWindow();

};

// use the _CLASSDEF macro to declare reference and pointer
// types related to the new TAppWindow and TChildWindow classes
_CLASSDEF(TAppWindow)
_CLASSDEF(TChildWindow)

// expand the functionality of TWindow by deriving class TAppWindow
class TAppWindow : public TWindow
{
public:
  BYTE NumHelpWindows;

  TAppWindow(PTWindowsObject AParent, LPSTR ATitle);

  // handle the left mouse button click
  virtual void WMLButtonDown(RTMessage Msg)
      = [WM_FIRST + WM_LBUTTONDOWN];
```

continues

Listing 3.10. continued

```
    // handle the right mouse button click
    virtual void WMRButtonDown(RTMessage Msg)
        = [WM_FIRST + WM_RBUTTONDOWN];

    virtual void CMHelp(RTMessage Msg)
        = [CM_FIRST + CM_HELP];

    // handle the Cut menu option
    virtual void CMEditCut(RTMessage Msg)
        = [CM_FIRST + CM_EDITCUT];

    // handle the Copy menu option
    virtual void CMEditCopy(RTMessage Msg)
        = [CM_FIRST + CM_EDITCOPY];

    // handle the Paste menu option
    virtual void CMEditPaste(RTMessage Msg)
        = [CM_FIRST + CM_EDITPASTE];
    // handle closing the window
    virtual BOOL CanClose();

protected:
    // handle painting the window
    virtual void Paint(HDC DC, PAINTSTRUCT& P);

private:
    // display a message "Feature not implemented"
    void notImplemented();

};

class TChildWindow : public TWindow
{
public:
    BYTE WindowNumber;
    TChildWindow(PTWindowsObject AParent, LPSTR ATitle, BYTE WinNum);

protected:
    // handle painting the child window
    virtual void Paint(HDC DC, PAINTSTRUCT& P);
};
```

Creating Basic Windows

```cpp
TChildWindow::TChildWindow(PTWindowsObject AParent,
                          LPSTR ATitle, BYTE WinNum) :
                TWindow(AParent, ATitle)
{
  WindowNumber = WinNum;

  if (WindowNumber % 2) {
  // assign attributes of odd-numbered child-windows
     Attr.Style |= WS_CHILD | WS_CAPTION  | WS_SYSMENU |
                   WS_BORDER | WS_OVERLAPPEDWINDOW |
                   WS_CLIPSIBLINGS;
     Attr.X = 90 + 10 * (WindowNumber / 2);
     Attr.Y = 90 + 10 * (WindowNumber / 2);
     Attr.H = 200;
     Attr.W = 200;
  }
  else {
  // assign attributes of even-numbered child-windows
     Attr.Style |= WS_CHILD | WS_CAPTION  | WS_SYSMENU |
                   WS_BORDER | WS_CLIPSIBLINGS;
     Attr.X = 290 + 10 * (1 + WindowNumber / 2);
     Attr.Y = 90 + 10 * (1 + WindowNumber / 2);
     Attr.H = 100;
     Attr.W = 100;
  }
};

void TChildWindow::Paint(HDC DC, PAINTSTRUCT& P)
{

  const MAX_LINES = 3;
  const LINE_INCR = 20;
  char line[3][40] = {"This is the help line #1",
                      "This is the help line #2",
                      "This is the help line #3"};

  for (BYTE i = 0; i < MAX_LINES; i++)
    TextOut(DC, 0, i * LINE_INCR,
            line[i], strlen(line[i]));
}

TAppWindow::TAppWindow(PTWindowsObject AParent, LPSTR ATitle) :
                TWindow(AParent, ATitle)
```

continues

Listing 3.10. continued

```
{
  AssignMenu("MAINMENU");
  Attr.Style |= WS_MAXIMIZE;
  NumHelpWindows = 0;
}

void TAppWindow::WMLButtonDown(RTMessage Msg)
{
   MessageBox(HWindow, "You clicked the left button!",
            "Mouse Click Event!", MB_OK);
}

void TAppWindow::WMRButtonDown(RTMessage Msg)
{
  MessageBeep(0);
  SendMessage(HWindow, WM_CLOSE, 0, 0);
}

BOOL TAppWindow::CanClose()
{
  return MessageBox(HWindow, "Want to close this application",
                    "Query", MB_YESNO | MB_ICONQUESTION) == IDYES;
}

void TAppWindow::CMHelp(RTMessage Msg)
{
  char WindowTitle[30];

  // build help window title to include the window number
  sprintf(WindowTitle, "HELP #%d", ++NumHelpWindows);
  if (GetApplication()->MakeWindow(
          new TChildWindow(this, WindowTitle, NumHelpWindows)
                                   ) == NULL) {
    MessageBox(HWindow, "Failed to create child window",
               "Error", MB_OK);
    NumHelpWindows--; // decrement window number
  }
}

void TAppWindow::CMEditCut(RTMessage Msg)
{
  notImplemented();
}
```

```cpp
void TAppWindow::CMEditCopy(RTMessage Msg)
{
  notImplemented();
}

void TAppWindow::CMEditPaste(RTMessage Msg)
{
  notImplemented();
}

void TAppWindow::notImplemented()
{
  MessageBox(HWindow, "This feature is not implemented",
             "Information", MB_OK);
}

void TAppWindow::Paint(HDC DC, PAINTSTRUCT& P)
{

  const MAX_LINES = 3;
  const LINE_INCR = 20;
  char line[3][40] = {"This is line 1",
                      "This is line 2",
                      "This is line 3"};

  for (BYTE i = 0; i < MAX_LINES; i++)
    TextOut(DC, 0, i * LINE_INCR,
            line[i], strlen(line[i]));
}

void TWinApp::InitMainWindow()
{
  MainWindow = new TAppWindow(NULL, Name);
}

int PASCAL WinMain(HINSTANCE hInstance, HINSTANCE hPrevInstance,
                   LPSTR lpCmdLine, int nCmdShow)
{
  TWinApp WinApp("A Menu-Driven OWL Application", hInstance,
                 hPrevInstance, lpCmdLine, nCmdShow);
  WinApp.Run(); // run OWL application
  return WinApp.Status; // return application status
}
```

Listing 3.10 contains the declarations of three classes: `TWinApp`, `TAppWindow`, and `TChildWindow`. The last two classes represent the parent and child windows, respectively. Notice that the `_CLASSDEF` macro is used with both window classes.

Notice the child window class first. `TChildWindow` is a descendant of `TWindow` and declares the `WindowNumber` data member, a class constructor, and the `Paint` member function. The `TChildWindow` constructor assigns the argument for parameter `WinNum` to the data member `WindowNumber`. Next, the constructor examines whether `WindowNumber` contains an odd or even integer. Each condition leads to a different set of values that are assigned to the data member `Attr`. All windows use the style of `WS_CHILD`, `WS_CAPTION`, `WS_SYSMENU`, and `WS_BORDER`. Consequently, all the child windows have a caption, a Control menu, and a border. The odd numbered child windows contain the `WS_OVERLAPPEDWINDOW` style that creates a thick frame for resizing. The program creates the odd- and even-numbered child windows with different locations and sizes. The statements that assign the locations of the child windows use the `WindowNumber` member to ensure that the child windows appear stacked.

The `TChildWindow::Paint` member function displays three simple lines of text that symbolize help text (with some stretch of the imagination). Incidentally, the `Paint` member function of the parent and child windows contains very similar code.

The parent window class `TAppWindow` contains the `NumHelpWindows` data member and a number of familiar member functions. The `NumHelpWindows` member keeps track of the highest index for the help window instance created. The `class` constructor initializes `NumHelpWindows` with 0.

The most relevant `TAppWindow` member function is `CMHelp`. This function responds to the help menu command by creating a new child window with the `MakeWindow` member function, as follows:

```
sprintf(WindowTitle, "HELP #%d", ++NumHelpWindows);
if (GetApplication()->MakeWindow(
        new TChildWindow(this, WindowTitle, NumHelpWindows)
                          ) == NULL) {
  MessageBox(HWindow, "Failed to create child window",
            "Error", MB_OK);
  NumHelpWindows--; // decrement window number
}
```

The `MakeWindow` function creates an instance of `TChildWindow`. The parent-child link is established by the first argument of `MakeWindow`. The other arguments of `MakeWindow` assign the child window its title and number. If the `MakeWindow` fails to create a child window, it returns a NULL result and displays an error message box.

Creating Basic Windows

To create the WINOBJ1.EXE ObjectWindows application you must create a resource file that contains the WINOBJ1.CPP, MENU3.RC, and OWL.DEF files. Compile and run the program. Click the Help menu to create a few child windows. You should promptly move each child window as you create it. Experiment with closing individual child windows with the Close option in the Control menu. Finally, close the parent window while at least one child window is open. Notice that the child windows close as well. Figure 3.5 contains a sample session with the WINOBJ1.EXE application.

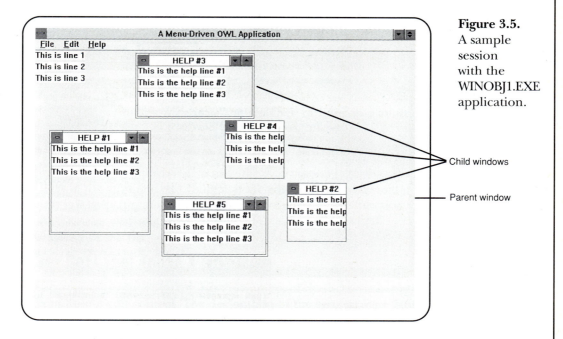

Figure 3.5. A sample session with the WINOBJ1.EXE application.

Scrolling Through Text

One of the versatile features of Windows is the ability to scroll information that cannot be contained in the current viewing portion of the screen. The scroll bars are the visual components of a window that assist in scrolling through the window's contents. A window can have a vertical scroll bar, horizontal scroll bar, or both. A scroll bar contains an arrow box at each end and a scroll thumb. The arrow boxes enable you to scroll the window's contents toward either end or side. The thumb serves two purposes. First, it indicates your position relative to the entire width or length of the information. Second, you can drag

it with the mouse to quickly move in or zoom in on a portion of the viewed information.

Scroll bars also support the auto scrolling and track mode features. *Auto scrolling* enables you to scroll the window's contents by pressing the mouse button inside the window and then dragging the mouse outside the window. This action causes the window's contents to scroll in the direction that you drag the mouse. In addition, the speed of scrolling is proportional to the distance between the mouse cursor and the closest window frame. The further the distance, the faster the window scrolls, and vice versa. The *track mode* affects the scrolling of the window's information when you drag the scroll bar thumb. When the track mode is enabled, the contents of the window are promptly updated with the thumb movement. When the track mode is disabled, the contents of the window are updated only after you release the thumb. Disabling the track mode is beneficial when incrementally updating the window's contents is time consuming. In this case, it is more practical to update the window once, after you have released the scroll bar thumb.

The scrolling effect is supported by a visual interface and an internal "engine." You can easily include visual scroll bars in a window by incorporating the `WS_VSCROLL` and `WS_HSCROLL` styles in the `Style` data member of the window's `Attr` data member. For example, to create a window with both vertical and horizontal scroll bars, use the following statement:

```
// both vertical and horizontal scroll bars
Attr.Style |= WS_VSCROLL | WS_HSCROLL;
```

The `WS_VSCROLL` and `WS_HSCROLL` constants add only the visual aspect of the scroll bars. The functionality is provided by the `TWindow::Scroller` data member (which is of type `PTScroller`). By default, the `Scroller` data member is assigned NULL by the `TWindow` constructors. To create a scroller object, create an instance of `TScroller` in the constructor of your application's window class.

The `TScroller` class contains a number of data members that store and update the information regarding the scrolled window. `AutoMode` and `TrackMode` are two Boolean data members that store the status of the auto scrolling and track mode. These data members are set to TRUE by default. You can access these members to initialize the scrolling mode. You can also change the settings of these members at your discretion.

Other data members you need to know are `XUnit`, `YUnit`, `XLine`, `YLine`, `XPage`, `YPage`, `XPos`, `YPos`, `XRange`, and `YRange`:

- The `XUnit` and `YUnit` members store the number of pixels that constitute the "logical" vertical and horizontal lines, respectively.

> **Caution:** When you want to use the `TextOut` API function to write text, consider the total number of pixels required by the character height and the line spacing. For example, if the character height is 12 pixels and the line space requires 10 pixels, then set `YUnit` to 22. Assign the character width to the `XUnit` data member.

- The `XLine` data member stores the number of `XUnit` pixels (or logical vertical lines) to scroll horizontally when you click the horizontal scroll bar arrows. The default value is 1.

- The `YLine` data member stores the number of `YUnit` pixels (or logical horizontal lines) to scroll vertically when you click the vertical scroll bar arrows. The default value is 1.

- The `XPage` member stores the number of `XUnit` pixels to scroll horizontally when you click the horizontal scroll bar thumb area. By default, the value of `XPage` is calculated by the `SetPageSize`.

- The `YPage` member stores the number of `YUnit` pixels to scroll vertically when you click the vertical scroll bar thumb area. By default, the value of `YPage` is calculated by the `SetPageSize`.

- The `XPos` and `YPos` members return the scroller's current horizontal and vertical positions, respectively.

- The `XRange` is the total number of horizontal lines (in `XUnits`) that the window can scroll.

- The `YRange` is the total number of vertical lines (in `YUnits`) that the window can scroll.

The `TScroller` class has the following constructor that enables you to specify values for the `XUnit`, `YUnit`, `XRange`, and `YRange` data members:

```
TScroller(PTWindow TheWindow, int TheXUnit, int TheYUnit,
         long TheXRange, long TheYRange);
```

The `TScroller` class also contains other member functions that enable you to set or change some of the its data members after the `TScroller` instance is created. Before discussing these member functions, I'll present a simple scrolling window application. Listing 3.11 shows the source code for the WINSCRL1.CPP application, which enables you to scroll through the 100 lines of text created with `TextOut`. The main window has both vertical and horizontal scroll bars and a menu with a single item, Exit.

Listing 3.11. The source code for the WINSCRL1.CPP program file.

```
#include <stdio.h>
#include <string.h>
#include <owl.h>

/*
   declare the constants that manage the character width
   and height, the line height, and the number of columns
   and rows
*/
const MAX_LINES = 100;
const LINE_WIDTH = 25;
const LINE_SPACING_HEIGHT = 10;
const CHAR_HEIGHT = 10;
const CHAR_WIDTH = 8;
const LINE_HEIGHT = CHAR_HEIGHT + LINE_SPACING_HEIGHT;

// declare the custom application class as
// a subclass of TApplication

class TWinApp : public TApplication
{
public:
  TWinApp(LPSTR     AName,            // application name
          HINSTANCE hInstance,        // instance handle
          HINSTANCE hPrevInstance,    // previous instance handle
          LPSTR     lpCmdLine,        // command-line arguments
          int       nCmdShow) :       // display command
          TApplication(AName, hInstance, hPrevInstance,
                       lpCmdLine, nCmdShow) {};

protected:
  virtual void InitMainWindow();

};

// use the _CLASSDEF macro to declare reference and pointer
```

Creating Basic Windows

```cpp
// types related to the new TAppWindow class
_CLASSDEF(TAppWindow)

// expand the functionality of TWindow by deriving class TAppWindow
class TAppWindow : public TWindow
{
public:

  TAppWindow(PTWindowsObject AParent, LPSTR ATitle);

  // handle closing the window
  virtual BOOL CanClose();

protected:
  // return the name of this class
  LPSTR GetClassName() { return "TAppWindow"; }

  // assign the attributes to the Windows class WNDCLASS
  virtual void GetWindowClass(WNDCLASS& W);

  // handle painting the window
  void Paint(HDC DC, PAINTSTRUCT& P);
};

TAppWindow::TAppWindow(PTWindowsObject AParent, LPSTR ATitle) :
                 TWindow(NULL, ATitle)
{
  AssignMenu("EXITMENU");
  Attr.Style |= WS_VSCROLL | WS_HSCROLL;
  Scroller = new TScroller(this,
                           CHAR_WIDTH, LINE_HEIGHT,
                           LINE_WIDTH, MAX_LINES);
  // disable the autoscroll and track modes
  Scroller->AutoMode = FALSE;
  Scroller->TrackMode = FALSE;
}}

void TAppWindow::GetWindowClass(WNDCLASS& W)
{
  TWindow::GetWindowClass(W);
  // select a white background color
  W.hbrBackground = (HBRUSH)(COLOR_HIGHLIGHTTEXT + 1);
}

void TAppWindow::Paint(HDC DC, PAINTSTRUCT& P)
```

continues

Listing 3.11. continued

```
{
  char aLine[LINE_WIDTH + 1];

  // draw MAX_LINES lines of text
  for (BYTE i = 0; i < MAX_LINES; i++) {
    sprintf(aLine, "This is line number %d", i+1);
    TextOut(DC, 0, i * LINE_HEIGHT, aLine, strlen(aLine));
  }
}

BOOL TAppWindow::CanClose()
{
  return MessageBox(HWindow, "Want to close this application",
                    "Query", MB_YESNO | MB_ICONQUESTION) == IDYES;
}

void TWinApp::InitMainWindow()
{
  MainWindow = new TAppWindow(NULL, Name);
}

int PASCAL WinMain(HINSTANCE hInstance, HINSTANCE hPrevInstance,
                   LPSTR lpCmdLine, int nCmdShow)
{
  TWinApp WinApp("A Simple Text Scroller Window",
                 hInstance, hPrevInstance, lpCmdLine, nCmdShow);
  WinApp.Run(); // run OWL application
  return WinApp.Status; // return application status
}
```

The program declares a set of global constants to specify the maximum number of lines, the line width, the line spacing, the character height, the character width, and the total height of a text line.

The application declares two classes, TWinApp and TAppWindow. The TAppWindow implements the scrollable window. The window's constructor performs the following tasks:

- Invokes the constructor of its parent class.
- Assigns the EXITMENU menu resource to the window's menu.

- Sets the `Attr.Style` data member to create a window with vertical and horizontal scroll bars.

- Creates an instance of `TScroller` by using the arguments `CHAR_WIDTH` for `TheXUnit`, `LINE_HEIGHT` for `TheYUnit`, `LINE_WIDTH` for `TheXRange`, and `MAX_LINES` for `TheYRange`. The scroll bar instance is accessed by the inherited `TWindow::Scroller` data member. The `Scroller` pointer controls any further manipulation of the scroll bars.

To complement the action of the scroll bars, the `TAppWindow` class declares a new version of the `Paint` member function. This new version calls the `TextOut` function to draw the lines. The drawing of the text line is systematic, relying on the clipping feature of the window to display only those lines that can be seen. The values of `Scroller->XPos` and `Scroller->YPos` determine which lines are clipped. The `Paint` function draws the first text line at the logical line number 0, the second text line at the logical line number 1, and so on.

To create the WINSCRL1.EXE ObjectWindows application, first create a resource file that contains the WINSCRL1.CPP, WINDOW1.RC, and OWL.DEF files. Compile and run the program. The application displays a number of leading lines contained in a scrollable window. Use the vertical scroll bar to scroll up or down, slowly or quickly. You will witness the result of the cooperation among the `Paint` member function and the member functions of the `TScroller` instance. Figure 3.6 shows a sample session with the WINSCRL1.EXE program.

The Auto Scroll and Track Modes

The last application enables both the auto scroll and track modes by default. This section presents a modified version that enables you to toggle the auto scroll and track modes with menu options. You then can test the effect of enabling and disabling these scrolling modes.

Figure 3.6.
A sample session with the WINSCRL1.EXE program.

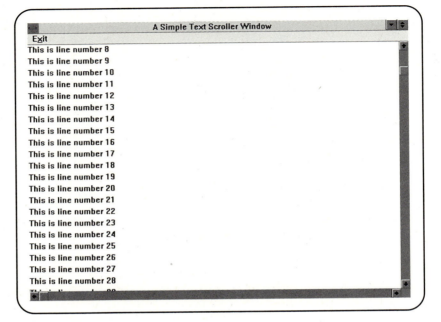

Notes: ObjectWindows enables you to set and modify the auto scrolling mode by assigning TRUE or FALSE to the Boolean member Scroll->AutoMode. Similarly, you can set and toggle the track mode by manipulating the Boolean member Scroll->TrackMode. Some applications tolerate enabling the track mode, such as programs that view single pages of .BMP or any other graphics image. On the other hand, some applications run more smoothly when you disable the track mode altogether, such as an electronic Rolodex application that displays personal contacts information. In between these two extreme cases is a third case wherein the track mode is conditionally enabled or disabled. For example, a file viewer utility disables the track mode when you view a large text file and enables the track mode when you view a small file.

The next program uses the WINSCRL2.H header file (Listing 3.12), the WINSCRL2.RC resource file (Listing 3.13), and the WINSCRL2.CPP program file (Listing 3.14).

The header file (Listing 3.12) defines the constants for the commands that toggle the auto scrolling and track modes. The resource file script (Listing 3.13) defines the menu resource for the application. The menu has two main items, Exit and Toggle. The latter item is a pop-up menu with options that toggle the two scrolling modes.

Listing 3.12. The source code for the WINSCRL2.H header file.

```
#define CM_AUTOSCROLL 201
#define CM_TRACKMODE 202
```

Listing 3.13. The script of the resource file WINSCRL2.RC.

```
#include <windows.h>
#include <owlrc.h>
#include "winscrl2.h"

EXITMENU MENU LOADONCALL MOVEABLE PURE DISCARDABLE
BEGIN
    MENUITEM "E&xit", CM_EXIT
    POPUP "&Toggle"
    BEGIN
      MENUITEM "&Auto scrolling", CM_AUTOSCROLL
      MENUITEM "&Track mode", CM_TRACKMODE
    END
END
```

Listing 3.14 shows the source code for the ObjectWindows application. I developed the WINSCRL2.CPP file from the WINSCRL1.CPP file by adding the `#include "winscrl2.h"` directive and the `CMAutoScroll` and `CMTrackMode` member functions.

Listing 3.14. The source code for the WINSCRL2.CPP program file.

```
#include <stdio.h>
#include <string.h>
#include <owl.h>
#include "winscrl2.h"

/*
  declare the constants that manage the character width
```

continues

Listing 3.14. continued

```
  and height, the line height, and the number of columns
  and rows
*/
const MAX_LINES = 100;
const LINE_WIDTH = 25;
const LINE_SPACING_HEIGHT = 10;
const CHAR_HEIGHT = 10;
const CHAR_WIDTH = 8;
const LINE_HEIGHT = CHAR_HEIGHT + LINE_SPACING_HEIGHT;

// declare the custom application class as
// a subclass of TApplication

class TWinApp : public TApplication
{
public:
  TWinApp(LPSTR     AName,           // application name
          HINSTANCE hInstance,        // instance handle
          HINSTANCE hPrevInstance,    // previous instance handle
          LPSTR     lpCmdLine,        // command-line arguments
          int       nCmdShow) :       // display command
          TApplication(AName, hInstance, hPrevInstance,
                       lpCmdLine, nCmdShow) {};

protected:
  virtual void InitMainWindow();

};

// use the _CLASSDEF macro to declare reference and pointer
// types related to the new TAppWindow class
_CLASSDEF(TAppWindow)

// expand the functionality of TWindow by deriving class TAppWindow
class TAppWindow : public TWindow
{
public:

  TAppWindow(PTWindowsObject AParent, LPSTR ATitle);

  // handle toggling the autoscroll feature
  virtual void CMAutoScroll(RTMessage Msg)
      = [CM_FIRST + CM_AUTOSCROLL];

  // handle toggling the track mode feature
```

```
    virtual void CMTrackMode(RTMessage Msg)
       = [CM_FIRST + CM_TRACKMODE];

    // handle closing the window
    virtual BOOL CanClose();

protected:
    // return the name of this class
    LPSTR GetClassName() { return "TAppWindow"; }

    // assign the attributes to the Windows class WNDCLASS
    virtual void GetWindowClass(WNDCLASS& W);

    // handle painting the window
    virtual void Paint(HDC DC, PAINTSTRUCT& P);
};

TAppWindow::TAppWindow(PTWindowsObject AParent, LPSTR ATitle) :
                TWindow(AParent, ATitle)
{
   AssignMenu("EXITMENU");
   Attr.Style |= WS_VSCROLL | WS_HSCROLL;
   Scroller = new TScroller(this,
                            CHAR_WIDTH, LINE_HEIGHT,
                            LINE_WIDTH, MAX_LINES);
}

void TAppWindow::GetWindowClass(WNDCLASS& W)
{
   TWindow::GetWindowClass(W);
   // select a white background color
   W.hbrBackground = (HBRUSH)(COLOR_HIGHLIGHTTEXT + 1);
}

void TAppWindow::Paint(HDC DC, PAINTSTRUCT& P)
{
   char aLine[LINE_WIDTH + 1];

   // draw MAX_LINES lines of text
   for (BYTE i = 0; i < MAX_LINES; i++) {
      sprintf(aLine, "This is line number %d", i+1);
      TextOut(DC, 0, i * LINE_HEIGHT, aLine, strlen(aLine));
   }
}
void TAppWindow::CMAutoScroll(RTMessage Msg)
```

continues

Listing 3.14. continued

```
{
  // toggle the AutoMode data member
  Scroller->AutoMode = (Scroller->AutoMode == TRUE) ? FALSE : TRUE;
  // display a message that conveys the current status
  // of the autoscrolling mode
  if (Scroller->AutoMode)
    MessageBox(HWindow, "Autoscrolling mode is now ON",
               "Information", MB_OK | MB_ICONINFORMATION);
  else
      MessageBox(HWindow, "Autoscrolling mode is now OFF",
               "Information", MB_OK | MB_ICONINFORMATION);
}

void TAppWindow::CMTrackMode(RTMessage Msg)
{
  // toggle the TrackMode data member
  Scroller->TrackMode = (Scroller->TrackMode == TRUE) ? FALSE : TRUE;
  // display a message that conveys the current status
  // of the track mode
  if (Scroller->TrackMode)
    MessageBox(HWindow, "Track mode is now ON",
               "Information", MB_OK | MB_ICONINFORMATION);
  else
      MessageBox(HWindow, "Track mode is now OFF",
               "Information", MB_OK | MB_ICONINFORMATION);
}

BOOL TAppWindow::CanClose()
{
  return MessageBox(HWindow, "Want to close this application",
                    "Query", MB_YESNO | MB_ICONQUESTION) == IDYES;
}

void TWinApp::InitMainWindow()
{
  MainWindow = new TAppWindow(NULL, Name);
}

int PASCAL WinMain(HINSTANCE hInstance, HINSTANCE hPrevInstance,
                   LPSTR lpCmdLine, int nCmdShow)
{
  TWinApp WinApp("A Simple Text Scroller Window",
```

```
                    hInstance, hPrevInstance, lpCmdLine, nCmdShow);
    WinApp.Run(); // run OWL application
    return WinApp.Status; // return application status
}
```

The `TAppWindow` class constructor disables the auto scroll and track mode. This action reverses the default settings assigned by the `TScroller` constructor.

The `CMAutoScroll` member function traps the `CM_AUTOSCROLL` command and performs two basic tasks: it toggles the `Scroller-AutoMode` data member and displays a message that reveals the current status of the auto scrolling mode.

The `CMTrackMode` member function traps the `CM_TRACKMODE` command and also performs two basic tasks: it toggles the `Scroller->TrackMode` data member and displays a message that reveals the current status of the track mode.

To compile the WINSCRL2.EXE file, you must create a project file that includes the WINSCRL2.CPP, WINSCRL2.RC, and OWL.DEF files. Compile and run the program. Initially, the auto scrolling and track modes are disabled. Test both features and then toggle either or both modes. Test the scrolling bar mode for its new state. Figure 3.7 shows a sample session with the WINSCRL2.EXE program.

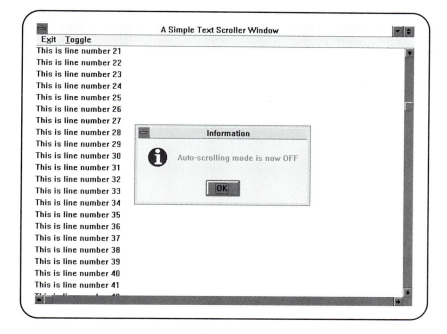

Figure 3.7. A sample session with the WINSCRL2.EXE application.

Changing the Scroll Bar Metrics

The `TScroller` constructor accepts arguments that assign values to the `XUnit`, `YUnit`, `XRange`, and `YRange` data members. Often, the arguments for these members are adequate for the application instance. However, in some applications this information is either not known ahead of time or might differ at run-time. The next example explores the possibility of displaying text with different values for the data members `XUnit`, `YUnit`, `XLine`, `YLine`, `XPage`, `YPage`, `XRange`, and `YRange`.

ObjectWindows enables you to set new values for `XUnit` and `YUnit` by using the `SetUnits` member function. This function has the following declaration:

```
void SetUnits(int TheXUnit, int TheYUnit);
```

You can also set new values for `XRange` and `YRange` with the `SetRange` member function. The declaration of this function is

```
void SetRange(long TheXRange, long TheYRange);
```

> **Tip:** Setting the `XPage` and `YPage` data members is a bit trickier, because whenever you change the size of the window, the `WM_SIZE` message invokes the window's `WMSize` member function, which in turn calls the scroller's `SetPageSize` member function. The `SetPageSize` function sets the values of `XPage` and `YPage` according to the current window size and the values of data members `XUnit` and `YUnit`. Consequently, to set your own values for `XPage` and `YPage`, you must declare in your window class a virtual member function `WMSize` that responds to the `WM_SIZE` message. The declared `WMSize` can then customize the setting of the scroller's `XPage` and `YPage` members.

You can also set the values of `XLine` and `YLine` by directly accessing them with the scroller pointer. The default value of 1 is adequate for most applications. You rarely will need to change these settings.

To simulate the variations in text, the next application enables you to select from three sets of text. The first set contains 100 lines, with each line height set at 20 pixels. The second set contains 200 lines, with each line height set at 17 pixels. The third set contains 50 lines, with each line height set at 15 pixels.

When you first run the application, the window contains no text. You can select a specific set of text lines from a pop-up menu item. The other menu options enable you to toggle the auto scrolling and track modes (a feature similar to the last program) and exit the program.

The variant text application uses the WINSCRL3.H file (Listing 3.15) to define a number of constants for the menu commands. The program also uses the menu resource defined in Listing 3.16.

Listing 3.15. The source code for the WINSCRL3.H header file.

```
#define CM_AUTOSCROLL 201
#define CM_TRACKMODE 202
#define CM_SELECTSET1 203
#define CM_SELECTSET2 204
#define CM_SELECTSET3 205
```

Listing 3.16. The script for the resource file WINSCRL3.RC.

```
#include <windows.h>
#include <owlrc.h>
#include "winscrl3.h"

EXITMENU MENU LOADONCALL MOVEABLE PURE DISCARDABLE
BEGIN
    MENUITEM "E&xit", CM_EXIT
    POPUP "&Toggle"
    BEGIN
      MENUITEM "&Auto scrolling", CM_AUTOSCROLL
      MENUITEM "&Track mode", CM_TRACKMODE
    END
    POPUP "&Select Line Set"
    BEGIN
      MENUITEM "Set 1", CM_SELECTSET1
      MENUITEM "Set 2", CM_SELECTSET2
      MENUITEM "Set 3", CM_SELECTSET3
    END
END
```

Listing 3.17. The source code for the WINSCRL3.CPP program file.

```cpp
#include <stdio.h>
#include <string.h>
#include <owl.h>
#include "winscrl3.h"

// declare the custom application class as
// a subclass of TApplication

class TWinApp : public TApplication
{
public:
   TWinApp(LPSTR     AName,           // application name
           HINSTANCE hInstance,       // instance handle
           HINSTANCE hPrevInstance,   // previous instance handle
           LPSTR     lpCmdLine,       // command-line arguments
           int       nCmdShow) :      // display command
           TApplication(AName, hInstance, hPrevInstance,
                     lpCmdLine, nCmdShow) {};

protected:
   virtual void InitMainWindow();

};

// use the _CLASSDEF macro to declare reference and pointer
// types related to the new TAppWindow class
_CLASSDEF(TAppWindow)

// expand the functionality of TWindow by deriving class TAppWindow
class TAppWindow : public TWindow
{
public:

   TAppWindow(PTWindowsObject AParent, LPSTR ATitle);

   // handle toggling the autoscroll feature
   virtual void CMAutoScroll(RTMessage Msg)
      = [CM_FIRST + CM_AUTOSCROLL];

   // handle toggling the track mode feature
   virtual void CMTrackMode(RTMessage Msg)
      = [CM_FIRST + CM_TRACKMODE];
```

```cpp
    // handle selecting the first set of lines
    virtual void CMSelectSet1(RTMessage Msg)
       = [CM_FIRST + CM_SELECTSET1];

    // handle selecting the second set of lines
    virtual void CMSelectSet2(RTMessage Msg)
       = [CM_FIRST + CM_SELECTSET2];

    // handle selecting the third set of lines
    virtual void CMSelectSet3(RTMessage Msg)
       = [CM_FIRST + CM_SELECTSET3];

    // handle closing the window
    virtual BOOL CanClose();

protected:
    // declare protected data members that store the data
    // for the various set of lines
    int SetOfLinesIndex;
    long MaxLines;
    long LineWidth;
    int LineSpacingHeight;
    int CharHeight;
    int CharWidth;
    int LineHeight;

    // store the current values for the SetPageSize member
    int xPage;
    int yPage;

    // return the name of this class
    LPSTR GetClassName() { return "TAppWindow"; }

    // assign the attributes to the Windows class WNDCLASS
    virtual void GetWindowClass(WNDCLASS& W);

    // handle painting the window
    virtual void Paint(HDC DC, PAINTSTRUCT& P);

    // handle setting the page sizes
    virtual void WMSize(RTMessage Msg)
       = [WM_FIRST + WM_SIZE];
};
```

continues

Listing 3.17. continued

```cpp
TAppWindow::TAppWindow(PTWindowsObject AParent, LPSTR ATitle) :
                      TWindow(AParent, ATitle)
{
  AssignMenu("EXITMENU");
  Attr.Style |= WS_VSCROLL | WS_HSCROLL;
  Scroller = new TScroller(this, 1, 1, 10, 10);
  // set the index of the selected set of text to 0
  SetOfLinesIndex = 0;
  // set arbitrary values to xPage and yPage
  xPage = 10;
  yPage = 10;
}

void TAppWindow::GetWindowClass(WNDCLASS& W)
{
  TWindow::GetWindowClass(W);
  // select a white background color
  W.hbrBackground = (HBRUSH)(COLOR_HIGHLIGHTTEXT + 1);
}

void TAppWindow::Paint(HDC DC, PAINTSTRUCT& P)
{
  char aLine[40];
  char formatStr[40];

  switch (SetOfLinesIndex) {
    case 0:
      return; // exit the function
    case 1:
      strcpy(formatStr, "This is line number %d of set 1");
      break;
    case 2:
      strcpy(formatStr, "This is line number %d of set 2");
      break;
    case 3:
      strcpy(formatStr, "This is line number %d of set 3");
      break;
  }
  // draw MaxLines lines of text
  for (BYTE i = 0; i < MaxLines; i++) {
    sprintf(aLine, formatStr, i+1);
    TextOut(DC, 0, i * LineHeight, aLine, strlen(aLine));
  }
}
```

```cpp
void TAppWindow::CMAutoScroll(RTMessage Msg)
{
  // toggle the AutoMode data member
  Scroller->AutoMode = (Scroller->AutoMode == TRUE) ? FALSE : TRUE;
  // display a message that conveys the current status
  // of the autoscrolling mode
  if (Scroller->AutoMode)
    MessageBox(HWindow, "Autoscrolling mode is now ON",
               "Information", MB_OK | MB_ICONINFORMATION);
  else
      MessageBox(HWindow, "Autoscrolling mode is now OFF",
               "Information", MB_OK | MB_ICONINFORMATION);
}

void TAppWindow::CMTrackMode(RTMessage Msg)
{
  // toggle the TrackMode data member
  Scroller->TrackMode = (Scroller->TrackMode == TRUE) ? FALSE : TRUE;
  // display a message that conveys the current status
  // of the track mode
  if (Scroller->TrackMode)
    MessageBox(HWindow, "Track mode is now ON",
               "Information", MB_OK | MB_ICONINFORMATION);
  else
      MessageBox(HWindow, "Track mode is now OFF",
               "Information", MB_OK | MB_ICONINFORMATION);
}

BOOL TAppWindow::CanClose()
{
  return MessageBox(HWindow, "Want to close this application",
                    "Query", MB_YESNO | MB_ICONQUESTION) == IDYES;
}

void TAppWindow::CMSelectSet1(RTMessage Msg)
{
  // assign the data to describe the first set of lines
  SetOfLinesIndex = 1;
  MaxLines = 100;
  LineWidth = 25;
  LineSpacingHeight = 10;
  CharHeight = 10;
  CharWidth = 8;
  LineHeight = CharHeight + LineSpacingHeight;
  // set new values for XRange and YRange
```

continues

Listing 3.17. continued

```cpp
    Scroller->SetRange(LineWidth, MaxLines);
    // set new values for XUnit and YUnit
    Scroller->SetUnits(CharWidth, LineHeight);
    // assign new values to the xPage and yPage data members.
    // These values are copied by the SetPageSize function into
    // the TScroller::XPage and TScroller::YPage data members
    // whenever the window is resized.
    xPage = 10;
    yPage = MaxLines / 4;
    // assign values to the XLine and YLine data members.
    // These values are actually the default settings.
    Scroller->XLine = 1;
    Scroller->YLine = 1;
    // clear the window
    InvalidateRect(HWindow, NULL, TRUE);
}

void TAppWindow::CMSelectSet2(RTMessage Msg)
{
    // assign the data to describe the second set of lines
    SetOfLinesIndex = 2;
    MaxLines = 200;
    LineWidth = 40;
    LineSpacingHeight = 7;
    CharHeight = 10;
    CharWidth = 8;
    LineHeight = CharHeight + LineSpacingHeight;
    // set new values for XRange and YRange
    Scroller->SetRange(LineWidth, MaxLines);
    // set new values for XUnit and YUnit
    Scroller->SetUnits(CharWidth, LineHeight);
    // assign new values to the xPage and yPage data members.
    // These values are copied by the SetPageSize function into
    // the TScroller::XPage and TScroller::YPage data members
    // whenever the window is resized.
    xPage = 10;
    yPage = MaxLines / 4;
    // assign values to the XLine and YLine data members.
    // These values are rather unusual and are for demonstration
    // purpose only.
    Scroller->XLine = 2;
    Scroller->YLine = 2;
    // clear the window
    InvalidateRect(HWindow, NULL, TRUE);
```

```cpp
}

void TAppWindow::CMSelectSet3(RTMessage Msg)
{
  // assign the data to describe the third set of lines
  SetOfLinesIndex = 3;
  MaxLines = 50;
  LineWidth = 30;
  LineSpacingHeight = 5;
  CharHeight = 10;
  CharWidth = 8;
  LineHeight = CharHeight + LineSpacingHeight;
  // set new values for XRange and YRange
  Scroller->SetRange(LineWidth, MaxLines);
  // set new values for XUnit and YUnit
  Scroller->SetUnits(CharWidth, LineHeight);
  // assign new values to the xPage and yPage data members.
  // These values are copied by the SetPageSize function into
  // the TScroller::XPage and TScroller::YPage data members
  // whenever the window is resized.
  xPage = 10;
  yPage = MaxLines / 4;
  // assign values to the XLine and YLine data members.
  // These values are actually the default settings.
  Scroller->XLine = 1;
  Scroller->YLine = 1;
  // clear the window
  InvalidateRect(HWindow, NULL, TRUE);
}

void TAppWindow::WMSize(RTMessage Msg)
{
  // call parent's member function
  TWindow::WMSize(Msg);
  // override the assignments made to XPage and YPage
  Scroller->XPage = xPage;
  Scroller->YPage = yPage;
}

void TWinApp::InitMainWindow()
{
  MainWindow = new TAppWindow(NULL, Name);
}
```

continues

Listing 3.17. continued

```
int PASCAL WinMain(HINSTANCE hInstance, HINSTANCE hPrevInstance,
                   LPSTR lpCmdLine, int nCmdShow)
{
  TWinApp WinApp("A Simple Text Scroller Window",
                 hInstance, hPrevInstance, lpCmdLine, nCmdShow);
  WinApp.Run(); // run OWL application
  return WinApp.Status; // return application status
}
```

The program supports the various sets of text by using the following special members of the TAppWindow class:

- The protected data members store the information related to the currently displayed text. The SetOfLinesIndex member stores the index of the current set of text. Other members are MaxLines, LineWidth, LineSpacingHeight, CharHeight, CharWidth, and LineHeight. The names of the data members resemble the names of constants that appear in the last program. The difference is that the line-related information is now a data member and not a constant.

- The protected data members xPage and yPage store the values used by the application's WMSize member function to set the XPage and YPage members of the scroller.

> **Caution:** Note that the names of the xPage and yPage data members and the XPage and YPage data members differ only in case. This is acceptable, because C++ is a case-sensitive language. However, in practice, you should avoid naming data members so that they differ only in case.

- The Paint member function employs the value of SetOfLinesIndex to select the format string used in building the displayed text lines. In addition, the function uses the MaxLines and LineHeight data members to obtain the number of lines and the total line height.

- A family of CMSelectSetx member functions assigns different values to the MaxLines, LineWidth, and LineSpacingHeight data members. Each routine sets the new XRange and YRange members by calling the scroller's SetRange member function. The member functions also set the XUnit and YUnit data members by invoking the scroller's SetUnits member function. The functions also assign values to the xPage and yPage data members, as well as the scroller's data members XLine and YLine. The assignments for the XLine and YLine are for the sake of demonstration. The last statement in these member functions calls the **InvalidateRect** API function to clear the window before displaying another set of text. Without calling the **InvalidateRect** function, the new set of lines simply overwrites the old set.

The application uses the WMSize member function to set the scroller's XPage and YPage members to their respective values. The WMSize function first calls the parent's WMSize member function and then sets the values for the scroller's XPage and YPage members.

Also notice that the TAppWindow constructor initializes TScroller with arbitrary values—values that the program does not use when displaying text.

To compile the WINSCRL3.EXE file, you must create a project file that includes the WINSCRL3.CPP, WINSCRL3.RC, and OWL.DEF files. Compile and run the program. Initially, the window displays no text. Use the menu options to select a set of text lines. Scroll down through the text and select another set. What do you notice? The new set starts with the same line number where the previous set left off. For example, if the first line in the window is line 20 of set 1 and you switch to set 2, you will also see line 20 of set 2. The next example deals with "correcting" this feature. Figure 3.8 shows a sample session with the WINSCRL3.EXE application.

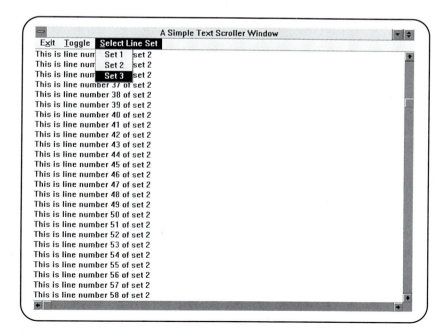

Figure 3.8. A sample session with the WINSCRL3.EXE application.

Internally Induced Scrolling

The WINSCRL3.EXE application presented in the last section has a special feature. When you choose a different set of text lines, the application does not reset the vertical scroll bar position at the top. In addition, the application's implementation of the `Paint` member function is rather inefficient. The function systematically attempts to paint all of the lines without taking the following two conditions into account:

- The current location of the vertical scroll bar thumb
- The height of the window's workspace

As result, there are many calls to the `TextOut` API function that result in clipping the requested lines because they are located outside the current viewing portion of the window.

In this section, I discuss the scroll bar member functions that enable you to internally position or shift the scroll bars. I also discuss the techniques that fine-tune the `Paint` member function.

The `TScroller` class uses the `ScrollTo` member function to scroll at a specific location. The `ScrollTo` function has the following declaration:

```
virtual void ScrollTo(long X, long Y);
```

The `ScrollTo` function first checks the arguments for `X` and `Y` (which are expressed in `XUnit` and `YUnit` pixels) and then moves to the specified location. Keep in mind that the first vertical and horizontal lines are both numbered 0.

The `TScroller` class also offers the `ScrollBy` member function that enables you to shift the scroll bars in either direction. The `ScrollBy` function has the following declaration:

```
void ScrollBy(long Dx, long Dy);
```

The parameter `Dx` specifies the shift in the horizontal scroll bar. Assigning a 0 argument to `Dx` maintains the current position of the horizontal scroll bar thumb. Positive and negative arguments for `Dx` move the horizontal scroll bar thumb to the right and to the left, respectively. The parameter `Dy` specifies the shift in the vertical scroll bar. Assigning a 0 argument to `Dy` maintains the current position of the vertical scroll bar thumb. Positive and negative arguments for `Dy` move the vertical scroll bar thumb down and up, respectively.

Creating Basic Windows

The next ObjectWindows application adds the pop-up Scroll To and Scroll By main menu items to the menu of the previous application. The Scroll To menu item enables you to scroll to the top, to the bottom, or to a user specified line. The last option uses an input dialog box. The Scroll By menu item enables you to scroll up or down by a number of lines that you specify. These two options also utilize an input dialog box and each of them stores your last input separately.

The next application uses the WINSCRL4.H header file in Listing 3.18, the resource file script WINSCRL4.RC in Listing 3.19, and the WINSCRL4.CPP source code in Listing 3.20.

The WINSCRL4.H header file defines the command constants used by the menu resource defined in the WINWSCRL4.RC file. Notice that the .RC resource file contains the `#include <inputdia.dlg>` directive that provides the input dialog box resource. The WINSCRL4.RC resource file expands the WINSCRL3.RC resource file by adding the Scroll To and Scroll By pop-up menu items.

Listing 3.18. The source code for the WINSCRL4.H header file.

```
#define CM_AUTOSCROLL 201
#define CM_TRACKMODE 202
#define CM_SELECTSET1 203
#define CM_SELECTSET2 204
#define CM_SELECTSET3 205
#define CM_SCROLLTOTOP 206
#define CM_SCROLLTOBOTTOM 207
#define CM_SCROLLTOLINE 208
#define CM_SCROLLUPBY 209
#define CM_SCROLLDOWNBY 210
```

Listing 3.19. The script for the WINSCRL4.RC resource file.

```
#include <windows.h>
#include <owlrc.h>
#include "winscrl4.h"
#include <inputdia.dlg>

EXITMENU MENU LOADONCALL MOVEABLE PURE DISCARDABLE
BEGIN
    MENUITEM "E&xit", CM_EXIT
    POPUP "&Toggle"
```

continues

Listing 3.19. continued

```
    BEGIN
      MENUITEM "&Auto scrolling", CM_AUTOSCROLL
      MENUITEM "&Track mode", CM_TRACKMODE
    END
    POPUP "&Select Line Set"
    BEGIN
      MENUITEM "Set 1", CM_SELECTSET1
      MENUITEM "Set 2", CM_SELECTSET2
      MENUITEM "Set 3", CM_SELECTSET3
    END
    POPUP "Scroll T&o"
    BEGIN
      MENUITEM "&Top", CM_SCROLLTOTOP
      MENUITEM "&Bottom", CM_SCROLLTOBOTTOM
      MENUITEM "&Line...", CM_SCROLLTOLINE
    END
    POPUP "Scroll &By"
    BEGIN
      MENUITEM "&Up...", CM_SCROLLUPBY
      MENUITEM "&Down...", CM_SCROLLDOWNBY
    END
END
```

Listing 3.20 shows the source code for the ObjectWindows application. The source code uses the `#include` directive to include the INPUTDIA.H header file that contains the declaration of the `TInputDialog` class. The program uses a modal instance of `TInputDIalog` to prompt for input when you select various menu items.

Listing 3.20. The source code for the WINSCRL4.CPP program file.

```
#include <stdlib.h>
#include <stdio.h>
#include <string.h>
#include <owl.h>
#include <inputdia.h>
#include "winscrl4.h"

// declare the custom application class as
// a subclass of TApplication
```

```cpp
class TWinApp : public TApplication
{
public:
  TWinApp(LPSTR     AName,           // application name
          HINSTANCE hInstance,       // instance handle
          HINSTANCE hPrevInstance,   // previous instance handle
          LPSTR     lpCmdLine,       // command-line arguments
          int       nCmdShow) :      // display command
          TApplication(AName, hInstance, hPrevInstance,
                     lpCmdLine, nCmdShow) {};

protected:
  virtual void InitMainWindow();

};

// use the _CLASSDEF macro to declare reference and pointer
// types related to the new TAppWindow class
_CLASSDEF(TAppWindow)

// expand the functionality of TWindow by deriving class TAppWindow
class TAppWindow : public TWindow
{
public:

  TAppWindow(PTWindowsObject AParent, LPSTR ATitle);

  // handle toggling the autoscroll feature
  virtual void CMAutoScroll(RTMessage Msg)
     = [CM_FIRST + CM_AUTOSCROLL];

  // handle toggling the track mode feature
  virtual void CMTrackMode(RTMessage Msg)
     = [CM_FIRST + CM_TRACKMODE];

  // handle selecting the first set of lines
  virtual void CMSelectSet1(RTMessage Msg)
     = [CM_FIRST + CM_SELECTSET1];

  // handle selecting the second set of lines
  virtual void CMSelectSet2(RTMessage Msg)
     = [CM_FIRST + CM_SELECTSET2];

  // handle selecting the third set of lines
  virtual void CMSelectSet3(RTMessage Msg)
     = [CM_FIRST + CM_SELECTSET3];
```

continues

Listing 3.20. continued

```
    // handle scrolling to the top
    virtual void CMScrollToTop(RTMessage Msg)
        = [CM_FIRST + CM_SCROLLTOTOP];

    // handle scrolling to the bottom
    virtual void CMScrollToBottom(RTMessage Msg)
        = [CM_FIRST + CM_SCROLLTOBOTTOM];

    // handle scrolling to a user-specified line
    virtual void CMScrollToLine(RTMessage Msg)
        = [CM_FIRST + CM_SCROLLTOLINE];

    // handle scrolling up by a user-specified number of lines
    virtual void CMScrollUpBy(RTMessage Msg)
        = [CM_FIRST + CM_SCROLLUPBY];

    // handle scrolling down by a user-specified number of lines
    virtual void CMScrollDownBy(RTMessage Msg)
        = [CM_FIRST + CM_SCROLLDOWNBY];

    // handle closing the window
    virtual BOOL CanClose();

protected:
    // declare protected data members that store the data
    // for the various set of lines
    int SetOfLinesIndex;
    long MaxLines;
    long LineWidth;
    int LineSpacingHeight;
    int CharHeight;
    int CharWidth;
    int LineHeight;

    // store the current values for the SetPageSize member
    int xPage;
    int yPage;

    // return the name of this class
    LPSTR GetClassName() { return "TAppWindow"; }

    // assign the attributes to the Windows class WNDCLASS
    virtual void GetWindowClass(WNDCLASS& W);
```

Creating Basic Windows

```cpp
  // handle painting the window
  virtual void Paint(HDC DC, PAINTSTRUCT& P);

  // handle resizing the window
  virtual void WMSize(RTMessage Msg)
    = [WM_FIRST + WM_SIZE];
};

TAppWindow::TAppWindow(PTWindowsObject AParent, LPSTR ATitle) :
                      TWindow(AParent, ATitle)
{
  AssignMenu("EXITMENU");
  Attr.Style |= WS_VSCROLL | WS_HSCROLL;
  Scroller = new TScroller(this, 1, 1, 10, 10);
  // set the index of the selected set of text to 0
  SetOfLinesIndex = 0;
  // set arbitrary values to xPage and yPage
  xPage = 10;
  yPage = 10;
}


void TAppWindow::GetWindowClass(WNDCLASS& W)
{
  TWindow::GetWindowClass(W);
  // select a white background color
  W.hbrBackground = (HBRUSH)(COLOR_HIGHLIGHTTEXT + 1);
}

void TAppWindow::Paint(HDC DC, PAINTSTRUCT& P)
{
  char aLine[40];
  char formatStr[40];
  int yp = Scroller->YPos;
  int xwide;
  int yu = Scroller->YUnit;

  switch (SetOfLinesIndex) {
    case 0:
      return; // exit the function
    case 1:
      strcpy(formatStr, "This is line number %d of set 1");
      break;
    case 2:
      strcpy(formatStr, "This is line number %d of set 2");
      break;
```

continues

Listing 3.20. continued

```
    case 3:
      strcpy(formatStr, "This is line number %d of set 3");
      break;
  }
  // draw lines of text starting with line YPos
  for (int y = yp; y < (yp + Attr.H / yu); y++) {
    sprintf(aLine, formatStr, y+1);
    TextOut(DC, 0, y * yu, aLine, strlen(aLine));
  }
}

void TAppWindow::CMAutoScroll(RTMessage Msg)
{
  // toggle the AutoMode data member
  Scroller->AutoMode = (Scroller->AutoMode == TRUE) ? FALSE : TRUE;
  // display a message that conveys the current status
  // of the autoscrolling mode
  if (Scroller->AutoMode)
    MessageBox(HWindow, "Autoscrolling mode is now ON",
               "Information", MB_OK | MB_ICONINFORMATION);
  else
      MessageBox(HWindow, "Autoscrolling mode is now OFF",
               "Information", MB_OK | MB_ICONINFORMATION);
}

void TAppWindow::CMTrackMode(RTMessage Msg)
{
  // toggle the TrackMode data member
  Scroller->TrackMode = (Scroller->TrackMode == TRUE) ? FALSE : TRUE;
  // display a message that conveys the current status
  // of the track mode
  if (Scroller->TrackMode)
    MessageBox(HWindow, "Track mode is now ON",
               "Information", MB_OK | MB_ICONINFORMATION);
  else
      MessageBox(HWindow, "Track mode is now OFF",
               "Information", MB_OK | MB_ICONINFORMATION);
}

void TAppWindow::CMScrollToTop(RTMessage Msg)
{
  Scroller->ScrollTo(0, 0);
}
```

```cpp
void TAppWindow::CMScrollToBottom(RTMessage Msg)
{
   Scroller->ScrollTo(0, MaxLines-1);
}

void TAppWindow::CMScrollToLine(RTMessage Msg)
{
 static int MoveToLine = 1;
 char s[10];

 sprintf(s, "%d", MoveToLine);
 if (GetApplication()->ExecDialog(
        new TInputDialog(this, "Numeric Input", "Go to line?",
                         s, sizeof(s))) == IDOK)
    {
       MoveToLine = atoi(s);
       Scroller->ScrollTo(0, MoveToLine-1);
    }
}

void TAppWindow::CMScrollUpBy(RTMessage Msg)
{
 static MoveUpBy = 1;
 char s[10];

 sprintf(s, "%d", MoveUpBy);
 if (GetApplication()->ExecDialog(
        new TInputDialog(this, "Numeric Input", "Scroll up by?",
                         s, sizeof(s))) == IDOK)
    {
       MoveUpBy = atoi(s);
       Scroller->ScrollBy(0, -MoveUpBy);
    }
}

void TAppWindow::CMScrollDownBy(RTMessage Msg)
{
 static MoveDownBy = 1;
 char s[10];

 sprintf(s, "%d", MoveDownBy);
 if (GetApplication()->ExecDialog(
        new TInputDialog(this, "Numeric Input", "Scroll down by?",
                         s, sizeof(s))) == IDOK)
    {
```

continues

Listing 3.20. continued

```
      MoveDownBy = atoi(s);
      Scroller->ScrollBy(0, MoveDownBy);
    }
}

BOOL TAppWindow::CanClose()
{
  return MessageBox(HWindow, "Want to close this application",
                    "Query", MB_YESNO | MB_ICONQUESTION) == IDYES;
}

void TAppWindow::CMSelectSet1(RTMessage Msg)
{
  // assign the data to describe the first set of lines
  SetOfLinesIndex = 1;
  MaxLines = 100;
  LineWidth = 25;
  LineSpacingHeight = 10;
  CharHeight = 10;
  CharWidth = 8;
  LineHeight = CharHeight + LineSpacingHeight;
  // set new values for XRange and YRange
  Scroller->SetRange(LineWidth, MaxLines);
  // set new values for XUnit and YUnit
  Scroller->SetUnits(CharWidth, LineHeight);
  // assign new values to the xPage and yPage data members.
  // These values are copied by the SetPageSize function into
  // the TScroller::XPage and TScroller::YPage data members
  // whenever the window is resized.
  xPage = 10;
  yPage = MaxLines / 4;
  // assign values to the XLine and YLine data members.
  // These values are actually the default settings.
  Scroller->XLine = 1;
  Scroller->YLine = 1;
  // clear the window
  InvalidateRect(HWindow, NULL, TRUE);
  // scroll to the top
  Scroller->ScrollTo(0, 0);
}

void TAppWindow::CMSelectSet2(RTMessage Msg)
{
```

```cpp
  // assign the data to describe the second set of lines
  SetOfLinesIndex = 2;
  MaxLines = 200;
  LineWidth = 40;
  LineSpacingHeight = 7;
  CharHeight = 10;
  CharWidth = 8;
  LineHeight = CharHeight + LineSpacingHeight;
  // set new values for XRange and YRange
  Scroller->SetRange(LineWidth, MaxLines);
  // set new values for XUnit and YUnit
  Scroller->SetUnits(CharWidth, LineHeight);
  // assign new values to the xPage and yPage data members.
  // These values are copied by the SetPageSize function into
  // the TScroller::XPage and TScroller::YPage data members
  // whenever the window is resized.
  xPage = 10;
  yPage = MaxLines / 4;
  // assign values to the XLine and YLine data members.
  // These values are rather unusual and are for demonstration
  // purpose only.
  Scroller->XLine = 2;
  Scroller->YLine = 2;
  // clear the window
  InvalidateRect(HWindow, NULL, TRUE);
  // scroll to the top
  Scroller->ScrollTo(0, 0);
}

void TAppWindow::CMSelectSet3(RTMessage Msg)
{
  // assign the data to describe the third set of lines
  SetOfLinesIndex = 3;
  MaxLines = 50;
  LineWidth = 30;
  LineSpacingHeight = 5;
  CharHeight = 10;
  CharWidth = 8;
  LineHeight = CharHeight + LineSpacingHeight;
  // set new values for XRange and YRange
  Scroller->SetRange(LineWidth, MaxLines);
  // set new values for XUnit and YUnit
  Scroller->SetUnits(CharWidth, LineHeight);
  // assign new values to the xPage and yPage data members.
  // These values are copied by the SetPageSize function into
```

continues

Listing 3.20. continued

```
  // the TScroller::XPage and TScroller::YPage data members
  // whenever the window is resized.
  xPage = 10;
  yPage = MaxLines / 4;
  // assign values to the XLine and YLine data members.
  // These values are actually the default settings.
  Scroller->XLine = 1;
  Scroller->YLine = 1;
  // clear the window
  InvalidateRect(HWindow, NULL, TRUE);
  // scroll to the top
  Scroller->ScrollTo(0, 0);
}

void TAppWindow::WMSize(RTMessage Msg)
{
  // call parent's WMSize function member
  TWindow::WMSize(Msg);
  // assign new values for the scroller's XPage and YPage members
  Scroller->XPage = xPage;
  Scroller->YPage = yPage;
}

void TWinApp::InitMainWindow()
{
  MainWindow = new TAppWindow(NULL, Name);
}

int PASCAL WinMain(HINSTANCE hInstance, HINSTANCE hPrevInstance,
                   LPSTR lpCmdLine, int nCmdShow)
{
  TWinApp WinApp("A Simple Text Scroller Window",
                 hInstance, hPrevInstance, lpCmdLine, nCmdShow);
  WinApp.Run(); // run OWL application
  return WinApp.Status; // return application status
}
```

The application implements the featured functionality of the new menu items by adding new member functions (compared to the WINSCRL3.CPP source code). The `CMScrollToTop` function displays the top part of the viewed text. The `CMScrollToBottom` moves the viewed text to the bottom to display the last line. The `CMScrollToLine` function invokes a dialog box that prompts you for the line number you want to view. The line you request (if valid) appears at the top of the window. The `ScrollUpBy` and `ScrollDownBy` member functions enable you to move up or down in the viewed text. These functions invoke a dialog box to prompt you for the line number to go to, or the number of lines to move. Incidentally, the `ScrollUpBy` function expects that you enter a positive integer. The function internally uses the negative value of your input to scroll upward.

Now that I have introduced you to the new member functions of the `TAppWindow` class, I'll describe the statements in these functions.

The `CMScrollToTop` function has a single statement that invokes the scroller's `ScrollTo` function with the arguments of 0, and 0 for the `X` and `Y` parameters. This call displays the first line of text.

The `CMScrollToBottom` function displays the last line in the window by calling `Scroller->ScrollTo(0, MaxLines-1)`. The second function argument subtracts one, because the application user regards the first line at line number 1 and not number 0 (the internal index).

The `CMScrollToLine` function invokes a modal input dialog box to request an input. The following call to function `TModule::ExecDialog` executes an "on the fly" dialog box (more about this in Chapter 5, "ObjectWindows Controls"):

```
GetApplication()->ExecDialog(
        new TInputDialog(this, "Numeric Input", "Go to line?",
                        s, sizeof(s)))
```

Specifying the first argument as `this` links the dialog box to the current window so that `this` points to the caller window. The dialog box appears with the title Numeric Input and the prompt message `Go to line?`. The last two arguments of `ExecDialog` supply the default input. With the static local variable `MoveToLine`, the `CMScrollToLine` function stores the last value you enter (it supplies an initial value of 1). The `sprintf` function converts the value stored in variable `MoveToLine` to the string `s`. The input dialog box displays the latter string as the default input.

The `if` statement in `CMScrollToLine` tests whether the value returned by the `ExecDialog` function is IDOK. The dialog box returns the IDOK value when you click the OK button or press Enter (while the OK button is the default button). If the tested condition is TRUE, the function converts the contents of string `s` into an integer and stores that integer in the local variable `MoveToLine`. The function then invokes the scroller's `ScrollTo` function, which moves to the line you specify.

The `CMScrollUpBy` and `CMScrollDownBy` member functions are very similar to the `CMScrollToLine` function. These member functions also invoke the `TModule::ExecDialog` dialog box and use local static variables to maintain your last input. Notice that the `CMScrollUpBy` function uses the negative value of the local variable `MoveUpBy` as the argument to the `ScrollBy` function call to scroll the viewed text upward.

Concerning the optimization of the `Paint` member function, notice the code for the loop displaying the text line:

```
for (int y = yp; y < (yp + Attr.H / yu); y++) {
  sprintf(aLine, formatStr, y+1);
  TextOut(DC, 0, y * yu, aLine, strlen(aLine));
}
```

The local variable `yp` stores the value of `Scroller->YPos`, the current position of vertical scroll bar. The local variable `yu` stores the value of `Scroller->YUnit`. The `for` loop uses the variable `y` as its control variable. The variable `y` is initialized with `yp`, the first line to display. The upper limit for the loop uses an expression that calculates the first line that is *not* displayed. Remember that `Attr.H` stores the current height of the window. Dividing that value by `yu` yields the number of lines to display. Then, adding `yp` to that ratio yields the expression you want. Also notice that the `Y` coordinate argument for the **TextOut** API function is `y * yu`. This expression translates the number of logical scroll bar lines into pixels.

The `TScroller` class also provides the Boolean `IsVisibleRect` member function to test whether a specified rectangle is visible. The declaration of the `IsVisisbleRect` function is

```
BOOL IsVisibleRect(long X, long Y, int XExt, int YExt)
```

The parameters `X` and `Y` are the scroll bars lines (in `XUnit` and `YUnit` pixels) that define the top-left corner of the tested rectangle. The `XExt` and `YExt` specify the width and height of the tested rectangle (also expressed in `XUnit` and `YUnit` pixels). If you are using `IsVisibleRect` to test the visibility of graphics shapes, convert the `X` and `XExt` arguments from pixels to `XUnit` units. Likewise, convert the `Y` and `YExt` arguments from pixels to `YUnit` units.

To compile the WINSCRL4.EXE file, create a project file that includes the WINSCRL4.CPP, WINSCRL4.RC, and OWL.DEF files. Compile and run the program. Initially, the window displays no text. Select a set of text lines by using the menu options and scroll down. Then select another set of text and observe how the program resets the viewed text to the first line. Experiment with the options offered by the Scroll To and Scroll By pop-up menus. Figure 3.9 shows a sample session with the WINSCRL4.EXE application.

Creating Basic Windows

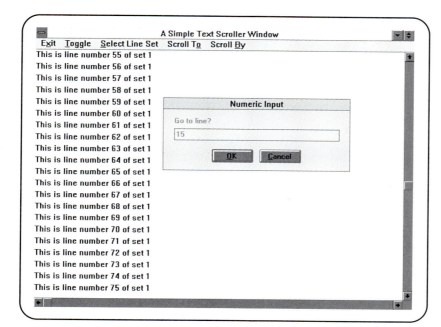

Figure 3.9.
A sample session with the WINSCRL4.EXE application.

Summary

This chapter discussed the mechanics of creating windows with a variety of attributes. You also saw how to display and manage simple text in a window, including the use of scroll bars. The chapter covered the following topics:

- ☐ Creating a read-only text window that displays information.
- ☐ Writing text in a window using the versatile `TextOut` API function.
- ☐ Creating windows with different styles, cursor shapes, program icons, default menus, and background colors.
- ☐ Registering a window class and examining its role in fine-tuning registration attributes.
- ☐ Making positional and incidental changes to the cursor shape at runtime.
- ☐ Creating child windows.
- ☐ Scrolling through text with scroll bars.

- Investigating the auto scroll and track modes of a scroller and how these scrolling modes affect scrolling behavior.
- Changing the scroll bar metrics. These metrics include the units, line size, page size, and ranges of a scroll bar.
- Performing internally induced scrolling with the `ScrollTo` and `ScrollBy` member functions.
- Optimizing the `Paint` member function to avoid wasting effort in drawing text lines that do not appear in the window.

This chapter also begins to explain the concepts of ownership and parent-child relationships among different objects. These concepts open the door to understanding how ObjectWindows and Windows work.

The next chapter is an epilogue to this one. It presents specialized window classes, namely `TEditWindow` and `TFileWindow`. These classes offer basic text editing features. The instances of `TFileWindow` provide you with a simple but functioning text editor.

Creating Basic Windows

CHAPTER 4

Windows Editing Classes

This chapter is an epilogue to the last one. In this chapter, I present two special descendants of `TWindow` that support basic text editing and basic text file editing. I also focus on these classes and show you how to expand their functionality through descendant classes. You will learn about the following topics:

- The `TEditWindow` text editor class
- The `TFileWindow` text file editor class
- The sending of output to the printer

The topic of printing emerges in examples I present that extend the functionality of the `TEditWindow` and `TFileWindow` classes. Although ObjectWindows classes do not involve printing devices, you should know how to send output to the printer.

The TEditWindow Class

The `TEditWindow` class offers the very basic functionality of a simple text editor. Although `TEditWindow` is a descendant of `TWindow`, it contains the `Editor` and `SearchStruct` data members that are typed `PTEdit` and `TSearchStruct`, respectively. The `Editor` data member is the pointer of a `TEdit` instance. Recall that the `TEdit` class is the descendant of `TStatic`. Therefore, the `Editor` member possesses most of the basic text editing features of the `TEditWindow` class. The `Editor` member provides an unframed multiline edit control located inside the main window.

The `SearchStruct` data member stores data related to the text search and replace operations. In fact, most member functions of `TEditWindow` handle the text search and replace tasks. From an object-oriented standpoint, the `TEditWindow` class formally inherits the members of `TWindow` (and its ancestor classes) and accesses the members of `TEdit` through containment (where a class has data members that are objects of another class). The `TEditWindow` class contributes the text search and replace functionality.

From a practical point of view, the `TEditWindow` is a minimally (better yet, barely) functioning class because it cannot communicate with the system devices. The only way to transport text in and out of the instances of `TEditWindow` is through the Clipboard!

To give you an example of the functionality of the TEditWindow class, I'll present the bare bones of a program that uses the class. Listing 4.1 shows the WINEDIT1.RC resource file and Listing 4.2 contains the source code for the WINEDIT1.CPP program sample. From the resource file, you can deduce that the program has three main menu items: Exit, Edit, and Search. The Edit and Search menu items are pop-up menus that offer various text editing and search/replace options.

Listing 4.1. The script of the resource file WINEDIT1.RC.

```
#include <windows.h>
#include <owlrc.h>

#include <stdwnds.dlg>
#include <editacc.rc>

COMMANDS MENU LOADONCALL MOVEABLE PURE DISCARDABLE
BEGIN
        MENUITEM "E&xit", CM_EXIT
        POPUP "&Edit"
        BEGIN
            MENUITEM    "&Undo\aAlt+BkSp", CM_EDITUNDO
            MENUITEM    SEPARATOR
            MENUITEM    "&Cut\aShift+Del", CM_EDITCUT
            MENUITEM    "C&opy\aIns", CM_EDITCOPY
            MENUITEM    "&Paste\aShift+Ins", CM_EDITPASTE
            MENUITEM    "&Delete\aDel", CM_EDITDELETE
            MENUITEM    "C&lear All\aCtrl+Del", CM_EDITCLEAR
        END
        POPUP "&Search"
        BEGIN
            MENUITEM    "&Find...", CM_EDITFIND
            MENUITEM    "&Replace...", CM_EDITREPLACE
            MENUITEM    "&Next\aF3", CM_EDITFINDNEXT
        END
END
```

Listing 4.2. The source code for the WINEDIT1.CPP program file.

```
#include <owl.h>
#include <editwnd.h>
```

Windows Editing Classes

```cpp
// declare the custom application class as
// a subclass of TApplication

class TWinApp : public TApplication
{
public:
  TWinApp(LPSTR     AName,          // application name
          HINSTANCE hInstance,       // instance handle
          HINSTANCE hPrevInstance,   // previous instance handle
          LPSTR     lpCmdLine,       // command-line arguments
          int       nCmdShow) :      // display command
          TApplication(AName, hInstance, hPrevInstance,
                       lpCmdLine, nCmdShow) {};

protected:
  virtual void InitMainWindow();
  virtual void InitInstance();
};


// use the _CLASSDEF macro to declare reference and pointer
// types related to the new TAppWindow class
_CLASSDEF(TAppWindow)

// expand the functionality of TEditWindow by deriving
// class TAppWindow
class TAppWindow : public TEditWindow
{
public:
  TAppWindow(PTWindowsObject AParent, LPSTR ATitle) :
                 TEditWindow(AParent, ATitle)
                 { AssignMenu("COMMANDS"); };


  virtual BOOL CanClose();
};

BOOL TAppWindow::CanClose()
{
  return MessageBox(HWindow, "Want to close this application",
                    "Query", MB_YESNO | MB_ICONQUESTION) == IDYES;
}

void TWinApp::InitMainWindow()
```

continues

Listing 4.2. continued

```
{
  MainWindow = new TAppWindow(NULL, Name);
}

void TWinApp::InitInstance()
{
  TApplication::InitInstance();
  HAccTable = LoadAccelerators(hInstance, "EDITCOMMANDS");
}

int PASCAL WinMain(HINSTANCE hInstance, HINSTANCE hPrevInstance,
                   LPSTR lpCmdLine, int nCmdShow)
{
  TWinApp WinApp("A Simple OWL Text Editor Application", hInstance,
                 hPrevInstance, lpCmdLine, nCmdShow);
  WinApp.Run(); // run OWL application
  return WinApp.Status; // return application status
}
```

The sample program declares an application class and a window class. The window class, TAppWindow, is a descendant of TEditWindow and adds very little functionality to its parent class. Notice that the application class declares its own version of InitInstance. This member function calls TApplication::InitInstance and loads the accelerator keys by using the **LoadAccelerators** API function and the name of the accelerator resource (EDITCOMMANDS, in this case).

Compile and run the program. Type text and perform the various text editing and search/replace operations. The functionality of TEditWindow is certainly promising, but it obviously lacks a reasonable way to receive and send text. The Clipboard is the only tool that currently helps exchange text with the WINEDIT1.EXE program.

The Free-Form Calculator

At first the TEditWindow class seems to be a practically crippled class in desperate need of file I/O to complete its functionality. This perception is certainly valid. In fact, this perception is shared by the creators of the ObjectWindows classes, who also provide TFileWindow, a descendant of TEditWindow, which adds the much-needed file I/O. On the other hand, you should not be quick to

Windows Editing Classes

conclude that all the `TEditWindow` descendant classes require file or device I/O capability to offer some useful features. To prove this point, I present an example of a "self-contained" application that is a descendant of `TEditWindow`. By *self-contained,* I mean a program that can function with minimal or no communication with the environment. The application is a free-form calculator application that enables you to type operands and operators, perform basic math, and use calculator-like memory registers to store and recall text (individual numbers or operations).

Figure 4.1 shows the free-form calculator, which is basically a text editor with special menu items.

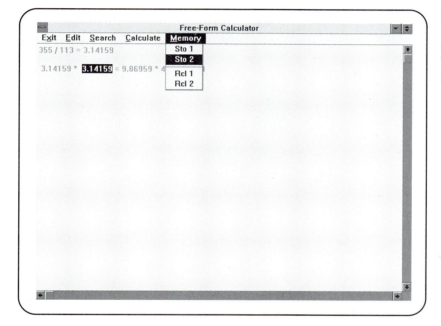

Figure 4.1. A sample session with the WINEDIT2.EXE application.

To execute a mathematical operation, perform the following steps:

1. Type the first operand, the operator, and the second operand. Separate these items with spaces. The program currently supports only the four basic mathematical operations.
2. Select text that contains a set of operands and an operator.
3. Invoke the Calculate menu item to execute the operation.

4. If the mathematical operation is evaluated successfully, the result is inserted at the cursor location. The program inserts an equal sign between the second operand and the result. If any errors occur, the program displays an error message box.

You can also perform chained calculations by appending an operator and a new operand after the result of a previous operation. Follow steps 2 through 4 to obtain the result for this new operation.

The free-form calculator also contains a Memory menu item with pop-up options that enables you to store and recall text (using the Clipboard) with two calculator-like memory registers (these can also store any text). To store an item, simply select it and invoke one of the two store menu items. To recall a stored text, move the cursor to the location where you want the text inserted and invoke one of the recall menu items.

Listing 4.3 contains the source code for the WINEDIT2.H header file. This file declares constants that define some program parameters and custom commands. The MAX_MEM_LEN constant defines the number of characters that can be stored in each memory-register string. The MAX_MEM constant defines the number of memory-register strings.

Listing 4.3. The source code for the WINEDIT2.H header file.

```
#define MAX_MEM_LEN 80
#define MAX_MEM 2
#define CM_CALCULATE 201
#define CM_STO1 202
#define CM_STO2 203
#define CM_RCL1 204
#define CM_RCL2 205
```

Listing 4.4 shows the script for the WINEDIT2.RC resource file. Unlike WINEDIT1.RC, this resource file includes the `#include "winedit2.h"` directive and the additional Calculate and Memory menu items.

Listing 4.4. The script for the WINEDIT2.RC resource file.

```
#include <windows.h>
#include <owlrc.h>
#include "winedit2.h"

#include <stdwnds.dlg>
```

```
#include <editacc.rc>

COMMANDS MENU LOADONCALL MOVEABLE PURE DISCARDABLE
BEGIN
      MENUITEM "E&xit", CM_EXIT
      POPUP "&Edit"
      BEGIN
        MENUITEM   "&Undo\aAlt+BkSp", CM_EDITUNDO
        MENUITEM   SEPARATOR
        MENUITEM   "&Cut\aShift+Del", CM_EDITCUT
        MENUITEM   "C&opy\aIns", CM_EDITCOPY
        MENUITEM   "&Paste\aShift+Ins", CM_EDITPASTE
        MENUITEM   "&Delete\aDel", CM_EDITDELETE
        MENUITEM   "C&lear All\aCtrl+Del", CM_EDITCLEAR
      END
      POPUP "&Search"
      BEGIN
        MENUITEM   "&Find...", CM_EDITFIND
        MENUITEM   "&Replace...", CM_EDITREPLACE
        MENUITEM   "&Next\aF3", CM_EDITFINDNEXT
      END
      MENUITEM "&Calculate", CM_CALCULATE
      POPUP "&Memory"
      BEGIN
        MENUITEM "Sto 1", CM_STO1
        MENUITEM "Sto 2", CM_STO2
        MENUITEM SEPARATOR
        MENUITEM "Rcl 1", CM_RCL1
        MENUITEM "Rcl 2", CM_RCL2
      END
END
```

Listing 4.5 shows the source code for the WINEDIT2.CPP program file. The application declares TAppWindow as a descendant of TEditWindow. The TAppWindow class contains a collection of member functions to implement the application's functionality.

Listing 4.5. The source code for the WINEDIT2.CPP program file.

```
#include <string.h>
#include <stdio.h>
```

continues

Listing 4.5. continued

```cpp
#include <stdlib.h>
#include <owl.h>
#include <editwnd.h>
#include "winedit2.h"

// declare the custom application class as
// a subclass of TApplication

class TWinApp : public TApplication
{
public:
  TWinApp(LPSTR     AName,           // application name
          HINSTANCE hInstance,       // instance handle
          HINSTANCE hPrevInstance,   // previous instance handle
          LPSTR     lpCmdLine,       // command-line arguments
          int       nCmdShow) :      // display command
          TApplication(AName, hInstance, hPrevInstance,
                  lpCmdLine, nCmdShow) {};

protected:
  virtual void InitMainWindow();
  virtual void InitInstance();
};


// use the _CLASSDEF macro to declare reference and pointer
// types related to the new TAppWindow class
_CLASSDEF(TAppWindow)

// expand the functionality of TEditWindow by deriving
// class TAppWindow
class TAppWindow : public TEditWindow
{
public:
  TAppWindow(PTWindowsObject AParent, LPSTR ATitle);

  // handle the Calculate command
  virtual void CMCalculate(RTMessage Msg)
    = [CM_FIRST + CM_CALCULATE];

  // handle storing a string in memory # 1
  virtual void CMSto1(RTMessage Msg)
    = [CM_FIRST + CM_STO1];
```

```cpp
  // handle storing a string in memory # 2
  virtual void CMSto2(RTMessage Msg)
    = [CM_FIRST + CM_STO2];

  // handle recalling a string from memory # 1
  virtual void CMRcl1(RTMessage Msg)
    = [CM_FIRST + CM_RCL1];

  // handle recalling a string from memory # 2
  virtual void CMRcl2(RTMessage Msg)
    = [CM_FIRST + CM_RCL2];

  virtual BOOL CanClose();

protected:
  char memoryStr[MAX_MEM][MAX_MEM_LEN+1];
  void Sto(int memIndex);
};

TAppWindow::TAppWindow(PTWindowsObject AParent, LPSTR ATitle) :
                TEditWindow(AParent, ATitle)
{
  AssignMenu("COMMANDS");
  // assign "0" to the memory-register strings
  for (int i = 0; i < MAX_MEM; i++)
    strcpy(memoryStr[i], "0");
};


void TAppWindow::CMCalculate(RTMessage Msg)
{
  int startPos, endPos;
  char calcStr[81];
  char operand1[81], operand2[81], mathOp[11];
  double x, y, z;
  BOOL mathError = FALSE;

  // get the character indices for the selected text
  Editor->GetSelection(startPos, endPos);
  // if there is no selected text, exit
  if (startPos == endPos) return;
  // get the selected text
  Editor->GetSubText(calcStr, startPos, endPos);
  // obtain the first operand
```

continues

Listing 4.5. continued

```
    strcpy(operand1, strtok(calcStr, " "));
    // obtain the operator
    strcpy(mathOp, strtok(NULL, " "));
    // obtain the second operand
    strcpy(operand2, strtok(NULL, " "));
    // missing data?
    if (!(operand1 && mathOp && operand2)) {
      MessageBox(HWindow, "Incomplete expression", "Error", MB_OK);
      return;
    }
    // convert operands to numeric values
    x = atof(operand1);
    y = atof(operand2);

    // execute the requested math operation
    if (!strcmp(mathOp, "+"))
      z = x + y;
    else if (!strcmp(mathOp, "-"))
      z = x - y;
    else if (!strcmp(mathOp, "*"))
      z = x * y;
    else if (!strcmp(mathOp, "/")) {
      if (y != 0)
        z = x / y;
      else
        mathError = TRUE;
    }
    else
      mathError = TRUE;

    // if there are no errors, show the result
    if (!mathError) {
      // convert numeric result into a string
      sprintf(calcStr, " = %g", z);
      // move the insertion point to the end of the selected text
      Editor->SetSelection(endPos, endPos);
      // now insert the result
      Editor->Insert(calcStr);
    }
    else
      // display an error message
      MessageBox(HWindow, "Math error", "Error", MB_OK);
}
```

```cpp
void TAppWindow::CMSto1(RTMessage Msg)
{
  Sto(0);
}

void TAppWindow::CMSto2(RTMessage Msg)
{
  Sto(1);
}

void TAppWindow::Sto(int memIndex)
{
  int startPos, endPos;

  // get the character indices for the selected text
  Editor->GetSelection(startPos, endPos);
  // if there is no selected text, exit
  if (startPos == endPos) return;
  // is the selected text longer than the string capacity?
  if ((endPos - startPos + 1) > MAX_MEM_LEN)
    endPos = startPos + MAX_MEM_LEN - 1;
  // get the selected text
  Editor->GetSubText(memoryStr[memIndex], startPos, endPos);
}

void TAppWindow::CMRcl1(RTMessage Msg)
{
  Editor->Insert(memoryStr[0]);
}

void TAppWindow::CMRcl2(RTMessage Msg)
{
  Editor->Insert(memoryStr[1]);
}

BOOL TAppWindow::CanClose()
{
  return MessageBox(HWindow, "Want to close this application",
                    "Query", MB_YESNO | MB_ICONQUESTION) == IDYES;
}

void TWinApp::InitMainWindow()
{
  MainWindow = new TAppWindow(NULL, Name);
```

continues

Listing 4.5. continued

```
}

void TWinApp::InitInstance()
{
  TApplication::InitInstance();
  HAccTable = LoadAccelerators(hInstance, "EDITCOMMANDS");
}

int PASCAL WinMain(HINSTANCE hInstance, HINSTANCE hPrevInstance,
                   LPSTR lpCmdLine, int nCmdShow)
{
  TWinApp WinApp("Free-Form Calculator", hInstance,
                 hPrevInstance, lpCmdLine, nCmdShow);
  WinApp.Run(); // run OWL application
  return WinApp.Status; // return application status
}
```

The `CMCalculate` member function evaluates the selected expression using the following steps:

1. Obtains the indices for the selected text by invoking the `TEdit::GetSelection` member function by using the inherited `Editor` data member. In fact, the inherited `Editor` data member helps carry out all text editing operations.

2. Compares the values of the first and last character positions of the selected text. If these positions are equal, no text is selected and the `CMCalculate` function exits without any further action.

3. Retrieves the selected text by using the `TEdit::GetSubText` member function. The retrieved text is assigned to the string `calcStr`, the first argument of `GetSubText`. The other arguments of `GetSubText` are the character positions that defined the selected text and were obtained in the first task.

4. Obtains the operands and operator with the `strtok` string function.

5. Verifies that none of the strings is NULL. Verifies that no NULL strings exist. If there are any NULL strings, the `CMCalculate` function displays an error message and exits.

6. Converts the operands into numeric values assigned to the local variables `x` and `y`.

Windows Editing Classes

7. Uses a series of if statements to execute the appropriate operations and assigns the result to the local variable z. The local Boolean variable mathError (which is initialized as FALSE) is assigned TRUE if any error occurs.

8. If no error occurs, uses sprintf to convert the numeric result into a string image and stores that string in calcStr.

9. Sets the insertion point at the end of the originally selected text by using the TEdit::SetSelection member function. The two arguments for the SetSelection function are both endPos (the original location where the selected text ends).

10. Inserts the string image of the result by using the TEdit::Insert member function.

The CMSto1 and CMSto2 member functions store the selected text in the protected data member memoryStr. Both these member functions call the Sto member function, which actually performs the storage task. The Sto member function performs the following tasks:

1. Obtains the character positions for the selected text.

2. Compares the values of the first and last character positions of the selected text. If they are equal, no text is selected and the Sto function exits without any further action.

3. Checks the selected text to determine whether it is longer than the capacity of a memoryStr array member. If this condition is true, the function sets the local variable endPos to fit the string member capacity.

4. Stores the selected text (or portions of it) in the member memIndex of the string array memoryStr.

The CMRcl1 and CMRcl2 member functions retrieve the characters stored in the memoryStr string array. The tasks of these routines are very simple and include a single statement that calls the TEdit::Insert member function.

To compile the WINEDIT2.EXE program, create a project file that includes the WINEDIT2.CPP, WINEDIT2.RC, and OWL.DEF files. Compile and run the program. Enter simple mathematical expressions and evaluate them by using the Calculate menu item. Experiment with chaining calculations, and storing and recalling results.

The free-form calculator is not your usual kind of Windows application, but it provides an example of a resourceful way to use a descendant class of TEditWindow without device or file I/O.

The Typewriter Application

The descendants of `TEditWindow` can offer more practical applications if they provide more common ways to communicate with the environment. Here is a short list of suggested applications:

- A text editor dedicated to work on a specific text file that is frequently edited. You simply invoke the application that automatically reads the client text file. When you exit, the client file is updated if necessary. This kind of application might be too specialized for programmers like you and me. However, it can find a niche with new Windows users at the office.

- A text editor that systematically appends text to a special log file. In this type of application, the text that you enter has chronological significance, so you want to record the time and sequence that you entered the text. When you exit, the application adds a time and date stamp and automatically appends the text to the log file.

- A typewriter application. This application enables you to write short discardable memos and print them. No file output is needed, because the written memos need not be stored.

In this section I implement the typewriter application with a descendant of `TEditWindow`. The application works very simply. Type the text and when you are ready to print, simply select a print menu item. That's all!

Although the notion of such an application seems simple by DOS application standards, printing in Windows is a new ball game. Why? Windows needs to streamline printing jobs that can be requested by multiple applications (or their multiple instances) running concurrently. Printing under Windows dictates a new set of rules. This application sheds some light on printing simple text under Windows. Even though ObjectWindows does not handle printing, the task is too important to ignore altogether.

Listings 4.6 to 4.8 contain the typewriter application's header file, resource script, and program files, respectively. The header and script files offer new insight on how to print under ObjectWindows. The program file contains the relevant code, namely the `CMPrint`, `GetPrtDC`, and `PrintPage` member functions of the `TAppWindow` class.

Listing 4.6. The source code for the WINEDIT3.H header file.

```
#define CM_PRINT 201
```

Listing 4.7. The script of the WINEDIT3.RC resource file.

```
#include <windows.h>
#include <owlrc.h>
#include "winedit3.h"

#include <stdwnds.dlg>
#include <editacc.rc>

COMMANDS MENU LOADONCALL MOVEABLE PURE DISCARDABLE
BEGIN
    MENUITEM "E&xit", CM_EXIT
    POPUP "&Edit"
    BEGIN
        MENUITEM    "&Undo\aAlt+BkSp", CM_EDITUNDO
        MENUITEM    SEPARATOR
        MENUITEM    "&Cut\aShift+Del", CM_EDITCUT
        MENUITEM    "C&opy\aIns", CM_EDITCOPY
        MENUITEM    "&Paste\aShift+Ins", CM_EDITPASTE
        MENUITEM    "&Delete\aDel", CM_EDITDELETE
        MENUITEM    "C&lear All\aCtrl+Del", CM_EDITCLEAR
    END
    POPUP "&Search"
    BEGIN
        MENUITEM    "&Find...", CM_EDITFIND
        MENUITEM    "&Replace...", CM_EDITREPLACE
        MENUITEM    "&Next\aF3", CM_EDITFINDNEXT
    END
    MENUITEM "&Print", CM_PRINT
END
```

Listing 4.8. The source code for the WINEDIT3.CPP program file.

```
#include <string.h>
#include <stdlib.h>
```

continues

Listing 4.8. continued

```
#include <owl.h>
#include <editwnd.h>
#include "winedit3.h"

// declare the custom application class as
// a subclass of TApplication

class TWinApp : public TApplication
{
public:
  TWinApp(LPSTR    AName,           // application name
          HINSTANCE hInstance,       // instance handle
          HINSTANCE hPrevInstance,   // previous instance handle
          LPSTR    lpCmdLine,       // command-line arguments
          int      nCmdShow) :      // display command
          TApplication(AName, hInstance, hPrevInstance,
                   lpCmdLine, nCmdShow) {};

protected:
  virtual void InitMainWindow();
  virtual void InitInstance();
};


// use the _CLASSDEF macro to declare reference and pointer
// types related to the new TAppWindow class
_CLASSDEF(TAppWindow)

// expand the functionality of TEditWindow by deriving
// class TAppWindow
class TAppWindow : public TEditWindow
{
public:
  TAppWindow(PTWindowsObject AParent, LPSTR ATitle) :
              TEditWindow(AParent, ATitle)
              { AssignMenu("COMMANDS"); };

  // handle printing the document
  virtual void CMPrint(RTMessage Msg)
    = [CM_FIRST + CM_PRINT];

  virtual BOOL CanClose();
```

```cpp
private:
  // get printer handle
  HDC GetPrtDC();
  // print the pages
  void PrintPage(HDC hPrtDC, char* text);
};

void TAppWindow::CMPrint(RTMessage Msg)
{
  char PrtMsg[] = "Typewriter Output";
  HDC hPrtDC;
  int textLen = Editor->GetTextLen() + 1;
  char *textStr = new char[textLen];

  // get the text
  Editor->GetText(textStr, textLen);
  // get the handle of the printer
  hPrtDC = GetPrtDC();
  // start the printing process
  if (hPrtDC) {
    if (Escape(hPrtDC, STARTDOC, sizeof(PrtMsg)-1, PrtMsg, NULL) > 0)
    {
      // print the pages
      PrintPage(hPrtDC, textStr);
      if (Escape(hPrtDC, NEWFRAME, 0, NULL, NULL) > 0)
        Escape(hPrtDC, ENDDOC, 0, NULL,NULL);
    }
  }
  // delete the printer handle and the dynamic string
  DeleteDC(hPrtDC);
  delete textStr;
}

HDC TAppWindow::GetPrtDC()
{
  const int PrinterDataSize = 80;
  char PrinterData[PrinterDataSize];
  char *DevicePtr, *DriverPtr, *OutputPtr;

  // get the profile of the printer from the WIN.INI file's
  // [windows] section, keyword "device"
  GetProfileString("windows", "device", ",,,",
                   PrinterData, PrinterDataSize);
  // get the related pointers
  DevicePtr = strtok(PrinterData, ",");
```

continues

Listing 4.8. continued

```
    DriverPtr = strtok(NULL, ",");
    OutputPtr = strtok(NULL, ",");
    // all device-related pointers are set?
    if (DevicePtr && DriverPtr && OutputPtr)
      // return handle
      return CreateDC(DriverPtr, DevicePtr, OutputPtr, NULL);
    else
      return NULL;
}

void TAppWindow::PrintPage(HDC hPrtDC, char* text)
{
  const LINE_HEIGHT = 50;
  const MAX_LINES = 60;
  char *p1 = text;
  char *p2 = text;
  int lineNumber = 0;

  // loop until the p2 pointer sees the end-of-string
  while (*p2 != '\0') {
    // is the accessed character not an '\r'?
    if (*p2 != '\r')
      p2++; // increment pointer
    else {
      // print a line
      TextOut(hPrtDC, 0, lineNumber++ * LINE_HEIGHT, p1, p2 - p1);
      // is the current page full?
      if (lineNumber >= MAX_LINES) {
        // eject page
        Escape(hPrtDC, NEWFRAME, 0, NULL, NULL);
        lineNumber = 0; // reset line number counter
      }
      // reset pointers
      p2 += 2;
      p1 = p2;
    }
  }
  // any pending text?
  if (p1 < p2) {
      if (lineNumber >= MAX_LINES) {
        // eject page
        Escape(hPrtDC, NEWFRAME, 0, NULL, NULL);
        lineNumber = 0; // reset line number counter
      }
```

```
        // print the last line
        TextOut(hPrtDC, 0, lineNumber * LINE_HEIGHT, p1, p2 - p1);
    }
}

BOOL TAppWindow::CanClose()
{
  return MessageBox(HWindow, "Want to close this application",
                    "Query", MB_YESNO | MB_ICONQUESTION) == IDYES;
}

void TWinApp::InitMainWindow()
{
  MainWindow = new TAppWindow(NULL, Name);
}

void TWinApp::InitInstance()
{
  TApplication::InitInstance();
  HAccTable = LoadAccelerators(hInstance, "EDITCOMMANDS");
}

int PASCAL WinMain(HINSTANCE hInstance, HINSTANCE hPrevInstance,
                   LPSTR lpCmdLine, int nCmdShow)
{
  TWinApp WinApp("Typewriter Application", hInstance,
                 hPrevInstance, lpCmdLine, nCmdShow);
  WinApp.Run(); // run OWL application
  return WinApp.Status; // return application status
}
```

The CMPrint function handles the print commands (generated by the Print menu item) and declares a number of local variables. The PrtMsg string contains the title of the print job used by the Windows Print Manager. The textLen variable stores the length of the entire document text. This length sizes up the dynamic string textStr that stores the document text. The CMPrint function performs the following tasks:

1. Stores the document text in the dynamic string textStr.

2. Obtains the handle for the printer by invoking the GetPrtDC member function.

3. If the printer handle is not NULL, starts the printing process. This involves the special API function **Escape**. The first call to **Escape** uses the

printer handler and the STARTDOC command. This command informs the Print Manager that a new print job has begun. For more information regarding the special **Escape** API function, consult the online help.

4. Prints the pages by calling the `PrintPage` member function.

5. Calls the **Escape** API function with the NEWFRAME command to eject the last page.

6. Calls the **Escape** API function with the ENDDOC command to inform the Print Manager that the print job has ended.

7. Deletes the printer handle.

8. Deallocates the dynamic memory of string `textStr`.

The `CMPrint` member function invokes the `GetPrtDC` and `PrintPage` member functions. The `GetPrtDC` function is vital in getting a handle for the printer. This function works by obtaining printer information from the WIN.INI file and using that information to create a device context. The `GetPrtDC` function performs the following tasks:

1. Calls the API function **GetProfileString** to obtain information from the WIN.INI file. The first function specifies the section name, the [windows] section in this case. The second argument searches for the device keyword. The sought information is retrieved with the `PrinterData` string.

2. Obtains pointers to the names of the device, driver, and output port.

3. If the names of the device, driver, and output port are valid, calls the API function **CreateDC** to create and return the device context for the printer. Otherwise, the function returns a NULL handle.

The `PrintPage` member function performs a line-by-line text output. The function defines local constants for the line height and number of lines per page. These values work fine on my HP LaserJet III, but you might need to alter these constants for your printer. `PrintPage` uses pointers `p1` and `p2` to track the first and last character of a text line. The document uses pairs of '\r' and '\n' to delimit lines. The `PrintPage` function detects line breaks by looking for the '\r' character. When such a character is found, the function uses the **TextOut** API function to print the current text line. Notice that the coordinates for printing a text line are 0 and the expression `lineNumber * LINE_HEIGHT`. The function also monitors the number of lines and issues a form feed when a page is full. The **Escape** function along with the NEWFRAME command ejects the page from the printer. The `PrintPage` function also handles printing the last line, which ends with a NULL character instead of the '\r' and '\n' character pairs.

To compile the WINEDIT3.EXE program, you need a project file that includes the WINEDIT3.CPP, WINEDIT3.RC, and OWL.DEF files. Compile and run the program. Type some text and select the Print menu item to print the current text. Adjust the line height and number of lines per page constants, if needed, to obtain a better output from your printer.

> **Tip:** Borland C++ 3.1 offers the PRINTER.H header file in the directory \BORLANDC\OWL\EXAMPLES\OWLPRINT. This header file declares four printer-related classes: `TPrintout`, `TPrinter`, `TPrinterSetupDlg`, and `TPrinterAbortDlg`. These classes are useful in making the process of printing under Windows easier. I have presented the more low-level approach for printing to give you a better feel of the complexity of the process and to show you how to gain maximum control over printing.

The TFileWindow Class

ObjectWindows declares a `TFileWindow` class as a descendant of `TEditWindow`. The derived class adds the capability to create a new file, open an existing file, save the current text to the current file, or save the current text to a new file. Thus `TFileWindow` offers features for file I/O, text editing, and text search/replace that are available in the Turbo C++ for Windows IDE, as well as in most Windows text editors.

The incorporated file I/O features make the `TFileWindow` class more practical. The next application has a descendant of `TFileWindow` that deliberately does not add any new functionality, so that you can simply get a feel for the capabilities of `TFileWindow`. The result is a working text editor that you can actually use to perform simple and routine text editing chores.

Listing 4.9 shows the code for the WINFILE1.RC resource file. The file includes other resource files that provide the descendant of `TFileWindow` with the various input and file dialog boxes needed.

Listing 4.9. The source code for the WINFILE1.RC resource file.

```
#include <windows.h>
#include <owlrc.h>

#include <inputdia.dlg>
#include <filedial.dlg>
#include <stdwnds.dlg>

#include <editacc.rc>
#include <fileacc.rc>

#include <editmenu.rc>
#include <filemenu.rc>
```

This listing does the following:

- ☐ The INPUTDIA.DLG resource file supports the input dialog box.
- ☐ The FILEDIAL.DLG resource file supports the Open and Save file dialog box.
- ☐ The STDWNDS.DLG resource file supports the standard (or common) dialog boxes, including the Find and Replace dialog boxes.
- ☐ The EDITACC.RC and FILEACC.RC resource files define the accelerator keys used by the edit and file manipulation menu items.
- ☐ EDITMENU.RC and FILEMENU.RC are resource files for the edit and file manipulation menus.

Listing 4.10 contains the source code for the WINFILE1.CPP program file. As I mentioned before, the window class `TAppWindow` is a descendant of `TFileWindow` that does not declare any new member functions. The program creates an instance of `TAppWindow` that offers the simple text editor. The `InitInstance` member function loads the accelerator keys for the file manipulation commands.

Listing 4.10. The source code for the WINFILE1.CPP program file.

```
#include <owl.h>
#include <filewnd.h>

// declare the custom application class as
// a subclass of TApplication
```

```
class TWinApp : public TApplication
{
public:
  TWinApp(LPSTR    AName,         // application name
          HINSTANCE hInstance,     // instance handle
          HINSTANCE hPrevInstance, // previous instance handle
          LPSTR    lpCmdLine,     // command-line arguments
          int      nCmdShow) :    // display command
          TApplication(AName, hInstance, hPrevInstance,
                   lpCmdLine, nCmdShow) {};

protected:
  virtual void InitMainWindow();
  virtual void InitInstance();
};


// use the _CLASSDEF macro to declare reference and pointer
// types related to the new TAppWindow class
_CLASSDEF(TAppWindow)

// expand the functionality of TFileWindow by deriving
// class TAppWindow
class TAppWindow : public TFileWindow
{
public:
  TAppWindow(PTWindowsObject AParent, LPSTR ATitle, LPSTR AFilename)
          : TFileWindow(AParent, ATitle, AFilename)
                { AssignMenu("FileCommands"); };

};

void TWinApp::InitMainWindow()
{
  MainWindow = new TAppWindow(NULL, Name, "");
}

void TWinApp::InitInstance()
{
  TApplication::InitInstance();
  if (Status == 0)
    HAccTable = LoadAccelerators(hInstance, "FileCommands");
}
```

continues

Listing 4.10. continued

```
int PASCAL WinMain(HINSTANCE hInstance, HINSTANCE hPrevInstance,
                   LPSTR lpCmdLine, int nCmdShow)
{
  TWinApp WinApp("OWL Text Editor", hInstance,
                 hPrevInstance, lpCmdLine, nCmdShow);
  WinApp.Run(); // run OWL application
  return WinApp.Status; // return application status
}
```

To compile the WINFILE1.EXE program, you need a project file that includes the WINFILE1.CPP, WINFILE1.RC, and OWL.DEF files. Compile and run the program. What you have at your fingertips is a simple text editor. Figure 4.2 shows a sample session with the WINFILE1.EXE text editor.

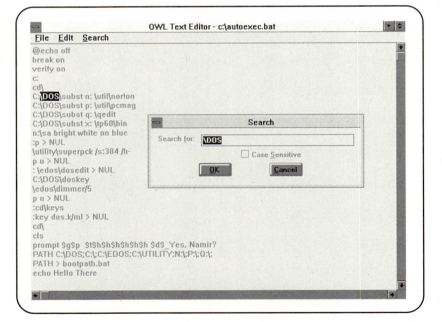

Figure 4.2.
A sample session with the WINFILE1.EXE text editor.

An Enhanced Text Editor

Now that you have experimented with the TFileWindow class features, this section presents an enhanced text editor to demonstrate how to extend TFileWindow's functionality. The new version can print the entire file, print only the selected text, and convert the selected text to uppercase or lowercase characters. These new features are accompanied by the addition and modification of menu items. I included the document Print menu item as part of the File pop-up menu item, and created a new pop-up menu for block-oriented operations. Figure 4.3 shows a sample session with the WINFILE2.EXE application.

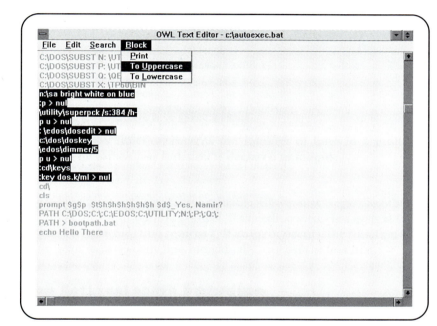

Figure 4.3. A sample session with the WINFILE2.EXE application.

Listing 4.11 shows the declarations of custom command constants used by the enhanced text editor.

Listing 4.11. The source code for the WINFILE2.H header file.

```
#define CM_PRINT      201
#define CM_BLOCKPRINT 202
#define CM_BLOCKUPPER 203
#define CM_BLOCKLOWER 204
```

Listing 4.12 shows the script for the FILEMNU1.RC resource file, which defines the menu resource for the application. This menu includes the Block pop-up menu item and its options: Print, Uppercase, and Lowercase.

Listing 4.12. The script for the FILEMNU1.RC resource file.

```
FILECOMMANDS MENU LOADONCALL MOVEABLE PURE DISCARDABLE
BEGIN
    POPUP "&File"
    BEGIN
        MENUITEM    "&New", CM_FILENEW
        MENUITEM    "&Open...", CM_FILEOPEN
        MENUITEM    "&Save", CM_FILESAVE
        MENUITEM    "Save &As...", CM_FILESAVEAS
        MENUITEM    SEPARATOR
        MENUITEM    "&Print", CM_PRINT
        MENUITEM    SEPARATOR
        MENUITEM    "E&xit", CM_EXIT
    END
    POPUP "&Edit"
    BEGIN
        MENUITEM    "&Undo\aAlt+BkSp", CM_EDITUNDO
        MENUITEM    SEPARATOR
        MENUITEM    "&Cut\aShift+Del", CM_EDITCUT
        MENUITEM    "C&opy\aCtrl+Ins", CM_EDITCOPY
        MENUITEM    "&Paste\aShift+Ins", CM_EDITPASTE
        MENUITEM    "&Delete\aDel", CM_EDITDELETE
        MENUITEM    "C&lear All\aCtrl+Del", CM_EDITCLEAR
    END
    POPUP "&Search"
    BEGIN
        MENUITEM    "&Find...", CM_EDITFIND
        MENUITEM    "&Replace...", CM_EDITREPLACE
        MENUITEM    "&Next\aF3", CM_EDITFINDNEXT
    END
    POPUP "&Block"
    BEGIN
        MENUITEM    "&Print", CM_BLOCKPRINT
        MENUITEM    "To &Uppercase", CM_BLOCKUPPER
        MENUITEM    "To &Lowercase", CM_BLOCKLOWER
    END
END
```

Listing 4.13 contains the script for the WINFILE2.RC resource file. The file is similar to WINFILE1.RC except that FILEMNU1.RC replaces FILEMENU.RC. Listing 4.14 shows the source code for the WINFILE2.CPP application.

Listing 4.13. The script for the WINFILE2.RC resource file.

```
#include <windows.h>
#include <owlrc.h>
#include "winfile2.h"

#include <inputdia.dlg>
#include <filedial.dlg>
#include <stdwnds.dlg>

#include <editacc.rc>
#include <fileacc.rc>

#include <editmenu.rc>
#include "filemnu1.rc"
```

Listing 4.14. The source code for the WINFILE2.CPP program file.

```
#include <string.h>
#include <owl.h>
#include <filewnd.h>
#include "winfile2.h"

// declare the custom application class as
// a subclass of TApplication

class TWinApp : public TApplication
{
public:
  TWinApp(LPSTR     AName,           // application name
          HINSTANCE hInstance,       // instance handle
          HINSTANCE hPrevInstance,   // previous instance handle
          LPSTR     lpCmdLine,       // command-line arguments
          int       nCmdShow) :      // display command
          TApplication(AName, hInstance, hPrevInstance,
                    lpCmdLine, nCmdShow) {};

protected:
  virtual void InitMainWindow();
  virtual void InitInstance();
};
```

continues

Listing 4.14. continued

```
// use the _CLASSDEF macro to declare reference and pointer
// types related to the new TAppWindow class
_CLASSDEF(TAppWindow)

// expand the functionality of TFileWindow by deriving
// class TAppWindow
class TAppWindow : public TFileWindow
{
public:
  TAppWindow(PTWindowsObject AParent, LPSTR ATitle, LPSTR AFilename)
            : TFileWindow(AParent, ATitle, AFilename)
                 { AssignMenu("FileCommands"); };

  // handle the print document command
  virtual void CMPrint(RTMessage Msg)
    = [CM_FIRST + CM_PRINT];

  // handle the block print command
  virtual void CMBlockPrint(RTMessage Msg)
    = [CM_FIRST + CM_BLOCKPRINT];

  // convert the selected text to uppercase
  virtual void CMBlockUpper(RTMessage Msg)
    = [CM_FIRST + CM_BLOCKUPPER];

  // convert the selected text to lowercase
  virtual void CMBlockLower(RTMessage Msg)
    = [CM_FIRST + CM_BLOCKLOWER];

private:
  // get printer handle
  HDC GetPrtDC();
  // print the pages
  void PrintPage(HDC hPrtDC, char* text);
};

void TAppWindow::CMPrint(RTMessage Msg)
{
  char PrtMsg[] = "File Editor Output";
  HDC hPrtDC;
  int textLen = Editor->GetTextLen() + 1;
  char *textStr = new char[textLen];

  // get the text
```

```cpp
    Editor->GetText(textStr, textLen);
    // get the handle of the printer
    hPrtDC = GetPrtDC();
    // start the printing process
    if (hPrtDC) {
      if (Escape(hPrtDC, STARTDOC, sizeof(PrtMsg)-1, PrtMsg, NULL) > 0)
      {
        // print the pages
        PrintPage(hPrtDC, textStr);
        if (Escape(hPrtDC, NEWFRAME, 0, NULL, NULL) > 0)
          Escape(hPrtDC, ENDDOC, 0, NULL,NULL);
      }
    }
    // delete the printer handle and the dynamic string
    DeleteDC(hPrtDC);
    delete textStr;
}

void TAppWindow::CMBlockPrint(RTMessage Msg)
{
    char PrtMsg[] = "File Editor Block Output";
    HDC hPrtDC;
    int startPos, endPos, textLen;
    char *textStr;

    // get the character position for the selected text
    Editor->GetSelection(startPos, endPos);
    // is there no selected text?
    if (startPos == endPos) return;
    // calculate the length of the selected text
    textLen = endPos - startPos + 1;
    // create dynamic string to store the selected text
    textStr = new char[textLen + 1];
    // obtain the selected text and store it in textStr
    Editor->GetSubText(textStr, startPos, endPos);
    // get the handle of the printer
    hPrtDC = GetPrtDC();
    // start the printing process
    if (hPrtDC) {
      if (Escape(hPrtDC, STARTDOC, sizeof(PrtMsg)-1, PrtMsg, NULL) > 0)
      {
        // print the pages
        PrintPage(hPrtDC, textStr);
        if (Escape(hPrtDC, NEWFRAME, 0, NULL, NULL) > 0)
```

continues

Listing 4.14. continued

```
        Escape(hPrtDC, ENDDOC, 0, NULL,NULL);
    }
  }
  // delete the printer handle and the dynamic string
  DeleteDC(hPrtDC);
  delete textStr;
}

void TAppWindow::CMBlockUpper(RTMessage Msg)
{
  int startPos, endPos, textLen;
  char *textStr;

  // get the character position for the selected text
  Editor->GetSelection(startPos, endPos);
  // is there no selected text?
  if (startPos == endPos) return;
  // calculate the length of the selected text
  textLen = endPos - startPos + 1;
  // create dynamic string to store the selected text
  textStr = new char[textLen + 1];
  // obtain the selected text and store it in textStr
  Editor->GetSubText(textStr, startPos, endPos);
  // convert characters of textStr to uppercase
  strupr(textStr);
  // insert back in document and replace selected text
  Editor->Insert(textStr);
  // delete the dynamic string
  delete textStr;
}

void TAppWindow::CMBlockLower(RTMessage Msg)
{
  int startPos, endPos, textLen;
  char *textStr;

  // get the character position for the selected text
  Editor->GetSelection(startPos, endPos);
  // is there no selected text?
  if (startPos == endPos) return;
  // calculate the length of the selected text
  textLen = endPos - startPos + 1;
  // create dynamic string to store the selected text
  textStr = new char[textLen + 1];
```

```
    // obtain the selected text and store it in textStr
    Editor->GetSubText(textStr, startPos, endPos);
    // convert characters of textStr to lowercase
    strlwr(textStr);
    // insert back in document and replace selected text
    Editor->Insert(textStr);
    // delete the dynamic string
    delete textStr;
}

HDC TAppWindow::GetPrtDC()
{
    const int PrinterDataSize = 80;
    char PrinterData[PrinterDataSize];
    char *DevicePtr, *DriverPtr, *OutputPtr;

    GetProfileString("windows", "device", ",,,",
                     PrinterData, PrinterDataSize);
    DevicePtr = strtok(PrinterData, ",");
    DriverPtr = strtok(NULL, ",");
    OutputPtr = strtok(NULL, ",");
    if (DevicePtr && DriverPtr && OutputPtr)
        return CreateDC(DriverPtr, DevicePtr, OutputPtr, NULL);
    else
        return NULL;
}

void TAppWindow::PrintPage(HDC hPrtDC, char* text)
{
    const LINE_HEIGHT = 50;
    const MAX_LINES = 60;
    char *p1 = text;
    char *p2 = text;
    int lineNumber = 0;

    while (*p2 != '\0') {
        if (*p2 != '\r')
            p2++;
        else {
            TextOut(hPrtDC, 0, lineNumber++ * LINE_HEIGHT, p1, p2 - p1);
            if (lineNumber >= MAX_LINES) {
                // eject page
                Escape(hPrtDC, NEWFRAME, 0, NULL, NULL);
                lineNumber = 0;
```

continues

Listing 4.14. continued

```
      }
      // reset pointers
      p2 += 2;
      p1 = p2;
    }
  }

  if (p1 < p2) {
    if (lineNumber >= MAX_LINES) {
      // eject page
      Escape(hPrtDC, NEWFRAME, 0, NULL, NULL);
      lineNumber = 0;
    }
    TextOut(hPrtDC, 0, lineNumber * LINE_HEIGHT, p1, p2 - p1);
  }
}

void TWinApp::InitMainWindow()
{
  MainWindow = new TAppWindow(NULL, Name, "");
}

void TWinApp::InitInstance()
{
  TApplication::InitInstance();
  if (Status == 0)
    HAccTable = LoadAccelerators(hInstance, "FileCommands");
}

int PASCAL WinMain(HINSTANCE hInstance, HINSTANCE hPrevInstance,
                   LPSTR lpCmdLine, int nCmdShow)
{
  TWinApp WinApp("OWL Text Editor", hInstance,
                 hPrevInstance, lpCmdLine, nCmdShow);
  WinApp.Run(); // run OWL application
  return WinApp.Status; // return application status
}
```

This application declares TAppWindow as a descendant of TFileWindow and contains a number of member functions. Some of the member functions, like CMPrint, GetPrtDC, and PrintPage, are identical to those in file WINEDIT3.CPP. The following discussion focuses on the new member functions: CMBlockPrint, CMBlockUpper, and CMBlockLower.

The `CMBlockPrint` member function is similar to `CMPrint`. The main difference is that `CMBlockPrint` copies the selected text, rather than the entire document text, to the dynamic string `textStr`. Therefore, the `CMBlockPrint` function starts with the steps needed to define the location of the selected text, obtains its size, and copies the selected text to string `textStr`. Obtaining the printer handle and printing is the same as in `CMPrint`.

The `CMBlockUpper` and `CMBlockLower` functions work in a similar fashion to convert the characters of the selected text to uppercase and lowercase, respectively. The `CMBlockUpper` member function performs the following tasks:

1. Obtains the start and end character positions of the selected text by invoking the `TEdit::GetSelection` member function.

2. Tests whether the obtained start and end character positions are identical. If this condition is true, no text is selected and the function exits.

3. Calculates the size of the selected text and uses that size to create the dynamic string that stores a copy of the selected text.

4. Retrieves a copy of the selected text by calling the `TEdit::GetSubText` member function. The function stores a copy in the dynamic string `textStr`.

5. Converts the characters of `textStr` to uppercase using the `strupr` function.

6. Inserts the characters of `textStr` back into the document and replaces the selected text.

7. Deallocates the space of the dynamic string `textStr`.

To compile the WINFILE2.EXE program, you need a project file that includes the WINFILE2.CPP, WINFILE2.RC, and OWL.DEF files. Compile and run the program. Experiment with printing a text file or parts of it with the block print feature. Also experiment with converting the characters of the selected text into uppercase and lowercase letters.

You can extend the WINFILE2.EXE application further by adding new command constants to the WINFILE2.H file, using a new menu structure in file FILEMNU1.RC, and adding the member functions for the new features in file WINFILE2.CPP.

Summary

This chapter presented two special descendants of TWindow: TEditWindow and TFileWindow. The first descendant class implements basic text editing features, and the second descendant class offers a working minimal text editor. You also learned about the following:

- ☐ Using a descendant of TEditWindow to create a self-contained application that uses a simple math expression interpreter.
- ☐ Using a descendant of TEditWindow to implement a simple typewriter application.
- ☐ Accessing the printer under Windows.
- ☐ Extending the TFileWindow class to include printing and block-oriented operations.

Windows Editing Classes

CHAPTER 5

ObjectWindows Controls

In Chapter 4, "Windows Editing Classes," I presented the `TFileWindow` class that implemented a basic text file editor. Using such an editor involves dialog boxes that contain various types of controls, such as the list box, edit control (also called the edit box), and push button, to name a few. You can include these controls in windows or, more frequently, in dialog boxes. This chapter and the next two examine these controls as they appear in windows and focus on the basic properties of these controls. Chapter 8 presents dialog boxes and explains how these controls work with these boxes. In this chapter you will learn about the following:

- Static text controls
- Edit controls
- Push button controls

If you understand the various controls and master how they behave and interact, you can implement highly interactive Windows applications. This chapter and the two that follow discuss the constructors and relevant member functions for the control classes.

The Static Text Control

The static text control provides a window or a dialog box with static text—one that the application user cannot easily change. Static text is not necessarily etched in stone. In fact, static text controls allow your ObjectWindows applications to alter text at will. You can still specify the text as unchangeable. The choice is ultimately yours. The `TStatic` class implements the static text control. Look at the class constructor and members.

The `TStatic` Class

The `TStatic` class, a descendant of `TControl`, offers static text that is defined by a display area, text to display, and text attributes. Of these three components, you can only change the displayed text during run-time.

The `TStatic` class has three constructors: two public and one protected. I will focus on the constructor that creates a `TStatic` instance from scratch. This constructor is declared as follows:

```
TStatic(PTWindowsObject AParent, int AnId, LPSTR ATitle, int X,
        int Y, int W, int H, WORD ATextLen,
        PTModule AModule = NULL);
```

The `AParent` parameter is the pointer to the parent window (or owner, if you prefer). The `AnId` is the ID for the static text control. This parameter is available for use with dialog boxes. Passing a –1 argument suits most applications. The –1 value indicates that you cannot access the control through its ID. You can still access a static text control by using a pointer. The `ATitle` parameter is a pointer to the string that supplies the static text characters. The `X`, `Y`, `W`, `H` parameters define the location and dimensions for the rectangular area that contains the static text. The `ATextLen` parameter specifies the leading number of characters that the `ATitle` pointer accesses and copies to the static text.

Normally, you create static text in a window or dialog box and do not need to access it or alter its attributes. In this case, you do not need to maintain a `PTStatic`-typed data member (in the application window class or dialog box) to access the `TStatic` instances. On the other hand, if you want to fine-tune the display attribute or access the static text characters at run-time, you need such a data member. The CTLSTAT1.CPP program, shown in Listing 5.2, shows an example of accessing a static text control using a `PTStatic` pointer.

As a type of window, the instances of `TStatic` can redefine the display style by accessing their `Attr.Style` member. Table 5.1 shows the various static text style values. The default setting of a static text instance is the expression `WS_VISIBLE | WS_GROUP | SS_LEFT`, which produces a visible left-justified static text.

Note: To specify different text alignment attributes, assign a new value to the `Attr.Style` member by using a pointer to the static text instance. The assignment statement must be placed inside the window (or dialog box) constructor after the creation of the static text instance.

The assignment statement is

```
// StaticPtr is a data member of the application window class
StaticPtr = new TStatic(this, -1, textStr, 10, 10,
                        100, 40, strlen(textStr));
StaticPtr->Attr.Style = (Attr.Style & ~SS_LEFT) | SS_CENTER;
```

Table 5.1. The static text style values.

Value	Meaning
SS_BLACKFRAME	Designates a box frame drawn with the color that matches the window frame. This color is black in the default Windows color scheme.
SS_BLACKRECT	Specifies a rectangle filled with the color that matches the window frame. This color is black in the default Windows color scheme.
SS_CENTER	Centers static text characters. The text is wrappable.
SS_GRAYFRAME	Specifies a box with a frame that is the same color as the screen background. This color is gray in the default Windows color scheme.
SS_GRAYRECT	Selects a rectangle filled with same color as the screen background. This color is gray in the default Windows color scheme.
SS_LEFT	Indicates left-justified text that is wrappable.
SS_LEFTNOWORDWRAP	Indicates left-justified text that is not wrappable.
SS_NOPREFIX	Specifies that the ampersand (&) in the static text string should not be a hot key designator character. Instead, the character appears as part of the static text character.
SS_RIGHT	Selects right-justified text that is wrappable.
SS_SIMPLE	Indicates that static text characters cannot be altered at run-time. In addition, the static text is displayed on a single line. Line breaks are ignored.

Caution: Normally, accessing Attr.Style outside the constructor of the owner window does not change the display attributes of the static text.

The string accessed by the ATitle pointer in the constructor can include the & to specify a hot key visually. To actually support the hot key, your application must load accelerator keys (more about this later in this chapter). The hot key character appears as an underlined character. The ampersand must be placed before the hot key. If the string contains multiple ampersand characters, only the last occurrence is affected. The other occurrences of the ampersand are

not displayed and are ignored. To display the &, you need to specify the SS_NOPREFIX style.

Now consider the component of the static text control that you can change during run-time: the text itself. If you specify the SS_SIMPLE style during the creation of a TStatic instance, you cannot alter its text. In this sense, the instance of TStatic is indeed etched in stone. The TStatic class enables you to set, query, and clear the characters of the static text. The following member functions assist in this process:

- The parameterless GetTextLen member function returns the length of the control's text.
- The GetText member function enables you to access the static text characters. The declaration of the GetText function is

    int GetText(LPSTR ATextString, int MaxChars)

    The ATextString parameter is a pointer to the string that receives a copy of the static text characters. The MaxChars parameter specifies the maximum number of static text characters to copy. The function result returns the actual number of characters copied to the string that the pointer ATextString accesses.
- The SetText member function overwrites the current static text characters with those characters in the string that the LPSTR-typed parameter ATextString accesses. The declaration of the SetText function is

    void SetText(LPSTR ATextString)

- The parameterless member function Clear writes an empty string to the static text buffer. Using the GetText, SetText, and Clear member functions, you can easily toggle between hiding and showing the static text at run-time.

Static Text Sampler

Here's a simple ObjectWindows application that samples various types of static text. This program (located in Listings 5.1 and 5.2) gives you a feel for the various display attributes and how you can use them to show the following types of static text:

- Default single- and multiline static text
- Simple static text
- Left-justified single- and multiline static text

- Centered single- and multiline static text
- Right-justified single- and multiline static text
- Long wrappable static text
- Long unwrappable static text
- The black frame and rectangle
- The gray frame and rectangle
- The white frame and rectangle
- The black frame that contains text
- The gray frame that contains text
- The white frame that contains text
- Static text that you can clear, set, and query

> **Tip:** Obviously, a large amount of static text cannot fit in a fixed window, so using scroll bars is indeed in order. This is another important feature demonstrated by the static text sampler—the capability to easily scroll through lines of static text. The key word here is "easily," because the application does not require the services of a Paint member function. (This is the case when you draw text lines with the TextOut API function.) In addition, static text is more flexible than drawn text when you are dealing with wrappable text and line breaks.

Listing 5.1 contains the script for the CTLSTAT1.RC resource file. This resource file reveals that the static text sampler program has two main menu items: Exit and Text. The first menu item enables you to exit the application, and the second menu item is a pop-up menu. This menu features three menu items that can manipulate the static text string, which is the last item in the scrollable window. These three menu items enable you to clear, set, and obtain a copy of the last static text string.

Listing 5.2 shows the source code for the CTLSTAT1.CPP program. I suggest that you first compile and run the static text sampler application.

Listing 5.1. The script for the CTLSTAT1.RC resource file.

```
#include <windows.h>
#include <owlrc.h>

#include <inputdia.dlg>

COMMANDS MENU LOADONCALL MOVEABLE PURE DISCARDABLE
BEGIN
     MENUITEM "E&xit", CM_EXIT
     POPUP "&Text"
     BEGIN
            MENUITEM "&Clear", CM_EDITCLEAR
            MENUITEM "&Set", CM_EDITPASTE
            MENUITEM "&Get" CM_EDITCOPY
     END
END
```

Listing 5.2. The source code for the CTLSTAT1.CPP program.

```
#include <string.h>
#include <owl.h>
#include <inputdia.h>
#include <static.h>

//---------- declare global "parameters" ------------
// X coordinate for the upper-left corner of
// the left column of static text
const XLstat = 25;
const Ystat = 25;
const Hstat = 30;
const Wstat = 250;
// X coordinate for the upper-left corner of
// the right column of static text
const XRstat = XLstat + Wstat + 50;
// spacing between static text area
const Ydelta = 10;
const MaxStaticLen = 80;

// declare the custom application class as
// a subclass of TApplication
class TWinApp : public TApplication
{
public:
```

```cpp
    TWinApp(LPSTR     AName,              // application name
            HINSTANCE hInstance,          // instance handle
            HINSTANCE hPrevInstance,      // previous instance handle
            LPSTR     lpCmdLine,          // command-line arguments
            int       nCmdShow) :         // display command
            TApplication(AName, hInstance, hPrevInstance,
                         lpCmdLine, nCmdShow) {};

protected:
   virtual void InitMainWindow();
};

// use the _CLASSDEF macro to declare reference and pointer
// types related to the new TAppWindow class
_CLASSDEF(TAppWindow)

// expand the functionality of TWindow by deriving class TAppWindow
class TAppWindow : public TWindow
{
public:
   PTStatic EditText;

   TAppWindow(PTWindowsObject AParent, LPSTR ATitle);

   // clears the static text
   virtual void CMEditClear(RTMessage Msg)
        = [CM_FIRST + CM_EDITCLEAR];

   // sets new static text
   virtual void CMEditPaste(RTMessage Msg)
        = [CM_FIRST + CM_EDITPASTE];

   // echoes the static text in a message box
   virtual void CMEditCopy(RTMessage Msg)
        = [CM_FIRST + CM_EDITCOPY];

   // handle closing the window
   virtual BOOL CanClose();

protected:
   // return the name of this class
   LPSTR GetClassName() { return "TAppWindow"; }

   // assign the attributes to the Windows class WNDCLASS
   virtual void GetWindowClass(WNDCLASS& W);
```

continues

Listing 5.2. continued

```
private:
  // get the Y coordinates for static text number i
  int getY(int i) { return --i * (Ystat + Hstat) + Ydelta; }
};

TAppWindow::TAppWindow(PTWindowsObject AParent, LPSTR ATitle) :
                      TWindow(AParent, ATitle)
{
  int i = 2;
  char s[MaxStaticLen+1];
  char longStr[161];
  char oneLine[] = "Single-line s&tatic text";
  char multLine[] = " Multiline\nstatic t&ext";

  AssignMenu("COMMANDS");
  // include the vertical and horizontal scroll bars
  Attr.Style |= WS_HSCROLL | WS_VSCROLL;
  // create scroller object
  Scroller = new TScroller(this, 8, 35, 80, 35);

  // set the default single-line static text
  strcpy(s, "Default single-line static text");
  new TStatic(this, -1, s, XLstat, Ystat, Wstat, Hstat, strlen(s));
  new TStatic(this, -1, oneLine, XRstat, Ystat, Wstat, Hstat,
              strlen(oneLine));

  // set the default multiline static text
  strcpy(s, "Default multiline static text");
  new TStatic(this, -1, s, XLstat, getY(i), Wstat, Hstat, strlen(s));
  new TStatic(this, -1, multLine, XRstat, getY(i++), Wstat, Hstat,
              strlen(multLine));

  // set the simple single-line static text
  strcpy(s, "Simple single-line static text");
  new TStatic(this, -1, s, XLstat, getY(i), Wstat, Hstat, strlen(s));
  EditText = new TStatic(this, -1, oneLine, XRstat, getY(i++),
                         Wstat, Hstat, strlen(oneLine));
  EditText->Attr.Style |= SS_SIMPLE;

  // set the simple multiline static text
  strcpy(s, "Simple multiline static text");
  new TStatic(this, -1, s, XLstat, getY(i), Wstat, Hstat, strlen(s));
  EditText = new TStatic(this, -1, multLine, XRstat, getY(i++),
                         Wstat, Hstat, strlen(multLine));
```

ObjectWindows Controls

```cpp
EditText->Attr.Style |= SS_SIMPLE;

// set the left-justified single-line static text
strcpy(s, "Left-justified single-line static text");
new TStatic(this, -1, s, XLstat, getY(i), Wstat, Hstat, strlen(s));
new TStatic(this, -1, oneLine, XRstat, getY(i++), Wstat, Hstat,
            strlen(oneLine));

// set the left-justified multiline static text
strcpy(s, "Left-justified multiline static text");
new TStatic(this, -1, s, XLstat, getY(i), Wstat, Hstat, strlen(s));
new TStatic(this, -1, multLine, XRstat, getY(i++), Wstat, Hstat,
            strlen(multLine));

// set the left-justified long single-line static text
strcpy(s, "Left-justified long single-line static text");
new TStatic(this, -1, s, XLstat, getY(i), Wstat, Hstat, strlen(s));
strcpy(longStr, "This string is longer than the other strings.");
strcat(longStr, "  It illustrates text wrapping.");
new TStatic(this, -1, longStr, XRstat, getY(i++), Wstat, Hstat,
            strlen(longStr));

// set the left-justified long single-line static text
strcpy(s, "Unwrappable long single-line static text");
new TStatic(this, -1, s, XLstat, getY(i), Wstat, Hstat, strlen(s));
strcpy(longStr, "This string is longer than the other strings.");
strcat(longStr, "  It illustrates how to prevent text wrapping.");
EditText = new TStatic(this, -1, longStr, XRstat, getY(i++),
                       Wstat, Hstat, strlen(longStr));
EditText->Attr.Style |= SS_LEFTNOWORDWRAP;

// set the right-justified single-line static text
strcpy(s, "Right-justified single-line static text");
new TStatic(this, -1, s, XLstat, getY(i), Wstat, Hstat, strlen(s));
EditText = new TStatic(this, -1, oneLine, XRstat, getY(i++),
                       Wstat, Hstat, strlen(oneLine));
EditText->Attr.Style = (EditText->Attr.Style & ~SS_LEFT) | SS_RIGHT;

// set the right-justified multiline static text
strcpy(s, "Right-justified multiline static text");
new TStatic(this, -1, s, XLstat, getY(i), Wstat, Hstat, strlen(s));
EditText = new TStatic(this, -1, multLine, XRstat, getY(i++),
                       Wstat, Hstat, strlen(multLine));
EditText->Attr.Style = (EditText->Attr.Style & ~SS_LEFT) | SS_RIGHT;
```

continues

Listing 5.2. continued

```
// set the centered single-line static text
strcpy(s, "Centered single-line static text");
new TStatic(this, -1, s, XLstat, getY(i), Wstat, Hstat, strlen(s));
EditText = new TStatic(this, -1, oneLine, XRstat, getY(i++),
                    Wstat, Hstat, strlen(oneLine));
EditText->Attr.Style = (EditText->Attr.Style & ~SS_LEFT) |
                    SS_CENTER;

// set the centered multiline static text
strcpy(s, "Centered multiline static text");
new TStatic(this, -1, s, XLstat, getY(i), Wstat, Hstat, strlen(s));
EditText = new TStatic(this, -1, multLine, XRstat, getY(i++),
                    Wstat, Hstat, strlen(multLine));
EditText->Attr.Style = (EditText->Attr.Style & ~SS_LEFT) |
                    SS_CENTER;

// set the centered single-line static text with no prefix
strcpy(s, "Centered single-line static text with no prefix");
new TStatic(this, -1, s, XLstat, getY(i), Wstat, Hstat, strlen(s));
EditText = new TStatic(this, -1, oneLine, XRstat, getY(i++),
                    Wstat, Hstat, strlen(oneLine));
EditText->Attr.Style = (EditText->Attr.Style & ~SS_LEFT) |
                    SS_CENTER | SS_NOPREFIX;

// show a black frame
strcpy(s, "Black frame style");
new TStatic(this, -1, s, XLstat, getY(i), Wstat, Hstat, strlen(s));
EditText = new TStatic(this, -1, oneLine, XRstat, getY(i++),
                    Wstat, Hstat, strlen(oneLine));
EditText->Attr.Style |= SS_BLACKFRAME;

// show a black frame with text
strcpy(s, "Black frame with text");
new TStatic(this, -1, s, XLstat, getY(i), Wstat, Hstat, strlen(s));
new TStatic(this, -1, oneLine, XRstat, getY(i), Wstat, Hstat,
            strlen(oneLine));
EditText = new TStatic(this, -1, oneLine, XRstat, getY(i++),
                    Wstat, Hstat, strlen(oneLine));
EditText->Attr.Style |= SS_BLACKFRAME;

// show a black rectangle
strcpy(s, "Black rectangle style");
new TStatic(this, -1, s, XLstat, getY(i), Wstat, Hstat, strlen(s));
```

ObjectWindows Controls

```
    EditText = new TStatic(this, -1, oneLine, XRstat, getY(i++),
                        Wstat, Hstat, strlen(oneLine));
    EditText->Attr.Style |= SS_BLACKRECT;

    // show a gray frame
    strcpy(s, "Gray frame style");
    new TStatic(this, -1, s, XLstat, getY(i), Wstat, Hstat, strlen(s));
    EditText = new TStatic(this, -1, oneLine, XRstat, getY(i++),
                        Wstat, Hstat, strlen(oneLine));
    EditText->Attr.Style |= SS_GRAYFRAME;

    // show a gray frame with text
    strcpy(s, "Gray frame with text");
    new TStatic(this, -1, s, XLstat, getY(i), Wstat, Hstat, strlen(s));
    new TStatic(this, -1, oneLine, XRstat, getY(i), Wstat, Hstat,
             strlen(oneLine));
    EditText = new TStatic(this, -1, oneLine, XRstat, getY(i++),
                        Wstat, Hstat, strlen(oneLine));
    EditText->Attr.Style |= SS_GRAYFRAME;

    // show a gray rectangle
    strcpy(s, "Gray rectangle style");
    new TStatic(this, -1, s, XLstat, getY(i), Wstat, Hstat, strlen(s));
    EditText = new TStatic(this, -1, oneLine, XRstat, getY(i++),
                        Wstat, Hstat, strlen(oneLine));
    EditText->Attr.Style |= SS_GRAYRECT;

    // show a white frame
    strcpy(s, "White frame style");
    new TStatic(this, -1, s, XLstat, getY(i), Wstat, Hstat, strlen(s));
    EditText = new TStatic(this, -1, oneLine, XRstat, getY(i++),
                        Wstat, Hstat, strlen(oneLine));
    EditText->Attr.Style |= SS_WHITEFRAME;

    // show a white frame with text
    strcpy(s, "White frame with text");
    new TStatic(this, -1, s, XLstat, getY(i), Wstat, Hstat, strlen(s));
    new TStatic(this, -1, oneLine, XRstat, getY(i), Wstat, Hstat,
             strlen(oneLine));
    EditText = new TStatic(this, -1, oneLine, XRstat, getY(i++),
                        Wstat, Hstat, strlen(oneLine));
    EditText->Attr.Style |= SS_WHITEFRAME;

    // show a white rectangle
    strcpy(s, "White rectangle style");
```

continues

Listing 5.2. continued

```
    new TStatic(this, -1, s, XLstat, getY(i), Wstat, Hstat, strlen(s));
    EditText = new TStatic(this, -1, oneLine, XRstat, getY(i++),
                        Wstat, Hstat, strlen(oneLine));
    EditText->Attr.Style |= SS_WHITERECT;

    // show editable static text
    strcpy(s, "Editable static text");
    new TStatic(this, -1, s, XLstat, getY(i), Wstat, Hstat, strlen(s));
    strcpy(s, "Sample &static text");
    EditText = new TStatic(this, -1, s, XRstat, getY(i++), Wstat, Hstat,
                         strlen(s));
};

void TAppWindow::CMEditClear(RTMessage Msg)
{
  EditText->Clear();
}

void TAppWindow::CMEditPaste(RTMessage Msg)
{
 int size = EditText->GetTextLen() + 1;
 char s[MaxStaticLen+1];

 // get the current text
 EditText->GetText(s, size);
 if (GetApplication()->ExecDialog(
        new TInputDialog(this, "Text Input",
                         "Enter new static text",
                         s, sizeof(s))) == IDOK)
    // update static text
    EditText->SetText(s);
}

void TAppWindow::CMEditCopy(RTMessage Msg)
{
  int size = EditText->GetTextLen() + 1;
  char *s = new char[size+1];
  EditText->GetText(s, size);
  MessageBox(HWindow, s, "Copy of static text", MB_OK);
}

BOOL TAppWindow::CanClose()
{
```

```
    return MessageBox(HWindow, "Want to close this application",
                      "Query", MB_YESNO | MB_ICONQUESTION) == IDYES;
}

void TAppWindow::GetWindowClass(WNDCLASS& W)
{
  TWindow::GetWindowClass(W);
  // select a white background color
  W.hbrBackground = (HBRUSH)(COLOR_HIGHLIGHTTEXT + 1);
}

void TWinApp::InitMainWindow()
{
  MainWindow = new TAppWindow(NULL, Name);
}

int PASCAL WinMain(HINSTANCE hInstance, HINSTANCE hPrevInstance,
                   LPSTR lpCmdLine, int nCmdShow)
{
  TWinApp WinApp("Static Text Sampler", hInstance,
                 hPrevInstance, lpCmdLine, nCmdShow);
  WinApp.Run(); // run OWL application
  return WinApp.Status; // return application status
}
```

Figures 5.1 and 5.2 show the upper and lower portions of the CTLSTAT1.EXE application's scrollable window. The main window contains two columns of static text. The left column contains the text that explains the type of static text shown in the right column. On my system, the main window has a white background and the static text instances have a blue background. This contrast in color enables you to detect visually the area that the TStatic constructor specifies in creating the numerous static text instances.

Scroll through the various kinds of static text and observe the following:

- ☐ The single and multiline default static text have the same appearance as the left-justified single and multiline static text, respectively.

- ☐ The simple static text has a background color that extends only with the text characters.

- ☐ Attempting to display simple multiline static text fails because the SS_LEFTNOWORDWRAP style that is used prevents the display of multiline text. In fact, the line break character appears with the rest of the text.

Figure 5.1.
The upper portion of the scrollable window in a sample session with the CTLSTAT1.EXE application.

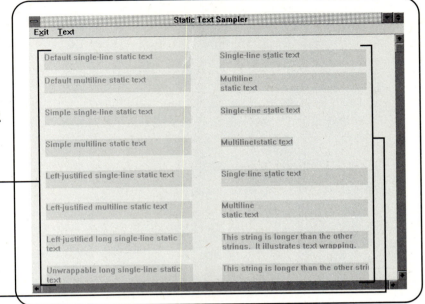

Types of text

Examples

Figure 5.2.
The lower portion of the scrollable window in a sample session with the CTLSTAT1.EXE application.

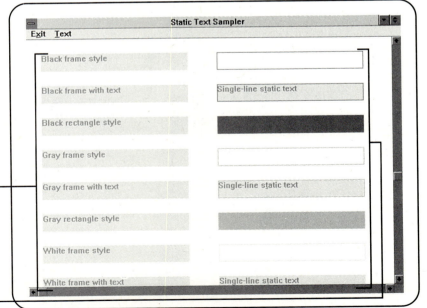

Types of text

Examples

ObjectWindows Controls

- The normal left-justified long static text succeeds in wrapping to the next line in the constructor-defined rectangle.
- The left-justified long static text with the SS_LEFTNOWORDWRAP style does not wrap and is truncated instead.
- All the lines of the multiline right-justified static text are right-justified, not just the first line.
- All the lines of the multiline centered static text are centered.
- The characters of the static text with the black, gray, and white rectangle styles are invisible.

> **Caution:** As I just mentioned, these characters of the static text with the black, gray, and white frame styles are basically invisible. However, using a simple programming trick (which I'll present later in this chapter), you can still display text inside these frames.

When you reach the end of the scrollable window, you see the special static text that can be manipulated. Use the Text pop-up menu option Get to display a copy of that static text in a message box. You can use the Set menu item to type a new set of characters using an input dialog box. Finally, try the Clear option to erase the last static text.

Here's how the static text sampler works. Listing 5.2 shows the application source code. The program declares a number of global constants (which I regard as parameters) to specify the location, size, and spacing for the static text instances. I included these constants in the program file because they speed up recompiling (if you use the precompiled headers option) in case you want to experiment with changing the values assigned to these constants. The listing declares the application class TWinApp and the window class TAppWindow. The instances of TAppWindow own and manage the set of TStatic instances.

The TAppWindow class declares a single data member, EditText, to point to an instance of TStatic. This data member serves two purposes. First, when the window creates the various static instances, it uses EditText to assign nondefault styles to certain instances of static text. Second, when the window is completely initialized, EditText points to the last TStatic instance, the one you can edit. This approach allows the pointer EditText to access the TStatic member functions Clear, GetTextLen, SetText, and SetText.

The TAppWindow class has a constructor and four public, two protected, and one private member functions. The private GetY member function calculates the

y coordinates for the static text. The protected member functions `GetClassName` and `GetWindowClass` enable the application to select a nondefault background color for the window. The first three public member functions handle the messages sent by the various options of the Text pop-up menu.

The `TAppWindow` constructor declares a number of local variables. The variable `i` stores the row index of the static text. The other variable stores various strings. The variable `oneLine` contains a sample single-line text, and the `multLine` variable stores a string with a line break.

The constructor performs the following tasks:

- ☐ Loads the COMMANDS menu resource.

- ☐ Incorporates the vertical and horizontal scroll bars by including the `WS_HSCROLL` and `WS_VSCROLL` in the window's `Attr.Style` data member.

- ☐ Creates an instance of the scroller class `TScroller`.

- ☐ Constructs a sample default single-line static text. The x coordinate for the "commenting text" (the left column) is `XLstat`. The x coordinate for the sampled static text (the right column) is `XRstat`.

- ☐ Creates a sample default multiline static text. Notice that the y coordinates for the two `TStatic` instances are obtained by calling `getY(i)` and `getY(i++)`. Using the variable `i` and the member function `getY` greatly simplifies the building of the static text set. This approach enables you to move, delete, and insert new groups of static text without worrying about changing coordinates.

- ☐ Generates a representative simple single-line static text. Notice that the constructor uses the `EditText` member to access the second `TStatic` instance in this group. The pointer `EditText` enables the constructor to include the `SS_SIMPLE` style.

- ☐ Attempts to create a sample simple multiline static text. The attempt fails, resulting in the display of a single-line simple static text.

- ☐ Creates a sample left-justified single and multiline static text. Notice that in creating these two static text instances, the constructor does not need the `EditText` pointer because the `SS_LEFT` style is the default style.

- ☐ Generates a long left-justified single-line static text. Because the default style supports wrappable static text, the constructor does not need to alter the `Attr.Style` member of the second `TStatic` instance.

- Creates a long left-justified single-line static text string that does not wrap. The constructor uses the EditText to access the second TStatic instance and include the SS_LEFTNOWORDWRAP style.
- Generates a sample right-justified single and multiline static text string. The constructor uses the EditText member and bitwise operators to remove the SS_LEFT style and include the SS_RIGHT style.
- Creates a sample centered single- and multiline static text string. The constructor uses the EditText member and bitwise operators to remove the SS_LEFT style and include the SS_CENTER style.
- Generates a sample centered single-line static text string with no prefix. The constructor uses the EditText member and bitwise operators to remove the SS_LEFT style and include the SS_CENTER and SS_NOPREFIX styles.
- Creates a black frame by specifying the SS_BLACKFRAME style in the EditText->Attr.Style. Notice that the characters of the oneLine variable are not visible.
- Generates a black frame that contains text.

> **Tip:** The programming trick here is to first create the visible text instance and then create the black frame. Creating the frame before the text instance results in the frame blocking out the text. (Incidentally, the same trick does not work with the rectangle style.)

- Creates gray and white frames and rectangles. You can create the frames with or without text inside them, using the same trick that I mentioned previously.
- Creates static text you can edit.

The CMEditClear member function handles the command sent by the Clear menu item. The function simply invokes the TStatic::Clear member function to delete the static text characters.

The CMEditPaste member function enables you to type new static text characters. The function uses the local variable size to store the size of the static text. The variable size is initialized with the expression EditText->GetTextLen() + 1. Adding 1 to the result of GetTextLen() accounts for the ampersand character. The CMEditPaste function obtains a copy of the static text characters by calling the GetText function. The static text characters are stored in the string variable s, which is used in the input dialog box. The function writes the new static text characters by invoking the `SetText` function with the variable `s` as its argument.

The `CMEditCopy` member function obtains a copy of the static text characters by using the `TStatic::GetTextLen` and `TStatic::GetText` member functions. The **MessageBox** API function then displays the copied characters in a message box.

The Edit Control

ObjectWindows offers the `TEdit` class, which implements an edit control. You have encountered this control in some of the earlier programs that use the input dialog box. The edit control enables you to type and edit text in the input dialog box. Chapter 4, "Windows Editing Classes," introduced the `TEdit`-typed data member `Editor` declared in the `TEditWindow` class. The examples in Chapter 4 provided you with a good feel for the functionality of the `TEdit` class. This section discusses this functionality in more detail, because to implement customized text editors in your ObjectWindows application, you must become quite familiar with the `TEdit` member functions.

The TEdit Class

The `TEdit` class, a descendant of class `TStatic`, implements a versatile edit control that supports single- and multiline text and can cut, copy, paste, delete, and clear text. The edit control can also undo the last text changes and exchange text with the Clipboard. The `TEdit` class has three constructors (two are public and the other is protected). This section focuses on the constructor that enables you to create `TEdit` instances from scratch. This constructor is declared as follows:

```
TEdit(PTWindowsObject AParent, int AnId, LPSTR AText, int X,
      int Y, int W, int H, WORD ATextLen, BOOL Multiline,
      PTModule AModule = NULL);
```

The `AParent` parameter is the pointer to the parent (or owner) object. The `AnId` parameter is an integer ID for the edit control. The `AText` parameter is the pointer to the string that supplies the `TEdit` instance with its initial text. The `ATextLen` parameter specifies the number of characters accessed by `AText` that actually appear in the edit control. The parameters `X`, `Y`, `W`, and `H` specify the coordinates and dimensions of the edit control. The `BOOL MultiLine` parameter

ObjectWindows Controls

indicates whether the edit control is single-line (using the argument FALSE) or multiline (using the argument TRUE).

The `TEdit` constructor assigns default styles to the instances of the `TEdit` class. Table 5.2 lists the `ES_xxxx` style values for the multiline edit control. The default styles for all `TEdit` instances are `WS_CHILD`, `WS_VISIBLE`, `WS_TABSTOP`, `ES_LEFT`, `ES_AUTOHSCROLL`, and `WS_BORDER`. These styles produce an edit control that has a frame and displays left-justified text that can be scrolled horizontally if the entire text does not fit in the frame. When you supply the argument TRUE to the `Multiline` parameter of the constructor, `ES_MULTILINE`, `ES_AUTOVSCROLL`, `WS_HSCROLL`, and `WS_VSCROLL` are included as additional defaults. These additional default styles support multiple text lines, scroll the text vertically, and include vertical and horizontal scroll bars.

Table 5.2. The values for the multiline edit control styles.

Value	Meaning
ES_AUTOHSCROLL	Enables the text to automatically scroll to the right by 10 characters when the user types a character at the end of the line. When the user presses the Enter key, the text scrolls back all the way to the left.
ES_AUTOVSCROLL	Lets the text scroll up by one page when the user presses the Enter key on the last visible line.
ES_CENTER	Centers the text in a multiline edit control.
ES_LEFT	Left-justifies text.
ES_LOWERCASE	Converts to lowercase all of the letters that the user types.
ES_MULTILINE	Specifies a multiline edit control that recognizes line breaks (designated by the sequence of carriage return and line feed characters).
ES_NOHIDESEL	Prevents the typical action of an edit control, which is to hide the selected text by default when it loses focus and show the selection when it gains focus again.
ES_RIGHT	Right-justifies text.
ES_UPPERCASE	Converts to uppercase all of the letters that the user types.

The next subsections discuss the various categories of text-editing features that the edit control supports.

Menu-Driven Commands and the Clipboard

The TEdit class includes a set of protected member functions that handle common text-editing commands. These commands are available in typical menu options such as Cut, Copy, Paste, Clear, Undo, and Delete. Table 5.3 shows the TEdit member functions and the menu commands that respond to them. The table also shows the public member functions of TEdit that are called by the response member functions.

Table 5.3. The protected **TEdit** member functions that support basic text-editing menu commands.

Response Member Function	Menu Command Function(s)	Calls Member
CMEditCut	CM_EDITCUT	Cut
CMEditCopy	CM_EDITCOPY	Copy
CMEditPaste	CM_EDITPASTE	Paste
CMEditClear	CM_EDITCLEAR	Clear
CMEditDelete	CM_EDITDELETE	Delete Selection
CMEditUndo	CM_EDITUNDO	Undo

Edit Controls for Text Queries

The TEdit class has a family of text query member functions. These functions enable you to retrieve the entire control text or parts of it. They also enable you to obtain information on the text statistics (number of lines, length of lines, and so on). This section describes the relevant query member functions.

The GetText Function

The GetText member function, which is inherited from TStatic, enables you to retrieve all or the leading part of the text in an edit control. The GetText function is declared as follows:

```
int GetText(LPSTR ATextString, int MaxChars);
```

ObjectWindows Controls

The `MaxChars` parameter specifies the number of leading control characters to return. These characters are copied to the string accessed by the pointer `ATextString`. The function result returns the actual number of characters copied.

>
>
> **Caution:** When you obtain the text for a multiline edit control, take into account the pairs of carriage return and line feed characters at the end of each line. This information is relevant when you count the number of characters to process.

The GetNumLines Function

The `GetNumLines` function returns the number of lines in a multiline edit control. The `GetNumLines` function is declared as follows:

```
int GetNumLines();
```

The `GetNumLines` function returns valuable information regarding the number of lines in the multiline edit control. If the edit control has no text (it has one empty line), the function returns 1. If an error occurs, the function returns 0. If you plan to access any line individually, call `GetNumLines` first.

The GetLineLength Function

The `GetLineLength` function returns the number of characters in a specified line of a multiline edit control. The declaration of the `GetLineLength` function is

```
int GetLineLength(int LineNumber);
```

The parameter `LineNumber` specifies the target line by number. When you pass an argument of –1 to `LineNumber`, the function returns one of the following values:

- ☐ The length of the line containing the caret, if there is no selected text.
- ☐ The length of the line minus the number of selected characters, when text is selected on the line.
- ☐ The length of the lines minus the number of selected characters, when the selected text stretches across multiple lines.

The `GetLine` Function

The Boolean `GetLine` function retrieves the text of a specified line. The declaration of the `GetLine` function is

```
BOOL GetLine(LPSTR ATextString, int StrSize, int LineNumber);
```

The function returns TRUE if the sought text is found and retrieved in its entirety. If either of these conditions fails, the function returns FALSE. The parameter `ATextString` is the pointer to the string buffer that receives a copy of the specified text line. The `StrSize` parameter specifies the number of characters to copy. The `LineNumber` parameter selects the target line.

If you use a static string to retrieve a copy of a text line, the `GetLineLength` function should tell you whether you have enough string space. If you use a dynamic string, the result of `GetLineLength` helps you create an adequately sized dynamic string to copy the target text line.

The `GetSubText` Function

The `GetSubText` function enables you to retrieve a copy of text that is specified by the starting and ending character positions. The declaration of `GetSubText` is

```
void GetSubText(LPSTR ATextString, int StartPos, int EndPos);
```

The `ATextString` function is the pointer to the string receiving the characters from position `StartPos` to `EndPos`. The `GetSubText` function enables you to extract text that spans over multiple lines.

The `GetSelection` Function

The `GetSelection` function obtains the starting and ending character positions of the selected text. The general declaration of the `GetSelection` member function is

```
void GetSelection(Rint StartPos, Rint EndPos);
```

The `StartPos` and `EndPos` parameters are references that return the character positions defining the span of the selected text. If no text is selected, the values returned by the `StartPos` and `EndPos` are equal and refer to the position of the caret (the current insertion point). Therefore, you can query the existence of any selected text by simply comparing the values of the arguments for the `StartPos` and `EndPos` parameters.

The GetLineIndex Function

The `GetLineIndex` function serves two purposes, depending on its argument. The declaration of the `GetLineIndex` function is

```
int GetLineIndex(int LineNumber);
```

The main purpose of this function is to return the number of characters that appear before the line number specified by the `LineNumber` parameter. The second purpose of the function is to return the line number containing the caret when the argument for `LineNumber` is –1.

The GetLineFromPos Function

The `GetLineFromPos` member function is a versatile function that returns the line number of a character position. When the character position is supplied, this function is valuable in locating an edited line. The declaration of the `GetLineFromPos` functions is

```
int GetLineFromPos(int CharPos);
```

The `CharPos` parameter supplies the character position. If the argument for `CharPos` is greater than the actual position of the last character, the function returns the number of the last line. When the argument for `CharPos` is –1, the function returns the line number that contains the first selected character.

The IsModified Function

The Boolean `IsModified` member function takes no argument and returns TRUE if the text in the edit control has been changed. Otherwise it yields FALSE. The `IsModified` function plays a valuable role in monitoring any text changes in an edit control. If the text was read from a text file, the application can query the `IsModified` function whether it is necessary to save the text in the edit control.

The ClearModify Function

The `ClearModify` function takes no arguments and simply resets the text change flag. Consequently, any previous text changes are ignored by the `IsModified` function, which returns FALSE after calling `ClearModify` (and before making any new text changes).

The Search Function

The `Search` member function searches for a specific string in the edit control text. The declaration of the `Search` member function is

```
int Search(int StartPos, LPSTR AText, BOOL CaseSensitive);
```

The `StartPos` parameter specifies the position of the first searched character. If you supply the argument −1 to `StartPos`, the search starts from the end of the currently selected text or, if no text is selected, from the position of the caret. `AText` is the pointer to the search string. The Boolean `CaseSensitive` parameter indicates whether the search is case-sensitive.

Altering the Edit Controls

Now look at the member functions of `TEdit` that alter the edit control text. These member functions delete text, insert text, and replace selected text.

Deleting Text

The `TEdit` member functions `Clear`, `DeleteLine`, `DeleteSelection`, and `DeleteSubText` delete text in various ways:

- ☐ The `Clear` function (inherited from the `TStatic` class) deletes the entire text of an edit control. You can also use the `Clear` and `SetText` functions to emulate hiding and showing text in an edit control.

- ☐ The Boolean `DeleteLine` member function deletes a specified line or the current line. The function returns TRUE if the target line was successfully deleted, and yields FALSE otherwise. The declaration of `DeleteLine` function is

    ```
    BOOL DeleteLine(int LineNumber);
    ```

    The `LineNumber` parameter specifies the line to delete. If you assign `LineNumber` an argument of −1, the function deletes the current line.

- ☐ The parameterless Boolean `DeleteSelection` function simply deletes the selected text. The function returns TRUE if there is selected text to delete, and yields FALSE if no text is selected.

- ☐ The Boolean `DeleteSubText` function deletes a range of characters that you specify. The function returns TRUE if the deletion is successful and FALSE otherwise. The declaration of the `DeleteSubText` function is

    ```
    BOOL DeleteSubText(int StartPos, int EndPos);
    ```

The `StartPos` and `EndPos` parameters specify the character positions that define the text to delete. The `DeleteSubText` function provides more control over deleting text than the other functions.

Inserting and Overwriting Text

`TEdit` offers the following functions to insert text and overwrite the selected text:

- The Boolean `SetSelection` function defines a block of characters as new selected text. The function returns TRUE if it succeeds in selecting the specified text. The declaration of the `SetSelection` function is

    ```
    BOOL SetSelection(int StartPos, int EndPos);
    ```

    The parameters `StartPos` and `EndPos` define the range of characters that make up the new selected text.

- The `Insert` function inserts text at the current text insertion position. If text is selected, the `Insert` function replaces the selected text with the inserted text. The declaration of the `Insert` function is

    ```
    void Insert(LPSTR ATextString);
    ```

    `ATextString` is the pointer to the inserted string. The `Insert` function replaces any portion of the edit control text by creating that portion of the new, selected text (by using the `SetSelection` function) and then inserting the new text.

- The `SetText` function (inherited from the `TStatic` class) assigns a new text to the edit control. This function has the same effect as invoking the `Clear` and `Insert` functions.

The Command-Oriented Calculator Application (COCA)

Now look at an application that uses single and multiline edit controls. This section presents the command-oriented calculator application (COCA), which implements a floating-point calculator with edit controls rather than buttons. Figure 5.3 shows a sample session with the COCA (version 1) program.

Figure 5.3.
A sample session with the COCA (version 1) program.

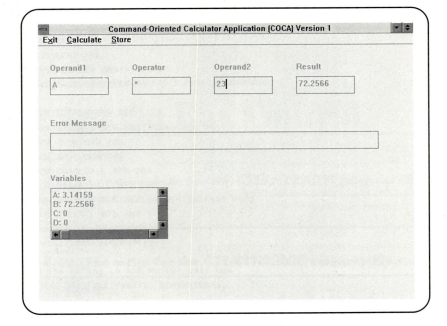

This type of interface is somewhat visually inferior to the typical button-populated Windows Calculator applet. However, the interface presented can support more mathematical functions without requiring additional buttons. Also, I will later replace the menu items and edit controls with the other controls. As the figure shows, the calculator consists of the following controls:

- Two edit controls for the first and second operands. These controls accept integers, floating-point numbers, and single-letter variables, A to Z.

- An edit control for the operator. The current version of the calculator supports the four basic math operations and the exponentiation (using the ^ character).

- An edit control for the result of the math operation.

- An edit control that displays any error messages.

- A multiline edit control that stores a number from the Result edit control in one of 26 single-letter variables named A to Z. The multi-edit line displays the current values stored in these variables and enables you to view and edit these numbers. You can use the vertical scroll bar to inspect the values in the different variables.

- Multiple static text controls that label the various edit controls. Of particular interest is the static control for the Error Message box. Clicking the accompanying static text clears the Error Message box of any text.
- A menu with three main menu items: Exit, Calculate, and Store. With the Exit menu item, you can exit the application. The Calculate menu item performs a calculation that uses the numbers in the operand edit controls and the operator in operator edit control. The Store menu item stores the number from the Result edit control in the variable with the line that contains the text insertion point.

The calculator application demonstrates the following:

- The use of a single-line edit control for simple input.
- The use of a multiline edit control to view and edit information.
- The line-oriented text access and editing.
- The simulation of static text that responds to mouse clicks.

You should first compile and run the application to get a feel for how the Calculator application works. Try typing different numeric operands and their supported operators and click the Calculate menu item. Each time, the result appears in the Result box, overwriting the previous result. Try dividing a number by zero to experiment with the error-handling features.

Using the single-letter variables is easy. All these variables are initialized at 0, so to use them, store a nonzero value. Perform an operation and then click inside the Variables edit box. Select the first line that contains the variable A. Now click the Store menu item (or press Alt-S) and watch the number in the Result box appear in the first line of the Variables edit box. The name of the variable and the colon and space characters that follow reappear with the new text line. Now replace the contents of the Operand1 edit box with the variable A, and then click the Calculate menu item. The Result edit box displays the result of the latest operation.

When you store a number in a variable, the insertion point moves to the next line. Therefore, you can store the same result in neighboring variables by repeatedly pressing Alt-S.

Listing 5.3 shows the source code for the CTLEDIT1.H header file. The header file declares the command constants for the Calculate and Store menu items. Listing 5.4 contains the script for the CTLEDIT1.RC resource file.

Listing 5.3. The source code for the CTLEDIT1.H header file.

```
#define CM_CALC 201
#define CM_STORE 202
```

Listing 5.4. The script for the CTLEDIT1.RC resource file.

```
#include <windows.h>
#include <owlrc.h>
#include "ctledit1.h"

COMMANDS MENU LOADONCALL MOVEABLE PURE DISCARDABLE
BEGIN
    MENUITEM "E&xit", CM_EXIT
    MENUITEM "&Calculate", CM_CALC
    MENUITEM "&Store", CM_STORE
END
```

Listing 5.5 contains the source code for the CTLEDIT1.CPP program file. The program contains two sets of constants. The first set declares the constants for height, width, vertical spacing, and horizontal spacing that are used in dimensioning the various controls. The second set of constants declares the ID_*xxxx* values used in creating the various edit control instances.

Listing 5.5. The source code for the CTLEDIT1.CPP program file.

```
#include <stdlib.h>
#include <ctype.h>
#include <stdio.h>
#include <math.h>
#include <string.h>
#include <owl.h>
#include <static.h>
#include <edit.h>
#include "ctledit1.h"

// declare the constants that represent the sizes of the controls
const Wlbl = 100;
const Hlbl = 20;
const LblVertSpacing = 5;
const LblHorzSpacing = 40;
const Wbox = 100;
```

```cpp
    const Hbox = 30;
    const BoxVertSpacing = 30;
    const BoxHorzSpacing = 40;
    const WLongbox = 4 * (Wbox + BoxHorzSpacing);
    const Wvarbox = 2 * Wbox;
    const Hvarbox = 3 * Hbox - 10;
    const MaxEditLen = 30;
    const MAX_MEMREG = 26;

    // declare the ID_XXXX constants for the edit boxes
    #define ID_OPERAND1_EDIT 101
    #define ID_OPERATOR_EDIT 102
    #define ID_OPERAND2_EDIT 103
    #define ID_RESULT_EDIT 104
    #define ID_ERRMSG_EDIT 105
    #define ID_VARIABLE_EDIT 106

    // declare the custom application class as
    // a subclass of TApplication
    class TWinApp : public TApplication
    {
    public:
      TWinApp(LPSTR    AName,           // application name
              HINSTANCE hInstance,      // instance handle
              HINSTANCE hPrevInstance,  // previous instance handle
              LPSTR     lpCmdLine,      // command-line arguments
              int       nCmdShow) :     // display command
              TApplication(AName, hInstance, hPrevInstance,
                           lpCmdLine, nCmdShow) {};

    protected:
      virtual void InitMainWindow();
    };

    // use the _CLASSDEF macro to declare reference and pointer
    // types related to the new TAppWindow class
    _CLASSDEF(TAppWindow)

    // expand the functionality of TWindow by deriving class TAppWindow
    class TAppWindow : public TWindow
    {
    public:

      TAppWindow(PTWindowsObject AParent, LPSTR ATitle);
```

continues

Listing 5.5. continued

```
    // handle clicking the left mouse button
    virtual void WMLButtonDown(RTMessage Msg)
      = [WM_FIRST + WM_LBUTTONDOWN];

    // handle  the calculation
    virtual void CMCalc(RTMessage Msg)
      = [CM_FIRST + CM_CALC];

    // handle storing the result in a variable
    virtual void CMStore(RTMessage Msg)
      = [CM_FIRST + CM_STORE];

    // handle closing the window
    virtual BOOL CanClose();

protected:
    PTEdit Operand1Box;
    PTEdit OperatorBox;
    PTEdit Operand2Box;
    PTEdit ResultBox;
    PTEdit ErrMsgBox;
    PTEdit VariableBox;

    // math error flag
    BOOL InError;

    // coordinates for the Error Message static text area
    int MSG_xulc, MSG_yulc, MSG_xlrc, MSG_ylrc;

    // obtain a number of a Variable edit box line
    double getVar(int lineNum);

    // store a number in the selected text of
    // the Variable edit box line
    void putVar(double x);

};

TAppWindow::TAppWindow(PTWindowsObject AParent, LPSTR ATitle) :
                    TWindow(AParent, ATitle)
{
  char s[81];
  char bigStr[6 * MAX_MEMREG + 1];
  char c;
```

ObjectWindows Controls

```cpp
    int x0 = 20;
    int y0 = 30;
    int x = x0, y = y0;

    // load the menu resource
    AssignMenu("COMMANDS");

    // create the first set of labels for the edit boxes
    strcpy(s, "Operand1");
    new TStatic(this, -1, s, x, y, Wlbl, Hlbl, strlen(s));
    strcpy(s, "Operator");
    x += Wlbl + LblHorzSpacing;
    new TStatic(this, -1, s, x, y, Wlbl, Hlbl, strlen(s));
    strcpy(s, "Operand2");
    x += Wlbl + LblHorzSpacing;
    new TStatic(this, -1, s, x, y, Wlbl, Hlbl, strlen(s));
    x += Wlbl + LblHorzSpacing;
    strcpy(s, "Result");
    new TStatic(this, -1, s, x, y, Wlbl, Hlbl, strlen(s));

    // create the operand1, operator, operand2, and result
    // edit boxes
    x = x0;
    y += Hlbl + LblVertSpacing;
    Operand1Box = new TEdit(this, ID_OPERAND1_EDIT, "", x, y,
                            Wbox, Hbox, 0, FALSE);
    // force conversion of letters to uppercase
    Operand1Box->Attr.Style |= ES_UPPERCASE;
    x += Wbox + BoxHorzSpacing;
    OperatorBox = new TEdit(this, ID_OPERATOR_EDIT, "", x, y,
                            Wbox, Hbox, 0, FALSE);
    x += Wbox + BoxHorzSpacing;
    Operand2Box = new TEdit(this, ID_OPERAND2_EDIT, "", x, y,
                            Wbox, Hbox, 0, FALSE);
    // force conversion of letters to uppercase
    Operand2Box->Attr.Style |= ES_UPPERCASE;
    x += Wbox + BoxHorzSpacing;
    ResultBox = new TEdit(this, ID_RESULT_EDIT, "", x, y, Wbox, Hbox,
                          0, FALSE);

    // create the static text and edit box for the error message
    x = x0;
    y += Hbox + BoxVertSpacing;
    // store the coordinates for the static text area
    MSG_xulc = x;
```

continues

255

Listing 5.5. continued

```
  MSG_yulc = y;
  MSG_xlrc = x + Wlbl;
  MSG_ylrc = y + Hlbl;
  strcpy(s, "Error Message");
  new TStatic(this, -1, s, x, y, Wlbl, Hlbl, strlen(s));
  y += Hlbl + LblVertSpacing;
  ErrMsgBox = new TEdit(this, ID_ERRMSG_EDIT, "", x, y,
                        WLongbox, Hbox, 0, FALSE);
  // create the static text and edit box for the single-letter
  // variable selection
  y += Hbox + BoxVertSpacing;
  strcpy(s, "Variables");
  new TStatic(this, -1, s, x, y, Wlbl, Hlbl, strlen(s));
  y += Hlbl + LblVertSpacing;
  // build the initial contents of the Variable edit box
  for (c = 'A'; c <= 'Z'; c++) {
    sprintf(s, "%c: 0\r\n", c);
    strcat(bigStr, s);
  }
  VariableBox = new TEdit(this, ID_VARIABLE_EDIT, bigStr, x, y,
                          Wvarbox, Hvarbox, 0, TRUE);
  // force conversion of letters to uppercase
  VariableBox->Attr.Style |= ES_UPPERCASE;

  // clear the InError flag
  InError = FALSE;

  // enable keyboard handler
  EnableKBHandler();
}

void TAppWindow::WMLButtonDown(RTMessage Msg)
{
  int x = Msg.LP.Lo;
  int y = Msg.LP.Hi;
  char s[MaxEditLen+1];
  char line[MaxEditLen+1];
  double z;

  if (x >= MSG_xulc && x <= MSG_xlrc &&
      y >= MSG_yulc && y <= MSG_ylrc)
    ErrMsgBox->Clear();
}
```

```
void TAppWindow::CMCalc(RTMessage Msg)
{
  double x, y, z;
  char opStr[MaxEditLen+1];
  char s[MaxEditLen+1];

  // obtain the string in the Operand1 edit box
  Operand1Box->GetText(s, MaxEditLen);
  // does the Operand1Box contain the name
  // of a single-letter variable?
  if (isalpha(s[0]))
    // obtain value from the Variable edit control
    x = getVar(s[0] - 'A');
  else
    // convert the string in the edit box
    x = atof(s);

  // obtain the string in the Operand2 edit box
  Operand2Box->GetText(s, MaxEditLen);
  // does the Operand2Box contain the name
  // of a single-letter variable?
  if (isalpha(s[0]))
    // obtain value from the Variable edit control
    y =getVar(s[0] - 'A');
  else
    // convert the string in the edit box
    y = atof(s);

  // obtain the string in the Operator edit box
  OperatorBox->GetText(opStr, MaxEditLen);

  // clear the error message box
  ErrMsgBox->Clear();
  InError = FALSE;

  // determine the requested operation
  if (strcmp(opStr, "+") == 0)
    z = x + y;
  else if (strcmp(opStr, "-") == 0)
    z = x - y;
  else if (strcmp(opStr, "*") == 0)
    z = x * y;
  else if (strcmp(opStr, "/") == 0) {
    if (y != 0)
      z = x / y;
```

continues

Listing 5.5. continued

```
    else {
      z = 0;
      InError = TRUE;
      ErrMsgBox->SetText("Division-by-zero error");
    }
  }
  else if (strcmp(opStr, "^") == 0) {
    if (x > 0)
      z = exp(y * log(x));
    else {
      InError = TRUE;
      ErrMsgBox->SetText(
        "Cannot raise the power of a negative number");
    }
  }
  else {
    InError = TRUE;
    ErrMsgBox->SetText("Invalid operator");
  }
  // display the result if no error has occurred
  if (!InError) {
    sprintf(s, "%g", z);
    ResultBox->SetText(s);
  }
}

void TAppWindow::CMStore(RTMessage Msg)
{
  char varName[MaxEditLen+1];
  char result[MaxEditLen+1];

  // get the string in the Result edit box
  ResultBox->GetText(result, MaxEditLen);

  // store the result in the selected text of
  // the Variable edit box
  putVar(atof(result));
}

double TAppWindow::getVar(int lineNum)
{
  int lineSize;
  char s[MaxEditLen+1];
```

```cpp
    if (lineNum >= MAX_MEMREG) return 0;
    // get the size of the target line
    lineSize = VariableBox->GetLineLength(lineNum);
    // get the line
    VariableBox->GetLine(s, lineSize+1, lineNum);
    // delete the first three characters
    strcpy(s, (s+3));
    // return the number stored in the target line
    return atof(s);
}

void TAppWindow::putVar(double x)
{
    int startPos, endPos;
    int lineNum;
    int lineSize;
    char s[MaxEditLen+1];

    // locate the character position of the cursor
    VariableBox->GetSelection(startPos, endPos);
    // turn off the selected text
    if (startPos != endPos)
        VariableBox->SetSelection(startPos, startPos);
    // get the line number where the cursor is located
    lineNum = VariableBox->GetLineFromPos(startPos);
    // get the line size of line lineNum
    lineSize = VariableBox->GetLineLength(lineNum);
    // obtain the text of line lineNum
    VariableBox->GetLine(s, lineSize+1, lineNum);
    // delete line lineNum
    VariableBox->DeleteLine(lineNum);
    // build the new text line
    sprintf(s, "%c: %g\r\n", s[0], x);
    // insert it
    VariableBox->Insert(s);
}

BOOL TAppWindow::CanClose()
{
    return MessageBox(HWindow, "Want to close this application",
                      "Query", MB_YESNO | MB_ICONQUESTION) == IDYES;
}

void TWinApp::InitMainWindow()
{
```

continues

Listing 5.5. continued

```
  MainWindow = new TAppWindow(NULL, Name);
}

int PASCAL WinMain(HINSTANCE hInstance, HINSTANCE hPrevInstance,
                   LPSTR lpCmdLine, int nCmdShow)
{
  TWinApp WinApp("Command-Oriented Calculator Application (COCA) Version 1",
                 hInstance, hPrevInstance, lpCmdLine, nCmdShow);
  WinApp.Run(); // run OWL application
  return WinApp.Status; // return application status
}
```

The COCA program declares an application class and a window class. The TAppWindow window class owns the static text and edit controls. The class declares a number of data members and member functions.

The TAppWindow contains the following groups of data members:

- Pointers to the various TEdit instances. Each pointer accesses one of the edit controls that appear in the program.
- The Boolean data member InError. This flags any error.
- The MSG_xxxx data members. These store the coordinates for the rectangle that contains the Error Message static text. The mouse click response member function WMLButtonDown examines whether the mouse is clicked inside that rectangle. If so, the member function clears the Error Message edit control text.

The TAppWindow class contains a constructor and a number of message response member functions that handle the mouse click and respond to the menu options.

The window class constructor performs the following tasks:

1. Loads the menu resource COMMANDS.
2. Creates the static text controls that label the Operand1, Operator, Operand2, and Result edit controls by invoking the TStatic constructor. The local variable x is increased by (Wlbl + LblHorzSpacing) to calculate the x coordinate for the next static text control. This approach is easier than plugging numbers into the TStatic constructor.

3. Creates the edit boxes for the operands, operator, and the result. The instances for these controls are accessed by the `Operand1Box`, `OperatorBox`, `Operand2Box`, and `ResultBox` data members. Each `TEdit` instance is created with its own `ID_xxxx` constant and a empty edit box. The edit boxes have the same size. The constructor modifies the style of the operand edit controls to include the `ES_UPPERCASE` style. When you type single-letter variable names in these edit controls, this style automatically converts the names to uppercase. The argument for the `ATextLen` parameter in the single-line controls is 0 to indicate that the amount of text to store is unlimited. The argument for the `MultiLine` parameter is FALSE to indicate that these controls are single-line edit boxes.

4. Calculates the top-left and bottom-right corner of the rectangle containing the Error Message text and stores them in the `MSG_xxxx` data members.

5. Creates the error message static text control and the edit control.

6. Creates the Variables multiline edit control. This task begins by using the string variable `bigStr` to build the contents of the Variables box. The `TEdit` constructor uses the `bigStr` variable as the initial text for the control. The argument for the `ATextLen` parameter is 0 to indicate that the amount of text to store is unlimited. The argument for the `MultiLine` parameter is TRUE, which indicates that the control is a multiline edit box. The style of the Variables edit control is also set to convert the letters into uppercase.

7. Sets the `InError` data member to FALSE.

8. Enables the keyboard handler by invoking the inherited `TWindow::EnableKBHandler` member function. With the keyboard handler enabled, you can use the Tab key to move between the various controls.

The constructor uses the local variables x and y and the control size constants to simplify calculation of the coordinates for the various controls. This approach enables you to modify the application without getting lost in a trail of numbers.

The `WMLButtonDown` member function performs a simple task. It checks whether the mouse click occurs in the rectangle occupied by the error message static text control. If this condition is TRUE, the function clears the error message box by invoking the `Clear` function.

The `CMCalc` member function responds to the Calculate menu command and performs the calculation by using the operands and operators that appear in their respective edit controls. The `CMCalc` function performs the following tasks:

1. Gets the first operand from the Operand1 edit box. The control may contain the name of a single-letter variable (A to Z) or a floating-point number. The function uses the GetText function to store a copy of the edit control text in the local variable s. The function then examines the first character in variable s. If that character is a letter, the first operand is a single-letter variable. Consequently, the function calls the protected member function getVar to obtain the value associated with that variable. If the first character is not a letter, the function uses the atof function to convert the contents of variable s into a double-typed number. In both cases, the function stores in variable x the operand that is first in numeric order.

2. Gets the second operand in a manner identical to the first one. The function stores in variable y the operand that is second in numeric order.

3. Copies the text in the Operator edit box into the local variable opStr.

4. Clears the error message text box and sets the InError data member to FALSE.

5. Determines the requested operation by using a series of if and if-else statements. The operators supported are +, -, *, /, and ^ (raise to a power). If the function detects an error, it sets the InError data member to TRUE and displays a message in the error message box.

6. Displays the result in the Result box if the InError data member is FALSE. The function first converts the result from double to a string and then writes to the Result box using the SetText function.

The CMStore member function stores the contents of the Result box in a single-letter variable. The function first obtains the string in the Result edit box by calling the GetText function. Then, the function invokes the protected member function putVar to actually store the result string at the current insertion point in the Variables edit box.

The getVar member function returns the number stored at line number lineNum of the Variables edit box. The function performs the following tasks:

1. Exits and returns 0 if lineNum is greater than or equal to the constant MAX_MEMREG.

2. Gets the size of the target line by making the GetLineLength(lineNum) call.

3. Retrieves the strings of line number lineNum by calling the GetLine function.

4. Deletes the first three characters of the retrieved line. This step should leave the string with the number stored in the target line.

5. Returns the double-typed number obtained by calling the `atof` function and supplying it with argument `s`.

The `putVar` member function stores the number from the Result box in the variable located on the same line containing the text insert position. The function performs the following tasks:

  1. Locates the character position of the cursor by calling the `GetSelection` function. The function returns the first and last character positions in the local variables `startPos` and `endPos`.

  2. Turns off any selected text. The function compares the values in the variables `startPos` and `endPos`. If these values do not match, `putVar` invokes the `SetSelection` function and supplies it with `startPos` as both the first and second arguments. This invocation of `SetSelection` turns off the selected text.

  3. Uses the `GetLineFromPos` function to obtain the line number where the cursor is located.

  4. Uses the `GetLineLength` function to obtain the size of the target line.

  5. Retrieves the text in the target line by calling the `GetLine` function.

  6. Deletes the target line by using the `DeleteLine` function.

  7. Builds the string for the new line.

  8. Inserts the new line by calling the `Insert` function.

The Push Button Control

Psychologically, the push button (also known as the command button) control is perhaps the most powerful control compared to other controls. The word *button* might remind you of the nuclear button in the hands of super-power leaders. You never hear about the nuclear list box or the nuclear check box. In a sense, the push button control represents the fundamental notion of a control—you click the control and something happens.

The ObjectWindows Library implements the `TButton` class, the instances of which create push button controls. There are basically two types of push button controls, default and nondefault. The default button appears with slightly thicker edges than the nondefault button. Pressing the Enter key is equivalent to clicking the default button. Only one default button can exist in a group. You can select a new default button by pressing the Tab key. This feature works only when the buttons are in a dialog box. If a nondialog box window owns a push button control, it can only visually display a default button—the functionality is not supported. You can simulate this feature by monitoring the push button that has the focus and changing the button style accordingly.

The TButton Class

The TButton class is a descendant of TControl that declares a rather small number of member functions. The TButton class declares two Boolean data members, IsDef and IsCurrentDefPB. Public member IsDef indicates whether a push button is the default button. The protected member IsCurrentDefPB signals whether the button is the current default button.

The most relevant member functions of TButton are its three constructors. I will focus on the constructor that enables you to create a push button control from scratch:

```
TButton(PTWindowsObject AParent, int AnId, LPSTR AText,
        int X, int Y, int W, int H, BOOL IsDefault,
        PTModule AModule = NULL);
```

The AParent parameter is the pointer to the owner window. The AnId parameter is a unique ID for the TButton instance. This same ID handles messages that the button control sends to its parent window. The AText parameter is the pointer to the button's caption. The X, Y, W, and H parameters define the location and dimensions of the TButton instance. The Boolean parameter IsDefault specifies whether the button is the default button.

Handling Button Messages

When you click a button, the control sends the BN_CLICKED notification message to its parent window. The parent window responds to this message by invoking a message response member function based on the button's ID. For example, if a button is created with an ID of ID_EXIT_BTN, the message handler function is

```
virtual void HandleExitBtn(RTMessage Msg)
        = [ID_FIRST +  ID_EXIT_BTN];
```

Manipulating Buttons

You can disable, enable, show, and hide a button (as well as any other control) with Windows API functions. A disabled button features a faded gray caption and does not respond to mouse clicks. Although the `TButton` class does not implement member functions for this type of visual manipulation, they are important and should be included here. With the `EnableWindow` API function, you can enable or disable a button. The API function accepts two arguments, the handle for the button and a Boolean argument that specifies whether the button is enabled (when the argument is TRUE) or disabled (when the argument is FALSE). Here are some sample calls to the `EnableWindow` function:

```
EnableWindow(AButton->HWindow, FALSE); // disable button
EnableWindow(AButton->HWindow, TRUE); // enable button
```

You can query the enabled state of a button by using the Boolean `IsWindowEnabled` API function, which takes one argument, the handle for the tested button. Here is a sample call to `IsWindowEnabled`:

```
// toggle the enabled state of a button
if (IsWindowEnabled(AButton->HWindow)
    EnableWindow(AButton->HWindow, FALSE); // disable button
else
    EnableWindow(AButton->HWindow, TRUE); // enable button
```

You can hide and show a button with the `ShowWindow` API function. The function takes two arguments: the handle for the button and either the `SW_HIDE` constant to hide the button or the `SW_SHOW` constant to show the button. The Boolean `IsWindowVisible` API function queries the visibility of a button. This function takes one argument, the handle for the queried button. The following is a sample call to the `ShowWindow` and `IsWindowVisible` functions:

```
// toggle the visibility of a button
if (IsWindowVisible(AButton->HWindow)
    ShowWindow(AButton->HWindow, SW_HIDE); // hide button
else
    ShowWindow(AButton->HWindow, SW_SHOW); // show button
```

These short examples manipulate individual push buttons with pointers to the `TButton` instances. But, what about manipulating multiple buttons or buttons that meet certain criteria? The answer lies in the `ForEach`, `FirstThat`, and `LastThat` iterator member functions that are declared in the `Object` class. These iterators work with special functions that have the following general declaration:

returnType iteratorFunctionName(Pvoid P, Pvoid Param)

returnType varies with the function's purpose. The function must typecast the parameter P to the pointer of the manipulated class. The parameter Param is the pointer to additional information needed by the iterated function. The following is an example of an iterated function that disables a button:

```
void DisableButton(Pvoid P, Pvoid Param)
{
    EnableWindow(PTButton(P)->HWindow, FALSE);
}
```

Other parts of the program can then call the DisabledButton in an application window class member function to disable all of the buttons in the window child list. The call might look like the following statement:

```
void TAppWindow::CMDisableAllBtn(RTMessage Msg)
{
    ForEach(DisableButton, NULL);
}
```

A slightly more elaborate code for the CMDisableAllBtn function can exclude certain buttons from being disabled.

The Modified Calculator Application

The first version of the Calculator application uses menu items to execute calculations, store results, and exit the application. Here is a new version that uses push buttons to perform these same tasks. Figure 5.4 updates you on the user interface of this new Calculator version.

The basic features of this new application version are the same as the previous one. The differences are minor. First, the visual interface has changed as follows:

- The menu is reduced to a single menu item Exit.

- There are three push buttons with the captions Calc, Store, and Exit. The first two buttons replace the Calculate and Store menu items eliminated from the first version.

The following are new features for the operations supported by the new Calculator version:

- The Store push button is disabled if the application attempts to execute an invalid operator. This feature demonstrates the disabling of a push button when a certain condition arises (in this case, a specific calculation error).

☐ The Store push button is enabled if you click the Error Message static text and when you successfully execute a math operation.

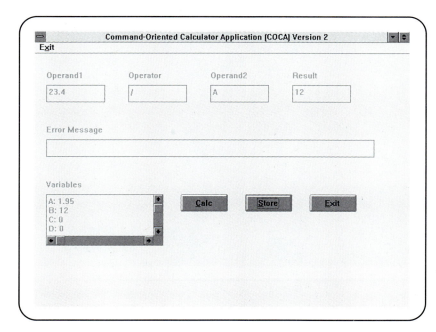

Figure 5.4. A sample session with the COCA (version 2) program.

The application demonstrates the following features:

☐ Using push buttons.

☐ Disabling and enabling push buttons.

☐ Associating accelerator keys with push buttons. This feature allows the program to maintain hot keys that are the same accelerator keys used by the menu items of the previous version.

The code associated with version 2 of COCA contains significant additions and changes. Listing 5.6 shows the source code for the CTLBTN1.H header file. This header file contains the ID_xxxx constants that define the various push button IDs.

Listing 5.7 contains the script for the CTLBTN1.RC resource file. The resource file reveals a single item menu resource. In addition, the resource file also declares the accelerator key resources. These resources support the hot keys Alt-C, Alt-S, and Alt-E that are associated with their respective button IDs. Listing 5.8 shows the source code for the CTLBTN1.CPP program file.

Listing 5.6. The source code for the CTLBTN1.H header file.

```
#define ID_CALC_BTN 107
#define ID_STORE_BTN 108
#define ID_EXIT_BTN 109
```

Listing 5.7. The script for the CTLBTN1.RC resource file.

```
#include <windows.h>
#include <owlrc.h>
#include "ctlbtn1.h"

BUTTONS ACCELERATORS
BEGIN
     "c", ID_CALC_BTN, ALT
     "s", ID_STORE_BTN, ALT
     "e", ID_EXIT_BTN, ALT
END


EXITMENU MENU LOADONCALL MOVEABLE PURE DISCARDABLE
BEGIN
        MENUITEM "E&xit", CM_EXIT
END
```

Listing 5.8. The source code for the CTLBTN1.CPP program file.

```
#include <stdlib.h>
#include <ctype.h>
#include <stdio.h>
#include <math.h>
#include <string.h>
#include <owl.h>
#include <static.h>
#include <edit.h>
#include <button.h>
#include "ctlbtn1.h"
```

ObjectWindows Controls

```cpp
// declare the constants that represent the sizes of the controls
const Wlbl = 100;
const Hlbl = 20;
const LblVertSpacing = 2;
const LblHorzSpacing = 40;
const Wbox = 100;
const Hbox = 30;
const BoxVertSpacing = 30;
const BoxHorzSpacing = 40;
const WLongbox = 4 * (Wbox + BoxHorzSpacing);
const Wvarbox = 2 * Wbox;
const Hvarbox = 3 * Hbox - 10;
const Hbtn = 30;
const Wbtn = 80;
const BtnHorzSpacing = 30;
const MaxEditLen = 30;
const MAX_MEMREG = 26;

// declare the ID_XXXX constants for the edit boxes
#define ID_OPERAND1_EDIT 101
#define ID_OPERATOR_EDIT 102
#define ID_OPERAND2_EDIT 103
#define ID_RESULT_EDIT 104
#define ID_ERRMSG_EDIT 105
#define ID_VARIABLE_EDIT 106

// declare the custom application class as
// a subclass of TApplication
class TWinApp : public TApplication
{
public:
  TWinApp(LPSTR     AName,           // application name
          HINSTANCE hInstance,       // instance handle
          HINSTANCE hPrevInstance,   // previous instance handle
          LPSTR     lpCmdLine,       // command-line arguments
          int       nCmdShow) :      // display command
          TApplication(AName, hInstance, hPrevInstance,
                       lpCmdLine, nCmdShow) {};

protected:
  virtual void InitMainWindow();
  virtual void InitInstance();
};
```

continues

Listing 5.8. continued

```
// use the _CLASSDEF macro to declare reference and pointer
// types related to the new TAppWindow class
_CLASSDEF(TAppWindow)

// expand the functionality of TWindow by deriving class TAppWindow
class TAppWindow : public TWindow
{
public:

  TAppWindow(PTWindowsObject AParent, LPSTR ATitle);

  // handle clicking the left mouse button
  virtual void WMLButtonDown(RTMessage Msg)
    = [WM_FIRST + WM_LBUTTONDOWN];

  // handle the calculation
  virtual void HandleCalcBtn(RTMessage Msg)
    = [ID_FIRST + ID_CALC_BTN];

  // handle the accelerator key for the Calculate button
  virtual void CMCalcBtn(RTMessage Msg)
    = [CM_FIRST + ID_CALC_BTN];

  // handle storing the result in a variable
  virtual void HandleStoreBtn(RTMessage Msg)
    = [ID_FIRST + ID_STORE_BTN];

  // handle the accelerator key for the Store button
  virtual void CMStoreBtn(RTMessage Msg)
    = [CM_FIRST + ID_STORE_BTN];

  // handle exiting the application
  virtual void HandleExitBtn(RTMessage Msg)
    = [ID_FIRST + ID_EXIT_BTN];

  // handle the accelerator key for the Exit button
  virtual void CMExitBtn(RTMessage Msg)
    = [CM_FIRST + ID_EXIT_BTN];

  // enable a push button control
  virtual void EnableButton(PTButton Btn)
  { EnableWindow(Btn->HWindow, TRUE); }

  // disable a push button control
```

```
    virtual void DisableButton(PTButton Btn)
    { EnableWindow(Btn->HWindow, FALSE); }

    // handle closing the window
    virtual BOOL CanClose();

protected:
  PTEdit Operand1Box;
  PTEdit OperatorBox;
  PTEdit Operand2Box;
  PTEdit ResultBox;
  PTEdit ErrMsgBox;
  PTEdit VariableBox;
  PTButton CalcBtn;
  PTButton StoreBtn;
  PTButton ExitBtn;

    // math error flag
    BOOL InError;

    // coordinates for the Error Message static text area
    int MSG_xulc, MSG_yulc, MSG_xlrc, MSG_ylrc;
    // obtain a number of a Variable edit box line
    double getVar(int lineNum);

    // store a number in the selected text of
    // the Variable edit box line
    void putVar(double x);

};

TAppWindow::TAppWindow(PTWindowsObject AParent, LPSTR ATitle) :
                    TWindow(AParent, ATitle)
{
  char s[81];
  char bigStr[6 * MAX_MEMREG + 1];
  char c;
  int x0 = 20;
  int y0 = 30;
  int x = x0, y = y0;

  // load the menu resource
  AssignMenu("EXITMENU");

  // create the first set of labels for the edit boxes
```

continues

Listing 5.8. continued

```
            strcpy(s, "Operand1");
            new TStatic(this, -1, s, x, y, Wlbl, Hlbl, strlen(s));
            strcpy(s, "Operator");
            x += Wlbl + LblHorzSpacing;
            new TStatic(this, -1, s, x, y, Wlbl, Hlbl, strlen(s));
            strcpy(s, "Operand2");
            x += Wlbl + LblHorzSpacing;
            new TStatic(this, -1, s, x, y, Wlbl, Hlbl, strlen(s));
            x += Wlbl + LblHorzSpacing;
            strcpy(s, "Result");
            new TStatic(this, -1, s, x, y, Wlbl, Hlbl, strlen(s));

            // create the operand1, operator, operand2, and result
            // edit boxes
            x = x0;
            y += Hlbl + LblVertSpacing;
            Operand1Box = new TEdit(this, ID_OPERAND1_EDIT, "", x, y,
                                   Wbox, Hbox, 0, FALSE);

            // force conversion of letters to uppercase
            Operand1Box->Attr.Style |= ES_UPPERCASE;
            x += Wbox + BoxHorzSpacing;
            OperatorBox = new TEdit(this, ID_OPERATOR_EDIT, "", x, y,
                                    Wbox, Hbox, 0, FALSE);
            x += Wbox + BoxHorzSpacing;
            Operand2Box = new TEdit(this, ID_OPERAND2_EDIT, "", x, y,
                                    Wbox, Hbox, 0, FALSE);
            // force conversion of letters to uppercase
            Operand2Box->Attr.Style |= ES_UPPERCASE;
            x += Wbox + BoxHorzSpacing;
            ResultBox = new TEdit(this, ID_RESULT_EDIT, "", x, y, Wbox, Hbox,
                                  0, FALSE);

            // create the static text and edit box for the error message
            x = x0;
            y += Hbox + BoxVertSpacing;
            // store the coordinates for the static text area
            MSG_xulc = x;
            MSG_yulc = y;
            MSG_xlrc = x + Wlbl;
            MSG_ylrc = y + Hlbl;
            strcpy(s, "Error Message");
            new TStatic(this, -1, s, x, y, Wlbl, Hlbl, strlen(s));
```

ObjectWindows Controls

```
    y += Hlbl + LblVertSpacing;
    ErrMsgBox = new TEdit(this, ID_ERRMSG_EDIT, "", x, y,
                        WLongbox, Hbox, 0, FALSE);
    // create the static text and edit box for the single-letter
    // variable selection
    y += Hbox + BoxVertSpacing;
    strcpy(s, "Variables");
    new TStatic(this, -1, s, x, y, Wlbl, Hlbl, strlen(s));
    y += Hlbl + LblVertSpacing;
    // build the initial contents of the Variable edit box
    for (c = 'A'; c <= 'Z'; c++) {
      sprintf(s, "%c: 0\r\n", c);
      strcat(bigStr, s);
    }
    VariableBox = new TEdit(this, ID_VARIABLE_EDIT, bigStr, x, y,
                        Wvarbox, Hvarbox, 0, TRUE);
    // force conversion of letters to uppercase
    VariableBox->Attr.Style |= ES_UPPERCASE;

    // create the Calc push button
    x += Wvarbox + BtnHorzSpacing;
    CalcBtn = new TButton(this, ID_CALC_BTN, "&Calc",
                        x, y, Wbtn, Hbtn, FALSE);

    // create the Store Btn
    x += Wbtn + BtnHorzSpacing;
    StoreBtn = new TButton(this, ID_STORE_BTN, "&Store",
                        x, y, Wbtn, Hbtn, FALSE);

    // Create the Exit Btn
    x += Wbtn + BtnHorzSpacing;
    ExitBtn = new TButton(this, ID_EXIT_BTN, "&Exit",
                        x, y, Wbtn, Hbtn, FALSE);

    // clear the InError flag
    InError = FALSE;

    // enable keyboard handler
    EnableKBHandler();
}

void TAppWindow::WMLButtonDown(RTMessage Msg)
{
    int x = Msg.LP.Lo;
    int y = Msg.LP.Hi;
    char s[MaxEditLen+1];
```

continues

Listing 5.8. continued

```
  char line[MaxEditLen+1];
  double z;

  if (x >= MSG_xulc && x <= MSG_xlrc &&
      y >= MSG_yulc && y <= MSG_ylrc) {
    ErrMsgBox->Clear();
    // enable the Store button
    EnableButton(StoreBtn);
  }
}

void TAppWindow::HandleCalcBtn(RTMessage Msg)
{
  double x, y, z;
  char opStr[MaxEditLen+1];
  char s[MaxEditLen+1];

  // obtain the string in the Operand1 edit box
  Operand1Box->GetText(s, MaxEditLen);
  // does the Operand1Box contain the name
  // of a single-letter variable?
  if (isalpha(s[0]))
    // obtain value from the Variable edit control
    x = getVar(s[0] - 'A');
  else
    // convert the string in the edit box
    x = atof(s);

  // obtain the string in the Operand2 edit box
  Operand2Box->GetText(s, MaxEditLen);
  // does the Operand2Box contain the name
  // of a single-letter variable?
  if (isalpha(s[0]))
    // obtain value from the Variable edit control
    y =getVar(s[0] - 'A');
  else
     // convert the string in the edit box
    y = atof(s);

  // obtain the string in the Operator edit box
  OperatorBox->GetText(opStr, MaxEditLen);

  // clear the error message box
  ErrMsgBox->Clear();
```

```
    InError = FALSE;

    // determine the requested operation
    if (strcmp(opStr, "+") == 0)
      z = x + y;
    else if (strcmp(opStr, "-") == 0)
      z = x - y;
    else if (strcmp(opStr, "*") == 0)
      z = x * y;
    else if (strcmp(opStr, "/") == 0) {
      if (y != 0)
        z = x / y;
      else {
        z = 0;
        InError = TRUE;
        ErrMsgBox->SetText("Division-by-zero error");
      }
    }
    else if (strcmp(opStr, "^") == 0) {
      if (x > 0)
        z = exp(y * log(x));
      else {
        InError = TRUE;
        ErrMsgBox->SetText(
          "Cannot raise the power of a negative number");
      }
    }
    else {
      InError = TRUE;
      ErrMsgBox->SetText("Invalid operator");
    }
    // display the result if no error has occurred
    if (!InError) {
      sprintf(s, "%g", z);
      ResultBox->SetText(s);
      // enable the Store button
      EnableButton(StoreBtn);
    }
    else
      // disable the Store button
      DisableButton(StoreBtn);
}

void TAppWindow::CMCalcBtn(RTMessage Msg)
{
```

continues

Listing 5.8. continued

```cpp
    HandleCalcBtn(Msg);
}

void TAppWindow::HandleStoreBtn(RTMessage Msg)
{
  char varName[MaxEditLen+1];
  char result[MaxEditLen+1];

  // get the string in the Result edit box
  ResultBox->GetText(result, MaxEditLen);

  // store the result in the selected text of
  // the Variable edit box
  putVar(atof(result));
}

void TAppWindow::CMStoreBtn(RTMessage Msg)
{
  HandleStoreBtn(Msg);
}

void TAppWindow::HandleExitBtn(RTMessage Msg)
{
  SendMessage(HWindow, WM_CLOSE, NULL, NULL);
}

void TAppWindow::CMExitBtn(RTMessage Msg)
{
  SendMessage(HWindow, WM_CLOSE, NULL, NULL);
}

double TAppWindow::getVar(int lineNum)
{
  int lineSize;
  char s[MaxEditLen+1];

  if (lineNum >= MAX_MEMREG) return 0;
  // get the size of the target line
  lineSize = VariableBox->GetLineLength(lineNum);
  // get the line
  VariableBox->GetLine(s, lineSize+1, lineNum);
  // delete the first three characters
  strcpy(s, (s+3));
  // return the number stored in the target line
```

```
    return atof(s);
}

void TAppWindow::putVar(double x)
{
  int startPos, endPos;
  int lineNum;
  int lineSize;
  char s[MaxEditLen+1];

  // locate the character position of the cursor
  VariableBox->GetSelection(startPos, endPos);
  // turn off the selected text
  if (startPos != endPos)
    VariableBox->SetSelection(startPos, startPos);
  // get the line number where the cursor is located
  lineNum = VariableBox->GetLineFromPos(startPos);
  // get the line size of line lineNum
  lineSize = VariableBox->GetLineLength(lineNum);
  // obtain the text of line lineNum
  VariableBox->GetLine(s, lineSize+1, lineNum);
  // delete line lineNum
  VariableBox->DeleteLine(lineNum);
  // build the new text line
  sprintf(s, "%c: %g\r\n", s[0], x);
  // insert it
  VariableBox->Insert(s);
}

BOOL TAppWindow::CanClose()
{
  return MessageBox(HWindow, "Want to close this application",
                    "Query", MB_YESNO | MB_ICONQUESTION) == IDYES;
}

void TWinApp::InitMainWindow()
{
  MainWindow = new TAppWindow(NULL, Name);
}

void TWinApp::InitInstance()
{
  TApplication::InitInstance();
  HAccTable = LoadAccelerators(hInstance, "BUTTONS");
}
```

continues

Listing 5.8. continued

```
int PASCAL WinMain(HINSTANCE hInstance, HINSTANCE hPrevInstance,
                LPSTR lpCmdLine, int nCmdShow)
{
  TWinApp WinApp("Command-Oriented Calculator Application (COCA) Version 2",
               hInstance, hPrevInstance, lpCmdLine, nCmdShow);
  WinApp.Run(); // run OWL application
  return WinApp.Status; // return application status
}
```

Here are the additions and changes made to convert version 1 into version 2:

- ☐ The section that declares the constants for the control sizes adds new constants to specify the size and dimension of each push button.

- ☐ The application class `TWinApp` includes the `InitInstance` member function. This member function loads the hot keys from the BUTTONS resource.

- ☐ The Main window class `TAppWindow` adds new data members. These new members are pointers to the three push button instances. As for the member functions, the new application version retains the `WMLButtonDown`, `CanClose`, `getVar`, and `putVar` member functions from the previous version. All the other member functions are new or have different names.

- ☐ The `TAppWindow` constructor loads the menu resource and creates instances for the static text, edit box, and push buttons. The additional code in the constructor creates the push button instances using the following statements:

  ```
  CalcBtn = new TButton(this, ID_CALC_BTN, "&Calc",
                     x, y, Wbtn, Hbtn, FALSE);

  StoreBtn = new TButton(this, ID_STORE_BTN, "&Store",
                     x, y, Wbtn, Hbtn, FALSE);

  ExitBtn = new TButton(this, ID_EXIT_BTN, "&Exit",
                     x, y, Wbtn, Hbtn, FALSE);
  ```

The constructor creates each `TButton` instance with a unique ID and caption. The caption uses the ampersand character to underline the hot key. The last argument in all of the previous three statements supplies FALSE to the `IsDefault` parameter. Although these argument values explicitly specify that no button is the default button, they are not really relevant, because the buttons are created in a nondialog window. You can use a TRUE value and still get the same result.

The `WMLButtonDown` member function in this application version adds a single statement to enable the Store button.

The `HandleCalcBtn` member function responds to the notification message sent by Calc button. The message ID is `ID_FIRST + ID_CALC_BTN`. The latter identifier is the ID of the Calc button that also helps create the Calc button instance. The statements in the `HandleCalcBtn` are very similar to the `CMCalc` member function in the first version of COCA. A few additional statements enable or disable the Store button by calling the `EnableButton` and `DisableButton` member functions (more about these functions later in this subsection).

The `CMCalcBtn` member function handles the command messages sent by the Alt-C hot key. The function is declared in a manner similar to declaring menu-item command handlers. The message ID is specified as `CM_FIRST + ID_CALC_BTN`. `CM_FIRST` indicates that the function responds to a command message. `ID_CALC_BTN` is the ID associated with Alt-C in the resource file (which is also the ID for the Calc button). The `CMCalcBtn` function simply invokes the `HandleCalcBtn` member function to execute the requested calculation.

The `HandleStoreBtn` member function works much like the `CMStore` member function in the previous version. The `CMStoreBtn` member function intercepts the Alt-S hot key in the form of the command message with the ID number `ID_STORE_BTN`. The `CMStoreBtn` function simply calls the `HandleStoreBtn` member function.

The `HandleExitBtn` member function responds to the Exit button's notification message. The function sends the `WM_CLOSE` message to the parent window. The `CMExitBtn` member function intercepts the Alt-E hot key in the form of a command message with the ID number `ID_EXIT_BTN`. The `CMExitBtn` function also sends a `WM_CLOSE` message to the parent window.

The `EnableButton` and `DisableButton` member functions enable and disable a push button, respectively, by calling the **`EnableWindow`** API function. Other member functions with the `StoreBtn` argument call these functions.

The Button Manipulation Tester

In object-oriented terms, the window and its controls are distinct objects that communicate with each other. Typically, a push button sends a notification message to its parent window. The window can respond to that message using the ID of the button that sent the message. It is also possible for the window to send a message to a push button. Such messages are sent to buttons with the

WS_OWNERDRAW style. The owner window draws these buttons, typically, to reflect whether that control has become the current default button or a nondefault button.

This subsection discusses the interaction between windows and buttons from a practical standpoint (that is, as allowed by message response member functions and Windows API functions). I use the term *influence* to indicate that one object is affecting another. This interaction can occur between the following objects:

- ◼ A button influences a window. This kind of interaction involves sending a notification message to the parent window.

- ◼ A window influences a button. This kind of interaction involves sending a message to the button, invoking a Windows API function to alter the button, or using the `FirstThat` or `LastThat` iterators. In the latter case, the window attempts to influence any button that meets specific criteria.

- ◼ A window influences multiple buttons. This kind of interaction typically involves the `ForEach` iterator member function.

- ◼ One button influences another button. This kind of interaction involves using Windows API functions or sending a message to the parent window. In the latter case, the parent window is involved in the operation.

- ◼ One button influences other buttons. This kind of interaction expands on the last kind and usually involves using the `ForEach` iterator.

If this discussion strikes you as a bit abstract, do not be concerned. The next ObjectWindows application illustrates these concepts. Figure 5.5 shows a sample session with the CTLBTN2.EXE application and gives you an idea about the program's rather simple interface.

The program contains the following components:

- ◼ The Button1 and Button2 push buttons that display simple message boxes. These controls represent typical buttons that send messages to the parent window.

- ◼ The Toggle1 push button that toggles the enabled state of the Button1 push button. This control is an example of a button that influences a single specific button.

- ◼ The Toggle All push button that toggles the enabled state of the other three buttons. This control illustrates how a button influences other buttons.

☐ The menu that contains the Exit, Button 1, and All Buttons menu items. The Button 1 pop-up menu item has options to enable, disable, show, and hide the Button1 push button. This pop-up menu enables the parent window to influence a single specific button. The All Buttons pop-up menu item has options that enable, disable, show, and hide all four push buttons. With this pop-up menu item, the parent window can influence all the buttons.

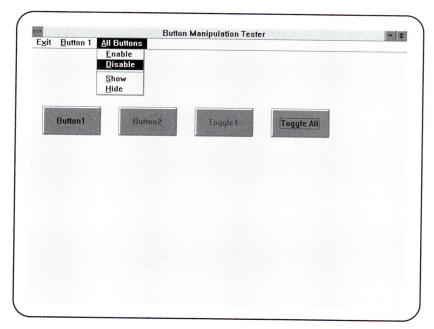

Figure 5.5. A sample session with the CTLBTN2.EXE application.

Compile and run the program. Click the various buttons to experience their functionality. In addition, use the Button 1 or All Buttons menu options to manipulate the various push buttons.

Now look at the code that animates the CTLBTN2.EXE application. Listing 5.9 shows the source code for the CTLBTN2.H header file. The file contains the declarations for the button ID_*xxxx* numbers as well as the menu command constants CM_*xxxx*.

Listing 5.10 contains the script for the CTLBTN2.RC resource file. The resource file defines the menu resource for the application.

Listing 5.9. The source code for the CTLBTN2.H header file.

```
#define ID_BTN1 201
#define ID_BTN2 202
#define ID_TOGGLE1 203
#define ID_TOGGLEALL 204

#define CM_ENABLE_BTN 201
#define CM_DISABLE_BTN 202
#define CM_SHOW_BTN 203
#define CM_HIDE_BTN 204
#define CM_ENABLEALL_BTN 205
#define CM_DISABLEALL_BTN 206
#define CM_SHOWALL_BTN 207
#define CM_HIDEALL_BTN 208
```

Listing 5.10. The script for the CTLBTN2.RCC resource file.

```
#include <windows.h>
#include <owlrc.h>
#include "ctlbtn2.h"

MAINMENU MENU LOADONCALL MOVEABLE PURE DISCARDABLE
BEGIN
     MENUITEM "E&xit", CM_EXIT
     POPUP "&Button 1"
     BEGIN
         MENUITEM "&Enable", CM_ENABLE_BTN
         MENUITEM "&Disable", CM_DISABLE_BTN
         MENUITEM SEPARATOR
         MENUITEM "&Show", CM_SHOW_BTN
         MENUITEM "&Hide", CM_HIDE_BTN
     END
     POPUP "&All Buttons"
     BEGIN
         MENUITEM "&Enable", CM_ENABLEALL_BTN
         MENUITEM "&Disable", CM_DISABLEALL_BTN
         MENUITEM SEPARATOR
         MENUITEM "&Show", CM_SHOWALL_BTN
         MENUITEM "&Hide", CM_HIDEALL_BTN
     END
END
```

Listing 5.11 contains the source code for the CTLBTN2.CPP program file. This program file declares three constants for sizing the buttons. The code also contains a number of special iterator functions to enable, disable, show, hide, and toggle the push button controls. To access the control's `HWindow` handler, the various iterated functions typecast the `P` parameter to the `PTButton` pointer type. The `ToggleButton` iterated function has some additional code that prevents the Toggle All button from disabling itself. The first statement compares the control's ID (accessed by the `Attr.Id` data member) with `ID_TOGGLEALL`, the ID of the Toggle All button. If the tested condition is TRUE, the iterated function exits without toggling the enabled state of the Toggle All button.

Listing 5.11. The source code for the CTLBTN2.CPP program file.

```
#include <owl.h>
#include <button.h>
#include "ctlbtn2.h"

// declare the constants that represent the size
// of the push button controls
const Hbtn = 50;
const Wbtn = 100;
const BtnHorzSpacing = 30;

// special functions that are mainly for use with
// with the parent class iterator ForEach

// enable a button
void EnableButton(Pvoid P, Pvoid Param)
{
  EnableWindow(PTButton(P)->HWindow, TRUE);
}

// disable a button
void DisableButton(Pvoid P, Pvoid Param)
{
  EnableWindow(PTButton(P)->HWindow, FALSE);
}

// show a button
void ShowButton(Pvoid P, Pvoid Param)
{
```

continues

Listing 5.11. continued

```
  ShowWindow(PTButton(P)->HWindow, SW_SHOW);
}

// hide a button
void HideButton(Pvoid P, Pvoid Param)
{
  ShowWindow(PTButton(P)->HWindow, SW_HIDE);
}

// toggle a button
void ToggleButton(Pvoid P, Pvoid Param)
{
  PTButton BtnPtr = PTButton(P);

  if (BtnPtr->Attr.Id == ID_TOGGLEALL) return;
  if (IsWindowEnabled(BtnPtr->HWindow))
    EnableWindow(BtnPtr->HWindow, FALSE);
  else
    EnableWindow(BtnPtr->HWindow, TRUE);
}

// declare the custom application class as
// a subclass of TApplication
class TWinApp : public TApplication
{
public:
   TWinApp(LPSTR     AName,          // application name
           HINSTANCE hInstance,      // instance handle
           HINSTANCE hPrevInstance,  // previous instance handle
           LPSTR     lpCmdLine,      // command-line arguments
           int       nCmdShow) :     // display command
           TApplication(AName, hInstance, hPrevInstance,
                        lpCmdLine, nCmdShow) {};

protected:
   virtual void InitMainWindow();
};

// use the _CLASSDEF macro to declare reference and pointer
// types related to the new TAppWindow class
_CLASSDEF(TAppWindow)

// expand the functionality of TWindow by deriving class TAppWindow
class TAppWindow : public TWindow
```

```cpp
{
public:

  TAppWindow(PTWindowsObject AParent, LPSTR ATitle);

  // ---------------- Menu Commands ---------------

  // handle Button1 | Enable menu item
  virtual void CMEnableBtn(RTMessage Msg)
    = [CM_FIRST + CM_ENABLE_BTN];

  // handle Button1 | Disable menu item
  virtual void CMDisableBtn(RTMessage Msg)
    = [CM_FIRST + CM_DISABLE_BTN];

  // handle the Button1 | Show menu item
  virtual void CMShowBtn(RTMessage Msg)
    = [CM_FIRST + CM_SHOW_BTN];

  // handle the Button1 | Hide menu item
  virtual void CMHideBtn(RTMessage Msg)
    = [CM_FIRST + CM_HIDE_BTN];

  // handle All Buttons | Enable menu item
  virtual void CMEnableAllBtn(RTMessage Msg)
    = [CM_FIRST + CM_ENABLEALL_BTN];

  // handle All Buttons | Disable menu item
  virtual void CMDisableAllBtn(RTMessage Msg)
    = [CM_FIRST + CM_DISABLEALL_BTN];

  // handle All Buttons | Show menu item
  virtual void CMShowAllBtn(RTMessage Msg)
    = [CM_FIRST + CM_SHOWALL_BTN];

  // handle the All Buttons | Hide menu item
  virtual void CMHideAllBtn(RTMessage Msg)
    = [CM_FIRST + CM_HIDEALL_BTN];

  // -------------- Button Messages --------------

  // handle Button1
  virtual void HandleButton1Btn(RTMessage Msg)
    = [ID_FIRST + ID_BTN1];
```

continues

Listing 5.11. continued

```cpp
  // handle Button2
  virtual void HandleButton2Btn(RTMessage Msg)
    = [ID_FIRST + ID_BTN2];

  // handle Toggle1 button
  virtual void HandleToggle1Btn(RTMessage Msg)
    = [ID_FIRST + ID_TOGGLE1];

  // handle Toggle1 button
  virtual void HandleToggleAllBtn(RTMessage Msg)
    = [ID_FIRST + ID_TOGGLEALL];

  // handle closing the window
  virtual BOOL CanClose();

protected:
  PTButton Button1Btn;
  PTButton Button2Btn;
  PTButton Toggle1Btn;
  PTButton ToggleAllBtn;
};

TAppWindow::TAppWindow(PTWindowsObject AParent, LPSTR ATitle) :
                      TWindow(AParent, ATitle)
{
  int x0 = 20;
  int y0 = 100;
  int x = x0, y = y0;

  // load the menu resource
  AssignMenu("MAINMENU");

  Button1Btn = new TButton(this, ID_BTN1, "Button1",
                           x, y, Wbtn, Hbtn, FALSE);
  x += Wbtn + BtnHorzSpacing;

  Button2Btn = new TButton(this, ID_BTN2, "Button2",
                           x, y, Wbtn, Hbtn, FALSE);
  x += Wbtn + BtnHorzSpacing;

  Toggle1Btn = new TButton(this, ID_TOGGLE1, "Toggle1",
                           x, y, Wbtn, Hbtn, FALSE);
  x += Wbtn + BtnHorzSpacing;
```

```cpp
    ToggleAllBtn = new TButton(this, ID_TOGGLEALL, "Toggle All",
                               x, y, Wbtn, Hbtn, FALSE);
}

void TAppWindow::CMEnableBtn(RTMessage Msg)
{
  EnableButton(Button1Btn, NULL);
}

void TAppWindow::CMDisableBtn(RTMessage Msg)
{
  DisableButton(Button1Btn, NULL);
}

void TAppWindow::CMShowBtn(RTMessage Msg)
{
  ShowButton(Button1Btn, NULL);
}

void TAppWindow::CMHideBtn(RTMessage Msg)
{
  HideButton(Button1Btn, NULL);
}

void TAppWindow::CMEnableAllBtn(RTMessage Msg)
{
  ForEach(EnableButton, NULL);
}

void TAppWindow::CMDisableAllBtn(RTMessage Msg)
{
  ForEach(DisableButton, NULL);
}

void TAppWindow::CMShowAllBtn(RTMessage Msg)
{
  ForEach(ShowButton, NULL);
}

void TAppWindow::CMHideAllBtn(RTMessage Msg)
{
  ForEach(HideButton, NULL);
}
```

continues

Listing 5.11. continued

```
void TAppWindow::HandleButton1Btn(RTMessage Msg)
{
  MessageBox(HWindow, "Button 1", "You Clicked", MB_OK);
}

void TAppWindow::HandleButton2Btn(RTMessage Msg)
{
  MessageBox(HWindow, "Button 2", "You Clicked", MB_OK);
}

void TAppWindow::HandleToggle1Btn(RTMessage Msg)
{
  ToggleButton(Button1Btn, NULL);
}

void TAppWindow::HandleToggleAllBtn(RTMessage Msg)
{
  ForEach(ToggleButton, NULL);
}

BOOL TAppWindow::CanClose()
{
  return MessageBox(HWindow, "Want to close this application",
                    "Query", MB_YESNO | MB_ICONQUESTION) == IDYES;
}

void TWinApp::InitMainWindow()
{
  MainWindow = new TAppWindow(NULL, Name);
}

int PASCAL WinMain(HINSTANCE hInstance, HINSTANCE hPrevInstance,
                   LPSTR lpCmdLine, int nCmdShow)
{
  TWinApp WinApp("Button Manipulation Tester",
                 hInstance, hPrevInstance, lpCmdLine, nCmdShow);
  WinApp.Run(); // run OWL application
  return WinApp.Status; // return application status
}
```

The program file declares the application and window classes. The TAppWindow class declares data members to access the TButton instances. The class also declares a constructor and two sets of member functions, the first handles the menu command messages and the second handles the button messages.

The class constructor loads the MAINMENU resource and creates the various TButton instances. The pointer of each TButton instance is assigned to a data member. Each TButton constructor is supplied with a unique button ID and caption.

The class member functions that handle the menu command messages either directly call the iterated functions or use the ForEach iterator. The HandleButton1Btn and HandleButton1Btn member functions invoke the **MessageBox** API function to display simple messages. The HandleToggle1Btn member function calls the iterated function ToggleButton and supplies it with the Button1Btn argument for the parameter P. The HandleToggleAllBtn member function uses the ForEach iterator and supplies the iterator with ToggleButton as the first argument.

Summary

This chapter examined the static text, edit box, and push button controls. These and other controls animate Windows applications and provide a more consistent user interface. You learned about the following topics:

- Creating static text controls and manipulating their text at run-time.
- Creating single- and multiline edit box controls.
- Creating, using, and manipulating push button controls. The control manipulation includes enabling, disabling, showing, and hiding the push button controls at run-time.

Chapter 6, "Grouped Controls," presents the grouped controls, namely the classes for group, check box, and radio controls. These controls are used to fine-tune the execution of a specific task, such as searching and replacing text in a text editor.

CHAPTER 6

Grouped Controls

Windows supports the check box and radio button controls that act as software switches. These controls appear in typical search and replace dialog boxes and influence certain aspects of the text search or replacement. These aspects include the scope, direction, and case-sensitivity of searching or replacing text. This chapter examines the check box and radio button controls, as well as a special group box control that visually and logically groups these controls. You will learn about the following topics:

- The check box control
- The radio button control
- The group control

The topics discussed also demonstrate how to respond to the messages sent by these controls and how to use the ForEach iterator to manipulate the check box and radio button controls.

The Check Box Control

The check box control is a special button that toggles a check mark. The control instances appear with a small rectangular button and a title that appears, by default, to the right side of the square. When you click the square, you toggle the control's check mark. Think of the check box as a binary digit that can be either set or cleared. The instances of a check box can appear inside or outside a group box and are mutually nonexclusive—toggling any check box does not affect the check state of other check boxes.

> **Tip:** Placing check boxes inside groups serves two purposes:
>
> - The group box provides a visual grouping that clarifies the purpose of the check boxes to the application user.
>
> - When you place check boxes in a group box, your ObjectWindows application can detect any change in the checked state of the check boxes.

Earlier I compared the check box control with a binary digit that can be set or cleared. Actually, Windows enables you to specify a check box with three states: checked, unchecked, and grayed. The grayed state fills the control's rectangular button with a gray color. This third state can indicate that the check box control is either disabled or in an indeterminate state.

The TCheckBox Class

ObjectWindows offers the TCheckBox, a descendant of TButton, as the class that provides the instances of check box controls. The TCheckBox class has three constructors and a small number of member functions that set and query the check state of each TCheckBox instance. I will focus on the following constructor, because it enables you to create a TCheckBox instance from scratch:

```
TCheckBox(PTWindowsObject AParent, int AnId, LPSTR ATitle,
         int X, int Y, int W, int H, PTGroupBox AGroup,
         PTModule AModule = NULL);
```

The AParent parameter is the pointer to the parent window or dialog box. The AnId parameter specifies the unique ID for the control. The ATitle parameter is the pointer to the string that contains the control's title. The parameters X, Y, W, and H define the location and size of the control. The AGroup parameter is the pointer to the group box that contains the check box instance. If the check box is not located inside a group box, this parameter is supplied a NULL argument. The constructor creates the TCheckBox instances with the BS_AUTOCHECK style and an unchecked box. You can override this style by specifying, in its constructor, other styles, which are listed in Table 6.1. The following are examples of overriding the default check box style:

```
// make the title appear to the left of the button
Check1->Attr.Style |= BS_LEFTTEXT;

// make the check box nonautomatic
Check2->Attr.Style &= ~BS_AUTOCHECK;
Check2->Attr.Style |= BS_CHECK;

// make the check box a three-state control with
// text that appears to the left of the button
Check2->Attr.Style &= ~BS_AUTOCHECK;
Check2->Attr.Style |= BS_AUTO3STATE | BS_LEFTTEXT;
```

The check box styles shown in Table 6.1 indicate that there are two basic modes for managing the check state of a check box control: automatic and nonautomatic (or manual, if you prefer). In the automatic mode (specified by BS_AUTOCHECK and BS_AUTO3STATE), Windows toggles the check state when you click the control. In manual mode, your application code manages the check state of the check box.

Table 6.1. The check box control styles.

Style	Meaning
BS_CHECKBOX	Specifies a check box with the title to the right of the rectangular button.
BS_AUTOCHECKBOX	Same as BS_CHECKBOX, except the button automatically toggles when you click it.
BS_3STATE	Same as BS_CHECKBOX, except the control has three states: checked, unchecked, and grayed.
BS_AUTO3STATE	Same as BS_3STATE, except the button automatically toggles when you click it.
BS_LEFTTEXT	Sets the control's title to the left of the button.

The TCheckBox class provides member functions that set and query the state of the check box. The GetCheck member function returns a state of the check box control and is declared as follows:

```
WORD GetCheck();
```

The function returns a WORD-typed result that can be compared with the OWL-predefined constants BF_CHECKED, BF_UNCHECKED, or BF_GRAYED to conclude the control's check state.

TCheckBox offers four member functions to set the check state of a check box control: Check, Uncheck, Toggle, and SetCheck. The first three functions return a void type and are without parameters. The Check member function forces a check of the box's state. The Uncheck function performs the reverse action. The Toggle function toggles the check state of a check box control. For a dual-state control, the Toggle function toggles the state between checked and unchecked. For a three-state control, the Toggle function changes the check state as follows: from unchecked to checked, from checked to grayed, and from grayed to unchecked.

Tip: You can create a descendant of `TCheckBox` that overrides the `Toggle` member function to supply your applications with a different sequence for changing the check state for three-state controls.

With the `SetCheck` member function, you can set the check state to a specific value. The function is more useful with a three-state check box. The declaration of the `SetCheck` function is

`void SetCheck(WORD CheckFlag);`

The parameter `CheckFlag` takes one of the predefined constants (`BF_CHECKED`, `BF_UNCHKED`, or `BF_GRAYED`) as an argument.

Responding to Check Box Messages

When you click a check box, it sends a notification message to its parent window. You can access the `BN_CLICKED` notification message code with the `LP.Hi` data member of the message parameter. If your ObjectWindows application must respond to the notification message, you need a message response member function that is based on the check box ID number. For example, to respond to the notification message sent by the check box with the ID `ID_DEGREE_CHK`, you need the following member function:

```
TAppWindow : public TWindow
{
public:
    double angleFactor;

    // constructors here

    virtual void HandleDegreeChk(RTMessage Msg)
        = [ID_FIRST + ID_DEGREE_CHK];

    // other member functions
};

void TAppWindow::HandleDegreeChk(RTMessage Msg)
{
    angleFactor = 4 * atan(1) / 180;
}
```

The Radio Button Control

Radio buttons are controls that typically enable you to select an option from two or more items. This kind of control includes a circular button and a title that appears, by default, to the right of the button. When you check a radio button, a tiny filled circle appears inside the circular button. Radio buttons must be placed in group boxes that visually and logically group them. You can select only one radio button from each group. Therefore, radio buttons are mutually exclusive.

The TRadioButton Class

ObjectWindows offers the TRadioButton class as a descendant of the TCheckBox class because the radio button is a more specialized version of the check box. The TRadioButton class has three constructors and a small number of member functions that set and query the check state of each TRadioButton instance. I will focus on the following constructor because it enables you to create a TRadioButton instance from scratch:

```
TRadioButton(PTWindowsObject AParent, int AnId, LPSTR ATitle,
             int X, int Y, int W, int H, PTGroupBox AGroup,
             PTModule AModule = NULL);
```

The parameters of these constructors are identical to those of the TCheckBox constructor presented in the previous section. Table 6.2 contains the radio button styles. The constructor creates a radio button with the BS_AUTORADIOBUTTON style, which is necessary to create mutually exclusive radio buttons.

Table 6.2. The check box control styles.

Style	Meaning
BS_RADIOBUTTON	Specifies a radio button with the title to the right of the circular button.
BS_AUTORADIOBUTTON	Same as BS_RADIOBUTTON, except the button automatically toggles when you click it.
BS_LEFTTEXT	Sets the control's title to the left of the button.

To query and modify the check state of a radio button, you can use the member functions `GetCheck`, `Check`, `Uncheck`, `Toggle`, and `SetCheck` that are inherited from the `TCheckBox` class.

The radio button controls send the same type of notification messages to their parent windows as the check box controls. You handle these messages for radio buttons the same way as you handle the messages for check boxes.

The Group Control

The group box control is a special container control that encloses radio buttons and check boxes. The group box performs the following:

- Visually groups radio buttons and check boxes. This grouping clearly relates these controls to each other for the application user.
- Logically groups multiple radio buttons so that when you select one radio button, the other buttons in the same group are automatically deselected.
- Sends a group notification message to the parent window when you click any check box or radio button inside a group box. This feature provides your application with a single, centralized notification mechanism.

The `TGroupBox` Class

ObjectWindows provides the `TGroupBox`, a descendant of `TControl`, as the class that implements the group box controls. The class has three constructors. I will focus on the following constructor because it enables you to create a group box control from scratch:

```
TGroupBox(PTWindowsObject AParent, int AnId, LPSTR ATitle, int X,
         int Y, int W, int H, PTModule AModule = NULL);
```

The `AParent` parameter is the pointer to a parent window or dialog box. The `AnId` parameter specifies the unique ID for the group box control. The `ATitle` parameter is the pointer to the string that contains the group's title. The parameters `X`, `Y`, `W`, and `H` define the location and size of the group box. The `TGroupBox` class also declares the Boolean `NotifyParent` data member. The class constructor sets the `NotifyParent` member to TRUE, creates the group box with a `BS_GROUPBOX` style, and removes the `WS_TABSTOP` style. As a result, a group box

Grouped Controls

notifies its parent window when a selection change occurs in any control within the boxes. To disable parent notification, simply assign FALSE to the `NotifyParent` data member.

Responding to Group Box Messages

The group box controls send notification messages to their parent when the `NotifyParent` data member is TRUE and when a member control selection is altered. The parent window can process the notification message using the ID of the group control. For example, to respond to the notification message sent by the group box with the ID `ID_ANGLE_GRP`, you need the following member function:

```
TAppWindow : public TWindow
{
public:
    PTGroupBox AngleGrp;   // Angle group box control
    // the following controls are contained in
    // the Angle group box control
    PTRadioButton RadianRbt;  // Radian radio button
    PTRadioButton DegreeRbt;  // Degree radio button
    PTRadioButton GradianRbt; // Gradian radio button

    double angleFactor;

    // constructors here

    virtual void HandleAngleGrp(RTMessage Msg)
        = [ID_FIRST + ID_ANGLE_GRP];

    // other member functions
};

void TAppWindow::HandleAngleGrp(RTMessage Msg)
{
    static double pi = 4 * atan(1);

    if (RadianRbt->GetCheck() == BF_CHECKED)
        angleFactor = 1;
    else if (DegreeRbt->GetCheck() == BF_CHECKED)
        angleFactor = pi / 180;
```

```
            else if (GradianRbt->GetCHeck() == BF_CHECKED)
                angleFactor = pi / 180 / 0.9;
}
```

This code demonstrates how the group notification message response function can replace the individual response function for each of the three radio button controls.

The `TGroup` class contains the `SelectionChanged` member function that sends the notification messages to the parent window. You can override this function with a descendant of `TGroupBox` that handles the selection changes in a different manner.

The Updated Calculator Application

The operations of the Calculator application presented in the last chapter can be expanded to include trigonometric functions. Trigonometric functions frequently offer you the choice of angle modes: radians, degrees, or gradians (100 gradians equal 90 degrees). A group box that contains angle mode radio buttons suits the demonstration of the operations of these controls. Check boxes are added to fine-tune other operational aspects of the calculator (more about this later in this section).

The updated calculator application (COCA version 3) demonstrates the following:

- ☐ Using a check box control.
- ☐ Using a radio button.
- ☐ Responding to a radio button notification message.
- ☐ Responding to a group box notification message.
- ☐ Using a check box control to alter the action of response message function that handles the group box notification message.
- ☐ Using the `ForEach` iterator to manipulate multiple check boxes and edit boxes.
- ☐ Selecting the initial check box.
- ☐ Selecting the initial radio button.

Figure 6.1 shows the Command-Oriented Calculator Application (COCA), in its latest form.

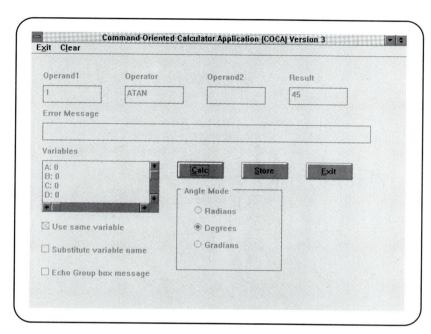

Figure 6.1. The Command-Oriented Calculator Application (COCA), version 3.

The new version of the calculator application contains the following controls:

- The single-line edit controls labeled Operand1, Operator, Operand2, Result, and Error Message.
- The multiline edit control labeled Variables.
- The static text controls that label the previous edit boxes.
- The Calc, Store, and Exit push buttons.
- The Angle Mode group box that contains the Radians, Degrees, and Gradians radio buttons.
- The Use same variable check box that makes the Store commands retain the same variable for storing future results.
- The Substitute variable name check box that replaces the names of the single-letter variables (which can appear in either operand edit box)

with their values. The replacement occurs after you click the Calc push button.

- The `Echo Group box message` check box that allows the group notification message handler to display a message box when you select another radio button.

- The menu that contains the Exit and Clear main menu items. The Clear item is a pop-up menu with the Edit Controls and Check Boxes menu items. The Edit Controls menu item clears the contents of the edit controls except the Variables edit box. The Check Boxes menu item unchecks the three check boxes.

Experimenting with the Application

Compile and run the Calculator application to get a good feel for the features supported by the radio buttons, check boxes, and the group box. When the application's window appears, maximize it to get a full view. The Angle Mode group box shows the initial selection of the Degrees radio button. In addition, the `Use same variable` check box appears checked and the `Store button` check box is disabled. The current application version supports the SIN, COS, TAN, ASIN, ACOS, and ATAN trigonometric functions, which you can enter in the Operator edit box.

As an exercise, enter the number 45 in the Operand1 edit box and enter TAN in the Operator edit box. Click the Calc button to obtain the tangent of 45 degrees in the Result edit box (a value of 1). Store the result in variable A by clicking the Store button.

Now replace the number 45 with the pound sign character (#) in the Operand1 edit box. Then add an A to the beginning of the TAN string in the Operator box and click the Calc button. The # character is replaced by 1, the previous number in the Result edit box. The Result edit box now shows the number 45, the arctangent of 1. The # character is a new feature that I added to the program—by entering the # character, you can use the result from the previous calculation in either or both operand edit boxes. Click the Store button again. The application stores the number 45 in variable A, overwriting the previous result. Now click the `Use same variable` check box and click the Store button a few times. The number in the Result edit box is stored in multiple variables.

Check the `Echo Group box message` check box and then click any radio button. The application displays a message box that contains information on converting different angles. Selecting a different radio button yields a different message. These messages are responses to the Angle Mode group notification message.

Experiment with selecting different angle modes. Each time enter a value in the Operand1 edit box and type a trigonometric function. Notice that the results differ for the same arguments as the angle mode varies. Remember that the inverse sine and cosine functions accept arguments between −1 and 1. If the application detects invalid arguments for these two functions, it displays error messages.

Finally, use the Clear|Edit Control and Clear|Check Boxes menu items to clear the edit boxes (except the Variables edit box) and the check boxes.

I have omitted the feature that clears the error message and enables the Store button when you click the Error Message label.

The Application's Code

Listing 6.1 contains the source code for the CTLGRP1.H header file.

Listing 6.1. The source code for the CTLGRP1.H header file.

```
#define ID_CALC_BTN 107
#define ID_STORE_BTN 108
#define ID_EXIT_BTN 109

#define CM_CLEARBOX 201
#define CM_CLEARCHK 202
```

Listing 6.2 shows the script for the CTLGRP1.RC resource file. The resource file contains the accelerator keys and the menu resources.

Listing 6.2. The script for the CTLGRP1.RC resource file.

```
#include <windows.h>
#include <owlrc.h>
#include "ctlgrp1.h"
```

continues

Listing 6.2. continued

```
BUTTONS ACCELERATORS
BEGIN
    "c", ID_CALC_BTN, ALT
    "s", ID_STORE_BTN, ALT
    "e", ID_EXIT_BTN, ALT
END

EXITMENU MENU LOADONCALL MOVEABLE PURE DISCARDABLE
BEGIN
    MENUITEM 'E&xit", CM_EXIT
    POPUP "C&lear"
    BEGIN
        MENUITEM "&Edit Controls", CM_CLEARBOX
        MENUITEM "&Check Boxes", CM_CLEARCHK
    END
END
```

Listing 6.3 contains the source code for the CTLGRP1.CPP program file. The program contains #include statements, declaration of constants, iterated functions, and the classes for the application and its window.

Listing 6.3. The source code for the CTLGRP1.CPP program file.

```
#include <stdlib.h>
#include <ctype.h>
#include <stdio.h>
#include <math.h>
#include <string.h>
#include <owl.h>
#include <static.h>
#include <edit.h>
#include <button.h>
#include <groupbox.h>
#include <radiobut.h>
#include <checkbox.h>

// declare the constants that represent the sizes of the controls
const Wlbl = 100;
const Hlbl = 20;
const LblVertSpacing = 2;
const LblHorzSpacing = 40;
const Wbox = 100;
```

Grouped Controls

```cpp
const Hbox = 30;
const BoxVertSpacing = 10;
const BoxHorzSpacing = 40;
const WLongbox = 4 * (Wbox + BoxHorzSpacing);
const Wvarbox = 2 * Wbox;
const Hvarbox = 3 * Hbox - 10;
const Hbtn = 30;
const Wbtn = 80;
const BtnHorzSpacing = 30;
const BtnVertSpacing = 10;
const Hgrp = 130;
const Wgrp = 180;
const GrpHorzSpacing = 30;
const GrpVertSpacing = 10;
const Hchk = 20;
const Wchk = 200;
const ChkHorzSpacing = 30;
const ChkVertSpacing = 5;
const Hrbt = 30;
const Wrbt = 80;
const RbtHorzSpacing = 30;
const RbtVertSpacing = 30;
const RbtLeftMargin = 30;

const MaxEditLen = 30;
const MAX_MEMREG = 26;

// declare the ID_XXXX constants for the edit boxes
#define ID_OPERAND1_EDIT 101
#define ID_OPERATOR_EDIT 102
#define ID_OPERAND2_EDIT 103
#define ID_RESULT_EDIT 104
#define ID_ERRMSG_EDIT 105
#define ID_VARIABLE_EDIT 106

// include file has IDs for the buttons in the range of 107 to 109
#include "ctlgrp1.h"

#define ID_VAR_CHK 110
#define ID_SUBST_CHK 111
#define ID_ECHO_CHK 112
#define ID_ANGLE_GRP 113
#define ID_RADIAN_RBT 114
#define ID_DEGREE_RBT 115
#define ID_GRADIAN_RBT 116
```

continues

Listing 6.3. continued

```
const double pi = 4 * atan(1);
const double DegToRad = pi / 180;
const double GradToRad = 0.9 * DegToRad;

// declare iterated function to clear the edit controls
// except the Variables edit control
void ClearEditControls(Pvoid P, Pvoid Param)
{
  PTEdit pEdit = PTEdit(P);
  int i = pEdit->Attr.Id;

  // if the instance Id is an edit control (except
  // for the VariableBox control) clear its text
  if (i >= ID_OPERAND1_EDIT && i <= ID_ERRMSG_EDIT)
       pEdit->Clear();
}

// declare the iterated function to clear the check boxes
void ClearCheckBoxes(Pvoid P, Pvoid Param)
{
  PTCheckBox pCheck = PTCheckBox(P);
  int i = pCheck->Attr.Id;

  if (i >= ID_VAR_CHK && i <= ID_ECHO_CHK)
       pCheck->Uncheck();
}

// declare the custom application class as
// a subclass of TApplication
class TWinApp : public TApplication
{
public:
  TWinApp(LPSTR     AName,           // application name
          HINSTANCE hInstance,       // instance handle
          HINSTANCE hPrevInstance,   // previous instance handle
          LPSTR     lpCmdLine,       // command-line arguments
          int       nCmdShow) :      // display command
          TApplication(AName, hInstance, hPrevInstance,
                    lpCmdLine, nCmdShow) {};

protected:
  virtual void InitMainWindow();
  virtual void InitInstance();
};
```

Grouped Controls

```cpp
// use the _CLASSDEF macro to declare reference and pointer
// types related to the new TAppWindow class
_CLASSDEF(TAppWindow)

// expand the functionality of TWindow by deriving class TAppWindow
class TAppWindow : public TWindow
{
public:

  TAppWindow(PTWindowsObject AParent, LPSTR ATitle);

  // initialize the instances of TAppWindow
  virtual void InitAppWindow();

  // handle clearing the edit controls
  virtual void CMClearBox(RTMessage Msg)
    = [CM_FIRST + CM_CLEARBOX];

  // handle clearing the check box controls
  virtual void CMClearChk(RTMessage Msg)
    = [CM_FIRST + CM_CLEARCHK];

  // handle the calculation
  virtual void HandleCalcBtn(RTMessage Msg)
    = [ID_FIRST + ID_CALC_BTN];

  // handle the accelerator key for the Calculate button
  virtual void CMCalcBtn(RTMessage Msg)
    = [CM_FIRST + ID_CALC_BTN];

  // handle storing the result in a variable
  virtual void HandleStoreBtn(RTMessage Msg)
    = [ID_FIRST + ID_STORE_BTN];

  // handle the accelerator key for the Store button
  virtual void CMStoreBtn(RTMessage Msg)
    = [CM_FIRST + ID_STORE_BTN];

  // handle exiting the application
  virtual void HandleExitBtn(RTMessage Msg)
    = [ID_FIRST + ID_EXIT_BTN];

  // handle the accelerator key for the Exit button
  virtual void CMExitBtn(RTMessage Msg)
```

continues

Listing 6.3. continued

```
    = [CM_FIRST + ID_EXIT_BTN];

  // handle the Angle Mode group box message
  virtual void HandleAngleModeGrp(RTMessage Msg)
    = [ID_FIRST + ID_ANGLE_GRP];

  // handle selecting the Radians radio button
  virtual void HandleRadianRbt(RTMessage Msg)
    = [ID_FIRST + ID_RADIAN_RBT];

  // handle selecting the Degrees radio button
  virtual void HandleDegreeRbt(RTMessage Msg)
    = [ID_FIRST + ID_DEGREE_RBT];

  // handle selecting the Gradians radio button
  virtual void HandleGradianRbt(RTMessage Msg)
    = [ID_FIRST + ID_GRADIAN_RBT];

  // enable a push button control
  virtual void EnableButton(PTButton Btn)
  { EnableWindow(Btn->HWindow, TRUE); }

  // disable a push button control
  virtual void DisableButton(PTButton Btn)
  { EnableWindow(Btn->HWindow, FALSE); }

  // handle closing the window
  virtual BOOL CanClose();

protected:
  PTEdit Operand1Box;
  PTEdit OperatorBox;
  PTEdit Operand2Box;
  PTEdit ResultBox;
  PTEdit ErrMsgBox;
  PTEdit VariableBox;
  PTButton CalcBtn;
  PTButton StoreBtn;
  PTButton ExitBtn;
  PTGroupBox AngleModeGrp;
  PTRadioButton RadianRbt;
  PTRadioButton DegreeRbt;
  PTRadioButton GradianRbt;
  PTCheckBox AutoVarSubstChk;
```

```cpp
    PTCheckBox UseSameVarChk;
    PTCheckBox EchoGroupChk;

    // math error flag
    BOOL InError;

    // the factor that converts between angles the
    // currently selected angle mode and radians
    double angleFactor;

    // obtain a number of a Variable edit box line
    double getVar(int lineNum);

    // store a number in the selected text of
    // the Variable edit box line
    void putVar(double x);
};

TAppWindow::TAppWindow(PTWindowsObject AParent, LPSTR ATitle) :
                    TWindow(AParent, ATitle)
{
  char s[81];
  char bigStr[6 * MAX_MEMREG + 1];
  char c;
  int x0 = 20;
  int y0 = 5;
  int x = x0, y = y0;
  int x1, y1;

  // load the menu resource
  AssignMenu("EXITMENU");

  // create the first set of labels for the edit boxes
  strcpy(s, "Operand1");
  new TStatic(this, -1, s, x, y, Wlbl, Hlbl, strlen(s));
  strcpy(s, "Operator");
  x += Wlbl + LblHorzSpacing;
  new TStatic(this, -1, s, x, y, Wlbl, Hlbl, strlen(s));
  strcpy(s, "Operand2");
  x += Wlbl + LblHorzSpacing;
  new TStatic(this, -1, s, x, y, Wlbl, Hlbl, strlen(s));
  x += Wlbl + LblHorzSpacing;
  strcpy(s, "Result");
  new TStatic(this, -1, s, x, y, Wlbl, Hlbl, strlen(s));
```

continues

Listing 6.3. continued

```c
// create the operand1, operator, operand2, and result
// edit boxes
x = x0;
y += Hlbl + LblVertSpacing;
Operand1Box = new TEdit(this, ID_OPERAND1_EDIT, "", x, y,
                        Wbox, Hbox, 0, FALSE);

// force conversion of letters to uppercase
Operand1Box->Attr.Style |= ES_UPPERCASE;
x += Wbox + BoxHorzSpacing;
OperatorBox = new TEdit(this, ID_OPERATOR_EDIT, "", x, y,
                        Wbox, Hbox, 0, FALSE);
// force conversion of letters to uppercase
OperatorBox->Attr.Style |= ES_UPPERCASE;
x += Wbox + BoxHorzSpacing;
Operand2Box = new TEdit(this, ID_OPERAND2_EDIT, "", x, y,
                        Wbox, Hbox, 0, FALSE);
// force conversion of letters to uppercase
Operand2Box->Attr.Style |= ES_UPPERCASE;
x += Wbox + BoxHorzSpacing;
ResultBox = new TEdit(this, ID_RESULT_EDIT, "", x, y, Wbox,
                      Hbox, 0, FALSE);

// create the static text and edit box for the error message
x = x0;
y += Hbox + BoxVertSpacing;
strcpy(s, "Error Message");
new TStatic(this, -1, s, x, y, Wlbl, Hlbl, strlen(s));
y += Hlbl + LblVertSpacing;
ErrMsgBox = new TEdit(this, ID_ERRMSG_EDIT, "", x, y,
                      WLongbox, Hbox, 0, FALSE);
// create the static text and edit box for the single-letter
// variable selection
y += Hbox + BoxVertSpacing;
strcpy(s, "Variables");
new TStatic(this, -1, s, x, y, Wlbl, Hlbl, strlen(s));
y += Hlbl + LblVertSpacing;
// build the initial contents of the Variable edit box
for (c = 'A'; c <= 'Z'; c++) {
  sprintf(s, "%c: 0\r\n", c);
  strcat(bigStr, s);
}
VariableBox = new TEdit(this, ID_VARIABLE_EDIT, bigStr, x, y,
                        Wvarbox, Hvarbox, 0, TRUE);
```

Grouped Controls

```cpp
// force conversion of letters to uppercase
VariableBox->Attr.Style |= ES_UPPERCASE;

// create the Calc push button
x += Wvarbox + BtnHorzSpacing;
x1 = x;
y1 = y;
CalcBtn = new TButton(this, ID_CALC_BTN, "&Calc",
                      x, y, Wbtn, Hbtn, FALSE);

// create the Store Btn
x += Wbtn + BtnHorzSpacing;
StoreBtn = new TButton(this, ID_STORE_BTN, "&Store",
                       x, y, Wbtn, Hbtn, FALSE);

// create the Exit Btn
x += Wbtn + BtnHorzSpacing;
ExitBtn = new TButton(this, ID_EXIT_BTN, "&Exit",
                      x, y, Wbtn, Hbtn, FALSE);

// create the "Use same variable" check box
x = x0;
y += Hvarbox + BoxVertSpacing;
UseSameVarChk = new TCheckBox(this, ID_VAR_CHK,
                              "Use same variable",
                              x, y, Wchk, Hchk, NULL);

// create the "Substitute variable name" check box
y += Hchk + ChkVertSpacing;
AutoVarSubstChk = new TCheckBox(this, ID_SUBST_CHK,
                                "Substitute variable name",
                                x, y, Wchk, Hchk, NULL);

// create the "Echo Group box message" check box
y += Hchk + ChkVertSpacing;
EchoGroupChk = new TCheckBox(this, ID_ECHO_CHK,
                             "Echo Group box message",
                             x, y, Wchk, Hchk, NULL);

// create the Angle Mode group box
y = y1 + Hbtn + BtnVertSpacing;
x = x1;
AngleModeGrp = new TGroupBox(this, ID_ANGLE_GRP, " Angle Mode ",
                             x, y, Wgrp, Hgrp);
```

continues

Listing 6.3. continued

```
  // create the Radians radio button
  y += RbtVertSpacing;
  RadianRbt = new TRadioButton(this, ID_RADIAN_RBT, "Radians",
                               RbtLeftMargin + x, y, Wrbt, Hrbt,
                               AngleModeGrp);
  // create the Degrees radio button
  y += RbtVertSpacing;
  DegreeRbt = new TRadioButton(this, ID_DEGREE_RBT, "Degrees",
                               RbtLeftMargin + x, y, Wrbt, Hrbt,
                               AngleModeGrp);
  // create the Gradians radio button
  y += RbtVertSpacing;
  GradianRbt = new TRadioButton(this, ID_GRADIAN_RBT, "Gradians",
                                RbtLeftMargin + x, y, Wrbt, Hrbt,
                                AngleModeGrp);

  // clear the InError flag
  InError = FALSE;

  // enable keyboard handler
  EnableKBHandler();
}

void TAppWindow::InitAppWindow()
{

  // disable the Store button control
  EnableWindow(StoreBtn->HWindow, FALSE);

  // check the Degrees radio button
  DegreeRbt->Check();
  angleFactor = DegToRad;

  // check the "Use Same Var" check button
  UseSameVarChk->Check();
}

void TAppWindow::CMClearBox(RTMessage Msg)
{
  ForEach(ClearEditControls, NULL);
}

void TAppWindow::CMClearChk(RTMessage Msg)
{
```

```cpp
  ForEach(ClearCheckBoxes, NULL);
}

void TAppWindow::HandleCalcBtn(RTMessage Msg)
{
  double x, y, z, result;
  char opStr[MaxEditLen+1];
  char s[MaxEditLen+1];

  // convert the string in the Result box to a double
  ResultBox->GetText(s, MaxEditLen);
  result = atof(s);

  // obtain the string in the Operand1 edit box
  Operand1Box->GetText(s, MaxEditLen);
  // does the Operand1Box contain the name
  // of a single-letter variable?
  if (isalpha(s[0])) {
    // obtain value from the Variable edit control
    x = getVar(s[0] - 'A');
    // substitute the variable name with its value
    if (AutoVarSubstChk->GetCheck() == BF_CHECKED) {
      sprintf(s, "%g", x);
      Operand1Box->SetText(s);
    }
  }
  // translate the # character into the value in the Result box
  else if (s[0] == '#')
    x = result;
  else
    // convert the string in the edit box
    x = atof(s);

  // obtain the string in the Operand2 edit box
  Operand2Box->GetText(s, MaxEditLen);
  // does the Operand2Box contain the name
  // of a single-letter variable?
  if (isalpha(s[0])) {
    // obtain value from the Variable edit control
    y =getVar(s[0] - 'A');
    // substitute the variable name with its value
    if (AutoVarSubstChk->GetCheck() == BF_CHECKED) {
      sprintf(s, "%g", y);
      Operand2Box->SetText(s);
```

continues

Listing 6.3. continued

```
    }
  }
  // translate the # character into the value in the Result box
  else if (s[0] == '#')
    y = result;
  else
    // convert the string in the edit box
    y = atof(s);

  // obtain the string in the Operator edit box
  OperatorBox->GetText(opStr, MaxEditLen);

  // clear the error message box
  ErrMsgBox->Clear();
  InError = FALSE;

  // determine the requested operation
  if (strlen(opStr) == 1) {
    if (strcmp(opStr, "+") == 0)
      z = x + y;
    else if (strcmp(opStr, "-") == 0)
      z = x - y;
    else if (strcmp(opStr, "*") == 0)
      z = x * y;
    else if (strcmp(opStr, "/") == 0) {
      if (y != 0)
        z = x / y;
      else {
        z = 0;
        InError = TRUE;
        ErrMsgBox->SetText("Division-by-zero error");
      }
    }
    else if (strcmp(opStr, "^") == 0) {
      if (x > 0)
        z = exp(y * log(x));
      else {
        InError = TRUE;
        ErrMsgBox->SetText(
          "Cannot raise the power of a negative number");
      }
    }
    else {
      InError = TRUE;
```

```
      ErrMsgBox->SetText("Invalid operator");
    }
  }
  else if (strcmp(opStr, "SIN") == 0) {
    z = sin(angleFactor * x);
  }
  else if (strcmp(opStr, "COS") == 0) {
    z = cos(angleFactor * x);
  }
  else if (strcmp(opStr, "TAN") == 0) {
    z = tan(angleFactor * x);
  }
  else if (strcmp(opStr, "ASIN") == 0) {
    if (fabs(x) <= 1)
      z = asin(x) / angleFactor;
    else {
      InError = TRUE;
      ErrMsgBox->SetText(
            "Invalid argument for the asin(x) function");
    }
  }
  else if (strcmp(opStr, "ACOS") == 0) {
    if (fabs(x) <= 1)
      z = acos(x) / angleFactor;
    else {
      InError = TRUE;
      ErrMsgBox->SetText(
            "Invalid argument for the acos(x) function");
    }
  }
  else if (strcmp(opStr, "ATAN") == 0) {
    z = atan(x) / angleFactor;
  }
  else {
    InError = TRUE;
    ErrMsgBox->SetText("Invalid math function");
  }

  // display the result if no error has occurred
  if (!InError) {
    sprintf(s, "%g", z);
    ResultBox->SetText(s);
    // enable the Store button
    EnableButton(StoreBtn);
```

continues

Listing 6.3. continued

```
  }
  else
    // disable the Store button
    DisableButton(StoreBtn);
}

void TAppWindow::CMCalcBtn(RTMessage Msg)
{
  HandleCalcBtn(Msg);
}

void TAppWindow::HandleStoreBtn(RTMessage Msg)
{
  char varName[MaxEditLen+1];
  char result[MaxEditLen+1];

  // get the string in the Result edit box
  ResultBox->GetText(result, MaxEditLen);

  // store the result in the selected text of
  // the Variable edit box
  putVar(atof(result));
}

void TAppWindow::CMStoreBtn(RTMessage Msg)
{
  HandleStoreBtn(Msg);
}

void TAppWindow::HandleExitBtn(RTMessage Msg)
{
  SendMessage(HWindow, WM_CLOSE, NULL, NULL);
}

void TAppWindow::CMExitBtn(RTMessage Msg)
{
  SendMessage(HWindow, WM_CLOSE, NULL, NULL);
}

void TAppWindow::HandleAngleModeGrp(RTMessage Msg)
{
  char angleStr[81];

  // exit if the EchoGroup check box is not checked
```

```cpp
    if (EchoGroupChk->GetCheck() != BF_CHECKED) return;
    // build the text of the message
    if (DegreeRbt->GetCheck() == BF_CHECKED)
      sprintf(angleStr, "1 radian = %g degrees", 1 / DegToRad);
    else if (GradianRbt->GetCheck() == BF_CHECKED)
      sprintf(angleStr, "1 radian = %g gradians", 1 / GradToRad);
    else
      sprintf(angleStr, "1 radian = %g degrees = %g gradians",
              1 / DegToRad, 1 / GradToRad);
    MessageBox(HWindow, angleStr, "Group Box Message",
               MB_OK | MB_ICONINFORMATION);
}

void TAppWindow::HandleRadianRbt(RTMessage Msg)
{
  angleFactor = 1;
}

void TAppWindow::HandleDegreeRbt(RTMessage Msg)
{
  angleFactor = DegToRad;
}

void TAppWindow::HandleGradianRbt(RTMessage Msg)
{
  angleFactor = GradToRad;
}


BOOL TAppWindow::CanClose()
{
  return MessageBox(HWindow, "Want to close this application",
                    "Query", MB_YESNO | MB_ICONQUESTION) == IDYES;
}

double TAppWindow::getVar(int lineNum)
{
  int lineSize;
  char s[MaxEditLen+1];

  if (lineNum >= MAX_MEMREG) return 0;
  // get the size of the target line
  lineSize = VariableBox->GetLineLength(lineNum);
  // get the line
```

continues

Listing 6.3. continued

```
    VariableBox->GetLine(s, lineSize+1, lineNum);
    // delete the first three characters
    strcpy(s, (s+3));
    // return the number stored in the target line
    return atof(s);
}

void TAppWindow::putVar(double x)
{
  int startPos, endPos;
  int lineNum;
  int lineSize;
  char s[MaxEditLen+1];

  // locate the character position of the cursor
  VariableBox->GetSelection(startPos, endPos);
  // turn off the selected text
  if (startPos != endPos)
    VariableBox->SetSelection(startPos, startPos);
  // get the line number where the cursor is located
  lineNum = VariableBox->GetLineFromPos(startPos);
  // get the line size of line lineNum
  lineSize = VariableBox->GetLineLength(lineNum);
  // obtain the text of line lineNum
  VariableBox->GetLine(s, lineSize+1, lineNum);
  // delete line lineNum
  VariableBox->DeleteLine(lineNum);
  // build the new text line
  sprintf(s, "%c: %g\r\n", s[0], x);
  // insert it
  VariableBox->Insert(s);
  // use the same variable?
  if (UseSameVarChk->GetCheck())
    // reset insertion point to the original position
    VariableBcx->SetSelection(startPos, startPos);
}

void TWinApp::InitMainWindow()
{
  MainWindow = new TAppWindow(NULL, Name);
}

void TWinApp::InitInstance()
{
```

```
  TApplication::InitInstance();
  HAccTable = LoadAccelerators(hInstance, "BUTTONS");
  // initialize the TAppWindow instance
  PTAppWindow(MainWindow)->InitAppWindow();
}

int PASCAL WinMain(HINSTANCE hInstance, HINSTANCE hPrevInstance,
                   LPSTR lpCmdLine, int nCmdShow)
{
  TWinApp WinApp(
    "Command-Oriented Calculator Application (COCA) Version 3",
                hInstance, hPrevInstance, lpCmdLine, nCmdShow);
  WinApp.Run(); // run OWL application
  return WinApp.Status; // return application status
}
```

The first set of constants specifies the sizes and spacings between the various controls. The macro-based constants define the IDs of the various controls. The last set of constants specifies the value of pi and also specifies the angle conversion factors between radians and degrees and between radians and gradians.

Note: This version of the application declares the `ClearEditControls` and `ClearCheckBoxes` as iterated functions to clear the specified edit boxes and all the check boxes. You might wonder how to use typecasting for pointers to controls when you have different kinds of controls in the window's child control list. Can straightforward typecasting work? The answer is, fortunately, yes. Let's check the code for each iterated function.

The `ClearEditControls` function clears all the edit boxes, except for the Variables box. The function performs the following tasks:

1. Declares `pEdit` as a `PTEdit` typecast of parameter `P`.
2. Declares the local variable `i` to store the control's ID by assigning it the expression `pEdit->Attr.Id`. This assignment is critical. If this programming method failed, such an assignment would hang or corrupt the system.

3. Tests whether the control's ID is in the range of the ID for the cleared edit boxes. The `if` statement serves two purposes. First, it excludes all controls that are not edit boxes. Second, it excludes the Variables edit box. When the tested condition is TRUE, the `Clear` member function is applied to clear the text of the client control.

The `ClearCheckBoxes` function works in a manner similar to that of `ClearEditBoxes`. The difference is that `ClearCheckBoxes` invokes the `Uncheck` member function when the control's ID matches that of any check box.

Tip: Coding iterated functions that work on specific controls of a certain type is easier when you declare the ID of these controls using consecutive numbers. This approach creates a suitable range of ID that can be quickly and efficiently examined.

The CTLGRP1.CPP file declares the `TAppWindow` application window class. The class contains many data members. Most of these members are pointers to the instances of the various controls used by the application. The application adds the `angleFactor` data member to store the angle conversion factor between the currently selected angle mode and radians.

The `TAppWindow` class declares a constructor and a number of member functions to support the essential program operations and special initialization. The constructor loads the menu resource and creates the various controls—namely, the static text controls, the edit controls, the push buttons, the check boxes, the radio buttons, and the group box. Of interest are the statements that create the check boxes, the group box, and the radio buttons:

- Each instance of `TCheckBox` involves a unique control ID and title, and unique coordinates. The last argument for the three `TCheckBox` constructor invocations is FALSE. This argument value indicates that each check box is created outside a group box.

- The group box instance is created with its own ID, title, and coordinates.

- Each radio button control is created with a unique ID, title, and coordinates. The last argument used in each invocation of the `TRadioButton` constructor is `AngleModeGrp`. This argument is the pointer to the group box that contains these radio buttons.

The `TAppWindow` class declares the various member functions needed to implement the program's functionality. The `CMClearBox` and `CMClearChk` member functions respond to their respective menu command messages, clear the designated edit boxes, and uncheck all the check boxes. Each function invokes the `ForEach` operator and specifies the appropriate iterated function.

The `HandleCalcBtn` member function performs calculations and any character substitution, as well as the following tasks:

- Converts the string in the Result box to a double and stores that value in the local variable result.

- Obtains the value for the first operand stored in variable x. The Operand1 edit box contains either a string image of a number, the name of a single-letter variable, or the # character:

    The statements that support the first option determine whether the Operand1 box contains a letter. If this condition is true, the statements invoke the `getVar` member function and assign the result to variable x. In addition, the code checks whether the `Substitute variable name` check box is checked. If it is, the name of the variable in the Operand1 box is replaced with its value.

    The statements that support the second option compare the first character in the Operand1 box with the # character. If the two characters match, the value stored in the local variable result is assigned to the variable x.

    The statements that support the third option simply convert the string in the Operand1 edit box to a double and assign it to the local variable x.

- Obtains the second operand in a manner very similar to the first one. The second operand is stored in the local variable y.

- Acquires the operator or function from the Operator edit box.

- Performs the requested operation or function evaluation. A set of `if` statements determines the requested operation. The statements also include argument error checking. If any error occurs, the function assigns TRUE to the `InError` data member and displays a message in the error message edit box.

- Displays the result in the Result edit box if no error has occurred.

The member functions `CMCalcBtn`, `HandleStoreBtn`, `CMStoreBtn`, `HandleExitBtn`, `CMExitBtn`, `putVar`, and `getVar` are the same as in the second version of the COCA program (file CTLBTN2.CPP).

The `HandleAngleMode` member function responds to the group box notification message. The function first verifies whether the `Echo Group box message` check box is not checked. If this condition is true, the member function simply exits. Otherwise, the function determines which radio button is checked and accordingly builds an angle conversion message. The function then invokes the `MessageBox` API function to display the previous message.

The `HandleRadianRbt`, `HandleDegreeRbt`, and `HandleGradianRbt` member functions respond to the individual notification messages sent by the three radio buttons. Each member function assigns an angle conversion factor to the `angleFactor` data member. Using these member functions is more efficient than systematically examining the check states of the radio buttons in the `HandleCalcBtn` member function. This approach alters the value in `angleFactor` only when you select a new angle mode.

The `TAppWindow` class includes the `InitAppWindow` member function that initializes the following controls:

- ☐ Disables the Store button.
- ☐ Checks the Degrees radio button.
- ☐ Checks the `Use same variable` check box.

The `TWinApp::InitInstance` member function performs this initialization by using a `PTAppWindow` typecast with the `MainWindow` pointer (that has the type `PTWindowsObject`). This typecasting permits the window to access the public `InitAppWindow` member function of the application window class and perform the required initialization.

Summary

This chapter discussed the special switch controls—namely, the group box, check box, and radio button controls. You learned how to do the following:

- ☐ Create each type of control.
- ☐ Set and query the check state for the check box and radio button controls.

- Respond to notification messages that these controls send to their parent window.
- Selectively manipulate controls.
- Initialize controls.

This chapter should also provide you with a clearer understanding of the child window linked-list—the one maintained by the application window and the group box controls. Such lists are vital in managing the various components of a Windows application, as well as the applications themselves.

Chapter 7 presents the scroll bar, list box, and combo box controls. These controls are value selectors because they enable you to select from a list or range of values.

Scroll Bars, List Boxes, and Combo Boxes

List controls are input tools that conveniently provide you with items to choose. List controls are popular because they liberate you from remembering the list members—especially when a computer program expects exact spelling. The various DOS utilities that display lists of files and directories are much easier to use than their counterparts, which assume you know all the names of your files and directories. List controls have gradually become a routine method for retrieving information. This chapter discusses the list box, the combo box (a list box control variant), and the scroll bar control. You will learn about the following topics:

- The scroll bar control
- The list control and its capability to support single or multiple selections
- The synchronized scrolling of list boxes
- The handling of multiple-selection list boxes
- The combo box control and its various styles

This chapter covers versatile controls that you can manipulate in various ways. Therefore, I present a number of test programs so you can examine most of the functionality supported by these controls.

The Scroll Bar Control

A Windows scroll bar can be a separate control and be incorporated in windows, lists, and combo boxes. The scroll bar control appears and behaves much like the scroll bar of a window. The control has a thumb box that keeps track of the current value and lets mouse clicks move it by either single lines or pages. In addition, the scroll bar responds to cursor control keys, such as Home, End, Page Up, and Page Down. The main purpose of the scroll bar control is to enable you to select quickly and efficiently an integer value in a predefined range of values. Windows, for example, uses scroll bars to fine-tune the color palette, the keyboard rate, and the mouse sensitivity.

> **Note:** You might view the scroll bar control as convenient but not terribly versatile, especially compared to the list box and the combo box controls. As I demonstrate later in this chapter, you can find indistinct uses for the scroll bar control by using the scroll bar values as indices for other types of data.

The TScrollBar Class

ObjectWindows offers `TScrollBar`, a descendant of `TControl`, as the class that models the scroll bar controls. The `TScrollBar` class (which is not to be confused with `TScroller`) declares two data members and a number of member functions to set and query the control's current position and range of values. The two data members are `LineMagnitude` and `PageMagnitude`. These members store the magnitude of change in the thumb box position when you move the box by a line or a page. The default values for the `LineMagnitude` and `PageMagnitude` data members are 1 and 10, respectively.

The `TScrollBar` class contains three constructors. I will focus on the constructor that enables you to create instances of `TScrollBar` from scratch:

```
TScrollBar(PTWindowsObject AParent, int AnId, int X, int Y,
          int W, int H, BOOL IsHScrollBar,
          PTModule AModule = NULL);
```

The `AParent` parameter is the pointer to the parent window. The `AnId` parameter specifies the unique ID for the control. The `X`, `Y`, `W`, and `H` parameters specify the location and dimensions of the control. The Boolean parameter `IsHScrollBar` specifies whether the control is a horizontal or vertical scroll bar. When the argument for `IsHScrollBar` is TRUE, the control is created with the `SBS_HORZ` style. By contrast, when the argument for `IsHScrollBar` is FALSE, the control is created with the `SBS_VERT` style.

The `TScrollBar` class offers the following member functions to query and set the scroll bar thumb box position:

- The first member function that you most likely will use after creating a `TScrollBar` instance is `SetRange`. This function enables you to set the range of values for the scroll bar. The declaration of the `SetRange` function is

  ```
  void SetRange(int LoVal, int HiVal);
  ```

  The arguments for the `LoVal` and `HiVal` parameters designate the new range of values for the scroll bar control.

☐ With the `GetRange` member function, you can query the current range of values for the scroll bar. The declaration of the `GetRange` function is

    void GetRange(Rint LoVal, Rint HiVal);

The reference parameters `LoVal` and `HiVal` return the current range of values for the scroll bar control.

☐ The parameterless `GetPosition` member function returns the current position of the thumb box.

☐ The `SetPosition` member function moves the thumb box to the specified position. If the requested position is outside the current scroll bar range, the thumb box is moved to the closest position. The `SetPosition` function is declared as follows:

    void SetPosition(int ThumbPos);

The parameter `ThumbPos` specifies the new thumb box position.

☐ The `DeltaPos` member function alters the position of the thumb box by a specified magnitude. The declaration of the `DeltaPos` function is

    int DeltaPos(int Delta);

The parameter `Delta` specifies the change in the thumb box position. Positive arguments for `Delta` move the thumb box down in a vertical scroll bar and right in a horizontal scroll bar; negative arguments for `Delta` move the thumb box up in a vertical scroll bar and left in a horizontal scroll bar. The `DeltaPos` function returns the new thumb box position.

☐ The group of protected message response member functions `SBLineUp`, `SBLineDown`, `SBPageUp`, `SBPageDown`, `SBThumbPosition`, `SBThumbTrack`, `SBTop`, and `SBBottom` handle the thumb box notification messages listed in Table 7.1.

Note: The parent window of a scroll bar control responds to the notification messages of that control by using the child-ID response member functions. The various notification messages, shown in Table 7.1, are stored in the `wParam` data member of the message parameter. This storage scheme is different from that of other controls. In addition, the notification messages of the scroll bar control are based on the `WM_VSCROLL` and `WM_HSCROLL` messages and not the `WM_COMMAND` message (as with other controls).

Table 7.1. The scroll bar notification messages.

Message	Meaning
SB_LINEUP	Moves the thumb box one line up for a vertical scroll bar and one line left for a horizontal scroll bar.
SB_LINEDOWN	Moves the thumb box one line down for a vertical scroll bar and one line right for a horizontal scroll bar.
SB_PAGEUP	Moves the thumb box one page up for a vertical scroll bar and one page left for a horizontal scroll bar.
SB_PAGEDOWN	Moves the thumb box one page down for a vertical scroll bar and one page right for a horizontal scroll bar.
SB_THUMBPOSITION	Moves the thumb box.
SB_THUMBTRACK	Tracks the thumb box.

Responding to Scroll Bar Notification Messages

The following is a sample template response member function:

```
#define ID_SCROLLER 101

class TAppWindow : public TWindow
{
public:

    // other declarations

    // handle the scroll bar notification messages
    virtual void HandleScroller(RTMessage Msg)
        = [ID_FIRST + ID_SCROLLER];

    // other declarations
};
```

Scroll Bars, List Boxes, and Combo Boxes

```
void TAppWindow::HandleScroller(RTMessage Msg)
{
    switch (Msg.WParam) {
        case SB_LINEUP:
            // response statements here
            break;
        case SB_LINEDOWN:
            // response statements here
            break;
        case SB_PAGEUP:
            // response statements here
            break;
        case SB_PAGEDOWN:
            // response statements here
            break;
    }
}
```

The Countdown Timer

Now examine the countdown timer application (shown in Figure 7.1), a small test program that uses the scroll bar control.

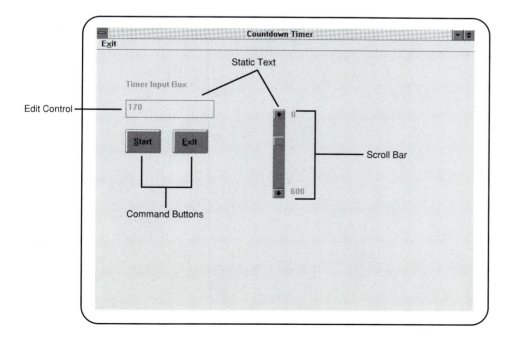

Figure 7.1. A sample session with the CTLLST1.EXE application.

The countdown timer application includes the following controls:

- The Timer Input Box edit control, which accepts input for the timer and displays the current timer value.
- The Static text control, which labels the edit box.
- The Start button, which triggers the countdown timer.
- The Exit Button.
- The timer scroll bar control with a default range of 0 to 600 seconds.
- The static text controls that label the range of values for the timer scroll bar.

You can set the number of seconds in one of two ways: you can type that value in the edit box or use the scroll bar. When you move the scroll bar thumb box, the current thumb position appears in the edit box. To trigger the count time process, click the Start button or press the Alt-S key. The countdown process takes the value stored in the edit box and converts it into the maximum number of seconds to count down. If the edit box is empty, contains 0, or has nonnumerical text, the program assigns a default of 15 seconds. The program also assigns that value to the static text that specifies the maximum scroll bar value. During the countdown, the application decrements the number of seconds in the edit box and moves the scroll bar's thumb box upward. When the countdown ends, the program sounds a beep, restores the maximum limit of the scroll bar, and restores the maximum limit static text.

The countdown timer application demonstrates the following aspects of scroll bar manipulation:

- Setting and altering the scroll bar range of values.
- Moving and changing the scroll bar thumb box position. The program shows how these tasks are performed internally or with the mouse.
- Using the scroll bar to supply a value.

The Timer's Code

Now examine the code for the countdown timer application. Listing 7.1 shows the source code for the CTLLST1.H header file.

Listing 7.1. The source code for the CTLLST1.H header file.

```
#define ID_START_BTN 201
#define ID_EXIT_BTN 202
#define ID_INPUT_BOX 203
#define ID_TIMER_SCR 304
```

Listing 7.2 shows the script for the CTLLST1.RC resource file. The resource file contains the accelerator keys and menu resources. The program uses a menu with the single menu item Exit.

Listing 7.2. The script for the CTLLST1.RC resource file.

```
#include <windows.h>
#include <owlrc.h>
#include "ctllst1.h"

BUTTONS ACCELERATORS
BEGIN
    "s", ID_START_BTN, ALT
    "e", ID_EXIT_BTN, ALT
END


EXITMENU MENU LOADONCALL MOVEABLE PURE DISCARDABLE
BEGIN
    MENUITEM "E&xit", CM_EXIT
END
```

Listing 7.3 includes the source code for the CTLLST1.CPP program file. The listing contains the declaration for the application and window classes.

Listing 7.3. The source code for the CTLLST1.CPP program file.

```
#include <stdlib.h>
#include <ctype.h>
#include <stdio.h>
#include <math.h>
#include <string.h>
#include <owl.h>
#include <static.h>
```

continues

Listing 7.3. continued

```
#include <edit.h>
#include <button.h>
#include <scrollba.h>
#include "ctllst1.h"

// current timer limit is 10 minutes
const MaxTimer = 600;
const MaxEditLen = 10;

// declare the custom application class as
// a subclass of TApplication
class TWinApp : public TApplication
{
public:
  TWinApp(LPSTR     AName,           // application name
          HINSTANCE hInstance,       // instance handle
          HINSTANCE hPrevInstance,   // previous instance handle
          LPSTR     lpCmdLine,       // command-line arguments
          int       nCmdShow) :      // display command
          TApplication(AName, hInstance, hPrevInstance,
                  lpCmdLine, nCmdShow) {};

protected:
  virtual void InitMainWindow();
  virtual void InitInstance();
};

// use the _CLASSDEF macro to declare reference and pointer
// types related to the new TAppWindow class
_CLASSDEF(TAppWindow)

// expand the functionality of TWindow by deriving class TAppWindow
class TAppWindow : public TWindow
{
public:

  TAppWindow(PTWindowsObject AParent, LPSTR ATitle);

  // set the initial timer range
  virtual void InitTimerRange()
    { TimerScr->SetRange(0, MaxTimer); }

  // handle starting the timer
  virtual void HandleStartBtn(RTMessage Msg)
```

```cpp
      = [ID_FIRST + ID_START_BTN];

    // handle starting the timer
    virtual void CMStartBtn(RTMessage Msg)
      = [CM_FIRST + ID_START_BTN];

    // handle exiting the program
    virtual void HandleExitBtn(RTMessage Msg)
      = [ID_FIRST + ID_EXIT_BTN];

    // handle exiting the program
    virtual void CMExitBtn(RTMessage Msg)
      = [CM_FIRST + ID_EXIT_BTN];

    // handle moving the scroll bar
    virtual void HandleTimerScr(RTMessage Msg)
      = [ID_FIRST + ID_TIMER_SCR];

    // handle closing the window
    virtual BOOL CanClose();

protected:
    PTEdit InputBox;
    PTButton StartBtn;
    PTButton ExitBtn;
    PTScrollBar TimerScr;
    PTStatic TimerTxt;

private:
    // delays the program for about ms milliseconds
    void delay(DWORD ms);
};

TAppWindow::TAppWindow(PTWindowsObject AParent, LPSTR ATitle) :
                       TWindow(AParent, ATitle)
{
    char s[81];
    int x = 50, y = 50;

    // load the menu resource
    AssignMenu("EXITMENU");

    // create the timer input box and its label
    strcpy(s, "Timer Input Box");
    new TStatic(this, -1, s, x, y, 150, 30, strlen(s));
```

continues

Listing 7.3. continued

```
    y += 30 + 5;
    InputBox = new TEdit(this, ID_INPUT_BOX, "",
                         x, y, 150, 30, 0, FALSE);
    // create the Start button
    y += 30 + 20;
    StartBtn = new TButton(this, ID_START_BTN, "&Start",
                           x, y, 60, 40, FALSE);
    // create the Exit button
    x += 60 + 20;
    ExitBtn  = new TButton(this, ID_EXIT_BTN, "&Exit",
                           x, y, 60, 40, FALSE);
    // create the timer scroll bar
    x = 300;
    y = 100;
    TimerScr = new TScrollBar(this, ID_TIMER_SCR,
                              x, y, 20, 150, FALSE);
    // create the static text controls that label the
    // minimum and maximum values
    x += 20 + 10;
    new TStatic(this, -1, "0", x, y, 80, 20, 2);
    y += 130;
    sprintf(s, "%d", MaxTimer);
    TimerTxt = new TStatic(this, -1, s, x, y,
                           80, 20, strlen(s));
    // enable the keyboard handler
    EnableKBHandler();
}

void TAppWindow::HandleStartBtn(RTMessage Msg)
{
    char s[MaxEditLen+1];
    int x;

    // get the text in the edit box
    InputBox->GetText(s, MaxEditLen);
    // convert the string into an integer
    x = atoi(s);
    // if x is 0 assign it 15
    x = (x != 0) ? x : 15;
    // set the maximum timer static text
    sprintf(s, "%d", x);
    TimerTxt->SetText(s);
    // set the new range
    TimerScr->SetRange(0, x);
```

```
    // set the thumb position to the maximum position
    TimerScr->SetPosition(x);
    // countdown loop
    while (x > 0) {
      delay(980);
      x--;
      // update the thumb position
      TimerScr->DeltaPos(-1);
      sprintf(s, "%d", x);
      // echo thumb position in the edit box
      InputBox->SetText(s);
    }
    MessageBeep(0); // beep
    // restore the default timer limits
    sprintf(s, "%d", MaxTimer);
    TimerScr->SetRange(0, MaxTimer);
    TimerScr->SetPosition(MaxTimer);
    TimerTxt->SetText(s);
}

void TAppWindow::CMStartBtn(RTMessage Msg)
{
  HandleStartBtn(Msg);
}

void TAppWindow::HandleExitBtn(RTMessage Msg)
{
  SendMessage(HWindow, WM_CLOSE, NULL, NULL);
}

void TAppWindow::CMExitBtn(RTMessage Msg)
{
  SendMessage(HWindow, WM_CLOSE, NULL, NULL);
}

void TAppWindow::HandleTimerScr(RTMessage Msg)
{
    int x = TimerScr->GetPosition();
    char s[MaxEditLen+1];
    // convert the thumb position into a string
    sprintf(s, "%d", x);
    // insert the string in the edit box
    InputBox->SetText(s);
}
```

continues

Listing 7.3. continued

```
BOOL TAppWindow::CanClose()
{
  return MessageBox(HWindow, "Want to close this application",
                    "Query", MB_YESNO | MB_ICONQUESTION) == IDYES;
}

void TAppWindow::delay(DWORD ms)
{
  DWORD time1 = GetTickCount();
  do {
    ;
  } while ((GetTickCount() - time1) < ms);
}

void TWinApp::InitMainWindow()
{
  MainWindow = new TAppWindow(NULL, Name);
}

void TWinApp::InitInstance()
{
  TApplication::InitInstance();
  HAccTable = LoadAccelerators(hInstance, "BUTTONS");
  // set the maximum range of the timer scroll bar
  PTAppWindow(MainWindow)->InitTimerRange();
}

int PASCAL WinMain(HINSTANCE hInstance, HINSTANCE hPrevInstance,
                   LPSTR lpCmdLine, int nCmdShow)
{
  TWinApp WinApp(" Countdown Timer", hInstance, hPrevInstance,
                 lpCmdLine, nCmdShow);
  WinApp.Run(); // run OWL application
  return WinApp.Status; // return application status
}
```

The application window class TAppWindow declares a number of data members that are pointers to the application's controls. The TAppWindow class declares a constructor and seven member functions.

The TAppWindow class constructor creates the application window and performs the following tasks:

Scroll Bars, List Boxes, and Combo Boxes

1. Loads the menu resource.
2. Creates the timer edit box and static text that labels it.
3. Creates the push button controls marked Start and Exit.
4. Creates the timer scroll bar control. The `TScrollBar` constructor uses the argument `ID_TIMER_SCR` to specify the controls' ID. The last argument in the `TScrollBar` constructor call is FALSE and indicates that the scroll bar is vertical.
5. Creates the static text controls that label the range of scroll bar values. The lower value is always 0. The upper limit is set initially with the global constant `MaxTimer`.
6. Enables the keyboard handler.

The `HandleStartBtn` member function implements the functionality that triggers the timer countdown. The function carries out the following tasks:

1. Retrieves the text in the edit box and stores it in the local variable `s`.
2. Converts the characters in variable `s` into an `int` type and stores the result in the local variable `x`.
3. Examines the value of `x`. If it is zero, the function assigns 15 to variable `x`.
4. Sets the maximum timer limit static text to the string image of the value in variable `x`.
5. Sets the range of the timer scroll bar by invoking the `TScrollBar::SetRange` member function with the arguments of `0` and `x`.
6. Moves the thumb position to the bottom of the scroll bar by using the `TScrollBar::SetPosition` member function. The argument for that function call is `x`.
7. Starts the countdown loop. This loop invokes the delay function and requests that the program wait for 980 milliseconds. This value allows for some processing time. The loop then changes the thumb box position by moving it one value upward. This step requires the `TScrollBar::DeltaPos` member function with an argument of –1. The loop then sets a string image of the current thumb box position in the edit box. This task causes the edit box to show the countdown time in seconds.
8. Beeps when the countdown loop terminates.
9. Restores the default upper range of the scroll bar timer to 600 and updates the maximum limit static text accordingly.

The `CMStartBtn` member function traps the command message generated by the Alt-S key. The function merely calls the `HandleStartBtn` member function.

The `HandleExitBtn` and `CMExitBtn` member functions send a `WM_CLOSE` message to the application window.

The `HandleTimeScr` member function responds to the notification message that the scroll bar control sends to its parent window. The function converts the current thumb box position into a string and writes it in the edit box. Thus the `HandleTimerScr` function updates the contents of the edit box when you move the thumb box.

The delay member function uses the `GetTickCount` API function to simulate the requested delay.

The List Box Controls

List boxes are input controls that provide a list of items from which the application user can choose. List boxes are typically framed and include a vertical scroll bar. When you select an item by clicking it, the selection is highlighted. Microsoft suggests the following simple guidelines for making a selection:

- A single click selects a new or an additional item. A separate button control retrieves the selected item.
- A double click is a shortcut for selecting an item and retrieving it.

A list box control supports multiple selections only if you specify the multiple-selection style when you create the control. Making multiple selections is convenient when you want to process the selected items in a similar manner. For example, selecting multiple files for deletion speeds up the process and reduces your effort.

The `TListBox` Class

ObjectWindows offers a versatile class of `TListBox`, a descendant of `TControl`, to implement list box controls. The `TListBox` class features a rich set of member functions that enable you to easily manipulate and query both the contents of the list box and the selected item. Like many other ObjectWindows classes, `TListBox` has three constructors. I will focus on the one that enables you to create class instances from scratch:

Scroll Bars, List Boxes, and Combo Boxes

```
TListBox(PTWindowsObject AParent, int AnId, int X, int Y,
        int W, int H, PTModule AModule = NULL);
```

The `AParent` parameter is the pointer to the parent window. The `AnId` parameter specifies the unique ID for the control. The `X`, `Y`, `W`, and `H` parameters specify the location and dimensions of the control. The class constructor creates the instance with the `LBS_STANDARD` style, which sets the `WS_BORDER`, `WS_VSCROLL`, `LBS_SORT`, and `LBS_NOTIFY` styles. Table 7.2 shows some of the list box styles that are relevant to ObjectWindows.

> **Tip:** You can remove the `LBS_SORT` style from the list box control to maintain a list of items that is not automatically sorted. Such a list enables you to maintain items chronologically in the order in which they are entered into the list. You can also use such a list to maintain the items sorted in descending order. In this case, you must preserve the list items in that order. Removing the `WS_VSCROLL` style results in a list box without the vertical scroll bar. The next section presents a demonstration program that uses this type of list box to implement the synchronized scrolling of multiple list boxes.

Table 7.2. The list box control styles.

Style	Meaning
LBS_EXTENDESEL	Enables you to extend multiple selections in the list box by using the Shift key.
LBS_MULTICOLUMN	Designates a multicolumn list box that scrolls horizontally. The message `LB_SETCOLUMNWIDTH` sets the number of columns. Employing this control style requires the use of Windows API functions.
LBS_MULTIPLESEL	Supports multiple selections in a list box.
LBS_NOINTEGRALHEIGHT	Suppresses the list box from showing parts of an item.
LBS_NOREDRAW	Prevents the list box from being updated when the selection has changed. Sending the `WM_SETREDRAW` message can alter this style to allow the list box update.
LBS_NOTIFY	Notifies the parent window when you click or double-click the list box.

continues

Table 7.2. continued

Style	Meaning
LBS_SORT	Specifies that the items inserted in the list box be automatically sorted in an ascending order.
LBS_STANDARD	Sets the WS_BORDER, WS_VSCROLL, LBS_SORT, and LBS_NOTIFY styles.
LBS_WANTKEYBOARDINPUT	Enables list box owners to receive WM_VKEYTOITEM or WM_CHARTOITEM messages when they press a key while the list box has the focus. This style enables an application to manipulate the items in the list box.

The TListBox class offers the following member functions, which set and query ordinary and selected list members:

- The AddString member function adds a string to the list box and is declared as follows:

    int AddString(LPSTR AString);

    The AString parameter is the pointer to the added string. The function also returns the position (list box positions start with 0) of the added string in the control. If any error occurs when the string is added, the function yields a –1 value. If the LBS_SORT style is set, the string is inserted so that the list order is maintained. If the LBS_SORT style is not set, the added string is inserted at the end of the list.

- The DeleteString member function removes a list member from a specified position and is declared as follows:

    int DeleteString(int Index)

    The Index parameter specifies the position of the item to delete. The function returns the number of remaining list members. If an error occurs, DeleteString yields a negative result. The remaining items "bump up" to fill the vacant entry.

- The parameterless ClearList member function clears the list of strings from the list box control in one swoop. This function resets the contents of a list box before building a new list.

- The FindExactString member function searches for a item that exactly matches a specified string. The declaration of the FindExactString function is

Scroll Bars, List Boxes, and Combo Boxes

```
int FindExactString(LPSTR AString, int SearchIndex);
```

The `AString` parameter is the pointer to the searched string. `SearchIndex` specifies the first position to be searched. The function then searches the entire list beginning with position `SearchIndex` and resuming at the beginning of the list if necessary. The search stops when either a list member matches the search string or the entire list is searched. Passing an argument of –1 to `SearchIndex` forces the function to start searching from the beginning. The function returns the position of the matching list item or a negative result if no match is found or when an error occurs.

> **Tip:** Using the `FindExactString` function's interesting search method, you can speed up the search by specifying a position that comes closely before the most likely location for a match. The beauty of this method is that if you specify a position that is actually beyond that of the string you seek, you will not miss finding that string, because the function resumes searching at the beginning of the list.
>
> Another benefit of `FindExactString` is that it can find duplicate strings.

- ☐ The `FindString` member function is a more relaxed version of the `FindExtactString` function. The `FindString` function hunts for a list item that starts with the same search string characters. The declaration of the `FindString` function is

    ```
    int FindString(LPSTR AString, int SearchIndex);
    ```

    Other aspects of the `FindString` function match those of the `FindExactString` function.

- ☐ The parameterless `GetCount` member function returns the number of items in the list box. The function returns a negative value if an error occurs.

- ☐ The parameterless `GetSelCount` member function returns the number of selected items in the list box. For single-selection list boxes, the function returns either 0 or 1.

- ☐ The parameterless `GetSelIndex` member function returns the position of the selected item in a single-selection list box. If no item is selected, the function yields a negative value. This function is for single-selection list boxes only.

- The `GetSelIndexes` member function returns the number and positions of the selected items in a multiple-selection list box. The declaration of the `GetSelIndexes` function is

    int GetSelIndexes(Pint Indexes, int MaxCount);

    The `Indexes` parameter, which is the pointer to an array of integers, stores the positions of the selected items. The `MaxCount` parameter specifies the size of the array accessed by the `Indexes` pointer. The function returns the current number of selections.

- The `GetSelString` member function obtains part or all of the selected item in a single-selection list box. The declaration for the `GetSelString` function is

    int GetSelString(LPSTR AString, int MaxChars);

    The `AString` parameter is the pointer to the string that receives characters from the current selection. The `MaxChars` parameter indicates the maximum number of characters to obtain. The function returns the length of the retrieved string or a negative value if an error occurs.

- The `GetString` member function obtains part or all of an item in a list box. The declaration for the `GetString` function is

    int GetString(LPSTR AString, int Index);

    The `AString` parameter is the pointer to the string that receives characters from the selected items. The `Index` parameter specifies the target list item. The function returns the length of the retrieved string or a negative value if an error occurs.

- The `GetStringLen` member function returns the length of a list item specified by its position in the list. The declaration of the `GetStringLen` function is

    int GetStringLen(int Index);

    The parameter `Index` specifies the index of the target list item. The function returns the length of the target item or a negative result if an error occurs.

- The `InsertString` member function inserts a string in a list box. The declaration of the `InsertString` function is

    int InsertString(LPSTR AString, int Index);

The `AString` parameter is the pointer to the inserted string. The `Index` parameter specifies the requested insertion position. The function returns the actual insertion position or yields a negative value if an error occurs. If the argument for `Index` is –1, the string is simply appended to the end of the list.

Caution: Normally, you should use the `InsertString` member function with list boxes that have the `LBS_SORT` style removed. Using this function with ordered list box will probably corrupt the sort order of the list.

- The `SetSelIndex` member function chooses a list item as the new selection in a single-selection list box. The declaration of the `SetSelIndex` function is

    ```
    int SetSelIndex(int Index);
    ```

    The parameter `Index` specifies the position of the new selection. To clear any selection from a list box, pass a –1 argument to the `Index` parameter. The function returns a negative value if an error occurs.

- The `SetSelIndexes` member function sets or clears the selections in a multiple-selection list box. The declaration of the `SetSelIndexes` function is

    ```
    int SetSelIndexes(Pint Indexes, int NumSelections,
            BOOL ShouldSet);
    ```

    The `Indexes` parameter is a pointer to the array of integers that stores the positions for the multiple selections. The parameter `NumSelections` specifies the number of selections. The Boolean parameter `ShouldSet` indicates whether to select or deselect the items in the list box. If you assign a TRUE argument to `ShouldSet`, the function selects the items with positions that are indicated by the integer array. By contrast, if you assign FALSE to `ShouldSet`, the indicated items are deselected. The function returns the number of items that were actually selected or deselected. If an error occurs, the function yields a negative value. To select or deselect all the list items, pass a negative argument to the `NumSelections` parameter.

> **Tip:** You can use the `GetSelIndexes` member function to store snapshots of specific multiple selections in different integer arrays. Later, you can restore these snapshot multiple-selections with the `SetSelIndexes` member function. Thus the integer arrays involved in this process define selection sets. This technique assumes that while these snapshots are taken and restored, the list box items remain fixed.

■ The `SetSelString` member function selects the item that matches a search string. The declaration of the `SetSelString` function is

```
int SetSelString(LPSTR AString, int SearchIndex);
```

The parameter `AString` points to the search string. The `SearchIndex` parameter specifies the first list position to search. The `SetSelString` function works like `FindExactString`, with the added feature of selecting the list item that matches the search string. The function returns the position of the new selection or a negative number if an error occurs.

■ The `SetSelStrings` member function selects and deselects multiple-selection list items that match an array of search strings. The declaration of the `SetSelStrings` function is

```
int SetSelStrings(LPSTR *Prefixes, int NumSelections,
    BOOL ShouldSet);
```

The `Prefixes` parameter is a pointer to the array of search strings. The `NumSelections` parameter specifies the number of selections. The Boolean parameter `ShouldSet` indicates whether the list items that match the members of the string search array are selected or deselected. The function searches for a list item that matches each member of the search array. Each time, the function searches the list, starting at the beginning, until either a matching item is found or the entire list is searched. To select or deselect all the list items, pass a negative argument to the `NumSelections` parameter. The function returns the number of list items that were successfully selected or deselected.

Responding to List Box Notification Messages

As a result of changes in a list box, Windows sends `WM_COMMAND` notification messages to the parent window. To respond to the notification message, the

Scroll Bars, List Boxes, and Combo Boxes

window class must use child-ID response-handling member functions. Table 7.3 shows the various list box notification messages.

Table 7.3. The list box notification messages.

Message	Meaning
LBN_CHANGE	A list item is selected with a click.
LBN_DBLCLK	A list item is selected with a double-click.
LBN_SETFOCUS	The list box has gained focus.
LBN_KILLFOCUS	The list box has lost focus.
LBN_ERRSPACE	The list box cannot allocate more dynamic memory to accommodate new list items.

These notification messages are located in the high word of the LParam of the message parameter (that is, the LP.Hi data member). The notification response member functions can handle one or more notification messages by matching the LP.Hi member with the LBN_XXXX values. Here is a sample skeleton code for responding to the list box message:

```
#define ID_LISTBOX 101

class TAppWindow : public TWindow
{
public:

    // other declarations

    // handle the list box notification messages
    virtual void HandleListBox(RTMessage Msg)
        = [ID_FIRST + ID_LISTBOX];

    // other declarations
};

void TAppWindow::HandleListBox(RTMessage Msg)
{
    switch (Msg.LP.Hi) {
        case LBN_SELCHANGE:
            // response statements here break;
        case LBN_DBLCLK:
            // response statements here break;
```

343

```
        case LBN_SETFOCUS:
            // response statements here break;
    }
}
```

The Simple List Manipulation Tester

Here's a simple list manipulation tester that demonstrates how to set and query normal and selected strings. The program also demonstrates how to set and query the current selection in a single-selection list box. Figure 7.2 shows the program's interface and a sample session.

Figure 7.2. A sample session with the CTLLST2.EXE application.

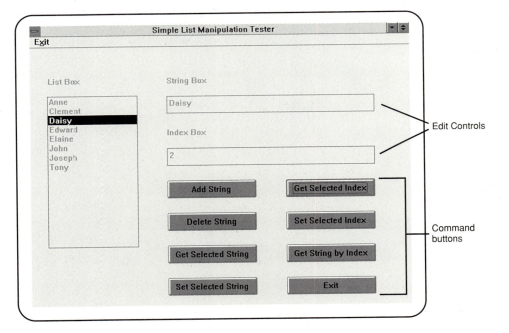

The list tester program demonstrates how to use most of the TListBox member functions presented earlier in this section. The program contains the following controls, which offer the indicated test features:

- A list box control.
- A String Box edit control, which enables you to type and retrieve a list member.

- An Index Box edit control, which enables you to type and retrieve the position of the current selection.
- An Add String push button, which adds the content of the String Box to the list box. The program does not enable you to add duplicate names. If you attempt to do so, the program displays a warning message.
- A Delete String push button, which deletes the selection currently in the list box. The program automatically selects another list member.
- A Get Selected String push button, which copies the current list selection to the String Box.
- A Set Selected String push button, which overwrites the current selection with the string in the String Box.
- A Get Selected Index push button, which writes the position of the current selection in the Index Box.
- A Set Selected Index push button, which uses the integer value in the Index Box as the position of the new list box selection.
- A Get String button, which copies into the String Box the string with the position that appears in the Index Box.
- The Exit push button.

These controls accomplish various aspects of manipulating a sorted list box and its members. The program is coded to retain a current selection and to prevent the insertion of duplicate names.

Now compile and run the program. When the program starts running, it places a set of names in the list box. The program is straightforward and easy to run. Experiment with the various push button controls to add, delete, and obtain strings.

The Single-List Application Code

Listings 7.4 and 7.5 show the script for the CTLLST2.RC resource file and the source code for the CTLLST2.CPP program file, respectively. The resource file contains a single-item menu resource. I avoided using hot keys to make the program a bit shorter.

Listing 7.4. The script for the CTLLST2.RC resource file.

```
#include <windows.h>
#include <owlrc.h>

EXITMENU MENU LOADONCALL MOVEABLE PURE DISCARDABLE
BEGIN
      MENUITEM "E&xit", CM_EXIT
END
```

Listing 7.5. The source code for the CTLLST2.CPP program file.

```
#include <stdlib.h>
#include <ctype.h>
#include <stdio.h>
#include <math.h>
#include <string.h>
#include <owl.h>
#include <static.h>
#include <edit.h>
#include <button.h>
#include <listbox.h>

const LowVertSpacing = 5;
const HiVertSpacing = 10;
const HorzSpacing = 50;
const Wctl = 150;
const Hctl = 30;
const Wbox = 2 * Wctl + HorzSpacing;
const Hlst = Hctl + LowVertSpacing + 4 * (Hctl + HiVertSpacing);
const MaxEditLen = 10;

// declare the ID constants for the various controls
#define ID_STRING_LST 101
#define ID_STRING_EDIT 102
#define ID_INDEX_EDIT 103
#define ID_ADDSTR_BTN 104
#define ID_DELSTR_BTN 105
#define ID_GETSELSTR_BTN 106
#define ID_SETSELSTR_BTN 107
#define ID_GETSELIDX_BTN 108
#define ID_SETSELIDX_BTN 109
#define ID_EXIT_BTN 110
#define ID_GETSTR_ETN 111
```

```cpp
// declare the custom application class as
// a subclass of TApplication
class TWinApp : public TApplication
{
public:
  TWinApp(LPSTR    AName,           // application name
          HINSTANCE hInstance,      // instance handle
          HINSTANCE hPrevInstance,  // previous instance handle
          LPSTR    lpCmdLine,       // command-line arguments
          int      nCmdShow) :      // display command
          TApplication(AName, hInstance, hPrevInstance,
                   lpCmdLine, nCmdShow) {};

protected:
  virtual void InitMainWindow();
  virtual void InitInstance();
};

// use the _CLASSDEF macro to declare reference and pointer
// types related to the new TAppWindow class
_CLASSDEF(TAppWindow)

// expand the functionality of TWindow by deriving class TAppWindow
class TAppWindow : public TWindow
{
public:

  TAppWindow(PTWindowsObject AParent, LPSTR ATitle);

  // initialize the String list box
  void InitStringLst();

  // handle adding a string to the list box
  virtual void HandleAddStrBtn(RTMessage Msg)
    = [ID_FIRST + ID_ADDSTR_BTN];

  // handle deleting a string from the list box
  virtual void HandleDelStrBtn(RTMessage Msg)
    = [ID_FIRST + ID_DELSTR_BTN];

  // handle getting the selected text
  virtual void HandleGetSelStrBtn(RTMessage Msg)
    = [ID_FIRST + ID_GETSELSTR_BTN];

  // handle setting the selected text
```

continues

Listing 7.5. continued

```
    virtual void HandleSetSelStrBtn(RTMessage Msg)
      = [ID_FIRST + ID_SETSELSTR_BTN];

    // handle getting the index of the selected text
    virtual void HandleGetSelIdxBtn(RTMessage Msg)
      = [ID_FIRST + ID_GETSELIDX_BTN];

    // handle setting the index of the selected text
    virtual void HandleSetSelIdxBtn(RTMessage Msg)
      = [ID_FIRST + ID_SETSELIDX_BTN];

    // handle getting a string from the list box
    virtual void HandleGetStrBtn(RTMessage Msg)
      = [ID_FIRST + ID_GETSTR_BTN];

    // handle setting a string in the list box
    virtual void HandleExitBtn(RTMessage Msg)
      = [ID_FIRST + ID_EXIT_BTN];

    // handle closing the window
    virtual BOOL CanClose();

protected:
    PTListBox StringLst;
    PTEdit StringBox;
    PTEdit IndexBox;
    PTButton AddStrBtn;
    PTButton DelStrBtn;
    PTButton GetSelStrBtn;
    PTButton SetSelStrBtn;
    PTButton GetSelIdxBtn;
    PTButton SetSelIdxBtn;
    PTButton GetStrBtn;
    PTButton ExitBtn;

    char dataStr[MaxEditLen+1];  // string for StringBox
    char indexStr[MaxEditLen+1]; // string for IndexBox
};

TAppWindow::TAppWindow(PTWindowsObject AParent, LPSTR ATitle) :
                    TWindow(AParent, ATitle)
{
  char s[81];
  int x0 = 30;
```

Scroll Bars, List Boxes, and Combo Boxes

```
    int x1 = x0 + Wctl + HorzSpacing;
    int x2 = x1 + Wctl + HorzSpacing;
    int y0 = 50;
    int x = x0;
    int y = y0;
    int y1;

    // load the menu resource
    AssignMenu("EXITMENU");

    // create the list box and its label
    strcpy(s, "List Box");
    new TStatic(this, -1, s, x, y, Wctl, Hctl, strlen(s));
    y += Hctl + LowVertSpacing;
    StringLst = new TListBox(this, ID_STRING_LST, x, y, Wctl, Hlst);

    // create the edit boxes and their labels
    x = x1;
    y = y0;
    strcpy(s, "String Box");
    new TStatic(this, -1, s, x, y, Wctl, Hctl, strlen(s));
    y += Hctl + LowVertSpacing;
    StringBox = new TEdit(this, ID_STRING_EDIT, "",
                          x, y, Wbox, Hctl, 0, FALSE);

    y += Hctl + HiVertSpacing;
    strcpy(s, "Index Box");
    new TStatic(this, -1, s, x, y, Wctl, Hctl, strlen(s));
    y += Hctl + LowVertSpacing;
    IndexBox = new TEdit(this, ID_INDEX_EDIT, "", x, y, Wbox, Hctl,
                         0, FALSE);

    // create the button controls
    y += Hctl + HiVertSpacing;
    y1 = y;
    AddStrBtn = new TButton(this, ID_ADDSTR_BTN, "Add String",
                            x, y, Wctl, Hctl, FALSE);

    y += Hctl + HiVertSpacing;
    DelStrBtn = new TButton(this, ID_DELSTR_BTN, "Delete String",
                            x, y, Wctl, Hctl, FALSE);

    y += Hctl + HiVertSpacing;
    GetSelStrBtn = new TButton(this, ID_GETSELSTR_BTN,
                               "Get Selected String",
```

continues

Listing 7.5. continued

```
                                x, y, Wctl, Hctl, FALSE);

  y += Hctl + HiVertSpacing;
  SetSelStrBtn = new TButton(this, ID_SETSELSTR_BTN,
                             "Set Selected String",
                             x, y, Wctl, Hctl, FALSE);

  // create the secord row of buttons
  y  = y1;
  x = x2;
  GetSelIdxBtn = new TButton(this, ID_GETSELIDX_BTN,
                             "Get Selected Index",
                             x, y, Wctl, Hctl, FALSE);

  y += Hctl + HiVertSpacing;
  SetSelIdxBtn = new TButton(this, ID_SETSELIDX_BTN,
                             "Set Selected Index",
                             x, y, Wctl, Hctl, FALSE);

  y += Hctl + HiVertSpacing;
  GetStrBtn = new TButton(this, ID_GETSTR_BTN,
                          "Get String by Index",
                          x, y, Wctl, Hctl, FALSE);

  y += Hctl + HiVertSpacing;
  ExitBtn = new TButton(this, ID_EXIT_BTN, "Exit",
                        x, y, Wctl, Hctl, FALSE);

  // enable the keyboard handler
  EnableKBHandler();
}

void TAppWindow::HandleAddStrBtn(RTMessage Msg)
{
  int i;
  // get the string in the String box
  StringBox->GetText(dataStr, MaxEditLen);
  // exit if the string empty?
  if (dataStr[0] == '\0') return;
  // add the string if it is not already in the list box
  if (StringLst->FindExactString(dataStr, -1) < 0) {
    // add the string and store the position of the new string
    i = StringLst->AddString(dataStr);
    // make the added string the new selection
```

```cpp
      StringLst->SetSelIndex(i);
    }
    else
      // handle the duplicate-data error
      MessageBox(HWindow, "Cannot add duplicate names",
                          "Bad Data", MB_OK);
}

void TAppWindow::HandleDelStrBtn(RTMessage Msg)
{
  // get the index of the currently selected list member
  int i = StringLst->GetSelIndex();
  // delete the currently selected list member
  StringLst->DeleteString(i);
  // select another list member
  StringLst->SetSelIndex((i > 0) ? (i-1) : 0);
}

void TAppWindow::HandleGetSelStrBtn(RTMessage Msg)
{
  // get the selected list item
  StringLst->GetSelString(dataStr, MaxEditLen);
  /// store it in the String box
  StringBox->SetText(dataStr);
}

void TAppWindow::HandleSetSelStrBtn(RTMessage Msg)
{
  // get the index of the currently selected list member
  int i = StringLst->GetSelIndex();
  // get the string to replace the currently selected list item
  StringBox->GetText(dataStr, MaxEditLen);
  // is the candidate string not in the list?
  if (StringLst->FindExactString(dataStr, -1) < 0) {
    // delete the current selection
    StringLst->DeleteString(i);
    // insert the new selection
    i = StringLst->AddString(dataStr);
    // select the inserted string
    StringLst->SetSelIndex(i);
  }
  else
    MessageBox(HWindow, "Cannot add duplicate names",
                        "Bad Data", MB_OK);
}
```

continues

Listing 7.5. continued

```
void TAppWindow::HandleGetSelIdxBtn(RTMessage Msg)
{
  sprintf(indexStr, "%d", StringLst->GetSelIndex());
  IndexBox->SetText(indexStr);
}

void TAppWindow::HandleSetSelIdxBtn(RTMessage Msg)
{
  IndexBox->GetText(indexStr, MaxEditLen);
  StringLst->SetSelIndex(atof(indexStr));
}

void TAppWindow::HandleGetStrBtn(RTMessage Msg)
{
  int i;
  // get the index from the Index box
  IndexBox->GetText(indexStr, MaxEditLen);
  i = atof(indexStr);
  // get the target string from the list box
  StringLst->GetString(dataStr, i);
  // write the list member in the String box
  StringBox->SetText(dataStr);
}

void TAppWindow::HandleExitBtn(RTMessage Msg)
{
  SendMessage(HWindow, WM_CLOSE, NULL, NULL);
}

BOOL TAppWindow::CanClose()
{
  return MessageBox(HWindow, "Want to close this application",
                    "Query", MB_YESNO | MB_ICONQUESTION) == IDYES;
}

void TAppWindow::InitStringLst()
{
  // add data in the list box
  StringLst->AddString("Edward");
  StringLst->AddString("John");
  StringLst->AddString("Anne");
  StringLst->AddString("Elaine");
  StringLst->AddString("Joseph");
  StringLst->AddString("Clement");
```

```
  StringLst->AddString("Daisy");
  StringLst->AddString("Tony");
  // select the second item
  StringLst->SetSelIndex(1);
}

void TWinApp::InitMainWindow()
{
  MainWindow = new TAppWindow(NULL, Name);
}

void TWinApp::InitInstance()
{
  TApplication::InitInstance();
  PTAppWindow(MainWindow)->InitStringLst();
}

int PASCAL WinMain(HINSTANCE hInstance, HINSTANCE hPrevInstance,
                   LPSTR lpCmdLine, int nCmdShow)
{
  TWinApp WinApp("Simple List Manipulation Tester",
                 hInstance, hPrevInstance, lpCmdLine, nCmdShow);
  WinApp.Run(); // run OWL application
  return WinApp.Status; // return application status
}
```

The source code for the list tester declares two sets of constants. The first set contains the constants that dimension the sizes of the various controls. The second set of constants specifies the ID for the various controls.

The program listing declares an application class and a window class. The application window class `TAppWindow` declares a number of data members that are pointers to the controls owned by the window. The class also declares two strings to handle the contents of the String Box and Index Box edit controls. The `TAppWindow` class also declares a constructor and a number of member functions that respond to the notification messages sent by the various push button controls.

The `TAppWindow` constructor loads the menu resource, creates the instances for the application's controls, and enables the keyboard handler. All the controls are created with their default styles. For the list box, the control appears with a vertical scroll bar and automatically maintains a sorted list of strings.

The `InitStringLst` member function adds strings to the Names list box and selects the second list item. The application class `InitInstance` member function calls `InitStringLst` to initialize the list box with data.

The `HandleAddStrBtn` member function adds the string from the String Box in the list box control. The function performs the following tasks:

1. Obtains the string from the String Box edit control and stores it in the `dataStr` data member.

2. Exits if the `dataStr` member stores an empty string.

3. Verifies that the added string does not already exist in the list box. The function uses the `FindExactString` function to detect an attempt to add duplicate strings. If the `FindExactString` function returns a negative number, `HandleAddStrBtn` resumes with the subsequent tasks. Otherwise, the `HandleAddStrBtn` function displays a message informing you that you cannot add duplicate strings to the list box.

4. Adds the string of the `dataStr` member to the list box and assigns the position of the string to the local variable `i`. The function uses the `AddString` member to perform this task.

5. Designates the added string as the current selection by invoking the `SetSelIndex` function with the argument `i`.

The `HandleDelStrBtn` member function deletes the current selection by carrying out the following tasks:

1. Obtains the position of the current selection by invoking the `GetSelIndex` function. The function stores the selection position in the local variable `i`.

2. Deletes the selection by calling the `DeleteString` function and supplying it the argument `i`.

3. Selects another list item as the new selection at position `i - 1`. If the variable `i` already contains 0, the new first list item becomes the new selection.

The `HandleGetSelStrBtn` member function copies the current selection to the String Box edit control. The function performs the following tasks:

1. Copies the current selection to the `dataStr` member by calling the `GetSelString` function.

2. Overwrites the contents of the String Box with the characters of the `dataStr` member.

The `HandleSetSelStrBtn` member function overwrites the current selection with the string in the String Box edit control. Because the list maintains sorted items, the replacement string probably will have a different position than the original selection. The function performs the following tasks:

1. Obtains the position of the current selection by using the `GetSelIndex` function and assigns that value to the local variable `i`.
2. Copies the text from the String Box to the `dataStr` member.
3. Verifies that the string in `dataStr` is not already in the list box. This task involves the `FindExactString` function. If the string in `dataStr` is new to the list, the `FindExactString` function deletes the current selection (using the `DeleteString` function), adds `dataStr` (using the `AddString` function), and selects the added string (using the `SetSelIndex` function). However, if the string in `dataStr` has a matching list item, the `HandleSetSelStrBtn` function displays a message informing you that you cannot add duplicate strings in the list box. This warning also appears if you attempt to overwrite the current selection with the same string.

The `HandleGetSelIdxBtn` member function writes the position of the current selection to the Index Box edit box. The function uses the `GetSelIndex` function to obtain the sought position.

The `HandleSetSelIdxBtn` member function reads the value in the Index Box edit control and uses that value to set the new current selection. The function uses the `SetSelIndex` function to make the new selection.

The `HandleGetStrBtn` member function enables you to retrieve the list item with the position that appears in the Index Box edit control. The function performs the following tasks:

1. Copies the characters of the Index Box to the `indxStr` data member.
2. Converts the string from `indexStr` to the `int`-typed local variable `i`.
3. Copies the characters of the list item at position `i` to the `dataStr` member.
4. Writes the characters of `dataStr` in the String Box edit control.

Synchronized Scrolling of Lists

In the previous two chapters, I demonstrated how one control can influence and modify other controls. This section explores a special case for this kind of behavior—one that involves synchronized scrolling of two list boxes. The two list boxes should meet the following conditions:

- ☐ Both list boxes have the same height and contain the same number of items. An equal number of items enforces the one-on-one correspondence between the items of the two list boxes.
- ☐ At most, only one of the two list boxes can maintain sorted items.
- ☐ Changing the selection in one list box also must result in selecting the corresponding item in the other list box.
- ☐ The two list boxes must scroll simultaneously.

The first condition states that the each item in the two list boxes has a corresponding item in the other list. Moreover, you should be able to view the same number of items in both list boxes.

The second condition states that either both or at least one list box is unsorted. When the two list boxes are unsorted, you can insert and delete items from the two list boxes more easily. If one of the list boxes uses the LBS_SORT style, the items of the other unordered list must be added in an order that matches the sort order of the first list box.

The third and fourth conditions state that the two lists must maintain the same selection position and same the scroll bar position. Fulfilling this condition provides the application user with a nice interface.

The Synchronized Lists Program

Here's an ObjectWindows program that demonstrates the synchronized scrolling of lists. Figure 7.3 shows a sample session with the CTLLST3.EXE application, which supports the scrolling of synchronized lists.

Scroll Bars, List Boxes, and Combo Boxes

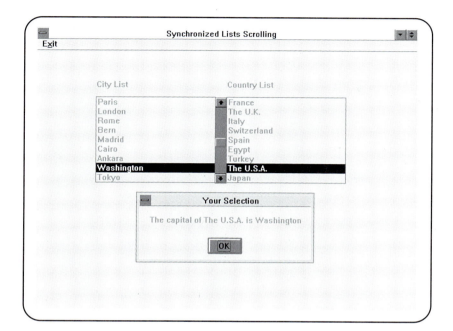

Figure 7.3.
A sample session with the CTLLST3.EXE application.

The program features a simple user interface: two list boxes with one vertical scroll bar located between them. The first list box contains the names of capitals, and the second list box contains the names of their corresponding countries. You cannot add, delete, or modify either list box. When you select a new capital, the corresponding country is also selected, and vice versa. When you move the thumb box of the scroll bar, both lists move simultaneously. If you double-click an item in either list, the application displays a message stating the capital of the currently selected country. To exit the program, use the Exit menu item.

Now compile and run the program. Experiment by scrolling the list boxes and making new selections. Also experiment with double-clicking items in either list. Try moving the scroll bar thumb box with the mouse or with the cursor control keys and watch the two lists move in sync.

> **Note:** Synchronizing the selections in both lists is a straightforward process. When you make a new selection, the list box notifies the parent window. The parent window in turn sets the same selection position in the other list box. Synchronizing the scroll bar movement requires some doing, however. The original program version displayed the vertical scroll bars of the list boxes. However, when the thumb boxes of these scroll bars moved, no notification messages were sent to the parent window, because the list's own scroll bar is part of the parent window and does not have a separate ID. Therefore, the two list boxes scrolled independently of each other, while maintaining the corresponding selection. This was not good enough.
>
> The first step to solve this problem is to remove the WS_VSCROLL style from both list boxes and maintain a selection at all times. The modified list boxes now scroll simultaneously, but the current selections change while scrolling.
>
> The second step of the solution is to create a vertical scroll bar control and place it between the list boxes. Because a scroll bar control sends a notification message to its parent window, you can move the current list selections in sync with the thumb box movement. Moreover, you also can move the thumb box when you scroll either list. This is the solution used in this application.

The Scrolling Lists Code

Now look at the code for the CTLLST3.EXE application. Listing 7.6 contains the source code for the CTLLST3.CPP program file. The CTLLST3.PRJ project file includes the CTLLST2.RC resource file and the OWL.DEF file.

Listing 7.6. The source code for the CTLLST3.CPP program file.

```
#include <stdlib.h>
#include <ctype.h>
#include <stdio.h>
#include <math.h>
#include <string.h>
#include <owl.h>
#include <static.h>
```

```cpp
#include <scrollba.h>
#include <listbox.h>

const Wtxt = 200;
const Htxt = 20;
const Wlst = 200;
const Hlst = 150;
const Wscr = 20;
const Hscr = Hlst;
const VertSpacing = 10;
const MaxString = 40;

// declare the ID constants for the various controls
#define ID_CITY_LST 101
#define ID_COUNTRY_LST 102
#define ID_SCROLL_SCR 103

// iterated function to update the selected list items
void updateSelection(Pvoid P, Pvoid Param)
{
  PTListBox pL = PTListBox(P);
  pL->SetSelIndex(*Pint(Param));
}

// declare the custom application class as
// a subclass of TApplication
class TWinApp : public TApplication
{
public:
  TWinApp(LPSTR     AName,           // application name
          HINSTANCE hInstance,       // instance handle
          HINSTANCE hPrevInstance,   // previous instance handle
          LPSTR     lpCmdLine,       // command-line arguments
          int       nCmdShow) :      // display command
          TApplication(AName, hInstance, hPrevInstance,
                    lpCmdLine, nCmdShow) {};

protected:
  virtual void InitMainWindow();
  virtual void InitInstance();
};

// use the _CLASSDEF macro to declare reference and pointer
// types related to the new TAppWindow class
_CLASSDEF(TAppWindow)
```

continues

Listing 7.6. continued

```
// expand the functionality of TWindow by deriving class TAppWindow
class TAppWindow : public TWindow
{
public:

  TAppWindow(PTWindowsObject AParent, LPSTR ATitle);

  // initialize the city and country lists
  virtual void InitLists();

  // handle the City list notification messages
  virtual void HandleCityLst(RTMessage Msg)
    = [ID_FIRST + ID_CITY_LST];

  // handle the Country list notification messages
  virtual void HandleCountryLst(RTMessage Msg)
    = [ID_FIRST + ID_COUNTRY_LST];

  // handle the scroll bar notification message
  virtual void HandleScrollScr(RTMessage Msg)
    = [ID_FIRST + ID_SCROLL_SCR];

  // handle closing the window
  virtual BOOL CanClose();

protected:
  PTListBox CityLst;
  PTListBox CountryLst;
  PTScrollBar ScrollScr;
};

TAppWindow::TAppWindow(PTWindowsObject AParent, LPSTR ATitle) :
                    TWindow(AParent, ATitle)
{
  char s[81];
  int x0 = 100;
  int y0 = 50;
  int x = x0;
  int y = y0;

  // load the menu resource
  AssignMenu("EXITMENU");
```

```cpp
  // create the city list box and its label
  strcpy(s, "City List");
  new TStatic(this, -1, s, x, y, Wtxt, Htxt, strlen(s));
  y += Htxt + VertSpacing;
  CityLst = new TListBox(this, ID_CITY_LST, x, y, Wlst, Hlst);
  // turn off the automatic sorting of the city list member
  CityLst->Attr.Style &= ~LBS_SORT;
  // hide the vertical scroll bar
  CityLst->Attr.Style &= ~WS_VSCROLL;
  y = y0 + Htxt + VertSpacing;
  x += Wlst;
  ScrollScr = new TScrollBar(this, ID_SCROLL_SCR,
                              x, y, Wscr, Hscr - 4, FALSE);
  x += Wscr;
  y = y0;
  // create the country list box and its label
  strcpy(s, "Country List");
  new TStatic(this, -1, s, x, y, Wtxt, Htxt, strlen(s));
  y += Htxt + VertSpacing;
  CountryLst = new TListBox(this, ID_COUNTRY_LST, x, y, Wlst, Hlst);
  // turn off the automatic sorting of the country list member
  CountryLst->Attr.Style &= ~LBS_SORT;
  // hide the vertical scroll bar
  CountryLst->Attr.Style &= ~WS_VSCROLL;
  // enable the keyboard handler
  EnableKBHandler();
}

void TAppWindow::InitLists()
{
  // add data in the city list box
  CityLst->AddString("Paris");
  CityLst->AddString("London");
  CityLst->AddString("Rome");
  CityLst->AddString("Bern");
  CityLst->AddString("Madrid");
  CityLst->AddString("Cairo");
  CityLst->AddString("Ankara");
  CityLst->AddString("Washington");
  CityLst->AddString("Tokyo");
  CityLst->AddString("Moscow");
  CityLst->AddString("Warsaw");
  CityLst->AddString("Seoul");
  CityLst->AddString("Lisbon");
  CityLst->AddString("Athens");
```

continues

Listing 7.6. continued

```
  // add data in the country list box
  CountryLst->AddString("France");
  CountryLst->AddString("The U.K.");
  CountryLst->AddString("Italy");
  CountryLst->AddString("Switzerland");
  CountryLst->AddString("Spain");
  CountryLst->AddString("Egypt");
  CountryLst->AddString("Turkey");
  CountryLst->AddString("The U.S.A.");
  CountryLst->AddString("Japan");
  CountryLst->AddString("Russia");
  CountryLst->AddString("Poland");
  CountryLst->AddString("South Korea");
  CountryLst->AddString("Portugal");
  CountryLst->AddString("Greece");
  // select the first item in both list boxes
  CityLst->SetSelIndex(0);
  CountryLst->SetSelIndex(0);
  // set the range of the scroll bar control
  ScrollScr->SetRange(0, CityLst->GetCount()-1);
}

void TAppWindow::HandleCityLst(RTMessage Msg)
{
  int i;
  char city[MaxString+1];
  char country[MaxString];
  char message[2*MaxString+1];

  // determine the type of notification message
  switch (Msg.LP.Hi) {
    case LBN_SELCHANGE:
      // get the current selection index in the city list
      i = CityLst->GetSelIndex();
      CountryLst->SetSelIndex(i); // update country selection
      ScrollScr->SetPosition(i);  // update scroll bar control
      break;
    case LBN_DBLCLK:
      // get the selected string in both list boxes
      CityLst->GetSelString(city, MaxString);
      CountryLst->GetSelString(country, MaxString);
      // build and display a message
      sprintf(message, "The capital of %s is %s", country, city);
      MessageBox(HWindow, message, "Your Selection", MB_OK);
```

```cpp
      break;
  }
}

void TAppWindow::HandleCountryLst(RTMessage Msg)
{
  int i;
  char city[MaxString+1];
  char country[MaxString];
  char message[2*MaxString+1];

  // determine the type of notification message
  switch (Msg.LP.Hi) {
    case LBN_SELCHANGE:
      // get the current selection index in the country list
      i = CountryLst->GetSelIndex();
      CityLst->SetSelIndex(i); // update city selection
      ScrollScr->SetPosition(i); // update scroll bar control
      break;
    case LBN_DBLCLK:
      // get the selected string in both list boxes
      CityLst->GetSelString(city, MaxString);
      CountryLst->GetSelString(country, MaxString);
      // build and display a message
      sprintf(message, "The capital of %s is %s", country, city);
      MessageBox(HWindow, message, "Your Selection", MB_OK);
      break;
  }
}

void TAppWindow::HandleScrollScr(RTMessage Msg)
{
  // get the thumb position of the scroll bar control
  int i = ScrollScr->GetPosition();
  // select the city and country items that have the same
  // index as the thumb position
  ForEach(updateSelection, &i);
}

BOOL TAppWindow::CanClose()
{
  return MessageBox(HWindow, "Want to close this application",
                    "Query", MB_YESNO | MB_ICONQUESTION) == IDYES;
}
```

continues

Listing 7.6. continued

```
void TWinApp::InitMainWindow()
{
  MainWindow = new TAppWindow(NULL, Name);
}

void TWinApp::InitInstance()
{
  TApplication::InitInstance();
  // add data in the city and country list boxes
  PTAppWindow(MainWindow)->InitLists();
}

int PASCAL WinMain(HINSTANCE hInstance, HINSTANCE hPrevInstance,
                LPSTR lpCmdLine, int nCmdShow)
{
  TWinApp WinApp("Synchronized Lists Scrolling",
               hInstance, hPrevInstance, lpCmdLine, nCmdShow);
  WinApp.Run(); // run OWL application
  return WinApp.Status; // return application status
}
```

The program listing declares two sets of constants. The first set declares the dimensions of the controls. The second set of constants defines the control ID values. The program also declares an iterated function to demonstrate that the method for scrolling two list boxes can easily be expanded to scroll more list boxes synchronously. The iterated function applies a `PTListBox` typecast to the first parameter, `P`. The function also uses the second parameter with the `SetSelIndex` function to access the new selection position.

The program listing declares an application class and a window class. The window class `TAppWindow` declares a number of data members that are pointers to the controls owned by the window. The `TAppWindow` class also declares a constructor and a number of member functions that respond to the notification messages sent by the various controls.

The `TAppWindow` constructor loads the menu resource, creates instances for the application's controls, and enables the keyboard handler. Both list boxes are created with the `LBS_SORT` and `WS_VSCROLL` styles removed.

The `InitAppWindow` member function inserts data into the city and country list boxes, selects the first item in both list boxes, and sets the range of the scroll bar control. The application class's `InitInstance` member function calls the `InitAppWindow` function as part of the initialization of the window instances.

The `HandleCityLst` member function responds to the notification message sent by the city list box, which contains the names of the capitals. The function uses a `switch` statement to examine the value in the `Msg.LP.Hi` member and determine the notification message. If the `LBN_SELCHANGE` notification message is sent, the `HandleCityLst` function synchronizes the selections of the two list boxes by performing the following tasks:

1. Obtains the position of the new selection in the city list and stores it in the local variable `i`.
2. Selects the country list item at position `i` as the new selection of that list.
3. Updates the position of the scroll bar thumb box to match the selection position common to both list boxes.

If the `LBN_DBLCLK` notification message is sent, the function displays a message that uses the currently selected items in both lists.

The `HandleCountryLst` member function is similar to the `HandleCityLst` function. `HandleCountryLst` handles the changing of the city list selection when you alter the country list selection.

The `HandleScrollScr` member function moves the list boxes in synchronization with the scroll bar thumb box. The function obtains the current thumb box position and invokes the `ForEach` iterator as follows:

```
ForEach(updateSelection, &i);
```

The first argument is the name of the iterated function and the second argument is the pointer to variable `i`, which stores the new selection position.

Handling Multiple-Selection Lists

In this section I demonstrate the use of multiple-selection lists and focus on getting and setting the selection strings and their indices.

Note: Before looking at the test program and discuss its code, you need to know that there are two ways to make multiple selections in a list box. These modes depend on whether you set the LBS_EXTENDEDSEL style when you create a TListBox instance.

By setting this style, you can quickly extend the range of selected items by holding down the Shift key and clicking the mouse. If you choose this style, you must select blocks of contiguous items in the list box manually (that is, with the mouse or cursor keys). Using the SetSelIndexes member function, you can make your program select noncontiguous items. However, this approach requires extra effort on behalf of the application user and a few extra controls to support this type of selection.

If you do not set the LBS_EXTENDEDSEL style, you can easily make dispersed selections by clicking the individual items you want to select. The downside of this selection mode is that, to select it, you must click every item, including neighboring items. Choose the selection mode that you feel best meets the user interface requirements for your ObjectWindows applications.

The Multiple-Selection List Tester

This section presents a program that demonstrates how to set and query multiple selections in a list box. Figure 7.4 shows a sample session with the CTLLST4.EXE application and also shows the application's controls.

The following are the controls used by the test program and the operation they support:

- ☐ A multiple-selection list with the LBS_MULTIPLESEL style selected (but not the LBS_EXTENDEDSEL style). The strings in the list box are sorted in ascending order.

- ☐ A multiline edit box control labeled Names Box containing the names of the selected strings.

- ☐ A push button with the caption Get Names that copies the list box selections in the Names Box edit control. Each selection appears on a separate line in the edit box. Every time you click this button, you lose the previous contents of the Names Box edit control.

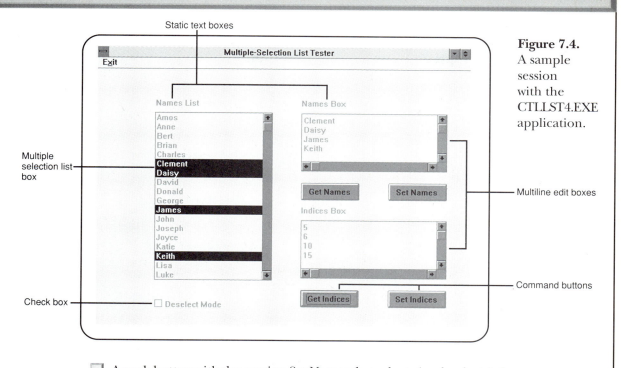

Figure 7.4. A sample session with the CTLLST4.EXE application.

- ☐ A push button with the caption Set Names that selects (or deselects) the list box items that match those in the Names Box edit control. The match does not have to be exact—the Names Box strings need only to match the first few characters of the list items.

- ☐ A multiline edit box control labeled Indices Box containing the indices of the selected strings.

- ☐ A push button with the caption Get Indices that writes the indices of the list box selections in the Indices Box edit control. The index of each selection appears on a separate line in the edit box. Every time you click this button, you lose the previous contents of the Indices Box edit control.

- ☐ A push button with the caption Set Indices. This push button selects (or deselects) the list box items by using the values in the Indices Box edit control.

- ☐ A check box control with the caption Deselect mode. This control determines whether the Set Names and Set Indices buttons select or deselect list items.

- ☐ The static text controls that label the list and edit boxes.

Now compile and run the program. The application initializes the list box with a number of names. This feature saves you the time and effort needed to enter the names yourself. Select a few list items and click the Get Names and Get Indices push buttons. The selected string and indices appear in the Names Box and Indices Box edit controls. To create partial names, edit the lines on the Names Box by deleting one or two trailing characters from each line. Click the Set Names push button. What do you see? The selections have not changed, because the strings in the Names Box still match the same list box selection.

Now type a new set of indices in the Indices Box and click the Set Indices push button. The program now displays a new set of selected items in the list box.

You can also make a new selection by deleting the text in the Names Box and typing names found in the list box. Click the Set Names button and view the new list box selections. When you are done experimenting with the program, click the Exit menu item or press Alt-X.

The Multiple-Selection List Tester Code

The multiple-selection list tester application drills the `GetSelIndexes`, `GetSelStrings`, `SetSelIndexes`, and `SetSelStrings` member functions of the `TListBox` class. Listing 7.7 contains the source code for the CTLLST4.CPP multiple-selection list tester program file.

Listing 7.7. The source code for the CTLLST4.CPP program file.

```
#include <stdlib.h>
#include <ctype.h>
#include <stdio.h>
#include <math.h>
#include <string.h>
#include <owl.h>
#include <static.h>
#include <edit.h>
#include <button.h>
#include <scrollba.h>
#include <listbox.h>
#include <checkbox.h>
```

```cpp
// declare the constants for the dimensions and spacing
// of the various controls
const Wtxt = 100;
const Htxt = 20;
const TxtVertSpacing = 20;
const Wlst = 200;
const Hlst = 300;
const LstHorzSpacing = 50;
const LstVertSpacing = 10;
const Wbox = 250;
const Hbox = 85;
const BoxVertSpacing = 10;
const Wbtn = 100;
const Hbtn = 20;
const BtnHorzSpacing = 50;
const BtnVertSpacing = 5;
const Wchk = 200;
const Hchk = 20;

const MaxString = 40;
const MaxSelections = 35; // maximum number of selections

// declare the ID constants for the various controls
#define ID_NAMES_LST 101
#define ID_NAMES_EDIT 102
#define ID_INDICES_EDIT 103
#define ID_GETNAMES_BTN 104
#define ID_SETNAMES_BTN 105
#define ID_GETINDICES_BTN 106
#define ID_SETINDICES_BTN 107
#define ID_SELECT_CHK 108

// declare the custom application class as
// a subclass of TApplication
class TWinApp : public TApplication
{
public:
  TWinApp(LPSTR     AName,           // application name
          HINSTANCE hInstance,       // instance handle
          HINSTANCE hPrevInstance,   // previous instance handle
          LPSTR     lpCmdLine,       // command-line arguments
          int       nCmdShow) :      // display command
          TApplication(AName, hInstance, hPrevInstance,
                       lpCmdLine, nCmdShow) {};
```

continues

Listing 7.7. continued

```
protected:
  virtual void InitMainWindow();
  virtual void InitInstance();
};

// use the _CLASSDEF macro to declare reference and pointer
// types related to the new TAppWindow class
_CLASSDEF(TAppWindow)

// expand the functionality of TWindow by deriving class TAppWindow
class TAppWindow : public TWindow
{
public:

  TAppWindow(PTWindowsObject AParent, LPSTR ATitle);

  // initialize the list box
  virtual void InitNamesLst();

  // class destructor to deallocate the dynamic space for
  // the names pointers.
  ~TAppWindow();

  // handle getting the selections
  virtual void HandleGetNamesBtn(RTMessage Msg)
    = [ID_FIRST + ID_GETNAMES_BTN];

  // handle setting the selections
  virtual void HandleSetNamesBtn(RTMessage Msg)
    = [ID_FIRST + ID_SETNAMES_BTN];

  // handle getting the selection indices
  virtual void HandleGetIndicesBtn(RTMessage Msg)
    = [ID_FIRST + ID_GETINDICES_BTN];

  // handle setting the selection indices
  virtual void HandleSetIndicesBtn(RTMessage Msg)
    = [ID_FIRST + ID_SETINDICES_BTN];

  // handle closing the window
  virtual BOOL CanClose();

protected:
  PTListBox NamesLst;
```

```
    PTEdit NamesBox;
    PTEdit IndicesBox;
    PTButton GetNamesBtn;
    PTButton SetNamesBtn;
    PTButton GetIndicesBtn;
    PTButton SetIndicesBtn;
    PTCheckBox SelectChk;

    // array of string pointers
    LPSTR names[MaxSelections];
    // array of integers to store the selection indices
    int indices[MaxSelections];
};

TAppWindow::TAppWindow(PTWindowsObject AParent, LPSTR ATitle) :
                    TWindow(AParent, ATitle)
{
  char s[81];
  int x0 = 100;
  int y0 = 10;
  int x = x0;
  int y = y0;

  // load the menu resource
  AssignMenu("EXITMENU");

  // create the name list box and its label
  strcpy(s, "Names List");
  new TStatic(this, -1, s, x, y, Wtxt, Htxt, strlen(s));
  y += Htxt + TxtVertSpacing;
  NamesLst = new TListBox(this, ID_NAMES_LST, x, y, Wlst, Hlst);
  // set the multiple-selection style
  NamesLst->Attr.Style |= LBS_MULTIPLESEL;
  // create the Deselect Mode check box
  y += Hlst + LstVertSpacing;
  SelectChk = new TCheckBox(this, ID_SELECT_CHK, "Deselect Mode",
                    x, y, Wchk, Hchk, NULL);

  x0 += Wlst + LstHorzSpacing;
  x = x0;
  y = y0;
  // creates the multiline Names Box edit control and its label
  strcpy(s, "Names Box");
  new TStatic(this, -1, s, x, y, Wtxt, Htxt, strlen(s));
```

continues

Listing 7.7. continued

```
    y += Htxt + TxtVertSpacing;
    NamesBox = new TEdit(this, ID_NAMES_EDIT, "",
                    x, y, Wbox, Hbox, 0, TRUE);

    // create the Get Names button
    y += Hbox + BoxVertSpacing;
    GetNamesBtn = new TButton(this, ID_GETNAMES_BTN, "Get Names",
                    x, y, Wbtn, Hbtn, FALSE);

    // create the Set Names button
    x += Wbtn + BtnHorzSpacing;
    SetNamesBtn = new TButton(this, ID_SETNAMES_BTN, "Set Names",
                    x, y, Wbtn, Hbtn, FALSE);

    x = x0;
    y += Hbtn + BtnVertSpacing;
    // create the multiline Indices Box edit control and its label
    strcpy(s, "Indices Box");
    new TStatic(this, -1, s, x, y, Wtxt, Htxt, strlen(s));
    y += Htxt + TxtVertSpacing;
    IndicesBox = new TEdit(this, ID_INDICES_EDIT, "",
                    x, y, Wbox, Hbox, 0, TRUE);

    // create the GetIndices button
    y += Hbox + BoxVertSpacing;
    GetIndicesBtn = new TButton(this, ID_GETINDICES_BTN, "Get Indices",
                    x, y, Wbtn, Hbtn, FALSE);

    // create the Set Indices button
    x += Wbtn + BtnHorzSpacing;
    SetIndicesBtn = new TButton(this, ID_SETINDICES_BTN, "Set Indices",
                    x, y, Wbtn, Hbtn, FALSE);

    // allocate the dynamic space for the array of strings accessed
    // by the array of pointers names
    for (int i = 0; i < MaxSelections; i++)
        names[i] = new char[MaxString + 1];

    // enable the keyboard handler
    EnableKBHandler();
}

TAppWindow::~TAppWindow()
{
```

Scroll Bars, List Boxes, and Combo Boxes

```cpp
  // deallocate the dynamic string space
  for (int i = 0; i < MaxSelections; i++)
    delete names[i];
}

void TAppWindow::InitNamesLst()
{
  // add names in the Names list box
  NamesLst->AddString("John");
  NamesLst->AddString("Robert");
  NamesLst->AddString("Melody");
  NamesLst->AddString("Charles");
  NamesLst->AddString("Olivia");
  NamesLst->AddString("Richard");
  NamesLst->AddString("James");
  NamesLst->AddString("Anne");
  NamesLst->AddString("Keith");
  NamesLst->AddString("Brian");
  NamesLst->AddString("Lisa");
  NamesLst->AddString("Margie");
  NamesLst->AddString("Thomas");
  NamesLst->AddString("Joseph");
  NamesLst->AddString("Donald");
  NamesLst->AddString("Bert");
  NamesLst->AddString("George");
  NamesLst->AddString("Ronald");
  NamesLst->AddString("Katie");
  NamesLst->AddString("Susan");
  NamesLst->AddString("Joyce");
  NamesLst->AddString("David");
  NamesLst->AddString("Paul");
  NamesLst->AddString("Mark");
  NamesLst->AddString("Luke");
  NamesLst->AddString("Amos");
  NamesLst->AddString("Matthew");
  NamesLst->AddString("Mary");
  NamesLst->AddString("Patrick");
  NamesLst->AddString("Clement");
  NamesLst->AddString("Daisy");
}

void TAppWindow::HandleGetNamesBtn(RTMessage Msg)
{
  char s[MaxString+1];
  // get the selected strings
```

continues

Listing 7.7. continued

```
  int n = NamesLst->GetSelStrings(names, MaxSelections, MaxString);
  // exit if n is negative
  if (n < 0) return;
  // clear the Names Box edit control
  NamesBox->SetText("");
  // insert the selected strings in the Names Box control
  for (int i = 0; i < n; i++) {
    sprintf(s, "%s\r\n", names[i]);
    NamesBox->Insert(s);
  }
}

void TAppWindow::HandleSetNamesBtn(RTMessage Msg)
{
  // get the number of lines in the Names Box edit control
  int n = NamesBox->GetNumLines();
  // get the select status from the Deselect Mode check box
  BOOL shouldSet =
    (SelectChk->GetCheck() == BF_UNCHECKED) ? TRUE : FALSE;
  // read the lines from the Names Box control
  for (int i = 0; i < n; i++) {
    NamesBox->GetLine(names[i], MaxString, i);
  }
  // select the strings in the Names List control using the
  // array of pointers names
  NamesLst->SetSelStrings(names, n, shouldSet);
}

void TAppWindow::HandleGetIndicesBtn(RTMessage Msg)
{
  char s[MaxString+1];
  // get the selected indices
  int n = NamesLst->GetSelIndexes(indices, MaxSelections);
  // exit if n is negative
  if (n < 0) return;
  // clear the Indices Box edit control
  IndicesBox->SetText("");
  // insert the selected indices in the Indices Box control
  for (int i = 0; i < n; i++) {
    sprintf(s, "%d\r\n", indices[i]);
    IndicesBox->Insert(s);
  }
}
```

```cpp
void TAppWindow::HandleSetIndicesBtn(RTMessage Msg)
{
  char s[MaxString + 1];
  // get the number of lines in the Indices Box edit control
  // subtract 1 for the extra blank line in the text box
  int n = IndicesBox->GetNumLines() - 1;
  // get the select status from the Deselect Mode check box
  BOOL shouldSet =
    (SelectChk->GetCheck() == BF_UNCHECKED) ? TRUE : FALSE;
  // read the lines from the Names Box control
  for (int i = 0; i < n; i++) {
    IndicesBox->GetLine(s, MaxString, i);
    indices[i] = atoi(s);
  }
  // select the strings in the Names List control using the
  // array of integers indices
  NamesLst->SetSelIndexes(indices, n, shouldSet);
}

BOOL TAppWindow::CanClose()
{
  return MessageBox(HWindow, "Want to close this application",
                    "Query", MB_YESNO | MB_ICONQUESTION) == IDYES;
}

void TWinApp::InitMainWindow()
{
  MainWindow = new TAppWindow(NULL, Name);
}

void TWinApp::InitInstance()
{
  TApplication::InitInstance();
  // add data in the Names List control
  PTAppWindow(MainWindow)->InitNamesLst();
}

int PASCAL WinMain(HINSTANCE hInstance, HINSTANCE hPrevInstance,
                   LPSTR lpCmdLine, int nCmdShow)
{
  TWinApp WinApp("Multiple-Selection List Tester",
                 hInstance, hPrevInstance, lpCmdLine, nCmdShow);
  WinApp.Run(); // run OWL application
  return WinApp.Status; // return application status
}
```

The program listing declares three sets of constants. The first set specifies the dimensions and spacing for the various application controls. The second set declares the maximum string size and maximum number of selections. The third set establishes the ID numbers for the various controls.

The test program declares an application class and a window class. The `TAppWindow` class declares two sets of data members. The first set represents pointers to the various controls used in the application. The second set of data members contains the array of string pointers, `names`, and the array of integers, `indices`. Both arrays have `MaxSelections` members.

The `TAppWindow` class declares a class constructor, destructor (something new), and a collection of member functions. The class destructor is needed to remove the dynamic strings created by the constructor.

The `TAppWindow` constructor loads the menu resources, creates the various controls, creates the array of dynamic strings, and enables the keyboard handler. The constructor sets the style for `TListBox` instance to include the `LBS_MULTIPLESEL` style. If you want the list box selections to extend with the Shift key, simply add ¦ `LBS_EXTENDEDSEL` to the style-setting expression.

The `InitAppWindow` member function inserts a number of names into the multiline list box. The application class's `InitInstance` member function invokes the `InitAppWindow` as part of the process of initializing new window instances.

The `HandleGetNamesBtn` member function responds to the notification message that is sent when the Get Names push button is clicked. The function performs the following tasks:

1. Invokes the `GetSelString` function to obtain the list box selections. These selections are copied to the string array that is accessed by the `names` array of pointers. The function call also specifies that up to `MaxSelections` can be copied and that up to `MaxString` characters can be copied to each string. The function result is assigned to the local variable `n`.

2. Exits the `HandleGetNamesBtn` function if the variable `n` stores a negative value.

3. Clears the text in the Names Box edit control.

4. Uses a loop to copy the strings (accessed by the `names` array) into separate lines in the Names Box edit control.

The `HandleSetNamesBtn` member function responds to the notification message of the Set Names push button control. The function carries out the following tasks:

1. Obtains the number of lines in the Names Box control.

2. Obtains the check state of the Deselect Mode check box. The function assigns a Boolean value (equivalent to the check state) to the local variable shouldSet.

3. Copies the lines of the Names Box control to the string array accessed by the array of pointers, names.

4. Selects the matching list items by calling the SetSelStrings function. The function call specifies the names, n, and shouldSet variables as the arguments for the Prefix, NumSelections, and ShouldSet parameters, respectively.

The HandleGetIndicesBtn member function responds to the notification message sent by the Get Indices push button control. The function performs the following tasks:

1. Invokes the GetSelIndexes function to obtain the list box selections. These selections are copied to the integer array indices. The function call also specifies that up to MaxSelections indices can be copied to the array indices. The function result is assigned to the local variable n.

2. Exits the HandleGetIndicesBtn function if the variable n stores a negative value.

3. Clears the text in the Indices Box edit control.

4. Uses a loop to convert the selection indices to their string images and displays these string separate lines in the Indices Box edit control.

The HandleSetIndicesBtn member function responds to the notification message of the Set Indices push button control. The function carries out the following tasks:

1. Obtains the number of lines in the Indices Box control. This task subtracts 1 from the result of the GetNumLines function, because there is always an extra blank line in the Indices Box control.

2. Obtains the check state of the Deselect Mode check box. The function assigns a Boolean value, equivalent to the check state, to the local variable shouldSet.

3. Copies each line of the Indices Box control to a temporary string, converts that string into an int value, and stores that integer in a member of the indices array.

4. Selects the matching list items by calling the `SetSelIndexes` function. The function call specifies the `indices`, `n`, and `shouldSet` variables as the arguments for the `Indexes`, `NumSelections`, and `ShouldSet` parameters, respectively.

The Combo Box Control

Windows supports the combo box control, which combines an edit box with a list box. Thus, with a combo box, you can select either an item in the list box component or type your own input. The list box part of the combo box contains convenient or frequently used selections. A combo box, unlike a list box, does not restrict your choice of items to the list box.

There are three kinds of combo boxes: simple, drop-down, and drop-down list. The simple combo box includes an edit box and a list box that is always displayed. The drop-down combo box differs from the simple type in that a list box appears only when you click the down scroll arrow. The drop-down list combo box provides a drop-down list that appears only when you click the down scroll arrow. This kind of combo box includes an edit box. However, you cannot change the edit box's contents.

The `TComboBox` Class

ObjectWindows offers the `TComboBox` class, a descendant of `TListBox`, to support combo box controls. `TComboBox` inherits the list manipulation functionality from the `TListBox` class. Combo boxes support only single-selection list boxes. The `TComboBox` class contains three constructors. I will focus on the constructor that enables you to create `TComboBox` instances from scratch. This constructor is declared as follows:

```
TComboBox(PTWindowsObject AParent, int AnId, int X, int Y, int W,
         int H, DWORD AStyle, WORD ATextLen,
         PTModule AModule = NULL);
```

The `AParent` parameter is the pointer to the parent window. The `AnId` parameter specifies the unique ID of the control. The `X`, `Y`, `W`, and `H` parameters specify the location and dimensions of the control. The `AStyle` parameter specifies the combo box style. The arguments for this parameter are either `CBS_SIMPLE` for a simple combo box, `CBS_DROPDOWN` for a drop-down combo box, or `CBS_DROPDOWNLIST` for a drop-down list combo box. The instances of `TComboBox` are created with default styles that include `WS_CHILD`, `WS_VISIBLE`, `WS_GROUP`, `WS_TABSTOP`, `CBS_SORT`, `CBS_AUTOHSCROLL`, and `WS_VSCROLL`. Table 7.4 lists the more frequently used styles for the combo box controls.

Table 7.4. The styles for the combo box control.

Style	Meaning
CBS_AUTOHSCROLL	Automatically scrolls the text in the edit control to the right when you enter a character at the end of the line. Removing this style limits the text to the characters that fit inside the rectangular boundary of the edit control.
CBS_DROPDOWN	Specifies a drop-down combo box.
CBS_DROPDOWNLIST	Designates a drop-down list combo box.
CBS_SIMPLE	Specifies a simple combo box.
CBS_SORT	Automatically sorts the items in the list box.

`TComboBox` implements a number of member functions that manipulate the text in the edit control and show or hide the list box. The member functions `Clear`, `SetText`, `GetText`, `GetTextLen`, `GetEditSel`, and `SetEditSel` manipulate the text in the edit control. The parameterless `ShowList` and `HideList` member functions show and hide the list box component of drop-down and drop-down list combo boxes. Member functions inherited from `TListBox` let you manipulate the contents of the list box.

The edit control manipulation member functions include the following:

- The parameterless `Clear` member function, which clears the text in edit control of a combo box.

- The `GetEditSel` member function, which returns the starting and ending positions of the selected text. The declaration of the `GetEditSel` function is

    ```
    int GetEditSel(Rint StartPos, Rint EndPos);
    ```

    `StartPos` and `EndPos` are reference parameters that return the starting and ending character positions of the selected text.

- The `GetText` member function, which copies the text in the edit control to a string. The declaration of the `GetText` function is

    ```
    int GetText(LPSTR AString, int MaxChars);
    ```

The parameter `AString` is the pointer to the string receiving up to `MaxChars` characters from the edit control. The function returns the actual number of characters that were copied.

- The parameterless `GetTextLen` member function, which returns the length of the text in the edit control of a combo box.

- The `SetEditSel` member function, which enables you to define the selected text in the edit control by specifying the starting and ending character positions of the selected text. The declaration of the `SetEditSel` function is

    ```
    int SetEditSel(int StartPos, int EndPos);
    ```

    The `StartPos` and `EndPos` parameters specify the newly selected text.

- The `SetText` member function, which selects the first item in the combo list box that begins with a specified string. The declaration of the `SetText` function is

    ```
    void SetText(LPSTR AString);
    ```

    The parameter `AString` is the pointer to the search string. The function searches for a list item with the first few characters that match the search string. If a match is found, the matching list member is selected. However, if no match is found, the search string appears as selected text in the edit control.

The member functions that show or hide the list box component of a drop-down or drop-down list combo boxes are

- The parameterless `ShowList` member function, which shows the list box associated with a combo box.

- The parameterless `HideList` member function, which hides the list box associated with a combo box.

Tip: You need the `ShowList` and `HideList` member functions only when you want to manipulate the visibility of the list box through notification messages sent by other controls, such as check boxes or push buttons.

Responding to Combo Box Notification Messages

Combo boxes send the same types of notification messages to their parent windows as list boxes do. The owner window can respond to the notification messages by using child-ID member functions.

> **Tip:** The combo box LBN_KILLFOCUS notification message offers an interesting feature. When you type any character in the edit box area of a combo box, the combo box sends the LBN_KILLFOCUS notification message to its owner. You can use this notification message to search for the first list item that matches the character you type. Thus you can use the LBN_KILLFOCUS message to make the combo box more interactive. The next application demonstrates this feature.

Combo Boxes as History List Boxes

A history list box is a special combo box that inserts new edit control strings into the list box in chronological order. History list boxes typically follow these rules of operation:

- ☐ The combo list box removes the CBS_SORT style to insert the list items chronologically. New items are inserted at position 0, pushing the older items further down the list. The oldest item is the one at the bottom of the list. Thus the history list box behaves like a queue structure.

- ☐ To prevent using up memory, history list boxes usually limit the number of items you can insert. This conservative scheme requires that the oldest list item be removed once the number of list item reaches a maximum limit.

- ☐ If the edit control contains a string without an exact match in the accompanying list box, the edit control string is inserted as a new member at position 0.

- ☐ If the edit control contains a string with an exact match in the accompanying list box, the matching list member is moved to position 0, which is the top of the list. Of course, this process involves first deleting the matching list member from its current position and then reinserting it at position 0.

A history list box is really a combo box that manipulates its edit control and list box items in a certain way. You don't need to drive a descendant of TComboBox to add new member functions.

The COCA Version 4 Application

The fourth version of the calculator application (COCA) is actually derived from the second version, not the third one (except that the feature of substituting the # character in the operand controls with the previous result is also included). Figure 7.5 shows a sample session with the CTLLST5.EXE application.

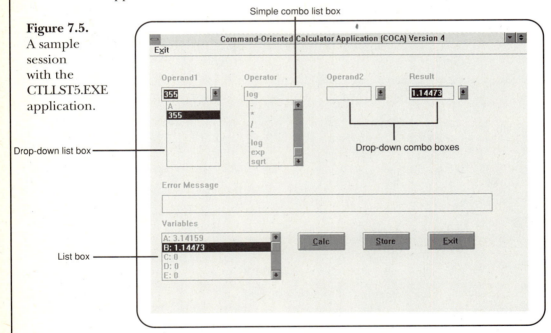

Figure 7.5. A sample session with the CTLLST5.EXE application.

In the CTLLST5.EXE application, the following controls are used:

- An Operand1 drop-down combo box, which operates like a history list box.
- An Operator simple combo box. This combo box contains the list of supported operators and functions. The functions are log, exp, and sqrt.

Scroll Bars, List Boxes, and Combo Boxes

The program handles the `LBN_KILLFOCUS` notification messages sent by this control to select the `log`, `exp`, and `sqrt` functions when you simply type the letters `l`, `e`, and `s`, respectively.

- An Operand2 drop-down combo box, which operates like a history list box.
- A Result drop-down combo box, which operates like a history list box.
- The error message edit box.
- The Variables list box, which supports a new variable name substitution feature. If you enter the @ character in the operand edit boxes and double-click a Variables list item, the number stored in that item replaces the @ character in operand edit boxes.
- The Calc push button control.
- The Store push button control, which stores the current result (the number in the edit control of the Result combo box) in the currently selected item of the Variables list box.
- The Exit push button control.

Now compile and run the program. Experiment by entering and executing numbers and operators or functions. Notice that the combo boxes for the operands and the result are entered in their accompanying list boxes in a chronological order. The operand combo boxes remember the last 35 different operands you entered. The Result combo box remembers the last 35 different results calculated. The Result combo box acts as a temporary transient memory. You can select older results and store them in the Variables list box. Experiment with selecting the supported functions by typing the first letter of the function's name. In addition, type the @ character in the edit box of either operand combo box and double-click an item in the Variables list box. This action immediately replaces the @ character with the number in the list box item that you double-clicked.

The Code for the COCA Version 4 Application

Now look at the code for the COCA version 4 application. Listing 7.8 shows the source code for the CTLLST5.H header file.

Listing 7.8. The source code for the CTLLST5.H header file.

```
#define ID_CALC_BTN 110
#define ID_STORE_BTN 111
#define ID_EXIT_BTN 112
```

Listing 7.9 contains the script for the CTLLST5.RC resource file. The resource file defines the accelerator keys and menu resources.

Listing 7.9. The script for the CTLLST5.RC resource file.

```
#include <windows.h>
#include <owlrc.h>
#include "ctllst5.h"

BUTTONS ACCELERATORS
BEGIN
     "c", ID_CALC_BTN, ALT
     "s", ID_STORE_BTN, ALT
     "e", ID_EXIT_BTN, ALT
END

EXITMENU MENU LOADONCALL MOVEABLE PURE DISCARDABLE
BEGIN
         MENUITEM "E&xit", CM_EXIT
END
```

Listing 7.10 shows the source code for the CTLLST5.CPP program file. The program listing declares three sets of constants. The first set specifies the dimensions and spacing for the various application controls. The second set declares the maximum string size and maximum number of selections. The third set establishes the ID numbers for the various controls.

Listing 7.10. The source code for the CTLLST5.CPP program file.

```
#include <stdlib.h>
#include <ctype.h>
#include <stdio.h>
#include <math.h>
#include <string.h>
#include <owl.h>
```

Scroll Bars, List Boxes, and Combo Boxes

```cpp
#include <static.h>
#include <edit.h>
#include <button.h>
#include <listbox.h>
#include <combobox.h>
#include "ctllst5.h"

// declare the constants that represent the sizes of the controls
const Wlbl = 100;
const Hlbl = 20;
const LblVertSpacing = 10;
const LblHorzSpacing = 40;
const Wbox = 100;
const Hbox = 25;
const BoxVertSpacing = 10;
const BoxHorzSpacing = 40;
const WLongbox = 4 * (Wbox + BoxHorzSpacing);
const Wlst = 200;
const Hlst = 100;
const LstVertSpacing = 10;
const LstHorzSpacing = 40;
const Hbtn = 30;
const Wbtn = 60;
const BtnHorzSpacing = 30;
const BtnVertSpacing = 10;
const Wcmb = 100;
const Hcmb = 120;
const CmbVertSpacing = 10;
const CmbHorzSpacing = 40;

const MaxEditLen = 30;
// maximum number of items in a combo box that doubles as
// history list box
const MaxHistory = 30;

// declare the ID_XXXX constants for the edit boxes
#define ID_OPERAND1_CMB 101
#define ID_OPERATOR_CMB 102
#define ID_OPERAND2_CMB 103
#define ID_RESULT_CMB 104
#define ID_ERRMSG_EDIT 105
#define ID_VARIABLE_LST 106

// declare the custom application class as
// a subclass of TApplication
class TWinApp : public TApplication
```

continues

385

Listing 7.10. continued

```
{
public:
   TWinApp(LPSTR     AName,           // application name
           HINSTANCE hInstance,       // instance handle
           HINSTANCE hPrevInstance,   // previous instance handle
           LPSTR     lpCmdLine,       // command-line arguments
           int       nCmdShow) :      // display command
           TApplication(AName, hInstance, hPrevInstance,
                     lpCmdLine, nCmdShow) {};

protected:
  virtual void InitMainWindow();
  virtual void InitInstance();
};

// use the _CLASSDEF macro to declare reference and pointer
// types related to the new TAppWindow class
_CLASSDEF(TAppWindow)

// expand the functionality of TWindow by deriving class TAppWindow
class TAppWindow : public TWindow
{
public:

  TAppWindow(PTWindowsObject AParent, LPSTR ATitle);

  // initialize the instances of TAppWindow
  virtual void InitAppWindow();

  // handle the notification messages from the Operator combo box
  virtual void HandleOperatorCmb(RTMessage Msg)
    = [ID_FIRST + ID_OPERATOR_CMB];

  // handle the calculation
  virtual void HandleCalcBtn(RTMessage Msg)
    = [ID_FIRST + ID_CALC_BTN];

  // handle the accelerator key for the Calculate button
  virtual void CMCalcBtn(RTMessage Msg)
    = [CM_FIRST + ID_CALC_BTN];

  // handle storing the result in a variable
  virtual void HandleStoreBtn(RTMessage Msg)
    = [ID_FIRST + ID_STORE_BTN];
```

Scroll Bars, List Boxes, and Combo Boxes

```cpp
    // handle the accelerator key for the Store button
    virtual void CMStoreBtn(RTMessage Msg)
      = [CM_FIRST + ID_STORE_BTN];

    // handle exiting the application
    virtual void HandleExitBtn(RTMessage Msg)
      = [ID_FIRST + ID_EXIT_BTN];

    // handle the accelerator key for the Exit button
    virtual void CMExitBtn(RTMessage Msg)
      = [CM_FIRST + ID_EXIT_BTN];

    // handle the Variables list box when it gets the focus
    virtual void HandleVariableLst(RTMessage Msg)
      = [ID_FIRST + ID_VARIABLE_LST];

    // enable a push button control
    virtual void EnableButton(PTButton Btn)
    { EnableWindow(Btn->HWindow, TRUE); }

    // disable a push button control
    virtual void DisableButton(PTButton Btn)
    { EnableWindow(Btn->HWindow, FALSE); }

    // handle closing the window
    virtual BOOL CanClose();

protected:
   PTComboBox Operand1Cmb;
   PTComboBox OperatorCmb;
   PTComboBox Operand2Cmb;
   PTComboBox ResultCmb;
   PTEdit ErrMsgBox;
   PTListBox VariableLst;
   PTButton CalcBtn;
   PTButton StoreBtn;
   PTButton ExitBtn;

   BOOL InError;

   // obtain a number of the Variable list box
   double getVar(int lineNum);

   // store a number in the selected item of the Variable list box
   void putVar(double x);
```

continues

Listing 7.10. continued

```
  // update the combo box with the text in the
  // accompanying edit box, assuming that the text
  // is not already in the box
  void updateComboBox(PTComboBox P);
};

TAppWindow::TAppWindow(PTWindowsObject AParent, LPSTR ATitle) :
                      TWindow(AParent, ATitle)
{
  char s[81];
  int x0 = 20;
  int y0 = 30;
  int x = x0, y = y0;

  // load the menu resource
  AssignMenu("EXITMENU");

  Attr.Style |= WS_MAXIMIZE;

  // create the first set of labels for the edit boxes
  strcpy(s, "Operand1");
  new TStatic(this, -1, s, x, y, Wlbl, Hlbl, strlen(s));
  strcpy(s, "Operator");
  x += Wlbl + LblHorzSpacing;
  new TStatic(this, -1, s, x, y, Wlbl, Hlbl, strlen(s));
  strcpy(s, "Operand2");
  x += Wlbl + LblHorzSpacing;
  new TStatic(this, -1, s, x, y, Wlbl, Hlbl, strlen(s));
  x += Wlbl + LblHorzSpacing;
  strcpy(s, "Result");
  new TStatic(this, -1, s, x, y, Wlbl, Hlbl, strlen(s));

  // create the Operand1, Operator, Operand2, and Result
  // combo list boxes
  x = x0;
  y += Hlbl + LblVertSpacing;
  Operand1Cmb = new TComboBox(this, ID_OPERAND1_CMB, x, y,
                              Wcmb, Hcmb, CBS_DROPDOWN, 0);
  Operand1Cmb->Attr.Style &= ~CBS_SORT;
  // create the Operator combo box
  x += Wcmb + CmbHorzSpacing;
  OperatorCmb = new TComboBox(this, ID_OPERATOR_CMB, x, y,
                              Wcmb, Hcmb, CBS_SIMPLE, 0);
  // force conversion of letters to uppercase
```

Scroll Bars, List Boxes, and Combo Boxes

```
    OperatorCmb->Attr.Style &= ~CBS_SORT;
    x += Wcmb + CmbHorzSpacing;
    Operand2Cmb = new TComboBox(this, ID_OPERAND2_CMB, x, y,
                        Wcmb, Hcmb, CBS_DROPDOWN, 0);
    Operand2Cmb->Attr.Style &= ~CBS_SORT;
    x += Wcmb + CmbHorzSpacing;
    ResultCmb = new TComboBox(this, ID_RESULT_CMB,
                        x, y, Wcmb, Hcmb, CBS_DROPDOWN, 0);
    ResultCmb->Attr.Style &= ~CBS_SORT;
    // create the static text and edit box for the error message
    x = x0;
    y += Hcmb + CmbVertSpacing;
    strcpy(s, "Error Message");
    new TStatic(this, -1, s, x, y, Wlbl, Hlbl, strlen(s));
    y += Hlbl + LblVertSpacing;
    ErrMsgBox = new TEdit(this, ID_ERRMSG_EDIT, "", x, y,
                        WLongbox, Hbox, 0, FALSE);
    // create the static text and list box for the single-letter
    // variable selection
    y += Hbox + BoxVertSpacing;
    strcpy(s, "Variables");
    new TStatic(this, -1, s, x, y, Wlbl, Hlbl, strlen(s));
    y += Hlbl + LblVertSpacing;
    VariableLst = new TListBox(this, ID_VARIABLE_LST,
                        x, y, Wlst, Hlst);
    // create the Calc push button
    x += Wlst + BtnHorzSpacing;
    CalcBtn = new TButton(this, ID_CALC_BTN, "&Calc",
                        x, y, Wbtn, Hbtn, FALSE);

    // create the Store Btn
    x += Wbtn + BtnHorzSpacing;
    StoreBtn = new TButton(this, ID_STORE_BTN, "&Store",
                        x, y, Wbtn, Hbtn, FALSE);

    // Create the Exit Btn
    x += Wbtn + BtnHorzSpacing;
    ExitBtn = new TButton(this, ID_EXIT_BTN, "&Exit",
                        x, y, Wbtn, Hbtn, FALSE);

    // clear the InError flag
    InError = FALSE;

    // enable keyboard handler
    EnableKBHandler();
```

continues

Listing 7.10. continued

```
}

void TAppWindow::InitAppWindow()
{
  char c;
  char s[MaxEditLen];

  // disable the Store button
  EnableWindow(StoreBtn->HWindow, FALSE);
  // build the initial contents of the Variable list box
  for (c = 'Z'; c >= 'A'; c--) {
    sprintf(s, "%c: 0", c);
    VariableLst->AddString(s);
  }
  // select the first item
  VariableLst->SetSelIndex(0);

  // add the operators in the Operator combo box
  OperatorCmb->AddString("+");
  OperatorCmb->AddString("-");
  OperatorCmb->AddString("*");
  OperatorCmb->AddString("/");
  OperatorCmb->AddString("^");
  OperatorCmb->AddString("log");
  OperatorCmb->AddString("exp");
  OperatorCmb->AddString("sqrt");
}

void TAppWindow::HandleOperatorCmb(RTMessage Msg)
{
  char s[MaxEditLen+1];
  int i;

  // is the notification message a kill focus message?
  if (Msg.LP.Hi == LBN_KILLFOCUS) {
    // get the text in the Operator combo box edit area
    OperatorCmb->GetText(s, MaxEditLen);
    // use it to search for a matching list item
    OperatorCmb->SetText(s);
  }
}

void TAppWindow::HandleCalcBtn(RTMessage Msg)
{
```

```cpp
int opIndex;
double x, y, z, result;
char opStr[MaxEditLen+1];
char s[MaxEditLen+1];

// convert the string in the Result combo box to a double
ResultCmb->GetText(s, MaxEditLen);
result = atof(s);

// obtain the string in the Operand1 combo box
Operand1Cmb->GetText(s, MaxEditLen);
// does the Operand1Cmb contain the name
// of a single-letter variable?
if (isalpha(s[0]))
  // obtain value from the Variable list box control
  x = getVar(toupper(s[0]) - 'A');
// translate the # character into the value
// in the Result combo box
else if (s[0] == '#')
  x = result;
else
  // convert the string in the edit box area
  x = atof(s);

// obtain the string in the Operand2 combo box
Operand2Cmb->GetText(s, MaxEditLen);
// does the Operand2Cmb contain the name
// of a single-letter variable?
if (isalpha(s[0]))
  // obtain value from the Variable list box
  y =getVar(toupper(s[0]) - 'A');
// translate the # character into the value in
// the Result combo box
else if (s[0] == '#')
  y = result;
else
   // convert the string in the edit box area
  y = atof(s);

// obtain the string in the Operator combo box
OperatorCmb->GetText(opStr, MaxEditLen);

// clear the error message box
ErrMsgBox->Clear();
InError = FALSE;
```

continues

Listing 7.10. continued

```
// determine the requested operation using the FindExactString
// member function of TListBox
opIndex = OperatorCmb->FindExactString(opStr, -1);
switch (opIndex) {
  case 0: // + operator
    z = x + y;
    break;
  case 1: // - operator
    z = x - y;
    break;
  case 2: // * operator
    z = x * y;
    break;
  case 3: // / operator
    if (y != 0)
      z = x / y;
    else {
      z = 0;
      InError = TRUE;
      ErrMsgBox->SetText("Division-by-zero error");
    }
    break;
  case 4: // ^ operator
    if (x > 0)
      z = exp(y * log(x));
    else {
      InError = TRUE;
      ErrMsgBox->SetText(
        "Cannot raise the power of a negative number");
    }
    break;
  case 5: // the natural logarithm function
    if (x > 0)
      z = log(x);
    else {
      InError = TRUE;
      ErrMsgBox->SetText(
        "Invalid argument for the log(x) function");
    }
    break;
  case 6: // the exponential function
    if (x < 230)
      z = exp(x);
    else {
```

```
        InError = TRUE;
         ErrMsgBox->SetText(
           "Invalid argument for the exp(x) function");
      }
      break;
    case 7: // the square root function
      if (x >= 0)
        z = sqrt(x);
      else {
        InError = TRUE;
         ErrMsgBox->SetText(
           "Invalid argument for the sqrt(x) function");
      }
      break;
    default:
      InError = TRUE;
      ErrMsgBox->SetText("Invalid operator");
      break;
  }

  // display the result if no error has occurred
  if (!InError) {
    sprintf(s, "%g", z);
    ResultCmb->SetText(s);
    updateComboBox(ResultCmb);
    // enable the Store button
    EnableButton(StoreBtn);
  }
  else
    // disable the Store button
    DisableButton(StoreBtn);

  // update the operand combo boxes
  updateComboBox(Operand1Cmb);
  updateComboBox(Operand2Cmb);
}

void TAppWindow::CMCalcBtn(RTMessage Msg)
{
  HandleCalcBtn(Msg);
}

void TAppWindow::HandleStoreBtn(RTMessage Msg)
{
  char varName[MaxEditLen+1];
```

continues

Listing 7.10. continued

```
  char result[MaxEditLen+1];

  // get the string in the edit box of the Result combo box
  ResultCmb->GetText(result, MaxEditLen);

  // store the result in the selected text of
  // the Variable list box
  putVar(atof(result));
}

void TAppWindow::CMStoreBtn(RTMessage Msg)
{
  HandleStoreBtn(Msg);
}

void TAppWindow::HandleExitBtn(RTMessage Msg)
{
  SendMessage(HWindow, WM_CLOSE, NULL, NULL);
}

void TAppWindow::CMExitBtn(RTMessage Msg)
{
  SendMessage(HWindow, WM_CLOSE, NULL, NULL);
}

void TAppWindow::HandleVariableLst(RTMessage Msg)
{
  char s[MaxEditLen+1];
  char operandText[MaxEditLen];

  // handle the various list box notification messages
  if (Msg.LP.Hi == LBN_DBLCLK) {
     VariableLst->GetSelString(s, MaxEditLen);
     strcpy(s, (s+3));
     // get the text in the Operand1 combo box
     Operand1Cmb->GetText(operandText, MaxEditLen);
     // is the first character in the Operand1 combo box a #?
     if (operandText[0] == '@')
        Operand1Cmb->SetText(s);
     // get the text in the Operand2 edit box
     Operand2Cmb->GetText(operandText, MaxEditLen);
     // is the first character in the Operand2 combo box a #?
     if (operandText[0] == '@')
        Operand2Cmb->SetText(s);
```

```cpp
    }
  }

  BOOL TAppWindow::CanClose()
  {
    return MessageBox(HWindow, "Want to close this application",
                    "Query", MB_YESNO | MB_ICONQUESTION) == IDYES;
  }

  double TAppWindow::getVar(int lineNum)
  {
    char s[MaxEditLen+1];

    if (lineNum >= VariableLst->GetCount()) return 0;
    VariableLst->GetString(s, lineNum);
    strcpy(s, (s+3));
    // return the number stored in the target line
    return atof(s);
  }

  void TAppWindow::putVar(double x)
  {
    char s[MaxEditLen+1];
    char c;
    int selectIndex = VariableLst->GetSelIndex();

    VariableLst->DeleteString(selectIndex);
    strcpy(s, "A:");
    c = selectIndex + 'A';
    // locate the character position of the cursor
    sprintf(s, "%c: %g", c, x);
    // insert it
    VariableLst->InsertString(s, selectIndex);
    VariableLst->SetSelIndex(selectIndex);
  }

  void TAppWindow::updateComboBox(PTComboBox P)
  {
    char s[MaxEditLen+1];
    int i;

    P->GetText(s, MaxEditLen);
    // is string s in the combo list
    i = P->FindExactString(s, -1);
    if (i == 0) return;
```

continues

Listing 7.10. continued

```
  else if (i < 0) {
    P->InsertString(s, 0);
    // delete extra history list members?
    while (P->GetCount() >= MaxHistory)
      P->DeleteString(P->GetCount()-1);
  }
  else {
    // delete the current selection
    P->DeleteString(i);
    // insert the string s at the first position
    P->InsertString(s, 0);
    // select the first combo box item
    P->SetSelIndex(0);
  }
}

void TWinApp::InitMainWindow()
{
  MainWindow = new TAppWindow(NULL, Name);
}

void TWinApp::InitInstance()
{
  TApplication::InitInstance();
  HAccTable = LoadAccelerators(hInstance, "BUTTONS");
  // initialize the window instance
  PTAppWindow(MainWindow)->InitAppWindow();
}

int PASCAL WinMain(HINSTANCE hInstance, HINSTANCE hPrevInstance,
                   LPSTR lpCmdLine, int nCmdShow)
{
  TWinApp WinApp(
    "Command-Oriented Calculator Application (COCA) Version 4",
               hInstance, hPrevInstance, lpCmdLine, nCmdShow);
  WinApp.Run(); // run OWL application
  return WinApp.Status; // return application status
}
```

The calculator program declares an application class and a window class. The TAppWindow class declares two sets of data members. The first set represents pointers to the various controls used in the application. The second set contains the InError data member, which flags any computational errors.

Scroll Bars, List Boxes, and Combo Boxes

The `TAppWindow` class declares a constructor and a collection of member functions to handle the various messages. The `TAppWindow` constructor performs the following tasks:

1. Loads the menu resource.
2. Creates instances for the various controls. The operand and result combo boxes are created with the `CBS_DROPDOWN` style. These same combo boxes remove the `CB_SORT` style so they can work as history list boxes. The Operator combo box is created with the `CBS_SIMPLE` style and maintains the ordered items in the accompanying list box. You use the default styles to create the Variables list box.
3. Sets the `InError` data member at FALSE.
4. Enables the keyboard handler.

The `InitAppWindow` member function initializes window instance by performing the following tasks:

1. Disabling the Store push button control.
2. Building the Variables list box.
3. Selecting the first item in the Variables list box.
4. Adding the supported operators and math functions in the list box component of the Operator combo box.

The application class's `InitInstance` member function calls `InitAppWindow` as part of the initialization of the window instance.

The `HandleOperatorCmb` member function responds to the `LBN_KILLFOCUS` notification message sent by the Operator combo box. The function carries out the following tasks:

1. Verifies that the notification message is `LBN_KILLFOCUS` by comparing that value with the `Msg.LP.HI` data member. If the two values match, the function performs the next tasks.
2. Obtains the text from the edit box by using the `GetText` function.
3. Invokes the `SetText` function to search for a list box member that matches the retrieved string. If the `SetText` call finds a match, the matching item appears as selected text in the edit control area of the combo box.

The `HandleCalcBtn` member function responds to the notification message of the Calc button and performs the requested calculation. The function performs the following tasks:

1. Obtains the string in the edit box of the Result combo box and converts it to a double type. The function stores the resulting floating point number in the local variable result.

2. Retrieves the string in the edit box of the Operand1 combo box.

3. Examines the operand string to determine whether it is a single-letter variable name, the # character (which is substituted by the value in the result variable), or the image of a number. The function performs the necessary conversion and stores the numerical value for the first operand in the local variable x.

4. Retrieves the string in the edit box of the Operand2 combo box. This string is processed in a manner similar to that of Operand1 combo box. The result is stored in variable y.

5. Obtains the string in the edit control of the Operator combo box.

6. Clears the Error Message edit control and assigns FALSE to the InError data member.

7. Finds the position of the invoked operator or math function in the Operator combo box list. HandleCalcBtn uses the member function TListBox::FindExtactString for this task.

8. Uses a switch statement to determine the requested operation or math function evaluation. Notice that this is the first time a version of the COCA program uses the switch statement. This decision-making statement should execute faster than the cascaded if statements (which use the strcmp function) found in the earlier versions. The switch statement either performs the requested task and assigns the result to variable z or flags an error.

9. If no error occurs, the function displays the result of the operation or function evaluation in the edit control box of the Result combo box. In addition, the function inserts the new result in the list box of the Result combo box by calling the updateComboBox member function. HandleCalcBtn also enables the Store button control if no error occurs and disables the button if an error occurs.

10. Inserts the new operands in the list boxes of their respective combo boxes. The function calls the updateComboBox member function twice to update both operand combo boxes. Notice that this update occurs regardless of the error condition. Moreover, if you request an evaluation of a math function, the list box of the Operand2 combo box remains unchanged, unless you enter a new and superfluous operand in that combo box.

`CMCalcBtn` responds to the command message sent by the Alt-C hot key. The function merely calls the `HandleCalcBtn` member function to provide the needed response.

The `HandleStoreBtn` member function responds to the notification message sent by the Store push button. The function stores the number found in the edit box of the Result combo box in the currently selected Variables list box item. `HandleStoreBtn` performs the following tasks:

1. Retrieves the string in the edit box of the Result combo box by using the `TComboBox::GetText` member function. The obtained string is copied to the local variable result.

2. Stores the obtained string in the Variables list box by calling the `putVar` member function with an argument of `atof(result)`.

The `CMStoreBtn` member function responds to the command message generated by the hot key Alt-S. The function simply calls the `HandleStoreBtn` member function to provide the required response.

The `HandleExitBtn` and `CMExitBtn` member functions offer the same response to the messages sent by the Exit button and the Alt-E hot key. Both functions send the `WM_CLOSE` message to the parent window.

The `HandleVariablesLst` member function responds to the `LBN_DBLCLK` notification messages sent by the Variables list box when you double-click a list item. The purpose of double-clicking is to replace the @ character with the number in the double-clicked item in either of the operand edit boxes. The function carries out the following tasks:

1. Verifies whether the notification message is `LBN_DBLCLK` by comparing that value with the `Msg.LP.HI` data member. If the two values match, the function performs the subsequent tasks.

2. Copies the characters of the new selection (chosen by the double-click action) to the local string variable s. The function calls the `GetSelString` function for this task.

3. Deletes the first three characters of variable s.

4. Retrieves a copy of the text in the edit control of the Operand1 combo box and stores it in the local variable `operandText`.

5. Sets the edit control of the Operand1 combo box to the string variable s if the first character in the string `operandText` is the @ character.

6. Repeats the last two tasks with the Operand2 combo box.

The protected `getVar` member function obtains the value from the Variables list box by specifying the item number. The function performs the following tasks:

1. Returns a 0 value if the item position exceeds the position of the last item in the Variables list box. This task uses the `GetCount` function to return the number of items in the list box.

2. Obtains the list item at the specified item position with the help of the `GetString` function.

3. Deletes the first three characters of the obtained list item.

4. Returns the expression `atof(s)`, which represents the doubletyped number stored in the selected list box item.

The protected `putVar` member function stores the `a` result in the selected Variable list item. The function carries out the following tasks:

1. Obtains the index of the current selection by calling the `GetSelIndex` function. The function stores the retrieved index in the local variable `selectIndex`.

2. Deletes the current selection by invoking the `DeleteString` function and supplying it the argument `selectIndex`.

3. Creates the string image of the new list item by using the `sprintf` function.

4. Inserts the new list item at the `selectIndex` position. This particular way of using `InsertString` to insert an item in a sorted list box does not corrupt the order of the item. Utilizing `InsertString` this way is the exception and not the rule.

5. Selects the newly inserted item. The same item remains selected but now has a different value associated with it.

Summary

This chapter introduced the scroll bar, list box, and combo box controls. These controls are all input objects. The chapter covered the following topics:

- The scroll bar control, which enables you to quickly select from a wide range of integers.

- ☐ The list box control, which provides you with a list of items from which to select.

- ☐ The creation of synchronized scrolling list boxes. At most, one of these lists can be sorted. You can use the scroll bar control to easily scroll these lists.

- ☐ The multiple-selection list box, which enables you to select multiple items in a list box for collective processing.

- ☐ The combo box controls and its various types: simple, drop-down, and drop-down list combo boxes. The LBN_KILLFOCUS notification message can make the combo boxes more interactive. In addition, you can make a history list box from a drop-down combo box.

List boxes and combo boxes are versatile input devices that benefit from a well-developed functionality supported by ObjectWindows. Consequently, you can do much with these controls. It's a matter of pushing your imagination to the limit.

CHAPTER 8

Dialog Boxes

Dialog boxes are special child windows with controls that display information or input data. Windows applications use dialog boxes to exchange information with the user. This chapter examines the modal and modeless dialog boxes supported by Windows. Modal dialog boxes require that you close them before you proceed any further with the application, because they are meant to perform a critical exchange of data. In fact, modal dialog boxes disable their parent windows while they have the focus. Modeless dialog boxes, on the other hand, do not do not require that you close them to continue using the application.

In this chapter, you will learn about the following topics:

- Constructing instances of class `TDialog`
- Executing a modal dialog box
- Minimizing the role of resource files
- Creating a modeless dialog box
- Creating a dialog box as a window
- Transferring control data
- Transferring data for dialog boxes
- Using the ObjectWindows `TInputDialog` class
- Using the ObjectWindows `TFileDialog` class
- Using the `TSearchDialog` class

Constructing Dialog Boxes

The `TDialog` class has three constructors. I focus on the two that create instances of class `TDialog` from resource files. These constructors are the following:

```
TDialog(PTWindowsObject AParent, LPSTR AName,
        PTModule AModule = NULL);
TDialog(PTWindowsObject AParent, int ResourceId,
        PTModule AModule = NULL);
```

The `AParent` parameter is the pointer to the parent window. If the application class creates the dialog box instance, the argument for `AParent` is NULL. The `AName` parameter is the pointer to the resource name that defines the dialog box. The `ResourceId` parameter represents the dialog box resource ID number, as defined in the resource file.

Caution: ObjectWindows does not support a constructor that creates dialog boxes from scratch. Instead, you must use a resource file or a stream to build new dialog boxes.

One advantage of using resources to define dialog boxes and their controls is that you can define the location, dimensions, style, and caption of a control outside the Windows application source code. Thus you can change the resource file, recompile it, and then incorporate it into the .EXE application file without recompiling the source file itself. This approach enables you to develop different resource versions with varying colors, styles, and even languages while maintaining a single copy of the application code. Using the Resource Workshop enables you to edit .RES compiled resource files easily. The visual editing features help you avoid the possible trial-and-error process that may be involved in using .RC resource files.

Executing Modal Dialog Boxes

Dialog boxes are created and destroyed much more frequently than windows. When a modal dialog box is created, it is immediately activated (executed).

This process calls a dialog box that remains until you click special exit buttons. Typically, these buttons are labeled OK and Cancel and send the special IDOK and IDCANCEL notification messages. Clicking the OK button is interpreted as confirming the data in the dialog box controls. Clicking the Cancel button is interpreted as rejecting the control's values and any changes you have made in these values since the dialog box was last executed. You can use alternative captions for the OK and Cancel buttons, but you must retain the same notification messages. Executing a dialog box involves the TModule::ExecuteDialog member function (which in turn calls the TDialog::Execute member function). The following is the general form for executing a modal dialog box:

```
GetModule()->ExecDialog(new TAppDialog(this, "AppDialog"))
GetModule()->ExecDialog(new TAppDialog(this, ID_DIALOG_BOX))
```

The ExecDialog member function returns an integer value that indicates whether the user exited the dialog box by pressing the OK or Cancel button. If you click the OK button (or an equivalent button that has the predefined IDOK resource ID), the ExecDialog member function returns IDOK. By contrast, if you click the Cancel button (or an equivalent button that has the predefined IDCANCEL resource ID), the ExecDialog function returns IDCANCEL. Normally, you compare the value returned by the ExecDialog function with IDOK (or IDCANCEL, whichever is more convenient for your application) to determine the steps, if any, to take based on your input. Because ObjectWindows applications delete the dialog box instance after they close, dialog boxes have to be created dynamically (on the heap).

> **Caution:** Do not use TDialog-type variables to create stack-based instances. The results are unpredictable, and a system hang is very possible.

> **Note:** Dialog boxes can contain additional buttons to manipulate the other controls or send information to other dialog boxes or the parent window.

Now look at a simple ObjectWindows program that uses a dialog box defined in the resource files. I used resource files to create alternate forms of the same dialog box—the first uses modern English, and the second uses old English. The simple application consists of an empty window with a single menu item,

Exit. When you click the Exit menu item (or press the Alt-X key) a dialog box appears that asks whether you want to exit the application. The dialog box contains a title, message, and the two buttons. (I purposely designed it to resemble the dialog boxes spawned by the `MessageBox` API function.) The program toggles the two versions of the dialog box. When you first click the Exit menu, the modern English version (with OK and Cancel buttons) appears, as shown in figure 8.1.

Figure 8.1.
A sample session with the DIALOG1.EXE application showing the dialog box with its modern English wording.

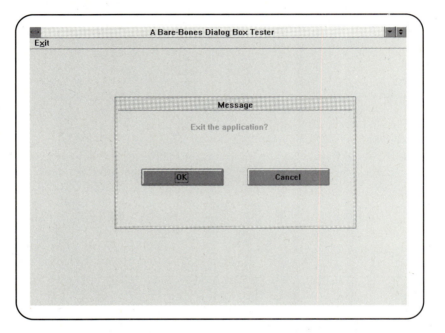

If you click the Cancel button and then click the Exit menu again, the old English version of the dialog box (with Yea and Nay buttons) appears, as shown in figure 8.2.

Every time you select the Cancel or Nay button and then click the Exit menu you toggle from one version of the dialog box to the other.

To exit the application, click the OK or Yea button, depending on the current dialog box version.

Now examine the code behind the application. Listing 8.1 shows the script for the DIALOG1.RC resource file.

Dialog Boxes

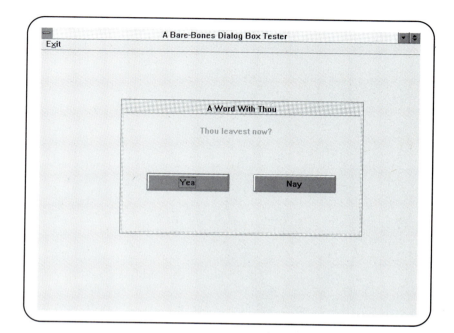

Figure 8.2.
A sample session with the DIALOG1.EXE application showing the dialog box with its old English wording.

Listing 8.1. The script for the DIALOG1.RC resource file.

```
#include <windows.h>
#include <owlrc.h>


EXITMENU MENU LOADONCALL MOVEABLE PURE DISCARDABLE
BEGIN
          MENUITEM "E&xit", CM_EXIT
END


NEW DIALOG DISCARDABLE LOADONCALL PURE MOVEABLE 30, 50, 200, 100
STYLE WS_POPUP | DS_MODALFRAME
CAPTION "Message"
BEGIN
    CTEXT "Exit the application?", 1, 10, 10, 170, 15
    CONTROL "OK", IDOK, "BUTTON", WS_CHILD | WS_VISIBLE |
      WS_TABSTOP | BS_DEFPUSHBUTTON, 20, 50, 70, 15
    CONTROL "Cancel", IDCANCEL, "BUTTON", WS_CHILD | WS_VISIBLE |
      WS_TABSTOP | BS_PUSHBUTTON, 110, 50, 70, 15
END

OLD DIALOG DISCARDABLE LOADONCALL PURE MOVEABLE 30, 50, 200, 100
STYLE WS_POPUP | DS_MODALFRAME
```

continues

Listing 8.1. continued

```
CAPTION "A Word With Thou"
BEGIN
     CTEXT "Thou leavest now?", 1, 10, 10, 170, 15
     CONTROL "Yea", IDOK, "BUTTON", WS_CHILD | WS_VISIBLE |
       WS_TABSTOP | BS_DEFPUSHBUTTON, 20, 50, 70, 15
     CONTROL "Nay", IDCANCEL, "BUTTON", WS_CHILD | WS_VISIBLE |
       WS_TABSTOP | BS_PUSHBUTTON, 110, 50, 70, 15
END
```

DIALOG1.RC defines the following resources:

- The menu resource, EXITMENU, which displays a single menu with the single item Exit.

- The dialog box resource, NEW, which contains a defined style, caption, and list of child controls. The specified style indicates that the dialog box is a modal pop-up child window. The specified caption is the string Message. The dialog box contains three controls: a centered static text (for the dialog box message), a default OK push button, and an ordinary Cancel button. The OK button has the resource ID of the predefined IDOK constant and the button style of BS_DEFPUSHBUTTON. The Cancel button has the resource ID of the predefined IDCANCEL constant and the button style of BF_PUSHBUTTON.

- The dialog box resource named OLD is similar to the NEW resource dialog box, except it uses old English wording. The Yea button has the resource ID of the predefined IDOK constant. The Nay button has the resource ID of the predefined IDCANCEL constant. These buttons are examples of exit buttons with atypical captions.

The resource definition of the dialog box and controls might be new to you. Chapter 11, "Controls Resource Script," discusses the resource files in more detail. CTEXT is a keyword that specifies centered text. The CONTROL keyword enables you to define any control and requires the caption, ID, control class, control style, location, and dimensions of the control.

Listing 8.2 shows the source code for the DIALOG1.CPP program file. The source code declares three classes: an application class, a window class, and a dialog box class. The latter is actually optional for this program because it does not add any new functionality to the parent TDialog class.

Listing 8.2. The source code for the DIALOG1.CPP program file.

```cpp
#include <owl.h>
#include <dialog.h>

// declare the custom application class as
// a subclass of TApplication

class TWinApp : public TApplication
{
public:
  TWinApp(LPSTR     AName,           // application name
          HINSTANCE hInstance,       // instance handle
          HINSTANCE hPrevInstance,   // previous instance handle
          LPSTR     lpCmdLine,       // command-line arguments
          int       nCmdShow) :      // display command
          TApplication(AName, hInstance, hPrevInstance,
                   lpCmdLine, nCmdShow) {};

protected:
  virtual void InitMainWindow();

};

// use the _CLASSDEF macro to declare reference and pointer
// types related to the new TAppWindow and TAppDialog classes
_CLASSDEF(TAppWindow)
_CLASSDEF(TAppDialog)

// expand the functionality of TDialog by deriving class TAppDialog
class TAppDialog : public TDialog
{
public:
  TAppDialog(PTWindowsObject AParent, LPSTR AName) :
    TDialog(AParent, AName) {};
};


// expand the functionality of TWindow by deriving class TAppWindow
class TAppWindow : public TWindow
{
public:
  TAppWindow(PTWindowsObject AParent, LPSTR ATitle) :
            TWindow(AParent, ATitle) { AssignMenu("EXITMENU"); };
```

continues

Listing 8.2. continued

```
  // Handle closing the window
  virtual BOOL CanClose();

};

BOOL TAppWindow::CanClose()
{
  static BOOL flag = FALSE;

  // toggle flag that selects alternate dialog box resources
  flag = (flag == TRUE) ? FALSE : TRUE;
  if (flag)
    // use modern English dialog box
    return (GetModule()->ExecDialog(
            new TAppDialog(this, "NEW")) == IDOK)
            ? TRUE : FALSE;
  else
    // use old English dialog box
    return (GetModule()->ExecDialog(
            new TAppDialog(this, "OLD")) == IDOK)
            ? TRUE : FALSE;

}

void TWinApp::InitMainWindow()
{
  MainWindow = new TAppWindow(NULL, Name);
}

int PASCAL WinMain(HINSTANCE hInstance, HINSTANCE hPrevInstance,
                   LPSTR lpCmdLine, int nCmdShow)
{
  TWinApp WinApp("A Bare-Bones Dialog Box Tester", hInstance,
                 hPrevInstance, lpCmdLine, nCmdShow);
  WinApp.Run(); // run OWL application
  return WinApp.Status; // return application status
}
```

The most relevant member function is `TAppWindow::CanClose`, which responds to the WM_CLOSE command message sent by the Exit menu item. The function uses the Boolean static local variable, `flag`, to toggle between the two dialog box resources NEW and OLD. The modern English dialog box is invoked in the following statement:

Dialog Boxes

```
return (GetModule()->ExecDialog(
        new TAppDialog(this, "NEW")) == IDOK)
        ? TRUE : FALSE;
```

The `ExecDialog` function accepts as an argument the pointer to the dynamically created instance of the `TAppDialog` class. The dialog box is executed, disabling the parent window until you click either push button control. The value returned by the `ExecDialog` member function is compared with the `IDOK` constant to return either TRUE or FALSE.

The instance of the old English version of the dialog box is created similarly, as shown in the statement that follows:

```
return (GetModule()->ExecDialog(
        new TAppDialog(this, "OLD")) == IDOK)
        ? TRUE : FALSE;
```

How do you close the dialog boxes? The answer lies with the `TDialog` class itself. When you click the OK (or Yea) button, it sends the `IDOK` notification message. The `TDialog::Ok` member function handles closing the window and returning the `IDOK` result for the `ExecDialog` function. By contrast, when you click the Cancel (or Nay) button, it sends the `IDCANCEL` notification message. The `TDialog::Cancel` member function intercepts this notification message and closes the dialog box, causing the `ExecDialog` function to return `IDCANCEL`.

How do the `Ok` and `Cancel` member functions in `TDialog` work? Listing 8.3 contains the source code for these functions and the functions they call. These member functions are found in the DIALOG.CPP file in the SOURCE directory.

Listing 8.3. The source code for the `Ok`, `Cancel`, `WMClose`, `CloseWindow`, and `ShutDown` member functions of the `TDialog` class.

```
void TDialog::Ok(TMessage&)
{
    CloseWindow(IDOK);
}

void TDialog::Cancel(TMessage&)
{
    ShutDownWindow();
}

void TDialog::WMClose(TMessage&)
{
```

continues

Listing 8.3. continued

```
        ShutDownWindow();
}

void TDialog::CloseWindow(int ARetValue)
{
    if ( IsModal )
    {
        if ( CanClose() )
        {
            TransferData(TF_GETDATA);
            ShutDownWindow(ARetValue);
        }
    }
    else    // !IsModal
        TWindowsObject::CloseWindow();
}

void TDialog::CloseWindow()
{
    if ( IsModal )
        CloseWindow(IDCANCEL);
    else    // !IsModal
        TWindowsObject::CloseWindow();
}

void TDialog::ShutDownWindow(int ARetValue)
{
    if ( IsModal )
        // Note that we can't delete a modal dialog here because
        // we're still in its Execute function.
        Destroy(ARetValue);
    else
        TWindowsObject::ShutDownWindow();
}

void TDialog::ShutDownWindow()
{
    if ( IsModal )
        // Note that we can't delete a modal dialog here because
        // we're still in its Execute function.
        Destroy(IDCANCEL);
    else
    TWindowsObject::ShutDownWindow();
}
```

The `Ok` function calls the `TDialog::CloseWindow(int)` member function (`TDialog` has two versions of this function) to close the dialog box conditionally and return an `IDOK` result. The `Cancel` function invokes the `TDialog::ShutDownWindow` member function to close the dialog box unconditionally. Listing 8.3 also includes the member function `TDialog::WMClose`, which responds to the `WM_CLOSE` messages. This function also calls the `ShutDownWindow` member function.

The `CloseWindow` member function with the `int`-type parameter first examines whether the dialog box instance is modal or modeless. If the dialog box is modal, the function calls the `CanClose` function. If the `CanClose` function returns TRUE, the `CloseWindow` function transfers the dialog box data (which is discussed later in this chapter) and calls the `ShutDownWindow(int)` member function to shut down the dialog box safely. If the dialog box is modeless, the `CloseWindow(int)` function calls the `TWindowsObject::CloseWindow()` member function.

The `TDialog` class defines another version of the `CloseWindow` member function. This version has no parameters and issues a `CloseWindow(IDCANCEL)` call to close the dialog box and return the `IDCANCEL` result for modal dialog boxes. If the dialog box is modeless, the `TDialog::CloseWindow` function invokes the member function `TWindowsObject::CloseWindow`.

The `ShutDownWindow(int)` member function unconditionally shuts down a dialog box. For a modal dialog box, the function calls the `TDialog::Destroy` member function and passes its argument to the `Destroy` function. In the case of a modeless dialog box, the `ShutDownWindow` function calls the member function `TWindowsObject::ShutDownWindow()`.

The `TDialog` class declares another version of the `ShutDownWindow` member function. This one has no parameters and invokes the `TDialog::Destroy` member function with an `IDCANCEL` argument when dealing with modal dialog boxes. In the case of a modeless dialog box, the `ShutDownWindow` function calls the member function `TWindowsObject::ShutDownWindow()`.

> **Note:** I described the preceding member functions to give you a clear idea of how they work and to show you that these functions do not have extensive code. You can modify the `CloseWindow` and `ShutDownWindow` member functions in descendants of `TDialog` to alter the sequence of tasks involved in closing a dialog box.

Minimizing Resource File Contribution

The DIALOG1.EXE program relies entirely on the resource file to define the dialog box and its controls. How can the role of the resource file be minimized? The answer lies mainly with the arguments of the constructors for the dialog box and its controls. In the last three chapters, I presented the constructors for the various controls that enable you to create instances from scratch. This capability is not implemented in the TDialog class; therefore, a resource file (or a stream) must be used. This section presents DIALOG2.CPP, a modified version of DIALOG1.CPP that uses only the resource file to define the dialog box. The static text and push button controls are created inside the program.

Listing 8.4 contains the script for the DIALOG2.RC resource file. Notice that the definitions of the dialog boxes are minimal—they do not define any controls.

Listing 8.4. The script for the DIALOG2.RC resource file.

```
#include <windows.h>
#include <owlrc.h>

EXITMENU MENU LOADONCALL MOVEABLE PURE DISCARDABLE
BEGIN
      MENUITEM "E&xit", CM_EXIT
END

NEW DIALOG DISCARDABLE LOADONCALL PURE MOVEABLE 30, 30, 200, 100
STYLE WS_POPUP | DS_MODALFRAME
CAPTION "Message"
BEGIN
END

OLD DIALOG DISCARDABLE LOADONCALL PURE MOVEABLE 30, 30, 200, 100
STYLE WS_POPUP | DS_MODALFRAME
CAPTION "A Word With Thou"
BEGIN
END
```

Listing 8.5 shows the source code for the DIALOG2.CPP program. This listing differs from DIALOG1.CPP in that it declares constants for sizing the controls in the dialog boxes and uses the `TAppDialog` constructor to create the instances of the various controls. The `TAppDialog` constructor first compares the name of the dialog resource with the string NEW to determine the wording to assign to the message text and button captions. The constructor then proceeds to create the message static text and the two buttons.

Listing 8.5. The source code for the DIALOG2.CPP program file.

```
#include <string.h>
#include <owl.h>
#include <static.h>
#include <button.h>
#include <dialog.h>

// declare constants for sizing and dimensioning controls
const Wtxt = 300;
const Htxt = 15;
const TxtVertSpacing = 30;
const Wbtn = 100;
const Hbtn = 25;
const BtnHozSpacing = 40;

// declare the maximum length of a caption
const MaxCaptionLen = 40;

// declare the custom application class as
// a subclass of TApplication

class TWinApp : public TApplication
{
public:
  TWinApp(LPSTR     AName,          // application name
          HINSTANCE hInstance,      // instance handle
          HINSTANCE hPrevInstance,  // previous instance handle
          LPSTR     lpCmdLine,      // command-line arguments
          int       nCmdShow) :     // display command
          TApplication(AName, hInstance, hPrevInstance,
                   lpCmdLine, nCmdShow) {};

protected:
  virtual void InitMainWindow();

};
```

continues

Listing 8.5. continued

```
// use the _CLASSDEF macro to declare reference and pointer
// types related to the new TAppWindow and TAppDialog classes
_CLASSDEF(TAppWindow)
_CLASSDEF(TAppDialog)

// expand the functionality of TDialog by deriving class TAppDialog
class TAppDialog : public TDialog
{
public:
  TAppDialog(PTWindowsObject AParent, LPSTR AName);

};


// expand the functionality of TWindow by deriving class TAppWindow
class TAppWindow : public TWindow
{
public:
  TAppWindow(PTWindowsObject AParent, LPSTR ATitle) :
             TWindow(AParent, ATitle)
             { AssignMenu("EXITMENU"); };

  // Handle closing the window
  virtual BOOL CanClose();

};

TAppDialog::TAppDialog(PTWindowsObject AParent, LPSTR AName)
                     : TDialog(AParent, AName)
{
  int x0 = 50;
  int y0 = 50;
  int x = x0, y = y0;
  char MessageText[MaxCaptionLen+1];
  char YesBtnCaption[MaxCaptionLen+1];
  char CancelBtnCaption[MaxCaptionLen+1];

  PTStatic S;

  // assign the text to the static text and captions,
  // based on the dialog box resource name
  if (_fstricmp(AName, "NEW") == 0) {
    // modern English wording
    strcpy(MessageText, "Exit the application?");
```

Dialog Boxes

```
    strcpy(YesBtnCaption, "OK");
    strcpy(CancelBtnCaption, "Cancel");
  }
  else {
    // old English wording
    strcpy(MessageText, "Thou leavest now?");
    strcpy(YesBtnCaption, "Yea");
    strcpy(CancelBtnCaption, "Nay");
  }

  // create the static text control
  S = new TStatic(this, -1, MessageText, x, y,
                  Wtxt, Htxt, strlen(MessageText));
  // set style to center the text
  S->Attr.Style |= SS_CENTER;
  S->Attr.Style &= ~SS_LEFT;

  // create the Yes button
  y += Htxt + TxtVertSpacing;
  x += 20;
  new TButton(this, IDOK, YesBtnCaption, x, y, Wbtn, Hbtn, TRUE);

  // create the Cancel button
  x += Wbtn + BtnHozSpacing;
  new TButton(this, IDCANCEL, CancelBtnCaption, x, y, Wbtn, Hbtn,
              FALSE);
}

BOOL TAppWindow::CanClose()
{
  static BOOL flag = FALSE;

  // toggle flag
  flag = (flag == TRUE) ? FALSE : TRUE;
  if (flag)
    return (GetModule()->ExecDialog(
            new TAppDialog(this, "NEW")) == IDOK)
            ? TRUE : FALSE;
  else
    return (GetModule()->ExecDialog(
            new TAppDialog(this, "OLD")) == IDOK)
            ? TRUE : FALSE;

}
```

continues

Listing 8.5. continued

```
void TWinApp::InitMainWindow()
{
  MainWindow = new TAppWindow(NULL, Name);
}

int PASCAL WinMain(HINSTANCE hInstance, HINSTANCE hPrevInstance,
                LPSTR lpCmdLine, int nCmdShow)
{
  TWinApp WinApp("A Bare-Bones Dialog Box Tester", hInstance,
              hPrevInstance, lpCmdLine, nCmdShow);
  WinApp.Run(); // run OWL application
  return WinApp.Status; // return application status
}
```

The code for the `CanClose` member function is identical to that of DIALOG1.CPP.

> **Tip:** The DIALOG2.CPP program demonstrates that you can create the dialog box controls inside the application rather than in the resource file. Which approach is better? The argument can swing toward the resource file. Then why use the approach demonstrated in this program? First, the location and sizes of the controls are easier to adjust using the coding style I present. Second, you recognize that it can be done—numerous approaches in programming with ObjectWindows seem logical and feasible at first, but turn out to be dead ends. Therefore, knowing that a certain technique actually works in ObjectWindows is a plus. On the other hand, resource files have the advantage of being language independent. Therefore, you can use the same resource files with C++, C, Pascal, and other Windows compilers.

Creating Modeless Dialog Boxes

Modeless dialog boxes are less restrictive than modal dialog boxes. You can shift the focus back to the parent window without having to close a modeless dialog box. Modeless dialog boxes are created and not executed. The `TModule::MakeWindow` member function is invoked to create a modeless dialog box safely. The dialog box creation process invokes the `TDialog::Create` member function.

The following are the general forms for creating a modeless dialog box:

```
PTAppDialog P;
P = new TAppDialog(this, "AppDialog");
GetModule()->MakeWindow(P);
ShowWindow(P->HWindow, SW_SHOW);

PTAppDialog P;
P = new TAppDialog(this, ID_DIALOG_BOX);
GetModule()->MakeWindow(P);
ShowWindow(P->HWindow, SW_SHOW);
```

This general form shows that the `MakeWindow` must be followed by a call to the **ShowWindow** API function so the modeless dialog box can be made visible. Modeless dialog boxes do not return a value. To close a modeless dialog box, invoke the `TDialog::ShutDownWindow()` member function.

Now examine an ObjectWindows program that creates multiple modeless dialog boxes and enables them to talk to each other. The program has a parent window that contains four push button controls, labeled Member 1, Member 2, Member 3, and Wizard. The first three buttons create modeless dialog boxes. Each modeless dialog box contains the following controls:

- An outgoing message edit box.
- A receiver ID edit box that enables you to specify the index of the receiving dialog box.
- An incoming message edit box.
- A sender ID edit box that specifies the index of the dialog box that sent the message.
- Static text controls that label the edit boxes.
- A Close push button control that closes the modeless dialog box.
- A Send push button control that sends the message in the outgoing edit box.

The Wizard button in the parent window creates a Wizard modal dialog box. This dialog box possesses the same controls found in the modeless dialog boxes and a Close All push button that closes all the dialog boxes, including itself.

The dialog boxes have indices of 0 to 3. Indices 1, 2, and 3 are designated for the modeless dialog boxes, and index 0 is assigned to the modal dialog box.

The dialog rules are simple. A dialog box can talk to an existing dialog box, including itself. Figure 8.3 shows a sample session with the DIALOG3.EXE program.

Figure 8.3. A sample session with the DIALOG3.EXE application.

Static Text

Edit boxes

Modal dialog box

Modeless dialog box

Note: You should compile and run the program. Click one or two member buttons and then click the Wizard button. When the Wizard modal dialog box is executed, it has the focus. You can switch to the other dialog boxes, because Windows supports switching of the focus to modeless dialog boxes created before a modal dialog box is executed. Of course, the parent window is disabled and, therefore, you cannot create any new modeless dialog boxes. Try sending text between the dialog boxes. You can close the modeless dialog boxes before or after you close the modal dialog box.

Dialog Boxes

The sample program demonstrates the following:

- How to create and manage a modeless dialog box.
- How modeless dialog boxes coexist with a modal dialog box.
- How to transfer data between different dialog boxes.
- How to manipulate the dialog box controls by copying text between edit boxes.

Now examine the code that implements this ObjectWindows program. Listing 8.6 shows the header file DIALOG3.H, which contains the ID_*xxxx* constants for the various controls of the window and the dialog boxes. In addition, the header file declares the WM_CLOSEALL message ID.

Listing 8.6. The source code for the DIALOG3.H header file.

```
#define ID_MEMBER1_BTN 201
#define ID_MEMBER2_BTN 202
#define ID_MEMBER3_BTN 203
#define ID_WIZARD_BTN 204

#define ID_SEND_BTN 205
#define ID_CLOSE_BTN 206
#define ID_CLOSEALL_BTN 207
#define ID_SEND_EDIT 208
#define ID_SENDID_EDIT 209
#define ID_GET_EDIT 208
#define ID_GETID_EDIT 209

#define WM_CLOSEALL 100
```

Listing 8.7 contains the script for the DIALOG3.RC resource file. This file defines the resources for the application's menu and four dialog boxes. Notice that the modeless dialog boxes have the WS_DLGFRAME style, and the modal dialog box has the DS_MODALFRAME style. Each dialog box resource also declares the caption that appears with the dialog box.

Listing 8.7. The script for the DIALOG3.RC resource file.

```
#include <windows.h>
#include <owlrc.h>

EXITMENU MENU LOADONCALL MOVEABLE PURE DISCARDABLE
BEGIN
    MENUITEM "E&xit", CM_EXIT
END


MEMBER1 DIALOG DISCARDABLE LOADONCALL PURE MOVEABLE 30, 30, 150, 150
STYLE WS_POPUP | WS_DLGFRAME
CAPTION "Member #1"
BEGIN
END

MEMBER2 DIALOG DISCARDABLE LOADONCALL PURE MOVEABLE 40, 40, 150, 150
STYLE WS_POPUP | WS_DLGFRAME
CAPTION "Member #2"
BEGIN
END

MEMBER3 DIALOG DISCARDABLE LOADONCALL PURE MOVEABLE 50, 50, 150, 150
STYLE WS_POPUP | WS_DLGFRAME
CAPTION "Member #3"
BEGIN
END

WIZARD DIALOG DISCARDABLE LOADONCALL PURE MOVEABLE 60, 60, 150, 150
STYLE WS_POPUP | DS_MODALFRAME
CAPTION "Wizard"
BEGIN
END
```

Listing 8.8 contains the source code for the DIALOG3.CPP program file. The program listing declares two sets of constants: one for sizing the controls, and the other for defining the edit box string limits and the maximum number of buttons in the application window. The program uses the `#include` directive to include the ID_*xxxx* and WS_*xxxx* constants declared in the header file DIALOG3.H.

Listing 8.8. The source code for the DIALOG3.CPP program file.

```cpp
#include <stdio.h>
#include <string.h>
#include <owl.h>
#include <static.h>
#include <edit.h>
#include <button.h>
#include <dialog.h>
#include "dialog3.h"

// declare constants for sizing and dimensioning controls
const Wtxt = 200;
const Htxt = 15;
const TxtVertSpacing = 5;
const Wbox = 200;
const Hbox = 30;
const BoxVertSpacing = 5;
const Wbtn = 70;
const Hbtn = 25;
const BtnHorzSpacing = 10;
const WinWbtn = 100;

// declare the maximum length of a caption
const MaxString = 80;
const MaxDialog = 4;

// use the _CLASSDEF macro to declare reference and pointer
// types related to the new TAppWindow and TAppDialog classes
_CLASSDEF(TAppWindow)
_CLASSDEF(TAppDialog)

// declare the custom application class as
// a subclass of TApplication
class TWinApp : public TApplication
{
public:
   TWinApp(LPSTR     AName,           // application name
           HINSTANCE hInstance,       // instance handle
           HINSTANCE hPrevInstance,   // previous instance handle
           LPSTR     lpCmdLine,       // command-line arguments
           int       nCmdShow) :      // display command
           TApplication(AName, hInstance, hPrevInstance,
                    lpCmdLine, nCmdShow) {};

protected:
```

continues

Listing 8.8. continued

```cpp
  virtual void InitMainWindow();

};


// expand the functionality of TDialog by deriving class TAppDialog
class TAppDialog : public TDialog
{
public:

  TAppDialog(PTWindowsObject AParent, LPSTR AName, int ADlgId);

  // Handle the Send button message
  virtual void HandleSendBtn(RTMessage Msg)
    = [ID_FIRST + ID_SEND_BTN];

  // Handle the Close button message
  virtual void HandleCloseBtn(RTMessage Msg)
    = [ID_FIRST + ID_CLOSE_BTN];

  // Handle the Close All button message
  virtual void HandleCloseAllBtn(RTMessage Msg)
    = [ID_FIRST + ID_CLOSEALL_BTN];

protected:
  PTEdit SendBox;
  PTEdit SendIdBox;
  PTEdit GetBox;
  PTEdit GetIdBox;
  PTButton SendBtn;
  PTButton CloseBtn;
  PTButton CloseAllBtn;

  // dialog's own ID
  int DlgId;

  // initialize a dialog box
  virtual void InitMember(BOOL IsMember = TRUE);
};

// expand the functionality of TWindow by deriving class TAppWindow
class TAppWindow : public TWindow
{
public:
```

```cpp
    PTAppDialog DlgPtr[MaxDialog];

    TAppWindow(PTWindowsObject AParent, LPSTR ATitle);

    // Handle creating the Member 1 modeless dialog box
    virtual void HandleMember1Btn(RTMessage Msg)
      = [ID_FIRST + ID_MEMBER1_BTN];

    // Handle creating the Member 2 modeless dialog box
    virtual void HandleMember2Btn(RTMessage Msg)
      = [ID_FIRST + ID_MEMBER2_BTN];

    // Handle creating the Member 3 modeless dialog box
    virtual void HandleMember3Btn(RTMessage Msg)
      = [ID_FIRST + ID_MEMBER3_BTN];

    // Handle creating the Wizard modal dialog box
    virtual void HandleWizardBtn(RTMessage Msg)
      = [ID_FIRST + ID_WIZARD_BTN];

protected:
    // handle any Member dialog box
    virtual void AMemberBtn(int AnId);

};

TAppDialog::TAppDialog(PTWindowsObject AParent, LPSTR AName,
                       int ADlgId) : TDialog(AParent, AName)
{
  DlgId = ADlgId;
  PTAppWindow(Parent)->DlgPtr[DlgId] = this;

  if (_fstricmp(AName, "WIZARD") == 0)
    InitMember(FALSE);
  else
    InitMember();
}

void TAppDialog::HandleSendBtn(RTMessage Msg)
{
  char MsgSent[MaxString+1];
  char ReceiverId[MaxString+1];
  char SenderId[MaxString+1];
  int i;
```

continues

Listing 8.8. continued

```
  // get the text in the Send edit control
  SendBox->GetText(MsgSent, MaxString);
  // get the index in the Receiver Id edit control
  SendIdBox->GetText(ReceiverId, MaxString);
  // convert string to an int
  i = atoi(ReceiverId);
  // is the value in i within range?
  if (i >= 0 && i <= MaxDialog) {
    // convert receiver dialog Id to a string
    sprintf(SenderId, "%d", DlgId);
    // if the receiver is an existing instance write the
    // sent message and the sender Id in the receiver's
    // Get and Get Id edit controls
    if (PTAppWindow(Parent)->DlgPtr[i]) {
      PTAppWindow(Parent)->DlgPtr[i]->GetIdBox->SetText(SenderId);
      PTAppWindow(Parent)->DlgPtr[i]->GetBox->SetText(MsgSent);
    }
  }
}

void TAppDialog::HandleCloseBtn(RTMessage Msg)
{
  PTAppWindow(Parent)->DlgPtr[DlgId] = NULL;
  ShutDownWindow();
}

void TAppDialog::HandleCloseAllBtn(RTMessage Msg)
{
  for (int i = 0; i < MaxDialog; i++)
    if (PTAppWindow(Parent)->DlgPtr[i]) {
      PTAppWindow(Parent)->DlgPtr[i]->ShutDownWindow();
      PTAppWindow(Parent)->DlgPtr[i] = NULL;
    }
}

void TAppDialog::InitMember(BOOL IsMember)
{
  int x = 50;
  int y = 10;
  char s[MaxString+1];

  // create the output message edit box and its label
  strcpy(s, "Outgoing Message");
  new TStatic(this, -1, s, x, y, Wtxt, Htxt, strlen(s));
```

```
    y += Htxt + TxtVertSpacing;
    SendBox = new TEdit(this, ID_SEND_EDIT, "", x, y, Wbox, Hbox,
                       0, FALSE);

    // create the output ID edit box and its label
    y += Hbox + BoxVertSpacing;
    strcpy(s, "ID number of recipient member");
    new TStatic(this, -1, s, x, y, Wtxt, Htxt, strlen(s));

    y += Htxt + TxtVertSpacing;
    SendIdBox = new TEdit(this, ID_SENDID_EDIT, "", x, y, Wbox, Hbox,
                         0, FALSE);

    // create the input message edit box and its label
    y += Hbox + BoxVertSpacing;
    strcpy(s, "Incoming Message");
    new TStatic(this, -1, s, x, y, Wtxt, Htxt, strlen(s));

    y += Htxt + TxtVertSpacing;
    GetBox = new TEdit(this, ID_GET_EDIT, "", x, y, Wbox, Hbox, 0, FALSE);

    y += Hbox + BoxVertSpacing;
    strcpy(s, "ID number of sender");
    new TStatic(this, -1, s, x, y, Wtxt, Htxt, strlen(s));

    // create the input ID message box and its label
    y += Htxt + TxtVertSpacing;
    GetIdBox = new TEdit(this, ID_GETID_EDIT, "", x, y, Wbox, Hbox,
                        0, FALSE);

    // create the Send button
    if (IsMember == FALSE)
      x -= 20;
    y += Hbox + BoxVertSpacing;
    SendBtn = new TButton(this, ID_SEND_BTN, "Send", x, y, Wbtn,
                         Hbtn, TRUE);

    // create the Close button
    x += Wbtn + BtnHorzSpacing;
    CloseBtn = new TButton(this, ID_CLOSE_BTN, "Close", x, y, Wbtn,
                          Hbtn, FALSE);

    if (IsMember == FALSE) {

      // create the Close All button
```

continues

Listing 8.8. continued

```
    x += Wbtn + BtnHorzSpacing;
    CloseAllBtn = new TButton(this, ID_CLOSEALL_BTN, "Close All",
                              x, y, Wbtn, Hbtn, FALSE);
  }
}

TAppWindow::TAppWindow(PTWindowsObject AParent, LPSTR ATitle) :
            TWindow(AParent, ATitle)
{
  int x = 50;
  int y = 50;

  AssignMenu("EXITMENU");

  // create window button controls
  new TButton(this, ID_MEMBER1_BTN, "Member 1",
              x, y, WinWbtn, Hbtn, FALSE);

  x += WinWbtn + BtnHorzSpacing;
  new TButton(this, ID_MEMBER2_BTN, "Member 2",
              x, y, WinWbtn, Hbtn, FALSE);

  x += WinWbtn + BtnHorzSpacing;
  new TButton(this, ID_MEMBER3_BTN, "Member 3",
              x, y, WinWbtn, Hbtn, FALSE);

  x += WinWbtn + BtnHorzSpacing;
  new TButton(this, ID_WIZARD_BTN, " Wizard",
              x, y, WinWbtn, Hbtn, FALSE);

  // clear dialog box pointers
  for (int i = 0; i < MaxDialog; i++)
    DlgPtr[i] = NULL;
}

void TAppWindow::HandleMember1Btn(RTMessage Msg)
{
  // create modeless dialog box if it does not already exist
  if (!DlgPtr[1])
    AMemberBtn(1);
}

void TAppWindow::HandleMember2Btn(RTMessage Msg)
{
```

```cpp
  // create modeless dialog box if it does not already exist
  if (!DlgPtr[2])
    AMemberBtn(2);
}

void TAppWindow::HandleMember3Btn(RTMessage Msg)
{
  // create modeless dialog box if it does not already exist
  if (!DlgPtr[3])
    AMemberBtn(3);
}

void TAppWindow::HandleWizardBtn(RTMessage Msg)
{
  // create modal dialog box
  GetModule()->ExecDialog(new TAppDialog(this, "WIZARD", 0));
}

void TAppWindow::AMemberBtn(int AnId)
{
  char s[10];

  // create a modeless Member dialog box
  sprintf(s, "MEMBER%d", AnId);
  GetModule()->MakeWindow(new TAppDialog(this, s, AnId));
  // show the modeless dialog box
  if (DlgPtr[AnId])
    ShowWindow(DlgPtr[AnId]->HWindow, SW_SHOW);
}

void TWinApp::InitMainWindow()
{
  MainWindow = new TAppWindow(NULL, Name);
}

int PASCAL WinMain(HINSTANCE hInstance, HINSTANCE hPrevInstance,
                   LPSTR lpCmdLine, int nCmdShow)
{
  TWinApp WinApp("A Modal & Modeless Dialog Box Tester", hInstance,
                 hPrevInstance, lpCmdLine, nCmdShow);
  WinApp.Run(); // run OWL application
  return WinApp.Status; // return application status
}
```

The application declares three classes: the application, window, and dialog box classes.

The application window class `TAppWindow` declares the public data member `DlgPtr`. This member is an array of pointers to the `TDialogApp` type. These pointers provide the required access to the edit boxes of the dialog boxes and also indicate whether their respective dialog boxes exist or not. You must use this type of pointer when dealing with a category of application that involves coexisting multiple dialog boxes. The application also uses pointers to detect the existence of specific dialog box instances and prevent the creation of duplicates.

The `TAppWindow` class declares a constructor and a group of member functions. The class constructor loads the menu resources, creates the four push button controls, and initializes the members of the `DlgPtr` array to NULL values.

The application window class declares member functions to handle notification messages sent by the window's push button controls. The member functions `HandleMember1Btn`, `HandleMember2Btn`, and `HandleMember3Btn` create their corresponding modeless dialog boxes. The code for these functions is similar. Each member function verifies that the corresponding member of the array `DlgPtr` is NULL before invoking the protected `AMemberBtn` member function to create a modeless dialog box.

The `AMemberBtn` member function creates and displays a modeless dialog box. The function performs the following tasks:

1. Builds the resource name for the required dialog box.

2. Creates the dialog box by using the `TModule::MakeWindow` member function.

3. Invokes the **ShowWindow** API function to display the modeless dialog box. This step involves checking first that the pointer to the dialog box is not NULL. A non-NULL pointer indicates that `MakeWindow` successfully created the object.

The `TAppWindow` class declares the `HandleWizardBtn` member function to create the Wizard modal dialog box. This function simply invokes the `TModule::ExecDialog` member function. The value of the `ExecDialog` function is discarded. Notice that this function does not check whether the data member `DlgPtr[0]` is NULL. This step is not needed because modal dialog box instances are unique and cannot have duplicates, as is the case with modeless dialog boxes. The pointer to the modal dialog box is still needed to access its edit box controls.

The program declares the application dialog box class `TAppDialog`. All the dialog boxes created in the application use this class. The dialog class includes a class constructor, data members, and a number of member functions.

The dialog class declares the `DlgId` data member that is a self-identifying index for the dialog box. The class also declares a group of pointers to access the various controls in the dialog box, especially the edit boxes.

The `TAppDialog` constructor differs from the constructor of its parent class because it has the additional parameter `ADlgId`. This parameter specifies the index number of the dialog box instance to be instantiated. The constructor performs the following tasks:

1. Stores the argument of the `ADlgId` parameter in the `DlgId` data member to inform the dialog box instance of its index number (a sort of social security number for the dialog boxes).

2. The constructor then assigns the pointer `this` to the `DlgPtr[DlgId]` member of the parent window class. This task demonstrates how to access a parent's data member. This approach also consolidates the pointer assignment—that is, the pointers are assigned with a single statement in a single member function—rather than having two separate statements in the `TAppWindow::AMemberBtn` and the `TAppWindow::HandleWizzardBtn` member functions.

3. Compares the name of the dialog box resource with the string `WIZARD`. If the two strings match, the constructor calls the `InitMember` member function and passes the argument FALSE. On the other hand, if the two strings do not match, the constructor invokes the `InitMember` function with no argument (causing the function to use the default parameter value of TRUE).

The `InitMember` member function helps construct the dialog box instances and creates the various edit boxes and button controls required by the dialog box instance. The `IsMember` function parameter determines whether to create a MemberX button or a Wizard button. If the argument for `IsMember` is TRUE, the function creates an additional push button with the caption Close All.

The dialog class uses the `HandleSendBtn` function to handle the notification messages sent by the Send push button of a dialog box. The function performs the following tasks so a dialog box can send text to an existing dialog box:

1. Obtains the text in the Outgoing Message edit control.

2. Obtains the index of the receiver dialog box from the Receiver ID edit box.

3. Converts the ID string to `int` and stores it in the local variable `i`.

4. Verifies that the value in variable `i` is valid before proceeding with the next tasks. If `i` contains an invalid value, the function takes no further action.

5. Converts the ID of the sender dialog box to a string and stores it in the local variable `SenderId`.

6. Verifies that the receiver dialog box exists by checking the address of the `DlgPtr[i]` member. If the receiver dialog box exists, the function writes the sender ID in the Sender ID edit box and writes the transmitted text in the Incoming Message edit box.

The dialog class declares two member functions for closing dialog boxes. The `HandleCloseBtn` member function closes a single dialog box by assigning NULL to the object's pointer and then invoking the `ShutDownWindow` member function. The `HandleCloseAllBtn` member function performs a similar operation on all of the existing dialog boxes.

The program in Listing 8.8 created the dialog box controls from scratch inside the `InitMember` member function. How would that function look if these same controls were declared in the resource file? The answer appears in Listing 8.9, which contains a version of `InitMember` that uses resource-tapping constructors to create the various controls. Because coordinates of the controls would be specified in the resource file, the new version of `InitMember` has no use for coordinate-tracking variables.

Listing 8.9. The alternative version for the `InitMember` member function if resources were used to create the dialog box controls.

```
void TAppDialog::InitMember(BOOL IsMember)
{
    char s[MaxString+1];

    // create the output message edit box and its label
    strcpy(s, "Outgoing Message");
    new TStatic(this, ID_STATIC1_TXT, strlen(s));
    SendBox = new TEdit(this, ID_SEND_EDIT, MaxEditLen);

    // create the output ID edit box and its label

    strcpy(s, "ID number of recipient member");
    new TStatic(this, ID_STATIC2_TXT, strlen(s));
    SendIdBox = new TEdit(this, ID_SENDID_EDIT, MaxEditLen);
```

```
    // create the input message edit box and its label
    strcpy(s, "Incoming Message");
    new TStatic(this, -1, s, x, y, Wtxt, Htxt, strlen(s));
    GetBox = new TEdit(this, ID_GET_EDIT, MaxEditLen);

    strcpy(s, "ID number of sender");
    new TStatic(this, ID_STATIC3_TXT, strlen(s));

    // create the input ID message box and its label
    GetIdBox = new TEdit(this, ID_GETID_EDIT, MaxEditLen);

    // create the Send button
    SendBtn = new TButton(this, ID_SEND_BTN);

    // create the Close button
    CloseBtn = new TButton(this, ID_CLOSE_BTN);

    if (IsMember == FALSE)
        // create the Close All button
        CloseAllBtn = new TButton(this, ID_CLOSEALL_BTN);
}
```

Using Dialog Boxes as Windows

A dialog box does not always have to be a child window. In fact, if the nature of your application requires the use of multiple controls and has little use for a typical parent window, you can create a dialog box instance that is a direct child of the application class instance. This approach correctly bypasses the classic parent window when that window really has nothing to offer the application.

A good example is the category of calculator applications. A calculator typically has many controls. Because using dialog boxes is more suitable, calculator applications are often implemented as dialog boxes. Unless you are collecting the results from the various calculator instances in a parent window (or doing some other meaningful management task) there is really no need for a parent window. Therefore, using a dialog box as the main window is more suitable than making it a child of a TWindow (or its descendants) instance.

In the previous chapters, I presented several versions of the Command-Oriented Calculator Application (COCA) with each version's controls attached to a window. This section presents a calculator version that uses a dialog box. This version is derived from COCA version 2. Versions 2 and 5 offer identical operations. Figure 8.4 shows a sample session with the DIALOG4.EXE program.

Figure 8.4. A sample session with the DIALOG4.EXE application.

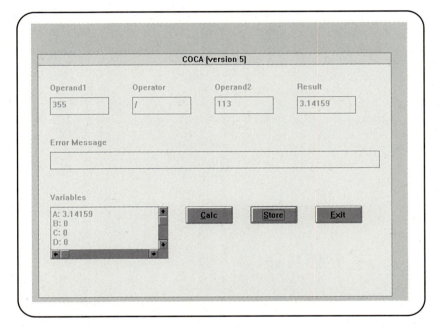

Listing 8.10 shows the header file DIALOG4.H.

Listing 8.10. The source code for the DIALOG4.H header file.

```
#define ID_CALC_BTN 107
#define ID_STORE_BTN 108
#define ID_EXIT_BTN 109
```

Listing 8.11 shows the script for the resource file DIALOG4.RC. The resource file defines the accelerator keys resources and the basic modeless dialog box resource.

Dialog Boxes

Listing 8.11. The script for the DIALOG4.RC resource file.

```
#include <windows.h>
#include <owlrc.h>
#include "dialog4.h"

BUTTONS ACCELERATORS
BEGIN
     "c", ID_CALC_BTN, ALT
     "s", ID_STORE_BTN, ALT
     "e", ID_EXIT_BTN, ALT
END

CALC DIALOG DISCARDABLE LOADONCALL PURE MOVEABLE 10, 10, 300, 200
STYLE WS_POPUP ¦ WS_DLGFRAME
CAPTION "COCA (version 5)"
CLASS "TAppWindow"
BEGIN
END
```

Listing 8.12 contains the source code for the DIALOG4.CPP program.

Listing 8.12. The source code for the DIALOG4.CPP program file.

```
#include <stdlib.h>
#include <ctype.h>
#include <stdio.h>
#include <math.h>
#include <string.h>
#include <owl.h>
#include <static.h>
#include <edit.h>
#include <button.h>
#include <dialog.h>
#include "dialog4.h"

// declare the constants that represent the sizes of the controls
const Wlbl = 100;
const Hlbl = 20;
const LblVertSpacing = 5;
const LblHorzSpacing = 40;
const Wbox = 100;
const Hbox = 30;
```

continues

435

Listing 8.12. continued

```
const BoxVertSpacing = 20;
const BoxHorzSpacing = 40;
const WLongbox = 4 * (Wbox + BoxHorzSpacing);
const Wvarbox = 2 * Wbox;
const Hvarbox = 3 * Hbox;
const Hbtn = 30;
const Wbtn = 80;
const BtnHorzSpacing = 30;
const MaxEditLen = 30;
const MAX_MEMREG = 26;

// declare the ID_XXXX constants for the edit boxes
#define ID_OPERAND1_EDIT 101
#define ID_OPERATOR_EDIT 102
#define ID_OPERAND2_EDIT 103
#define ID_RESULT_EDIT 104
#define ID_ERRMSG_EDIT 105
#define ID_VARIABLE_EDIT 106

// declare the custom application class as
// a subclass of TApplication
class TWinApp : public TApplication
{
public:
  TWinApp(LPSTR     AName,           // application name
          HINSTANCE hInstance,       // instance handle
          HINSTANCE hPrevInstance,   // previous instance handle
          LPSTR     lpCmdLine,       // command-line arguments
          int       nCmdShow) :      // display command
          TApplication(AName, hInstance, hPrevInstance,
                      lpCmdLine, nCmdShow) {};

protected:
  virtual void InitMainWindow();
  virtual void InitInstance();
};

// use the _CLASSDEF macro to declare reference and pointer
// types related to the new TAppWindow class
_CLASSDEF(TAppWindow)

// expand the functionality of TDialog by deriving class TAppWindow
class TAppWindow : public TDialog
{
```

```cpp
public:

  TAppWindow(PTWindowsObject AParent, LPSTR AName);

  // define the class name method
  virtual LPSTR GetClassName() { return "TAppWindow"; }

  virtual void GetWindowClass(WNDCLASS& W);

  // handle clicking the left mouse button
  virtual void WMLButtonDown(RTMessage Msg)
    = [WM_FIRST + WM_LBUTTONDOWN];

  // handle the calculation
  virtual void HandleCalcBtn(RTMessage Msg)
    = [ID_FIRST + ID_CALC_BTN];

  // handle the accelerator key for the Calculate button
  virtual void CMCalcBtn(RTMessage Msg)
    = [CM_FIRST + ID_CALC_BTN];

  // handle storing the result in a variable
  virtual void HandleStoreBtn(RTMessage Msg)
    = [ID_FIRST + ID_STORE_BTN];

  // handle the accelerator key for the Store button
  virtual void CMStoreBtn(RTMessage Msg)
    = [CM_FIRST + ID_STORE_BTN];

  // handle exiting the application
  virtual void HandleExitBtn(RTMessage Msg)
    = [ID_FIRST + ID_EXIT_BTN];

  // handle the accelerator key for the Exit button
  virtual void CMExitBtn(RTMessage Msg)
    = [CM_FIRST + ID_EXIT_BTN];

  // enable a push button control
  virtual void EnableButton(PTButton Btn)
  { EnableWindow(Btn->HWindow, TRUE); }

  // disable a push button control
  virtual void DisableButton(PTButton Btn)
  { EnableWindow(Btn->HWindow, FALSE); }
```

continues

Listing 8.12. continued

```
  // handle closing the window
  virtual BOOL CanClose();

protected:
  PTEdit Operand1Box;
  PTEdit OperatorBox;
  PTEdit Operand2Box;
  PTEdit ResultBox;
  PTEdit ErrMsgBox;
  PTEdit VariableBox;
  PTButton CalcBtn;
  PTButton StoreBtn;
  PTButton ExitBtn;

  // math error flag
  BOOL InError;

  // coordinates for the Error Message static text area
  int MSG_xulc, MSG_yulc, MSG_xlrc, MSG_ylrc;
  // obtain a number of a Variable edit box line
  double getVar(int lineNum);

  // store a number in the selected text of
  // the Variable edit box line
  void putVar(double x);

};

TAppWindow::TAppWindow(PTWindowsObject AParent, LPSTR AName) :
                      TDialog(AParent, AName)
{
  char s[81];
  char bigStr[6 * MAX_MEMREG + 1];
  char c;
  int x0 = 20;
  int y0 = 30;
  int x = x0, y = y0;

  // create the first set of labels for the edit boxes
  strcpy(s, "Operand1");
  new TStatic(this, -1, s, x, y, Wlbl, Hlbl, strlen(s));
  strcpy(s, "Operator");
  x += Wlbl + LblHorzSpacing;
  new TStatic(this, -1, s, x, y, Wlbl, Hlbl, strlen(s));
```

```
            strcpy(s, "Operand2");
            x += Wlbl + LblHorzSpacing;
            new TStatic(this, -1, s, x, y, Wlbl, Hlbl, strlen(s));
            x += Wlbl + LblHorzSpacing;
            strcpy(s, "Result");
            new TStatic(this, -1, s, x, y, Wlbl, Hlbl, strlen(s));

            // create the operand1, operator, operand2, and result
            // edit boxes
            x = x0;
            y += Hlbl + LblVertSpacing;
            Operand1Box = new TEdit(this, ID_OPERAND1_EDIT, "", x, y,
                                Wbox, Hbox, 0, FALSE);

            // force conversion of letters to uppercase
            Operand1Box->Attr.Style |= ES_UPPERCASE;
            x += Wbox + BoxHorzSpacing;
            OperatorBox = new TEdit(this, ID_OPERATOR_EDIT, "", x, y,
                                Wbox, Hbox, 0, FALSE);
            x += Wbox + BoxHorzSpacing;
            Operand2Box = new TEdit(this, ID_OPERAND2_EDIT, "", x, y,
                                Wbox, Hbox, 0, FALSE);
            // force conversion of letters to uppercase
            Operand2Box->Attr.Style |= ES_UPPERCASE;
            x += Wbox + BoxHorzSpacing;
            ResultBox = new TEdit(this, ID_RESULT_EDIT, "", x, y, Wbox, Hbox,
                              0, FALSE);

            // create the static text and edit box for the error message
            x = x0;
            y += Hbox + BoxVertSpacing;
            // store the coordinates for the static text area
            MSG_xulc = x;
            MSG_yulc = y;
            MSG_xlrc = x + Wlbl;
            MSG_ylrc = y + Hlbl;
            strcpy(s, "Error Message");
            new TStatic(this, -1, s, x, y, Wlbl, Hlbl, strlen(s));
            y += Hlbl + LblVertSpacing;
            ErrMsgBox = new TEdit(this, ID_ERRMSG_EDIT, "", x, y,
                              WLongbox, Hbox, 0, FALSE);
            // create the static text and edit box for the single-letter
            // variable selection
            y += Hbox + BoxVertSpacing;
            strcpy(s, "Variables");
```

continues

Listing 8.12. continued

```
  new TStatic(this, -1, s, x, y, Wlbl, Hlbl, strlen(s));
  y += Hlbl + LblVertSpacing;
  // build the initial contents of the Variable edit box
  for (c = 'A'; c <= 'Z'; c++) {
    sprintf(s, "%c: 0\r\n", c);
    strcat(bigStr, s);
  }
  VariableBox = new TEdit(this, ID_VARIABLE_EDIT, bigStr, x, y,
                          Wvarbox, Hvarbox, 0, TRUE);
  // force conversion of letters to uppercase
  VariableBox->Attr.Style |= ES_UPPERCASE;

  // create the Calc push button
  x += Wvarbox + BtnHorzSpacing;
  CalcBtn = new TButton(this, ID_CALC_BTN, "&Calc",
                        x, y, Wbtn, Hbtn, TRUE);

  // create the Store Btn
  x += Wbtn + BtnHorzSpacing;
  StoreBtn = new TButton(this, ID_STORE_BTN, "&Store",
                         x, y, Wbtn, Hbtn, FALSE);

  // Create the Exit Btn
  x += Wbtn + BtnHorzSpacing;
  ExitBtn = new TButton(this, ID_EXIT_BTN, "&Exit",
                        x, y, Wbtn, Hbtn, FALSE);

  // clear the InError flag
  InError = FALSE;

  // enable the keyboard handler
  EnableKBHandler();
}

void TAppWindow::GetWindowClass(WNDCLASS& W)
{
  TDialog::GetWindowClass(W);
  W.hCursor = LoadCursor(NULL, IDC_UPARROW);
}

void TAppWindow::WMLButtonDown(RTMessage Msg)
{
  int x = Msg.LP.Lo;
  int y = Msg.LP.Hi;
```

```
    char s[MaxEditLen+1];
    char line[MaxEditLen+1];
    double z;

    if (x >= MSG_xulc && x <= MSG_xlrc &&
        y >= MSG_yulc && y <= MSG_ylrc) {
      ErrMsgBox->Clear();
      // enable the Store button
      EnableButton(StoreBtn);
    }
}

void TAppWindow::HandleCalcBtn(RTMessage Msg)
{
  double x, y, z;
  char opStr[MaxEditLen+1];
  char s[MaxEditLen+1];

  // obtain the string in the Operand1 edit box
  Operand1Box->GetText(s, MaxEditLen);
  // does the Operand1Box contain the name
  // of a single-letter variable?
  if (isalpha(s[0]))
    // obtain value from the Variable edit control
    x = getVar(s[0] - 'A');
  else
    // convert the string in the edit box
    x = atof(s);

  // obtain the string in the Operand2 edit box
  Operand2Box->GetText(s, MaxEditLen);
  // does the Operand2Box contain the name
  // of a single-letter variable?
  if (isalpha(s[0]))
    // obtain value from the Variable edit control
    y =getVar(s[0] - 'A');
  else
     // convert the string in the edit box
    y = atof(s);

  // obtain the string in the Operator edit box
  OperatorBox->GetText(opStr, MaxEditLen);

  // clear the error message box
  ErrMsgBox->Clear();
```

continues

Listing 8.12. continued

```c
  InError = FALSE;

  // determine the requested operation
  if (strcmp(opStr, "+") == 0)
    z = x + y;
  else if (strcmp(opStr, "-") == 0)
    z = x - y;
  else if (strcmp(opStr, "*") == 0)
    z = x * y;
  else if (strcmp(opStr, "/") == 0) {
    if (y != 0)
      z = x / y;
    else {
      z = 0;
      InError = TRUE;
      ErrMsgBox->SetText("Division-by-zero error");
    }
  }
  else if (strcmp(opStr, "^") == 0) {
    if (x > 0)
      z = exp(y * log(x));
    else {
      InError = TRUE;
      ErrMsgBox->SetText(
        "Cannot raise the power of a negative number");
    }
  }
  else {
    InError = TRUE;
    ErrMsgBox->SetText("Invalid operator");
  }
  // display the result if no error has occurred
  if (!InError) {
    sprintf(s, "%g", z);
    ResultBox->SetText(s);
    // enable the Store button
    EnableButton(StoreBtn);
  }
  else
    // disable the Store button
    DisableButton(StoreBtn);
}

void TAppWindow::CMCalcBtn(RTMessage Msg)
```

```cpp
  {
    HandleCalcBtn(Msg);
  }

void TAppWindow::HandleStoreBtn(RTMessage Msg)
{
  char varName[MaxEditLen+1];
  char result[MaxEditLen+1];

  // get the string in the Result edit box
  ResultBox->GetText(result, MaxEditLen);

  // store the result in the selected text of
  // the Variable edit box
  putVar(atof(result));
}

void TAppWindow::CMStoreBtn(RTMessage Msg)
{
  HandleStoreBtn(Msg);
}

void TAppWindow::HandleExitBtn(RTMessage Msg)
{
  // use the dialog box member function
  CloseWindow();
}

void TAppWindow::CMExitBtn(RTMessage Msg)
{
  // send a WM_CLOSE message
  SendMessage(HWindow, WM_CLOSE, NULL, NULL);
}

double TAppWindow::getVar(int lineNum)
{
  int lineSize;
  char s[MaxEditLen+1];

  if (lineNum >= MAX_MEMREG) return 0;
  // get the size of the target line
  lineSize = VariableBox->GetLineLength(lineNum);
  // get the line
  VariableBox->GetLine(s, lineSize+1, lineNum);
  // delete the first three characters
```

continues

Listing 8.12. continued

```cpp
  strcpy(s, (s+3));
  // return the number stored in the target line
  return atof(s);
}

void TAppWindow::putVar(double x)
{
  int startPos, endPos;
  int lineNum;
  int lineSize;
  char s[MaxEditLen+1];

  // locate the character position of the cursor
  VariableBox->GetSelection(startPos, endPos);
  // turn off the selected text
  if (startPos != endPos)
    VariableBox->SetSelection(startPos, startPos);
  // get the line number where the cursor is located
  lineNum = VariableBox->GetLineFromPos(startPos);
  // get the line size of line lineNum
  lineSize = VariableBox->GetLineLength(lineNum);
  // obtain the text of line lineNum
  VariableBox->GetLine(s, lineSize+1, lineNum);
  // delete line lineNum
  VariableBox->DeleteLine(lineNum);
  // build the new text line
  sprintf(s, "%c: %g\r\n", s[0], x);
  // insert it
  VariableBox->Insert(s);
}

BOOL TAppWindow::CanClose()
{
  return MessageBox(HWindow, "Want to close this application",
                    "Query", MB_YESNO | MB_ICONQUESTION) == IDYES;
}

void TWinApp::InitMainWindow()
{
  MainWindow = new TAppWindow(NULL, "CALC");
}

void TWinApp::InitInstance()
{
```

```
  TApplication::InitInstance();
  HAccTable = LoadAccelerators(hInstance, "BUTTONS");
}

int PASCAL WinMain(HINSTANCE hInstance, HINSTANCE hPrevInstance,
                   LPSTR lpCmdLine, int nCmdShow)
{
  TWinApp WinApp(
    "Command-Oriented Calculator Application (COCA) Version 4",
               hInstance, hPrevInstance, lpCmdLine, nCmdShow);
  WinApp.Run(); // run OWL application
  return WinApp.Status; // return application status

}
```

This source code is very similar to that of file CTLBTN1.CPP. The differences are as follows:

- ☐ The program declares `TAppWindow` as a descendant of the `TDialog` class.
- ☐ The application instance creates an instance of `TAppWindow`, the dialog box class. Notice that the creation of the dialog box is very similar to that of the typical window and involves neither `ExecDialog` nor `MakeWindow`.
- ☐ The modeless calculator dialog box closes in response to `WM_CLOSE` messages sent by the Exit push button control.

Transferring Control Data

Dialog boxes serve mainly as pop-up windows that request input from the application's user. This input often includes a variety of settings that use radio buttons, check boxes, and edit boxes. Because dialog boxes are frequently executed or created, it makes sense to preserve the latest values in the dialog's controls for the next time it appears. The Search and Replace dialog boxes found in the Turbo C++ IDE and many other Windows editors are typical examples. These dialog boxes remember the settings of all or some of their controls from the last time the dialog box was executed.

The Transfer Buffer Type

To implement data transfer in dialog boxes (and also in windows), ObjectWindows offers a data transfer mechanism between the dialog box and a buffer. This buffer is usually a data member of the parent window. Therefore, the first step in supporting data transfer is to define a transfer buffer type. The buffer defines data fields for the controls with data that you want to transfer. These controls include the static text, edit box, list box, combo box, scroll bar, check box, and radio button. The group box and push button controls have no data to transfer and, therefore, do not enter into the declaration of the data transfer buffer type. The following is a sample data buffer type that includes a single instance of each allowable control:

```
struct TAppTransferBuffer {
    char StaticText[MaxSTaticLen];
    char EditBox[MaxEditLen];
    PTListBoxData ListBoxData;
    PTComboBoxData ComboBoxData;
    TScrollBarData ScrollBarData;
    WORD CheckBox;
    WORD RadioButton;
};
```

There are two simple rules to observe regarding the type and sequence of declared data members:

- Include only members for the controls with data that is transferred.
- Declare the buffer type members in the same order that you create the controls in the dialog box constructor.

Here are the various members of the data transfer buffer types:

- The `StaticText` member helps in transferring data between a static text control and the data buffer. The data member defines a character array that has to be equal to the number of characters in the static text control.

- The `EditBox` member assists in moving data between the edit box control and the data buffer. The data member defines a character array that must be equal to the number of characters in the edit box control.

- The `ListBoxData` member helps to transfer data between a list box control and the data buffer. `ListBoxData` is a pointer to the following `TListBoxData` class:

```
class _EXPORT TListBoxData
{
```

```
public:
    PArray Strings;
    PArray SelStrings;
    int SelCount;

    TListBoxData();
    ~TListBoxData();
    void AddString(Pchar AString, BOOL IsSelected = FALSE);
    void SelectString(LPSTR AString);
    void ResetSelections();
    int GetSelStringLength(int Index = 0);
    void GetSelString(LPSTR Buffer, int BufferSize,
                      int Index = 0);
};
```

The `Strings` data member is an array of `Strings` that contains the list items. `SelStrings` is an array of `Strings` that contains the list selections. In a single-selection list box, the `SelStrings` array has only one member. The `SelCount` data member stores the number of selections in the list box.

▢ The `ComboBoxData` member helps to move data between a combo box control and the data buffer. `ComboBoxData` is a pointer to the following `TComboBoxData` class:

```
class _EXPORT TComboBoxData
{
public:
    PArray Strings;
    Pchar Selection;

    TComboBoxData();
    ~TComboBoxData();
    void AddString(Pchar AString, BOOL IsSelected = FALSE);
};
```

The `Strings` data member is an array of `Strings` that contains the list items. `Selection` is a pointer to the selected item in the list box of the combo box control.

▢ The `ScrollBarData` member assists in transferring data between a scroll bar control and the data buffer. This member has the following `TScollBarData` structure type:

```
struct TScrollBarData {
    int LowValue;
    int HighValue;
    int Position;
};
```

- The `LowValue`, `HighValue`, and `Position` members store the scroll bar range and the current thumb position.
- The `CheckBox` member stores the current check state of a check box in a `WORD` type.
- The `RadioButton` member stores the current check state of a radio button in a `WORD` type.

The `Transfer` Member Function

The `TStatic`, `TListBox`, `TComboBox`, `TScrollBar`, and `TCheckBox` classes declare their own versions of the virtual `Transfer` member function. The `TEdit` class inherits the `TStatic::Transfer` member function. Similarly, the `TRadioButton` class inherits the `TCheckBox::Transfer` member function. The `Transfer` function contains the code to transfer data to and from the buffer. The general form of the `Transfer` function is

```
WORD Transfer(Pvoid DataPtr, WORD TransferFlag)
```

The `DataPtr` is a pointer to the transferred data. The `TransferFlag` is a transfer direction flag that can take the following values:

- `TF_SETDATA` to move data from the buffer to the control of the dialog box
- `TF_GETDATA` to move data from the control of the dialog box to the buffer
- `TF_SIZEDATA` to return the size of the transferred data, which is systematically supplied by the function's result type

Listing 8.13 contains the `Transfer` member functions for various controls. The listing shows how the current `Transfer` member functions are coded and how to write a `Transfer` member function.

Listing 8.13. The `Transfer` member functions for various controls.

```
WORD TStatic::Transfer(Pvoid DataPtr, WORD TransferFlag)
{
    if ( TransferFlag == TF_GETDATA )
        GetText((LPSTR)DataPtr, TextLen);
    else
        if ( TransferFlag == TF_SETDATA )
            SetText((LPSTR)DataPtr);
    return TextLen;
}
```

```cpp
WORD TListBox::Transfer(Pvoid DataPtr, WORD TransferFlag)
{
    int I, SelIndex;
    long Style;
    int *Selections;
    int MaxStringLen = 0, TmpStringLen = 0;
    Pchar TmpString;
    PTListBoxData ListBoxData = *(PTListBoxData _FAR *)DataPtr;

    Style = GetWindowLong(HWindow, GWL_STYLE);
    if ( TransferFlag == TF_GETDATA )
    {
      ListBoxData->ResetSelections();
      if ( (Style & LBS_MULTIPLESEL) != LBS_MULTIPLESEL )
      {
         SelIndex = (int)SendMessage(HWindow, LB_GETCURSEL, 0, 0);
         if ( SelIndex != LB_ERR )
         {
      MaxStringLen = GetStringLen(SelIndex);
      TmpString = new char[MaxStringLen + 1];
      GetString(TmpString, SelIndex);
      ListBoxData->SelectString(TmpString);
      delete TmpString;
         }
    }
    else
    {
            I = GetSelCount();
            if ( I > 0 )
            {
              Selections = new int[I];
              SendMessage(HWindow, LB_GETSELITEMS,
                        I, (long)(Selections));
              for (int SelIndex = 0; SelIndex < I; SelIndex++)
              {
                TmpStringLen = GetStringLen(Selections[SelIndex]);
                if ( TmpStringLen > MaxStringLen )
                    MaxStringLen = TmpStringLen;
              }
              TmpString = new char[MaxStringLen+1];
              for (SelIndex = 0; SelIndex < I; SelIndex++)
              {
                    GetString(TmpString, Selections[SelIndex]);
                    ListBoxData->SelectString(TmpString);
              }
```

continues

Listing 8.13. continued

```
                delete TmpString;
                }
        }
    }
    else if ( TransferFlag == TF_SETDATA )
    {
        ClearList();
        ListBoxData->Strings->forEach(DoAddForLB, this);

        if ( (Style & LBS_MULTIPLESEL) != LBS_MULTIPLESEL )
        {
            if ( ListBoxData->SelCount )
            {
                SelIndex = FindExactString(
                    (LPSTR)(PCchar)(RString)
                    (*ListBoxData->SelStrings)[0], -1);
                if ( SelIndex > -1 )
                    SetSelIndex(SelIndex);
            }
        }
        else
        {
            SendMessage(HWindow, LB_SETSEL,
                    0, -1); // Unselect all

            for (I = 0; I < ListBoxData->SelCount; ++I)
            {
                SelIndex = FindExactString(
                        (LPSTR)(PCchar)(RString)
                        (*ListBoxData->SelStrings)[I], -1);
                if ( SelIndex > -1 )
                    SendMessage(HWindow, LB_SETSEL,
                            1, SelIndex);
            }
        }
    }
    return sizeof(PTListBoxData);
}

WORD TComboBox::Transfer(Pvoid DataPtr, WORD TransferFlag)
{
    PTComboBoxData ComboBoxData = *(PTComboBoxData _FAR *)DataPtr;

    if ( TransferFlag == TF_GETDATA )
```

Dialog Boxes

```cpp
        {
            int StringSize = GetWindowTextLength(HWindow) + 1;
            if ( ComboBoxData->Selection )
                delete ComboBoxData->Selection;
            ComboBoxData->Selection= new char[StringSize];
            GetWindowText(HWindow, ComboBoxData->Selection,
                          StringSize);
        }
        else
            if ( TransferFlag == TF_SETDATA )
            {
                ClearList();
                ComboBoxData->Strings->forEach(DoAddForCB, this);

                int SelIndex = FindExactString(
                                ComboBoxData->Selection, -1);
                if ( SelIndex > -1 )
                    SetSelIndex(SelIndex);

                SetWindowText(HWindow, ComboBoxData->Selection);
            }
    return sizeof(PTComboBoxData);
}

WORD TCheckBox::Transfer(Pvoid DataPtr, WORD TransferFlag)
{
        WORD CheckFlag;

    if ( TransferFlag == TF_GETDATA )
    {
        CheckFlag = GetCheck();
        _fmemcpy(DataPtr, &CheckFlag, sizeof(CheckFlag));
    }
    else
        if ( TransferFlag == TF_SETDATA )
            SetCheck( *(WORD *)DataPtr );
    return sizeof(CheckFlag);
}

WORD TScrollBar::Transfer(Pvoid DataPtr, WORD TransferFlag)
{
    TScrollBarData *NewPtr = (TScrollBarData *)DataPtr;

    if ( TransferFlag == TF_GETDATA )
    {
```

continues

Listing 8.13. continued

```
            GetRange(NewPtr->LowValue, NewPtr->HighValue);
            NewPtr->Position = GetPosition();
    }
    else if ( TransferFlag == TF_SETDATA )
    {
            SetRange(NewPtr->LowValue, NewPtr->HighValue);
            SetPosition(NewPtr->Position);
    }
    return sizeof(TScrollBarData);
}
```

The Transfer Buffer

The transfer buffer is typically declared as a member of the parent window. The window class constructor is the member function that usually performs the initialization of the transfer buffer. The members of the buffer transfer types are assigned values to set the initial values and states of the controls. The buffer parts for the list box and combo box controls need a few extra steps. These steps involve at least creating the instances of the TListBoxData and TComboBoxData classes. The additional, optional steps involve adding and selecting list items. The following is a simple example:

```
// create the class instance
AppBuffer.ListBox = new TListBoxData()
// add strings to the list box buffer
AppBuffer.ListBox->AddString("List String #1");
AppBuffer.ListBox->AddString("List String #2");
AppBuffer.ListBox->AddString("List String #3");
// select the second list item
AppBuffer.ListBox->SelString("List String #2");

// create the class instance
AppBuffer.ComboBox = new TComboBoxData()
// add strings to the combo box buffer
AppBuffer.ComboBox->AddString("Combo String #1");
AppBuffer.ComboBox->AddString("Combo String #2");
AppBuffer.ComboBox->AddString("Combo String #3");
```

Once the data buffer is initialized, assign its address to the predefined pointer member TransferBuffer. Here's an example:

```
TransferBuffer = &AppBuffer;
```

This assignment establishes the connection between the buffer and the dialog box or window.

Data Transfer Rules

ObjectWindows establishes a protocol for transferring data between a control and its buffer. Here are the rules:

- ☐ The transfer of data for the controls of a dialog box is enabled by default, except for instances of the TStatic class.

- ☐ The transfer of data for the controls of a window is disabled by default.

- ☐ To disable the transfer mechanism for a dialog box control, use the DisableTransfer member function of that control class. Here's an example:

    ```
    ADlgCheckBox = new TCheckBox(this, ID_CHECK_BOX);
    ADlgCheckBox->DisableTransfer();
    ```

- ☐ To enable the transfer mechanism for a window control, use the EnableTransfer member function of that control class. Here's an example:

    ```
    AWindowCheckBox = new TCheckBox(this, ID_CHECK_BOX);
    AWindowCheckBox->EnableTransfer();
    ```

- ☐ Data is automatically transferred when a window (with at least one control that has enabled data transfer) is created or a dialog box is created or executed.

- ☐ The data of a modal dialog box is automatically transferred to the buffer when the dialog box receives a notification message of IDOK. A notification message of IDCANCEL blocks the transfer of data to the buffer.

- ☐ The data of a modal dialog box is automatically transferred to the buffer if the CloseWindow member function obtains a TRUE result by calling the CanClose member function.

- ☐ The TransferData member function with a single argument TF_GETDATA must be used to explicitly transfer data from a window or a modeless dialog box.

- ☐ You can transfer data to and from the buffer (to reset the controls of a window or dialog box) by invoking the TransferData member function with the TF_GETDATA or TF_SETDATA arguments.

Data Transfer Examples

This section presents examples of transferring data between dialog boxes and their buffers. These examples demonstrate how to transfer data with modal dialog boxes, modeless dialog boxes, and windows.

A Simple Modal Dialog Box

Here's an example of transferring data between the controls of a modal dialog box and a buffer. This simple application creates a sample dialog box that replaces text. Figure 8.5 shows the dialog box during a sample session with the DIALOG5.EXE application.

Figure 8.5.
A sample session with the DIALOG5.EXE application.

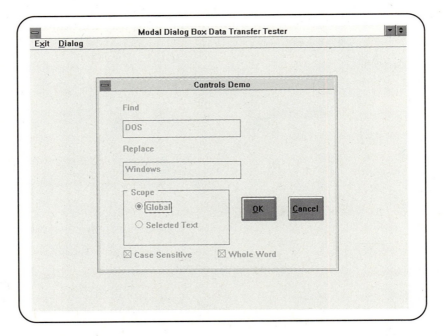

The dialog box includes the following controls:

- The Find edit box
- The Replace edit box
- The Scope group box that contains the Global and Selected Text radio button controls

- The Case Sensitive check box
- The Whole Word check box
- The OK push button control
- The Cancel push button control

This application includes a main menu with Exit and Dialog menu items. To invoke the dialog box, click the Dialog menu item or press Alt-D. When you invoke the dialog box for the first time, the controls have the following initial values and states:

- The Find edit box contains the string DOS.
- The Replace edit box contains the string Windows.
- The Global radio button is checked.
- The Case-Sensitive check box is checked.
- The Whole Word check box is checked.

Type new strings in the edit box and alter the check states of the radio buttons and check boxes. Now click the OK button (or press the Alt-O) to close the dialog box. Invoke the Dialog menu item again to open the dialog box. Notice that the controls of the dialog box have the same values and states as when you last closed the dialog box.

Now examine the code that implements the DIALOG5.EXE application. Listing 8.14 shows the source code for the DIALOG5.H header file. This file declares the ID_XXXX constants for the various controls as well as the CM_DIALOG constant for the Dialog menu command.

Listing 8.14. The source code for the DIALOG5.H header file.

```
#define CM_DIALOG 101

#define ID_DIALOG        200
#define ID_FIND_TXT      201
#define ID_FIND_EDIT     202
#define ID_REPLACE_TXT       203
#define ID_REPLACE_EDIT  204
#define ID_SCOPE_GRP     205
#define ID_GLOBAL_RBT        206
#define ID_SELTEXT_RBT       207
#define ID_CASE_CHK      208
#define ID_WHOLEWORD_CHK 209
```

Listing 8.15 contains the script for the DIALOG5.RC resource file. This file defines the resources for the accelerator keys, the menu, and the dialog box, including its controls.

Caution: You must define all the controls in a resource file to enable the data transfer mechanism supported by ObjectWindows. Creating the controls from scratch inside the dialog box constructor will not work.

Listing 8.15. The script for the DIALOG5.RC resource file.

```
#include <windows.h>
#include <owlrc.h>
#include "dialog5.h"

BUTTONS ACCELERATORS
BEGIN
     "o", IDOK, ALT
     "c", IDCANCEL, ALT
END

ID_DIALOG DIALOG DISCARDABLE LOADONCALL PURE MOVEABLE
                10, 10, 200, 150
STYLE WS_POPUP ¦ WS_CLIPSIBLINGS ¦
WS_CAPTION ¦ WS_SYSMENU ¦ DS_MODALFRAME
CAPTION "Controls Demo"
BEGIN
    CONTROL "Find", ID_FIND_TXT, "STATIC", WS_CHILD ¦ WS_VISIBLE ¦
        SS_LEFT, 20, 10, 100, 15

    CONTROL "", ID_FIND_EDIT, "EDIT", WS_CHILD ¦ WS_VISIBLE ¦
        WS_BORDER ¦ WS_TABSTOP, 20, 25, 100, 15

    CONTROL "Replace", ID_REPLACE_TXT, "STATIC", WS_CHILD ¦
        WS_VISIBLE ¦ SS_LEFT, 20, 45, 100, 15

    CONTROL "", ID_REPLACE_EDIT, "EDIT", WS_CHILD ¦ WS_VISIBLE ¦
        WS_BORDER ¦ WS_TABSTOP, 20, 60, 100, 15

    CONTROL " Scope ", ID_SCOPE_GRP, "BUTTON", WS_CHILD ¦
        WS_VISIBLE ¦ WS_GROUP ¦ BS_GROUPBOX, 20, 80, 90, 50
```

```
        CONTROL "Global", ID_GLOBAL_RBT, "BUTTON", WS_CHILD |
            WS_VISIBLE | WS_TABSTOP | BS_AUTORADIOBUTTON,
            30, 90, 50, 15

        CONTROL "Selected Text", ID_SELTEXT_RBT, "BUTTON", WS_CHILD |
            WS_VISIBLE | WS_TABSTOP | BS_AUTORADIOBUTTON,
            30, 105, 60, 15

        CONTROL "Case Sensitive", ID_CASE_CHK, "BUTTON", WS_CHILD |
            WS_VISIBLE | WS_TABSTOP | BS_AUTOCHECKBOX,
            20, 130, 80, 15

        CONTROL "Whole Word", ID_WHOLEWORD_CHK, "BUTTON", WS_CHILD |
            WS_VISIBLE | WS_TABSTOP | BS_AUTOCHECKBOX,
            100, 130, 80, 15

        CONTROL, "&OK", IDOK, "BUTTON", WS_CHILD | WS_VISIBLE |
            WS_TABSTOP | BS_DEFPUSHBUTTON, 120, 90, 30, 20

        CONTROL "&Cancel", IDCANCEL, "BUTTON", WS_CHILD | WS_VISIBLE |
            WS_TABSTOP | BS_PUSHBUTTON, 160, 90, 30, 20
END

MAINMENU MENU LOADONCALL MOVEABLE PURE DISCARDABLE
BEGIN
        MENUITEM "E&xit", CM_EXIT
        MENUITEM "&Dialog", CM_DIALOG
END
```

Notice that the controls are created with the CONTROL keyword (which is used to create controls in general). This keyword requires the caption, ID, control class name, style, location, and dimensions of the control. Chapter 11, "Controls Resource Script," discusses the resource file control script in more detail and presents other keywords that create the controls with default styles. For now, use the CONTROL keyword.

Notice in the dialog box resource definition that the OK and Cancel push buttons have the predefined IDOK and IDCANCEL IDs, respectively. Also notice that the OK button has the default push button style, and the Cancel button has the normal push button style. In addition, notice that the group box, radio buttons, and check boxes have the BUTTON class name. The styles associated with these controls suggest their intended use.

Listing 8.16 shows the source code for the DIALOG5.CPP program file. The program declares the data transfer type TAppTransferBuf and includes members for the edit boxes, radio buttons, and check boxes.

Listing 8.16. The source code for the DIALOG5.CPP program file.

```
#include <string.h>
#include <owl.h>
#include <static.h>
#include <edit.h>
#include <checkbox.h>
#include <groupbox.h>
#include <radiobut.h>
#include <button.h>
#include <dialog.h>
#include "dialog5.h"

const MaxEditLen = 30;

struct TAppTransferBuf {
  char FindBoxBuff[MaxEditLen];
  char ReplaceBoxBuff[MaxEditLen];
  WORD GlobalRbtBuff;
  WORD SelTextRbtBuff;
  WORD CaseChkBuff;
  WORD WholeWordChkBuff;
};

// declare the custom application class as
// a subclass of TApplication
class TWinApp : public TApplication
{
public:
  TWinApp(LPSTR     AName,          // application name
          HINSTANCE hInstance,      // instance handle
          HINSTANCE hPrevInstance,  // previous instance handle
          LPSTR     lpCmdLine,      // command-line arguments
          int       nCmdShow) :     // display command
          TApplication(AName, hInstance, hPrevInstance,
                  lpCmdLine, nCmdShow) {};

protected:
  virtual void InitMainWindow();
  virtual void InitInstance();
```

```
};

// use the _CLASSDEF macro to declare reference and pointer
// types related to the new TAppWindow and TAppDialog classes
_CLASSDEF(TAppWindow)
_CLASSDEF(TAppDialog)

// expand the functionality of TDialog by deriving class TAppDialog
class TAppDialog : public TDialog
{
public:

  TAppDialog(PTWindowsObject AParent, int ResourceId);


protected:
  PTGroupBox ScopeGrp;
};

// expand the functionality of TWindow by deriving class TAppWindow
class TAppWindow : public TWindow
{
public:
  TAppTransferBuf AppBuffer;

  TAppWindow(PTWindowsObject AParent, LPSTR ATitle);

  // handle the dialog command
  virtual void CMDialog(RTMessage Msg)
    = [CM_FIRST + CM_DIALOG];

  // handle closing the window
  virtual BOOL CanClose();
};

TAppDialog::TAppDialog(PTWindowsObject AParent, int ResourceId) :
                    TDialog(AParent, ResourceId)
{
  new TStatic(this, ID_FIND_TXT, MaxEditLen);
  new TEdit(this, ID_FIND_EDIT, MaxEditLen);
  new TStatic(this, ID_REPLACE_TXT, MaxEditLen);
  new TEdit(this, ID_REPLACE_EDIT, MaxEditLen);
  ScopeGrp = new TGroupBox(this, ID_SCOPE_GRP);
  new TRadioButton(this, ID_GLOBAL_RBT, ScopeGrp);
  new TRadioButton(this, ID_SELTEXT_RBT, ScopeGrp);
```

continues

Listing 8.16. continued

```
    new TCheckBox(this, ID_CASE_CHK, NULL);
    new TCheckBox(this, ID_WHOLEWORD_CHK, NULL);
    // assign the address of the dialog transfer buffer
    // to member TransferBuffer
    TransferBuffer = (void far*)&(((TAppWindow *)Parent)->
                                   AppBuffer);
}

TAppWindow::TAppWindow(PTWindowsObject AParent, LPSTR ATitle)
                     : TWindow(AParent, ATitle)
{
  AssignMenu("MAINMENU");

  // fill buffer with 0's
  memset(&AppBuffer, 0x0, sizeof(AppBuffer));
  strcpy(AppBuffer.FindBoxBuff, "DOS");
  strcpy(AppBuffer.ReplaceBoxBuff, "Windows");
  AppBuffer.GlobalRbtBuff = BF_CHECKED;
  AppBuffer.CaseChkBuff = BF_CHECKED;
  AppBuffer.WholeWordChkBuff = BF_CHECKED;
};

void TAppWindow::CMDialog(RTMessage Msg)
{
  char msgStr[256];

  if (GetModule()->ExecDialog(
       new TAppDialog(this, ID_DIALOG)) == IDOK) {
    strcpy(msgStr, "Find String: ");
    strcat(msgStr, AppBuffer.FindBoxBuff);
    strcat(msgStr, "\n");
    strcat(msgStr, "\n");
    strcat(msgStr, "Replace String: ");
    strcat(msgStr, AppBuffer.ReplaceBoxBuff);
    MessageBox(HWindow, msgStr, "Dialog Box Data", MB_OK);
  }
}

BOOL TAppWindow::CanClose()
{
  return MessageBox(HWindow, "Want to close this application",
                    "Query", MB_YESNO | MB_ICONQUESTION) == IDYES;
}
```

```
void TWinApp::InitMainWindow()
{
  MainWindow = new TAppWindow(NULL, Name);
}

void TWinApp::InitInstance()
{
  TApplication::InitInstance();
  HAccTable = LoadAccelerators(hInstance, "BUTTONS");
}

int PASCAL WinMain(HINSTANCE hInstance, HINSTANCE hPrevInstance,
                   LPSTR lpCmdLine, int nCmdShow)
{
  TWinApp WinApp(
    "Modal Dialog Box Data Transfer Tester",
              hInstance, hPrevInstance, lpCmdLine, nCmdShow);
  WinApp.Run(); // run OWL application
  return WinApp.Status; // return application status
}
```

The program listing declares three classes: an application class, a window class, and a dialog box class.

The application dialog box class `TAppDialog` declares a class constructor and a pointer to the Scope group box control. The class constructor creates the instances of the various controls in the dialog box by using resource-tapping constructors. Notice that the order of creating these controls matches the order of their corresponding buffer members in the `TAppTransferBuf` structure. Using resource-tapping constructors reduces the number of statements and does not require the services of the coordinate-tracking variables. The last statement assigns the address of the data buffer (which is a data member in the parent window class, `TAppWindow`) to the predefined `TransferBuffer` pointer. This statement connects the controls of the dialog box and the data buffer.

The application window class `TAppWindow` declares a public data transfer buffer (`AppBuffer`), a class constructor, and two member functions. To enable dialog box class constructor to access the `AppBuffer` data member, you must declare the member public.

The `TAppWindow` constructor loads the menu resource and then initializes the data buffer. The call to the `memset` function fills the `AppBuffer` member with zeros. You should systematically call the `memset` function to perform a basic initialization of the buffer before assigning specific values to its controls. The constructor then assigns the DOS and Windows strings to the Find and Replace edit boxes' buffers, respectively. The constructor also assigns BF_CHECKED to the GlobalRbtBuff, CaseChkBuff, and WholeWordChkBuf members.

The TAppWindow class declares the CMDialog member function to handle the command message sent by the Dialog menu item. This function executes an instance of the application dialog box by using the ExecDialog member function and compares the result of that function with IDOK. If the two items match, the CMDialog function builds and displays a message string that reflects the current Find and Replace text.

A Complex Modal Dialog Box

The preceding example shows the data transfer between the simple controls of a modal dialog box. Now modify the example and use drop-down list combo boxes rather than edit boxes. To do this, you must allocate dynamic portions of the transfer buffer by using pointers to the TComboBoxData class. Figure 8.6 shows a sample session with the new version of the dialog box.

Figure 8.6. A sample session with DIALOG6.EXE application.

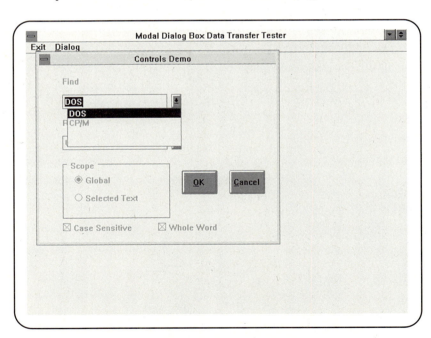

Dialog Boxes

The Find and Replace combo boxes enable you to select an item from their drop-down lists.

Listing 8.17 shows the source code for the DIALOG6.H header file. This file declares the ID_xxxx constants for the various controls as well as the CM_DIALOG constant for the Dialog menu command.

Listing 8.17. The source code for the DIALOG6.H header file.

```
#define CM_DIALOG 101

#define ID_DIALOG        200
#define ID_FIND_TXT      201
#define ID_FIND_CMB      202
#define ID_REPLACE_TXT   203
#define ID_REPLACE_CMB   204
#define ID_SCOPE_GRP     205
#define ID_GLOBAL_RBT    206
#define ID_SELTEXT_RBT   207
#define ID_CASE_CHK      208
#define ID_WHOLEWORD_CHK 209
```

Listing 8.18 contains script for the DIALOG6.RC resource file. The resource file defines the accelerator keys, menu, and dialog box resources. Notice that the dialog box resource definition for the new drop-down list combo boxes uses the class type COMBOBOX. In addition, the combo box controls are higher than the edit boxes they replace. This provides the space for the list box component of each combo box.

Listing 8.18. The script for the DIALOG6.RC resource file.

```
#include <windows.h>
#include <owlrc.h>
#include "dialog6.h"

BUTTONS ACCELERATORS
BEGIN
  "o", IDOK, ALT
  "c", IDCANCEL, ALT
END

ID_DIALOG DIALOG DISCARDABLE LOADONCALL PURE MOVEABLE 10, 10, 200, 150
STYLE WS_POPUP | WS_CLIPSIBLINGS | WS_CAPTION | WS_SYSMENU | DS_MODALFRAME
```

continues

Listing 8.18. continued

```
CAPTION "Controls Demo"
BEGIN
  CONTROL "Find", ID_FIND_TXT, "STATIC", WS_CHILD | WS_VISIBLE |
    SS_LEFT, 20, 10, 100, 15

  CONTROL "", ID_FIND_CMB, "COMBOBOX", WS_CHILD | WS_VISIBLE |
    WS_BORDER | WS_TABSTOP | CBS_DROPDOWNLIST, 20, 25, 100, 50

  CONTROL "Replace", ID_REPLACE_TXT, "STATIC", WS_CHILD | WS_VISIBLE |
    SS_LEFT, 20, 45, 100, 15

  CONTROL "", ID_REPLACE_CMB, "COMBOBOX", WS_CHILD | WS_VISIBLE |
    WS_BORDER | WS_TABSTOP | CBS_DROPDOWNLIST, 20, 60, 100, 50

  CONTROL " Scope ", ID_SCOPE_GRP, "BUTTON", WS_CHILD | WS_VISIBLE
    | WS_GROUP | BS_GROUPBOX, 20, 80, 90, 50

  CONTROL "Global", ID_GLOBAL_RBT, "BUTTON", WS_CHILD | WS_VISIBLE
    | WS_TABSTOP | BS_AUTORADIOBUTTON, 30, 90, 50, 15

  CONTROL "Selected Text", ID_SELTEXT_RBT, "BUTTON", WS_CHILD |
    WS_VISIBLE | WS_TABSTOP | BS_AUTORADIOBUTTON, 30, 105, 60, 15

  CONTROL "Case Sensitive", ID_CASE_CHK, "BUTTON", WS_CHILD |
    WS_VISIBLE | WS_TABSTOP | BS_AUTOCHECKBOX, 20, 130, 80, 15

  CONTROL "Whole Word", ID_WHOLEWORD_CHK, "BUTTON", WS_CHILD |
    WS_VISIBLE | WS_TABSTOP | BS_AUTOCHECKBOX, 100, 130, 80, 15

  CONTROL "&OK", IDOK, "BUTTON", WS_CHILD | WS_VISIBLE | WS_TABSTOP
    | BS_DEFPUSHBUTTON, 120, 90, 30, 20

  CONTROL "&Cancel", IDCANCEL, "BUTTON", WS_CHILD | WS_VISIBLE
    | WS_TABSTOP | BS_PUSHBUTTON, 160, 90, 30, 20
END

MAINMENU MENU LOADONCALL MOVEABLE PURE DISCARDABLE
BEGIN
    MENUITEM "E&xit", CM_EXIT
    MENUITEM "&Dialog", CM_DIALOG
END
```

Dialog Boxes

Listing 8.19 shows the source code for the DIALOG6.CPP program file. The program listing declares a modified version of the data transfer buffer type. This new version replaces the character array members with two `PTComboBoxData` pointers to access the buffer components for the combo box controls.

Listing 8.19. The source code for the DIALOG6.CPP program file.

```
#include <string.h>
#include <owl.h>
#include <static.h>
#include <combobox.h>
#include <checkbox.h>
#include <groupbox.h>
#include <radiobut.h>
#include <button.h>
#include <dialog.h>
#include "dialog6.h"

const MaxEditLen = 30;

struct TAppTransferBuf {
  PTComboBoxData FindCmbBuff;
  PTComboBoxData ReplaceCmbBuff;
  WORD GlobalRbtBuff;
  WORD SelTextRbtBuff;
  WORD CaseChkBuff;
  WORD WholeWordChkBuff;
};

// declare the custom application class as
// a subclass of TApplication
class TWinApp : public TApplication
{
public:
  TWinApp(LPSTR    AName,           // application name
          HINSTANCE hInstance,      // instance handle
          HINSTANCE hPrevInstance,  // previous instance handle
          LPSTR    lpCmdLine,       // command-line arguments
```

continues

Listing 8.19. continued

```
                   int       nCmdShow) :      // display command
              TApplication(AName, hInstance, hPrevInstance,
                         lpCmdLine, nCmdShow) {};

protected:
  virtual void InitMainWindow();
  virtual void InitInstance();
};

// use the _CLASSDEF macro to declare reference and pointer
// types related to the new TAppWindow and TAppDialog classes
_CLASSDEF(TAppWindow)
_CLASSDEF(TAppDialog)

// expand the functionality of TDialog by deriving class TAppDialog
class TAppDialog : public TDialog
{
public:

  TAppDialog(PTWindowsObject AParent, int ResourceId);

protected:
  PTGroupBox ScopeGrp;
};

// expand the functionality of TWindow by deriving class TAppWindow
class TAppWindow : public TWindow
{
public:
  TAppTransferBuf AppBuffer;

  TAppWindow(PTWindowsObject AParent, LPSTR ATitle);

  // handle the dialog command
  virtual void CMDialog(RTMessage Msg)
    = [CM_FIRST + CM_DIALOG];

  // handle closing the window
  virtual BOOL CanClose();
};

TAppDialog::TAppDialog(PTWindowsObject AParent, int ResourceId) :
                    TDialog(AParent, ResourceId)
{
```

Dialog Boxes

```
  new TStatic(this, ID_FIND_TXT, MaxEditLen);
  new TComboBox(this, ID_FIND_CMB, MaxEditLen);
  new TStatic(this, ID_REPLACE_TXT, MaxEditLen);
  new TComboBox(this, ID_REPLACE_CMB, MaxEditLen);
  ScopeGrp = new TGroupBox(this, ID_SCOPE_GRP);
  new TRadioButton(this, ID_GLOBAL_RBT, ScopeGrp);
  new TRadioButton(this, ID_SELTEXT_RBT, ScopeGrp);
  new TCheckBox(this, ID_CASE_CHK, NULL);
  new TCheckBox(this, ID_WHOLEWORD_CHK, NULL);
  // assign the address of the dialog transfer buffer
  // to member TransferBuffer
  TransferBuffer = (void far*)&((TAppWindow *)Parent)->
                                  AppBuffer;
}

TAppWindow::TAppWindow(PTWindowsObject AParent, LPSTR ATitle)
                     : TWindow(AParent, ATitle)
{
  AssignMenu("MAINMENU");

  // fill buffer with 0's
  memset(&AppBuffer, 0x0, sizeof(AppBuffer));
  AppBuffer.GlobalRbtBuff = BF_CHECKED;
  AppBuffer.CaseChkBuff = BF_CHECKED;
  AppBuffer.WholeWordChkBuff = BF_CHECKED;
  AppBuffer.FindCmbBuff = new TComboBoxData();
  AppBuffer.FindCmbBuff->AddString("DOS");
  AppBuffer.FindCmbBuff->AddString("DOS 5.0");
  AppBuffer.FindCmbBuff->AddString("DOS 4.0");
  AppBuffer.FindCmbBuff->AddString("DOS 3.3");
  AppBuffer.ReplaceCmbBuff = new TComboBoxData();
  AppBuffer.ReplaceCmbBuff->AddString("Windows");
  AppBuffer.ReplaceCmbBuff->AddString("Windows 3.1");
  AppBuffer.ReplaceCmbBuff->AddString("Windows 3.0");
  AppBuffer.ReplaceCmbBuff->AddString("Windows NT");
};

void TAppWindow::CMDialog(RTMessage Msg)
{
  char s[MaxEditLen];
  char msgStr[256];

  if (GetModule()->ExecDialog(
      new TAppDialog(this, ID_DIALOG)) == IDOK) {
    strcpy(s, AppBuffer.FindCmbBuff->Selection);
    strcpy(msgStr, "Find String: ");
```

continues

Listing 8.19. continued

```
    strcat(msgStr, s);
    strcat(msgStr, "\n\n");
    strcpy(s, AppBuffer.ReplaceCmbBuff->Selection);
    strcat(msgStr, "Replace String: ");
    strcat(msgStr, s);
    strcat(msgStr, "\n");
    MessageBox(HWindow, msgStr, "Dialog Box Data",
               MB_OK | MB_ICONINFORMATION);
  }
}

BOOL TAppWindow::CanClose()
{
  return MessageBox(HWindow, "Want to close this application",
                    "Query", MB_YESNO | MB_ICONQUESTION) == IDYES;
}

void TWinApp::InitMainWindow()
{
  MainWindow = new TAppWindow(NULL, Name);
}

void TWinApp::InitInstance()
{
  TApplication::InitInstance();
  HAccTable = LoadAccelerators(hInstance, "BUTTONS");
}

int PASCAL WinMain(HINSTANCE hInstance, HINSTANCE hPrevInstance,
                   LPSTR lpCmdLine, int nCmdShow)
{
  TWinApp WinApp(
    "Modal Dialog Box Data Transfer Tester",
               hInstance, hPrevInstance, lpCmdLine, nCmdShow);
  WinApp.Run(); // run OWL application
  return WinApp.Status; // return application status
}
```

The DIALOG6.CPP listing has the same classes and data members as DIALOG5.CPP. The difference is in the code for the constructors and member functions.

The `TAppDialog` class constructor creates the instances for the various controls in the dialog box. Like the `TAppDialog` constructor in DIALOG5.CPP, this version also uses resource-tapping constructors to create the various controls. After the controls are created, the `TAppDialog` constructor assigns the address of the buffer `AppBuffer` to the `TransferBuffer` pointer.

The application window class constructor loads the menu resource and then initializes the data transfer buffer. This process involves the creation of two instances of `TComboBoxData` for the Find and Replace combo box buffers. The constructor uses the `TComboBoxData:AddString` member function to add the items in the dropdown list of both combo box controls.

The `CMDialog` member function executes the dialog box and compares `IDOK` with the result of the `ExecDialog` function. If the two values match, the function displays the selected Find and Replace strings in a separate message box.

A Modeless Dialog Box

This subsection presents an ObjectWindows application that transfers data for a modeless dialog box. The program also demonstrates how you can transfer data by using a special push button control. This application uses a modified version of the original Replace dialog box (the one that uses edit boxes), presented earlier in this section. This new version, DIALOG7.EXE, is very similar to DIALOG5.EXE and differs in that the dialog box is modeless and includes an extra Send push button.

When you click the Send button (see Figure 8.7), the dialog box copies the text in its Find and Replace edit boxes to the edit boxes in the parent window, which are also labeled Find and Replace. Operationally, this program produces an effect similar to DIALOG3.EXE, which contained the Member x modeless dialog boxes and the Wizard dialog box. The dialog boxes in DIALOG3.EXE transferred text directly, without using any data buffer. However, this application demonstrates an alternative method that involves a data buffer.

When you click the Dialog menu item in the program, the application opens a modeless dialog box. The dialog box displays the `DOS` and `Windows` strings in the Find and Replace edit boxes, respectively. The Global radio button, Case Sensitive check box, and the Selected check box are all initially selected. Type new text in either or both edit boxes and click the OK push button. This action closes the dialog box and echoes the text of the dialog box in the edit boxes of the window. Reopen the dialog box to check whether it retains your last input. Now type new text in both edit boxes and click the Send button. Watch the text echo in the window's edit boxes.

Figure 8.7.
A sample session with the DIALOG7.EXE application.

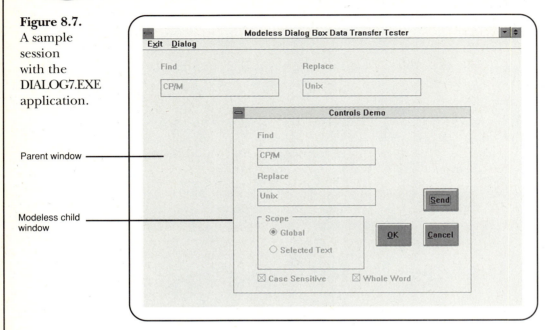

Parent window

Modeless child window

Now examine the code that implements the application. Listing 8.20 shows the source code for the DIALOG7.H header file. This file declares the constant for the ID_*xxxx* controls in both the modeless dialog box and the parent window.

Listing 8.20. The source code for the DIALOG7.H header file.

```
#define CM_DIALOG 101

// dialog box control ID
#define ID_DIALOG         200
#define ID_FIND_TXT       201
#define ID_FIND_EDIT      202
#define ID_REPLACE_TXT    203
#define ID_REPLACE_EDIT   204
#define ID_SCOPE_GRP      205
#define ID_GLOBAL_RBT     206
#define ID_SELTEXT_RBT    207
#define ID_CASE_CHK       208
#define ID_WHOLEWORD_CHK  209
#define ID_SEND_BTN       210
```

Dialog Boxes

```
// application window control ID
#define ID_FIND_BOX      301
#define ID_REPLACE_BOX   302
```

Listing 8.21 shows the script for the DIALOG7.RC resource file. The resource file defines the resources for the accelerator keys, menu, and modeless dialog box.

Listing 8.21. The script for the DIALOG7.RC resource file.

```
#include <windows.h>
#include <owlrc.h>
#include "dialog7.h"

BUTTONS ACCELERATORS
BEGIN
  "o", IDOK, ALT
  "c", IDCANCEL, ALT
  "s", ID_SEND_BTN, ALT
END

ID_DIALOG DIALOG DISCARDABLE LOADONCALL PURE MOVEABLE 10, 10, 200, 150
STYLE WS_POPUP | WS_CLIPSIBLINGS | WS_CAPTION | WS_SYSMENU | WS_DLGFRAME
CAPTION "Controls Demo"
BEGIN
  CONTROL "Find", ID_FIND_TXT, "STATIC", WS_CHILD | WS_VISIBLE |
    SS_LEFT, 20, 10, 100, 15

  CONTROL "", ID_FIND_EDIT, "EDIT", WS_CHILD | WS_VISIBLE |
    WS_BORDER | WS_TABSTOP, 20, 25, 100, 15

  CONTROL "Replace", ID_REPLACE_TXT, "STATIC", WS_CHILD | WS_VISIBLE |
    SS_LEFT, 20, 45, 100, 15

  CONTROL "", ID_REPLACE_EDIT, "EDIT", WS_CHILD | WS_VISIBLE |
    WS_BORDER | WS_TABSTOP, 20, 60, 100, 15

  CONTROL " Scope ", ID_SCOPE_GRP, "BUTTON", WS_CHILD | WS_VISIBLE
    | WS_GROUP | BS_GROUPBOX, 20, 80, 90, 50

  CONTROL "Global", ID_GLOBAL_RBT, "BUTTON", WS_CHILD | WS_VISIBLE
    | WS_TABSTOP | BS_AUTORADIOBUTTON, 30, 90, 50, 15
```

continues

Listing 8.21. continued

```
    CONTROL "Selected Text", ID_SELTEXT_RBT, "BUTTON", WS_CHILD ¦
      WS_VISIBLE ¦ WS_TABSTOP ¦ BS_AUTORADIOBUTTON, 30, 105, 60, 15

    CONTROL "Case Sensitive", ID_CASE_CHK, "BUTTON", WS_CHILD ¦
      WS_VISIBLE ¦ WS_TABSTOP ¦ BS_AUTOCHECKBOX, 20, 130, 80, 15

    CONTROL "Whole Word", ID_WHOLEWORD_CHK, "BUTTON", WS_CHILD ¦
      WS_VISIBLE ¦ WS_TABSTOP ¦ BS_AUTOCHECKBOX, 100, 130, 80, 15

    CONTROL, "&OK", IDOK, "BUTTON", WS_CHILD ¦ WS_VISIBLE ¦ WS_TABSTOP
      ¦ BS_DEFPUSHBUTTON, 120, 90, 30, 20

    CONTROL "&Cancel", IDCANCEL, "BUTTON", WS_CHILD ¦ WS_VISIBLE ¦
      WS_TABSTOP, 160, 90, 30, 20

    CONTROL "&Send", ID_SEND_BTN, "BUTTON", WS_CHILD ¦ WS_VISIBLE ¦
      WS_TABSTOP, 160, 60, 30, 20

END

MAINMENU MENU LOADONCALL MOVEABLE PURE DISCARDABLE
BEGIN
    MENUITEM "E&xit", CM_EXIT
    MENUITEM "&Dialog", CM_DIALOG
END
```

Listing 8.22 contains the source code for the DIALOG7.CPP program file. The listing declares a group of constants for sizing and spacing the controls in the window application. The listing also contains the declaration of the data transfer buffer type, which is identical to that shown in program DIALOG5.EXE.

Listing 8.22. The source code for the DIALOG7.CPP program file.

```
#include <string.h>
#include <owl.h>
#include <static.h>
#include <edit.h>
#include <checkbox.h>
#include <groupbox.h>
```

```
#include <radiobut.h>
#include <button.h>
#include <dialog.h>
#include "dialog7.h"

// declare constants for sizing and dimensioning the
// application window's controls
const Wtxt = 200;
const Htxt = 20;
const TxtVertSpacing = 10;
const Wbox = 200;
const Hbox = 30;
const BoxHorzSpacing = 40;

const MaxEditLen = 30;

// declare the data transfer buffer structure
struct TAppTransferBuf {
  char FindBoxBuff[MaxEditLen];
  char ReplaceBoxBuff[MaxEditLen];
  WORD GlobalRbtBuff;
  WORD SelTextRbtBuff;
  WORD CaseChkBuff;
  WORD WholeWordChkBuff;
};

// declare the custom application class as
// a subclass of TApplication
class TWinApp : public TApplication
{
public:
  TWinApp(LPSTR     AName,           // application name
          HINSTANCE hInstance,       // instance handle
          HINSTANCE hPrevInstance,   // previous instance handle
          LPSTR     lpCmdLine,       // command-line arguments
          int       nCmdShow) :      // display command
          TApplication(AName, hInstance, hPrevInstance,
                       lpCmdLine, nCmdShow) {};

protected:
  virtual void InitMainWindow();
  virtual void InitInstance();
```

continues

Listing 8.22. continued

```
};

// use the _CLASSDEF macro to declare reference and pointer
// types related to the new TAppWindow and TAppDialog classes
_CLASSDEF(TAppWindow)
_CLASSDEF(TAppDialog)

// expand the functionality of TDialog by deriving class TAppDialog
class TAppDialog : public TDialog
{
public:

  TAppDialog(PTWindowsObject AParent, int ResourceId);

  virtual void Ok(RTMessage Msg)
    =[ID_FIRST + IDOK];

  virtual void Cancel(RTMessage Msg)
    =[ID_FIRST + IDCANCEL];

  virtual void HandleSendBtn(RTMessage Msg)
    =[ID_FIRST + ID_SEND_BTN];

  virtual void CMSendBtn(RTMessage Msg)
    =[CM_FIRST + ID_SEND_BTN];

protected:
  PTGroupBox ScopeGrp;
};

// expand the functionality of TWindow by deriving class TAppWindow
class TAppWindow : public TWindow
{
public:
  BOOL DialogActive;
  TAppTransferBuf AppBuffer;

  TAppWindow(PTWindowsObject AParent, LPSTR ATitle);

  // handle the dialog command
  virtual void CMDialog(RTMessage Msg)
    = [CM_FIRST + CM_DIALOG];
```

```cpp
    // handle a message sent by the Send button of
    // the dialog box
    virtual void HandleSendBtn(RTMessage Msg)
      = [WM_FIRST + ID_SEND_BTN];

    // handle closing the window
    virtual BOOL CanClose();

protected:
  PTAppDialog DlgPtr;
  PTEdit FindBox;
  PTEdit ReplaceBox;
};

TAppDialog::TAppDialog(PTWindowsObject AParent, int ResourceId) :
                      TDialog(AParent, ResourceId)
{
  new TStatic(this, ID_FIND_TXT, MaxEditLen);
  new TEdit(this, ID_FIND_EDIT, MaxEditLen);
  new TStatic(this, ID_REPLACE_TXT, MaxEditLen);
  new TEdit(this, ID_REPLACE_EDIT, MaxEditLen);
  ScopeGrp = new TGroupBox(this, ID_SCOPE_GRP);
  new TRadioButton(this, ID_GLOBAL_RBT, ScopeGrp);
  new TRadioButton(this, ID_SELTEXT_RBT, ScopeGrp);
  new TCheckBox(this, ID_CASE_CHK, NULL);
  new TCheckBox(this, ID_WHOLEWORD_CHK, NULL);
  // assign the address of the dialog transfer buffer
  // to member TransferBuffer
  TransferBuffer = (void far*)&(((TAppWindow *)Parent)->
                                AppBuffer);
}

void TAppDialog::Ok(RTMessage Msg)
{
  TransferData(TF_GETDATA);
  SendMessage(Parent->HWindow, ID_SEND_BTN, NULL, NULL);
  PTAppWindow(Parent)->DialogActive = FALSE;
  TDialog::Ok(Msg);
}

void TAppDialog::Cancel(RTMessage Msg)
{
  PTAppWindow(Parent)->DialogActive = FALSE;
  TDialog::Cancel(Msg);
}
```

continues

Listing 8.22. continued

```c
void TAppDialog::HandleSendBtn(RTMessage Msg)
{
  TransferData(TF_GETDATA);
  SendMessage(Parent->HWindow, ID_SEND_BTN, NULL, NULL);
}

void TAppDialog::CMSendBtn(RTMessage Msg)
{
  HandleSendBtn(Msg);
}

TAppWindow::TAppWindow(PTWindowsObject AParent, LPSTR ATitle)
                     : TWindow(AParent, ATitle)
{
  int x0 = 30;
  int y0 = 20;
  int x = x0;
  int y = y0;

  char s[MaxEditLen];

  AssignMenu("MAINMENU");

  strcpy(s, "Find");
  new TStatic(this, -1, s, x, y, Wtxt, Htxt, strlen(s));

  y += Htxt + TxtVertSpacing;
  FindBox = new TEdit(this, ID_FIND_BOX, "", x, y, Wbox, Hbox,
                      0, FALSE);

  x += Wbox + BoxHorzSpacing;
  y = y0;
  strcpy(s, "Replace");
  new TStatic(this, -1, s, x, y, Wtxt, Htxt, strlen(s));

  y += Htxt + TxtVertSpacing;
  ReplaceBox = new TEdit(this, ID_REPLACE_BOX, "", x, y,
                         Wbox, Hbox, 0, FALSE);

  // fill buffer with 0's
  memset(&AppBuffer, 0x0, sizeof(AppBuffer));
  strcpy(AppBuffer.FindBoxBuff, "DOS");
  strcpy(AppBuffer.ReplaceBoxBuff, "Windows");
  AppBuffer.GlobalRbtBuff = BF_CHECKED;
```

```cpp
  AppBuffer.CaseChkBuff = BF_CHECKED;
  AppBuffer.WholeWordChkBuff = BF_CHECKED;

  DialogActive = FALSE;

  // enable the keyboard handler
  EnableKBHandler();
};

void TAppWindow::CMDialog(RTMessage Msg)
{
  if (DialogActive) return;
  DlgPtr = new TAppDialog(this, ID_DIALOG);
  GetModule()->MakeWindow(DlgPtr);
  ShowWindow(DlgPtr->HWindow, SW_SHOW);
  DialogActive = TRUE;
}

void TAppWindow::HandleSendBtn(RTMessage Msg)
{
  FindBox->SetText(AppBuffer.FindBoxBuff);
  ReplaceBox->SetText(AppBuffer.ReplaceBoxBuff);
}

BOOL TAppWindow::CanClose()
{
  return MessageBox(HWindow, "Want to close this application",
                    "Query", MB_YESNO | MB_ICONQUESTION) == IDYES;
}


void TWinApp::InitMainWindow()
{
  MainWindow = new TAppWindow(NULL, Name);
}

void TWinApp::InitInstance()
{
  TApplication::InitInstance();
  HAccTable = LoadAccelerators(hInstance, "BUTTONS");
}

int PASCAL WinMain(HINSTANCE hInstance, HINSTANCE hPrevInstance,
                   LPSTR lpCmdLine, int nCmdShow)
{
```

continues

Listing 8.22. continued

```
TWinApp WinApp(
  "Modeless Dialog Box Data Transfer Tester",
           hInstance, hPrevInstance, lpCmdLine, nCmdShow);
WinApp.Run(); // run OWL application
return WinApp.Status; // return application status
}
```

The application declares three classes: the application class, the window class, and the dialog box class. The TAppDialog class declares a class constructor, the ScopeGrp data member, and a set of member functions.

The TAppDialog constructor in this program is identical to that of the DIALOG5.EXE program. The constructor creates the dialog box controls and sets the TransferBuffer pointer.

The TAppDialog class declares member functions to handle each push button. The virtual OK member function responds to the IDOK notification message sent by the OK button. The function performs the following tasks:

1. Transfers the data from the controls to the buffer by calling the TransferData member function with a TF_GETDATA argument.
2. Sends an ID_SEND_BTN message to the parent window by using the **SendMessage** API function.
3. Sets the parent window data member, DialogActive, at FALSE.
4. Invokes the parent class Ok member function.

The Cancel member function handles the IDCANCEL notification message sent by the Cancel button. The function performs the following two tasks:

- Sets the parent window data member, DialogActive, at FALSE.
- Invokes the parent class's Cancel member function.

The HandleSendBtn member function handles the ID_SEND_BTN notification message sent by the Send button. The function performs the following tasks:

- Transfers the data from the controls to the buffer by calling the TransferData member function with a TF_GETDATA argument.
- Sends an ID_SEND_BTN message to the parent window by using the **SendMessage** API function.

The CMSendBtn member function handles the ID_SEND_BTN command message generated by the hot key Alt-S. The function simply calls the **HandleSendBtn** member function.

The application window class `TAppWindow` declares two public data members, three protected data members, a constructor, and three member functions. The Boolean `DialogActive` data member indicates whether the dialog box instance exists. Using this flag ensures that one instance of the modeless dialog box exists. The `AppBuffer` data member is the data transfer buffer. The window class declares three protected pointers. The `FindBox` and `ReplaceBox` pointers access the edit box instances. The `DlgPtr` pointer is the pointer to the dialog box instance.

The `TAppWindow` constructor performs the following tasks:

1. Loads the menu resource
2. Creates the static text instance that labels the Find edit box
3. Creates the Find edit box
4. Creates the static text instance that labels the Replace edit box
5. Creates the Replace edit box
6. Initializes the buffer by filling it with zeros
7. Assigns values to the edit box buffers, the check box buffers, and the Global radio button buffer
8. Sets the `DialogActive` data member to FALSE
9. Enables the keyboard handler

The application window class declares the `CMDialog` member function to create a modeless dialog box. The function performs the following tasks:

1. Returns TRUE if dialog box is active (that is, the `DialogActive` member is TRUE).
2. Creates a `TAppDialog` instance that is accessed by the `DlgPtr` pointer.
3. Creates the modeless dialog box by invoking the `TModule::MakeWindow` member function. The function call uses the `DlgPtr` pointer as its argument.
4. Calls the **ShowWindow** API function to display the dialog box.
5. Sets the **DialogActive** data member at TRUE.

The `HandleSendBtn` member function responds to the message sent by the Send button in the dialog box by copying the `FindBoxBuff` and `ReplaceBoxBuff` buffer members to the Find and Replace edit boxes in the window.

Initialization of Window Controls

Transferring data to the controls of a window is a very suitable way to initialize the window's various controls. Chapter 7, "Scroll Bars, List Boxes, and Combo Boxes," presented a number of applications that include list and combo boxes that are initialized with data. The technique that achieved this initialization involved calling special member functions from the application class's `InitInstance` member function. Assigning initial values to the controls inside the window constructor (that also created these controls) does not work. Using the data transfer mechanism can actually rectify the situation.

This subsection presents a modified version of the CTLLST5.CPP program, which creates and maintains synchronized scrolling lists. The program inserts city and country names in their respective list boxes by using member functions called in `InitInstance`. The new version, shown in Listing 8.23, inserts the initial list items in the window class constructor. The `TAppWindow` constructor and the `InitLists` member function of DIALOG8.CPP differ from that of CTLLST5.CPP, so focus on these two members.

Listing 8.23. The source code for the DIALOG8.CPP program file.

```
#include <stdlib.h>
#include <ctype.h>
#include <stdio.h>
#include <math.h>
#include <string.h>
#include <owl.h>
#include <static.h>
#include <scrollba.h>
#include <listbox.h>

const Wtxt = 200;
const Htxt = 20;
const Wlst = 200;
const Hlst = 150;
const Wscr = 20;
const Hscr = Hlst;
const VertSpacing = 10;
const MaxString = 40;

// declare the ID constants for the various controls
#define ID_CITY_LST 101
```

```
#define ID_COUNTRY_LST 102
#define ID_SCROLL_SCR 103

struct TransferStruct {
  PTListBoxData CityData;
  PTListBoxData CountryData;
};


// iterated function to update the selected list items
void updateSelection(Pvoid P, Pvoid Param)
{
  PTListBox pL = PTListBox(P);
  pL->SetSelIndex(*Pint(Param));
}

// declare the custom application class as
// a subclass of TApplication
class TWinApp : public TApplication
{
public:
  TWinApp(LPSTR     AName,          // application name
          HINSTANCE hInstance,      // instance handle
          HINSTANCE hPrevInstance,  // previous instance handle
          LPSTR     lpCmdLine,      // command-line arguments
          int       nCmdShow) :     // display command
          TApplication(AName, hInstance, hPrevInstance,
                       lpCmdLine, nCmdShow) {};

protected:
  virtual void InitMainWindow();
  virtual void InitInstance();
};

// use the _CLASSDEF macro to declare reference and pointer
// types related to the new TAppWindow class
_CLASSDEF(TAppWindow)

// expand the functionality of TWindow by deriving class TAppWindow
class TAppWindow : public TWindow
{
public:

  TAppWindow(PTWindowsObject AParent, LPSTR ATitle);
```

continues

Listing 8.23. continued

```cpp
  // initialize the city and country lists
  virtual void InitLists();

  // handle the City list notification messages
  virtual void HandleCityLst(RTMessage Msg)
    = [ID_FIRST + ID_CITY_LST];

  // handle the Country list notification messages
  virtual void HandleCountryLst(RTMessage Msg)
    = [ID_FIRST + ID_COUNTRY_LST];

  // handle the scroll bar notification message
  virtual void HandleScrollScr(RTMessage Msg)
    = [ID_FIRST + ID_SCROLL_SCR];

  // handle closing the window
  virtual BOOL CanClose();

protected:
  PTListBox CityLst;
  PTListBox CountryLst;
  PTScrollBar ScrollScr;
  TransferStruct AppBuffer;
};

TAppWindow::TAppWindow(PTWindowsObject AParent, LPSTR ATitle) :
                    TWindow(AParent, ATitle)
{
  char s[81];
  int x0 = 100;
  int y0 = 50;
  int x = x0;
  int y = y0;

  // load the menu resource
  AssignMenu("EXITMENU");

  // create the city list box and its label
  strcpy(s, "City List");
  new TStatic(this, -1, s, x, y, Wtxt, Htxt, strlen(s));
  y += Htxt + VertSpacing;
  CityLst = new TListBox(this, ID_CITY_LST, x, y, Wlst, Hlst);
  // turn off the automatic sorting of the city list member
  CityLst->Attr.Style &= ~LBS_SORT;
```

Dialog Boxes

```cpp
   // hide the vertical scroll bar
   CityLst->Attr.Style &= ~WS_VSCROLL;
   y = y0 + Htxt + VertSpacing;
   x += Wlst;
   ScrollScr = new TScrollBar(this, ID_SCROLL_SCR,
                              x, y, Wscr, Hscr - 4, FALSE);
   x += Wscr;
   y = y0;
   // create the country list box and its label
   strcpy(s, "Country List");
   new TStatic(this, -1, s, x, y, Wtxt, Htxt, strlen(s));
   y += Htxt + VertSpacing;
   CountryLst = new TListBox(this, ID_COUNTRY_LST, x, y, Wlst, Hlst);
   // turn off the automatic sorting of the country list member
   CountryLst->Attr.Style &= ~LBS_SORT;
   // hide the vertical scroll bar
   CountryLst->Attr.Style &= ~WS_VSCROLL;

   // add data in the city list box
   AppBuffer.CityData = new TListBoxData();
   CityLst->EnableTransfer();
   AppBuffer.CityData->AddString("Paris");
   AppBuffer.CityData->AddString("London");
   AppBuffer.CityData->AddString("Rome");
   AppBuffer.CityData->AddString("Bern");
   AppBuffer.CityData->AddString("Madrid");
   AppBuffer.CityData->AddString("Cairo");
   AppBuffer.CityData->AddString("Ankara");
   AppBuffer.CityData->AddString("Washington");
   AppBuffer.CityData->AddString("Tokyo");
   AppBuffer.CityData->AddString("Moscow");
   AppBuffer.CityData->AddString("Warsaw");
   AppBuffer.CityData->AddString("Seoul");
   AppBuffer.CityData->AddString("Lisbon");
   AppBuffer.CityData->AddString("Athens");

   AppBuffer.CountryData = new TListBoxData();
   CountryLst->EnableTransfer();
   // add data in the country list box
   AppBuffer.CountryData->AddString("France");
   AppBuffer.CountryData->AddString("The U.K.");
   AppBuffer.CountryData->AddString("Italy");
   AppBuffer.CountryData->AddString("Switzerland");
   AppBuffer.CountryData->AddString("Spain");
   AppBuffer.CountryData->AddString("Egypt");
```

continues

Listing 8.23. continued

```
    AppBuffer.CountryData->AddString("Turkey");
    AppBuffer.CountryData->AddString("The U.S.A.");
    AppBuffer.CountryData->AddString("Japan");
    AppBuffer.CountryData->AddString("Russia");
    AppBuffer.CountryData->AddString("Poland");
    AppBuffer.CountryData->AddString("South Korea");
    AppBuffer.CountryData->AddString("Portugal");
    AppBuffer.CountryData->AddString("Greece");
    TransferBuffer = &AppBuffer;

    // enable the keyboard handler
    EnableKBHandler();
}

void TAppWindow::InitLists()
{
    // select the first item in both list boxes
    CityLst->SetSelIndex(0);
    CountryLst->SetSelIndex(0);
    // set the range of the scroll bar control
    ScrollScr->SetRange(0, CityLst->GetCount()-1);
}

void TAppWindow::HandleCityLst(RTMessage Msg)
{
    int i;
    char city[MaxString+1];
    char country[MaxString];
    char message[2*MaxString+1];

    // determine the type of notification message
    switch (Msg.LP.Hi) {
      case LBN_SELCHANGE:
        // get the current selection index in the city list
        i = CityLst->GetSelIndex();
        CountryLst->SetSelIndex(i); // update country selection
        ScrollScr->SetPosition(i);  // update scroll bar control
        break;
      case LBN_DBLCLK:
        // get the selected string in both list boxes
        CityLst->GetSelString(city, MaxString);
        CountryLst->GetSelString(country, MaxString);
        // build and display a message
        sprintf(message, "The capital of %s is %s", country, city);
```

```cpp
        MessageBox(HWindow, message, "Your Selection", MB_OK);
        break;
   }
}

void TAppWindow::HandleCountryLst(RTMessage Msg)
{
  int i;
  char city[MaxString+1];
  char country[MaxString];
  char message[2*MaxString+1];

  // determine the type of notification message
  switch (Msg.LP.Hi) {
    case LBN_SELCHANGE:
      // get the current selection index in the country list
      i = CountryLst->GetSelIndex();
      CityLst->SetSelIndex(i); // update city selection
      ScrollScr->SetPosition(i); // update scroll bar control
      break;
    case LBN_DBLCLK:
      // get the selected string in both list boxes
      CityLst->GetSelString(city, MaxString);
      CountryLst->GetSelString(country, MaxString);
      // build and display a message
      sprintf(message, "The capital of %s is %s", country, city);
      MessageBox(HWindow, message, "Your Selection", MB_OK);
      break;
   }
}

void TAppWindow::HandleScrollScr(RTMessage Msg)
{
  // get the thumb position of the scroll bar control
  int i = ScrollScr->GetPosition();
  // select the city and country items that have the same
  // index as the thumb position
  ForEach(updateSelection, &i);
}

BOOL TAppWindow::CanClose()
{
  return MessageBox(HWindow, "Want to close this application",
                    "Query", MB_YESNO | MB_ICONQUESTION) == IDYES;
}
```

continues

Listing 8.23. continued

```
void TWinApp::InitMainWindow()
{
  MainWindow = new TAppWindow(NULL, Name);
}

void TWinApp::InitInstance()
{
  TApplication::InitInstance();
  // make the initial selections in the list boxes
  PTAppWindow(MainWindow)->InitLists();
}

int PASCAL WinMain(HINSTANCE hInstance, HINSTANCE hPrevInstance,
                   LPSTR lpCmdLine, int nCmdShow)
{
  TWinApp WinApp(" Transferring Data to Window Controls",
                 hInstance, hPrevInstance, lpCmdLine, nCmdShow);
  WinApp.Run(); // run OWL application
  return WinApp.Status; // return application status
}
```

The `TAppWindow` constructor in DIALOG8.CPP adds the statements that initialize the City and Country list boxes. The initialization steps of both list boxes are very similar, so I'll focus on the steps for initializing the City list box:

1. Create an instance of the `TListBoxData` class. The `AppBuffer.CityData` pointer accesses the `TListBoxData` instance.

2. Enable the data transfer for the City list box by invoking the member function `EnableTransfer` as follows:

   `CityLst->EnableTransfer();`

3. Insert the initial data in the dynamic buffer space by calling the `TListBoxData::AddString` function.

When the buffer for both list boxes is supplied with the initial values, the constructor assigns the address of the data buffer to the `TransferBuffer` pointer.

DIALOG8.CPP declares the `TransferStruct` data transfer buffer type as follows:

```
struct TransferStruct {
    PTListBoxData CityData;
    PTListBoxData CountryData;
};
```

The current version of the `InitLists` member function has a few statements (compared to the long set of statements in the earlier program version) that select the first items in both list boxes and sets the range for the scroll bar control.

Declaring the TInputDialog Class

Some of the programs presented in earlier chapters required input dialog boxes to obtain input. These programs executed instances of the ObjectWindows `TInputDialog` class. This class declares three data members, a constructor, and a set of member functions. The `TInputDialog` class is declared as follows:

```
class _EXPORT TInputDialog : public TDialog
{
public:
    LPSTR Prompt;
    LPSTR Buffer;
    WORD BufferSize;

    TInputDialog(PTWindowsObject AParent, LPSTR ATitle,
             LPSTR APrompt, LPSTR ABuffer, WORD ABufferSize,
             PTModule AModule = NULL);
    void TransferData(WORD Direction);

    static PTStreamable build();

protected:
    virtual void SetupWindow();
    TInputDialog(StreamableInit) : TDialog(streamableInit) {};
    virtual void write (Ropstream os);
    virtual Pvoid read (Ripstream is);

private:
    virtual const Pchar streamableName() const
        { return "TInputDialog"; }
};
```

The `Buffer` and `Prompt` data members are pointers to the text buffer and prompting string, respectively. The `BufferSize` member stores the size of the buffer that returns the user's input.

The class constructor requires the parameters for the parent window, the pointer to the dialog box title, the pointer to the prompt string, the pointer to the text buffer, and the buffer size. The constructor calls the `TDialog` constructor to pass the `AParent` parameter, the resource identifier `SD_INPUTDIALOG`, and the `AModule` parameter. The `SD_INPUTDIALOG` identifier is the name of the dialog box resource defined in the INPUTDIA.DLG resource file, supplied by Borland.

The most noteworthy `TInputDialog` member function is the `TransferData` function. This function transfers data between the edit control of the input dialog box and the text buffer. If the caller passes the argument `TF_SETDATA` to the `Direction` parameter, the function transfers data from the text buffer to the edit control. The function moves data in the reverse direction when a caller passes the `TF_GETDATA` argument.

Consider a simple guessing game that uses the input dialog box to prompt you to guess a secret number. The game includes a main menu with the Exit and Game menu items. To start the game, you click the Game menu item or press Alt-G. The program generates a secret number between 0 and 1,000 and gives you 10 guesses. To help you refine your guess, the program displays hints in the dialog box that tell you whether your last guess was higher or lower than the secret number. You can stop the game at any time by clicking the Cancel button. In this case, the program displays the secret number. Also, if you fail to guess the number after 10 trials, the program displays the secret number. If you do manage to guess the number, the program displays a congratulatory message. Figure 8.8 shows a sample session with the DIALOG9.EXE application.

Look at the source code for the number guessing game. Listing 8.24 shows the source code for the DIALOG9.H header file, which contains a single constant declaration.

Listing 8.24. The source code for the DIALOG9.H header file.

```
#define CM_GAME 101
```

Listing 8.25 shows the script for the DIALOG9.RC resource file. The file includes the INPUTDIA.DLG resource file required to define the ObjectWindows input dialog box.

Dialog Boxes

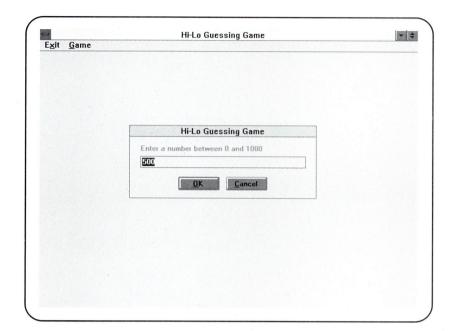

Figure 8.8.
A sample session with the DIALOG9.EXE application.

Listing 8.25. The script for the DIALOG9.RC resource file.

```
#include <windows.h>
#include <owlrc.h>
#include <inputdia.dlg>
#include "dialog9.h"


MAINMENU MENU LOADONCALL MOVEABLE PURE DISCARDABLE
BEGIN
    MENUITEM "E&xit", CM_EXIT
    MENUITEM "&Game", CM_GAME
END
```

Listing 8.26 shows the source code for the DIALOG9.CPP program file. The program listing declares two classes: the application class and the window class.

Listing 8.26. The source code for the DIALOG9.CPP program file.

```
#include <stdlib.h>
#include <stdio.h>
#include <string.h>
#include <owl.h>
#include <inputdia.h>
#include "dialog9.h"

const MaxBuffer = 81;

// declare the custom application class as
// a subclass of TApplication
class TWinApp : public TApplication
{
public:
  TWinApp(LPSTR     AName,           // application name
          HINSTANCE hInstance,       // instance handle
          HINSTANCE hPrevInstance,   // previous instance handle
          LPSTR     lpCmdLine,       // command-line arguments
          int       nCmdShow) :      // display command
          TApplication(AName, hInstance, hPrevInstance,
                    lpCmdLine, nCmdShow) {};

protected:
  virtual void InitMainWindow();
};

// use the _CLASSDEF macro to declare reference and pointer
// types related to the new TAppWindow class
_CLASSDEF(TAppWindow)

// expand the functionality of TWindow by deriving class TAppWindow
class TAppWindow : public TWindow
{
public:

  TAppWindow(PTWindowsObject AParent, LPSTR ATitle)
    : TWindow(AParent, ATitle) { AssignMenu("MAINMENU"); }

  // handle the Game menu item
  virtual void CMGame(RTMessage Msg)
    = [CM_FIRST + CM_GAME];
```

```cpp
    // handle closing the window
    virtual BOOL CanClose();

};


void TAppWindow::CMGame(RTMessage Msg)
{
  char s[MaxBuffer];
  int n, m;
  int MaxIter = 10;
  int iter = 0;
  BOOL ok = TRUE;

  randomize();
  n = random(1001);

  strcpy(s, "500");
  // execute the opening dialog box
  if (GetApplication()->ExecDialog(
      new TInputDialog(this, "Hi-Lo Guessing Game",
                       "Enter a number between 0 and 1000",
                       s, sizeof(s))) == IDOK) {
    m = atoi(s);
    iter++;
    // loop to obtain the other guesses
    while (m != n && iter < MaxIter && ok == TRUE) {
      // is the user's guess higher?
      if (m > n)
        ok = ((GetApplication()->ExecDialog(
                   new TInputDialog(this,
                       "Hi-Lo Guessing Game",
                       "Enter a lower guess",
                     s, sizeof(s))) == IDOK) ? TRUE : FALSE);

      else
        ok = ((GetApplication()->ExecDialog(
                   new TInputDialog(this,
                       "Hi-Lo Guessing Game",
                       "Enter a higher guess",
                     s, sizeof(s))) == IDOK) ? TRUE : FALSE);
      m = atoi(s);
      iter++;
    }
```

continues

Listing 8.26. continued

```
        // did the user guess the secret number
        if (iter < MaxIter && ok == TRUE) {
          MessageBeep(0);
          MessageBeep(0);
          MessageBox(HWindow, "You guessed it!",
                     "Congratulations!", MB_OK);
        }
        else {
          sprintf(s, "The secret number is %d", n);
          MessageBox(HWindow, s, "Sorry!", MB_OK);
        }
    }
}

BOOL TAppWindow::CanClose()
{
  return MessageBox(HWindow, "Want to close this application",
                    "Query", MB_YESNO | MB_ICONQUESTION) == IDYES;
}

void TWinApp::InitMainWindow()
{
  MainWindow = new TAppWindow(NULL, Name);
}

int PASCAL WinMain(HINSTANCE hInstance, HINSTANCE hPrevInstance,
                   LPSTR lpCmdLine, int nCmdShow)
{
  TWinApp WinApp("Hi-Lo Guessing Game",
                 hInstance, hPrevInstance, lpCmdLine, nCmdShow);
  WinApp.Run(); // run OWL application
  return WinApp.Status; // return application status
}
```

The most relevant part of the program is the member function CMGame, which executes the number guessing game. The function performs the following tasks:

1. Randomizes the seed for the random number generating function.

2. Obtains a random number in the range of 0 to 1,000 and stores that number in the local variable n.

3. Assigns the string `500` to the text buffer (implemented by the local variable `s`.)
4. Executes the open dialog box by calling the `ExecDialog` member function to create an instance of the `TInputDialog` class. If the `ExecDialog` function returns `IDOK`, the game resumes by executing the next tasks.
5. Converts the contents of the text buffer into `int` and stores that value in the local variable `m`.
6. Increments the iteration counter variable `iter`.
7. Loops to obtain other guesses while the following conditions are true:

    ☐ The contents of variables `m` and `n` differ.

    ☐ The number of iterations is less than the maximum limit.

    ☐ The Boolean ok flag is TRUE, indicating that you did not click the Cancel button of the dialog box.

    The loop displays one of two dialog box versions depending on whether the last number you entered is less than or greater than the secret number. The loop also converts your input into the integer stored in variable `m` and increments the loop iteration counter.

8. Displays a congratulatory message if you guess the secret number within the allowed number of iterations. Otherwise, the program displays the secret number.

Using the TFileDialog Class

The `TFileWindow` class that I presented in Chapter 4 supports a simple text editor. This text editor utilizes instances of the `TFileDialog` class to open or save text to a file. The `TFileDialog` class has the following declaration:

```
class _EXPORT TFileDialog : public TDialog
{
public:
    LPSTR FilePath;
    char PathName[MAXPATH];
    char Extension[MAXEXT];
    char FileSpec[FILESPEC];

    TFileDialog(PTWindowsObject AParent, int ResourceId,
```

```
                    LPSTR AFilePath, PTModule AModule = NULL);
    virtual BOOL CanClose();
    void SelectFileName();
    void UpdateFileName();
    BOOL UpdateListBoxes();

    static PTStreamable build();

protected:
    virtual void SetupWindow();
    virtual void HandleFName(RTMessage Msg)
        = [ID_FIRST + ID_FNAME];
    virtual void HandleFList(RTMessage Msg)
        = [ID_FIRST + ID_FLIST];
    virtual void HandleDList(RTMessage Msg)
        = [ID_FIRST + ID_DLIST];

    TFileDialog(StreamableInit) : TDialog(streamableInit) {};

private:
    virtual const Pchar streamableName() const
        { return "TFileDialog"; }
};
```

The class constructor includes the parameters for the parent window pointer, file dialog box resource ID, and file path. The arguments for the resource ID parameter are predefined as either SD_FILEOPEN, to open a file, or SD_FILESAVE, to save a file.

The TFileDialog class offers adequate functionality. In most cases, you do not have to create descendants to modify the class operations.

The following simple demonstration program uses the TFileDialog class. The program displays the file date stamp, time stamp, and size for a file you select using the file dialog box. The program includes a main menu with the Exit and File Stats menu items. When you click the File Stats menu item, a file dialog box pops up. Initially, the file mask (or wildcard) is set to *.* to select all the files. You can type another filename wildcard or select another drive and directory. Select a file and then double-click the selection, click the OK button, or just press the Enter key. The name, time stamp, date stamp, and size of the file you selected appears in a message dialog box. To view the statistics of another file, click the File Stats menu item again. Figure 8.9 shows a sample session with the DIALOG10.EXE application.

Dialog Boxes

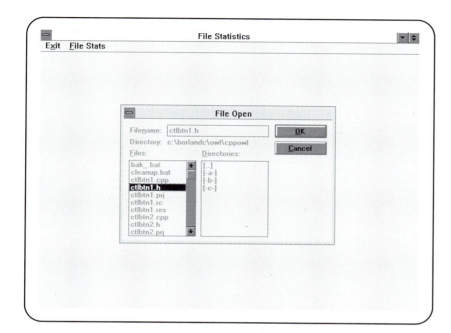

Figure 8.9. A sample session with the DIALOG10.EXE application.

Now look at the listings involved with this simple application. Listing 8.27 contains the source code for the DIALOG10.H header file with its single constant declaration.

Listing 8.27. The source code for the DIALOG10.H header file.

```
#define CM_FILESTAT 101
```

Listing 8.28 contains the script for the DIALOG10.RC resource file. This resource file must include the FILEDIAL.DLG resource file that defines the file dialog box resource.

Listing 8.28. The script for the DIALOG10.RC resource file.

```
#include <windows.h>
#include <owlrc.h>
#include <filedial.dlg>
#include "dialog10.h"
```

continues

Listing 8.28. continued

```
MAINMENU MENU LOADONCALL MOVEABLE PURE DISCARDABLE
BEGIN
      MENUITEM "E&xit", CM_EXIT
      MENUITEM "&File Stats", CM_FILESTAT
END
```

Listing 8.29 shows the source code for the DIALOG10.CPP program file. The program listing declares two classes, one for the application and the other for the application window. The most relevant member function is `TAppWindow::CmFileStat`.

Listing 8.29. The source code for the DIALOG10.CPP program file.

```
#include <stdlib.h>
#include <stdio.h>
#include <string.h>
#include <io.h>
#include <dos.h>
#include <dir.h>
#include <owl.h>
#include <filedial.h>
#include "dialog10.h"

const MaxBuffer = 81;

// declare the custom application class as
// a subclass of TApplication
class TWinApp : public TApplication
{
public:
  TWinApp(LPSTR     AName,          // application name
          HINSTANCE hInstance,      // instance handle
          HINSTANCE hPrevInstance,  // previous instance handle
          LPSTR     lpCmdLine,      // command-line arguments
          int       nCmdShow) :     // display command
          TApplication(AName, hInstance, hPrevInstance,
                    lpCmdLine, nCmdShow) {};

protected:
  virtual void InitMainWindow();
};
```

Dialog Boxes

```cpp
// use the _CLASSDEF macro to declare reference and pointer
// types related to the new TAppWindow class
_CLASSDEF(TAppWindow)

// expand the functionality of TWindow by deriving class TAppWindow
class TAppWindow : public TWindow
{
public:

  TAppWindow(PTWindowsObject AParent, LPSTR ATitle)
    : TWindow(AParent, ATitle) { AssignMenu("MAINMENU"); }

  // handle the Game menu item
  virtual void CMFileStat(RTMessage Msg)
    = [CM_FIRST + CM_FILESTAT];

  // handle closing the window
  virtual BOOL CanClose();

};


void TAppWindow::CMFileStat(RTMessage Msg)
{
  char selFile[MaxBuffer];
  char s[255];
  char format[81];
  ffblk fileInfo;
  unsigned Hour, Minute, Second, Day, Month, Year,
           uDate, uTime;


  _fstrcpy(selFile, "*.*");
  if (GetApplication()->ExecDialog(
    new TFileDialog(this, SD_FILEOPEN, selFile)) == IDOK) {
    // get the file information
    findfirst(selFile, &fileInfo, FA_ARCH);
    // build the format string
    strcpy(format, "Filename: %s\n");
    strcat(format, "Time Stamp: %u:%u:%u\n");
    strcat(format, "Date Stamp: %u/%u/%u\n");
    strcat(format, "Size: %ld\n");
    uTime = unsigned(fileInfo.ff_ftime);
    // get the seconds
    Second = 2 * (uTime & 0x1f);
```

continues

Listing 8.29. continued

```
    // get the minutes
    Minute = (uTime >> 5) & 0x3f;
    // get the hours
    Hour = (uTime >> 11) & 0x1f;
    uDate = unsigned(fileInfo.ff_fdate);
    // get the day
    Day =  uDate & 0x1f;
    // get the month
    Month = (uDate >> 5) & 0xf;
    // get the year
    Year = (uDate >> 9) & 0x7f;
    sprintf(s, format, fileInfo.ff_name, Hour, Minute, Second,
            Month, Day, Year + 1980U, fileInfo.ff_fsize);
    MessageBox(HWindow, s, "File Statistics", MB_OK);
  }
}

BOOL TAppWindow::CanClose()
{
  return MessageBox(HWindow, "Want to close this application",
                    "Query", MB_YESNO ¦ MB_ICONQUESTION) == IDYES;
}

void TWinApp::InitMainWindow()
{
  MainWindow = new TAppWindow(NULL, Name);
}

int PASCAL WinMain(HINSTANCE hInstance, HINSTANCE hPrevInstance,
                   LPSTR lpCmdLine, int nCmdShow)
{
  TWinApp WinApp("File Statistics",
                 hInstance, hPrevInstance, lpCmdLine, nCmdShow);
  WinApp.Run(); // run OWL application
  return WinApp.Status; // return application status
}
```

The `TAppWindow::CmFileStat` function performs the following tasks:

1. Assigns the default filename wildcard `*.*` to the `selFile` variable.

2. Invokes the `ExecDialog` function that executes a `TFileDialog` instance. The class creates the `SD_FILEOPEN` resource, which is suitable for this type of

application in which the program is not really opening a file for I/O operations. The local variable `selFile` provides the argument for the `AFilePath` parameter. If the `ExecDIalog` function returns `IDOK`, `CMFileStat` performs the remaining tasks.

3. Invokes the `findfirst` function to obtain the information for the file specified in the `selFile` variable.
4. Builds the output format string.
5. Extracts the time and date components from the `ffblk`-type `fileInfo` variable.
6. Creates the output string by using the `sprintf` function.
7. Displays the output in a message dialog box.

The TSearchDialog Class

ObjectWindows implements a highly specified class that supports Search and Replace dialog boxes. The `TSearchDialog` class is a descendant of `TDialog` and declares only a class constructor, as follows:

```
class _EXPORT TSearchDialog : public TDialog
{
public:
    TSearchDialog(PTWindowsObject AParent, int ResourceId,
                TSearchStruct _FAR &SearchStruct,
                PTModule AModule = NULL);
    };
```

Instances of `TSearchDialog` use two dialog box resources. The first is selected by the `SD_SEARCH` ID and performs text search. The second resource is selected by the `SD_REPLACE` ID and performs text replacement. The instances of `TSearchDialog` rely on the `TSearchStruct` structure, as follows:

```
struct _CLASSTYPE TSearchStruct {
    char SearchText[81];
    BOOL CaseSensitive;
    char ReplaceText[81];
    BOOL ReplaceAll;
    BOOL PromptOnReplace;
};
```

The `TSearchDialog` instance supports case-sensitive, replace all, and prompt-before-replace options.

The `TSearchDialog` is a highly specialized class that is typically integrated in the `TEditWindow` and `TFileWindow` text editor classes. In most cases, the functionality of the `TSearchDialog` class is adequate for ObjectWindows applications.

Summary

This chapter presented you with useful dialog boxes that serve as input tools. You learned about

- Constructing instances of class `TDialog`.
- Executing a modal dialog box using the `ExecDialog` member function.
- Minimizing the role of resource files by defining the dialog box object in a resource file and the rest of the controls inside the ObjectWindows application.
- Creating, displaying, and closing a modeless dialog box by using the `MakeWindow` member function, the **ShowWindow** API function, and the `ShutDownWindow` member function.
- Creating a command-oriented calculator version by using a dialog box as a window. In this case, the dialog box is a child of the application.
- Transferring control data. This involves declaring the data transfer buffer type, declaring the buffer, creating the controls in a sequence that matches their buffers, and establishing the buffer link.
- Transferring data for dialog boxes. Examples showed you how to transfer data for modal and modeless dialog boxes, and how to initialize window controls.
- Using the ObjectWindows `TInputDialog` class, which enables you to prompt the user for input.
- Using the ObjectWindows `TFileDialog` class that enables your ObjectWindows applications to select a file in any directory and any drive.
- Using the `TSearchDialog` class, which supports the text search and replace operations.

Dialog Boxes

501

CHAPTER 9

MDI Windows

You might have noticed that many Windows applications (such as the Windows Program Manager, Windows File Manager, and even the Turbo C++ for Windows 3.0 IDE) implement a special Windows interface with multiple windows. This is a standard Windows interface called the Multiple Document Interface (MDI). The MDI standard is also part of the Common User Access (CUA) standard set by IBM. Each MDI-compliant application enables you to open child windows for file-specific tasks, such as editing text, managing a database, or working with a spreadsheet. In this chapter, you will learn about the following topics regarding the management of MDI windows and objects:

- ☐ The basic features and components of an MDI-compliant application
- ☐ The basics of building an MDI-compliant application
- ☐ The TMDIFrame class
- ☐ The basics of building an MDI frame window
- ☐ The TMDIClient class
- ☐ The basics of building an MDI child window
- ☐ The management of messages in an MDI-compliant application

The MDI Application Features and Components

An MDI-compliant application consists of the following objects:

☐ The visible MDI frame window that contains all other MDI objects. The MDI frame window is an instance of the TMDIFrame class or its descendants. Each MDI application has one MDI frame window.

- The invisible MDI client window that performs underlying management of the MDI child windows, which are dynamically created and removed. The MDI client window is an instance of the TMDIClient class. Each MDI application has one MDI client window.

- The dynamic and visible MDI child window. An MDI application dynamically creates and removes multiple instances of MDI child windows. An MDI child window is an instance of TWindow or its descendant. These windows are located, moved, resized, maximized, and minimized inside the area defined by the MDI frame window. At any given time (and while there is at least one MDI child window), there is only one active MDI child window.

When you maximize an MDI child window, it occupies the area defined by the MDI frame window. When you minimize an MDI child window, the icon of that window appears at the bottom area of the MDI frame window.

Note: The MDI frame window has a menu that manipulates the MDI child windows and their contents. The MDI child windows cannot have a menu, but can contain controls. Otherwise, you can think of an MDI child window as an instance of TWindow or its descendants.

Basics of Building an MDI Application

Before elaborating on the creation of the various components that make up an MDI application, I will focus on the basic strategy involved. In the last section, you learned that the basic ingredients for an MDI application are the TMDIFrame, TMDIClient, and TWindow (or TWindow descendant) classes. The TMDIFrame class supports the following tasks:

- Creating and handling the MDI client window
- Creating and handling the MDI child windows
- Managing menu selections

The MDIClient class handles the underlying management of MDI child windows. The TWindow class offers the functionality for MDI child windows.

504

At this stage you might ask, "Do I typically derive descendants for all three classes to create an MDI application?" The answer is no. You normally have to derive descendants only for the TMDIFrame and TWindow classes. The functionality of the TMDIClient class is adequate for most MDI-compliant applications.

The TMDIFrame Class

ObjectWindows offers the TMDIFrame class, a descendant of TWindow, to implement the MDI frame window of an MDI application. The following is the declaration of the TMDIFrame class:

```
class _EXPORT TMDIFrame : public TWindow
{
public:
    PTMDIClient ClientWnd;       // MDI client window
    int ChildMenuPos;            // menu position for child menu
    PTWindow ActiveChild;

    TMDIFrame(LPSTR ATitle, LPSTR MenuName, PTModule AModule = NULL);
    TMDIFrame(LPSTR ATitle, int MenuId, PTModule AModule = NULL);
    TMDIFrame(HWND AnHWindow, HWND ClientHWnd,
              PTModule AModule = NULL);
    virtual ~TMDIFrame();

    virtual void InitClientWindow()
        { ClientWnd = new TMDIClient(this); }

    virtual PTMDIClient GetClient()
        { return ClientWnd; }

    virtual PTWindowsObject InitChild()
        { return new TWindow(this, ""); }

    virtual PTWindowsObject CreateChild();

    virtual void TileChildren()
        { ClientWnd->TileChildren(); }

    virtual void CascadeChildren()
        { ClientWnd->CascadeChildren(); }

    virtual void ArrangeIcons()
        { ClientWnd->ArrangeIcons(); }
```

```cpp
        virtual BOOL CloseChildren();
        static PTStreamable build();

    protected:
        virtual void GetWindowClass(WNDCLASS _FAR & AWndClass);
        virtual LPSTR GetClassName()
            { return "OWLMDIFrame"; }
        virtual void SetupWindow();

        virtual void WMActivate(RTMessage Msg)
            { TWindow::WMActivate(Msg);
              if ( ActiveChild )
                ActiveChild->ActivationResponse(
                    Msg.WParam, IsIconic(ActiveChild->HWindow)); }

        virtual void CMCreateChild(RTMessage) =
                    [CM_FIRST + CM_CREATECHILD]
            { CreateChild(); }

        virtual void CMTileChildren(RTMessage) =
                    [CM_FIRST + CM_TILECHILDREN]
            { TileChildren(); }

        virtual void CMCascadeChildren(RTMessage) =
                    [CM_FIRST + CM_CASCADECHILDREN]
            { CascadeChildren(); }

        virtual void CMArrangeIcons(RTMessage) =
                    [CM_FIRST + CM_ARRANGEICONS]
            { ArrangeIcons(); }

        virtual void CMCloseChildren(RTMessage) =
                    [CM_FIRST + CM_CLOSECHILDREN]
            { CloseChildren(); }

        TMDIFrame(StreamableInit) : TWindow(streamableInit) {};
        virtual void write (Ropstream os);
        virtual Pvoid read (Ripstream is);

    private:
        virtual const Pchar streamableName() const
            { return "TMDIFrame"; }
    };
```

The TMDIFrame class contains public, protected, and private members. Many of its member functions have single inline statements that invoke inherited member functions, sibling member functions, or Windows API functions.

The TMDIFrame class declares three data members: ActiveChild, ChildMenuPos, and ClientWnd. The ActiveChild member is the pointer to the currently active MDI child window and therefore enables you to access and manipulate the contents of that window. ChildMenuPos contains the position of the MDI child window. The first three class constructors assign 0 to the ChildMenuPos. This value places the first MDI child window at the top-left corner of the MDI frame window. ClientWnd is the pointer to the MDI client window instance owned by the MDI frame window instance.

The TMDIFrame class has four constructors (one more than the typical number of ObjectWindows constructor classes). The first two constructors require a title and a resource menu ID number or name. The third constructor creates a class instance by specifying window handles. The fourth constructor creates an instance from a stream.

The MDI frame class declares a number of member functions that handle Windows and menu command messages for activating an MDI child window, arranging the MDI child icons, cascading and tiling MDI children, closing MDI children, and creating an MDI child window. These message response functions use sibling member functions. Table 9.1 lists the predefined menu ID constants and the TMDIFrame member functions that respond to them. Note that it's your choice whether to use these constants in your menus.

Table 9.1. The predefined menu command messages for manipulating MDI children.

Action	Menu ID Constant	Responding TMDIFrame Member Function
Tile	CM_TILECHILDREN	CMTileChildren
Cascade	CM_CASCADECHILDREN	CMCascadeChildren
Arrange icons	CM_ARRANGEICONS	CMArrangeIcons
Close all	CM_CLOSECHILDREN	CMCloseChildren

When you create class descendants, you might want to modify a number of member functions in the `TMDIFrame` class. The list of such member functions includes `CreateChild`, `SetupWindow`, `CanClose`, and `CloseChildren`. These functions enable you to modify how you create, set up, and close MDI children.

Building MDI Frame Windows

The usual approach to creating the objects that make up an ObjectWindows application starts by creating the application instance and then its main window instance. In the case of an MDI-compliant application, the application's main window is typically a descendant of the `TMDIFrame` class. The `InitMainWindow` member function of the application class creates this window. Looking at the first two `TMDIFrame` constructors, you can tell that creating the main MDI window involves a title and menu resource—there is no pointer to a parent window because MDI frame windows have no parent windows. The MDI frame window, unlike most descendants of the `TWindow` class, needs to be associated with a menu. This menu typically includes the items shown in Table 9.1 needed to manipulate the MDI children. In addition, the menu of the MDI frame window is dynamically and automatically updated to include the current MDI children.

The constructor of the descendant of `TMDIFrame` (called the *application frame class*) can, in many cases, simply invoke the parent class constructor. This invocation occurs if the steps taken by the class constructor are adequate for creating the MDI frame window instance. Wherever you want to modify the behavior of the application frame class, you must include the required statements. Such statements might alter the initial value assigned to the `ChildMenuPos` or assign initial values to data members declared in the application frame class.

The `SetupWindow` member function invokes the `InitClientWindow` to create the `TMDIClient` instance, which is accessed by the data member `ClientWnd`. For example, you can modify the `SetupWindow` function to automatically create the first child MDI window.

The TMDIClient Class

ObjectWindows offers the TMDIClient class, a descendant of TWindow, to implement the invisible MDI client window. The following is the declaration of the TMDIClient class:

```
class _EXPORT TMDIClient : public TWindow
{
public:
    LPCLIENTCREATESTRUCT ClientAttr;

    TMDIClient(PTMDIFrame AParent, PTModule AModule = NULL);
    TMDIClient(PTMDIFrame AParent, HWND AnHWindow,
               PTModule AModule = NULL);
    virtual ~TMDIClient();

    virtual void ArrangeIcons()
    { SendMessage(HWindow, WM_MDIICONARRANGE, 0, 0); }

    virtual void CascadeChildren()
    { SendMessage(HWindow, WM_MDICASCADE, 0, 0); }

    virtual void TileChildren()
    { SendMessage(HWindow, WM_MDITILE, 0, 0); }

    static PTStreamable build();

protected:
    virtual LPSTR GetClassName()
        { return "MDICLIENT"; }

    virtual void WMPaint(RTMessage Msg) = [WM_FIRST + WM_PAINT]
        { DefWndProc(Msg); }

    virtual void WMMDIActivate(RTMessage Msg) =
                [WM_FIRST + WM_MDIACTIVATE]
        { DefWndProc(Msg); }

    TMDIClient(StreamableInit) : TWindow(streamableInit) {}
    virtual void write (Ropstream os);
    virtual Pvoid read (Ripstream is);
```

```
private:
    virtual const Pchar streamableName() const
        { return "TMDIClient"; }
};
```

The `TMDIClient` class constructors require a pointer to the parent MDI frame window. The second constructor contains the `AnHWindow` parameter to pass a handle of an existing window. This window becomes the MDI client window to the specified MDI frame window. This process requires that the window argument be removed from its current position in the ObjectWindows library's list of windows to avoid erroneous dual references.

Building MDI Child Windows

Building MDI child windows is very similar to building application windows in the programs presented earlier. The differences are as follows:

- An MDI child window cannot have its own menu. The menu of the MDI frame window manipulates the currently active MDI child window or all of the MDI children.
- An MDI child window can have controls (unusual but certainly allowed).

> **Caution:** The keyboard handler must not be enabled in an MDI child window. It actually causes the reverse effect in the MDI children and antagonizes the proper operations of the MDI application.

Managing MDI Messages

The message loop first directs the command messages to the active MDI child window so it can respond. If that window does not respond, the message is then sent to the parent MDI frame window. The active MDI child window responds to the notification messages sent by its controls, just as any window or dialog box would.

A Simple Text Viewer

Now look at a simple MDI-compliant application. Because MDI applications are frequently used as text viewers and text editors, the next application emulates a simple text viewer. I say "emulates" because the application actually displays random text rather than text you can retrieve from a file. This approach keeps the program simple and helps you focus on implementing the various MDI objects. Figure 9.1 shows a sample session with the MDIWIN1.EXE program. The MDI application has a simple menu containing Exit and MDI Children options.

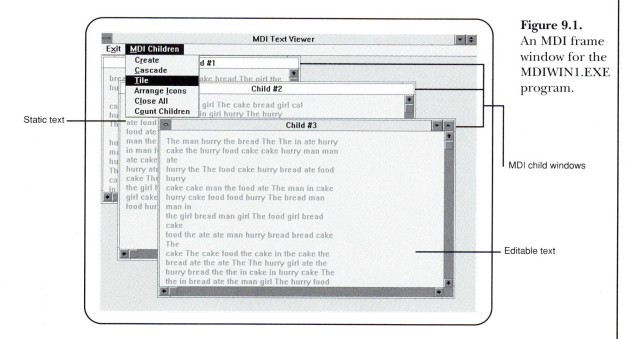

Figure 9.1.
An MDI frame window for the MDIWIN1.EXE program.

Compile and run the application. Experiment with creating MDI children. Notice that the text in odd-numbered MDI child windows is static, although the text in even-numbered windows can be edited. (Note that a window is considered odd- or even-numbered based on the value of the ChildNum variable, and not necessarily the number in the window's title bar.) I implemented this feature to demonstrate how to create a simple form of text viewer and text editor (with no save option to keep the example short). Try to tile, cascade, maximize, and minimize these windows. Also test closing individual MDI child windows and closing all the MDI children.

Examine the code that implements this simple MDI application. Listing 9.1 shows the source code for the MDIWIN1.H header file. This file declares the command message constants and a control ID constant.

Listing 9.1. The source code for the MDIWIN1.H header file.

```
#define CM_COUNTCHILDREN 101
#define ID_TEXT_EDIT 102
```

Listing 9.2 contains the script for the MDIWIN1.RC resource file. The file defines the menu resource required by the MDI frame window. The menu has two menu items, Exit and MDI Children. The latter menu item is a pop-up menu with several options. The menu options, except the Count Children option, use predefined command message constants.

Listing 9.2. The script for the MDIWIN1.RC resource file.

```
#include <windows.h>
#include <owlrc.h>
#include "mdiwin1.h"

COMMANDS MENU LOADONCALL MOVEABLE PURE DISCARDABLE
BEGIN
     MENUITEM "E&xit", CM_EXIT
     POPUP "&MDI Children"
     BEGIN
        MENUITEM   "C&reate", CM_CREATECHILD
        MENUITEM   "&Cascade", CM_CASCADECHILDREN
        MENUITEM   "&Tile", CM_TILECHILDREN
        MENUITEM   "Arrange &Icons", CM_ARRANGEICONS
        MENUITEM   "C&lose All", CM_CLOSECHILDREN
        MENUITEM   "C&ount Children", CM_COUNTCHILDREN
     END
END
```

Listing 9.3 shows the source code for the MDIWIN1.CPP program file. The program listing declares a set of constants used to generate the random text in each MDI child window. Words, a global array of pointers, contains the program's rather limited vocabulary. The listing also declares the iterated function CountChildren used in counting the number of MDI children.

Listing 9.3. The source code for the MDIWIN1.CPP program file.

```cpp
#include <stdio.h>
#include <string.h>
#include <owl.h>
#include <mdi.h>
#include <static.h>
#include <edit.h>
#include "mdiwin1.h"

const MaxWords = 200;
const WordsPerLine = 10;
const NumWords = 10;
char* Words[NumWords] = { "The ", "man ", "ate ", "the ",
                          "food ", "in ", "hurry ", "girl ",
                          "cake ", "bread " };

// declare iterated function to help count the number
// of MDI child windows
void CountMDIChild(Pvoid P, Pvoid DataPtr)
{
 ++*(int *)DataPtr;
}

// create the pointer and reference types for the application
// MDI frame and child window types
_CLASSDEF(TAppMDIFrame)
_CLASSDEF(TAppMDIChild)

class TWinApp : public TApplication
{
public:
  TWinApp(LPSTR AName, HINSTANCE hInstance, HINSTANCE hPrevInstance,
          LPSTR lpCmdLine, int nCmdShow)
    : TApplication(AName, hInstance, hPrevInstance, lpCmdLine, nCmdShow) {};
  virtual void InitMainWindow();
};

class TAppMDIChild : public TWindow
{
public:
  // pointer to the edit box control
  PTEdit TextBox;

  TAppMDIChild(PTWindowsObject AParent, int ChildNum);
```

continues

Listing 9.3. continued

```
  // handle closing the MDI child window
  virtual BOOL CanClose();
};

class TAppMDIFrame : public TMDIFrame
{
public:
  // flag to quickly close all MDI children windows
  BOOL ExpressClose;

  TAppMDIFrame(LPSTR ATitle, LPSTR MenuName) :
      TMDIFrame(ATitle, MenuName) { ExpressClose = FALSE; };

  // create a new MDI child window
  virtual PTWindowsObject CreateChild();

  // close all MDI children
  virtual BOOL CloseChildren();

  // get the number of MDI children
  int GetChildCount();

  // handle the command for counting the MDI children
  virtual void CMCountChildren(RTMessage Msg)
    = [CM_FIRST + CM_COUNTCHILDREN];

  // handle closing the MDI frame window
  virtual BOOL CanClose();
};

// TAppMDIChild's constructor instantiates a check box
TAppMDIChild::TAppMDIChild(PTWindowsObject AParent, int ChildNum)
    : TWindow(AParent, "")
{
  char s[1024];

  // set the scrollers in the window
  Attr.Style |= WS_VSCROLL | WS_HSCROLL;
  // create the TScroller instance
  Scroller = new TScroller(this, 200, 15, 10, 50);

  // set MDI child window title
  sprintf(s, "%s%i", "Child #", ChildNum);
  Title = _fstrdup(s);
```

```
    // randomize the seed for the random-number generator
    randomize();

    // assign a null string to the variable s
    strcpy(s, "");
    // build the list of random words
    for (int i = 0; i < MaxWords; i++) {
      if (i > 0 && i % WordsPerLine == 0)
        strcat(s, "\r\n");
      strcat(s, Words[random(NumWords)]);
    }
    // create a static text object in the child window if the
    // ChildNum variable stores an odd number.  Otherwise,
    // create an edit box control
    if (ChildNum % 2 == 0) {
      // create the edit box
      TextBox = new TEdit(this, ID_TEXT_EDIT, s,
                          10, 10, 300, 200, 0, TRUE);
      // remove borders and scroll bars
      TextBox->Attr.Style &= ~WS_BORDER;
      TextBox->Attr.Style &= ~WS_VSCROLL;
      TextBox->Attr.Style &= ~WS_HSCROLL;
    }
    else
      // create static text
      new TStatic(this, -1, s, 10, 10, 300, 400, strlen(s));

}

BOOL TAppMDIChild::CanClose()
{
  // return TRUE if the ExpressClose member of the
  // parent MDI frame window is TRUE
  if (PTAppMDIFrame(Parent)->ExpressClose == TRUE)
    return TRUE;
  else
    // prompt the user and return the prompt result
    return MessageBox(HWindow, "Close this MDI window?",
                 "Query", MB_YESNO | MB_ICONQUESTION) == IDYES;
}

PTWindowsObject TAppMDIFrame::CreateChild()
{
  return GetApplication()->MakeWindow(
    new TAppMDIChild(this, GetChildCount()+1));
```

continues

Listing 9.3. continued

```
}

BOOL TAppMDIFrame::CloseChildren()
{
  BOOL result;
  // set the ExpressClose flag
  ExpressClose = TRUE;
  // invoke the parent class CloseChildren() member function
  result = TMDIFrame::CloseChildren();
  // clear the ExpressClose flag
  ExpressClose = FALSE;
  return result;
}

int TAppMDIFrame::GetChildCount()
{
  int NumMDIChild = 0;

  ForEach(CountMDIChild, &NumMDIChild);
  return NumMDIChild;
}

//  display a message box that shows the number of children
void TAppMDIFrame::CMCountChildren(RTMessage)
{
  char msgStr[81];

  sprintf(msgStr, "There are %i MDI children", GetChildCount());
  MessageBox(HWindow, msgStr, "Information",
             MB_OK | MB_ICONINFORMATION);
}

BOOL TAppMDIFrame::CanClose()
{
  return MessageBox(HWindow, "Close this application",
                    "Query", MB_YESNO | MB_ICONQUESTION) == IDYES;
}

void TWinApp::InitMainWindow()
{
  MainWindow = new TAppMDIFrame(Name, "COMMANDS");
}
```

```
int PASCAL WinMain(HINSTANCE hInstance, HINSTANCE hPrevInstance,
                LPSTR lpCmdLine, int nCmdShow)
{
  TWinApp WinApp("MDI Text Viewer", hInstance, hPrevInstance,
                lpCmdLine, nCmdShow);
  WinApp.Run();
  return WinApp.Status;
}
```

The program listing declares three classes: the application class (TWinApp), the MDI frame class (TAppMDIFrame), and the MDI child window class (TAppMDIChild).

The code for the application class resembles the ones in previous programs, with one exception. The InitMainWindow member function creates an instance of the MDI frame class, TAppMDIFrame. The TAppMDIFrame constructor call contains the name of the application and the name of the menu resource, COMMANDS, as arguments.

The TAppMDIFrame class declares a public data member, a constructor, and a group of member functions. The Boolean data member ExpressClose assists in quickly closing all the windows—this process bypasses the confirmation normally requested when you close an individual MDI child window. The class constructor invokes the TMDIFrame constructor and assigns FALSE to the ExpressClose data member.

The CreateChild member function is a function required by all descendants of the TMDIFrame class. CreateChild creates a new MDI child window by invoking the MakeWindow member function and specifying the TAppMDIChild class. The second argument of the MakeWindow call is the MDI child window number, which you can obtain by calling the GetChildCount member function.

The CloseChildren member function alters the behavior of the inherited CloseChildren function. The new version performs the following tasks:

- Assigns TRUE to the ExpressClose data member.
- Invokes the parent class CloseChildren and stores the result of that function call in the local variable result.
- Assigns FALSE to the ExpressClose data member.
- Returns the value stored in the variable result.

The CMCountChildren member function responds to the menu command message CM_COUNTCHILDREN. This function invokes the GetChildCount function and displays the properly formatted result in a message dialog box.

The MDI child window class declares the `TextBox` data member, a constructor, and the `CanClose` member function. The `TextBox` member is the pointer to the `TEdit` instance, which is created to store the random text in the MDI child window.

The `TAppMDIChild` constructor performs the following tasks:

- ☐ Sets the window style to include the vertical and horizontal scrolls.
- ☐ Creates an instance of `TScroller` to animate the window's scroll bars.
- ☐ Sets the window title to include the MDI child window number.
- ☐ Randomizes the seed for the random number generator function, `random`.
- ☐ Creates the random text and stores it in the local string variable `s`.
- ☐ If the MDI child window number is even, it creates a multiline instance of `TEdit`. This instance contains a copy of the text stored in variable `s`. In addition, the constructor disables the border, vertical scroll bar, and horizontal scroll bar styles. These scroll bars are not needed, because the MDI child window itself contains scroll bars. In the case of an odd-numbered MDI child window number, the constructor creates static text using the characters in variable `s`.

The `CanClose` member function regulates closing an MDI child window. When you close such a window using the Close option in its own system menu, the function requires your confirmation. If the request to close comes from the Close All menu command in the parent window, the MDI child window closes without confirmation.

The Revised Text Viewer

I will now expand the MDIWIN1.EXE program to demonstrate other aspects of managing MDI windows. The next application also creates MDI children that contain edit box controls with random text. However, each MDI child window has the following additional controls:

- ☐ An `->UpperCase` pushbutton control that converts the text in the MDI child window into uppercase.
- ☐ A `->LowerCase` pushbutton control that converts the text in the MDI child window into lowercase.

☐ A Can Close check box. This box replaces the confirmation dialog box that appears when you want to close the MDI child window. The check box enables you to predetermine whether the MDI child window can be closed.

The application menu adds a new pop-up menu item, Current MDI Child. This menu item has options that work on the current MDI child window. The menu options enable you to clear, convert to uppercase, convert to lowercase, or rewrite the characters in the MDI child window. The new pop-up menu shows how you can manipulate MDI children with custom menus.

Compile and run the application. Create a few MDI children and use their push button controls to toggle the case of the characters inside these windows. Also use the Current MDI Child menu options to manipulate the text further in the currently active MDI child window. Try to close the MDI children when the Can Close check box is both marked and unmarked. Only the MDI children close individually when the Can Close control is checked. Use the Close All option in the MDI Children pop-up menu and watch all the MDI children close, regardless of the check state of the Can Close control. Figure 9.2 shows a sample session with the MDIWIN2.EXE program.

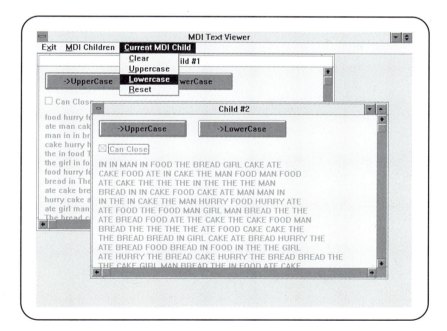

Figure 9.2.
A sample session with the MDIWIN2.EXE program.

Listing 9.4 shows the source code for the MDIWIN2.H header file. This file contains the constants for the menu commands and the control IDs.

Listing 9.4. The source code for the MDIWIN2.H header file.

```
#define CM_COUNTCHILDREN 101
#define CM_CLEAR 102
#define CM_UPPERCASE 103
#define CM_LOWERCASE 104
#define CM_RESET 105

#define ID_TEXT_EDIT 106
#define ID_CANCLOSE_CHK 107
#define ID_UPPERCASE_BTN 108
#define ID_LOWERCASE_BTN 109
```

Listing 9.5 contains the script for the MDIWIN2.RC resource file and shows the resource for the expanded menu.

Listing 9.5. The script for the MDIWIN2.RC resource file.

```
#include <windows.h>
#include <owlrc.h>
#include "mdiwin2.h"

COMMANDS MENU LOADONCALL MOVEABLE PURE DISCARDABLE
BEGIN
    MENUITEM "E&xit", CM_EXIT
    POPUP "&MDI Children"
    BEGIN
      MENUITEM   "C&reate", CM_CREATECHILD
      MENUITEM   "&Cascade", CM_CASCADECHILDREN
      MENUITEM   "&Tile", CM_TILECHILDREN
      MENUITEM   "Arrange &Icons", CM_ARRANGEICONS
      MENUITEM   "C&lose All", CM_CLOSECHILDREN
      MENUITEM   "C&ount Children", CM_COUNTCHILDREN
    END
    POPUP "&Current MDI Child"
    BEGIN
      MENUITEM   "&Clear", CM_CLEAR
      MENUITEM   "&Uppercase", CM_UPPERCASE
      MENUITEM   "&Lowercase", CM_LOWERCASE
      MENUITEM   "&Reset", CM_RESET
```

        END

    END

Listing 9.6 contains the source code for the MDIWIN2.CPP program file. The program listing declares two sets of constants. The first set sizes and spaces the controls of each MDI child window. The second set of constants manages the random text. The program also declares the variable AppBuffer as a single 1K text buffer. I chose to make the buffer global rather than a class data member mainly to reduce the buffer space—the application classes need only one shared buffer at any time. The program listing declares the iterated function CountMDIChildren. This is another component carried over from the program in the MDIWIN1.CPP file.

Listing 9.6. The source code for the MDIWIN2.CPP program file.

```
#include <stdio.h>
#include <string.h>
#include <owl.h>
#include <mdi.h>
#include <button.h>
#include <edit.h>
#include <checkbox.h>
#include "mdiwin2.h"

// declare constants for sizing and spacing the controls
// in the MDI child window
const Wbtn = 50 * 3;
const Hbtn = 30;
const BtnHorzSpacing = 20;
const BtnVertSpacing = 10;
const Wchk = 200 * 3;
const Hchk = 20;
const ChkVertSpacing = 10;
const Wbox = 300 * 3;
const Hbox = 200 * 3;

// declare the constants for the random text that appears
// in the MDI child window
const MaxWords = 200;
const WordsPerLine = 10;
const NumWords = 10;
```

continues

Listing 9.6. continued

```
const BufferSize = 1024;
char AppBuffer[BufferSize];
char* Words[NumWords] = { "The ", "man ", "ate ", "the ",
                          "food ", "in ", "hurry ", "girl ",
                          "cake ", "bread " };

// declare iterated function to help count the number
// of MDI child windows
void CountMDIChild(Pvoid P, Pvoid DataPtr)
{
 ++*(int *)DataPtr;
}

// create the pointer and reference types for the application
// MDI frame and child window types
_CLASSDEF(TAppMDIFrame)
_CLASSDEF(TAppMDIChild)

class TWinApp : public TApplication
{
public:
  TWinApp(LPSTR AName, HINSTANCE hInstance, HINSTANCE hPrevInstance,
          LPSTR lpCmdLine, int nCmdShow)
    : TApplication(AName, hInstance, hPrevInstance, lpCmdLine, nCmdShow) {};
  virtual void InitMainWindow();
};

class TAppMDIChild : public TWindow
{
public:
  // pointer to the edit box control
  PTEdit TextBox;

  TAppMDIChild(PTWindowsObject AParent, int ChildNum);

  // handle the UpperCase button
  virtual void HandleUpperCaseBtn(RTMessage Msg)
    = [ID_FIRST + ID_UPPERCASE_BTN]
      { CMUpperCase(Msg); }

  // handle the LowerCase button
  virtual void HandleLowerCaseBtn(RTMessage Msg)
    = [ID_FIRST + ID_LOWERCASE_BTN]
      { CMLowerCase(Msg); }
```

```cpp
    // handle clear the active MDI child
    virtual void CMClear(RTMessage Msg)
      = [CM_FIRST + CM_CLEAR]
        { TextBox->Clear(); }

    // handle converting the text of the active
    // MDI child to uppercase
    virtual void CMUpperCase(RTMessage Msg)
      = [CM_FIRST + CM_UPPERCASE];

    // handle converting the text of the active
    // MDI child to lowercase
    virtual void CMLowerCase(RTMessage Msg)
      = [CM_FIRST + CM_LOWERCASE];

    // handle resetting the text of the active MDI child
    virtual void CMReset(RTMessage Msg)
      = [CM_FIRST + CM_RESET];

    // reset the text in an MDI child window
    virtual void InitText();

    // handle closing the MDI child window
    virtual BOOL CanClose();

protected:
    PTCheckBox CanCloseChk;
};

class TAppMDIFrame : public TMDIFrame
{
public:
    // flag to quickly close all MDI children windows
    BOOL ExpressClose;

    TAppMDIFrame(LPSTR ATitle, LPSTR MenuName) :
      TMDIFrame(ATitle, MenuName) { ExpressClose = FALSE; };

    // create a new MDI child window
    virtual PTWindowsObject CreateChild();

    // close all MDI children
    virtual BOOL CloseChildren();
```

continues

Listing 9.6. continued

```
  // get the number of MDI children
  int GetChildCount();

  // handle the command for counting the MDI children
  virtual void CMCountChildren(RTMessage Msg)
    = [CM_FIRST + CM_COUNTCHILDREN];

  // handle closing the MDI frame window
  virtual BOOL CanClose();

};

// TAppMDIChild's constructor instantiates a check box
TAppMDIChild::TAppMDIChild(PTWindowsObject AParent, int ChildNum)
  : TWindow(AParent, "")
{
  char s[41];
  int x0 = 10;
  int y0 = 10;
  int x = x0;
  int y = y0;

  // set the scrollers in the window
  Attr.Style |= WS_VSCROLL | WS_HSCROLL;
  // create the TScroller instance
  Scroller = new TScroller(this, 200, 15, 10, 50);

  // set MDI child window title
  sprintf(s, "%s%i", "Child #", ChildNum);
  Title = _fstrdup(s);

  // create the push button controls
  new TButton(this, ID_UPPERCASE_BTN, "->UpperCase",
              x, y, Wbtn, Hbtn, TRUE);
  x += Wbtn + BtnHorzSpacing;
  new TButton(this, ID_LOWERCASE_BTN, "->LowerCase",
              x, y, Wbtn, Hbtn, FALSE);

  x = x0;
  y += Hbtn + BtnVertSpacing;
  CanCloseChk = new TCheckBox(this, ID_CANCLOSE_CHK, "Can Close",
                              x, y, Wchk, Hchk, NULL);
  y += Hchk + ChkVertSpacing;
```

```
  InitText();
  // create the edit box
  TextBox = new TEdit(this, ID_TEXT_EDIT, AppBuffer,
                      x, y, Wbox, Hbox, 0, TRUE);
  // remove borders and scroll bars
  TextBox->Attr.Style &= ~WS_BORDER;
  TextBox->Attr.Style &= ~WS_VSCROLL;
  TextBox->Attr.Style &= ~WS_HSCROLL;

  // NOTE: DO NOT enable the keyboard handler!
}

void TAppMDIChild::CMUpperCase(RTMessage Msg)
{
  TextBox->GetText(AppBuffer, BufferSize);
  strupr(AppBuffer);
  TextBox->SetText(AppBuffer);
}

void TAppMDIChild::CMLowerCase(RTMessage Msg)
{
  TextBox->GetText(AppBuffer, BufferSize);
  strlwr(AppBuffer);
  TextBox->SetText(AppBuffer);
}

void TAppMDIChild::CMReset(RTMessage Msg)
{
  InitText();
  TextBox->SetText(AppBuffer);
}

BOOL TAppMDIChild::CanClose()
{
  // return TRUE if the ExpressClose member of the
  // parent MDI frame window is TRUE
  if (PTAppMDIFrame(Parent)->ExpressClose == TRUE)
    return TRUE;
  else
  // do not close the MDI child window if the Can Close is not checked
  if (CanCloseChk->GetCheck() == BF_UNCHECKED)
    return FALSE;
  else
    return TRUE;
}
```

continues

Listing 9.6. continued

```
void TAppMDIChild::InitText()
{
  // randomize the seed for the random-number generator
  randomize();

  // assign a null string to the buffer
  AppBuffer[0] = '\0';
  // build the list of random words
  for (int i = 0;
       i < MaxWords && strlen(AppBuffer) <= (BufferSize - 10);
       i++) {
    if (i > 0 && i % WordsPerLine == 0)
      strcat(AppBuffer, "\r\n");
    strcat(AppBuffer, Words[random(NumWords)]);
  }
}

PTWindowsObject TAppMDIFrame::CreateChild()
{
  return GetApplication()->MakeWindow(
      new TAppMDIChild(this, GetChildCount()+1));
}

BOOL TAppMDIFrame::CloseChildren()
{
  BOOL result;
  // set the ExpressClose flag
  ExpressClose = TRUE;
  // invoke the parent class CloseChildren() member function
  result = TMDIFrame::CloseChildren();
  // clear the ExpressClose flag
  ExpressClose = FALSE;
  return result;
}

int TAppMDIFrame::GetChildCount()
{
  int NumMDIChild = 0;

  ForEach(CountMDIChild, &NumMDIChild);
  return NumMDIChild;
}
```

```
// display a message box that shows the number of children
void TAppMDIFrame::CMCountChildren(RTMessage)
{
  char msgStr[81];

  sprintf(msgStr, "There are %i MDI children", GetChildCount());
  MessageBox(HWindow, msgStr, "Information",
             MB_OK | MB_ICONINFORMATION);
}

BOOL TAppMDIFrame::CanClose()
{
  return MessageBox(HWindow, "Close this application",
                    "Query", MB_YESNO | MB_ICONQUESTION) == IDYES;
}

void TWinApp::InitMainWindow()
{
  MainWindow = new TAppMDIFrame(Name, "COMMANDS");
}

int PASCAL WinMain(HINSTANCE hInstance, HINSTANCE hPrevInstance,
                   LPSTR lpCmdLine, int nCmdShow)
{
  TWinApp WinApp("MDI Text Viewer", hInstance, hPrevInstance,
                 lpCmdLine, nCmdShow);
  WinApp.Run();
  return WinApp.Status;
}
```

This revised application maintains the same three classes described in the original version of the program. However, the MDI child class contains different members in this updated version. The new members manage the response to the control notification messages as well as the Current MDI Child menu command messages.

The `TAppMDIChild` constructor performs the following tasks:

- ☐ Sets the window style to include the vertical and horizontal scrolls.
- ☐ Creates an instance of `TScroller` to animate the window's scroll bars.
- ☐ Sets the window title to include the MDI child window number.
- ☐ Creates the `->LowerCase` and `->UpperCase` push button controls.

- Creates the Can Close check box control.
- Calls the `InitText` member function to generate random text in the application buffer `AppBuffer`.
- Creates a multiline instance of `TEdit`. This instance contains a copy of the text stored in the application buffer.
- Disables the border, vertical scroll bar, and horizontal scroll bar styles.

The `CMUpperCase` member function responds to the command message sent by the `UpperCase` menu option. This function copies the text in the MDI child window to the application buffer, converts the characters in the buffer to uppercase, and writes the buffer back to the MDI child window.

The `CMLowerCase` member function responds to the command message sent by the Lowercase menu option. This function performs steps similar to those in `CMUpperCase`, except the text is converted to lowercase.

The `CanClose` member function responds to the `WM_CLOSE` message sent by the Close option in the system menu available in each MDI child window. If the MDI frame window's `ExpressClose` variable is TRUE, the function systematically returns TRUE. Otherwise, the function returns TRUE if the Can Close check box is checked and FALSE if the control is not checked.

The `InitText` member function is an auxiliary routine that fills the application buffer with random text. The function creates up to `MaxWords` words or until the buffer limit is closely reached (within 10 bytes). Checking the number of characters in the buffer ensures that the program does not corrupt the memory while attempting to add `MaxWords` words to the buffer.

The `HandleUpperCaseBtn` and `HandleLowerCase` member functions respond to the notification messages sent by the push buttons of an MDI child window. These functions perform the same tasks as `CMUpperCase` and `CMLowerCase`, respectively. Therefore, the notification response functions call their respective command message response member functions.

The `CMClear` member function responds to the command message sent by the Clear menu option in the Current MDI Child menu item. The function simply invokes the `TextBox->Clear()` function call.

The `CMReset` member function responds to the command message sent by the Reset menu option in the Current MDI Child menu item. The function calls the `InitText` member function to create a new batch of random text and copies the buffer's text to the edit control of the MDI child window.

MDI Windows

> **Note:** The Current MDI Child pop-up menu contains four options that manipulate the currently active MDI child window. The command messages sent by these options are handled by the MDI child window instances and not the MDI frame instance. Normally, a parent (or frame) window responds to the messages sent by the menu items. In this case, the active MDI child window can intercept and respond to these messages. This modified, versatile order of handling command messages makes use of the fact that the menu-based messages reach the currently active MDI child window first. You can rewrite the program so the functions CMClear, CMUpperCase, CMLowerCase, and CMReset appear as member functions of the TAppMDIFrame class.

Summary

This chapter presented the Multiple Document Interface (MDI), which is an interface standard in Windows. The chapter discussed the following subjects:

- The basic features and components of an MDI-compliant application. These components include the MDI frame window, the invisible MDI client window, and the dynamically created MDI child window.
- The basics of building an MDI application.
- The TMDIFrame class that manages the MDI client window, the MDI child window, and the execution of the menu commands.
- The building of MDI frame windows as objects that are owned by the application and that own the MDI children.
- The TMDIClient class.
- The building of MDI child windows as an instance of a TWindow descendant.
- The management of messages in an MDI-compliant application. The currently active MDI child window has a higher priority for handling menu-based command messages than its parent, the MDI frame window.

CHAPTER 10

ObjectWindows Streams

The concept of streams finds its source in the UNIX operating system. UNIX regards every device as a file that sends, receives, or exchanges a stream of bytes. Although the term *streams* conveys the notion of sequential data flow, random-access streams can also support databases. Because UNIX is written in C, the standard file I/O libraries are based on the concept of streams. C++ has built on the concepts of streams and offers the << and >> operators to perform stream I/O. The designers of C++ created the C++ stream I/O libraries as a more flexible successor to the standard I/O, C libraries. Using overloaded operators, you can define << and >> operators to perform object I/O with streams. The benefit of these C++ operators is that they make the object I/O transparent to the client programmer—which is not possible with C. This chapter discusses the role of C++ streams in storing and retrieving both ObjectWindows and non-ObjectWindows instances. You will learn about the following topics:

- The ObjectWindows streams hierarchy
- Making a class streamable
- Storing ObjectWindows controls in a stream
- Constructing ObjectWindows controls from streams

The ObjectWindows Stream Hierarchy

ObjectWindows includes a small hierarchy to store and retrieve objects in streams. The source of the streamable class hierarchy, shown in Figure 10.1, is in the pstream class. The letter p in pstream stands for *persistent,* because the objects can persist long after their host program ends. Figure 10.1 indicates that the streamable classes take advantage of the multiple inheritance feature supported by C++. The TStreamable class is a friend class of the ipstream and opstream classes. This relationship is indicated by the dotted connectors.

Figure 10.1.
The streamable class hierarchy.

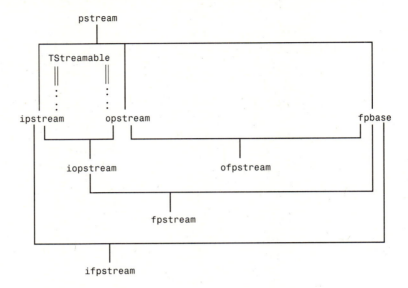

This section looks briefly at the various streamable classes, starting with the base class, pstream, and working down through the classes shown in Figure 10.1.

The pstream Class

The pstream class is the base class for managing streamable objects. The following is the declaration of the pstream class:

```
class _CLASSTYPE pstream
{
        friend class _CLASSTYPE TStreamableTypes;

public:

        enum StreamableError { peNotRegistered, peInvalidType };
        enum PointerTypes { ptNull, ptIndexed, ptObject };

        _Cdecl pstream(Pstreambuf sb) { init(sb); }
        virtual _Cdecl ~pstream() {}

        int _Cdecl rdstate() const { return state; }
        int _Cdecl eof() const { return state & ios::eofbit; }
        int _Cdecl fail() const
```

ObjectWindows Streams

```
                {
            return state & (ios::failbit | ios::badbit | ios::hardfail); }
        int _Cdecl bad() const
                    { return state & (ios::badbit | ios::hardfail); }
        int _Cdecl good() const { return state == 0; }

        void _Cdecl clear(int i = 0)
                        { state = (i & 0xFF) | (state & ios::hardfail); }
        _Cdecl operator Pvoid() const
                        { return fail() ? 0 : (void *)this; }
        int _Cdecl operator ! () const
                    { return fail(); }

        Pstreambuf _Cdecl rdbuf() const { return bp; }

        static void initTypes();
        static PTStreamableTypes types;

protected:
    _Cdecl pstream() {}
    void _Cdecl error(StreamableError) { abort(); }
void _Cdecl error(StreamableError, RCTStreamable) { abort(); }

    Pstreambuf bp;
    int state;

void _Cdecl init(Pstreambuf sbp) { state = 0; bp = sbp; }
    void _Cdecl setstate(int b) { state |= (b&0xFF); }
};
```

The `pstream` class declares the `bp`, `state`, and `types` data members. The `bp` member is a pointer to the stream buffer. The `state` data member stores the error state and is accessed with the `rdstate` member function. The `types` data member is a pointer to a database of all the registered types in an ObjectWindows application. The run-time system uses a stream manager that creates a database for all streamable classes. To add a new class to the streamable objects database, you must register that class. The registration of the various streamable ObjectWindows classes is already done in the header files. Therefore, you can focus only on registering the new classes that you create. These classes can be descendants of ObjectWindows classes or non-ObjectWindows classes.

The `pstream` class declares the `bad`, `good`, and `fail` member functions to query the error state of a stream. The `eof` member function detects the end of a stream. The `clear` member function sets the value of the `state` member to a given value (which is 0 by default).

The fpbase Class

The fpbase class, a descendant of pstream, supports the basic operations common to the object file stream I/O. The following is the declaration of the fpbase class:

```
class _CLASSTYPE fpbase : virtual public pstream
{
public:

    _Cdecl fpbase() { pstream::init(&buf); }
    _Cdecl fpbase(PCchar, int, int = filebuf::openprot);
    _Cdecl fpbase(int f) : buf (f) { pstream::init(&buf); }
    _Cdecl fpbase(int f, Pchar b, int len) : buf(f, b, len)
        { pstream::init(&buf); }
    _Cdecl ~fpbase() {}

    void _Cdecl open(PCchar, int, int = filebuf::openprot);
    void _Cdecl attach(int);
    void _Cdecl close();
    void _Cdecl setbuf(Pchar, int);
    Pfilebuf _Cdecl rdbuf() { return &buf; }

private:

    filebuf buf;
};
```

The fpbase class includes four constructors and one destructor. The constructors create a buffered instance of the fpbase class. One of the constructors enables you to attach an opened file to a stream. With the open member function, you can open a file and attach it to a stream after the stream instance is created. The close function closes the stream and its associated file. Combining open and close member functions enables you to reuse the same stream instance with different files, one at a time. The buffer associated with an instance of fpbase or its descendants can be set either by a constructor or by the setbuf member function.

The ipstream Class

The ipstream class, a descendant of pstream, offers support for buffered stream input. The declaration for the ipstream class is

```cpp
class _CLASSTYPE ipstream : virtual public pstream
{
public:

    _Cdecl ipstream(Pstreambuf sb) { pstream::init(sb); }
    _Cdecl ~ipstream() {}

    streampos _Cdecl tellg()
        { return bp->seekoff(0, ios::cur, ios::in); }

    Ripstream _Cdecl seekg(streampos);
    Ripstream _Cdecl seekg(streamoff, ios::seek_dir);

    uchar _Cdecl readByte() { return bp->sbumpc(); }
    void _Cdecl readBytes(Pvoid data, size_t sz)
        { bp->sgetn((char *)data, sz); }
    void _Cdecl freadBytes(void far *data, size_t sz);

    ushort _Cdecl readWord();
    Pchar _Cdecl readString();
    Pchar _Cdecl readString(Pchar, unsigned);
    char far *freadString();
    char far *freadString(char far *buf, unsigned maxLen);

    friend Ripstream _Cdecl _EXPFUNC operator >> (Ripstream,
        signed char _FAR &);
    friend Ripstream _Cdecl _EXPFUNC operator >> (Ripstream,
        unsigned char _FAR &);
    friend Ripstream _Cdecl _EXPFUNC operator >> (Ripstream,
        signed short _FAR &);
    friend Ripstream _Cdecl _EXPFUNC operator >> (Ripstream,
        unsigned short _FAR &);
    friend Ripstream _Cdecl _EXPFUNC operator >> (Ripstream,
        signed int _FAR &);
    friend Ripstream _Cdecl _EXPFUNC operator >> (Ripstream,
        unsigned int _FAR &);
    friend Ripstream _Cdecl _EXPFUNC operator >> (Ripstream,
        signed long _FAR &);
    friend Ripstream _Cdecl _EXPFUNC operator >> (Ripstream,
        unsigned long _FAR &);
    friend Ripstream _Cdecl _EXPFUNC operator >> (Ripstream,
        float _FAR &);
    friend Ripstream _Cdecl _EXPFUNC operator >> (Ripstream,
        double _FAR &);
    friend Ripstream _Cdecl _EXPFUNC operator >> (Ripstream,
```

```
                    long double _FAR &);

        friend Ripstream _Cdecl _EXPFUNC operator >> (Ripstream,
            RTStreamable);
        friend Ripstream _Cdecl _EXPFUNC operator >> (Ripstream,
            RPvoid);

    protected:

        _Cdecl ipstream() {}

        PCTStreamableClass _Cdecl readPrefix();
        Pvoid _Cdecl readData(PCTStreamableClass, PTStreamable);
        void _Cdecl readSuffix();

        PCvoid _Cdecl find(P_id_type id) { return objs.find(id); }
        void _Cdecl registerObject(PCvoid adr)
            { objs.registerObject(adr); }

    private:

        TPReadObjects objs;
};
```

The `ipstream` class offers member functions to read a byte (`readByte`), a word (`readWord`), a number of bytes (`readBytes`), a string (`readString`), a far string (`freadString`), and streamable data (`readData`). The member functions `seekg` and `tellg` move and return the current stream position, respectively. The `ipstream` class declares a set of friend >> operators to read the basic data types, such as `int`, `char`, `double`, and `long`.

The opstream Class

The `opstream` class, a descendant of `pstream`, offers support for buffered stream output. The `opstream` and `ipstream` classes complement each other by providing stream I/O. The following is the declaration for the `opstream` class:

```
class _CLASSTYPE opstream : virtual public pstream
{
public:

    _Cdecl opstream(Pstreambuf sb) { pstream::init(sb); }
    _Cdecl ~opstream() {}
```

```
            streampos _Cdecl tellp()
                    { return bp->seekoff(0, ios::cur, ios::out); }
            Ropstream _Cdecl seekp(streampos pos);
            Ropstream _Cdecl seekp(streamoff off, ios::seek_dir dir);
            Ropstream _Cdecl flush();

            void _Cdecl writeByte(uchar ch) { bp->sputc(ch); }
            void _Cdecl writeBytes(PCvoid data, size_t sz)
                    { bp->sputn((char *)data, sz); }
            void _Cdecl fwriteBytes(const void far *data, size_t sz);

            void _Cdecl writeWord(ushort sh)
                    { bp->sputn((char *)&sh, sizeof(ushort)); }

            void _Cdecl writeString(PCchar);
            void _Cdecl fwriteString(const char far * str);

            friend Ropstream _Cdecl _EXPFUNC operator << (Ropstream,
                                                          signed char);
            friend Ropstream _Cdecl _EXPFUNC operator << (Ropstream,
                                                          unsigned char);
            friend Ropstream _Cdecl _EXPFUNC operator << (Ropstream,
                                                          signed short);
            friend Ropstream _Cdecl _EXPFUNC operator << (Ropstream,
                                                          unsigned short);
            friend Ropstream _Cdecl _EXPFUNC operator << (Ropstream,
                                                          signed int);
            friend Ropstream _Cdecl _EXPFUNC operator << (Ropstream,
                                                          unsigned int);
            friend Ropstream _Cdecl _EXPFUNC operator << (Ropstream,
                                                          signed long);
            friend Ropstream _Cdecl _EXPFUNC operator << (Ropstream,
                                                          unsigned long);
            friend Ropstream _Cdecl _EXPFUNC operator << (Ropstream,
                                                          float);
            friend Ropstream _Cdecl _EXPFUNC operator << (Ropstream,
                                                          double);
            friend Ropstream _Cdecl _EXPFUNC operator << (Ropstream,
                                                          long double);

            friend Ropstream _Cdecl _EXPFUNC operator << (Ropstream,
                                                          RTStreamable);
            friend Ropstream _Cdecl _EXPFUNC operator << (Ropstream,
                                                          PTStreamable);
```

```
protected:

    _Cdecl opstream() {}
    void _Cdecl writePrefix(RCTStreamable);
    void _Cdecl writeData(RTStreamable);
    void _Cdecl writeSuffix(RCTStreamable)
        { writeByte(']'); }
    P_id_type _Cdecl find(PCvoid adr) { return objs.find(adr); }
    void _Cdecl registerObject(PCvoid adr)
        { objs.registerObject(adr); }

private:
    TPWrittenObjects objs;
};
```

The `opstream` class offers member functions to write a byte (`writeByte`), a word (`writeWord`), a number of bytes (`writeBytes`), a string (`writeString`), a far string (`fwriteString`), and streamable data (`writeData`). The two versions of the overloaded member function `seekp` move the current stream position. The `ipstream` class declares a set of friend << operators to write the basic data types, such as `int`, `char`, `double`, and `long`.

The `iopstream` Class

The `iopstream` class is a descendant of the `ipstream` and `opstream` classes that combines the features of these two classes (and their ancestors). The following is the declaration of the `iopstream` class:

```
class _CLASSTYPE iopstream : public ipstream, public opstream
{
public:

    _Cdecl iopstream(Pstreambuf sb) { pstream::init(sb); }
    _Cdecl ~iopstream() {}

protected:

    _Cdecl iopstream() {}
};
```

The `iopstream` class declares the constructors and a destructor. All of the members needed are inherited from the parent classes.

The ofpstream Class

The `ofpstream` class, a descendant of the classes `fpbase` and `opstream`, supports the writing of objects to file streams. The following is the declaration of the `ofpstream` class:

```
class _CLASSTYPE ofpstream : public fpbase, public opstream
{
public:

    _Cdecl ofpstream() {}
    _Cdecl ofpstream(PCchar, int = ios::out,
                     int = filebuf::openprot);
    _Cdecl ofpstream(int f) : fpbase(f) {}
    _Cdecl ofpstream(int f, Pchar b, int len)
           : fpbase(f, b, len) {}
    _Cdecl ~ofpstream() {}

    Pfilebuf _Cdecl rdbuf() { return fpbase::rdbuf(); }
    void _Cdecl open(PCchar, int = ios::out,
                     int = filebuf::openprot);
};
```

The class constructors help you create an output file stream instance and specify the associated buffer and the associated file. The second constructor helps you specify the name of the file, and the third and fourth constructors help you specify a file handle.

The `ofpstream` class declares the open member functions to open a file and attach it to the stream instance. The default I/O mode is output. However, you can specify other I/O modes, such as input and append. The `rdbuf` member function returns a pointer to the current file buffer.

The fpstream Class

The `fpstream` class, a descendant of the classes `fpbase` and `iopstream`, supports both reading and writing objects in file streams. The declaration of the `fpstream` class is

```
class _CLASSTYPE fpstream : public fpbase, public iopstream
{
public:
```

```
_Cdecl fpstream() {}
_Cdecl fpstream(PCchar, int, int = filebuf::openprot);
_Cdecl fpstream(int f) : fpbase(f) {}
_Cdecl fpstream(int f, Pchar b, int len) : fpbase(f, b, len) {}
_Cdecl ~fpstream() {}

Pfilebuf _Cdecl rdbuf() { return fpbase::rdbuf(); }
void _Cdecl open(PCchar, int, int = filebuf::openprot);
```

};

The class constructors help you create a file stream instance and specify the I/O mode, the associated buffer, and the associated file. The second constructor helps you specify the name of the file, and the third and fourth constructors help you specify a file handle.

The ifpstream Class

The `ifpstream` class, a descendant of the classes `fpbase` and `ipstream`, supports reading objects from file streams. The following is the declaration of the `ifpstream` class:

```
class _CLASSTYPE ifpstream : public fpbase, public ipstream
{
public:

    _Cdecl ifpstream() {}
    _Cdecl ifpstream(PCchar name, int mode = ios::in,
                     int prot = filebuf::openprot);
    _Cdecl ifpstream(int f) : fpbase(f) {}
    _Cdecl ifpstream(int f, Pchar b, int len) : fpbase(f, b, len) {}
    _Cdecl ~ifpstream() {}

    Pfilebuf _Cdecl rdbuf() { return fpbase::rdbuf(); }
    void _Cdecl open(PCchar, int = ios::in,
                     int = filebuf::openprot);
};
```

The class constructors help you create an input file stream instance and specify the associated buffer and the associated file. The second constructor helps you specify the name of the file, and the third and fourth constructors help you specify a file handle.

The `TStreamable` Class

Most ObjectWindows classes have descendants of the `Object` and `TStreamable` classes. The ObjectWindows classes include the `TScroller` class, the `TWindowsObject` class, and all the descendants of `TWindowsObject`. The `TStreamable` class is declared as follows:

```
class _CLASSTYPE TStreamable
{

    friend class _CLASSTYPE opstream;
    friend class _CLASSTYPE ipstream;

private:

    virtual const Pchar streamableName() const = 0;

protected:

    virtual Pvoid read(Ripstream) = 0;
    virtual void write(Ropstream) = 0;
};
```

The `TStreamable` class is an abstract class that declares classes `opstream` and `ipstream` as friends. The ObjectWindows classes previously mentioned defined the `read`, `write`, and `streamableName` member functions inherited from `TStreamable`. These classes also define their own versions of the << and >> operators, as well as the protected stream-based constructors. This is discussed in more detail later in this chapter.

Making a Class Streamable

The power of C++ streams unleashes the capability to write and read various nonobjects (that is, basic data types and structures) and objects. In the case of nonobjects, the stream I/O is essentially straightforward. In comparison, having a stream handle objects is more complicated because objects usually involve pointers and dynamically allocated space. In some cases, multiple pointers access the same object. ObjectWindows uses a stream manager to manage single and multiple pointer references safely. The manager ensures that, when an object with multiple pointer references is read from the streams, these pointers still access the same object (and not multiple copies of it).

Making a class streamable is a process that involves a number of steps. The following discussion describes how to make an existing (or separate) class streamable. To present a typical example of code, I call the base class `TAppBase` and the streamable class `TStrmAppBase`. The following steps will help you make a class streamable and use the << and >> operators with either references or pointers to class instances.

Step One: Using the __link Macro

Use the `__link` macro when the class contains data members that are pointers to classes defined outside the source file. The single argument of the `__link` macro is an identifier. You create this identifier by removing the first letter (`T`) of the name of the streamable class and then appending the string `Reg` to the class name. The general form of the `__link` macro is

```
__link(RegStrmAppBase)
```

Step Two: Declaring the Descendant Class

Declare a descendant class that inherits both the target class and `TStreamable`. The general form of the class declaration is

```
class TStrmAppBase : public TAppBase, public TStreamable
```

Step Three: Declaring Public Constructors

Declare at least one public constructor for the streamable class. Usually, such a constructor simply calls the public constructor of the parent `TAppBase` class.

Step Four: Declaring the Protected Stream Constructor

Declare a protected stream constructor that creates a class instance before its data members are read from the stream. The general syntax for the stream constructor is

```
TStrmAppBase(StreamableInit);
```

> **Caution:** The `StreamableInit` is actually a dummy enumerated type with a single enumerated value, `streamableInit`; therefore, watch out for the case-sensitive difference between the enumerated type and its member. The enumerated type distinguishes this constructor from the default parameterless class constructor. The body of the stream constructor should create a class instance that has suitable defaults.

Step Five: Declaring the `build` Member Function

Declare a static public member function `build` so that you can build an empty instance. This empty instance occupies the required dynamic space but has no meaningful data. Notice that the use of the function name `build` is intentional because it is synonymous with the word "construct." In addition, the member function is static to ensure that it can be accessed by uninstantiated object pointers. The declaration of the `build` member function is

```
static PTStreamable build();
```

The `build` member function invokes the protected stream constructor. The general form of the `build` function is

```
PTStreamable TStrmAppBase::build()
{
  return new TStrmAppBase(streamableInit);
}
```

Step Six: Declaring the write Member Function

Declare a protected virtual write member function that writes the components of a class instance to the stream. The general form for declaring the write member function is

`virtual void write(Ropstream os);`

The code in the write function can use the << operator or any other stream output member function, such as fwriteString, writeByte, and writeBytes. In ObjectWindows classes, the write member function often invokes the write function of the parent class. Such a call reduces the number of statements in the write member function. Listing 10.1 shows the write member function for the TWindowsObject, TWindow, and TDialog classes to give you an idea of how to code a write function.

Listing 10.1. The source code for the write member function for the TWindowsObject, TWindow, and TDialog classes.

```
void TWindowsObject::write(opstream& os)
{
    WORD SavedFlags;
    BOOL TitleIsNumeric;

    TitleIsNumeric = HIWORD(Title) == NULL;
    os << TitleIsNumeric;
    // if TitleIsNumeric is TRUE then it's probably
    // a dialog with Title == -1, i.e., unchanged from resource
    if (TitleIsNumeric)
      os << (long)(Title);
    else
      os.fwriteString(Title);

    SavedFlags = Flags;
    if (HWindow)
      SavedFlags |= WB_AUTOCREATE;

    os << Status << SavedFlags << CreateOrder;
    PutChildren(os);
}
```

```
void TWindow::write(Ropstream os)
{
    long SaveStyle;
    BOOL NameIsNumeric;
    TWindowsObject::write(os);
    if (!IsFlagSet(WB_FROMRESOURCE))
    {
       SaveStyle = Attr.Style & ~(WS_MINIMIZE | WS_MAXIMIZE);
       if (HWindow)
         if (IsIconic(HWindow))
           SaveStyle |= WS_MINIMIZE;
         else
           if (IsZoomed(HWindow))
             SaveStyle |= WS_MAXIMIZE;
       os << SaveStyle << Attr.ExStyle << Attr.X
          << Attr.Y << Attr.W << Attr.H
          << (long)(Attr.Param);
    }
    os << Attr.Id;

    NameIsNumeric = HIWORD(Attr.Menu) == NULL;
    os << NameIsNumeric;
    if (NameIsNumeric)
      os << (long)(Attr.Menu);
    else
      os.fwriteString(Attr.Menu);

    os << Scroller;
}

void TDialog::write(opstream& os)
{
    BOOL NameIsNumeric;

    TWindowsObject::write(os);
    NameIsNumeric = HIWORD(Attr.Name) == NULL;
    os << NameIsNumeric;
    if (NameIsNumeric)
      os << (long)(Attr.Name);
    else
      os.fwriteString(Attr.Name);
    os << IsModal;
}
```

Step Seven: Declaring the read Member Function

Declare a protected virtual read member function that reads the components of a class instance from the stream. The general form for declaring the read member function is

virtual Pvoid read(Ripstream is);

The code in the read function can use the >> operator or any other stream input member function, such as freadString, readByte, and readBytes. In ObjectWindows classes, the read member function often invokes the read function of the parent class. Such a call reduces the number of statements in the read member function. To give you an idea of how to code a read function, Listing 10.2 shows the read member function for the TWindowsObject, TWindow, and TDialog classes.

Listing 10.2. The source code for the read member function for the TWindowsObject, TWindow, and TDialog classes.

```
void *TWindowsObject::read(ipstream& is)
{
    BOOL TitleIsNumeric;

    HWindow = 0;
    Parent = NULL;
    SiblingList = NULL;
    ChildList = NULL;
    TransferBuffer = NULL;
    DefaultProc = NULL;

    Application = GetApplicationObject();
    // For now, set Module to Application.
    // This is not a general solution.
    Module = (PTModule)Application;

    Instance = MakeObjectInstance((PTWindowsObject)this);

    is >> TitleIsNumeric;
    // if TitleIsNumeric is TRUE then it's probably
    // a dialog with Title == -1,  i.e., unchanged from resource
    if (TitleIsNumeric)
        is >> (long)(Title);
    else
```

```cpp
        Title = is.freadString();

    is >> Status >> Flags >> CreateOrder;
    GetChildren(is);
    return this;
}

void *TWindow::read(ipstream& is)
{
    BOOL NameIsNumeric;
    TWindowsObject::read(is);

    if (IsFlagSet(WB_FROMRESOURCE))
    {
        DefaultProc = (FARPROC)DefWindowProc;
        memset(&Attr, 0x0, sizeof (Attr));
    }
    else
    {
        is >> Attr.Style >> Attr.ExStyle
           >> Attr.X >> Attr.Y >> Attr.W
           >> Attr.H >> (long)(Attr.Param);

        if (IsFlagSet(WB_MDICHILD))
            DefaultProc = (FARPROC)DefMDIChildProc;
        else
            DefaultProc = (FARPROC)DefWindowProc;
    }
    is >> Attr.Id;

    is >> NameIsNumeric;
    if (NameIsNumeric)
      is >> (long)(Attr.Menu);
    else
      Attr.Menu= is.freadString();

    is >> Scroller;
    if (Scroller)
        Scroller->Window = this;
    FocusChildHandle = 0;
    return this;
}

void *TDialog::read(ipstream& is)
{
```

continues

Listing 10.2. continued

```
    BOOL NameIsNumeric;

    TWindowsObject::read(is);

    is >> NameIsNumeric;
    if (NameIsNumeric)
      is >> (long)(Attr.Name);
    else
      Attr.Name = is.freadString();

    is >> IsModal;
    return this;
}
```

Step Eight: Declaring the `streamableName` Member Function

Declare the private member function `streamableName` to return the name of the streamable class. The general form for this function is

```
virtual const Pchar streamableName() const
    { return "TStrmAppBase"; }
```

Step Nine: Declaring the << and >> Operators

Declare two versions of the << and >> operators. These operators are declared outside the streamable class declaration. Each set handles the stream I/O for a reference and a pointer to a class instance. The following listing shows the general form for declaring these operators:

```
inline Ropstream operator << (Ropstream os, RTStrmAppBase cl)
    { return os << (RTStreamable)cl; }
inline Ropstream operator << (Ropstream os, PTStrmAppBase cl)
    { return os << (PTStreamable)cl; }
```

```
inline Ripstream operator >> (Ripstream is, RTStrmAppBase cl)
    { return is >> (RTStreamable)cl; }
inline Ripstream operator >> (Ripstream is, PTStrmAppBase cl)
    { return is >> (PTStreamable)cl; }
```

Step Ten: Registering the Streamable Class with the Stream Manager

Declare an instance of the `TStreamableClass` class that is involved in registering the streamable class with the stream manager. The general form for this declaration is

```
TStreamableClass RegStrmAppBase("TStrmAppBase",
                                TStrmAppBase::build, __DELTA(TStrmAppBase));
```

The identifier `RegStrmAppBase` is the same name used in the `__link` macro, mentioned in step 1. The arguments for the `TStreamableClass` instance are as follows:

- The name of the streamable class
- The fully qualified name of the `build` member function
- The `__DELTA` macro with the name of the streamable class

The macro calculates the offset from the base of the object to the `TStreamable` component of the object.

Making a Simple Class Streamable: An Example

Now you'll put into action the steps outlined in the previous section. This section presents an example of making a non-OWL class streamable. When the ObjectWindows program creates its window, it also creates a dynamic array of random x,y coordinates and writes that array to a stream.

The ObjectWindows program contains a multiline edit box and two push button controls, Exit and Read. The Exit button exits the application. The Read button performs two main tasks. First, it reads the dynamic array of points from the streams and writes it to the edit box control—one x,y coordinate per line. Second, it writes a new set of random coordinates to the stream. This new set of coordinates appears in the edit control the next time you click the Read button. This feature animates the program more than reading the same data from the stream does. Figure 10.2 shows a sample session with the STRM1.EXE program.

Figure 10.2.
A sample session with the STRM1.EXE program.

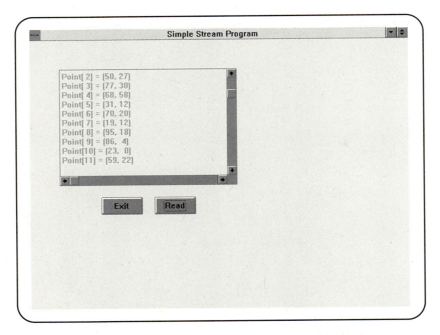

Look at the source code for the program, shown in Listing 10.3. The program declares three sets of constants. The first set declares the ID for the controls, the second of set spaces and dimensions the controls, and the third set declares the values used by the streamable classes.

Listing 10.3. The source code for the STRM1.CPP program.

```
#include <stdlib.h>
#include <stdio.h>
#include <string.h>
#include <owl.h>
```

```
#include <edit.h>
#include <button.h>
#include <objstrm.h>

// declare the control ID constants
#define ID_EXIT_BTN 101
#define ID_READ_BTN 102
#define ID_TEXT_EDIT 103

// declare constants for sizing and spacing the controls
const Wbox = 300;
const Hbox = 200;
const BoxVertSpacing = 20;
const Wbtn = 70;
const Hbtn = 30;
const BtnHorzSpacing = 20;
const BtnOffset = 70;

// miscellaneous constants
const DefPolySize = 10;
const TestSize = 14;
const char* streamFilename = "POLY.DAT";

// declare the Point data structure
struct Point {
  int x;
  int y;
};

// declare the class of dynamic array of points
class TPoints
{
public:
  TPoints(int MaxSize = DefPolySize);
  virtual int GetSize() { return arraySize; }
  virtual BOOL Store(int index, int X, int Y);
  virtual BOOL Recall(int Index, Rint X, Rint Y);

protected:
  Point* dataPtr;
  int arraySize;
};

_CLASSDEF(TPolygon)
```

continues

Listing 10.3. continued

```
// register the TPolygon class
__link(RegPolygon)

// declare the streamable class TPolygon that is derived
// from the TPoints and TStreamable classes
class TPolygon : public TPoints, public TStreamable
{
public:
  TPolygon(int MaxSize) : TPoints(MaxSize) {};

  static PTStreamable build();

protected:
  TPolygon(StreamableInit) : TPoints(DefPolySize) {};
  virtual void write(Ropstream os);
  virtual Pvoid read(Ripstream is);

private:
  virtual const Pchar streamableName() const
    { return "TPolygon"; }
};

inline Ropstream operator << (Ropstream os, RTPolygon cl)
    { return os << (RTStreamable )cl; }
inline Ropstream operator << (Ropstream os, PTPolygon cl)
    { return os << (PTStreamable)cl; }

inline Ripstream operator >> (Ripstream is, RTPolygon cl)
    { return is >> (RTStreamable)cl; }
inline Ripstream operator >> (Ripstream is, PTPolygon cl)
    { return is >> (PTStreamable)cl; }

TStreamableClass RegPolygon("TPolygon", TPolygon::build,
                                __DELTA(TPolygon));


// use the _CLASSDEF macro to declare reference and pointer
// types related to the new TAppWindow class
_CLASSDEF(TAppWindow)

// expand the functionality of TWindow by deriving class TAppWindow
class TAppWindow : public TWindow
{
public:
```

```cpp
    TAppWindow(PTWindowsObject AParent, LPSTR AName);

    virtual void HandleExitBtn(RTMessage Msg)
      = [ID_FIRST + ID_EXIT_BTN];

    virtual void HandleReadBtn(RTMessage Msg)
      = [ID_FIRST + ID_READ_BTN];

    BOOL CanClose();

protected:
   PTButton ExitBtn;
   PTButton ReadBtn;
   PTEdit TextBox;

   // write random data to a stream
   void writeRandomData();
};

// declare the custom application class as a subclass of TApplication
class TWinApp : public TApplication
{
public:
   TWinApp(LPSTR    AName,          // application name
           HINSTANCE hInstance,     // instance handle
           HINSTANCE hPrevInstance, // previous instance handle
           LPSTR     lpCmdLine,     // command-line arguments
           int       nCmdShow) :    // display command
           TApplication(AName, hInstance, hPrevInstance,
                        lpCmdLine, nCmdShow) {};

protected:
   virtual void InitMainWindow();
};

TPoints::TPoints(int MaxSize)
{
  // ensure that arraySize greater than 0
  arraySize = (MaxSize < 1) ? DefPolySize : MaxSize;
  // allocate dynamic data
  dataPtr = new Point[arraySize];
  // initialize the dynamic array
  memset(dataPtr, 0, arraySize * sizeof(Point));
}
```

continues

Listing 10.3. continued

```
BOOL TPoints::Store(int index, int X, int Y)
{
  // is index in the correct range?
  if (index >= 0 && index < arraySize) {
    // store the X and Y parameters
    (dataPtr + index)->x = X;
    (dataPtr + index)->y = Y;
    return TRUE;
  }
  else
    return FALSE;
}

BOOL TPoints::Recall(int index, Rint X, Rint Y)
{
  // is index in the correct range?
  if (index >= 0 && index < arraySize) {
    // retrieve the sought data
    X = (dataPtr + index)->x;
    Y = (dataPtr + index)->y;
    return TRUE;
  }
  else
    return FALSE;
}

PTStreamable TPolygon::build()
{
  return new TPolygon(streamableInit);
}

void TPolygon::write(Ropstream os)
{
  // write the current array size
  os << arraySize;
  // write the array elements
  for (int i = 0; i < arraySize; i++)
    os << (dataPtr + i)->x << (dataPtr + i)->y;
}

Pvoid TPolygon::read(Ripstream is)
{
  // read the array size
  is >> arraySize;
```

```
    // delete the current dynamic array
    delete dataPtr;
    // create a new dynamic array
    dataPtr = new Point[arraySize];
    // initialize the dynamic array
    memset(dataPtr, 0, arraySize * sizeof(Point));
    // assign data from the stream
    for (int i = 0; i < arraySize; i++)
      is >> (dataPtr + i)->x >> (dataPtr + i)->y;

    return this;
}

TAppWindow::TAppWindow(PTWindowsObject AParent, LPSTR AName) :
                   TWindow(AParent, AName)
{
  int x, y;

  x = 50;
  y = 50;
  // create the text box
  TextBox = new TEdit(this, ID_TEXT_EDIT, "", x, y, Wbox,
                      Hbox, 0, TRUE);
  // create the button controls
  y += Hbox + BoxVertSpacing;
  x += BtnOffset;
  ExitBtn = new TButton(this, ID_EXIT_BTN, "Exit", x, y, Wbtn,
                        Hbtn, FALSE);

  x += Wbtn + BtnHorzSpacing;
  ReadBtn = new TButton(this, ID_READ_BTN, "Read", x, y,
                        Wbtn, Hbtn, FALSE);

  // write random data to a stream
  writeRandomData();
}


void TAppWindow::HandleExitBtn(RTMessage Msg)
{
  SendMessage(HWindow, WM_CLOSE, NULL, NULL);
}

BOOL TAppWindow::CanClose()
{
```

continues

Listing 10.3. continued

```
  return MessageBox(HWindow, "Want to close this application",
                    "Query", MB_YESNO | MB_ICONQUESTION) == IDYES;
}

void TAppWindow::HandleReadBtn(RTMessage Msg)
{
  char bigStr[1024];
  char s[41];
  int X, Y;
  // purposely create an instance of TPolygon with a smaller size
  TPolygon Poly(TestSize / 2);

  // open the file stream for input
  ifpstream is(streamFilename);
  // input the instance of TPolygon
  is >> Poly;
  // close the stream
  is.close();

  // initialize buffer
  bigStr[0] ='\0';
  // loop to build the string for the edit box control
  for (int i = 0; i < Poly.GetSize(); i++) {
    Poly.Recall(i, X, Y); // recall the point at index i
    // format the recalled point
    sprintf(s, "Point[%2d] = (%2d, %2d)\r\n", i, X, Y);
    strcat(bigStr, s); // concatenate with the buffer string
  }
  // insert buffer text into the edit control
  TextBox->SetText(bigStr);

  // write random data to the stream
  writeRandomData();
}

void TAppWindow::writeRandomData()
{
  // create an instance of TPolygon
  TPolygon Poly(TestSize);

  randomize();
  // write random data in object Poly
  for (int i = 0; i < TestSize; i++)
    Poly.Store(i, random(100), random(100));
```

ObjectWindows Streams

```
  // open file stream for output
  ofpstream os(streamFilename);
  // write the Poly object to the stream
  os << Poly;
  // close the output stream
  os.close();
}

void TWinApp::InitMainWindow()
{
  MainWindow = new TAppWindow(NULL, "Simple Stream Program");
}

int PASCAL WinMain(HINSTANCE hInstance, HINSTANCE hPrevInstance,
                   LPSTR lpCmdLine, int nCmdShow)
{
  TWinApp WinApp(
    "Simple Stream I/O Program",
              hInstance, hPrevInstance, lpCmdLine, nCmdShow);
  WinApp.Run();  // run OWL application
  return WinApp.Status;  // return application status
}
```

Listing 10.3 declares the `Point` structure that represents the x,y coordinates. The program also declares the `TPoints` class to represent dynamic arrays of `TPoints`. The `TPoints` class declares two data members, `dataPtr` and `arraySize`. The `dataPtr` member is a pointer to the `Point` structure and accesses the dynamic array of `Point`-typed coordinates. The `arraySize` data member stores the number of dynamic array members.

The `TPoints` class declares a class constructor with a default size of `DefPolySize`. The class also declares a few member functions that obtain the number of array members, store data, and retrieve data from the dynamic array.

The listing also declares the streamable class `TPolygon`. This class is a descendant of `TPoints` and `TStreamable`. To declare the `TPolygon` class, you follow the steps described in the last section for making a class streamable:

```
// register the TPolygon class
__link(RegPolygon)

// declare the streamable class TPolygon that is derived
// from the TPoints and TStreamable classes
class TPolygon : public TPoints, public TStreamable
{
```

```
public:
  TPolygon(int MaxSize) : TPoints(MaxSize) {};

  static PTStreamable build();

protected:
  TPolygon(StreamableInit) : TPoints(DefPolySize) {};
  virtual void write(Ropstream os);
  virtual Pvoid read(Ripstream is);

private:
  virtual const Pchar streamableName() const
  { return "TPolygon"; }
};

inline Ropstream operator << (Ropstream os, RTPolygon cl)
    { return os << (RTStreamable)cl; }
inline Ropstream operator << (Ropstream os, PTPolygon cl)
    { return os << (PTStreamable)cl; }

inline Ripstream operator >> (Ripstream is, RTPolygon cl)
    { return is >> (RTStreamable)cl; }
inline Ripstream operator >> (Ripstream is, PTPolygon cl)
    { return is >> (PTStreamable)cl; }

TStreamableClass RegPolygon("TPolygon", TPolygon::build,
                            __DELTA(TPolygon));
```

Notice that both constructors invoke the `TPoints` constructor. In the case of the stream constructor, the `TPoints` constructor is called with the argument `DefPolySize` to create the dynamic array with a default size. `TPolygon` class declares the `write`, `read`, `build`, and `streamableName` member functions. Other declarations include those for the << operator, the >> operator, and the `TStreamableClass` instance, which register the `TPolygon` class with the stream manager.

The `write` member function writes the `arraySize` member to the output stream and then writes the array members. The function uses the << operator to write the `arraySize` member as well as the `x` and `y` members of the `Point` structures.

The `read` member function reads the array members from a stream by following these steps:

1. Reads the size of the array from the stream by using the >> operator.
2. Deletes the current dynamic array of coordinates.

3. Creates a new dynamic array by using the size obtained from the stream.
4. Initializes the array with zeros. (This is an optional but recommended step.)
5. Reads the coordinates from the stream. The function uses the >> operator to read the x and y members of each array element.

Caution: The read member function returns the pointer this. Every version of member function read that you write has to return the pointer this.

The build member function invokes the stream constructor to create a suitable class instance containing DefPolySize members. The size of the default array is not critical, because the read member function custom resizes it anyway.

The program also declares an application class and a window class. The application window class declares a constructor, a set of member functions, and a number of data members. The data members are pointers to the controls created by the constructor.

The TAppWindow constructor creates the edit box and push button controls and invokes the writeRandomData member function to write random coordinates to the stream.

The writeRandomData member function performs the following tasks:

1. Creates Poly, a local instance of the TPolygon class.
2. Randomizes the seed of the random number generator function.
3. Writes random data to the Poly object. This task uses the TPolygon::Store member function to store the random coordinates in the Poly object.
4. Opens the output stream by creating the instance os of the ofpstream class.
5. Writes the object Poly to the output stream os by using the << operator.
6. Closes the output stream by using the close member function.

The HandleReadBtn member function handles the notification message sent by the Read push button control. The member function performs the following tasks:

1. Declares local strings and variables.
2. Purposely declares `Poly` as an instance of `TPolygon` with an array smaller than the one stored in the stream.
3. Opens the stream for input by creating the instance `is` of the `ifpstream` class.
4. Reads the `Poly` object from the stream by using the `>>` operator. When the object is read, its size increases to match the size of the object read from the stream.
5. Closes the input stream.
6. Writes to the multiline edit box the formatted images of the coordinates.
7. Invokes the `writeRandomData` member function to write to the stream another set of random coordinates.

Storing Controls in a Stream

Resources provide a mechanism for defining controls outside Windows applications. A Windows program can then load the various resources during the creation of the various controls. The ObjectWindows streams provide an alternative mechanism for creating controls. Unlike the resources mechanism, this alternative mechanism involves two types of ObjectWindows applications:

- *Producers,* which produce the streams containing the controls.
- *Consumers,* which use streams to instantiate controls.

Multiple consumers can use a stream that has controls created by a producer. In this respect, streams play a role similar to resource files. However, resource files have a wider range of clients because Windows applications can use them even if they are coded in non-OOP languages such as C.

This section presents an example of a producer ObjectWindows application. The next section presents the corresponding consumer application. The producer application creates the controls for COCA version 2, which uses edit boxes and push button controls.

ObjectWindows Streams

Look at the code that implements the producer ObjectWindows application. Listing 10.4 shows the header file STRM2.H, which contains the declarations for the control ID constants. The header file also contains the constant streamFile, which declares the name of the object stream file.

Listing 10.4. The source code for the STRM2.H header file.

```
// declare the ID_XXXX constants for the edit boxes
#define ID_OPERAND1_EDIT 101
#define ID_OPERATOR_EDIT 102
#define ID_OPERAND2_EDIT 103
#define ID_RESULT_EDIT 104
#define ID_ERRMSG_EDIT 105
#define ID_VARIABLE_EDIT 106
#define ID_CALC_BTN 107
#define ID_STORE_BTN 108
#define ID_EXIT_BTN 109
#define ID_OPERAND1_TXT 110
#define ID_OPERATOR_TXT 111
#define ID_OPERAND2_TXT 112
#define ID_RESULT_TXT 113
#define ID_ERRMSG_TXT 114
#define ID_VARIABLE_TXT 115

const char* streamFile = "strm2.dat";
```

Listing 10.5 contains the source code for the STRM2A.CPP program.

Listing 10.5. The source code for the STRM2A.CPP program file.

```
#include <stdio.h>
#include <string.h>
#include <owl.h>
#include <static.h>
#include <edit.h>
#include <button.h>
#include <objstrm.h>
#include "strm2.h"

// declare the constants that represent the sizes of the controls
const Wlbl = 100;
const Hlbl = 20;
const LblVertSpacing = 10;
const LblHorzSpacing = 40;
```

continues

561

Listing 10.5. continued

```cpp
const Wbox = 100;
const Hbox = 30;
const BoxVertSpacing = 20;
const BoxHorzSpacing = 40;
const WLongbox = 4 * (Wbox + BoxHorzSpacing);
const Wvarbox = 2 * Wbox;
const Hvarbox = 3 * Hbox;
const Hbtn = 30;
const Wbtn = 80;
const BtnHorzSpacing = 30;
const MaxEditLen = 30;
const MAX_MEMREG = 26;

// declare the custom application class as
// a subclass of TApplication
class TWinApp : public TApplication
{
public:
   TWinApp(LPSTR     AName,           // application name
           HINSTANCE hInstance,        // instance handle
           HINSTANCE hPrevInstance,    // previous instance handle
           LPSTR     lpCmdLine,        // command-line arguments
           int       nCmdShow) :       // display command
           TApplication(AName, hInstance, hPrevInstance,
                        lpCmdLine, nCmdShow) {};

protected:
   virtual void InitMainWindow();
};

// use the _CLASSDEF macro to declare reference and pointer
// types related to the new TAppWindow class
_CLASSDEF(TAppWindow)

// expand the functionality of TWindow by deriving class TAppWindow
class TAppWindow : public TWindow
{
public:

   TAppWindow(PTWindowsObject AParent, LPSTR AName);

   virtual void HandleExitBtn(RTMessage Msg)
     = [ID_FIRST + ID_EXIT_BTN];
```

```
  protected:
    PTEdit Operand1Box;
    PTEdit OperatorBox;
    PTEdit Operand2Box;
    PTEdit ResultBox;
    PTEdit ErrMsgBox;
    PTEdit VariableBox;
    PTButton CalcBtn;
    PTButton StoreBtn;
    PTButton ExitBtn;
    PTStatic Operand1Txt;
    PTStatic OperatorTxt;
    PTStatic Operand2Txt;
    PTStatic ResultTxt;
    PTStatic ErrMsgTxt;
    PTStatic VariableTxt;
};

TAppWindow::TAppWindow(PTWindowsObject AParent, LPSTR AName) :
                      TWindow(AParent, AName)
{
    char bigStr[6 * MAX_MEMREG + 1];
    char c;
    char s[81];
    int x0 = 20;
    int y0 = 30;
    int x = x0, y = y0;

    // create the first set of labels for the edit boxes
    strcpy(s, "Operand1");
    Operand1Txt = new TStatic(this, -1, s, x, y, Wlbl,
                              Hlbl, strlen(s));
    strcpy(s, "Operator");
    x += Wlbl + LblHorzSpacing;
    OperatorTxt = new TStatic(this, -1, s, x, y, Wlbl,
                              Hlbl, strlen(s));
    strcpy(s, "Operand2");
    x += Wlbl + LblHorzSpacing;
    Operand2Txt = new TStatic(this, -1, s, x, y, Wlbl,
                              Hlbl, strlen(s));
    x += Wlbl + LblHorzSpacing;
    strcpy(s, "Result");
    ResultTxt = new TStatic(this, -1, s, x, y, Wlbl,
                            Hlbl, strlen(s));
```

continues

Listing 10.5. continued

```
// create the operand1, operator, operand2, and result
// edit boxes
x = x0;
y += Hlbl + LblVertSpacing;
Operand1Box = new TEdit(this, ID_OPERAND1_EDIT, "", x, y,
                        Wbox, Hbox, 0, FALSE);

// force conversion of letters to uppercase
Operand1Box->Attr.Style |= ES_UPPERCASE;
x += Wbox + BoxHorzSpacing;
OperatorBox = new TEdit(this, ID_OPERATOR_EDIT, "", x, y,
                        Wbox, Hbox, 0, FALSE);
x += Wbox + BoxHorzSpacing;
Operand2Box = new TEdit(this, ID_OPERAND2_EDIT, "", x, y,
                        Wbox, Hbox, 0, FALSE);
// force conversion of letters to uppercase
Operand2Box->Attr.Style |= ES_UPPERCASE;
x += Wbox + BoxHorzSpacing;
ResultBox = new TEdit(this, ID_RESULT_EDIT, "", x, y, Wbox, Hbox,
                      0, FALSE);

// create the static text and edit box for the error message
x = x0;
y += Hbox + BoxVertSpacing;
strcpy(s, "Error Message");
ErrMsgTxt = new TStatic(this, -1, s, x, y, Wlbl, Hlbl, strlen(s));
y += Hlbl + LblVertSpacing;
ErrMsgBox = new TEdit(this, ID_ERRMSG_EDIT, "", x, y,
                      WLongbox, Hbox, 0, FALSE);

// create the static text and edit box for the single-letter
// variable selection
y += Hbox + BoxVertSpacing;
strcpy(s, "Variables");
VariableTxt = new TStatic(this, -1, s, x, y, Wlbl,
                          Hlbl, strlen(s));

strcpy(bigStr, "");
// build the initial contents of the Variable edit box
for (c = 'A'; c <= 'Z'; c++) {
  sprintf(s, "%c: 0\r\n", c);
  strcat(bigStr, s);
}
y += Hlbl + LblVertSpacing;
```

```cpp
    VariableBox = new TEdit(this, ID_VARIABLE_EDIT, bigStr, x, y,
                            Wvarbox, Hvarbox, 0, TRUE);
    // force conversion of letters to uppercase
    VariableBox->Attr.Style |= ES_UPPERCASE;

    // create the Calc push button
    x += Wvarbox + BtnHorzSpacing;
    CalcBtn = new TButton(this, ID_CALC_BTN, "&Calc",
                          x, y, Wbtn, Hbtn, TRUE);

    // create the Store Btn
    x += Wbtn + BtnHorzSpacing;
    StoreBtn = new TButton(this, ID_STORE_BTN, "&Store",
                          x, y, Wbtn, Hbtn, FALSE);

    // Create the Exit Btn
    x += Wbtn + BtnHorzSpacing;
    ExitBtn = new TButton(this, ID_EXIT_BTN, "&Exit",
                          x, y, Wbtn, Hbtn, FALSE);
}

void TAppWindow::HandleExitBtn(RTMessage Msg)
{
    char bigStr[6 * MAX_MEMREG + 1];
    VariableBox->GetText(bigStr, 6 * MAX_MEMREG);

    // open output stream
    ofpstream os(streamFile);
    if (os.good()) {
        // write controls to the stream
        os << Operand1Txt << Operand1Box <<
              OperatorTxt << OperatorBox <<
              Operand2Txt << Operand2Box <<
              ResultTxt << ResultBox <<
              ErrMsgTxt << ErrMsgBox <<
              VariableTxt << VariableBox <<
              CalcBtn << StoreBtn << ExitBtn;
        // close the output stream
        os.close();
    }
    else
        MessageBox(HWindow, "Stream output error", "Error!",
                   MB_OK | MB_ICONEXCLAMATION);
    SendMessage(HWindow, WM_CLOSE, NULL, NULL);
}
```

continues

Listing 10.5. continued

```
void TWinApp::InitMainWindow()
{
  MainWindow = new TAppWindow(NULL, "Setup for COCA version 6");
}

int PASCAL WinMain(HINSTANCE hInstance, HINSTANCE hPrevInstance,
                LPSTR lpCmdLine, int nCmdShow)
{
  TWinApp WinApp(
    "Setup Program for COCA version 6",
              hInstance, hPrevInstance, lpCmdLine, nCmdShow);
  WinApp.Run(); // run OWL application
  return WinApp.Status; // return application status
}
```

Compile and run the STRM2A.CPP source code. The application builds the controls similar to that of COCA version 2. The difference is that in this application, only the Exit push button works. In fact, the Exit button performs two tasks. First, it writes the controls to the stream STRM2.DAT, and second, it exits the application. Click the Exit function to perform these two tasks.

Listing 10.5 declares constants used in dimensioning and spacing controls. The program declares two classes: an application class and a window class.

The TAppWindow application window class declares a constructor, the HandleExitBtn member function, and a collection of data members. These data members are pointers to the various controls, including the static text controls.

The TAppWindow class constructor creates the various controls, assigning each control to a pointer data member. The code for the constructor is similar to that of COCA version 2.

The HandleExitBtn member function is the most relevant part of the producer ObjectWindows application. The function performs the following tasks:

1. Copies the text in the multiline Variable edit box into the local variable bigStr.

2. Opens a file stream for output by creating an instance of class ofpstream.

3. Verifies that the good member function successfully opened the stream. If the condition is TRUE, the HandleExitBtn function writes the various controls to the file stream and closes the stream. The function uses the << operator and the pointers to write the various controls.

4. Displays an error message box if the stream was not correctly opened.
5. Closes the application window.

Constructing Controls from Streams

The producer ObjectWindows application presented in the preceding section writes the controls of a window to a file stream. This section introduces the corresponding consumer ObjectWindows application that reads the controls from the stream and proceeds much like the COCA version 2 program presented in Chapter 5, "ObjectWindows Controls" (except I removed the feature of clicking the Error Message static text to reset any error condition). In addition to providing the application's functionality, the new program version shows you how to read the controls from a file stream.

When you compile and run this consumer ObjectWindows application, it seems similar to COCA version 2. Figure 10.3 shows a sample session with the STRM2B.EXE program.

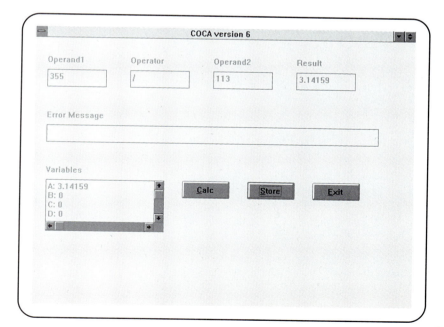

Figure 10.3. A sample session with the STRM2B.EXE program.

If you watch the hard disk's in-use light, you might notice a bit more activity than usual going on when the application starts running. After the application window appears, the program behaves much like COCA version 2.

Look at the code that implements the consumer ObjectWindows application. Listing 10.6 shows the script for the resource file STRM2B.RC. This resource file defines the accelerator keys resource for the push button controls. Listing 10.7 contains the source code for the STRM2B.CPP program file.

Listing 10.6. The script for the resource file STRM2B.RC.

```
#include <windows.h>
#include <owlrc.h>
#include "strm2.h"

BUTTONS ACCELERATORS
BEGIN
     "c", ID_CALC_BTN, ALT
     "s", ID_STORE_BTN, ALT
     "e", ID_EXIT_BTN, ALT
END
```

Listing 10.7. The source code for the STRM2B.CPP program file.

```
#include <stdlib.h>
#include <ctype.h>
#include <stdio.h>
#include <math.h>
#include <string.h>
#include <owl.h>
#include <static.h>
#include <edit.h>
#include <button.h>
#include <objstrm.h>
#include "strm2.h"

const MaxEditLen = 41;
const MAX_MEMREG = 26;

// declare the custom application class as
// a subclass of TApplication
class TWinApp : public TApplication
{
```

```
public:
   TWinApp(LPSTR     AName,            // application name
           HINSTANCE hInstance,        // instance handle
           HINSTANCE hPrevInstance,    // previous instance handle
           LPSTR     lpCmdLine,        // command-line arguments
           int       nCmdShow) :       // display command
          TApplication(AName, hInstance, hPrevInstance,
                       lpCmdLine, nCmdShow) {};

protected:
  virtual void InitMainWindow();
  virtual void InitInstance();
};

// use the _CLASSDEF macro to declare reference and pointer
// types related to the new TAppWindow class
_CLASSDEF(TAppWindow)

// expand the functionality of TWindow by deriving class TAppWindow
class TAppWindow : public TWindow
{
public:

  TAppWindow(PTWindowsObject AParent, LPSTR AName);

  // handle the calculation
  virtual void HandleCalcBtn(RTMessage Msg)
    = [ID_FIRST + ID_CALC_BTN];

  // handle the accelerator key for the Calculate button
  virtual void CMCalcBtn(RTMessage Msg)
    = [CM_FIRST + ID_CALC_BTN];

  // handle storing the result in a variable
  virtual void HandleStoreBtn(RTMessage Msg)
    = [ID_FIRST + ID_STORE_BTN];

  // handle the accelerator key for the Store button
  virtual void CMStoreBtn(RTMessage Msg)
    = [CM_FIRST + ID_STORE_BTN];

  // handle exiting the application
  virtual void HandleExitBtn(RTMessage Msg)
    = [ID_FIRST + ID_EXIT_BTN];
```

continues

Listing 10.7. continued

```
    // handle the accelerator key for the Exit button
    virtual void CMExitBtn(RTMessage Msg)
      = [CM_FIRST + ID_EXIT_BTN];

    // enable a push button control
    virtual void EnableButton(PTButton Btn)
    { EnableWindow(Btn->HWindow, TRUE); }

    // disable a push button control
    virtual void DisableButton(PTButton Btn)
    { EnableWindow(Btn->HWindow, FALSE); }

    // handle closing the window
    virtual BOOL CanClose();

protected:
    PTEdit Operand1Box;
    PTEdit OperatorBox;
    PTEdit Operand2Box;
    PTEdit ResultBox;
    PTEdit ErrMsgBox;
    PTEdit VariableBox;
    PTButton CalcBtn;
    PTButton StoreBtn;
    PTButton ExitBtn;
    PTStatic Operand1Txt;
    PTStatic OperatorTxt;
    PTStatic Operand2Txt;
    PTStatic ResultTxt;
    PTStatic ErrMsgTxt;
    PTStatic VariableTxt;

    // math error flag
    BOOL InError;

    // obtain a number of a Variable edit box line
    double getVar(int lineNum);

    // store a number in the selected text of
    // the Variable edit box line
    void putVar(double x);
};
```

ObjectWindows Streams

```cpp
TAppWindow::TAppWindow(PTWindowsObject AParent, LPSTR AName)
                    : TWindow(AParent, AName)
{
  // open the stream for input
  ifpstream is(streamFile);

  if (is.good()) {
    // build the instances for the controls
    Operand1Txt = PTStatic(TStatic::build());
    Operand1Box = PTEdit(TEdit::build());
    OperatorTxt = PTStatic(TStatic::build());
    OperatorBox = PTEdit(TEdit::build());
    Operand2Txt = PTStatic(TStatic::build());
    Operand2Box = PTEdit(TEdit::build());
    ResultTxt = PTStatic(TStatic::build());
    ResultBox = PTEdit(TEdit::build());
    ErrMsgTxt = PTStatic(TStatic::build());
    ErrMsgBox = PTEdit(TEdit::build());
    VariableTxt = PTStatic(TStatic::build());
    VariableBox = PTEdit(TEdit::build());
    CalcBtn = PTButton(TButton::build());
    StoreBtn = PTButton(TButton::build());
    ExitBtn = PTButton(TButton::build());

    // now read the various controls from the stream
    is >> Operand1Txt;
    Operand1Txt->SetParent(this);
    is >> Operand1Box;
    Operand1Box->Attr.Style |= WS_BORDER;
    Operand1Box->SetParent(this);
    is >> OperatorTxt;
    OperatorTxt->SetParent(this);
    is >> OperatorBox;
    OperatorBox->Attr.Style |= WS_BORDER;
    OperatorBox->SetParent(this);
    is >> Operand2Txt;
    Operand2Txt->SetParent(this);
    is >> Operand2Box;
    Operand2Box->Attr.Style |= WS_BORDER;
    Operand2Box->SetParent(this);
    is >> ResultTxt;
    ResultTxt->SetParent(this);
    is >> ResultBox;
    ResultBox->Attr.Style |= WS_BORDER;
    ResultBox->SetParent(this);
```

continues

Listing 10.7. continued

```
    is >> ErrMsgTxt;
    ErrMsgTxt->SetParent(this);
    is >> ErrMsgBox;
    ErrMsgBox->Attr.Style |= WS_BORDER;
    ErrMsgBox->SetParent(this);
    is >> VariableTxt;
    VariableTxt->SetParent(this);
    is >> VariableBox;
    VariableBox->Attr.Style |= WS_BORDER;
    VariableBox->SetParent(this);
    is >> CalcBtn;
    CalcBtn->SetParent(this);
    is >> StoreBtn;
    StoreBtn->SetParent(this);
    is >> ExitBtn;
    ExitBtn->SetParent(this);

    // close the input stream
    is.close();
  }

  // clear the InError flag
  InError = FALSE;

  // enable keyboard handler
  EnableKBHandler();
}

void TAppWindow::HandleCalcBtn(RTMessage Msg)
{
  double x, y, z;
  char opStr[MaxEditLen+1];
  char s[MaxEditLen+1];

  // obtain the string in the Operand1 edit box
  Operand1Box->GetText(s, MaxEditLen);
  // does the Operand1Box contain the name
  // of a single-letter variable?
  if (isalpha(s[0]))
    // obtain value from the Variable edit control
    x = getVar(s[0] - 'A');
  else
    // convert the string in the edit box
    x = atof(s);
```

```
  // obtain the string in the Operand2 edit box
  Operand2Box->GetText(s, MaxEditLen);
  // does the Operand2Box contain the name
  // of a single-letter variable?
  if (isalpha(s[0]))
    // obtain value from the Variable edit control
    y =getVar(s[0] - 'A');
  else
     // convert the string in the edit box
    y = atof(s);

  // obtain the string in the Operator edit box
  OperatorBox->GetText(opStr, MaxEditLen);

  // clear the error message box
  ErrMsgBox->Clear();
  InError = FALSE;

  // determine the requested operation
  if (strcmp(opStr, "+") == 0)
    z = x + y;
  else if (strcmp(opStr, "-") == 0)
    z = x - y;
  else if (strcmp(opStr, "*") == 0)
    z = x * y;
  else if (strcmp(opStr, "/") == 0) {
    if (y != 0)
      z = x / y;
    else {
      z = 0;
      InError = TRUE;
      ErrMsgBox->SetText("Division-by-zero error");
    }
  }
  else if (strcmp(opStr, "^") == 0) {
    if (x > 0)
      z = exp(y * log(x));
    else {
      InError = TRUE;
      ErrMsgBox->SetText(
        "Cannot raise the power of a negative number");
    }
  }
  else {
```

continues

Listing 10.7. continued

```
    InError = TRUE;
    ErrMsgBox->SetText("Invalid operator");
  }
  // display the result if no error has occurred
  if (!InError) {
    sprintf(s, "%g", z);
    ResultBox->SetText(s);
    // enable the Store button
    EnableButton(StoreBtn);
  }
  else
    // disable the Store button
    DisableButton(StoreBtn);
}

void TAppWindow::CMCalcBtn(RTMessage Msg)
{
  HandleCalcBtn(Msg);
}

void TAppWindow::HandleStoreBtn(RTMessage Msg)
{
  char varName[MaxEditLen+1];
  char result[MaxEditLen+1];

  // get the string in the Result edit box
  ResultBox->GetText(result, MaxEditLen);

  // store the result in the selected text of
  // the Variable edit box
  putVar(atof(result));
}

void TAppWindow::CMStoreBtn(RTMessage Msg)
{
  HandleStoreBtn(Msg);
}

void TAppWindow::HandleExitBtn(RTMessage Msg)
{
  // use the dialog box member function
  CloseWindow();
}
```

ObjectWindows Streams

```cpp
void TAppWindow::CMExitBtn(RTMessage Msg)
{
  // send a WM_CLOSE message
  SendMessage(HWindow, WM_CLOSE, NULL, NULL);
}

double TAppWindow::getVar(int lineNum)
{
  int lineSize;
  char s[MaxEditLen+1];

  if (lineNum >= MAX_MEMREG) return 0;
  // get the size of the target line
  lineSize = VariableBox->GetLineLength(lineNum);
  // get the line
  VariableBox->GetLine(s, lineSize+1, lineNum);
  // delete the first three characters
  strcpy(s, (s+3));
  // return the number stored in the target line
  return atof(s);
}

void TAppWindow::putVar(double x)
{
  int startPos, endPos;
  int lineNum;
  int lineSize;
  char s[MaxEditLen+1];

  // locate the character position of the cursor
  VariableBox->GetSelection(startPos, endPos);
  // turn off the selected text
  if (startPos != endPos)
    VariableBox->SetSelection(startPos, startPos);
  // get the line number where the cursor is located
  lineNum = VariableBox->GetLineFromPos(startPos);
  // get the line size of line lineNum
  lineSize = VariableBox->GetLineLength(lineNum);
  // obtain the text of line lineNum
  VariableBox->GetLine(s, lineSize+1, lineNum);
  // delete line lineNum
  VariableBox->DeleteLine(lineNum);
  // build the new text line
  sprintf(s, "%c: %g\r\n", s[0], x);
  // insert it
```

continues

Listing 10.7. continued

```
  VariableBox->Insert(s);
}

BOOL TAppWindow::CanClose()
{
  return MessageBox(HWindow, "Want to close this application",
                    "Query", MB_YESNO | MB_ICONQUESTION) == IDYES;
}

void TWinApp::InitMainWindow()
{
  MainWindow = new TAppWindow(NULL, "COCA version 6");
}

void TWinApp::InitInstance()
{
  TApplication::InitInstance();
  HAccTable = LoadAccelerators(hInstance, "BUTTONS");
}

int PASCAL WinMain(HINSTANCE hInstance, HINSTANCE hPrevInstance,
                   LPSTR lpCmdLine, int nCmdShow)
{
  TWinApp WinApp(
    "Command-Oriented Calculator Application (COCA) Version 6",
              hInstance, hPrevInstance, lpCmdLine, nCmdShow);
  WinApp.Run(); // run OWL application
  return WinApp.Status; // return application status
}
```

Looking at the source code, you might notice the absence of the rich set of constants I have typically used to dimension and space the controls. These constants are not needed in this program because the controls (including their location and sizes) are read from a file stream.

The program listing declares an application class and a window class. The most relevant part of the program is the window class constructor, which is new. The other member functions are similar to their counterparts in the COCA version 2 program. Therefore, I'll focus on the window class constructor as I discuss the use of streams to create the various controls.

The TAppWindow constructor creates the instances for the various controls in a new way, by using a file stream. The constructor carries out the following steps:

ObjectWindows Streams

1. Opens a file stream for input by creating an instance of the `ifpstream` class.

2. Uses the `good` member function to verify that the stream is correctly opened before proceeding with the next tasks.

3. Builds the empty instances of the various controls. You build each control by invoking its own build member function. This invocation includes the name of the class. The result of each invocation is typecast into a pointer type and assigned to the appropriate pointer data member.

4. Reads each control from the stream. After each control is read, the constructor places that control in the child list of the application window by invoking the member function `TWindowsObject::SetParent`.

> **Caution:** This is an important step, without which the controls do not appear in the window. In reading an edit box control, the `WS_BORDER` style is set; otherwise, the edit box control appears without a border.

5. Closes the input file stream.
6. Sets the `InError` data member to FALSE.
5. Enables the keyboard handler.

Summary

In this chapter, you learned about using streams to store and recall objects. Streams are very useful and versatile because they enable you to store different data types and objects and safely retrieve them later. This chapter covered the following topics:

- The ObjectWindows streams hierarchy. This family of classes offers support for both buffered and file stream I/O.

- Making a class streamable. This process involves declaring up to 10 items to register the class with the stream manager and provide the required member functions.

- Storing ObjectWindows controls in a stream. This chapter shows an example of a producer application that writes a set of different controls to an object file stream.
- Constructing ObjectWindows controls with streams. This chapter shows an example of how ObjectWindows controls are read from a stream and inserted in the child list of the parent window.

ObjectWindows Streams

CHAPTER 11

Controls Resource Script

The earlier chapters of this book presented the general syntax for the resources of menus and accelerator keys. Chapter 8, "Dialog Boxes," presented resources for dialog boxes and their controls, but did not go into detail regarding their syntax. This chapter focuses on the syntax for the controls resource script. The resource script itself is defined by Microsoft and is not part of the ObjectWindows class hierarchy. However, as you saw in Chapter 8, you create dialog box instances by using resources. You will learn about the following resources:

- The dialog box resource
- The DIALOG option statements
- The general control resource
- The resources for the default controls

The resource files require that you include the WINDOWS.H and OWLRC.H header files. In addition you can include your own header files that define command IDs and other constants used by the resource statements. If you are new to using the .RC resource file, you should know that resources have unique IDs that can be either strings or integers.

The Dialog Box Resource

The DIALOG statement defines the resource that can be utilized in a Windows program to build dialog boxes. The general syntax for the DIALOG statement is

```
nameID DIALOG [load-option][mem-option] x, y, width, height
    [option-statements]
    BEGIN
            control-statements
    END
```

The `menuID` is the unique name or integer ID of the dialog box resource. The keywords associated with resource files appear in uppercase. This is optional because they are not case-sensitive. However, you should use uppercase letters so you can easily distinguish between resource keywords and nonkeywords. The `load` options are

PRELOAD, which loads the resource immediately.

LOADONCALL, which loads the resource as needed. This is the default option.

The *mem* options are

FIXED, which keeps the resource in a fixed memory location.

MOVABLE, which moves the resource as necessary to compress memory. This option is selected by default.

DISCARDABLE, which discards the resource when it is no longer needed. This option is also selected by default.

The *x* and *y* parameters specify the location of the top-left corner of the dialog box. The width and height parameters define the dimensions of the dialog box.

The following example of a dialog box resource definition is from the DIALOG1.RC file:

```
#include <windows.h>
#include <owlrc.h>

NEW DIALOG DISCARDABLE LOADONCALL PURE MOVEABLE 30, 50, 200, 100 \
STYLE WS_POPUP | DS_MODALFRAME
CAPTION "Message"
BEGIN
    CTEXT "Exit the application?", 1, 10, 10, 170, 15
CONTROL "OK", IDOK, "BUTTON", WS_CHILD | WS_VISIBLE |
WS_TABSTOP | BS_DEFPUSHBUTTON, 20, 50, 70, 15 CONTROL "Cancel", IDCANCEL, \
"BUTTON", WS_CHILD | WS_VISIBLE | WS_TABSTOP | BS_PUSHBUTTON, 110, 50, 70, 15
END
```

The DIALOG Option Statements

The DIALOG option statements designate the special attributes of the dialog box, such as style, caption, and menu. These statements are optional. However, if you do not incorporate any statements in your dialog box resource definition, the result will be a dialog box with default attributes. The DIALOG option statements include the following items:

```
STYLE
CAPTION
MENU
CLASS
FONT
```

The following subsections explain each of these dialog box attributes.

The STYLE Statement

The STYLE statement specifies the window style of the dialog box. This attribute indicates whether the dialog box is a child window or a pop-up window. The default style for the dialog box has the WS_POPUP, WS_BORDER, and WS_SYSMENU styles. The general syntax for the STYLE statement is

`STYLE style`

The `style` parameter takes an integer value consisting of bitwise ORed style attributes. The following is an example of the STYLE option statement:

`STYLE WS_POPUP | DS_MODALFRAME`

The CAPTION Statement

The CAPTION statement defines the title for the dialog box. This title appears in the caption bar of the dialog box, if it has that bar. By default, the title is an empty string. The general syntax for the CAPTION statement is

`CAPTION title`

The `title` parameter is a string literal. An example of the CAPTION statement follows:

`CAPTION "Replace Text"`

The MENU Statement

The MENU statement specifies the menu that is attached to the dialog box. By default, the dialog box has no menu. The general syntax for the MENU statement is

MENU *menuName*

The *menuName* parameter is the name or number of the menu resource. The following is an example of the MENU statement:

```
#include <windows.h>
#include <owlrc.h>

YesNo MENU LOADONCALL MOVEABLE PURE DISCARDABLE
BEGIN
        MENUITEM "&Ok", IDOK
        MENUITEM "&Cancel", IDCANCEL
END

NEW DIALOG DISCARDABLE LOADONCALL PURE MOVEABLE 30, 50, 200, 100 STYLE \
WS_POPUP | DS_MODALFRAME
CAPTION "Message"
MENU YesNo
BEGIN
    CTEXT "Exit the application?", 1, 10, 10, 170, 15
CONTROL "OK", IDOK, "BUTTON", WS_CHILD | WS_VISIBLE |
 WS_TABSTOP | BS_DEFPUSHBUTTON, 20, 50, 70, 15 CONTROL "Cancel", IDCANCEL, \
 "BUTTON", WS_CHILD | WS_VISIBLE | WS_TABSTOP | BS_PUSHBUTTON, 110, 50, 70, 15
END
```

The CLASS Statement

The CLASS statement specifies the Windows registration class (and not the ObjectWindows class) of the dialog box. The general syntax for the CLASS statement is

CLASS *className*

The *className* parameter defines the integer or string name of the registration class. The following is an example of the CLASS statement:

CLASS "ChitChat"

The FONT Statement

The FONT statement specifies the font used by Windows to draw text in the dialog box. The specified font must be already loaded, either from WIN.INI or by invoking the **LoadFont** API function. The general syntax for the FONT statement is

FONT *pointSize*, *typeface*

The *pointSize* parameter is an integer that specifies the size of the font in points. The *typeface* parameter is a string that indicates the name of the font. An example of the FONT statement follows:

FONT 10, "Helv"

The Dialog Box Control Resources

The resource script supports two types of controls resources. The first is the CONTROL statement, which provides a general way for declaring the resource of a control. The other type is the modifiable default control resource. These resources use statements with keywords that are descriptive of the control they define. For example, the RADIOBUTTON statement defines the resource for a radio button. The next section presents the CONTROL statement. The sections after the next one present the statements that define the resources for specific controls.

The CONTROL Statement

The CONTROL statement enables you to define the resource for any standard or user-defined control owned by a dialog box. The general syntax for the CONTROL statement is

CONTROL *text*, *id*, *class*, *style*, *x*, *y*, *width*, *height*

The *text* parameter specifies a string literal for the text that appears in the control. The *id* parameter declares the control's unique ID. The *class* parameter is a string that indicates the name of the Windows registration class for the control. Table 11.1 shows the Windows registration class names for the various standard controls.

The *x*, *y*, *width*, and *height* parameters specify the location and dimensions of the control. These parameters are typically integer constants. You can also use the addition operator to build simple expressions.

Table 11.1. The Windows registration class names for the various standard controls.

Control	Registration Class Name
Check Box	BUTTON
Combo Box	COMBOBOX
Edit Box	EDIT
Group Box	BUTTON
List Box	LISTBOX
Push Button	BUTTON
Radio Button	BUTTON
Scroll Bar	SCROLLBAR
Static Text	STATIC

Note: The push button, check box, radio button, and group box each share the same registration class name. How are they distinguished from each other? The answer lies with the style parameter.

The style parameter, which is usually a bitwise ORed expression, sets all the styles associated with the control. There are no default style values.

The following are examples of using the CONTROL statement to create dialog box controls. These examples are taken from the DIALOG6.RC resource file.

```
ID_DIALOG DIALOG DISCARDABLE LOADONCALL PURE MOVEABLE 10, 10, 200, 150 \
STYLE WS_POPUP | WS_CLIPSIBLINGS | WS_CAPTION | WS_SYSMENU | DS_MODALFRAME
CAPTION "Controls Demo"
BEGIN
CONTROL "Find", ID_FIND_TXT, "STATIC", WS_CHILD | WS_VISIBLE |
        SS_LEFT, 20, 10, 100, 15

CONTROL "", ID_FIND_CMB, "COMBOBOX", WS_CHILD | WS_VISIBLE | WS_BORDER |
        WS_TABSTOP | CBS_DROPDOWN, 20, 25, 100, 50

CONTROL "Replace", ID_REPLACE_TXT, "STATIC", WS_CHILD | WS_VISIBLE |
        SS_LEFT, 20, 45, 100, 15
```

```
    CONTROL "", ID_REPLACE_CMB, "COMBOBOX", WS_CHILD | WS_VISIBLE | WS_BORDER |
        WS_TABSTOP | CBS_DROPDOWN, 20, 60, 100, 50

    CONTROL " Scope ", ID_SCOPE_GRP, "BUTTON", WS_CHILD | WS_VISIBLE
        | WS_GROUP | BS_GROUPBOX, 20, 80, 90, 50

    CONTROL "Global", ID_GLOBAL_RBT, "BUTTON", WS_CHILD | WS_VISIBLE
        | WS_TABSTOP | BS_AUTORADIOBUTTON, 30, 90, 50, 15

    CONTROL "Selected Text", ID_SELTEXT_RBT, "BUTTON", WS_CHILD | WS_VISIBLE |
        WS_TABSTOP | BS_AUTORADIOBUTTON, 30, 105, 60, 15

    CONTROL "Case Sensitive", ID_CASE_CHK, "BUTTON", WS_CHILD | WS_VISIBLE |
        WS_TABSTOP | BS_AUTOCHECKBOX, 20, 130, 80, 15

    CONTROL "Whole Word", ID_WHOLEWORD_CHK, "BUTTON", WS_CHILD | WS_VISIBLE |
        WS_TABSTOP | BS_AUTOCHECKBOX, 100, 130, 80, 15

    CONTROL "&OK", IDOK, "BUTTON", WS_CHILD | WS_VISIBLE | WS_TABSTOP
        | BS_DEFPUSHBUTTON, 120, 90, 30, 20

    CONTROL "&Cancel", IDCANCEL, "BUTTON", WS_CHILD | WS_VISIBLE |
        WS_TABSTOP, 160, 90, 30, 20
END
```

The LTEXT Statement

The LTEXT statement defines the resource of a static text control containing text that is flushed left. The general syntax for the LTEXT statement is

```
LTEXT text, id, x, y, width, height [, style]
```

The *text* parameter specifies the static control text. This text might include an & character to underline a hot key character. The *id* parameter defines the ID of the static control. The *x*, *y*, *width*, and *height* parameters specify the location and dimensions of the control. The optional *style* parameter specifies the additional styles for the resource. The default style is SS_LEFT and WS_GROUP. The style parameter can be the WS_TABSTOP style, the WS_GROUP style, or both.

The characters of the *text* parameter are left-justified. If the entire text does not fit in the specified width, the additional characters are wrapped to the beginning of the next line.

The following are examples of the LTEXT statement:

```
LTEXT "Current Drive:", ID_DRIVE_TXT, 10, 10, 50, 10

LTEXT "Current Dir:", ID_DIR_TXT, 10, 50, 50, 10, WS_TABSTOP | WS_GROUP
```

The RTEXT Statement

The RTEXT statement defines the resource of a static text control containing text that is flushed right. The general syntax for the RTEXT statement is

```
RTEXT text, id, x, y, width, height [, style]
```

The *text* parameter specifies the static control text. This text might include an ampersand (&) to underline a hot key character. The *id* parameter defines the ID of the static control. The *x*, *y*, *width*, and *height* parameters specify the location and dimensions of the control. The optional *style* parameter specifies the additional styles for the resource. The default style is SS_RIGHT and WS_GROUP. The style parameter can be the WS_TABSTOP style, the WS_GROUP style, or both.

The characters of the *text* parameter are right-justified. If the entire text does not fit in the specified width, the additional characters are wrapped to the next line and also are right-justified.

The following is an example of the RTEXT statement:

```
RTEXT "Current Drive:", ID_DRIVE_TXT, 70, 10, 50, 10
```

The CTEXT Statement

The CTEXT statement defines the resource of a static text control with centered text. The general syntax for the CTEXT statement is

```
CTEXT text, id, x, y, width, height [, style]
```

The *text* parameter specifies the static control text. This text might include an ampersand (&) to underline a hot key character. The *id* parameter defines the ID of the static control. The *x*, *y*, *width*, and *height* parameters specify the location and dimensions of the control. The optional *style* parameter specifies the additional styles for the resource. The default style is SS_CENTER and WS_GROUP. The *style* parameter can be the WS_TABSTOP style, the WS_GROUP style, or both.

The characters of the *text* parameter are centered. If the entire text does not fit in the specified width, the additional characters are wrapped to the next line and are also centered.

The following is an example of the CTEXT statement:

```
CTEXT "Current Drive:", ID_DRIVE_TXT, 10, 10, 50, 10
```

The CHECKBOX Statement

The CHECKBOX statement defines a check box control resource that has the BUTTON registration class. The general syntax for the CHECKBOX statement is

```
CHECKBOX text, id, x, y, width, height [, style]
```

The *text* parameter specifies the caption of the control. This text might include an ampersand (&) to underline a hot key character. The *id* parameter defines the ID of the check box control. The *x*, *y*, *width*, and *height* parameters specify the location and dimensions of the control. The optional *style* parameter specifies the additional styles for the resource. The default style is BS_CHECKBOX and WS_TABSTOP. The *style* parameter can be the WS_DISABLED style, the WS_TABSTOP style, or both.

The following is an example of the CHECKBOX statement:

```
CHECKBOX "Case-Sensitive", ID_CASE_CHK, 10, 10, 100, 10
```

The PUSHBUTTON Statement

The PUSHBUTTON statement defines a push button control resource that has the BUTTON registration class. The general syntax for the PUSHBUTTON statement is

```
PUSHBUTTON text, id, x, y, width, height [, style]
```

The *text* parameter specifies the caption of the control. This text might include an ampersand (&) to underline a hot key character. The *id* parameter defines the ID of the push button control. The *x*, *y*, *width*, and *height* parameters specify the location and dimensions of the control. The optional *style* parameter specifies the additional styles for the resource. The default style is BS_PUSHBUTTON and WS_TABSTOP. The style parameter can be the WS_TABSTOP style, the WS_DISABLED style, the WS_GROUP style, or any bitwise ORed combination of these styles.

The following is an example of the PUSHBUTTON statement:

```
PUSHBUTTON "Calculate", ID_CALC_BTN, 10, 10, 100, 10, WS_DISABLED
```

The DEFPUSHBUTTON Statement

The DEFPUSHBUTTON statement defines a default push button control resource that has the BUTTON registration class. The general syntax for the DEFPUSHBUTTON statement is

DEFPUSHBUTTON text, id, x, y, width, height [, style]

The text parameter specifies the caption of the control. This text might include an ampersand (&) to underline a hot key character. The id parameter defines the ID of the default push button control. The x, y, width, and height parameters specify the location and dimensions of the control. The optional style parameter specifies the additional styles for the resource. The default style is BS_DEFPUSHBUTTON and WS_TABSTOP. The style parameter can be the WS_TABSTOP style, the WS_DISABLED style, the WS_GROUP style, or any bitwise ORed combination of these styles.

The following is an example of the DEFPUSHBUTTON statement:

DEFPUSHBUTTON "Calculate", ID_CALC_BTN, 10, 10, 100, 10

The LISTBOX Statement

The LISTBOX statement defines a list box control resource that has the LISTBOX registration class. The general syntax for the LISTBOX statement is

LISTBOX id, x, y, width, height [, style]

The id parameter defines the ID of the list box control. The x, y, width, and height parameters specify the location and dimensions of the control. The optional style parameter specifies the additional styles for the resource. The default style is LBS_NOTIFY, WS_VSCROLL, and WS_BORDER. The style parameter can be the WS_BORDER style, the WS_VSCROLL style, or both.

The following is an example of the LISTBOX statement:

LISTBOX ID_OPERAND_LST, 10, 10, 100, 100

The GROUPBOX Statement

The GROUPBOX statement defines a group box control resource that has the BUTTON registration class. The general syntax for the GROUPBOX statement is

GROUPBOX text, id, x, y, width, height [, style]

The `text` parameter specifies the caption of the control. This text might include an ampersand (&) to underline a hot key character. The `id` parameter defines the ID of the group box control. The `x`, `y`, `width`, and `height` parameters specify the location and dimensions of the control. The optional `style` parameter specifies the additional styles for the resource. The default style is BS_GROUPBOX and WS_TABSTOP. The `style` parameter can be the WS_TABSTOP style, the WS_DISABLED style, or both.

The following is an example of the GROUPBOX statement:

```
GROUPBOX "Angle", ID_ANGLE_GRP, 10, 10, 200, 200
```

The RADIOBUTTON Statement

The RADIOBUTTON statement defines a radio button control resource that has the BUTTON registration class. The general syntax for the RADIOBUTTON statement is

```
RADIOBUTTON text, id, x, y, width, height [, style]
```

The `text` parameter specifies the caption of the control. This text might include an ampersand (&) to underline a hot key character. The `id` parameter defines the ID of the radio button control. The `x`, `y`, `width`, and `height` parameters specify the location and dimensions of the control. The optional `style` parameter specifies the additional styles for the resource. The default style is BS_RADIOBUTTON and WS_TABSTOP. The `style` parameter can be the WS_TABSTOP style, the WS_GROUP style, the WS_DISABLED style, or any bitwise ORed combination of these styles.

The following is an example of the RADIOBUTTON statement:

```
RADIOBUTTON "Degrees", ID_DEGREES_RBT, 10, 10, 100, 10
```

The EDITTEXT Statement

The EDITTEXT statement defines an edit box control resource that has the EDIT registration class. The general syntax for the EDITTEXT statement is

```
EDITTEXT id, x, y, width, height [, style]
```

The `id` parameter defines the ID of the edit box control. The `x`, `y`, `width`, and `height` parameters specify the location and dimensions of the control. The optional `style` parameter specifies the additional styles for the resource. The default style is WS_TABSTOP, ES_EDIT, and WS_BORDER. The style parameter can be the WS_TABSTOP style, the WS_GROUP style, the WS_VSCROLL style, the WS_HSCROLL style, the WS_DISABLED style, or any bitwise ORed combination of these styles.

The following is an example of the EDITTEXT statement:

EDITTEXT ID_INPUT_BOX, 10, 10, 200, 200

The COMBOBOX Statement

The COMBOBOX statement defines a combo box control resource that has the COMBOBOX registration class. The general syntax for the COMBOBOX statement is

COMBOBOX id, x, y, width, height [, style]

The id parameter defines the ID of the combo box control. The x, y, width, and height parameters specify the location and dimensions of the control. The optional style parameter specifies the additional styles for the resource. The default style is WS_TABSTOP and CBS_SIMPLE. The style parameter can be the WS_TABSTOP style, the WS_GROUP style, the WS_VSCROLL style, the WS_DISABLED style, or any bitwise ORed combination of these styles.

The following is an example of the COMBOBOX statement:

COMBOBOX ID_INPUT_BOX, 10, 10, 200, 200

The SCROLLBAR Statement

The SCROLLBAR statement defines a scroll bar control resource that has the SCROLLBAR registration class. The general syntax for the SCROLLBAR statement is

SCROLLBAR id, x, y, width, height [, style]

The id parameter defines the ID of the scroll bar control. The x, y, width, and height parameters specify the location and dimensions of the control. The optional style parameter specifies the additional styles for the resource. The default style is SBS_HORZ. The style parameter can be the WS_TABSTOP style, the WS_GROUP style, the WS_GROUP style, the WS_DISABLED style, or any bitwise ORed combination of these styles.

The following is an example of the SCROLLBAR statement:

SCROLLBAR ID_INDEX_SCR, 10, 10, 20, 200

Controls Resource Script

Summary

This chapter briefly introduced you to the resource statements that create the dialog box and its controls. You learned about the following topics:

- ☐ The DIALOG statement that defines a dialog box resource.
- ☐ The DIALOG option statements, including STYLE, CAPTION, MENU, CLASS, and FONT.
- ☐ The CONTROL statement that defines the resources for both standard and user-defined controls.
- ☐ The LTEXT statement that defines the resource for a left-justified static text control.
- ☐ The RTEXT statement that defines the resource for a right-justified static text control.
- ☐ The CTEXT statement that defines the resource for a centered-text static text control.
- ☐ The CHECKBOX statement that defines the resource for a check box control.
- ☐ The PUSHBUTTON statement that defines the resource for a push button control.
- ☐ The DEFPUSHBUTTON statement that defines the resource for a default push button control.
- ☐ The LISTBOX statement that defines the resource for a list box control.
- ☐ The GROUPBOX statement that defines the resource for a group box control.
- ☐ The RADIOBUTTON statement that defines the resource for a radio button control.
- ☐ The EDITTEXT statement that defines the resource for an edit box control.
- ☐ The COMBOBOX statement that defines the resource for a combo box control.
- ☐ The SCROLLBAR statement that defines the resource for a scroll bar control.

Index

Symbols

\# (pound sign) character, 300
`#define` directive, 57
`#include` directive, 173
& (ampersand) hot key character, 227-228
<< stream operators, 39-40
    declaring, 548-549
    friend, 538
>> stream operators, 39-40
    declaring, 548-549
    friend, 536

A

accelerators, defining, 76-77
ACCELERATORS statement, 76-77
`ActiveChild` data member, 507
`AddString` ObjectWindows function, 338
aligning text, *see* justifying text
`AMemberBtn` ObjectWindows function, 430
ampersand (&) hot key character, 227-228
API functions
    `CreateDC`, 208
    `DefWindowProc`, 51
    `DispatchMessage`, 65
    `EnableWindow`, 265
    `Escape`, 207-208
    GDI (Graphics Device Interface), 42-43
    `GetProfileString`, 208
    `GetTickCount`, 336
    `InvalidateRect`, 112
    invoking, 45-48
    `IsWindowEnabled`, 265
    `IsWindowVisible`, 265
    `LoadCursor`, 139
    `LoadIcon`, 123-124
    `MessageBeep`, 45-46
    `MessageBox`, 45-48
    `Polyline`, 45-46
    `PostMessage`, 56
    `SendDlgItemMessage`, 56-57
    `SendMessage`, 56
    `SetCursor`, 139
    `ShowWindow`, 265, 419
    system services interface, 44-45
    `TextOut`, 102
    `TranslateMessage`, 65
    Windows Manager interface, 41-42
`AppBuffer` public data member, 461
application frame class, 508
Application-exec API system services interface functions type, 45
applications
    adding menus, 72-81
    exiting, 95-99

 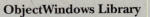

Guide to ObjectWindows Library

"Hello World" message, 54-55
minimal, 10-12, 62-63
    (MINWINAP.CPP,
    MINWINAP.EXE,
    MINWINAP.PRJ,
    OWL.DEL), 66-68
responding to menu-item
    selections, 81-88
running multiple instances, 89-95
arraySize data member, 557
AssignMenu ObjectWindows function,
    78, 103, 115
ATextString pointer, 228, 245
ATitle pointer, 226-227
Atom-management API system
    services interface functions
    type, 44
Attr data member, 20, 73
attributes, menu items, 75
auto scroll mode, 150
    toggling, 155-161
AutoMode data member, 150

B

background color of window
    classes, 125
bad ObjectWindows function, 533
BF_CHECKED constant, 293
BF_GRAYED constant, 293
BF_UNCHECKED constant, 293
Bitmap API GDI functions type, 43
bitwise OR operator, combining
    window styles, 113
black frames, 241
BNClicked ObjectWindows function,
    30-31
BOOL data type, 4
Borland Windows Custom Controls
    (BWCC), 40
bp data member, 533
BS_3STATE check box control
    style, 293

BS_AUTO3STATE check box control
    style, 293
BS_AUTOCHECKBOX check box control
    style, 293
BS_AUTORADIOBUTTON radio box control
    style, 295
BS_CHECKBOX check box control style,
    293
BS_LEFTTEXT
    check box control style, 293
    radio box control style, 295
BS_RADIOBUTTON radio box control
    style, 295
Buffer data member, 488
buffered stream input, supporting,
    534-538
buffered stream output, supporting,
    536-538
buffers, transfer, 454-462
    types, 446-448
BufferSize data member, 488
build ObjectWindows function, 559
    static public, 543
button manipulation tester
    (CTLBTN2.CPP, CTLBTN2.EXE,
    CTLBTN2.H, CTLBTN2.RC),
    279-289
BUTTON registration class, 586
buttons
    controls, 28
    default control, 29
    in command-oriented calculator
        application (COCA)
        (CTLGRP1.CPP, CTLGRP1.H,
        CTLGRP1.RC), 298-320
    push
        controls, 263-264
        handling messages, 264
        in command-oriented
            calculator application
            (COCA) (CTLBTN1.CPP,
            CTLBTN1.H,
            CTLBTN1.RC), 266-279

INDEX

interacting with windows, 279-289
manipulating, 265-266
radio, 30-31
controls, 295-296
Wizard, 419
BWCC (Borland Windows Custom Controls), 40
`BYTE` data type, 4

C

C++ streams, *see* streams, streamable
calculators
as dialog boxes, 434-445
COCA (command-oriented calculator application), 249-263, 266-279, 298-320, 382-400, 434-445
free-form (WINEDIT2.CPP, WINEDIT2.EXE, WINEDIT2.H, WINEDIT2.RC), 192-201
`Cancel` ObjectWindows function, 411-413, 478
`CanClose` ObjectWindows function, 96-99, 410, 413, 518, 528
`CAPTION` statement, 583
Caret API Windows Manager functions type, 42
`CBS_AUTOHSCROLL` style, 379
`CBS_DROPDOWN` style, 379
`CBS_DROPDOWNLIST` style, 379
`CBS_SIMPLE` style, 379
`CBS_SORT` style, 379
`char` data type, 4
check box controls, 291-294
`BUTTON` registration class, 586
defining resources, 589
transfer buffer types, 446-448
check boxes, 29-30
placing inside groups, 291
responding to messages, 294

`Check` ObjectWindows function, 293
`CheckBox` data member, 448
`CHECKBOX` statement, 589
child windows
creating, 141-149
MDI, 504
building, 510
`ChildMenuPos` data member, 507
`CLASS` statement, 584
`_CLASSDEF` macro, 9, 70, 148
classes
application
frame, 508
template derived from `TApplication`, 66-68
background, of window classes, 125
BWCC (Borland Windows Custom Controls), 40
descendant, 542
fpbase, 534
fpstream, 539-540
ifpstream, 540-541
iopstream, 538
ipstream, 534-536
`Object`, 8-9
ofpstream, 539
opstream, 536-538
pstream, 532-533
streamable
creating, 541-549
hierarchy, 531-541
`TApplication`, 10-12
`TAppMDIChild`, 518, 527-528
`TAppMDIFrame`, 517
`TAppWindow`, 69-72, 103, 111-112, 139, 148, 154-155, 170-171
`TButton`, 28, 264-289
`TCheckBox`, 29-30, 292-294
`TChildWindow`, 148
`TComboBox`, 26-28, 378-400
`TComboBoxData`, 447
`TControl`, 21

597

ObjectWindows Library

`TDialog`, 15-17, 404-433, 544-548
`TEdit`, 24-25, 242-263
`TEditWindow`, 31-32, 189-209
`TFileDialog`, 17, 493-499
`TFileWindow`, 33, 209-221
`TGroupBox`, 28, 296-298
`TInputDialog`, 18, 487-493
`TListBox`, 25-26, 336-355
`TListBoxData`, 446-447
`TMDIClient`, 36-37, 504-505, 509-510
`TMDIFrame`, 35-36, 504-508
`TModule`, 9-10
`TPoints`, 557
`TPolygon`, 557-558
`TRadioButton`, 30-31, 295-296
`TScrollBar`, 222-223, 324-336
`TScroller`, 37-39, 150-152
`TSearchDialog`, 18-19, 499-500
`TStatic`, 23-24, 225-242
`TStreamable`, 541
`TStreamableClass`, 549
`TWinApp`, 139
`_TWinApp_`, 63, 66-68
`TWindow`, 19-21, 504-505, 544-548
`TWindowsObject`, 12-15, 544-548
window, 120-133
`_CLASSTYPE` identifier macro, 8
`Clear` ObjectWindows function, 228, 248, 379, 533
`ClearCheckBoxes` ObjectWindows function, 318
`ClearEditControls` ObjectWindows function, 317-318
`ClearList` ObjectWindows function, 338
`ClearModify` ObjectWindows function, 247
clicking mouse, displaying message boxes, 69-72
client windows, 34-37
    MDI, 504, 509-510
`ClientWnd` data member, 507

Clipboard,
    API Windows Manager functions type, 42
    messages, 51
    searching and replacing text through, 189-192
Clipping API GDI functions type, 43
`close` ObjectWindows function, 534
`CloseChildren` ObjectWindows function, 517
`CloseWindow` ObjectWindows function, 411-413
closing windows, 95-99
`CM_ARRANGEICONS` constant, 507
`CM_AUTOSCROLL` command, 161
`CM_CASCASDECHILDREN` constant, 507
`CM_CLOSECHILDREN` constant, 507
`CM_EDITCLEAR` command, 107, 244
`CM_EDITCOPY` command, 244
`CM_EDITCUT` command, 244
`CM_EDITDELETE` command, 244
`CM_EDITPASTE` command, 244
`CM_EDITUNDO` command, 244
`CM_EXIT` command, 107
`CM_FIRST` constant, 56
`CM_HELPx` constants, 126
`CM_INTERNAL` constant, 56
`CM_LONGMENU` command, 83
`CM_SHORTMENU` command, 83
`CM_TILECHILDREN` constant, 507
`CM_TRACKMODE` command, 161
`CM_xxxx` constants, 77
`CMArrangeIcons` ObjectWindows function, 507
`CMAutoScroll` ObjectWindows function, 161
`CMBlockLower` ObjectWindows function, 221
`CMBlockPrint` ObjectWindows function, 221
`CMBlockUpper` ObjectWindows function, 221

INDEX

`CMCalc` ObjectWindows function, 261-262
`CMCalcBtn` ObjectWindows function, 279, 399
`CMCalculate` ObjectWindows function, 200-201
`CMCascadeChildren` ObjectWindows function, 507
`CMClear` ObjectWindows function, 112, 528
`CMClearBox` ObjectWindows function, 319
`CMClearChk` ObjectWindows function, 319
`CMCloseChildren` ObjectWindows function, 507
`CMCountChildren` ObjectWindows function, 517
`CMDialog` ObjectWindows function, 462, 469, 479
`CMDisableAllBtn` ObjectWindows function, 266
`CMEditClear` ObjectWindows function, 241, 244
`CMEditCopy` ObjectWindows function, 88, 242-244
`CMEditCut` ObjectWindows function, 88, 244
`CMEditDelete` ObjectWindows function, 244
`CMEditPaste` ObjectWindows function, 88, 241-244
`CMEditUndo` ObjectWindows function, 244
`CMExit` ObjectWindows function, 88
`CMExitBtn` ObjectWindows function, 279, 336, 399
`CMGame` ObjectWindows function, 492-493
`CMHelp` ObjectWindows function, 88, 148
`CMHelp1` ObjectWindows function, 133
`CMHelp2` ObjectWindows function, 133
`CMLongMenu` ObjectWindows function, 88
`CMLowerCase` ObjectWindows function, 528
`CMPrint` ObjectWindows function, 207-208
`CMRcl1` ObjectWindows function, 201
`CMRcl2` ObjectWindows function, 201
`CMReset` ObjectWindows function, 528
`CMScrollToBottom` ObjectWindows function, 182-183
`CMScrollToLine` ObjectWindows function, 182-183
`CMScrollToTop` ObjectWindows function, 182-183
`CMSelectSetx` ObjectWindows functions, 170-171
`CMSendBtn` ObjectWindows function, 478
`CMShortMenu` ObjectWindows function, 88
`CMStartBtn` ObjectWindows function, 336
`CMSto1` ObjectWindows function, 201
`CMSto2` ObjectWindows function, 201
`CMStore` ObjectWindows function, 262
`CMStoreBtn` ObjectWindows function, 279, 399
`CMTileChildren` ObjectWindows function, 507
`CMTrackMode` ObjectWindows function, 161
`CMUpperCase` ObjectWindows function, 528
`CMxxxx` ObjectWindows functions, 32-33
COCA, *see* command-oriented calculator application

599

Color-palette API GDI functions
type, 43
COLOR_xxxx constants, 125
combo box controls, 26-28, 378-380
   COMBOBOX registration class, 586
   defining resources, 592
   transfer buffer types, 446-448
combo boxes
   as history list boxes, 381-382
   responding to notification
      messages, 381
COMBOBOX
   registration class, 586
   statement, 592
ComboBoxData data member, 447
command buttons, *see* push buttons
command-oriented calculator
   application (COCA)
      version 1 (CTLEDIT1.CPP,
         CTLEDIT1.H, CTLEDIT1.RC),
         249-263
      version 2 (CTLBTN1.CPP,
         CTLBTN1.H, CTLBTN1.RC),
         266-279
      version 3 (CTLGRP1.CPP,
         CTLGRP1.H, CTLGRP1.RC),
         298-320
      version 4 (CTLLST5.CPP,
         CTLLST5.EXE, CTLLST5.H,
         CTLLST5.RC), 382-400
      version 5 (DIALOG4.H,
         DIALOG4.RC), 434-445
commands
   CM_AUTOSCROLL, 161
   CM_EDITCLEAR, 107, 244
   CM_EDITCOPY, 244
   CM_EDITCUT, 244
   CM_EDITDELETE, 244
   CM_EDITPASTE, 244
   CM_EDITUNDO, 244
   CM_EXIT, 107
   CM_LONGMENU, 83
   CM_SHORTMENU, 83
   CM_TRACKMODE, 161
   ENDDOC, 208
   NEWFRAME, 208
   STARTDOC, 208
   text-editing menu-driven, 244
Communications API system
   services interface functions
   type, 45
constants, 55-56
   BF_CHECKED, 293
   BF_GRAYED, 293
   BF_UNCHECKED, 293
   CM_ARRANGEICONS, 507
   CM_CASCASDECHILDREN, 507
   CM_CLOSECHILDREN, 507
   CM_HELPx, 126
   CM_TILECHILDREN, 507
   CM_xxxx, 77
   COLOR_xxxx, 125
   ID_xxxx, 267
   IDCANCEL, 408
   IDOK, 408
   LINE_INCR, 106
   MAX_MEM, 194
   MAX_MEM_LEN, 194
   WS_HSCROLL, 150
   WS_VSCROLL, 150
constructors
   for streamable classes
      protected, 543
      public, 542
   resourcetapping, 432
   TAppDialog class, 415, 431, 469
   TAppMDIChild class, 518, 527-528
   TAppWindow
      class, 69, 119-120, 161,
         240-241, 260-261, 278,
         334-335, 397, 479, 486-487,
         576-577
      scrollable window, 154-155
   TButton class, 264
   TCheckBox class, 292
   TComboBox class, 378

INDEX

TDialog class, 16, 404
TEdit class, 242
TFileDialog class, 17
TGroupBox class, 296-297
TInputDialog class, 18, 488
TListBox class, 336-337
TMDIClient class, 510
TMDIFrame class, 507
TRadioButton class, 31, 295
TScrollBar class, 324
TScroller class, 151
TSearchDialog class, 19
TStatic class, 24, 226
TWinApp class, 94
TWindow class, 115-116
consumer programs, 560
  (STRM2B.CPP, STRM2B.EXE, STRM2B.RC), 567-577
CONTROL keyword, 408, 457-461
control manipulation messages, 52
control notification messages, 52
CONTROL statement, 585-587
controls, 21
  button, 28
  BWCC (Borland Windows Custom Controls), 40
  check box, 291-294
  combo box, 26-28, 378-400
  constructing from streams, 567-577
  dialog box
    defining within programs, 414-418
    modeless, 419
    resources, 585-592
  edit, 242-263
  group box, 296-298
  grouping, 28
  list box, 25-26, 336-355
  push button, 263-289
  radio button, 30-31, 295-296
  scroll bar, 323-336
  static text, 225-242

storing in streams, 560-567
transferring data, 445-487
window, initializing, 480-487
window-content editing, 24-25
Coord data member, 111
Coordinate API GDI functions type, 43
countdown timer application (CTLLST1.CPP, CTLLST1.H, CTLLST1.RC), 327-336
Create ObjectWindows function, 21, 419
CreateChild ObjectWindows function, 517
CreateDC API function, 208
CS_CLASSDC window class style, 123
CS_DBLCLKS window class style, 123
CS_HREDRAW window class style, 123
CS_NOCLOSE window class style, 123
CS_OWNDC window class style, 123
CS_PARENTDC window class style, 123
CS_VREDRAW window class style, 123
CTEXT
  keyword, 408
  statement, 588-589
CTLBTN1.CPP program, (COCA), 268-278
CTLBTN1.H program, (COCA), 268
CTLBTN1.RC program, (COCA), 267-268
CTLBTN2.CPP program, (button manipulation tester), 283-288
CTLBTN2.EXE program, (button manipulation tester), 280-281
CTLBTN2.H program, (button manipulation tester), 282
CTLBTN2.RC program, (button manipulation tester), 282
CTLEDIT1.CPP program, (COCA), 252-260
CTLEDIT1.H program, (COCA), 252

601

ObjectWindows Library

CTLEDIT1.RC program, (COCA), 252
CTLGRP1.CPP program, (COCA), 302-317
CTLGRP1.H program, (COCA), 301
CTLGRP1.RC program, (COCA), 301-302
CTLLST1.CPP program, (countdown timer application), 329-334
CTLLST1.H program, (countdown timer application), 329
CTLLST1.RC program, (countdown timer application), 329
CTLLST2.CPP program, (list manipulation tester), 346-353
CTLLST2.RC program, (list manipulation tester), 346
CTLLST3.CPP program, (synchronized lists), 358-364
CTLLST3.EXE program, (synchronized lists), 356-358
CTLLST4.CPP program, (multiple-selection list tester), 368-375
CTLLST4.EXE program, (multiple-selection list tester), 366-368
CTLLST5.CPP program, (COCA), 384-396
CTLLST5.EXE program, (COCA), 382-383
CTLLST5.H program, (COCA), 384
CTLLST5.RC program, (COCA), 384
CTLSTAT1.CPP program, (static text sampler), 230-237
CTLSTAT1.EXE program, (static text sampler), 237
CTLSTAT1.RC program, (static text sampler), 229-230
Cursor API Windows Manager functions type, 42
cursor resource, 124-125
cursors, changing shapes at run-time, 134-141

D

data members
  ActiveChild, 507
  AppBuffer, 461
  arraySize, 557
  Attr, 20, 73
  AutoMode, 150
  bp, 533
  Buffer, 488
  BufferSize, 488
  CheckBox, 448
  ChildMenuPos, 507
  ClientWnd, 507
  ComboBoxData, 447
  Coord, 111
  dataPtr, 557
  declaring as transfer buffers, 446
  DlgPtr, 430
  EditBox, 446
  Editor, 32, 189
  EditText, 239
  ExpressClose, 517
  ExStyle, 114
  Group, 30
  H, 115-116
  hPrevInstance, 95
  Id, 115
  InError, 260
  IsCurrentDefPB, 29, 264
  IsDef, 264
  IsDefPB, 29
  IsReplaceOp, 32
  LineHeight, 170
  LineMagnitude, 22, 324
  Lines, 111
  ListBoxData, 446-447
  LParam, 54
  MaxLines, 170
  memoryStr, 201
  Menu, 115-116
  Message, 53
  MSG_XXXX, 260

602

INDEX

NotifyParent, 296-297
NumHelpWindows, 148
numStrings, 111
PageMagnitude, 22, 324
Param, 115
Prompt, 488
RadioButton, 448
Receiver, 53
Result, 54
Scroll->AutoMode, 156
Scroll->TrackMode, 156
ScrollBarData, 447-448
Scroller, 20, 37, 150
SearchStruct, 32, 189
SelCount, 447
SetOfLinesIndex, 170
state, 533
StaticText, 446
Strings, 447
Style, 113-116, 150
TextBox, 518
TrackMode, 150
types, 533
W, 115-116
WindowNumber, 148
WParam, 53
X, 115-116
XLine, 151, 162
XPage, 151, 162, 170
XPos, 151
XRange, 151, 162
XUnit, 151, 162
Y, 115-116
YLine, 151, 162
YPage, 151, 162, 170
YPos, 151
YRange, 151, 162
YUnit, 151, 162
ZERO, 8
data types, 3, 4
   applying data-typing
      convention, 6
   HANDLE, 62

HINSTANCE, 62
TWindowAttr, 20, 73, 113
data-typing convention, 5, 6
dataPtr data member, 557
DataPtr pointer, 448
Debugging API system services
   interface functions type, 45
declaring
   << and >> operators, 39, 548-549
   API functions
      LoadIcon, 124
      MessageBeep, 46
      MessageBox, 47
      Polyline, 46
      PostMessage, 56
      SendDlgItemMessage, 56
      SendMessage, 56
   class constructors
      TComboBox, 378
      TEdit, 242
      TStatic, 226
   classes
      descendant, 542
      fpbase, 534
      fpstream, 539-540
      ifpstream, 540
      iopstream, 538
      ipstream, 534-536
      Object, 8
      ofpstream, 539
      opstream, 536-538
      pstream, 532-533
      streamable, protected
         constructors for, 543
      TApplication, 10-11
      TButton, 29
      TCheckBox, 29-30
      TComboBox, 27-28
      TControl, 21
      TDialog, 15-16
      TEdit, 24-25
      TEditWindow, 31-32
      TFileDialog, 17, 493-495

TFileWindow, 33
TGroupBox, 28
TInputDialog, 18, 487-488
TListBox, 25-26
TMDIClient, 36-37, 509-510
TMDIFrame, 34-36, 505-506
TModule, 9-10
TPolygon, 557-558
TRadioButton, 31
TScrollBar, 22
TScroller, 37-39
TSearchDialog, 18-19, 499
TStatic, 23
TStreamable, 541
TStreamableClass, 549
TWindow, 19-20
TWindowsObject, 12-15
data members, 446
ObjectWindows functions
   AddString, 338
   build, 543
   DeleteLine, 248
   DeleteString, 338
   DeleteSubText, 248
   DeltaPos, 325
   FindExactString, 338
   FindString, 339
   GetCheck, 293
   GetEditSel, 379
   GetLine, 246
   GetLineFromPos, 247
   GetLineIndex, 247
   GetLineLength, 245
   GetNumLines, 245
   GetRange, 325
   GetSelection, 246
   GetSelIndexes, 340
   GetSelString, 340
   GetString, 340
   GetStringLen, 340
   GetSubText, 246
   GetText, 228, 244, 379
   Insert, 249
   InsertString, 340
   IsVisibleRect, 184
   message response, 54
   Paint, 103
   read, 546
   ScrollBy, 172
   ScrollTo, 172
   Search, 248
   SetCheck, 294
   SetEditSel, 380
   SetPosition, 325
   SetRange, 162, 324
   SetSelection, 249
   SetSelIndex, 341
   SetSelIndexes, 341
   SetSelString, 342
   SetSelStrings, 342
   SetText, 228, 380
   SetUnits, 162
   streamableName, 548
   write, 544
structures
   POINT, 5
   RECT, 5
   TMessage, 53
   WNDCLASS, 122
TransferStruct data transfer buffer type, 486
TWindowAttr data type, 20, 73, 113
default
   control buttons, 29
   push buttons, defining control resources, 590
DEFPUSHBUTTON statement, 590
DefWindowProc API function, 51
DeleteLine ObjectWindows function, 248
DeleteSelection ObjectWindows function, 248
DeleteString ObjectWindows function, 338
DeleteSubText ObjectWindows function, 248-249

INDEX

deleting text, 248-249
`DeltaPos` ObjectWindows function, 23, 325
descendant classes, 542
`Destroy` ObjectWindows function, 17
Device-context API GDI functions type, 43
dialog boxes, 15-17
  as windows, 433-445
  attributes, setting, 582-585
  constructing, 404
  controls
    defining within programs, 414-418
    resources, 585-592
  file, 493-499
  Find, 210
  input, 210, 487-493
    with scrolling, 173
  inputting text, 18
  modal, 404-413
    Wizard, 419
  modeless, 418-433
  Open and Save file, 210
  Replace, 210
  resources, 581-582
  Search and Replace, 18-19, 499-500
  selecting files for input/output, 17
  static text objects, 23-24
  `TModule::ExecDialog`, 183
  transferring control data, 445
    modal dialog boxes, 454-469
    modeless dialog boxes, 469-479
    rules, 453
    transfer buffer type, 446-448
    transfer buffers, 452-453
    `Transfer` ObjectWindows function, 448-452
`DIALOG`
  option statements, 582-585
  statement, 581-582

Dialog-box API Windows Manager functions type, 41
DIALOG.CPP program, 411
DIALOG1.CPP program, (modern/old English dialog boxes), 409-410
DIALOG1.RC program, (modern/old English dialog boxes), 407-408
DIALOG2.CPP program, (modern/old English dialog boxes), 415-418
DIALOG2.RC program, (modern/old English dialog boxes), 414
DIALOG3.CPP program, (modeless dialog boxes), 423-429
DIALOG3.H program, (modeless dialog boxes), 421
DIALOG3.RC program, (modeless dialog boxes), 422
DIALOG4.CPP program, (COCA), 435-445
DIALOG4.H program, (COCA), 434
DIALOG4.RC program, (COCA), 435
DIALOG5.CPP program, (modal dialog box data transfer), 458-461
DIALOG5.EXE program, (modal dialog box data transfer), 454, 455
DIALOG5.H program, (modal dialog box data transfer), 455
DIALOG5.RC program, (modal dialog box data transfer), 456-457
DIALOG6.CPP program, (modal dialog box data transfer), 465-468
DIALOG6.H program, (modal dialog box data transfer), 463
DIALOG6.RC program, (modal dialog box data transfer), 463-464
DIALOG7.CPP program, (modeless dialog box data transfer), 472-478
DIALOG7.EXE program, (modeless dialog box data transfer), 469
DIALOG7.H program, (modeless dialog box data transfer), 470-471
DIALOG7.RC program, (modeless dialog box data transfer), 471-472

ObjectWindows Library

DIALOG8.CPP program, (synchronized lists), 480-486
DIALOG9.CPP program, (number guessing game), 490-492
DIALOG9.EXE program, (number guessing game), 488
DIALOG9.H program, (number guessing game), 488
DIALOG9.RC program, (number guessing game), 489
DIALOG10.CPP program, (file statistics), 496-498
DIALOG10.EXE program, (file statistics), 494-495
DIALOG10.H program, (file statistics), 495
DIALOG10.RC program, (file statistics), 495-496
directives
    #define, 57
    #include, 173
DisableButton ObjectWindows function, 279
DisabledButton ObjectWindows function, 266
DisableTransfer ObjectWindows function, 453
DispatchMessage API function, 65
Display and movement API Windows Manager functions type, 41
DlgPtr public data member, 430
DLLs (dynamic-link libraries), modeling, 9-10
DoSearch ObjectWindows function, 32
Drawing-attribute API GDI functions type, 43
Drawing-tool API GDI functions type, 43
drop-down
    combo boxes, 378
    list combo boxes, 378
DWORD data type, 4

E

edit box controls
    defining resources, 591-592
    EDIT registration class, 586
    transfer buffer types, 446-448
edit controls, 242-244
    altering, 248-249
    for text queries, 244-248
    in command-oriented calculator application (COCA) (CTLEDIT1.CPP, CTLEDIT1.H, CTLEDIT1.RC), 249-263
EDIT registration class, 586
EDITACC.RC program, 210
EditBox data member, 446
editing
    window contents, controls, 24-25
    windows for text, 31-32
    see also text editors
EDITMENU.RC program, 210
Editor data member, 32, 189
EditText data member, 239
EDITTEXT statement, 591-592
Ellipse and polygon API GDI functions type, 43
EnableButton ObjectWindows function, 279
EnableTransfer ObjectWindows function, 453
EnableWindow API function, 265
ENDDOC command, 208
enhanced text editor (WINFILE2.CPP, WINFILE2.EXE, WINFILE2.H, WINFILE2.RC), 212-221
Environment API GDI functions type, 43
eof ObjectWindows function, 533
Error API Windows Manager functions type, 42
ES_AUTOHSCROLL multiline edit control style value, 243

INDEX

ES_AUTOVSCROLL multiline edit control style value, 243
ES_CENTER multiline edit control style value, 243
ES_LEFT multiline edit control style value, 243
ES_LOWERCASE multiline edit control style value, 243
ES_MULTILINE multiline edit control style value, 243
ES_NOHIDESEL multiline edit control style value, 243
ES_RIGHT multiline edit control style value, 243
ES_UPPERCASE multiline edit control style value, 243
Escape API function, 207-208
ExecDialog ObjectWindows function, 183, 405, 411
Execute ObjectWindows function, 10, 16, 405
ExecuteDialog ObjectWindows function, 10, 16, 405
exiting applications, 95-99
EXITMENU menu resource, 103, 408
_EXPORT macro, 10
ExpressClose data member, 517
ExStyle data member, 114

F

fail ObjectWindows function, 533
FAR data type, 4
_FAR macro, 9
FARPROC data type, 4
file dialog boxes, 493-499
File I/O API system services interface functions type, 45
file statistics (DIALOG10.EXE, DIALOG10.H), 494-499
file streams, 534
  reading and writing objects to, 539-540
  reading objects from, 540-541
  writing objects to, 539
FILEACC.RC program, 210
FILEDIAL.DLG program, 210
FILEMENU.RC program, 210
FILEMNU1.RC program, 214
files
  dialog boxes for input/output selection, 17
  handling text in, 33
  .RC extension, 74
Find dialog box, 210
FindExactString ObjectWindows function, 338-339
FindString ObjectWindows function, 339
flag static local variable, 410
flags, TransferFlag transfer direction, 448
FONT statement, 584-585
fonts, dialog box text, 584-585
Fonts API GDI functions type, 43
ForEach iterator, 365
fpbase class, 534
fpstream class, 539-540
frame windows, MDI, 34-36, 503-508
frames, black, 241
freadString ObjectWindows function, 536
free-form calculator (WINEDIT2.CPP, WINEDIT2.EXE, WINEDIT2.H, WINEDIT2.RC), 192-201
friend << operators, 538
friend >> operators, 536
functions
  API, *see* API functions
  iterated, 317-318
  ObjectWindows, *see* ObjectWindows functions
  WinMain, 62-63
fwriteString ObjectWindows function, 538

G

games, number guessing, 488-493
GDI (Graphics Device Interface)
    functions, 42-43
`GetCheck` ObjectWindows
    function, 293
`GetChildCount` ObjectWindows
    function, 517
`GetClassName` ObjectWindows
    function, 121, 240
`GetCount` ObjectWindows
    function, 339
`GetEditSel` ObjectWindows
    function, 379
`GetLine` ObjectWindows
    function, 246
`GetLineFromPos` ObjectWindows
    function, 247
`GetLineIndex` ObjectWindows
    function, 247
`GetLineLength` ObjectWindows
    function, 245
`GetNumLines` ObjectWindows
    function, 245-248
`GetPosition` ObjectWindows
    function 22, 325
`GetProfileString` API function, 208
`GetPrtDC` ObjectWindows
    function, 208
`GetRange` ObjectWindows function, 22, 325
`GetSelCount` ObjectWindows
    function, 339
`GetSelection` ObjectWindows
    function, 221, 246
`GetSelIndex` ObjectWindows
    function, 339
`GetSelIndexes` ObjectWindows
    function, 340
`GetSelString` ObjectWindows
    function, 340
`GetString` ObjectWindows
    function, 340

`GetStringLen` ObjectWindows
    function, 340
`GetSubText` ObjectWindows function, 221, 246
`GetText` ObjectWindows function, 24, 228, 244-245, 379-380
`GetTextLen` ObjectWindows function, 24, 228, 380
`GetTickCount` API function, 336
`getVar` ObjectWindows function, 241, 262-263
    protected, 400
`GetWindowClass` ObjectWindows
    function, 121-122, 132-133, 140, 240
`getY` ObjectWindows function, 240
`GetY` private ObjectWindows
    function, 239
`good` ObjectWindows function, 533
Graphics Device Interface (GDI)
    functions, 42-43
group box controls, 296-298
    `BUTTON` registration class, 586
    defining resources, 590-591
`Group` data member, 30
`GROUPBOX` statement, 590-591
grouping
    check boxes, 291
    controls, 28

H

`H` data member, 115-116
`HANDLE` data type, 4, 62
`HandleAddStrBtn` ObjectWindows
    function, 354
`HandleAngleMode` ObjectWindows
    function, 320
`HandleButton1Btn` ObjectWindows
    function, 289
`HandleCalcBtn` ObjectWindows
    function, 279, 319, 397-398
`HandleCityLst` ObjectWindows
    function, 365

INDEX

HandleCloseAllBtn ObjectWindows function, 432
HandleCloseBtn ObjectWindows function, 432
HandleCountryLst ObjectWindows function, 365
HandleDegreeRbt ObjectWindows function, 320
HandleDelStrBtn ObjectWindows function, 354
HandleExitBtn ObjectWindows function, 279, 336, 399, 566-567
HandleGetIndicesBtn ObjectWindows function, 377
HandleGetNamesBtn ObjectWindows function, 376
HandleGetSelIdxBtn ObjectWindows function, 355
HandleGetSelStrBtn ObjectWindows function, 354-355
HandleGetStrBtn ObjectWindows function, 355
HandleGradianRbt ObjectWindows function, 320
HandleLowerCase ObjectWindows function, 528
HandleMember1Btn ObjectWindows function, 430
HandleMember2Btn ObjectWindows function, 430
HandleMember3Btn ObjectWindows function, 430
HandleOperatorCmb ObjectWindows function, 397
HandleRadianRbt ObjectWindows function, 320
HandleReadBtn ObjectWindows function, 559-560
handles
    HBRUSH, 125
    HCURSOR, 124
    HICON, 123
HandleScrollScr ObjectWindows function, 365
HandleSendBtn ObjectWindows function, 431-432, 478-479
HandleSetIndicesBtn ObjectWindows function, 377-378
HandleSetNamesBtn ObjectWindows function, 376-377
HandleSetSelIdxBtn ObjectWindows function, 355
HandleSetSelStrBtn ObjectWindows function, 355
HandleStartBtn ObjectWindows function, 335
HandleStoreBtn ObjectWindows function, 279, 399
HandleTimeScr ObjectWindows function, 336
HandleToggle1Btn ObjectWindows function, 289
HandleToggleAllBtn ObjectWindows function, 289
HandleUpperCaseBtn ObjectWindows function, 528
HandleVariablesLst ObjectWindows function, 399
HandleWizardBtn ObjectWindows function, 430
Hardware API Windows Manager functions type, 41
HBRUSH handle, 125
HCURSOR handle, 124
HDC data type, 4
"Hello World" message application, 54-55
HICON handle, 123
HideList ObjectWindows function, 380
hierarchies of classes
    ObjectWindows, 6-39
    streamable, 531-541
HINSTANCE data type, 4, 62
history list boxes, 381-382
Hook API Windows Manager functions type, 42

hot keys
    & character, 227-228
    menu items, defining, 75
hPrevInstance data member, 95
HWND data type, 4

I

I/O, stream, 534-538
icon resource, 123-124
Id data member, 115
ID_FIRST constant, 55
ID_INTERNAL constant, 55
ID_XXXX constants, 267
IDABORT identifier, 48
IDC_ARROW cursor type value, 124
IDC_CROSS cursor type value, 124
IDC_IBEAM cursor type value, 124
IDC_ICON cursor type value, 124
IDC_SIZE cursor type value, 124
IDC_SIZENESW cursor type value, 124
IDC_SIZENS cursor type value, 124
IDC_SIZENWSE cursor type value, 125
IDC_SIZEWE cursor type value, 125
IDC_UPARROW cursor type value, 125
IDC_WAIT cursor type value, 125
IDCANCEL constant, 408
IDCANCEL identifier, 48
IDI_APPLICATION icon value, 123
IDI_ASTERISK icon value, 123
IDI_EXCLAMATION icon value, 123
IDI_HAND icon value, 123
IDI_QUESTION icon value, 123
IDIGNORE identifier, 48
IdleAction ObjectWindows
    function, 12
IDNO identifier, 48
IDOK
    constant, 408
    identifier, 48
IDRETRY identifier, 48
IDYES identifier, 48
ifpstream class, 540-541

inactive menu items, 76
incidental cursor change, 134
InError data member, 260
Information API Windows Manager
    functions type, 42
InitApplication ObjectWindows
    function, 11, 63
InitAppWindow ObjectWindows
    function, 320, 365, 397
initialization messages, 50
Initialization-file API system services
    interface functions type, 44
initializing
    City list box, 486
    window controls, 480-487
InitInstance ObjectWindows
    function, 11, 63-64, 192, 210,
    320, 365
InitMainWindow ObjectWindows
    function, 11, 64, 508, 517
InitMember ObjectWindows function,
    431-433
InitStringLst ObjectWindows
    function, 354
InitText ObjectWindows
    function, 528
Input API Windows Manager
    functions type, 41
input
    dialog boxes, 210, 487-493
        with scrolling, 173
    messages, 50-51
INPUTDIA.DLG program, 210
Insert ObjectWindows function, 249
InsertString ObjectWindows
    function, 340-341
int data type, 4
InvalidateRect API function, 112
iopstream class, 538
ipstream class, 534-536
isA ObjectWindows function, 8-10
IsCurrentDefPB data member, 29
    protected, 264

`IsDef` public data member, 264
`IsDefPB` data member, 29
`IsModified` ObjectWindows function, 247
`IsReplaceOp` data member, 32
`IsVisibleRect` ObjectWindows function, 184
`IsWindowEnabled` API function, 265
`IsWindowVisible` API function, 265
iterated functions, 317-318
iterators, `ForEach`, 365

J-K

justifying text
    centered, 588-589
    left, 587-588
    right, 588
keys
    accelerator, defining, 76-77
    hot
        & character, 227-228
        for menu items, 75
keywords
    `CONTROL`, 408, 457-461
    `CTEXT`, 408

L

`LBN_CHANGE` message, 343
`LBN_DBLCLK` message, 343
`LBN_ERRSPACE` message, 343
`LBN_KILLFOCUS` message, 343, 381
`LBN_SETFOCUS` message, 343
`LBS_EXTENDESEL` style, 337
`LBS_MULTICOLUMN` style, 337
`LBS_MULTIPLESEL` style, 337
`LBS_NOINTEGRALHEIGHT` style, 337
`LBS_NOREDRAW` style, 337
`LBS_NOTIFY` style, 337
`LBS_SORT` style, 337-338
`LBS_STANDARD` style, 337-338
`LBS_WANTKEYBOARDINPUT` style, 338

Line-output API GDI functions type, 43
`LINE_INCR` constant, 106
`LineHeight` data member, 170
`LineMagnitude` data member, 22, 324
`Lines` data member, 111
`__link` macro, 542
list box controls, 25-26, 336-342
    defining resources, 590
    list manipulation tester, 344-355
    `LISTBOX` registration class, 586
    responding to notification messages, 342-344
    transfer buffer types, 446-448
list boxes
    City, initializing, 486
    history, 381-382
    multiple-selection, 365-378
    single-selection, 344-355
    synchronized scrolling (CTLLST3.CPP, CTLLST3.EXE, DIALOG8.CPP), 356-365, 480-487
list manipulation tester (CTLLST2.CPP, CTLLST2.RC), 344-355
`LISTBOX`
    registration class, 586
    statement, 590
`ListBoxData` data member, 446-447
Listing 2.1. The source code in the MINWINAP.CPP file., 67-68
Listing 2.2. The source code of file SECAPP.CPP., 70-72
Listing 2.3. The source code for the MENU1.RC resource file., 78-79
Listing 2.4. The contents of the MENUS.H header file., 79
Listing 2.5. The source code of the MENU1.CPP., 79-81
Listing 2.6. The resource script in file MENU2.RC., 82-83

ObjectWindows Library

Listing 2.7. The contents of the MENU2.H header file., 84
Listing 2.8. The source code in the file MENU2.CPP., 84-87
Listing 2.9. The resource script in file MENU3.RC., 89-90
Listing 2.10. The source code for the file MENU3.CPP., 91-94
Listing 2.11. The source code for the MENU4.CPP program file., 97-98
Listing 3.1. The script for the resource file WINDOW1.RC., 103
Listing 3.2. The source code for the WINDOW1.CPP program file., 103-105
Listing 3.3. The script for the resource file WINDOW2.RC., 107
Listing 3.4. The source code for the WINDOW2.CPP program file., 108-110
Listing 3.5. The source code for the WINDOW3.CPP program file., 117-119
Listing 3.6. The source code for the WINDOW4.H header file., 126
Listing 3.7. The script for the resource file WINDOW4.RC., 126-127
Listing 3.8. The source code for the WINDOW4.CPP program file., 127-132
Listing 3.9. The source code for the WINDOW5.CPP program file., 134-139
Listing 3.10. The source code for the WINOBJ1.CPP program file., 143-148
Listing 3.11. The source code for the WINSCRL1.CPP program file., 152-154
Listing 3.12. The source code for the WINSCRL2.H header file., 157
Listing 3.13. The script of the resource file WINSCRL2.RC., 157
Listing 3.14. The source code for the WINSCRL2.CPP program file., 157-161
Listing 3.15. The source code for the WINSCRL3.H heading file., 163
Listing 3.16. The script for the resource file WINSCRL3.RC., 163
Listing 3.17. The source code for the WINSCRL3.CPP program file., 164-170
Listing 3.18. The source code for the WINSCRL4.H header file., 173
Listing 3.19. The script for the WINSCRL4.RC resource file., 173-174
Listing 3.20. The source code for the WINSCRL4.CPP program file., 174-182
Listing 4.1. The script of the resource file WINEDIT1.RC., 190
Listing 4.2. The source code for the WINEDIT1.CPP program file., 190-192
Listing 4.3. The source code for the WINEDIT2.H header file., 194
Listing 4.4. The script for the WINEDIT2.RC resource file., 194-195
Listing 4.5. The source code for the WINEDIT2.CPP program file., 195-200
Listing 4.6. The source code for the WINEDIT3.H header file., 203
Listing 4.7. The script of the WINEDIT3.RC resource file., 203
Listing 4.8. The source code for the WINEDIT3.CPP program file., 203-207
Listing 4.9. The source code for the WINFILE1.RC resource file., 210

INDEX

Listing 4.10. The source code for the WINFILE1.CPP program file., 210-212

Listing 4.11. The source code for the WINFILE2.H header file., 213

Listing 4.12. The script for the FILEMNU1.RC resource file., 214

Listing 4.13. The script for the WINFILE2.RC resource file., 214-215

Listing 4.14. The source code for the WINFILE2.CPP program file., 215-220

Listing 5.1. The script for the CTLSTAT1.RC resource file., 230

Listing 5.2. The source code for the CTLSTAT1.CPP program., 230-237

Listing 5.3. The source code for the CTLEDIT1.H header file., 252

Listing 5.4. The script for the CTLEDIT1.RC resource file., 252

Listing 5.5. The source code for theCTLEDIT1.CPP program file., 252-260

Listing 5.6. The source code for the CTLBTN1.H header file., 268

Listing 5.7. The script for the CTLBTN1.RC resource file., 268

Listing 5.8. The source code for the CTLBTN1.CPP program file., 268-278

Listing 5.9. The source code for the CTLBTN2.H header file., 282

Listing 5.10. The script for the CTLBTN2.RC resource file., 282

Listing 5.11. The source code for the CTLBTN2.CPP program file., 283-288

Listing 6.1. The source code for the CTLGRP1.H header file., 301

Listing 6.2. The script for the CTLGRP1.RC resource file., 301-302

Listing 6.3. The source code for the CTLGRP1.CPP program file., 302-317

Listing 7.1. The source code for the CTLLST1.H header file., 329

Listing 7.2. The script for the CTLLST1.RC resource file., 329

Listing 7.3. The source code for the CTLLST1.CPP program file., 329-334

Listing 7.4. The script for the CTLLST2.RC resource file., 346

Listing 7.5. The source code for the CTLLST2.CPP program file., 346-353

Listing 7.6. The source code for the CTLLST3.CPP program file., 358-364

Listing 7.7. The source code for the CTLLST4.CPP program file., 368-375

Listing 7.8. The source code for the CTLLST5.H header file., 384

Listing 7.9. The script for the CTLLST5.RC resource file., 384

Listing 7.10. The source code for the CTLLST5.CPP program file., 384-396

Listing 8.1. The script for the DIALOG1.RC resource file., 407-408

Listing 8.2. The source code for the DIALOG1.CPP program file., 409-410

Listing 8.3. The source code for the Ok, Cancel, WMClose, CloseWindow, and ShutDown member functions of the TDialog class., 411-412

Listing 8.4. The script for the DIALOG2.RC resource file., 414

Listing 8.5. The source code for the DIALOG2.CPP program file., 415-418

613

Guide to ObjectWindows Library

Listing 8.6. The source code for the DIALOG3.H header file., 421
Listing 8.7. The script for the DIALOG3.RC resource file., 422
Listing 8.8. The source code for the DIALOG3.CPP program file., 423-429
Listing 8.9. The alternative version for the InitMember member function if resources were used to create the dialog box controls., 432-433
Listing 8.10. The source code for the DIALOG4.H header file., 434
Listing 8.11. The script for the DIALOG4.RC resource file., 435
Listing 8.12. The source code for the DIALOG4.CPP program file., 435-445
Listing 8.13. The Transfer member functions for various controls., 448-452
Listing 8.14. The source code for the DIALOG5.H header file., 455
Listing 8.15. The script for the DIALOG5.RC resource file., 456-457
Listing 8.16. The source code for the DIALOG5.CPP program file., 458-461
Listing 8.17. The source code for the DIALOG6.H header file., 463
Listing 8.18. The script for the DIALOG6.RC resource file., 463-464
Listing 8.19. The source code for the DIALOG6.CPP program file., 465-468
Listing 8.20. The source code for the DIALOG7.H header file., 470-471
Listing 8.21. The script for the DIALOG7.RC resource file., 471-472
Listing 8.22. The source code for the DIALOG7.CPP program file., 472-478
Listing 8.23. The source code for the DIALOG8.CPP program file., 480-486
Listing 8.24. The source code for the DIALOG9.H header file., 488
Listing 8.25. The script for the DIALOG9.RC resource file., 489
Listing 8.26. The source code for the DIALOG9.CPP program file., 490-492
Listing 8.27. The source code for the DIALOG10.H header file., 495
Listing 8.28. The script for the DIALOG10.RC resource file., 495-496
Listing 8.29. The source code for the DIALOG10.CPP program file., 496-498
Listing 9.1. The source code for the MDIWIN1.H header file., 512
Listing 9.2. The script for the MDIWIN1.RC resource file., 512
Listing 9.3. The source code for the MDIWIN1.CPP program file., 513-517
Listing 9.4. The source code for the MDIWIN2.H header file., 520
Listing 9.5. The script for the MDIWIN2.RC resource file., 520-521
Listing 9.6. The source code for the MDIWIN2.CPP program file., 521-527
Listing 10.1. The source code for the write member function for the TWindowsObject, TWindow, and TDialog classes., 544-545
Listing 10.2. The source code for the read member function for the TWindowsObject, TWindow, and TDialog classes., 546-548

Listing 10.3. The source code for the STRM1.CPP program., 550-557
Listing 10.4. The source code for the STRM2.H header file., 561
Listing 10.5. The source code for the STRM2A.CPP program file., 561-566
Listing 10.6. The script for the resource file STRM2B.RC., 568
Listing 10.7. The source code for the STRM2B.CPP program file., 568-576
`LoadCursor` API function, 139
`LoadIcon` API function, 123-124
`LONG` data type, 4
`long` data type, 4
`LowMemory` ObjectWindows function, 10
`LParam` data member, 54
`LPSTR` data type, 4
`lpszMenuName` pointer, 126
`LPVOID` data type, 4
`LTEXT` statement, 587-588

M

macros
   `_CLASSDEF`, 9, 70, 148
   `_CLASSTYPE` identifier, 8
   `_EXPORT`, 10
   `_FAR`, 9
   `__link`, 542
`MAINMENU` menu resource, 111, 289
MakeWindow ObjectWindows function, 10, 17, 142, 148, 419
Mapping API GDI functions type, 43
`MAX_MEM` constant, 194
`MAX_MEM_LEN` constant, 194
`MaxLines` data member, 170
MDI (Multiple Document Interface) applications, 34
   building basics, 504-505
   child windows, 510

client windows, 36-37, 509-510
components and features, 503-504
frame windows, 34-36, 505-508
messages, 53
   managing, 510
text viewer program, 511-518
   revised, 518-529
MDIWIN1.CPP program, (text viewer), 513-517
MDIWIN1.EXE program, (text viewer), 511
MDIWIN1.H program, (text viewer), 512
MDIWIN1.RC program, (text viewer), 512
MDIWIN2.CPP program, (text viewer), 521-527
MDIWIN2.EXE program, (text viewer), 519
MDIWIN2.H program, (text viewer), 520
MDIWIN2.RC program, (text viewer), 520-521
Memory-management API system services interface functions type, 44
`memoryStr` protected data member, 201
Menu API Windows Manager functions type, 41
`Menu` data member, 115-116
`MENU` statement, 74-75, 583-584
MENU1.CPP program, (nested menu), 79-81
MENU1.RC program, (nested menu), 77-79
MENU2.CPP program, (long/short menus), 84-87
MENU2.EXE program, (long/short menus), 88
MENU2.H program, (long/short menus), 84

MENU2.PRJ program, (long/short menus), 88
MENU2.RC program, (long/short menus), 81-83
MENU3.CPP program, (multiple instances), 91-94
MENU3.EXE program, (multiple instances), 95
MENU3.RC program, (multiple instances), 89-90
MENU4.CPP program, (closing window), 97-98
`MENUITEM SEPARATOR` statement, 76
`MENUITEM` statement, 75
menus
   accelerators, defining, 76-77
   adding to applications, 72-74
   attached to dialog boxes, 583-584
   attributes, defining, 75
   inactive items, 76
   item names, defining, 75
   nested, 79-81
   pop-up, 76
   resource contents, defining, 74-75
   responding to item selections, 81-88
MENUS.H program, 79
Message API Windows Manager functions type, 41
`Message` data member, 53
`MessageBeep` API function, 45-46
`MessageBox` API function, 45-48
`MessageLoop` ObjectWindows function, 11, 64-65
messages, 48-49
   button, handling, 264
   check box, responding to, 294
   Clipboard, 51
   combo box notification, 381
      `LBN_KILLFOCUS`, 381
   control
      manipulation, 52
      notification, 52
   group box, responding to, 297-298
   "Hello World", 54-55
   initialization, 50
   input, 50-51
   list box notification, 343
   MDI (Multiple Document Interface), 53
      managing, 510
   nonclient area, 52
   responding to, 53-56
   scroll bar notification, 52, 326
   sending, 56-57
   system, 51
      information, 52
   user-defined, 57
   Windows-management, 49-50
Metafile API GDI functions type, 43
minimal ObjectWindows application (MINWINAP.CPP, MINWINAP.EXE, MINWINAP.PRJ, OWL.DEL), 66-68
MINWINAP.CPP program, (minimal ObjectWindows application), 67-68
MINWINAP.EXE program, (minimal ObjectWindows application), 67-68
MINWINAP.PRJ program, (minimal ObjectWindows application), 67
modal dialog boxes
   data transfer
      (DIALOG5.CPP, DIALOG5.EXE, DIALOG5.H, DIALOG5.RC), 454-462
      (DIALOG6.CPP, DIALOG6.H, DIALOG6.RC), 462-469

INDEX

executing, 404-413
Wizard, 419
modeless dialog boxes
  creating, 418-433
  data transfer (DIALOG7.CPP, DIALOG7.EXE, DIALOG7.H, DIALOG7.RC), 469-479
modern/old English dialog boxes (DIALOG1.CPP, DIALOG1.RC, DIALOG2.CPP, DIALOG2.RC), 405-418
modes, auto scroll and track, 150, 155-161
Module-management API system services interface functions type, 44
mouse, displaying message boxes when clicking, 69-72
MoveToLine static local variable, 183
MSG_XXXX data members, 260
multiline edit control styles, 243
Multiple Document Interface, *see* MDI
multiple instances, running, 89-95
multiple-selection list tester (CTLLST4.CPP, CTLLST4.EXE), 366-378

N

nameOf ObjectWindows function, 8-10
naming menu items, 75
nested menus, 79-81
NEW dialog box resource, 408
NEWFRAME command, 208
NF_FIRST constant, 55
NF_INTERNAL constant, 56
nonclient area messages, 52
NotifyParent data member, 296-297
notImplemented private ObjectWindows function, 88

number guessing game (DIALOG9.CPP, DIALOG9.EXE, DIALOG9.H, DIALOG9.RC), 488-493
NumHelpWindows data member, 148
numStrings data member, 111

O

Object class, 8-9
ObjectWindows
  functions
    AddString, 338
    AMemberBtn, 430
    AssignMenu, 78, 103, 115
    bad, 533
    BNClicked, 30-31
    build, 543, 559
    Cancel, 411-413, 478
    CanClose, 96-99, 410, 413, 518, 528
    Check, 293
    Clear, 228, 248, 379, 533
    ClearCheckBoxes, 318
    ClearEditControls, 317-318
    ClearList, 338
    ClearModify, 247
    close, 534
    CloseChildren, 517
    CloseWindow, 411-413
    CMArrangeIcons, 507
    CMAutoScroll, 161
    CMBlockLower, 221
    CMBlockPrint, 221
    CMBlockUpper, 221
    CMCalc, 261-262
    CMCalcBtn, 279, 399
    CMCalculate, 200-201
    CMCascadeChildren, 507
    CMClear, 112, 528
    CMClearBox, 319
    CMClearChk, 319

617

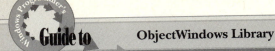
ObjectWindows Library

CMCloseChildren, 507
CMCountChildren, 517
CMDialog, 462, 469, 479
CMDisableAllBtn, 266
CMEditClear, 241, 244
CMEditCopy, 88, 242-244
CMEditCut, 88, 244
CMEditDelete, 244
CMEditPaste, 88, 241-244
CMEditUndo, 244
CMExit, 88
CMExitBtn, 279, 336, 399
CmFileStat, 498-500
CMGame, 492-493
CMHelp, 88, 148
CMHelp1, 133
CMHelp2, 133
CMLongMenu, 88
CMLowerCase, 528
CMPrint, 207-208
CMRcl1, 201
CMRcl2, 201
CMReset, 528
CMScrollToBottom, 182-183
CMScrollToLine, 182-183
CMScrollToTop, 182-183
CMSelectSet*x* family, 170-171
CMSendBtn, 478
CMShortMenu, 88
CMStartBtn, 336
CMSto1, 201
CMSto2, 201
CMStore, 262
CMStoreBtn, 279, 399
CMTileChildren, 507
CMTrackMode, 161
CMUpperCase, 528
CM*xxxx* family, 32-33
Create, 21, 419
CreateChild, 517
DeleteLine, 248

DeleteSelection, 248
DeleteString, 338
DeleteSubText, 248-249
DeltaPos, 23, 325
Destroy, 17
DisableButton, 279
DisabledButton, 266
DisableTransfer, 453
DoSearch, 32
EnableButton, 279
EnableTransfer, 453
eof, 533
ExecDialog, 183, 405, 411
Execute, 10, 16, 405
ExecuteDialog, 10, 16, 405
fail, 533
FindExactString, 338-339
FindString, 339
freadString, 536
fwriteString, 538
GetCheck, 293
GetChildCount, 517
GetClassName, 121, 240
GetCount, 339
GetEditSel, 379
GetLine, 246
GetLineFromPos, 247
GetLineIndex, 247
GetLineLength, 245
GetNumLines, 245-248
GetPosition, 22, 325
GetPrtDC, 208
GetRange, 22, 325
GetSelCount, 339
GetSelection, 221, 246
GetSelIndex, 339
GetSelIndexes, 340
GetSelString, 340
GetString, 340
GetStringLen, 340
GetSubText, 221, 246

INDEX

GetText, 24, 228, 244-245, 379-380
GetTextLen, 24, 228, 380
getVar, 241, 262-263, 400
GetWindowClass, 121-122, 132-133, 140, 240
getY, 240
GetY, 239
good, 533
HandleAddStrBtn, 354
HandleAngleMode, 320
HandleButton1Btn, 289
HandleCalcBtn, 279, 319, 397-398
HandleCityLst, 365
HandleCloseAllBtn, 432
HandleCloseBtn, 432
HandleCountryLst, 365
HandleDegreeRbt, 320
HandleDelStrBtn, 354
HandleExitBtn, 279, 336, 399, 566-567
HandleGetIndicesBtn, 377
HandleGetNamesBtn, 376
HandleGetSelIdxBtn, 355
HandleGetSelStrBtn, 354-355
HandleGetStrBtn, 355
HandleGradianRbt, 320
HandleLowerCase, 528
HandleMember1Btn, 430
HandleMember2Btn, 430
HandleMember3Btn, 430
HandleOperatorCmb, 397
HandleRadianRbt, 320
HandleReadBtn, 559-560
HandleScrollScr, 365
HandleSendBtn, 431-432, 478-479
HandleSetIndicesBtn, 377-378
HandleSetNamesBtn, 376-377
HandleSetSelIdxBtn, 355

HandleSetSelStrBtn, 355
HandleStartBtn, 335
HandleStoreBtn, 279, 399
HandleTimeScr, 336
HandleToggle1Btn, 289
HandleToggleAllBtn, 289
HandleUpperCaseBtn, 528
HandleVariablesLst, 399
HandleWizardBtn, 430
HideList, 380
IdleAction, 12
InitApplication, 11, 63
InitAppWindow, 320, 365, 397
InitInstance, 11, 63-64, 192, 210, 320, 365
InitMainWindow, 11, 64, 508, 517
InitMember, 431-433
InitStringLst, 354
InitText, 528
Insert, 249
InsertString, 340-341
isA, 8-10
IsModified, 247
IsVisibleRect, 184
LowMemory, 10
MakeWindow, 10, 17, 142, 148, 419
message response, 54
MessageLoop, 11, 64-65
nameOf, 8-10
notImplemented, 88
Ok, 411-413
OK virtual, 478
open, 534
Paint, 102-106, 112, 148, 170, 184
PrintPage, 208-209
ProcessAppMsg, 12
ProcessDlgMsg, 12
promptToQuit, 88

619

ObjectWindows Library

putVar, 263, 400
rdbuf, 539
read, 558-559
read protected virtual, 546-548
readByte, 536
readBytes, 536
readData, 536
readString, 536
readWord, 536
RestoreMemory, 10
Run, 12, 63-65
SB*xxxx* family, 23
scroll bar notification
   response, 326-327
ScrollBy, 172
ScrollDownBy, 183-184
ScrollTo, 172
ScrollUpBy, 183-184
Search, 248
seekg, 536
seekp, 538
selectCursor, 140
SelectionChanged, 28, 298
selectNextCursor, 140
selectPrevCursor, 140
SetCheck, 294
SetEditSel, 380
SetPageSize, 162
SetPosition, 23, 325
SetRange, 23, 162, 324
SetSelection, 249
SetSelIndex, 341
SetSelIndexes, 341-342
SetSelString, 342
SetSelStrings, 342
SetText, 24, 228, 249, 380
SetUnits, 162
SetupWindow, 508
ShowList, 380
ShutDown, 411-412
ShutDownWindow, 413, 419

Sto, 201
streamableName, 548
TEdit class text-editing, 244
tellg, 536
Toggle, 293-294
ToggleButton, 289
Transfer virtual, 448-452
TransferData, 453, 488
Uncheck, 293
ValidWindow, 10
WMClose, 411-413
WMLButtonDown, 70-72, 111,
   261, 279
WMMouseMove message
   response, 140
WMMove, 139
WMRButtonDown, 70-72
WMSize, 162
WMSize virtual, 162
WM*xxxx* family, 32
write, 558
write protected virtual,
   544-545
writeByte, 538
writeBytes, 538
writeData, 538
writeRandomData, 559
writeString, 538
writeWord, 538
hierarchy of classes, 6-7
   Object, 8-9
   TApplication, 10-12
   TButton, 28
   TCheckBox, 29-30
   TComboBox, 26-28
   TControl, 21
   TDialog, 15-17
   TEdit, 24-25
   TEditWindow, 31-32
   TFileDialog, 17
   TFileWindow, 33

TGroupBox, 28
TInputDialog, 18
TListBox, 25-26
TMDIClient, 36-37
TMDIFrame, 34-36
TModule, 9-10
TRadioButton, 30-31
TScrollBar, 22-23
TScroller, 37-39
TSearchDialog, 18-19
TStatic, 23-24
TWindow, 19-21
TWindowsObject, 12-15
minimal application (MINWINAP.CPP, MINWINAP.EXE, MINWINAP.PRJ, OWL.DEL), 66-68
ofpstream class, 539
Ok ObjectWindows function, 411-413
OK virtual ObjectWindows function, 478
OLD dialog box resource, 408
old English/modern dialog boxes (DIALOG1.CPP, DIALOG1.RC, DIALOG2.CPP, DIALOG2.RC), 405-418
Open and Save file dialog box, 210
open ObjectWindows function, 534
operators
    << stream, 39-40
        declaring, 548-549
        friend, 538
    >> stream, 39-40
        declaring, 548-549
        friend, 536
    bitwise OR, combining window styles, 113
opstream class, 536-538
Optimization-tool API system services interface functions type, 45

OS interrupt API system services interface functions type, 44
OWL.DEF program, 67, 70
OWL.H program, 68

P

PageMagnitude data member, 22, 324
Paint ObjectWindows function, 102-106, 112, 148, 170
    optimizing, 184
Painting API Windows Manager functions type, 41
Param data member, 115
PCchar data type, 6
PCclass data-typing convention, 5
Pchar data type, 6
Pclass data-typing convention, 5
PCvoid data type, 6
persistent streams, 531
Pint data type, 6
POINT structure, 5, 557
pointers
    ActiveChild, 507
    ATextString, 228, 245
    ATitle, 226, 227
    bp, 533
    Buffer, 488
    ClientWnd, 507
    ComboBoxData, 447
    DataPtr, 448, 557
    ListBoxData, 446
    lpszMenuName, 126
    Prompt, 488
    PTButton, 283
    TextBox, 518
    TransferBuffer, 452
    types, 533
polygons, plotting, 45-48
Polyline API function, 45-46
pop-up menus, 76

ObjectWindows Library

`POPUP` statement, 76
positional cursor change, 134
`PostMessage` API function, 56
pound sign (#) character, 300
Printer-control API GDI functions type, 43
Printer-escape API GDI functions type, 43
PRINTER.H program, 209
printing typewriter memos, 202-209
`PrintPage` ObjectWindows function, 208-209
`ProcessAppMsg` ObjectWindows function, 12
`ProcessDlgMsg` ObjectWindows function, 12
producer programs (STRM2.CPP, STRM2.H), 560-567
programs
   consumer, 560, 567-577
   CTLBTN1.CPP (COCA), 268-278
   CTLBTN1.H (COCA), 268
   CTLBTN1.RC (COCA), 267-268
   CTLBTN2.CPP (button manipulation tester), 283-288
   CTLBTN2.EXE (button manipulation tester), 280-281
   CTLBTN2.H (button manipulation tester), 282
   CTLBTN2.RC (button manipulation tester), 282
   CTLEDIT1.CPP (COCA), 252-260
   CTLEDIT1.H (COCA), 252
   CTLEDIT1.RC (COCA), 252
   CTLGRP1.CPP (COCA), 302-317
   CTLGRP1.H (COCA), 301
   CTLGRP1.RC (COCA), 301-302
   CTLLST1.CPP (countdown timer application), 329-334
   CTLLST1.H (countdown timer application), 329
   CTLLST1.RC (countdown timer application), 329
   CTLLST2.CPP (list manipulation tester), 346-353
   CTLLST2.RC (list manipulation tester), 346
   CTLLST3.CPP (synchronized lists), 358-364
   CTLLST3.EXE (synchronized lists), 356-358
   CTLLST4.CPP (multiple-selection list tester), 368-375
   CTLLST4.EXE (multiple-selection list tester), 366-368
   CTLLST5.CPP (COCA), 384-396
   CTLLST5.EXE (COCA), 382-383
   CTLLST5.H (COCA), 384
   CTLLST5.RC (COCA), 384
   CTLSTAT1.CPP (static text sampler), 230-237
   CTLSTAT1.EXE (static text sampler), 237
   CTLSTAT1.RC (static text sampler), 229-230
   DIALOG.CPP, 411
   DIALOG1.CPP (modern/old English dialog boxes), 409-410
   DIALOG1.RC (modern/old English dialog boxes), 407-408
   DIALOG2.CPP (modern/old English dialog boxes), 415-418
   DIALOG2.RC (modern/old English dialog boxes), 414
   DIALOG3.CPP (modeless dialog boxes), 423-429
   DIALOG3.H (modeless dialog boxes), 421
   DIALOG3.RC (modeless dialog boxes), 422
   DIALOG4.CPP (COCA), 435-445
   DIALOG4.H (COCA), 434

INDEX

DIALOG4.RC (COCA), 435
DIALOG5.CPP (modal dialog box data transfer), 458-461
DIALOG5.EXE (modal dialog box data transfer), 454, 455
DIALOG5.H (modal dialog box data transfer), 455
DIALOG5.RC (modal dialog box data transfer), 456-457
DIALOG6.CPP (modal dialog box data transfer), 465-468
DIALOG6.H (modal dialog box data transfer), 463
DIALOG6.RC (modal dialog box data transfer), 463-464
DIALOG7.CPP (modeless dialog box data transfer), 472-478
DIALOG7.EXE (modeless dialog box data transfer), 469
DIALOG7.H (modeless dialog box data transfer), 470-471
DIALOG7.RC (modeless dialog box data transfer), 471-472
DIALOG8.CPP (synchronized lists), 480-486
DIALOG9.CPP (number guessing game), 490-492
DIALOG9.EXE (number guessing game), 488
DIALOG9.H (number guessing game), 488
DIALOG9.RC (number guessing game), 489
DIALOG10.CPP (file statistics), 496-498
DIALOG10.EXE (file statistics), 494-495
DIALOG10.H (file statistics), 495
DIALOG10.RC (file statistics), 495-496
EDITACC.RC, 210
EDITMENU.RC, 210
FILEACC.RC, 210
FILEDIAL.DLG, 210
FILEMENU.RC, 210
FILEMNU1.RC, 214
INPUTDIA.DLG, 210
MDI, *see* MDI
MDIWIN1.CPP (text viewer), 513-517
MDIWIN1.EXE (text viewer), 511
MDIWIN1.H (text viewer), 512
MDIWIN1.RC (text viewer), 512
MDIWIN2.CPP (text viewer), 521-527
MDIWIN2.EXE (text viewer), 519
MDIWIN2.H (text viewer), 520
MDIWIN2.RC (text viewer), 520-521
MENU1.CPP (nested menu), 79-81
MENU1.RC (nested menu), 77-79
MENU2.CPP (long/short menus), 84-87
MENU2.EXE (long/short menus), 88
MENU2.H (long/short menus), 84
MENU2.PRJ (long/short menus), 88
MENU2.RC (long/short menus), 81-83
MENU3.CPP (multiple instances), 91-94
MENU3.EXE (multiple instances), 95
MENU3.RC (multiple instances), 89-90
MENU4.CPP (closing window), 97-98

 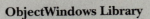

ObjectWindows Library

MENUS.H, 79
MINWINAP.CPP (minimal ObjectWindows application), 67-68
MINWINAP.EXE (minimal ObjectWindows application), 67-68
MINWINAP.PRJ (minimal ObjectWindows application), 67
OWL.DEF, 67, 70
OWL.H, 68
PRINTER.H, 209
producer, 560-567
SECAPP.CPP, 70-72
SECAPP.EXE, 70-72
SECAPP.PRJ, 70
self-contained, 193
STDWNDS.DLG, 210
STRM1.CPP (streamable class), 550-557
STRM1.EXE (streamable class), 550
STRM2.CPP (producer program), 561-566
STRM2.H (producer program), 561
STRM2B.CPP (consumer program), 568-576
STRM2B.EXE (consumer program), 567
STRM2B.RC (consumer program), 568
WINDOW1.CPP, 103-105
WINDOW1.EXE, 106
WINDOW1.RC, 102-103
WINDOW2.CPP, 108-110
WINDOW2.EXE, 112
WINDOW2.RC, 107
WINDOW3.CPP, 116-119
WINDOW3.EXE, 120
WINDOW4.CPP (window class registration), 127-132
WINDOW4.EXE (window class registration), 133
WINDOW4.H (window class registration), 126
WINDOW4.RC (window class registration), 126-127
WINDOW5.CPP (changing cursor), 134-139
WINDOW5.EXE (changing cursor), 140
WINEDIT1.CPP (text editor), 190-192
WINEDIT1.RC (text editor), 190
WINEDIT2.CPP (free-form calculator), 195-200
WINEDIT2.EXE (free-form calculator), 201
WINEDIT2.H (free-form calculator), 194
WINEDIT2.RC (free-form calculator), 194-195
WINEDIT3.CPP (typewriter application), 203-207
WINEDIT3.EXE (typewriter application), 209
WINEDIT3.H (typewriter application), 203
WINEDIT3.RC (typewriter application), 203
WINFILE1.CPP (text editor), 210-212
WINFILE1.EXE (text editor), 212
WINFILE1.RC (text editor), 210
WINFILE2.CPP (enhanced text editor), 215-220
WINFILE2.EXE (enhanced text editor), 221

WINFILE2.H (enhanced text editor), 213
WINFILE2.RC (enhanced text editor), 214-215
WINOBJ1.CPP (child window creation), 142-147
WINOBJ1.EXE (child window creation), 149
WINSCRL1.CPP (scrolling window), 152-154
WINSCRL1.EXE (scrolling window), 155
WINSCRL2.CPP (toggle auto scroll/track modes), 157-161
WINSCRL2.EXE (toggle auto scroll/track modes), 161
WINSCRL2.H (toggle auto scroll/track modes), 157
WINSCRL2.RC (toggle auto scroll/track modes), 157
WINSCRL3.CPP (variant text), 164-170
WINSCRL3.EXE (variant text), 171
WINSCRL3.H (variant text), 163
WINSCRL3.RC (variant text), 163
WINSCRL4.CPP, 174-182
WINSCRL4.EXE, 184
WINSCRL4.H, 173
WINWSCRL4.RC, 173-174
Prompt data member, 488
promptToQuit private ObjectWindows function, 88
Property API Windows Manager functions type, 42
protected constructors for streamable classes, 543
pstream class, 532-533
PTButton pointer, 283

public constructors for streamable classes, 542
push button controls, 263-264
   button manipulation tester, 279-289
   BUTTON registration class, 586
   defining resources, 589-590
   handling button messages, 264
   in command-oriented calculator application (COCA), 266-279
   manipulating buttons, 265-266
PUSHBUTTON statement, 589
putVar ObjectWindows function, 263
   protected, 400
Pvoid data type, 6
PWORD data type, 4

Q

queries
   multiple list-box selections, 366-378
   normal and selected strings, 344-355
   ordinary and selected list members, 338-342
   text, 244-248

R

radio button controls, 30-31, 295-296
   BUTTON registration class, 586
   defining resources, 591
   transfer buffer types, 446-448
RadioButton data member, 448
RADIOBUTTON statement, 591
.RC file extension, 74
RCclass data-typing convention, 5
Rclass data-typing convention, 5

`RCObject` data type, 6
`rdbuf` ObjectWindows function, 539
`read` ObjectWindows function, 558-559
    protected virtual, 546-548
read-only text, displaying in windows, 101-106
`readByte` ObjectWindows function, 536
`readBytes` ObjectWindows function, 536
`readData` ObjectWindows function, 536
reading
    and writing objects to file streams, 539-540
    objects from file streams, 540-541
`readString` ObjectWindows function, 536
`readWord` ObjectWindows function, 536
`Receiver` data member, 53
`RECT` structure, 5
Rectangle API Windows Manager functions type, 42
Region API GDI functions type, 43
registering window classes, 120-133
registration classes
    controls names, 586
    of dialog boxes, 584
Replace dialog box, 210
resource files, minimizing contributions to dialog box definitions, 414-418
Resource-management API system services interfaces functions type, 44
resources, 73-74
    cursor, 124-125
    dialog box, 581-582
        controls, 585-592

    `NEW`, 408
    `OLD`, 408
    icon, 123-124
    menu
        building, 74-77
        `EXITMENU`, 103, 408
        `MAINMENU`, 111, 289
resource-tapping constructors, 432
`RestoreMemory` ObjectWindows function, 10
`Result` data member, 54
`Rint` data type, 6
`Ripstream` data type, 6
`Ropstream` data type, 6
`RPclass` data-typing convention, 5
`RPvoid` data type, 6
`RTEXT` statement, 588
`Run` ObjectWindows function, 12, 63-65

S

`SB_LINEDOWN` message, 326
`SB_LINEUP` message, 326
`SB_PAGEDOWN` message, 326
`SB_PAGEUP` message, 326
`SB_THUMBPOSITION` message, 326
`SB_THUMBTRACK` message, 326
`SBxxxx` member functions, 23
scroll bar controls, 323-326
    countdown timer application, 327-336
    defining resources, 592
    responding to notification messages, 326-327
    `SCROLLBAR` registration class, 586
    transfer buffer types, 446-448
scroll bar notification messages, 52
scroll bars, 22-23
    changing metrics, 162-171

INDEX

`Scroll->AutoMode` data member, 156
`Scroll->TrackMode` data member, 156
`SCROLLBAR` registration class, 586
`SCROLLBAR` statement, 592
`ScrollBarData` data member, 447-448
`ScrollBy` ObjectWindows function, 172
`ScrollDownBy` ObjectWindows function, 183-184
`Scroller` data member, 20, 37, 150
scrolling
    internally inducing, 172-184
    list boxes, synchronizing, 356-365, 480-487
    windows, 37-39, 149-155
Scrolling API Windows Manager functions type, 41
`ScrollTo` ObjectWindows function, 172
`ScrollUpBy` ObjectWindows function, 183-184
Search and Replace dialog boxes, 18-19, 499-500
`Search` ObjectWindows function, 248
searching and replacing text through Clipboard, 189-192
`SearchStruct` data member, 32, 189
SECAPP.CPP program, 70-72
SECAPP.EXE program, 70-72
SECAPP.PRJ program, 70
`seekg` ObjectWindows function, 536
`seekp` ObjectWindows function, 538
Segment API system services interface functions type, 44
`SelCount` data member, 447
`selectCursor` protected ObjectWindows function, 140
`SelectionChanged` ObjectWindows function, 28, 298
`selectNextCursor` protected ObjectWindows function, 140

`selectPrevCursor` protected ObjectWindows function, 140
self-contained programs, 193
`SendDlgItemMessage` API function, 56-57
`SendMessage` API function, 56
`SetCheck` ObjectWindows function, 294
`SetCursor` API function, 139
`SetEditSel` ObjectWindows function, 380
`SetOfLinesIndex` data member, 170
`SetPageSize` ObjectWindows function, 162
`SetPosition` ObjectWindows function, 23, 325
`SetRange` ObjectWindows function, 23, 162, 324
`SetSelection` ObjectWindows function, 249
`SetSelIndex` ObjectWindows function, 341
`SetSelIndexes` ObjectWindows function, 341-342
`SetSelString` ObjectWindows function, 342
`SetSelStrings` ObjectWindows function, 342
`SetText` ObjectWindows function, 24, 228, 249, 380
`SetUnits` ObjectWindows function, 162
`SetupWindow` ObjectWindows function, 508
short data type, 4
`ShowList` ObjectWindows function, 380
`ShowWindow` API function, 265, 419
`ShutDown` ObjectWindows function, 411-412

627

ShutDownWindow ObjectWindows function, 413, 419
simple combo boxes, 378
Sound API system services interface functions type, 45
SS_BLACKFRAME static text style value, 227
SS_BLACKRECT static text style value, 227
SS_CENTER static text style value, 227
SS_GRAYFRAME static text style value, 227
SS_GRAYRECT static text style value, 227
SS_LEFT static text style value, 227
SS_LEFTNOWORDWRAP static text style value, 227
SS_NOPREFIX static text style value, 227
SS_RIGHT static text style value, 227
SS_SIMPLE static text style value, 227
STARTDOC command, 208
state data member, 533
statements
    ACCELERATORS, 76-77
    CAPTION, 583
    CHECKBOX, 589
    CLASS, 584
    COMBOBOX, 592
    CONTROL, 585-587
    CTEXT, 588-589
    DEFPUSHBUTTON, 590
    DIALOG, 581-582
    DIALOG option, 582-585
    EDITTEXT, 591-592
    FONT, 584-585
    GROUPBOX, 590-591
    LISTBOX, 590
    LTEXT, 587-588
    MENU, 74-75, 583-584
    MENUITEM, 75
    MENUITEM SEPARATOR, 76
    POPUP, 76
    PUSHBUTTON, 589
    RADIOBUTTON, 591
    RTEXT, 588
    SCROLLBAR, 592
    STYLE, 583
    WinApp.Run, 63
static text controls, 225-242
    STATIC registration class, 586
    text
        centered, 588-589
        flush left, 587-588
        flush right, 588
    transfer buffer types, 446-448
static text objects, 23-24
static text sampler (CTLSTAT1.CPP, CTLSTAT1, EXE, CTLSTAT1.RC), 228-242
StaticText data member, 446
STDWNDS.DLG program, 210
Sto ObjectWindows function, 201
stream
    managers, registering streamable classes with, 549
    operators, *see* << operators, >> operators
streamable classes (STRM1.CPP, STRM1.EXE), 549-560
    creating, 541-549
    hierarchy, 531-532
        fpbase, 534
        fpstream, 539-540
        ifpstream, 540-541
        iopstream, 538
        ipstream, 534-536
        ofpstream, 539
        opstream, 536-538
        pstream, 532-533

streamableName private
   ObjectWindows function, 548
streams, 531
   constructing controls from,
      567-577
   file, 534
      reading and writing objects to,
         539-540
      reading objects from, 540-541
      writing objects to, 539
   I/O, 534-538
   persistent, 531
   storing controls in, 560-567
String-manipulation API system
   services interface functions
   type, 44
strings, querying normal and
   selected, 344-355
Strings data member, 447
STRM1.CPP program, (streamable
   class), 550-557
STRM1.EXE program, (streamable
   class), 550
STRM2.CPP program, (producer
   program), 561-566
STRM2.H program, (producer
   program), 561
STRM2B.CPP program, (consumer
   program), 568-576
STRM2B.EXE program, (consumer
   program), 567
STRM2B.RC program, (consumer
   program), 568
structures
   POINT, 5, 557
   RECT, 5
   TMessage, 53-54
   TSearchStruct, 19, 499
   WNDCLASS, 121-123
Style data member, 113-116, 150
STYLE statement, 583

styles
   check box control, 293
      overriding, 292
   combo box control, 379
   dialog box windows, 583
   list box control, 337-338
   radio button control, 295
   static text, 227
   window, 113-115
   window class, 122-123
synchronized lists (CTLLST3.CPP,
   CTLLST3.EXE, DIALOG8.CPP),
   356-365, 480-487
System API Windows Manager
   functions type, 42
system
   information messages, 52
   messages, 51
   services interface functions, 44-45

T

TAppDialog class
   constructor, 415
   DIALOG3.CPP program, 431-432
   DIALOG5.CPP program, 461
TApplication class, 10-12
TAppMDIChild class constructor, 518,
   527-528
TAppMDIFrame class, 517
TAppWindow class, 69-72, 148
   constructor, 119-120, 161
   CTLBTN1.CPP program, 278
   CTLEDIT1.CPP program,
      260-263
   CTLGRP1.CPP program, 318-320
   CTLLST1.CPP program, 334-336
   CTLLST4.CPP program, 376
   CTLLST5.CPP program, 396-397
   CTLSTAT1.CPP program,
      239-241

ObjectWindows Library

DIALOG3.CPP program, 430
DIALOG5.CPP program, 461-462
DIALOG7.CPP program, 479
STRM2B.CPP program, 576-577
WINDOW1.CPP program, 103
WINDOW2.CPP program, 111-112
WINDOW5.CPP program, 139
WINSCRL1.CPP program, 154-155
WINSCRL3.CPP program, 170-171
Task API system services interface functions type, 44
`TButton` class, 28, 264
 button manipulation tester (CTLBTN2.CPP, CTLBTN2.EXE, CTLBTN2.H, CTLBTN2.RC), 279-289
 command-oriented calculator application (COCA) (CTLBTN1.CPP, CTLBTN1.H, CTLBTN1.RC), 266-279
 handling button messages, 264
 manipulating buttons, 265-266
`TCheckBox` class, 29-30, 292-294
`TChildWindow` class, 148
`TComboBox` class, 26-28, 378-380
`TComboBoxData` class, 447
`TControl` class, 21
`TDialog` class, 15-17
 constructing dialog boxes, 404
 minimizing resource file contributions, 414-418
 modal dialog boxes, 404-413
 modeless dialog boxes, 418-433
 `read` ObjectWindows function in, 546-548
 `write` ObjectWindows function in, 544-545
`TEdit` class, 24-25

command-oriented calculator application (COCA) (CTLEDIT1.CPP, CTLEDIT1.H, CTLEDIT1.RC), 249-263
 text-deleting functions, 248-249
 text-editing functions, 244
 text-inserting/overwriting functions, 249
`TEditWindow` class, 31-32
 application uses, 202
 basic text editor (WINEDIT1.CPP, WINEDIT1.RC), 189-192
 free-form calculator (WINEDIT2.CPP, WINEDIT2.EXE, WINEDIT2.H, WINEDIT2.RC), 192-201
 typewriter application (WINEDIT3.CPP, WINEDIT3.EXE, WINEDIT3.H, WINEDIT3.RC), 202-209
`tellg` ObjectWindows function, 536
templates
 application class derived from `TApplication`, 63, 66-68
 application instances derived from `TApplication`, 63
text
 deleting, 248-249
 dialog boxes
   fonts, 584-585
   for inputting, 18
 editing, menu-driven commands, 244
 handling in files, 33
 inserting and overwriting, 249
 queries, 244-248
 read-only, displaying in windows, 101-106
 scrolling, 149-155

INDEX

static
   centered, 588-589
   controls, *see* static text controls
   flush left, 587-588
   flush right, 588
   objects, 23-24
   variant (WINSCRL3.CPP, WINSCRL3.EXE, WINSCRL3.H, WINSCRL3.RC), 163-171
   windows for inputting and editing, 31-32
   writing in windows, 107-112
Text API GDI functions type, 43
text editors, 202
   basic (WINEDIT1.CPP, WINEDIT1.RC), 189-192
   (WINFILE1.CPP, WINFILE1.EXE, WINFILE1.R), 209-212
   enhanced (WINFILE2.CPP, WINFILE2.EXE, WINFILE2.H, WINFILE2.RC), 212-221
   free-form calculator (WINEDIT2.CPP, WINEDIT2.EXE, WINEDIT2.H, WINEDIT2.RC), 192-201
   text viewer (MDIWIN1.CPP, MDIWIN1.EXE, MDIWIN1.H, MDIWIN1.RC), 511-518
   revised (MDIWIN2.CPP, MDIWIN2.EXE, MDIWIN2.H, MDIWIN2.RC), 518-529
TextBox data member, 518
TextOut API function, 102
TFileDialog class, 17, 493-499
TFileWindow class, 33
   basic text editor, 209-212
   enhanced text editor, 212-221
TGroupBox class, 28, 296-298

timer application (CTLLST1.CPP, CTLLST1.H, CTLLST1.RC), 327-336
TInputDialog class, 18, 487-493
titles, dialog boxes, 583
TListBox class, 25-26, 336-342
   list manipulation tester (CTLLST2.CPP, CTLLST2.RC), 344-355
   responding to notification messages, 342-344
TListBoxData class, 446-447
TMDIClient class, 36-37, 504-505, 509-510
TMDIFrame class, 34-36, 504-508
TMessage structure, 53-54
TModule class, 9-10
TModule::ExecDialog dialog box, 183
Toggle ObjectWindows function, 293-294
ToggleButton ObjectWindows function, 289
TPoints class, 557
TPolygon class, 557-558
track mode, 150
   toggling, 155-161
TrackMode data member, 150
TRadioButton class, 30-31, 295-296
transfer
   buffer types, 446-448
   buffers, 454-462
Transfer virtual ObjectWindows functions, 448-452
TransferBuffer pointer, 452
TransferData ObjectWindows function, 453, 488
TransferFlag transfer direction flag, 448
TransferStruct data transfer buffer type, declaring, 486
TranslateMessage API function, 65

631

transparent processes, 20
TScrollBar class, 22-23, 324-326
   countdown timer application (CTLLST1.CPP, CTLLST1.H, CTLLST1.RC), 327-336
   responding to notification messages, 326-327
TScroller class, 37-39, 150-152
TSearchDialog class, 18-19, 499-500
TSearchStruct structure, 19, 499
TStatic class, 23-24, 225-242
   text-query functions, 244-248
TStreamable class, 541
TStreamableClass class, 549
TWinApp class, WINDOW5.CPP program, 139
TWinApp class, 63, 66-68
TWindow class, 19-21, 504-505
   constructor, 115-116
   read ObjectWindows function in, 546-548
   write ObjectWindows function in, 544-545
TWindowAttr data type, 20, 73, 113
TWindowsObject class, 12-15
   read ObjectWindows function in, 546-548
   write ObjectWindows function in, 544-545
typecasting, 317-318
types data member, 533
typewriter application (WINEDIT3.CPP, WINEDIT3.EXE, WINEDIT3.H, WINEDIT3.RC), 202-209

U-V

UINT data type, 4
Uncheck ObjectWindows function, 293

user-defined messages, 57
Utility macros API system services interface functions type, 45
ValidWindow ObjectWindows function, 10
variables
   flag static local, 410
   MoveToLine static local, 183
   WinApp, 63
variant text application (WINSCRL3.CPP, WINSCRL3.EXE, WINSCRL3.H, WINSCRL3.RC), 163-171
void data type, 4

W

W data member, 115-116
WinApp variable, 63
WinApp.Run statement, 63
window classes, registering, 120-133
Window-creation API Windows Manager functions type, 41
WINDOW1.CPP program, 103-105
WINDOW1.EXE program, 106
WINDOW1.RC program, 102-103
WINDOW2.CPP program, 108-110
WINDOW2.EXE program, 112
WINDOW2.RC program, 107
WINDOW3.CPP program, 116-119
WINDOW3.EXE program, 120
WINDOW4.CPP program, (window class registration), 127-132
WINDOW4.EXE program, (window class registration), 133
WINDOW4.H program, (window class registration), 126
WINDOW4.RC program, (window class registration), 126-127
WINDOW5.CPP program, (changing cursor), 134-139

INDEX

WINDOW5.EXE program, (changing cursor), 140-141
WindowNumber data member, 148
windows, 19-21
    attaching menu attributes, 72-81
    categories, *see* window classes
    child, 141-149
        MDI, 504, 510
    class styles, 122-123
    client, 34-37
        MDI, 504, 509-510
    closing, 95-99
    controls, 21
        initializing, 480-487
    creating, 113-120
    dialog boxes as, 433-445
    editing contents, controls, 24-25
    frame, 34-36
        MDI, 503-508
    handling text in files, 33
    interacting with buttons, 279-289
    read-only text, displaying, 101-106
    registering, 21
    scrolling, 37-39, 149-155
    static text objects, 23-24
    styles, 113-115
    text input and editing, 31-32
    writing text in, 107-112
Windows Manager interface functions, 41-42
Windows-management messages, 49-50
WINEDIT1.CPP program, (text editor), 190-192
WINEDIT1.RC program, (text editor), 190
WINEDIT2.CPP program, (free-form calculator), 195-200
WINEDIT2.EXE program, (free-form calculator), 201
WINEDIT2.H program, (free-form calculator), 194
WINEDIT2.RC program, (free-form calculator), 194-195
WINEDIT3.CPP program, (typewriter application), 203-207
WINEDIT3.EXE program, (typewriter application), 209
WINEDIT3.H program, (typewriter application), 203
WINEDIT3.RC program, (typewriter application), 203
WINFILE1.CPP program, (text editor), 210-212
WINFILE1.EXE program, (text editor), 212
WINFILE1.RC program, (text editor), 210
WINFILE2.CPP program, (enhanced text editor), 215-220
WINFILE2.EXE program, (enhanced text editor), 221
WINFILE2.H program, (enhanced text editor), 213
WINFILE2.RC program, (enhanced text editor), 214-215
WinMain function, 62-63
WINOBJ1.CPP program, (child window creation), 142-148
WINOBJ1.EXE program, (child window creation), 149
WINSCRL1.CPP program, (scrolling window), 152-154
WINSCRL1.EXE program, (scrolling window), 155
WINSCRL2.CPP program, (toggle auto scroll/track modes), 157-161
WINSCRL2.EXE program, (toggle auto scroll/track modes), 161
WINSCRL2.H program, (toggle auto scroll/track modes), 157

633

Guide to ObjectWindows Library

WINSCRL2.RC program, (toggle auto scroll/track modes), 157
WINSCRL3.CPP program, (variant text), 164-170
WINSCRL3.EXE program, (variant text), 171
WINSCRL3.H program, (variant text), 163
WINSCRL3.RC program, (variant text), 163
WINSCRL4.CPP program, 174-182
WINSCRL4.EXE program, 184
WINSCRL4.H program, 173
WINWSCRL4.RC program, 173-174
Wizard modal dialog box, 419
WM_ACTIVATE message, 50
WM_CLOSE message, 50
WM_COMMAND message, 51
WM_FIRST constant, 55
WM_HSCROLL message, 51, 325
WM_INITDIALOG message, 50
WM_INITMENU message, 50
WM_INITMENUPOPUP message, 50
WM_INTERNAL constant, 55
WM_KEYDOWN message, 51
WM_KEYUP message, 51
WM_LBUTTONDBLCLK message, 51
WM_LBUTTONDOWN message, 51
WM_LBUTTONUP message, 51
WM_MOUSEMOVE message, 51
WM_MOVE message, 50
WM_PAINT message, 50
WM_QUIT message, 50
WM_RBUTTONDBLCLK message, 51
WM_RBUTTONDOWN message, 51
WM_RBUTTONUP message, 51
WM_SIZE message, 50
WM_TIMER message, 51
WM_USER constant, 55
WM_VSCROLL message, 51, 325

WMClose ObjectWindows function, 411-413
WMLButtonDown ObjectWindows function, 70-72, 111, 261, 279
WMMouseMove message response ObjectWindows function, 140
WMMove public ObjectWindows function, 139
WMRButtonDown ObjectWindows function, 70-72
WMSize ObjectWindows function, 162
  virtual, 162
WM*xxxx* ObjectWindows functions, 32
WNDCLASS structure, 121-123
WORD data type, 4
workspace, 34
WParam data member, 53
write ObjectWindows function, 558
  protected virtual, 544-545
writeByte ObjectWindows function, 538
writeBytes ObjectWindows function, 538
writeData ObjectWindows function, 538
writeRandomData ObjectWindows function, 559
writeString ObjectWindows function, 538
writeWord ObjectWindows function, 538
writing
  and reading objects to, 539-540
  objects to file streams, 539
WS_BORDER window style, 114
WS_CAPTION window style, 114
WS_CHILD window style, 114
WS_CHILDWINDOW window style, 114
WS_CLIPCHILDREN window style, 114
WS_CLIPSIBLINGS window style, 114

WS_DISABLED window style, 114
WS_HSCROLL
    constant, 150
    window style, 114
WS_ICONIC window style, 114
WS_MAXIMIZEBOX window style, 114
WS_MAXIMIZED window style, 114
WS_MINIMIZE window style, 114
WS_MINIMIZEBOX window style, 114
WS_OVERLAPPED window style, 114
WS_POPUP window style, 114
WS_POPUPWINDOW window style, 114
WS_SYSMENU window style, 115
WS_THICKFRAME window style, 115
WS_VISIBLE window style, 115
WS_VSCROLL
    constant, 150
    style, 337
    window style, 115

X-Z

X data member, 115-116
XLine data member, 151
    changing values, 162
XPage data member, 151
    changing values, 162
xPage protected data member, 170
XPos data member, 151
XRange data member, 151
    changing values, 162
XUnit data member, 151
    changing values, 162

Y data member, 115-116
YLine data member, 151
    changing values, 162
YPage data member, 151
    changing values, 162
yPage protected data member, 170
YPos data member, 151

YRange data member, 151
    changing values, 162
YUnit data member, 151
    changing values, 162

ZERO data member, 8